THE CURRICULUM OF THE COMMON SCHOOL

THE UNIVERSITY OF CHICAGO PRESS · CHICAGO

THE BAKER & TAYLOR COMPANY, NEW YORK; THE CAMBRIDGE UNIVERSITY
PRESS, LONDON; THE MARUZEN-KABUSHIKI-KAISHA, TOKYO, OSAKA,
KYOTO, FUKUOKA, SENDAI; THE COMMERCIAL PRESS, LIMITED, SHANGHAI

THE CURRICULUM OF THE COMMON SCHOOL

FROM THE BEGINNING OF THE PRIMARY
SCHOOL TO THE END OF THE
JUNIOR COLLEGE

By HENRY C. MORRISON

*A Fiftieth Anniversary Publication of the
University of Chicago Press*

THE UNIVERSITY OF CHICAGO PRESS
CHICAGO · ILLINOIS

To

M. M.

PREFACE

THIS volume is a development of the argument in instruction and education which first appeared some fifteen years ago in my *The Practice of Teaching in the Secondary School*. It is in method a sequel to *Basic Principles in Education*. In the latter work the evolutionary principle is the foundation, and it is carried out in the light of fundamental disclosures touching Man as part of the order of Nature which have emerged out of the investigations made in sundry scientific fields but notably anthropology and ethnology, general biology, general physiology, and to a considerable extent out of the conceptions of recent psychology pertaining to the nature of personality. It particularly takes account of recent laboratory and clinical disclosures bearing upon the brain and nervous system, so far as they affect our notions of the nature of education in the individual. That work adheres to the doctrine that the scientific approach to all educational and instructional problems is to be found in the formulation of a factually defensible theory of what education is, to take the place of forever running a race of opinion as to what education ought to be.

Following a similar method in the present work, and passing on from the chapters dealing with Personality in *Basic Principles*, it is here sought to find a defensible answer to the question, "What then must the content of General Education be?" or, in other words, "What must be the valid Curriculum of the Common School?"

To that end we recognize at once that the individual human is inescapably social in his educational status at any period of his development, as contrasted with his equally asocial nature at birth. The problem then becomes at the outset one of finding a workable definition of Society and of its elementary structure. Therein, I have followed for the most part Albion W. Small, William G. Sumner, and various historical jurists. From that point, following the evolutionary argument, and especially the doctrine of Emergent Evolution, which seems to me to have been implicit in the refutations of utilitarianism found in Herbert Spencer's *Ethics*, it has seemed clear to me that we arrive at positive conclusions as to what the cultural content of General Education must be, and by consequence the elements of the Curriculum of the Common School, up to the point of educational maturity, which I presume should be reached by age twenty-one or near the end of what we now call the junior college.

In the many years during which thought has been maturing, I have tried to impose upon myself the obligation of refusing hospitality to any presumptions whatever, or to be influenced by any sort of tradition. So much so that I have gladly gone on as if the final result might be to prove that an entirely new kind of Curriculum is essential or that the General Education of the masses is an impossibility. Now that the work is done, so far from proving anything of the sort, I have come out at a result in terms of courses to be taught which reveals that there is little or nothing contained in the work but has been taught somewhere, in some form, at some time, short of the junior year in college.

Again, I have declined to allow myself to be governed by the limitations of what is at present feasible, feeling sure that no such study as this would be entitled to any respect whatever if the author were constantly asking himself, "Can teachers be found to conduct these courses, or principals to administer them?" In some cases in the outcome I know full well that competent teachers cannot be found; they must be prepared and trained. Nevertheless, if works on public instruction forever permit one of the critical tests of their conclusions to be that the findings must be teachable by those who are now to be found in our schoolrooms, the result must be progressive degradation of the whole fabric of public instruction itself.

Nor have I allowed adventitious circumstances to interfere, notably whether, under our political institutions and laws, certain subjects can legally be taught at all or taught without interfering with the prejudices of large classes of citizens. I hold that such matters are not determinative of the results of inquiries conceived in a scientific spirit. So it is that, on the principles I have followed, I find that Religion is properly a part of the cultural content of General Education, and I devote a chapter to the subject, although I believe that Religion, even undenominational Religion, can probably not legally be taught in tax-supported schools.

Ever since the publication of *The Practice of Teaching*, I have had innumerable requests for lists of units. I have always refused to accede to such requests, well knowing that such lists are part of the art of teaching rather than of the science. In the preparation of the present work, however, I have been urged by former students who are now prominent schoolmasters to prepare such lists. There is a certain advantage in doing so, for after a course has seemed to be indicated by the reasoning which has been followed, it at once appears that definiteness is achieved if the course is, at least tentatively, defined by the list of units conceived to be implied. That has been done in every course which is susceptible of unit organization. The work therefore becomes quite as much a sequel to *The Practice of Teaching* as to *Basic Principles*—in the minds of most readers, probably more so.

The chapters of Civics, Politics, Commerce, and Industry may seem at first to be unduly encyclopedic in character, and perhaps some explanation is appropriate. This is the field which has been least common in schools, much of it appearing only in rare instances in response to the interest of some teacher. And yet it is, in my mind, the most important part of the book and the most imperatively needed in the instruction of our young people. Realizing that it is relatively strange to most teachers and schoolmasters, I have elaborated the subject matter, both for the sake of explaining why I believe it to be essential and for the sake of being as definite and lucid as I could touching what ought to be taught. I have some hope that in this way I may prove to be of some help to textbook-makers.

I suppose that it is quite likely that the present volume will in some quarters be received as a "plan" for adoption—or non-

adoption. Any such outcome is foreign to my purpose. I have not
been working at a plan. I have been rather endeavoring to work
out a critical study of what must in the nature of the social purposes of schools go into their standard programs of study, and
what ought to be left out. Much of it could be put in operation at
once, indeed already is in operation; some of it could be worked up
to in not many years; the residue could not well be placed in most
schools until after a period of teacher-training in subject matter.

It is pleasant to make acknowledgments. In all my books I
have felt a sort of primary obligation to those who have discussed
matters with me in my classes in the University of Chicago; there
have been many of them. I am grateful for much useful information and good advice which have come to me from former students.

I am under particular obligations to Dr. Wilbur L. Beauchamp
and to my sons, Hugh S. and Robert D. Morrison, for painstaking
and critical reading of several of the chapters and for useful
suggestions.

Perhaps most of all, I should acknowledge that the whole institutional conception in its relation to the Curriculum was suggested by the work of my colleague, Professor Charles H. Judd,
in his *Psychology of Social Institutions*.

Finally, I am grateful for the University of Chicago Press, and
to its editor, manager, and staff.

HENRY C. MORRISON

CHICAGO
February 1940

TABLE OF CONTENTS

CHAPTER I

EDUCATION IN THE COMMON SCHOOL

THE title of the present work is *The Curriculum of the Common School*. In the interest of definiteness some introductory explanation is called for, in order that we may have at the outset some common understanding touching what it is that we are talking about.

EDUCATION

The work apparently has to do with Education. The title chosen is meaningless, and the argument of the volume will not run, unless at the outset there is some clarity of ideas touching what is meant by the term "education" itself.

In a previous work I have sought to find an answer to the question, "What is Education?"—an answer based upon fact and principle scientifically determined.[1] The question posed was one which might well stand in the place of the ever recurrent and baseless query, "What ought Education to be?"

The conclusion of this earlier study was in substance that Education is nothing else than taking on the arts and sciences and moral attitudes which make up the fabric of Civilization. That it is not erudition or information and not even enlightenment alone, or mental training, or development of individual potentialities, or a process of generating a new and better civilization.

Adjustment.—Education is an organic or natural process, common in the broadest sense to pretty much the whole animal kingdom. It is a matter of individual learning how to get on in the world. It arises in all creatures which exist in a changeable environment in which there must be in the nature of the case solution of problems of some sort. It contrasts with tropistic behavior in some of the lower orders, where getting-on is a purely mechani-

---

[1] *Basic Principles in Education* (Boston: Houghton Mifflin Co., 1934).

I

cal matter. Nevertheless, education in humans is so fundamentally at a higher level, owing to man's possession of organs which enable him to produce a culture, chiefly exceedingly flexible hands and vocal apparatus, that we rightly accord to human education a difference in kind as well as in degree.

Learning how to get on in the world is *adjustment*, and so we speak of the adjustment theory of Education as contrasted with the eruditional theory or with theories in which it is held that Education is a matter of organic development of some sort. It ought, however, to be borne in mind that the adjustment theory is not to be understood as meaning that the individual has literally to learn somewhere every adjustment he must make. On the contrary, both in the race and in the individual the prize is not adjustment but *adaptability*, that is, the capacity to meet a very wide range of adjustments as the need arises. Hence, it has been said, with great penetration as I think, that "we do not learn what to do, but rather become the kind of people who will know what to do."

It follows that as the individual learns out of his experience of life he is always becoming something, in some way different from what he was before learning took place. The result is what we call *personality*, and every genuine learning product is an accretion to personality. So far as we can make out, the infant starts life with no personality and within a short space of time begins to learn— something—and thus personality begins to be drawn together. Personality is not a material entity, it is not located anywhere, it does not have to be located. It is simply the quality found in the attitudes and acquired abilities which characterize a given individual. It is frequently, in many of the books, as well as in popular use, confounded with physiological and psychological temperament, which is quite a different thing. It is sometimes confounded with the metaphysical concept which we call "the soul."

Maleducation.—Apart from effective upbringing and instruction, education is perhaps about as likely to go wrong as to go right. It must be borne in mind that Education is a natural process driven onward by natural laws, that those laws chiefly cluster about self-preservation and self-assertion, that the forces at work have nothing to do with ethics or right living in normal social relations. In simple terms the result of experience in the world, apart from upbringing and instruction, is in principle as likely to produce the worst of criminals as the best of citizens.

With this all in mind, we may practically dismiss the matter of maleducation, and when in this volume the term Education is used without qualifications, right or normal or ethical education will be meant.

INSTRUCTION

We turn then to Instruction, or the social process by which the community seeks to guarantee that the education of the rising generation shall be right education, of which the citizen and not the criminal or insane is the outcome. We shall consistently use the term to mean the process as carried on in schools. The correlative is Upbringing, by which the Family seeks to guarantee in its children right education.

We must linger here to point out how misuse of words confuses thought, often with really disastrous consequences in the Community. English-speaking peoples, including most of their books, do not discriminate between Instruction, the process, and Education, the product. Not infrequently leaders fail to make the distinction and thus turn their leadership to bad account.

Not long ago a publicist attracted considerable attention by noting that calls for the support of education were becoming tiresome, for, said he in substance, the very period during which most money has been spent on education with the promise that social betterment would follow is the very one during which social disruption has been most pronounced. I entirely agree with what he probably meant but not with what he said. If he had stated his meaning accurately, his thought would have been diametrically opposite to what he had in mind. He would in that case have said something like this: We willingly have contributed great sums of money for the support of schools and colleges. The sponsors told us that the effect would be social betterment, but in actuality there has been social disruption. The school people should be told that their *instruction* is not producing *education*. Therefore, they should be told that they can have no more money until they can mend their ways and show educational results.

The school, college, and university people are constantly led into the same verbal fallacy until they imagine that even a better building will automatically produce better results in education. Indeed, I sometimes suspect that they confound the material equipment with education.

We are constantly reminded that education is of no certain value since highly educated men not infrequently find their way into the penitentiaries. Of course, the statement is false in its terms. The men are where they are because of the failure of their schools and colleges in generating education. The men may have been extensively schooled, may have brilliantly acquired advanced degrees, but so far we have instruction only, and an instruction which evidently failed.

THE CURRICULUM

The basal framework of Instruction is the Curriculum. Without a curriculum, the school is in precisely the same situation as is a builder who bids on a project without plans and specifications and proceeds to erect with no better guidance. Evidently, if Instruction is to be systematically effective, the bedrock, the frame of reference, the plans and specification of the instruction provided, are in the Curriculum.

The term is an ancient one in pedagogy and originally it meant a race course, something to be "run through," a round of studies to be pursued and presumably learned. In our schools the term suffers from our habitual vagueness in matters of terminology. "Curriculum" is used when what is meant is "program of study" or "course of study" for a particular school.

Now the Curriculum is in its nature constant and universal. Programming, and especially teaching, are variable according to the circumstances of particular schools and individual pupils. Let us see.

P 8

We have seen that Education is a process of adjustment with the end of adaptability in a particular world. Now the world is common to all mankind. It is a world of physical and biological conditions, one of social conditions, one of moral and aesthetic values. Furthermore, so far as the anthropological disclosures tell us the story, human nature is at bottom the same the world over, however varied may be the cultural accumulations of different races and peoples, whatever may the spread in the extent to which different peoples have climbed the ladder of Civilization, and the differing extents to which Civilization may have been diffused among different populations. Hence the content of Education is at bottom the same the world over, and the framework upon which that content is hung, namely, the Curriculum, is the same in essentials. The *pedagogical problems* arise in the fields of programming and of teaching.

The thesis of the present work is then to follow the purposes set forth in *Basic Principles* and ascertain not what the Curriculum ought to be but rather *what the Curriculum is*.

THE COMMON SCHOOL

The foregoing being true, it follows in principle that The School is in its nature common to all mankind. The expression "Common School" is an old American use. In our early national period and down into years that are not yet remote the "common school" meant the school which covered the rudiments thought to be essential to the needs of all citizens. The expression makes a good term.

What was common school in early usage is still common school. The rudiments of culture in the simple society of 1840, however, were far short of what they have become in the complex society of 1940. Be that as it may, pupils in that old-time common school, ordinarily the "deestrick schule" of comedy, were in the habit of "attending winters" until, oftentimes, they got past their majority; or else they left when they had "got all they could out of that school."

We need not go into the growth of academies and high schools and the city graded school. All that belongs to another story. Suffice it to say that force of economic circumstances, in the release of child-hours in industry and the setting-up of educational requirements in employment, has brought back in large part, and is probably destined to bring back entirely, so far as enrolment is concerned, the picture of the old common school, in which elementary, junior high school, senior high school, and junior college are merged as of old into a single school organization.[2]

The Common Man.—The Curriculum of the Common School might further be defined as *The Content of the General Education of the Common Man.*

Demagogues have debauched the meaning of a fine term which lies, as I think, at the basis of what some of us still like to believe is the peculiar social contribution of America. The Common Man, in the use which will be followed in this book, is not the ignorant man, or the poor man, or the lowly, not the ordinary man, or the average man, but simply what all of us are in our nonvocational, nonphilosophical, nonspecialized, human nature. The child of the Common Man may be destined to eminence, to great achievement in any one of the walks of life, but in his humanity he is still Common Man and the son of Common Man. We are not told that eminence begets eminence.

GENERAL EDUCATION

The term "General Education" has been coming into common use to signify that education which is nonprofessional and nonspecialized. It is equivalent to the older term, "Liberal Education," which in reality meant education in the seven liberal arts.

Now Education itself is, of course, as long as life, at least potentially so. It normally begins as soon as the mother can penetrate the mind of her baby, and, providing personality develops early into a well-rounded structure,[3] it continues until the senescent changes have progressively destroyed the adaptive instrument which we call Mind. If, however, personal structure is not well

[2] I have sketched out the whole process of development in my Inglis Lecture entitled *The Evolving Common School* (Cambridge: Harvard University Press, 1933).

[3] For exact meaning see *Basic Principles*, chap. vii.

rounded and well integrated early in life, either subsequent learnings will tend to be spurious[4] or else the individual will tend to become intransigent for lack of apperceptive mass, that is to say ideational and volitional background capable of assimilating new ideas. It is probably equally true that certain organic temperaments will tend to become iconoclastic for lack of a balance wheel.

There is nothing in the nature of Education which excludes us from asserting that General Education as defined above also begins in infancy and extends into advanced old age. Only, it is convenient to use the term also to mean the general education which results from normal and effective instruction, and which begins to build up apart from instruction at educational maturity.

Here then is still another term, "Educational Maturity." It is factual and observable. It signifies that the individual has reached a stage at which he is in fact capable of directing widely his own further learning. The issue is positive: he is so capable or he is not. Many a student of forty or fifty has never matured educationally; he is dependent upon assignments. Many another is educationally mature by seventeen or eighteen years; he is capable of learning without assignments. In legal terms he has passed out of *status pupillaris*. Our age of majority fixed at twenty-one reflects that conception, and it assumes that people at age twenty-one are responsible persons. Age twenty-one is fully the end of the Junior College as average school age-groups now are.

The problem of the Common School is then to see that the civil expectations touching majority are realized, that the content of General Education is established in the persons of pupils, that the pupils themselves under discipline and teaching achieve veritable Educational Maturity.

[4] *Ibid.*, pp. 107 ff. and 151; see also *The Practice of Teaching in the Secondary School* (Chicago: University of Chicago Press, 1926; 2d ed., 1931), chaps. iii and iv. The factual material is presented in the first edition and summarized in the second edition of this work.

CHAPTER II

SOCIAL FOUNDATIONS

SINCE John Dewey's *School and Society* appeared, more than thirty-five years ago, American schoolmasters of the more thoughtful type have had little doubt that the school has a social function. Indeed, the word "social" has become something to conjure with. What is Society? and what is the legitimate meaning of the cognates of the word?

I. SOCIETY

For our purposes I shall take the definition written down by an eminent American sociologist in the last generation.

Society is, then, "that phase of the conditions of human life which consists of inevitable action and reaction between many individuals." It is also "living together in mutual relationships."[1]

So Society is, first of all, the name for a form of existence. We are conditioned by gravitation, by the laws of fluid behavior, by those of electricity and chemistry. That is to say, we cannot do as we please without entailing consequences. Similarly, we are conditioned by the structure and physiology of our own bodies. In the same sense and no other sense we are conditioned by the circumstance that we cannot escape living in relations with other humans.

Second, living together in mutual relationships means that sets of relationships get built up. That is Society too, and the different total sets of relationships are societies.

MISUSE OF THE TERM

Few words in the language are so lavishly misused, and by consequence sociological thought becomes almost devoid of logic, as it appears in conversation and in popular writings and in general literature. Let us look at a few instances.

[1] Albion W. Small, *General Sociology* (Chicago: University of Chicago Press, 1905), p. 405.

8

Social change, a cliché today, does not exist save as altered relationships between individuals are meant. A new invention is not a social change: it may or may not lead to social change.

The term "social justice," of which we are so fond just now, is meaningless, since it seems to refer to a new kind of justice. All justice is social, and you cannot divide up justice and sort it into different pigeonholes. If there is miserable injustice in holding slaves, that is enough; nothing whatever is gained by calling slaveholding social injustice.

And so on at great length.

Community.—In common use, the word "society" is most often employed where Community is meant. Nearly always, in the expression, "for the good of society," accurate use would say, "for the good of the Community" or "for the common good." A related misuse is to confound society with population or with people.

The State.—Again, "society" and "The State" are frequently used as if they meant the same thing.

Unions, guilds, corporations, etc.—The original meaning of the word in Latin is translatable into English as "union," "guild," "corporation," "company," "association." All these are often called "societies." They are social in their nature, but they are neither Society nor societies in the exact use of terms.

Social Progress.—So "social progress" is betterment in the relationships which constitute Society. The arbitrary distribution of wealth may be the opposite of social progress. The expansion of material culture is not necessarily social progress; it may or may not lead to social betterment. Specifically, social progress is ethical progress and nothing else.

SOCIETY AS GOING CONCERN

We shall have occasion to make much use of this expression. When inviduals live in communication with one another, whether it be in the same community or in different communities or in no community at all, under *common estimates* of the world of common experience and under *common expectation* of what each will do under certain sets of circumstances, then there is a *social order, a* society, and the society operates as a going concern, much as a business enterprise is said to be a going concern. So common estimates and common expectations are what constitute organized society. The State, which is social and part of the common estimates and expectations, may perform its civil functions, but for the most part things run along under the social formula which we have described. The society is an organism, not a living organism but a social organism. Such a social order is in the order of nature, and that gives us our reason for believing that there is such a thing as a General Sociology, even if its laws have not been formulated.

SOCIETY NOT SELF-CONSCIOUS

Finally, Society is not self-conscious. Despite the habitual ways of speaking and writing employed by many, Society requires nothing, decrees nothing, decides nothing, invents nothing. All these expressions flow from our inveterate habit of anthropomorphizing and personalizing everything. They imply that Society, or a particular society, is a self-conscious being of some sort, whereas it is no more self-conscious than is the circulation of the blood. Individuals invent, governments decree, courts decide, circumstances as well as powerful men or the law sometimes require, but not Society or societies. If it were otherwise, all the sociologists, economists, jurists, might as well burn their books, for there could be no such thing as social science if we were all of us subject to the caprice of a self-conscious being.

II. STRUCTURE OF SOCIETY

Can we then find characteristic sets of common estimates and common expectations, or rather relationships in which the latter inhere? The answer is "Yes," in the broadest sense four of them: folkways, mores, customs, and institutions.

A. FOLKWAYS

If two people approaching each other on the sidewalk begin to dodge back and forth in an embarrassed fashion in the effort to get safely past each other, it is because they are in part under social disruption: neither of them abides resolutely by the folk-way under which people keep to the right in passing. That is *folkway*, a form of common expectation. There are thousands of folkways. Nobody knows where the great folkways come from. The primitive will tell you that they "had them from their an-cestors," and our friend, the man on the street, will probably say, "I suppose we just got to doing things that way." Both of them are right. We just got to doing things that way, and the folkway thus established was handed down by tradition. Each of them— unless they are manufactured by advertisers—is the product of "the action and reaction between many individuals."

Whatever modifies folkways modifies society, for better or worse.

B. MORES

We sometimes use the expression "the public mind" or "the mind of America." We mean *the mores*. "Public mind" serves well enough, but for the considerable objection that there can be no such thing. The expression is a metaphor. Mind is part of the adaptive organism of individuals.

The mores—both singular and plural, although the Latin is plural, and use the English pronunciation, *mō-rees*—is the atti-tudes characteristic of a given population. We may say, for ex-ample, that good taste in dwelling-houses is in the local mores of this community, or civic decency in the mores of that. If we say, as unhappily we sometimes have to, that "you can never depend upon what anybody in that town tells you," we mean in sociologi-cal terms that veracity is not in the mores. Gross superstition may be in the mores of this region and a high level of intelligence in the mores of that.

And so common estimates are mainly in the mores. The esti-mates may be grossly wrong in fact, but they are estimates just the same; they are part of the structure of that society. It has sometimes been said that the mores can make anything right. That is not true, but it is true that the mores can and do make anything *seem* right. We are so inexorably social in our persons that most of us tend to conform to the mores in which we find ourselves. One of the hardest things in the world is to disagree with prevailing attitudes in the neighborhood.

Demoralization.—We frequently hear the word "demoralization," and we know well enough the connotation. It signifies that each does what seems right in his own eyes, believes what he desires to believe, avoids anything and everything which savors of duty—and salves his conscience by deriding the very notion of duty.

Such a community is without an actual mores. There is no common conviction in either Intelligence or Conscience or Taste. Civilization has not "collapsed," for Civilization no more collapses than does the multiplication table. Society as a going concern collapses, and there is nothing to go by.

The outcome in such demoralized communities is likely to be, in the first place, great increase in crime and especially in the more brutal crimes and, second, economic depression. Most depressions are to a greater or less extent the outcome of demoralization.

It is, however, nonetheless demoralization when despotism exalts The State and attempts to make what is in its nature institution take the place of ordered social structure.

C. CUSTOM

So far as I have been able to observe, most sociological writers take the position that the mores govern. To a certain extent that is true, for the common expectations and the common estimates do more or less determine conduct. But they determine conduct in the socially minded—the ethical—alone. There is nothing positive about folkways and mores by which the community can govern its irresponsibles.

So, instead of the mores acting as a compelling code of conduct, the juristic and political approaches assure us that positive control is in the customs out of which civil law has evolved.

In the history of the United States there is a great deal of sociological enlightenment coming from a source which is close at hand and recent enough not to have lost its dramatic aspects. Let us see.

In our frontier period, especially on the Plains and in the Mountains, horse-stealing was held to be peculiarly reprehensible. That was in the mores. In due season, horse thieves when caught were summarily hanged. That was *custom:* every individual knew what to expect. As organized Government grew up, it became *customary* to "let the law take its course." Thus custom merged into law.

When I say that custom is primitive law, I do not mean proto-law alone. On the contrary, a large part of positive control comes from custom still. Your friend queries, "Do you think I have got to?"—make a party call, for instance. He means, "Am I under the compulsion of custom so to do?" He has no idea of a statute and not much of moral obligation. If he says, "Ought I to make a call?" he raises an ethical question.

The bane of the social sciences is in the fact that they have but a scanty terminology, and when two words which mean two quite different things are used synonymously, we throw away useful terminological resources. So it is when custom is defined as "Social habit." Society has no habits; individuals do have habits. It is my habit to take a siesta but not my custom.

D. INSTITUTIONS

The fourth member of the elementary structure of ordered relationships between individuals is Institution. When a particular element in the folkways or mores, or a particular custom, becomes so important in experience that other elements in folkways and mores or a whole group of customs cluster around it and become integrated, then an institution is born—and Civilization becomes definitely launched.

There are many thousand such institutions—universal and national and even local, major and constituent, temporary and established.

Universal institutions.—When one of these, like Language or Number, appears everywhere or nearly everywhere in advancing societies, *and when we can rationally see that it is in principle a part of the method by which people can live together in harmony and cooperation,* then we have a right to conclude that it is universal and that peoples who have it not would be better off if they did have it. I think we can arrive at a serviceable definition of a universal institution, thus:

A universal institution is a system of popular usages or beliefs which originating in human nature, in the common sense and experience of mankind, has survived as a useful form of harmony and co-operation, has become organized, extended, and refined in the course of social evolution, and is, finally, capable of being rationally comprehended as a necessary element in the structure of all advancing societies.

"Institutions are the great culture carriers—the depositories of social heritage, the media of its operation and perpetuation. Without them there would be no enduring products of the intercourse and interstimulation of individuals and groups."[2]

We might well be content to rest the case of this whole volume on Hertzler's statement. Note, however, that there is no point in referring to "Social Institutions." All institutions in their nature are social and not physical or biological.

LEADERSHIP

So we turn away from the Structure of Society; but before passing on to the next topic we ought, I believe, to have in mind a matter which is not of Society but of the Community, not structural but functional. I mean *Leadership*, which in dynamic social existence is quite as important as structure.

Societies, or social orders, never become effective spontaneously. Like other organisms, they depend upon head dominance. Head dominance is found in the leadership of individuals.

In the last analysis leadership is determined by the mores. He is the leader whom the commons will follow. The leaders themselves, on the other hand, will tend to follow a single leader, local or regional or national as the case may be. Leaders are not appointed or elected; they arise.

The principle is supremely important in our theory of the School. For centuries men have seen, with greater or less clarity,

[2] J. O. Hertzler, *Social Institutions*, with the kind permission of McGraw-Hill Book Co., publishers.

that the quality of leadership in the Community depends upon the rate and extent to which Civilization is being bred into the mores. Modern despots recognize the principle when they propagandize their school systems.

Nor is political leadership the only form. The Community gets the kind of literature and music and painting which the content of the mores justifies. We are bedeviled with pseudo-science and charlatans in inverse proportion to the Intelligence in the mores. We get the kind of Government, especially in democracies, which the standard of Conscience and Political Intelligence in the mores requires.

Hence, while it is in no sense the function of schools to "educate for leadership," it is emphatically their business to educate the kind of followers who will follow the best leadership in all fields. The legitimate curriculum made effective in the kind of instruction administered does just that. But the curriculum is not aimed at right leadership; it is aimed at generating valid education.

III. CULTURE

Since we shall have to make large use of the term Culture, let us see what it is that we mean by it.

In his article on "Culture" in the *Encyclopedia of the Social Sciences* Malinowski has this to say: "Culture comprises inherited artifacts, goods, technical processes, ideas, habits, and values. Social organization cannot be readily understood except as a part of culture."

Dictionary meanings vary from refinement in manners and tastes to test tubes full of beef broth and raising potatoes. We shall use Malinowski's definition.

From the slingshot which the youth of the race has used from time immemorial, for the purpose of getting into mischief, to Shakespearean drama, we are dealing with culture and cultural products. A Paleolithic arrowhead is a cultural product, and so is the excellent mural drawing found in some prehistoric caves. The art of making the arrowhead is culture, and so is the art of drawing the deer or other animal. When men have learned to exchange spearpoints for tanned hides, the result is culture; and settling bills by exchange on London or New York is a variant of that culture.

An art museum is a cultural product, and so is what it contains. The New York Central Railway is a cultural product, and railways in general are culture. So is the United States Steel Corporation and its works, and so is the United States government. Water is not culture, but wines and liquors are cultural products. *Cannabis indica* is not a cultural but a natural product, but the narcotic drugs procured from it are dangerous cultural products.

Doubtless, the common meaning of culture carries the notion of pursuit of the higher arts and sciences, the tastes and graces of highly civilized life. These represent cultural acquisitions at a high level of Civilization. In that sense they are parts of the body of the Higher Culture.

In general, writers and speakers are prone to use "Culture" when they mean "Civilization," and the reverse.

Cultural environment.—The characteristic which chiefly marks off Man from the subhuman series is in the fact that he is organically capable of Culture enshrined in the cultural products which he leaves behind him. When men shaped stones roughly to serve as pounding instruments, they began the creation of a new kind of environment, over against the natural environment. And the law of adjustment is inexorable. People did not emerge into a highly institutionalized society, and come in contact with the cultural environment which that kind of society makes inevitable, without finding that the new environment requires adjustment to itself on pain of some kind of extinction, just as did the old environments. Any new cultural product whatever has a tendency to increase the complexity of Society and to dislocate the social order in which it appears.

Unutterable disaster is encountered when a barbarous invader, or the rise of barbarous classes in an old community, get their hands on the material culture with which they are not sufficiently civilized to be trusted.

IV. CIVILIZATION

It has just been said that people mistake Culture for Civilization and the reverse. What is Civilization?

Civilization has aptly been called *The Art of Living Together*. In the light of all we know regarding the genesis of Society and the history of social evolution, and having due regard to the etymology of terms, I do not believe that there is any better definition stated in simple form.

In this view of the matter Civilization has been evolving since an early period in prehistory. Further, on this planet, there can be but one Civilization—which presumably no people has as yet fully achieved—since human nature is at bottom the same everywhere, and at bottom in the great cosmic laws the environment is the same. When people speak of "different civilizations," consideration of their meaning will almost always disclose that what they have in mind is either different societies or else different cultures.

We are constantly confusing Civilization with the spread of Civilization among different peoples. A civilized individual is much the same person the world over regardless of time and place, race and nationality; but the number of such individuals in a given population may and does vary enormously.

Civilization is defined to be *an art*, and an art implies a technique and a structure. With our brief argument touching the Structure of Society in mind, it is scarcely to be doubted that the Structure of Civilization is anything else than the universal institutions which have to be the final element in social structure. In the chapters which are to constitute the bulk of the present volume we shall be engaged in identifying and studying the principal institutions. Meanwhile we can arrive at what will serve as a more exact definition:

Civilization is the art of living together in communities in harmony, and in co-operation in the presence of the natural and cultural environments.

If our argument be sound, it follows that a civilized individual at any stage of the world's development is the person who is in possession of the universal institutions available in his time. It cannot, however, be argued that Civilization itself is absolute, or that the Civilization which was in existence in the best days of Athens was at so high a level as the best of Civilization as it exists in the modern world.

Civilization, moreover, has content and effect as well as structure. I suggest that we can specify the observable measure in communities ancient and modern of the extent to which Civilization is present in their social structures. The terms of the measure would seem to be:

1. Justice is most evenly, promptly, and effectively administered.

2. The national defense against the external enemy and the internal criminal is most adequately provided for.

3. The perils of the geographical and biological environments are most effectively warded off.

4. Mental and bodily health in the population is at the maximum.

5. The national resources are most effectively conserved.

6. The distribution of wealth is at the maximum consistent with maximum total production.

Such a test would be good, for it would presume that pretty much the whole institutional fabric of Civilization was so extensively bred into the mores as to be dominant in individual and group conduct.

V. EVOLUTION

What assurance have we that the world as we know it, and especially the social world, is anything else than a meaningless flux of ever changing circumstances and ever changing adjustment. In other words, how do we know that the argument of the preceding pages of the present chapter presents a practical logic in its essentials rather than a fanciful delusion? Thinkers have over and over again adopted the meaningless-flux idea, and almost invariably they have appeared in decadent periods of history. The great thinkers, beginning with Socrates, who gave us the foundations of Ethics, Plato, who initiated us into Metaphysics, and Aristotle, who revised Metaphysics, gave us the foundations of Logic, and was in reality the founder of Science as we know Science, thought quite otherwise. So did Jesus and the Fathers of the Church. So did the jurists down the years who found the Law and Civil Government. All these found their assurance in the search for Reality and in the knowledge that Reality is eventually in Thought.

So the physical scientist has no doubt how his world is put together, or at least he has indestructible faith in the validity of the method by which he finds out.

The biologist for nearly a century past has found his conviction in the doctrine which holds that a given species or form of life is defined by what it has come to be. So it is that the medical man deals with us as Nature intended us to be, or so he says. In the last analysis, he removes our tonsils and our appendix because he knows that they belong to a stage of existence which has long passed away. He is patient with our stomachs and glands and tries to get them to do the work which it is normal for them to do. So all the biological callings pin their faith upon the confidence that what an organ or a process normally is has been determined by the history of that organ or process.

And so it is once more with the sociologist in his various fields. He has his choice between believing that there is no such thing as a logic in normal ways of living together and believing that there is a discoverable logic. But in all the sound studies of general sociologists, jurists, economists, political thinkers, there is search for normality in human relationships; and belief in the reality of normality can rest on no other terms than those upon which the biologist rests his belief, namely, the finding that normal social conditions are defined by what they have come to be.

Hence, we turn to Evolution as the method by which normality is sought, and in common use "normality" is about equivalent to "rightness."

The notion that there has been evolution in the scheme of things, unfolding from one state into another state, is as old as the Greeks at least, but it remained for biologists and sociologists in the nineteenth century to unravel the method and processes of evolution.

Herbert Spencer seems to me to have summarized evolution as a method of social thinking in the following passages:

Whatever is common to men's minds in all stages must be deeper down in thought than whatever is peculiar to men's minds in higher stages; and if the later product admits of being reached by modification and expansion of the earlier product, the implication is that it has been so reached.[3]

And again:

It has come to be a maxim of science that in the causes still at work, are to be identified the causes which, similarly at work during past times, have produced the state of things now existing.[4]

We should be intellectually helpless in a world of living things if we could not place ourselves securely upon the faith that life is life wherever we find it, that it is at bottom no different in the lowest forms from what it is in ourselves, however much it may differ from species to species in its manifestations. Biology justifies our faith.

We should be similarly helpless in our attempts to understand Society, if we had not faith that human nature, in its common-sense reactions, in its passions, and in its bodily controls, has always at bottom been what it is in us, despite the infinite variety of its manifestations among individuals. The anthropological record justifies our faith. Herein are the causes still at work which have always been at work in the presence of the same physical and biological forces. To be sure, we do not react to all *experiences* in the same way in which the savage reacts, but the difference is in the main, if not entirely, due to what we have learned with our human nature that he had not learned. The differences are cultural in their nature and not organic. Mentality does not evolve, or at best evolves after the slow methods of organic evolution; ideas do evolve, and they evolve rapidly because the method is learning.

FASHION

But the learning is racial learning and not individual learning. There is no consciousness in the Community in which learning is registered.

[3] *The Principle of Sociology* (3 vols.; New York: Appleton & Co., 1927), I, 305.
[4] *Ibid.*, II, 327.

Rather the method is variation, selection of advantageous variations, transmission, and survival. It is the same process which occurs in the evolution of plants and animals. Only here variation is what we are familiar with as Fashion; there it is variation in bodily form. There is fashion in pretty much everything in human behavior. We are aware of it chiefly in wearing apparel, dwelling-places, most of the material appurtenances of life; but it occurs also in scientific pursuits, in our perception of the beautiful, in conduct.

Now variation in bodily form grows less and less extreme as species become stabilized in adjustment, but it never ceases altogether. So in mature and well-integrated personality, fashionable variation appeals less and less. The mature, enlightened, civilized, personality inclines but slowly and not far to the left; and when reaction comes, he or she swings a little but not far to the right. One has only to observe the dress of cultivated ladies and observe how relatively stable their taste in dress is, while the infantile swing back and forth from the dress of small girls and the cosmetics of the Polynesian to hoop skirts and "waterfalls."

Still, honesty in business, perception of the beautiful in music, the scientific attitude, sense of personality —all of them and all the rest of the fabric of Civilization were at one time current fashion. Now there have been untold millions of variations in bodily structure for every one which has proved useful and has survived as advantageous, and of the latter there have been many, many thousands which proved to be but adjustments which fell short of the universal value in adaptability. Of the latter in the organic series, there are few indeed, perhaps ultimately only one.

So it is in social evolution. Fashionable variation at times runs wild, at least so it seems. Be that as it may, the survivals which have in the end proved to have universality and have given rise to universal institutions are few indeed.

In the end what has survived in this last sense has done so because it proved to be socially useful in all conceivable environments. *It was socially useful because it was right and not right because it was socially useful.*

The principle just enunciated refutes altogether the present doctrine of relativity in social structure. Whatever is morally valid is morally right in all times and all places.

THE GREAT ESCAPES

But evolution in what? What has been the content or subject matter of evolution?

Ten years ago or thereabout, there appeared a work entitled *This Economic World and How It May Be Improved.*[5] The theme of that work was what was called "the Great Escapes." I do not know that I have ever seen a phrase which, in my mind, so completely and graphically summarizes what social evolution has been. And so I would give it a scope much wider than that in which the authors employed it.

Perhaps the *pursuit of happiness* would be considered by most people to be the appropriate driving force in the evolution of Civilization. For my part I have never seen a definition of happiness which was dynamic enough in connotation to be a driving force in anything but the endless pursuit of pleasure.

But escape from the pangs of hunger, from the attacks of ravenous beasts, from the raids of only less ravenous men, from disease, from the fear of the unknown, from the dread of the destruction wrought by the elements, from the arbitrary power of capricious men and women, and, not the least, from the domination of the specialist—all these seem to me typical of what has chiefly forced mankind to learn all it could, all the way from the best way to kill a bear to the best way to avoid being devoured by destructive taxation.

In the whole story of social evolution the Great Escapes will explain most of the whole institutional development.

THE DOCTRINE OF EVOLUTION IN SOCIAL THINKING

The principles of evolution thus give us the only scientific approach to the tests of validity and normality. But they also give us basis for sound radical thinking.

[5] Thomas Nixon Carver and Hugh W. Lester, *This Economic World and How It May be Improved* (New York: A. W. Shaw & Co., 1928).

All the way along from the beginning of the history, adjustment to current circumstances has been the test of survival, in a larger sense adjustment to current circumstance evolving into creatures and cultures capable of effecting adjustment to any circumstances.

Nevertheless, ancient and obsolete adjustments linger on in the organism of Man and in the social structure as well, particularly in the civil and political structure. The latter make trouble, as much as or more than does a wisdom tooth.

The American county is an illustration. Prior to the age of rapid communication the county was an adjustment to the requirements of getting certain kinds of civil business done. But in an age in which in most of the states the state capital is nearer than was the county seat forty years ago, the county is merely a troublesome and expensive organ in the body politic.

The Law is full of these obsolete survivals, the most notable of which are the formalities surrounding the execution of contracts, which come down from a time when few could read and write and in which semimagical incantations were necessary to insure carrying out the agreement.

Latin and Greek in the Curriculum of the Common School make a patent instance. In the ages beginning with A.D. 1100, let us say, the only great literature was in Greek and Latin. The modern languages had not yet become literary tongues. So it was, with Latin at least, down to about 1700. The new science of the sixteenth and seventeenth centuries was in Latin. If you were going to keep up, you had to read Latin. Both the classical languages had a social meaning and utility, which Greek had lost by 1600 and Latin a century later.

Now a certain type of person who fancies himself a radical when he merely wants a change is not radical; he is merely juvenile. But the evolutionary method gives the intelligent radical a sound basis for his reasoning. The conservative, on the other hand, who is unwilling to change because he cannot foresee the consequences, if he were in possession of the evolutionary approach, would come to see that he is holding fast to what has not been good for a long time.

REGRESSION

In the large, organic evolution is protected from backward moves, because the method of transmission is biological heredity, and regressive progeny tend to get eliminated. In social evolution, however, the method of transmission is by upbringing and instruction, and a great deal of regression can take place in a single generation—will take place if the Home and the School fail. I have frequently called attention to the fact that each new generation in a mixed community always tends, apart from effective upbringing and instruction, to regress toward the lowest cultural level to be found among those with whom they associate. When radio, newspapers, and automobile expand the community, general regression in the Civilization present in the mores is an imminent possibility.

HAS CIVILIZATION CEASED EVOLVING?

The question inevitably arises: "What sort of an answer can we find in the principles which we have outlined and in the known facts of history?"

In the first place, we must always keep in mind the distinction between Civilization itself and the spread of Civilization in a given population. In the last four hundred years there has undoubtedly been great advance in this respect. And yet the Civilization which was recovered in the Renaissance of the twelfth century was in the main Civilization as we know it. It spread rapidly after the invention of printing and especially after the Industrial Revolution of the eighteenth century. And yet, in most that is fundamental in society, we constantly are made aware that the most enlightened of ancient times looked on most matters as do the most enlightened today.

Civilization changes but slowly and then for the most part in the development of the universal institutions; but, it must be remembered, the institutions themselves are in constant evolution. That process itself creates no problems, but the rapid consequent expansion of the cultural environment does make social problems. It would be hard to find an absolutely new major institution which has emerged out of nothing since recorded history began, but that gives us no assurance that the Art of Living Together will not in due season give us something new and more effective.

But whatever the future millenniums may hold in store we may be well assured of this, that the Civilization of the future will evolve out of experience found in the Civilization of the present and that there can be no progress at all, but rather regression, except in so far as Civilization as we know it is more and more bred into the mores through effective instruction of all the children of all the people.

VI. INSTITUTIONS AND THE CURRICULUM

If Civilization is the art of community existence and of conquest of the environment, and if the universal institutions are the fabric of the art, then it follows that the curriculum leading to General Education of the nonspecialized person must be constituted of the universal institutions which are good in all advancing societies.

The problem of the Curriculum of the Common School is reduced then to enumerating the universal institutions.

Such an undertaking must of course at first blush seem overambitious and perhaps impossible. And yet if we keep in mind our definition of universal institution, and follow the story carefully as it unfolds in the history of Culture, the task seems far from impossible, although it doubtless remains arduous. Certain criteria appear as we go on with the work.

Comprehensiveness of the term.—The initial difficulty doubtless arises from the fact that such arts and sciences as Language, Mathematics, the Natural Sciences, the Humanities, Commerce, and Industry are included as major institutions. It has been customary to accept civil and political enterprises as institutions— and I presume that there would probably appear little objection to including The State and Civil Government as major and comprehensive—but it is only recently that certain of the arts and sciences have come to be recognized as having institutional characteristics. Nevertheless, any definition which would account for the Family or Money and Credit as institutions would equally well account for Language and Mathematics. They assuredly exist as relationships between individuals, they are in origin in the nature of folkways, and they are folkways about which a great many others have clustered and become integrated.

The historical and rational tests. —Prima facie it seems absurd to contend that what has long been in the structure of societies is for that reason possessed of universal validity. Humans have cherished delusions for untold centuries only to discover that they were delusions. Nevertheless, when we find an indubitable method of holding a community together, quite regardless of the ideas people may have cherished about it, which has persisted from a remote antiquity, disappeared it may be and then returned, which has in historical fact expanded, become organized, and refined, and is still found in all societies which we rate as enlightened; then we must conclude that there must be something of reality in it.

Even so, however, there is no proof, but only plausibility. But if we turn the matter around and come to see how it is that there is inevitable *common expectation* and *common estimate* in the method of living which we are studying, we must conclude that it has social reality and validity.

Universality.—We may, however, list such methods of community existence and be permitted to call them institutions and still be without the essential scientific feature of universality.

Universality has already been defined as that which appears in all progressive societies. But what are progressive societies? It is flagrant begging the question to say that progressive societies are those in which Civilization is advancing, and then turn about and say that Civilization is the art of living in progressive societies.

Now the more philosophical evolutionists have frequently called attention to what we may call the "emergent principle" or the "trunk line." It may be illustrated thus:

I suppose that most of us "worm fishermen" regard with loathing the earthworm which we string on our hooks, as compared with the beautiful butterfly or moth which in its flight falls near the boat and is gobbled by a passing trout or bass. The worm belongs to a lower phylum, and the butterfly to a phylum which once attained about the highest point of adaptability of which that kind of form was capable—and stayed there. The worm, on the other hand, was capable of giving origin to higher forms which were in the trunk line which in the end led to the mammals and to Man. The principle of polarity, or the possibility of polarity, was emergent. It was valid and right. Evolution regarded from that point of view is revelatory.

On the other hand, when we study peoples like the Iroquois, the Maya, the Zuni, and some of the African peoples, and recognize in their social structure elements which we find more highly developed in the peoples among whom Art and Science and Religion and Law have reached the highest levels; and when in other primitive peoples we recognize nothing of the sort; we have a right to conclude that the peoples named were in the trunk line of progress, that their institutions were emergent, that they were advancing in the direction of universal validity.

"Universality" implies at first the notion that all the peoples in the world have been canvassed and that we find the institutions in question in all of them. That is the same as attributing scientific validity to the results of a party landslide in politics. It is the same as holding that what everybody believes must be true. Under that way of looking at the matter, it would be true that so long as the majority believed the Sun revolved about the Earth, the Sun in truth did revolve about the Earth; and that as soon as Copernicus and his followers proved the contrary and the majority accepted the teaching, then the Earth did begin to revolve about the Sun. At that, the reasoning would not be very different from what is found in a great deal of current popular ethics. No, Universality is found in reason based upon facts and not in the census tables.

Further criteria.—Perhaps the most difficult part of the problem of identifying the true major and universal institutions is met by adherence to the following criteria:

1. We must discriminate carefully between what is not only

universal but also of fundamental and comprehensive significance and what is no doubt universal but minor and constituent. Irrigation, for example, meets all the tests of universality, but it has no meaning apart from the major institution of Agriculture in Industry. Money and Credit are undoubtedly institutionally universal, but they have no meaning apart from the major and comprehensive Commerce.

2. We must discriminate between what is institution and what is a particular enterprise. Banks are often called institutions, but they are no more institutional than is a department store. Schools and colleges are often called institutions, but they are only educational enterprises. Banking is institution, constituent of Commerce. The School and the University, abstract nouns, are institutions constituent, as I think, of The State.

3. We must not confound institution with what is merely descriptive of community function, notably production, distribution, regulation, and reproduction.

4. It is easy to confound what is merely a symptom of an institution, or of Civilization, in personality or in the mores, with a particular institution.

That is notably true of Honesty, which cannot be tied down to any particular moral institution; it is rather a symptom of the presence of Conscience. So with Altruism, which seems to be exalted above Honesty itself nowadays. Altruism would have long ago developed institutional organization out of philanthropy if it had been institutional at all. It is rather a symptom of sublimated egoism in personality, one of the chief marks of maturity.

5. There must be discrimination between what is institution and what is only cultural product. The law of falling bodies or the electron theory of matter are such products; the institution is Science. The works of John Milton are cultural products; the institution is Literature.

6. Between what is institution and what is response to organic impulse. For example, concern for children is socially as important as any institution, but it is not institutional; it is only organic trait. It is apparent in birds and mammals as well as in

humans. Anything else is commonly called "unnatural," and so it is.

7. Between what is institution and what is prevalent ideology, theory of the universe if you will. Belief in ghosts is almost universal among primitives. Men for ages believed in a flat earth and a geocentric universe. These beliefs are not institutions and never were. Science is institution, major component of Civilization. As Science evolved out of mythology, beliefs of all sorts were brought under control and correction.

Defect in method.—Finally, when it comes to listing the institutions under the criteria which have been adopted, we are at a disadvantage which cannot be avoided by any method known to the author. One can be confident concerning those which he lists, but he can never be sure that he has listed them all. He can apply the principle of diminishing and finally disappearing investigational returns. He can test each of those which he suspects and afterward discards as being true institution. All this I have tried diligently to do. The list finally appears in the chapters which constitute most of the rest of the volume.

VII. INTELLIGENCE, CONSCIENCE, TASTE

Let us turn back for a moment to Hertzler's characterization of institutions: "Institutions are the great culture carriers—the depositories of social heritage, the media of its operation and perpetuation."

What is it that the institutions carry in the broadest and most comprehensive sense? We have repeatedly used the terms Intelligence, Conscience, and Taste. These are what is carried.

INTELLIGENCE

The verb *intellegere* signified "to perceive, understand, comprehend"; in particular, "to have an accurate knowledge of or skill in a thing, to be a connoisseur."

The connotation of Intelligence is reducible to "discernment," "power of discrimination," "ability to interpret and react to a novel situation." From the etymology, as well as from current use in at least half the passages to be found, the word implies a generalized product of learning. It is contrasted with mentality, ordinarily called "brightness," which is an organic trait.

If one is to acquire the power of discrimination in matters of health or business or citizenship, he must learn it and, it will always arise out of understanding principles of some sort. Mentality alone, apart from learning cannot accomplish that.

Intelligence becomes organized into Intellect, which is capacity to see the world understandingly and to react to it rationally instead of as a matter of prejudice and desire and caprice.

Education has nothing to do with mentality. Mentality remains the same kind of thing from the cradle to the grave, unless affected by intelligent medical intervention. It is unaffected by learning. But Intelligence is one of the chief outcomes of Education, one of the chief criteria by which we estimate the quality and extent of Education.

CONSCIENCE

All the way back into prehistory, some humans have been doing what they thought to be right without regard to hope of reward or fear of punishment. That I take it is the connotation of Conscience and its cognates.

We may define Conscience as sense of obligation without regard to the subject of obligation.

It arises out of experience in which common human nature is in contact with an external world which is also for the most part common. The mental process by which it arises appears to be not different from that which lies behind Intelligence, and indeed the whole body of the higher culture. We call it common sense. In the long run, variation and survival in the mores will thus yield an element in the quality of custom, and this element is what we mean by Conscience as defined above. Hence again, the rise of the subject matter of Conscience, namely, institutional morality. Conscience, like Intelligence, is a cultural trait.

The historian Lecky, in the prolonged chapter introductory to his *History of European Morals*, seems to take the view of Conscience thus set forth. Breasted, Egyptologist and historian of early culture, entitled one of his last publications *The Dawn of*

Conscience. His findings appear to be that Conscience is a cultural trait arising, like all such, out of social experience.

The contrary views have been two, in the main.

The most common, historically speaking, is what may be called the inward-monitor theory. In substance, I take it, the meaning is that each of us has a spiritual endowment, more or less acute—or even nonexistent—characteristic of him or her as individual, and called his or her conscience. The implication is, of course, that it is inborn, although not necessarily as part of the physical organism. It is parallel with intelligence as the early intelligence-testers conceived that term.

On the other hand is the holding of materialism in which individual conscience is in the nature of an instinct physiologically transmitted.

On the inward-monitor theory some individuals are "lost." On the biological theory they may be "moral imbeciles." On either theory there is no room for "character education" in the schools.

A phase of the biological doctrine is ancient indeed, and it bows to some great names of old. I mean the idea that Man is the "social animal" and even the "political animal." In truth, natural man is about as social as a puma. Consider any likely baby and judge for yourself. As political animal Man must belong to the same order as the polecat. True enough, the human organism makes it inevitable that the normal man will become social in some sense, and possible that he may become a statesman. Becoming is personal and education.

The tendency of medical men to invade fields for which their passports and warrants are insufficient has been a large factor in producing the doctrine of moral imbecility. It is undoubtedly true that real mental defectives are not likely to learn morality, or anything else; but that is far from justifying the contention that individuals are born with specific organic traits which make it impossible for them to become moral, while permitting them to become intelligent. It is true enough that some have temperamental traits which make it difficult for them to come to any sense of obligation, but that is not to say that the traits make it impossible. We further know that physical maladies may produce experience out of which are engendered abnormal personal traits, including moral traits; but it is a misuse of words to say that such traits or the consequences of such maladies are tantamount to imbecility.

TASTE

There may be Intelligence, but one's fitting into the scheme of things requires more than Intelligence. So the individual may be sanely conscientious, and yet a large part of Society lies outside of Conscience. Perhaps the best single word in English for summation of the characteristics of the civilized person is *Taste*. If that be true, then there is no Taste apart from Intelligence and Conscience, but the quality goes much farther. On the whole, since the beginning of things the Great Escapes have in the end taken the form of search for the Good, the Beautiful, the True. But there is always Good which is beyond moral goodness, and Truth which is beyond scientific truth.

The word is in common use, and its meaning, I take it, can be reduced pretty nearly to Sense of the Appropriate.

Even those who are but slenderly educated prize the quality as they understand it above all things. They may be ignorant and all but devoid of conscience, and yet you will hear men and women disapprove a course of action in the words, "I think it is in very bad taste." That explains, I suppose, the exceeding popularity of books on etiquette and the prestige of those writers who become arbiters of our elegancies—to our advantage no doubt. Most people dread being caught out in an infraction of good taste a great deal more than they dread infractions of the moral law or the reputation of ignorance.

But Taste is no more inborn than Intelligence and Conscience. It has to be learned as they have to be learned.

It is acquired in the first place through copying the behavior and sentiments of those whom we love and admire—parents, teachers, conspicuous members of the community. Herein is leadership which sets the standards. If leadership is composed of persons of inferior taste, then the rising generation will have little sense of the appropriate. If an alien and lower culture invades the community, then the rising generation will always tend to regress toward the lower level.

As normal and effective instruction goes on, the admirable in the culture of the race takes the place of the example and standards of the childhood group. We say that the individual is broadened.

Taste is not positive, whereas Intelligence fundamentally rests on the positive sciences; and Conscience on the emergent institutions of Morality. Taste comes rather out of immediate experience among human beings, or the vicarious experience extracted from books. It cannot be rationally or empirically derived, and yet it is knowledge in the same sense as that in which we have knowledge of the love of our dear ones. Not a dozen times in a long married life could either one of the pair produce evidence that would satisfy a logician or even a jury of the love of the other; and yet if they are happily married, each of them would be more certain of the love of the other than would either he or she be of the truth of the law of gravitation.

If it is true that Taste has no part in the methods which produce Intelligence, it is equally true that neither is Morality Taste, or Taste Morality. Over and over again we wrongly condemn practices which are offensive to our tastes as being immoral; and at least as often we rationalize our vices by wrapping them up in a web of sophistication and lifting them over into the domain of Taste—where they cannot be disputed.

So far as social integrity is concerned, Taste is probably fundamental to all else. In our ordinary associations we depend primarily on common expectations in matters of Taste. Therein is congeniality. Without it, cliques begin to form, dislikes become active and at times vindictive. In the end, rigid castes form in sheer self-protection.

Intelligence, Conscience, Taste—these are not institutions nor yet courses in a curriculum. They are rather symptomatic of the extent of Education in the person and of Civilization in the mores.

CHAPTER III

LANGUAGE

I N THE beginning was the Word." Civilization as we have studied it started its evolutionary journey in Language. If there is pain in consciousness, that is sensation and discomfort. If the victim says, "I am sick," he sets up a theory in Language and thus explains himself. He could not do so unless there were also in consciousness a generalized idea associated with the symbol "sick." The word is symbol of reality, and so Language can properly be called a "symbolic institution." Thus and thus alone can the sick man make himself intelligible to others. Intelligibility is in thought—not extended reflective thinking to be sure, but thought, a logic. Thus arises social experience out of which the Intelligence of the race emerges. The primitive in his imaginings can find ideas and words to stand for ideas, but there is no thought until he can utter a simple declarative sentence. When he can do that, he has set out on the road which leads to modern Science and Philosophy.

Ideas are the material of thought, but not thought itself. The latter does not appear until there are sentences and words expressive of relationships and qualities, that is to say, discourse. Anybody can test the truth of the statement by introspection. In reverie or contemplation, ideas follow one another in consciousness without thought; but as soon as one has a problem to think out, he tends to use unvoiced language. People sometimes say that they are "thinking aloud." That means that what is ordinarily unvoiced is in this case voiced. When we undertake to solve a problem of any considerable complexity, we seem to presume an audience. Thought is inescapably social in character and cultural in origin.

So it is that the individual who can handle an involved compound-complex sentence expressive of involved relationships is, other things being equal, at a higher level of intellect than is a person who cannot do so; but his intellect in this formal sense has been acquired through learning Language and practice with Language. There is no social value therein, however, save as others have been trained in their language up to the point at which they can share his language as thought. Therein is the real justification of Language in the Curriculum, and the vague notion that it is very useful to the individual is no justification at all.

It is almost universally assumed that our thoughts precede our language and that we learn to express them in language. The common notion seems to be that there is a ready-made dynamic entity called "mind" which secretes thought much as a gland secretes a hormone, and which learns to express the results of its thinking in various media, including Language. In the light of physiological and psychological investigation, over against the disclosures of social evolution, that view of mind is little better than animism. The mind is consciousness and certain adaptive processes which appear in consciousness and which make experience possible. That is about all we know about it, but we do know that. Thought evolves in the eternal process of variation and survival of fit forms, in the media of symbolisms. As we master the symbolisms, we enter into objective relations to the real environment in the thought or logic of the several institutions other than the symbolic institutions. We master thought, and awareness of thought is thinking. Thought is not mental but cultural. We do not learn how to think; we learn thought.

I. AS INSTITUTION

Language, an institution, is made possible by speech, an organic process in human beings. The normal infant learns to speak without being taught; in one form or another, he has to be taught his language, at least language which is above the level of crude dialect or patois If it were not for the fact that he lives in Society, he would not learn to speak at all, much less learn any language.

We have seen that Language evolves, as do all other institutions, through variation and survival of appropriate forms of expression. It becomes organized and refined and expanded, because it is inherently in the nature of Society itself as a body of relationships between individuals.

From Babylonian times at least, there is discernible a tendency to apply rational methods to an attempt to understand the structure of Language and thus more exactly to control its use. We call the result "Grammar." That step is long after the evolution of Language itself to institutional maturity, just as the discovery of organization in all the institutions, and formulation of the same, comes long after their emergence as cultural products.

When men had come to see that their language had a logic, and could understand and refine that logic through further experience, then was taken the essential step toward ease of transmission to oncoming generations. More than that, perhaps, came norms of order and coherency in thought-processes themselves, that is to say, straight thinking. Since Grammar is an account of the normal structure of the sentence, it is the beginning of Logic, which is concerned with discourse.

THE SPOKEN LANGUAGE

It must, however, be borne in mind that some sort of spoken discourse long antedated even the crude beginnings of written Language, and a long period still lay between that point and the emergence of the literary languages, that is to say, languages capable of being used for expression in the great Art of Literature. Even now, most people speak a dialect with little or no structure about it. Even those who speak a cultivated discourse ("speak like an educated person") employ in conversation a form of language which is different from the written language. In general, let anybody speak as he would write and the result seems stilted and pedantic—or is likely to.

Our children are children of the race; they learn their language as the race has learned it. The baby will learn any form as readily as he learns his mother-tongue. What they normally learn is literally the speech of the mother, for their early relationships are mostly with her. If the home uses altogether a spoken language which is in literary form, then the child will learn that. Coming along a near-by street, the other night, a couple of small children were playing on the sidewalk and in deep discussion about something—four or five years of age perhaps. One was heard to remark, "As one travels in other countries, and looking at it from that angle. . . . ." The rest was unhappily lost. Probably a professor's child. If the home uses a patois, then the child will do the same until association with cultivated adults, and more cultivated contemporaries, plus experience in the discourse of good writers, has brought about a more civilized usage.

The essence of Civilization is in the principle that in it are the universal common estimates and expectations; in the presence of advanced cultural accumulations, these can exist only on the basis of universal institutions in their refined stages. There is no other common denominator. Patois in the common speech comports only with a patois culture, and the modern cultural environment is far from patois. When one of the highly developed languages goes into regression, more or less social collapse occurs, for the reason that existing culture is based on Language in an advanced stage. Not much hope of lasting betterment in Society, if presumably educated individuals are incapable of either reading or listening to anything much beyond words of one syllable.

II. LANGUAGE IN THE CURRICULUM

That Language is an indefeasible element in the Curriculum of the Common School nobody seriously doubts. What Courses are implied is another matter, something to be investigated and argued. Nevertheless, the real justification of this element in the content of General Education is in the principle that it is a major, comprehensive, and universal institution and not that it is obviously useful. There is the same reason for teaching it that there is for teaching everything else which rightly enters into the Curriculum, and no better reason. It is primary, but otherwise no more essential. The Curriculum in English is in principle no different from that in any of the Indo-European and Semitic languages, in so far as they have well-developed literatures.

Applying the tests which we have already applied in seeking for the foundations of Civilization, and applying the doctrine of the Common School, it is not difficult to find the courses.

A. THE SPOKEN LANGUAGE

We have already noted that good spoken language is not likely to be bred into the persons of pupils didactically. The individual takes it on from example, as a matter of appreciation, in intercourse with people who do speak well. It is doubtless true that habits of grossly bad use must sometimes be broken up, even at the cost of minor inhibitions. In general, however, the influence of the school will appear in the example of cultivated speech in teachers, provided good discipline and the generation of cultural interests is breaking down native egoism.

Oral articulation.—Nevertheless, spoken language, as well as written language, is an instrument of communication and of thinking. Hence clarity of articulation and right pronunciation— especially the former—are of the essence of training. Harsh voices, mumbling, gabbling, are habits which singularly interfere with the institutional function of Language.

Now some of this is traceable to organic defect in the pupil, and that part is not remediable by pedagogical methods. Most of it is due to mere neglect and lack of language discipline. The only way to cure the fault is by making pupils aware of the necessity of clear speech and then unremittingly refusing to accept anything else.

Speech training.—There is evidently then justified the courses, or staff work, in speech training which we sometimes find. Since the requirement is universal, the course work should be universal. That does not mean, however, that it should necessarily apply to all pupils, for not all pupils need it. One does not chase a car if he is already comfortably seated therein.

Instruction in oral discourse.—In the presence of the cultural accumulations found in advanced communities, ability to arrange thought convincingly while addressing a neighbor or an audience, ability to "think on one's feet," is often of the essence of Language as institution. Only, the ability must be a product in education and not the artificial kind of thing which we sometimes see in the products of particular training. We see the latter in salesmen, all the way from the individual who "speaks his piece" in trying to locate an insurance policy on us to the nervous gymnastics of the boy who is selling magazines to "put himself through college." The term "rhetorician," carries an unhappy connotation for much the same reason perhaps.

Courses in "elocution," and in public speaking, are prone to produce an artificial effect, one which is felt to be artificial by people of sense. The heart of good speaking is in the fact that the speaker has something to say, that he knows what he is talking about, and has had experience enough in presenting a line of argument to generate the ability to do so without focal consciousness of his words.

Probably the best possible experience is found when pupils are habituated, from the early study periods in the beginning of the secondary school,[1] to standing on their feet and making competent oral recitations and reports in the various arts and sciences studied in school.

Hence, on the whole, there is neither need nor place for particular courses in this matter in the Common School.

B. READING

Obviously the primary content in the written Language is reading the written or printed page. That is the principal reason for calling the first functionally distinguishable school the "primary school."

By Reading as a Curriculum element we mean learning to read—only that and nothing more. We do not mean perfunctory scheduled exercises in reading which never come to anything save accidentally. Twenty-odd years ago, at least 25 per cent of the population of the United States was illiterate, so far as any effective use of reading is concerned, largely because they had spent their early days in schools in which there were classes in reading but none in teaching pupils to read.

Nor do we mean "improving ability in reading." We recognize

[1] Fourth grade and upward.

that reading goes on throughout the whole school and life-career and that pupils and students constantly learn to read new kinds of material. That does not, however, mean that new arts are learned. The application of the original art to new and broader sets of ideas is made possible not by "improving reading habits" but by taking on new ideational content in which to read.

Nobody ever effectively reads until he can look through the printed page to the ideas, or scenes, or movements, which form the subject matter, without focal consciousness of the words and other details of the language medium. It is convenient to call this attainment "reading at adaptation level."

C. WRITTEN EXPRESSION

Written expression begins with handwriting. If there should sometime be substituted for handwriting some mechanical medium, it would still be true that command of discourse expressed in visual symbols would begin with learning the manipulation of phonetic language in the new medium. For our purposes, we shall assume handwriting as we now know it.

1. *Handwriting.*—We need think of no separable course in Handwriting. The second of the three R's expands until at one end stands the pupil's struggles with letter forms and at the other end the mature person's command of written discourse.

Traditionally, handwriting has been penmanship, and the early stages have been preparatory to penmanship in some form or some degree and not to discourse-writing, which is one of the pupil's principal instruments in learning how to study and in completing his learning by reacting on what he has learned; that is to say, learning the thought or logic of the science which he is studying. Command of written expression is an art, and, like all arts, it is learned by doing. The common medium of expression is handwriting, and when handwriting is felt by the pupil to be a means of expressing ideas, then the learning is economical, genuine, and continuous. Hence handwriting is best learned, as is all written discourse, by practice in expressing ideas. The old copybooks, with their maxims to be copied, were in principle pedagogically sound.

This is not to say that legibility and facility are not desirable. The first is a matter of choosing good letter forms, good position at the desk, suitable pens and penholders, and in some pupils some degree of muscular drill; but these are as much a matter of training in written expression as is training in good use later on. Given the establishment of legibility in some cut-and-dried system of penmanship, in a course set apart for the subject, investigation shows over and over again that the learning product will lapse as mere lesson-learning, unless the pupil is required to use the best of which he is capable until the adaptation has formed. The latter is similar to adaptation level in reading; it is reached when the pupil writes as a matter of course without focal consciousness of the details of the writing. In the end, individual handwriting is what is implied by the individual's neuromuscular temperament. It is accordingly at maturity individuated and characteristic, but it still remains Handwriting.

Facility comes through practice.

Traditional admiration of the art of penmanship comes down to us from a time when true penmanship was a valued accomplishment for sundry vocational purposes. As such, even that value has largely disappeared on account of the universal use of typewriters. Something must be said as well for the control of schools through the Meddlesome-Matty theory of government. The typical school board could appreciate good penmanship, and that was about the only thing in the Curriculum that it could appreciate.

2. *Composition.*—Our traditional courses in the management of written discourse are: (1) a melange of grammar, usage, diction, and composition, called "language study" in the traditional elementary school; and (2) "composition," and sometimes "rhetoric," in the traditional high school.

Both of them, elementary- and high-school courses, are illy adapted, or not adapted at all, to the attainment of the major learning which is denoted by the expression "management of written discourse."

Here we have Composition as the name commonly used in

school practice. It is a poor term, for composition is but one side of the learning objective, the other side being diction. However, we shall use the common term.

Again, we still sometimes encounter the tradition brought down from the older university departments that written discourse falls into four principal forms—narration, description, exposition, and argumentation. So it does. As an inference, there arose the assumption that instruction in the high school ought to be centered on each of the four. Not so.

Narration and description belong to the literary craftsman; and to the Common Man, if at all, only as pleasing accomplishments. Neither professional study nor the mastery of pleasing accomplishments has any place in the Common School.

Argumentation is elementary Logic, and we shall come to Logic as a course in our study.

By far the greater part of our actual vital writing is exposition. More than that, if we recall that Language is thought, becoming able to develop the thread of explanatory discourse is training in thinking of the most practical and vital sort. Conversely, any adequate learning in any of the sciences is not only the emergence of new concepts, and chains of concepts which hold, but the actual, visible arrangement of such chains in discourse. It ought to be recalled that the real content of any science is its thought or logic and that the language of the science is its thought. So exposition in composition is both expression and impression. In so far, however, as the pupil learns the language of a science without clear apprehension of its ideational content in principles, he stereotypes the language.

Consequences of neglect.—In an extended career of dealing with graduate students and teachers, I have constantly been astonished at the inability of most of them to follow an argument. They are not convinced by argument—which by the way, they are apt to confuse with disputation—and I doubt that they have ever become aware that there is any such thing. They "like what you said" or "do not approve of what you said," but their mental content in either case tends to be affective and not rational. So it is apparently with the graduate public of which the students are probably rather better than a fair sample.

And yet I have frequently sat down with students, at least metaphorically, and taught them as I would teach high-school boys and girls. I do not recall an instance in which the effect was not one of raising the student to full intellectual status, at least so far as reading of science and the management of expository discourse are concerned.

So, when Composition is under discussion as an element in the Curriculum, exposition is in mind and that alone.

False leads.—The use of language is an art from the beginning; it has to be learned by doing. That principle at once rules out all such objectives as "How to accept an invitation," "How to write a business letter," "How to describe a football game," "How to tell of an outing." Such objectives are ruled out pedagogically, because the result will be artificial and spurious. They are ruled out institutionally in the Common School, because they are mere special accomplishments. If the educated pupil eventually joins the beau monde, which incidentally is not what is meant by "society," and wishes to find out how to acknowledge an invitation, he can doubtless find out how to do so. As to "business English," let us hope that he will become so far cultivated that he will never use it. As to the rest, if he cannot do what is needed, short of journalese, let him perish in his ignorance.

A single course.—Hence, there is but a single course in Composition, and that extends from the beginning of Handwriting to the competency characteristic of maturity. Its assimilative practice under supervision is always the expression of ideas, and practice is especially found in every course in which there is, or should be, writing to be done. Every teacher in such courses is of necessity a language teacher.

The practical objection at once arises, "How can a teacher of physics or chemistry or economics be also a teacher of language?" Thus the intellectual framework of departmentalized common schools. These teachers are employing some of the principles of the sciences in the instruction of pupils; they are not simply teaching physics, chemistry, and economics, as if the high school were a university. More than that, written discourse is one of the chief instruments of their teaching in science, for it is the one objective means of following the mind of the pupil. Finally, they have the material out of which discourse can be learned, and teachers of English language and literature have by comparison very little such material.

A different practical objection is in the remonstrance, "But our science teachers as a class are not competent writers themselves." That is unhappily true. The remonstrance is equivalent to a plea that illiterates should be allowed to teach. Nobody should be allowed to teach who is not an educated person, and an educated person writes well.

No doubt, even under the best of conditions, the administrative organization of schools should provide for the constructive supervision of all writing at the hands of those who are specifically occupied as teachers of the English language—or French, German, Scandinavian, Hebrew, or whatever is the language of the school.

D. USAGE

There is little social utility in written discourse, except there be certain valid canons touching composition and diction. The uncouth and the ignorant often speak compellingly without regard to style, but their discourse is seldom written unless it be deliberately so for its humorous content. It is not civilized discourse, nor is it capable of carrying the burden of sustained exposition—not civilized indeed for that very reason. The thought is simple and obvious, while the thought in the sustained discourse employed by the educated is far from simple and obvious; otherwise, it would not need to be written. Apart from the accepted canons of elementary style, there would be no common expectation between the writer and his reader.

Hence, in the evolution of discourse in the race, all the literary languages have developed common usages which on our principles are right usage and not mere convention. There are common usages in diction, including right use of words and spelling; devices for carrying thought in oral discourse over into written expression, and we call them punctuation; other devices in diction for making possible particular significance in words, and we call these capitalization. Perhaps it is not too much to say that the institutional function of usage is in the main to make possible in written discourse what is achieved in oral language through visible movement of the lips, facial expression, gesture, intonation, emphasis.

It is doubtless true that, given time enough under effective supervision and discipline, the pupil would arrive at good usage as the race has done, but the obstacle to that in practice is in the principle that, like other manifestations of laissez faire instruction, it would take a lifetime. Hence a systematic, organized course is called for.

The *Course in Usage* is set up to cover:

1. *The art of punctuation.*—Punctuation is an art and not a science. Save for certain conventions to mark off quotations, and quasi-quotations which are felt as such, and the kind of statement intended, punctuation is merely a phonetic device for carrying over into written discourse the pauses in articulation which we make impulsively in spoken discourse in order to make our meaning clear. Note how you would say it, and putting in commas and semicolons where you would naturally pause is a good rule. That would cover even the restrictive relative clause, which we always utter without the comma, phrases out of place, and all the rest. When the pupil has come to *feel* that, he has mastered the single unit of the course. Beyond that is skill and judgment which come from practice in writing. Save for the few conventions mentioned, easily memorized, there are few set rules for the use of comma, hyphen, dash, semicolon, and colon. Several generations of pupils have been bewildered by such rules. I suppose that most authors have been exasperated by editorial offices which rely on manuals when the former read their statements repunctuated and recapitalized until they mean what was never intended.

2. *Capitalization.*—Much the same observations apply to capitalization. Save for certain conventions agreed upon, the writer

comes to feel the use of capitals to express his exact meaning and to sense a similar use in what he reads.

3. *Sentence sense.*—Perhaps the most critical element in the usage course is the development of feeling for the integrity of a sentence, especially an involved sentence.

Pupils in the early stages of writing seem to have no difficulty here, as schools now are, for they write simple sentences, and usually each sentence is to them a paragraph. It follows, at least in my own observation and experience, that in early adolescence their composition is apt to suffer a slump. The phenomenon is probably due to the fact that by that time ideational content has expanded to the point at which complex sentences are needed, and the pupils do not know how to use them. Hence, they fall into the vice of the "run-on" sentence, and that proves to be a nuisance all the way up into the university. The result is of course confusion in composition and hence confusion in thought.

4. *Sundry elements in usage.*—I employ this expression to cover perhaps seventy or eighty common errors which the papers of pupils reveal, and which run all the way from bad use of partitives to awkward phrase and sentence structure. These have to be listed by the teachers in the particular school, the right use systematically taught, and the list handed over to teachers in all subject departments who handle written papers. Of necessity, most of the teaching has to be in the nature of individual tuition; and yet every school will show *types of errors* enough to make teaching units out of the types and do class teaching in them. It is of no use whatever to make up an artificial list theoretically derived, or to buy one ready made in a schoolbook. The list must grow out of the characteristic errors found in a particular school. Here the list may include about all the common errors and some original contributions; there the list may be short and not much teaching required.

5. *Use of manual and dictionary.*—In "language" or "composition" or "rhetoric" courses, it has long been the practice in our schoolbook-ridden country to make a text the course and lesson-learn it. Of course the result is spurious learning, save by chance

in the cases of a few pupils, since there is no discourse of the pupil's own into which the precepts can be bred. Be it remembered that discourse is personal in the individual from the time at which the infant begins to formulate speech to that at which the youth acquires command of his own discourse.

And yet recourse to a manual or manuals as suitable reference material is indispensable to the careful writer, whether he be layman or professional. But pupils must be inducted. Hence an important part of the course in Usage is making the pupil familiar with simple and illuminating manuals, and an important part of his training in Composition is the requirement that he shall use his manual as ready reference when such use is indicated.

So it is with the dictionary. If such use is not checked as part of the regular routine, pupils learn it but incidentally, and in considerable numbers escape with no knowledge at all. The latter do not know how to use the most common of ready-reference books.

Since the "alphabet method" in the teaching of reading became obsolete, pupils will sometimes appear a long way up in school with but a vague and uncertain command of the alphabet itself, particularly in respect to the sequence of letters. We know that most pupils do learn the alphabet incidentally, but this is the place to check up and make sure that they have learned.

Beyond that is the technology of diacritical marks and phonetic values of letters, pronunciation of unfamiliar words, the reading of the meaning of words.

6. *Right use of words.*—Properly speaking, right use of words is a matter of Usage, but pedagogically only a small part of the field can be covered in a systematic course. Save for a comparatively small number of words commonly misused, like "quite," "transpire," "infer" (when "imply" is meant), which indeed can be emphasized in a Usage course, this aspect of diction as a course would require something like learning a dictionary, and even then the instruction would be futile for the same reason that learning a textbook in Usage is always futile. Common misuse is not peculiar individual misuse, and pupils will misuse words in all sorts of curious ways.

Hence, the right use of words is a matter of slow growth under steady discipline whenever and wherever papers are taken up, and of steady inculcation in the use of the dictionary. As pupils emerge into the high-school and junior-college levels, unremitting attention to the tendency to use verbal stereotypes is called for.

Words are symbols of ideas; they are not thought as the sentence is thought. It is easy to fall in love with a word irrespective of the idea behind the word, and indeed irrespective of any idea at all. This is verbal stereotypy, a survival, I suppose, of the tendency which once appeared as fetish worship. When the individual acquires facility in stereotypy, as some do, it is amazing to see what an appearance of meaning can be set up when in reality there is no meaning at all. Jargon is stereotypy. Among the famous stereotypes of history are "glory," "patriotism," "equality," "democracy" (indeed in our stereotyping of this term, we bid fair to lose the reality altogether), "liberal," "tolerance," "possessive." All this is particularly apt to be true of pupils and college students—and not a few teachers—who have acquired a smattering of academic sociology, psychology, and education treated as an academic subject.

E. SPELLING

Spelling and Handwriting have been the two most abused of all the schoolroom subjects. The reason is not far to seek. They are visible and tangible. The vociferous untutored in the community are apt to discover in them their only possible scholastic interest and to cherish the ineradicable conviction that they are the touchstone of all culture. Hence the unfailing popularity of the schoolmaster who will inaugurate spelling contests, the prize-winner in which is a youth who has spelled correctly words which he never uses in his own discourse, never did use, and probably never will use. And yet some of our greatest literary artists were never able to spell with any degree of confidence.

Nevertheless, spelling is diction, and right spelling is of the essence of Language in Civilization. It is a form of common expectation.

Forty years ago, or thereabout, publicists became aware of the abuse of the old-time spelling-book and exposed its futility. With the easygoing disregard of logical inferences which has characterized so much of the prevailing philosophy of education, it was concluded that the teaching of spelling was superfluous, and thus an impetus was given to general laissez faire in all instruction. Happily the episode, or series of episodes, stimulated impartial scientific study—indeed it was one of the earlier points of departure in the whole scientific movement—and now the pedagogy of spelling rests upon as secure bases as any to be found in the schoolroom.

A systematic course in spelling is implied in which the unit is spelling sense, or the ability to sense the probable spelling of even unfamiliar words. The method is systematic drill in the spelling of words which are in the use vocabulary of pupils. Those of us who spell correctly with some degree of confidence were taught the spelling of only a small part of the words which we habitually use, but when we were children we learned to spell the words which we used, and in so doing we learned to spell, the nonsystematic and nonphonetic character of much of the spelling of English words to the contrary notwithstanding. Those of use who are at all advanced in years suffered a waste of time and energy by learning the spelling of words which were not in our use vocabulary at the time.

F. GRAMMAR

We have already seen the functional utility of Grammar and its place in the institution of Language. Grammar is not Logic, the science of valid thinking, but it is, pedagogically speaking, one of the two primary introductions to Logic which the pupil encounters. The other is right use of words. When Language had so far advanced in evolution that it was capable of being put together in continuous discourse, a systematic structure was implicated. That meant that its structure could be understood and formulated into a set of principles capable of being learned and transmitted. Doubtless the essential principles could be and were learned empirically in use, just as early Mathematics and Me-

chanics were learned; but Civilization began to advance rapidly
when empirical products were rationalized into thought systems,
partly because ordered Language was thus the more easily transmitted, and partly because thought could thus be more accurately
shared. Upon this last hangs the social significance and importance of Grammar. We should think it strange if it were proposed
to go back to the intuitive Arithmetic and Mechanics of the Egyptians. It is equally absurd to abandon the science of the sentence.

The weakening of Grammar as a regular school discipline was
no doubt in part due to the pedagogical laxity which arose out of
educational laissez faire at about the turn of the century. Moreover, when those who rested their case for Grammar on the dogma
of mental training lost faith in the dogma, they were left without
any case at all. Finally, the books supplied to pupils in the Civil
War period and later covered pretty much the whole scope of
Language as Language was understood. I well recall my own beginnings in the early eighties, when I had to commit to memory
the outline of Grammar, which was said to consist of pronunciation, orthography, etymology, syntax, and prosody—very much
as it might have been in the days of the Roman Republic. So far
as the actual course in Grammar went, I was taught syntax, and
I am profoundly grateful that I was taught that much thoroughly
and effectively.

Altogether, Grammar as taught was due for the attention of the
"liberalizing influences" of the nineties and early 1900's—and the
heart of the subject was liberalized out of existence.

The important part of Grammar is syntax, the structure of the
sentence, and what that implies in parts of speech; in gender,
number, person and case; in tense, mood, and forms of the verb.

G. LOGIC

Expository discourse is thought. So is Mathematics. So, in
their fields, are Physics, Chemistry, Biology, Economics, Law,
and all organized Science. But Logic, or at least practical Logic,
is the science of valid argument—of straight thinking in general—
or, still better, the corrective of false thinking. No doubt the

higher Logic is a branch of systematic philosophy and hence a unversity subject. There remains, however, the elementary Logic which deals with the sequence of argument and proof; with the two main branches of systematic thinking, the inductive and the deductive methods, and the limitations of each; with the common fallacies. I do not mean here Psychology masquerading as Logic, nor yet Epistemology or the theory of knowledge.

Besides the meaning thus attached to the term, we often also use "logic" as practically synonymous with "thought," as the way in which a body of ideas is put together. Thus we speak of the logic of Physics, and that is substantially synonymous with "Pure Physics," the logic of Commerce, or the logic of Education. We mean that there is something understandable about these branches of experience, that in them is part of the order of the universe.

Time was when the subject was taught in the secondary school, but it seems to have disappeared in favor of the intensely practical purpose of getting the offspring of the post–Civil War prosperity into college and into business. The leaders who might have led sanely were mostly dead or incapacitated. Perhaps if the secondary school of that period had maintained and improved its course, and the two generations of schoolmasters who have succeeded had persevered, by this time logical coherency might have been bred into the mores, and we might have been free from the charming insouciance which characterizes most of our present thought touching matters of public concern, not to say matters of scientific concern.

Logic as thus considered is pre-eminently of the Common School; it is but common sense refined, extended, and disciplined until it is capable of carrying the burden of a complex society resulting from an involved culture. Thinking logically is of necessity one of the critical marks of the educated person who has arrived at personal maturity. People seldom show the characteristic, not even those who hold college degrees. They constantly fall into the fallacies of thinking which have been identified as fallacies since the time of Socrates at the shortest. It is a rare individual, even among scientific men outside their own particular bailiwicks, who does not, for instance, fall into the most common of all fallacies by reasoning that because one event has happened after another the second in order of occurrence is caused by the first. Governments still fall with great regularity because the administration in power happened to be in power when a great natural calamity occurred.

Scarcely any student of public instruction would deny that the "scientific attitude" or the "positive attitude" is of primary importance as a trait in civilized, educated, man; and yet the scientific attitude never arises automatically out of the study of Science. When it does arise, it is a learning product in Logic, whether it originated in a systematic course in Logic, or was inculcated by some teacher who taught it as a specific objective, or appeared in the pupil by chance. It is by analysis, first of all, in the moral quality of Veracity. Second, it is awareness that nobody has a right to the expression of opinion unless he presumably knows what he is talking about. Third, it is a realization that the world is put together on rational grounds and that intellectual conviction ought to rest not only on principles clearly understood but on the compelling coherency of many principles, as thinking moves on in a chain of ratiocination.

Most people's convictions seem to be formed out of sheer dogmatic authority external to themselves; or out of slogans, "build-ups," and "smears"; or out of mere surmise, or out of fancy which is not even reputable surmise; or, probably most of all, out of prejudice, desire, or self-will. All this contributes to the anarchistic element to which democracy is prone. The people whose thinking runs in such channels lack, not mentality, but discipline in Logic.

Instruction.—It is as hard to imagine a good high-school or junior-college course in Logic without a textbook containing abundant exercises for practice as it would be to imagine a course in Algebra without printed matter to serve as study material. Even approximately good texts are hard to find. They tend to include many chapters on formal Logic which is out of place in an elementary course, or else the authors seem to be unable to distinguish between Logic and Psychology. I have examined all the texts I could get hold of, and I venture to suggest the following as seeming to come nearest to what the instructional situation requires:

1. *Beginners' Logic.* By Roy H. Dotterer. New York: Macmillan Co., 1924.
2. *The Principles of Logic.* By H. A. Aikins. New York: Henry Holt & Co., 1902.
3. *Elementary Lessons in Logic.* By W. Stanley Jevons. New York: Macmillan Co., 1891.
4. *Textbook of Logic.* By H. E. Cunningham. New York: Macmillan Co., 1924.

III. FOREIGN LANGUAGES IN THE COMMON SCHOOL

The final issue hangs upon the place of foreign languages in the Curriculum as essential to Language. School tradition says, "perhaps not essential but desirable." Earlier tradition said, "essential so far as Greek and Latin are concerned; these are the 'marks of an educated gentleman.' " Is tradition a valid criterion in this instance?

In the first place, our whole theory of education as based upon structural elements in civilized personality[2] leads to the conclusion that nothing in the Curriculum of the Common School is desirable which is not essential. The list of subjectively desirable things is endless. The legitimate function of the School as institution is to make the whole horizon of independent individual learnings possible, but not to teach everything. Moreover, if the major and universal institutions are the Curriculum, then nothing finds its way into the school which has not a major demonstrable social utility.

GREEK AND LATIN

As we have already seen,[3] prior to the time in our European background at which the modern European languages had evolved out of barbarous tongues and begun to accumulate national literatures, in science as well as in belles-lettres, Greek

[2] See my *Basic Principles in Education* (Boston: Houghton Mifflin Co., 1934), chap. viii.
[3] P. 23.

and Latin had not only important but essential social utility. More than that, the polish of the humanistic element in the Renaissance exalted Greek, and during the nineteenth century there sprang up a veritable cult of all things Greek—which, by the way, gave rise to a jargon all its own. Periodically, that cult is revived. The story for Latin was somewhat different, for Latin down to the end of the seventeenth century was the vernacular of science.

There never has been a time in our own national history in which the teaching of Greek and Latin as common-school instruction in Language was anything more than practicing upon the bones of a dead-and-gone humanism—save in the case of the extremely rare and cultivated teacher.

Values claimed.—It is inevitable, however, that the defenders of subject matter which has been under fire for so long would discover about all the instructional values that can be claimed for it; and it is worth while to review some of the claims.

A generation ago and earlier, the claim most often heard—apart from the "gentlemen's-education" claim—was that founded on some variant of mental discipline, sharpening the wits. Advances in educational psychology have so far discredited the whole theory of mental discipline—as distinguished from volitional and intellectual discipline—that the claim is seldom heard any more.

Next in order, probably, would come the claim that the study of Greek and Latin, and especially Latin, is an invaluable training in Language as institution. The large element of Latin in English, Latin as the parent-stock of the Romance languages, the severely grammatical form of the ancient tongues—all these are urged with force. On our principles the claim is just, at least for the English-speaking and Romance countries. Nevertheless, the issue of relative value comes in. If we make a dispassionate analysis of the language learnings which will accrue in four to six years in Latin—and less is scarcely worth the while—as set over against similar language learnings to be obtained from adequate instruction in any one of the European vernaculars, the supplementary results from Greek or Latin or both are far within the region of diminishing returns. That is to say, the additional value is not worth the time and effort.

Finally, the claim is sometimes urged that such intimate contact with the brilliant period in the evolution of Civilization which ran from about 500 B.C. to perhaps A.D. 200, as is made possible by familiarity with the thought of the ancients in their veritable language, is a most valuable part of the education of the modern man. The contention is undoubtedly sound, provided: (1) that pupils ever actually learn to read Latin and Greek, and the number who do so is negligible; and (2) that there is nothing else in the way of subject matter which has paramount claims.

But, granted that the claim has merit, the substantial results are much more readily attained through modern translations of the ancient classics, some of which for literary merit are comparable with the originals. That approach is indubitably part of instruction in Literature.

As university subjects.—In recent years there has been a notable increase in college courses in "beginning Latin." No doubt, thus far the movement is chiefly an instance of the secondary school in the university, but it points in the right direction. The University as institution is: (1) education in the professions, as distinguished from semiprofessions and crafts; (2) the systematic production of new knowledge and refinement of old knowledge; (3) the higher pursuit of culture for its own sake. Ancient languages, not merely Greek and Latin, qualify under all three heads. Nevertheless, while Language is used in the School as part of the development of personal character, in the university it is cultural pursuit for persons who are already presumably educated. There is no reason why Greek and Latin should not flourish in our universities as richly as they ever did anywhere—and indeed much more richly and vitally. Only, the traditional pedagogy will need to be modified in favor of one which will rapidly put students in possession of reading ability.

The arguments touching the use of the ancient languages in the Common School apply in the main to modern languages as well. In respect to Language as institution, there is probably less justification for them than for the ancient languages. As media for Literature, there is more justification.

Taking the Western world as a whole, French had prestige because in the eighteenth century it was the international language of the cultivated, just as English is today to a great extent the international language of Commerce. With us, French trickled down from the colleges of the nineteenth century as so much else did. It appeared in the colleges of the period under the influence of some accomplished gentlemen who were trying to wrench us out of our national provincialism, just as did German and Italian and Spanish for the same reason—and then it became the fateful college-entrance credit. Moreover, some of the old prestige was still left—and a good many were really interested. These professors, however, were not "teaching French"; they were rather using French in order to put students in contact with great literature. And so with college German and Italian.

In the case of German, there was an additional force at work, so far as the Common School was concerned, in the influence of the Germanic element in our population. For much the same reason, mercurial groups of Irishmen occasionally endeavor to revive Celtic. I do not recall any dramatic episode in our contacts with Spanish America which has failed to arouse a wave of high-school teaching of Spanish. Still, all in all, French and German have been our traditional modern languages in high school—and there is no reason which justifies either of them which does not equally well justify Italian and Scandinavian as well as Spanish.

The social utility of any other language than the vernacular in the Common School is small indeed. The utility arises in countries in which two or more languages are so far in common use that street signs, advertisements, and similar warnings have to be printed in more than one language, where there are about as many newspapers in one tongue as in the other or others, and especially where the vernacular is not the official language or yet a civilized tongue.

External learning.—Command of one or several foreign languages is often a matter of great individual utility. One desires to travel, to use foreign language vocationally, to become familiar with it or them as a matter of cultural interest. But these are all individual utilities, and that on our principles rules them out of the Common School. There is no social utility in trying to make the population polyglot, even if it were thought that it could be done. Hence the individual ought to look to private teaching for his instruction. Private teaching would probably come under the influence of supply and demand, and the results would in time be vastly better than is now the case in public schools. At present, the proportion of pupils who ever learn to read or speak a foreign language, after three years of study, is so small as to be negligible. If one desired command of French or Italian or German, and had to pay for it, he would be likely to claim shortage on a teacher who did not fulfil his contract.

As university subjects.—In recent years our colleges have sometimes followed the same course with modern languages as with ancient languages, that is to say, they have set up primary instruction. That is a legitimate university enterprise, where students desire to devote themselves to the pursuit of foreign literature and culture; provided, however, a systematic pedagogy is organized, such as has, for example, been done at the University of Chicago.

Otherwise, students who are sufficiently educated to be of right in a university at all, are fully capable of learning at least the European languages for themselves as their intellectual pursuits require. Indeed, eminent professors have long required their students to do just that.

But after all, the practical problem is a matter of economy. In this volume we are raising no questions touching the amount of time required. If it can be shown that subject matter is indeed an essential part of the transmission of an institution, is in truth a part of the content of General Education, then we are not con-

cerned with the amount of time it will require. We are attempting
to find a description of the Curriculum. Time requirements then
become problems to be solved in teaching and school organization.

Nevertheless, we are interested, when we seem to have shown
that a particular subject matter is no part of the content of
General Education, to point out the wasteful consequences of
teaching it. Now the typical pupil program in foreign languages
is still four course-years in Latin and three in a modern language.
There are commonly not exceeding sixteen course-years in a four-
year high-school program. Hence, such a pupil devotes nearly
one-half his high-school career to foreign language—and even
then actually learns a language in but a negligible number of instances. Thus the all-important social sciences and the foundations of modern machine culture are excluded. Such pupils are not
likely to become intelligent and useful members of the community, save by the chance that some other influence than the
school has operated in that direction.

IV. STANDARD PROGRAM OF STUDIES IN LANGUAGE

The Curriculum is the content of instruction without reference
to instructional ways and means. When we enter the field of systematic instruction, we first encounter the arrangement of a Program designed to achieve the content of the Curriculum under effective teaching. This section is entitled "Standard Program" in
Language. That means that it is the program suggested where
conditions are what they should be everywhere. In Language and
other parts of the Curriculum, it often happens that, on account of
various conditioning factors in the particular school, a school program designed to come as nearly as possible to the attainment of
the Curriculum objectives must be set up. Finally, many pupils
must have special programs designed to fit them as nearly as possible into progress toward the objectives. These are pupil programs. The whole matter is dealt with in the closing chapter, but
here we ask ourselves what sort of a picture would a Standard
Program in Language present. There are two good reasons for

doing so. First, the Language program is the most complex of all; and, second, it will serve as introduction to and explanation of the Unit Organizations which will be found in nearly all the courses.

It will be noted that three types of courses are presented:

a) *Set courses*, the kind, I suppose, most of us are familiar with. Grammar and Spelling are illustrations.

b) Courses which in the main are *part of the learning process in other courses*. Composition and a large part of Usage are the best illustrations.

c) Courses which are *disciplinary in character*, that is to say, courses which call for continuous constraint until a whole volitional attitude is established. In the nature of the case, the learning process in all language courses is disciplinary, in the sense that even after he has taken on the principles the immature pupil has to be required to practice them up to the point at which he becomes mature in the possession of good established habits.

SET COURSES

    I. Reading as primary school art

   II. Handwriting as primary school art, but treated also as introduction to Composition

 III. Speech Training for such pupils as reveal the need; sometimes the need goes to the extent of special corrective training as in the case of stammering

  IV. Spelling

   V. Usage

  VI. Grammar

 VII. Logic

COURSES IN OTHER COURSES

VIII. Composition growing out of Handwriting, which is a set course

  IX. Oral Discourse

   X. Right Use of Words

  XI. Logical Arrangement of Composition as a Whole—in science courses

DISCIPLINARY COURSES

 XII. Speech Training as applied to the correction of mumbling, gabbling, and similar bad habits

XIII. Right Discourse—usage, spelling, handwriting, wherever written papers are accepted

XIV. Straight Thinking, wherever in the latter Common School argumentation is presented

THE UNIT PRINCIPLE[4]

The unit principle implies that there is *something* in every course *to be taught* and *to be learned*. It contrasts with assigning and hearing lessons *about topics*. The art of Reading, for example, is a definite ability to be learned.

The principle itself applies to everything that can be taught, directly or indirectly; but the character or psychological quality of units to be learned differs from type to type as the types have been explained in the work above cited. In Language the unit is of a particular type which has been designated "language arts." While a course in Science or in one of the institutional arts will normally have several units, a language course never has more than one unit, one definite art to be mastered. The pupil learns to read, or he learns to write in grammatical form, or he acquires spelling sense, or he learns to manipulate word symbolic forms in an art which has the characteristics of handwriting, etc. Two courses in Language, however, are not language arts but rather sciences. They are Grammar and Logic. Each of them has several units.

A course is not an allotment of time.—It follows that a course is never an allotment of time, as is always the case where the topical organization is followed and still more so when there is no topic, but only pages in a schoolbook. In the latter case, it inevitably comes to pass that progress is estimated not by what a pupil has learned but by the time he has spent in learning *about* some topic, or in reciting textbook assignments to the teacher. Indeed the latter procedure is euphemistic of what actually comes to happen: in the end, there is no recitation but only questions by the teacher and answers by the pupils, and finally both questions and answers by the teacher.

In systematic teaching, where units to be learned are set up,

---

[4] See also the writer's *The Practice of Teaching in the Secondary School* (rev. ed.; Chicago: University of Chicago Press, 1931).

the teaching and learning time is not in the picture, but the thing to be mastered. Reading, for instance, is the first set course taught. Under skilful teaching, the learning process may require from less than one to perhaps three years, depending upon the mentality and upbringing of the pupil; but when the art is learned, it is the same art for the bright and the dull, for those who have learned in one year and those who have needed three. So it is with Handwriting. Spelling under diligent and skilful teaching may require six or seven years, but in the end spelling sense has been developed. Usage, on the contrary, will probably continue well into the high-school period, following the ideational development of the pupil.

Composition, on the other hand, will begin with Handwriting and will continue to actual maturity, normally somewhere in the junior college, for, since composition is thought, and thought is the heart of the educational process, established competency in Composition is one of the best symptoms of approaching maturity. When the pupil in his unsupervised writing writes as an educated person writes, he is nearing graduation time—graduation from the junior college as schools now are. We compare his writing with that of persons judged on other grounds to be educated. Of course, this is not the only test of maturity, even if it be the most penetrating. The pupil must have acquired the content in Intelligence and Taste presumed to arise out of the Arts and Sciences, out of Civics and Commerce and Industry and Health; and the established, or at least well-grounded, Conscience derived from discipline in the Moral Institutions.

The heart of the matter is that Composition cannot be a course running for a year or a half-year: in its nature, it follows the pupil's whole scholastic career.

Until we reach Grammar then, each language course is a single unit, in the nature of an art or an ability to be acquired and established.

UNITS IN GRAMMAR

Let us remind ourselves once more that we do not teach Grammar for the sake of good usage in speaking and writing. Usage is art and Grammar is science. The Curricular significance of

Grammar is that it is capable of breeding into personality intelligence touching the discourse used by civilized men and women. In the end, we teach Grammar because Language is thought, and Grammar is Language made normative. It is pre-eminently intellectual discipline, but not mental discipline.

Each of the several units suggested below is a crucial understanding to be taken on, and as such, an accretion to the pupil's intelligence. No one of the items thus set up is a topic for consideration in a limited time, but rather an understanding to be lived with and assimilated.

As is true of most science-type units, each unit in grammar shows an element organization. That does not mean that the unit title is a classificatory word covering a group of things to be taught, but rather that the elements are essential constituents of the unit itself. The unit is grasped by grasping the elements. For example, the unit, "The Noun." To understand common and proper nouns, case, number, and gender, is to understand the Noun.

THE UNITS IN GRAMMAR

I. The Simple Declarative Sentence
   1. Why declarative?
   2. Subject and predicate
   3. Noun, adjective, or pronoun in the predicate
   4. Direct and indirect object

II. Compound and Complex Sentences
   1. Clauses co-ordinate and subordinate
   2. Conjunctions
   3. Relative pronoun as connective
   4. Antecedent in subordinate clauses

III. The Noun
   1. Common and proper
   2. Number
   3. Gender
   4. Case
      (Because English has no inflected noun, save the vestiges found in the possessive, it is sometimes held that there is no occasion to study case in nouns. I hold this to be wrong. The function of a noun in the sentence makes its case. The fact that inflected forms appear in some languages does not make case.)

IV. The Pronoun
    1. Use in the sentence
    2. Kinds of pronouns, and pronominal forms
    3. Particular use of the relative as connective
    4. Antecedent in both personal and relative
    5. Case, number, person, and gender
 V. Adjectives and Adverbs as Qualifying Words
    1. Use in the sentence
    2. Contrasted
    3. Adjective and adverbial phrases and modifiers
    4. Comparison
VI. Conjunctions
    1. Use in the sentence
    2. Co-ordinate and subordinate
VII. Prepositions
    1. Contrast with conjunctions
    2. The prepositional phrase
    3. The base of prepositional phrase
    4. Case of the base
    5. Prepositional phrases as modifiers
VIII. The Verb
    1. Active and passive
    2. Transitive and intransitive
    3. Subjunctive, infinitive, and participial constructions
    4. Verb phrases
    5. Tense and tense forms
    6. Principal parts
    7. Auxiliary
IX. Agreement
    1. In number, gender, person, and case
    2. Pronouns, either personal or relative with antecedent
    3. Reason for agreement
 X. Phrases and Clauses as Modifiers
 XI. Phrases and Clauses as Substantives
XII. Parts of Speech Functionally Considered

To learn the parts of speech and to learn to identify them is of little intellectual account. Still it is useful even to memorize the names securely. That is traditionally done first. Here it is suggested that it be done last, after the pupil has long been familiar with the names and qualities.

The unit learning, however, is the perception that function determines definition, that a particular word may be by definition any part of speech, and still become noun, adjective, adverb—and even other part of speech, depending upon the use in a particular sentence.

UNITS IN LOGIC

Logic is but common sense refined and systematized. Indeed, some people who are well-nigh innocent of schooling, and who never so much as heard the word "logic," will often in the field of their experience reason with excellent logical coherency, especially when out of the discipline administered by the elders or won in the hard experience of life, they have sloughed off their native egoism and have taken on the fundamental volitional learnings. Nevertheless, in the extremely complex society found in advanced Civilization, untutored intellect does not suffice; a systematic course in Logic is indicated for all. In the school framework as we know it, such a course belongs in the secondary period at some time before the end of junior college, before age twenty-one if we are to continue to confer the franchise at that age.

In formulating the units which appear below, I have leaned heavily on the works mentioned on page 53, and especially on that of Dotterer, which appeals to me for its teaching arrangement; but that does not mean that the authors named are in any sense responsible for what I have done. Beyond these works, and many others as well, I have tried to raise in my own mind the elementary logical issues which appear in the daily life, as we see it in the thought of books and newspapers, in the conversation of our contemporaries, and especially the issues which have appeared in a considerable experience in teaching advanced students in a university. I have eliminated, so far as seemed to me safe, purely technical considerations, especially the whole body of symbolic logic.

The practical end to be served by universal instruction in Logic in the secondary period of the Common School is the final elimination of the monstrous fallacies commonly found in popular thinking, and which form the stock in trade of demagogues, charlatans, and propagandists. If the individual were perfectly schooled in Language and Logic, there would be no occasion for a consideration of fallacies by themselves. There would be no fallacies. It is, however, a help to have before us the most common fallacies, as students through the ages have detected them, listed them and named them, in their contemplation of the human intellectual comedy.

Extended comment on the units is unnecessary. The remarks on the unit principle as applied to the teaching of Grammar have equal force here. In one instance we find a true topic listed and that is not a unit; the heading "fallacies" is the title of a topic, the name for a collection of units. Each of the latter is simple and elementary, but each is a true unit.

THE UNITS IN LOGIC

I. Logic as the Science of Valid Argument
   1. Normative as distinguished from factual and descriptive science
   2. Validity as trustworthy form of reasoning

II. Primary Terminology of Logic
   1. Meaning and importance of *term* in reasoning
   2. Denotation and connotation of terms
   3. Proposition
   4. Judgment
   5. Premise and conclusion
   6. Collective and distributive
   7. Abstract and concrete

III. Immediate Inference
   1. Meaning
   2. Contraries and contradictories
   3. Subalterns
   4. Opposition
   5. Obversion
   6. Conversion and contraposition

IV. Mediate Inference
   1. Meaning
   2. The syllogism—categorical, hypothetical, disjunctive
   3. The categorical syllogism
      a) Four figures
      b) Middle term
      c) Reduction to hypothetical form
      d) Universally in premises

V. Ambiguity and Definition
    1. Exact meaning of words in the sense intended by the proponent
    2. Definition
    3. Characteristics of a good definition
    4. Definition and description

VI. Hypothesis
    1. Search for truth in particular propositions
    2. Reasonable inference from known facts—working hypothesis
    3. Contrast: fancy, suspicion, conjecture
    4. Circumstantial evidence
    5. Multiple hypothesis
    6. Test by implications—especially *reductio ad absurdum*
    7. Law of parsimony

VII. Induction
    1. Induction and deduction
    2. Mutuality of the two in the search for truth
    3. A priori reasoning
    4. Induction by simple enumeration
    5. Induction from fair sampling
    6. Mill's canons
    7. Experimental verification

VIII. Analogy and Classification
    1. Analogical reasoning
    2. Pitfalls
    3. Classification
    4. Extension and intension
    5. Genus and species
    6. Definition in terms of classification

IX. Fallacies
    1. Formal and material fallacies
    2. Ambigious middle
    3. Accident—"indicting a nation"
    4. Division
    5. Composition
    6. Relative terms
    7. Hypostatization—one of the two worst—verbal fetish—substituting the form for the substance—the particular for the general—the instrument for the purpose—the accident for the substance
    8. *Petitio principii*—begging the question
    9. *Ignoratio elenchi*—avoiding the issue—argumentative craft
      a) Argumentum ad hominem—"personalities"

    b) *Argumentum ad populum*—playing to the gallery
    c) *Argumentum ad verecundiam*—sentimentality; sob stuff
    d) *Argumentum ad ignorantiam*—what cannot be disproved must be true
    e) *Argumentum ad baculum*—bulldozing, the favorite device of disreputable lawyers
10. Complex question—Have you stopped beating your wife?
11. Neglected aspect—did not take all into account
12. *Post hoc, ergo propter hoc*—"after this, therefore on account of this." Grover Cleveland and Herbert Hoover were presidents at the times of the panics of 1893 and 1929, respectively; therefore, they caused the panics.
13. Accidental concomitance
14. The Baconian idols
    a) Idols of the Tribe—anthropomorphic views of the world, personification, false patriotism
    b) Idols of the Market Place—verbal stereotypes, slogans, clichés
    c) Idols of the Theater—partisan bias
    d) Idols of the Cave—individual prejudices

FINALLY

The units in Language once genuinely learned are bred into personality, become accretions to it and part of it. So is the institution bred into personality, and the person to that extent becomes a Civilized person. If there are persons enough to become influential the institution is bred into the mores. The units become behavior patterns, or, in the cases of Grammar and Logic, attitudes. We make a mistake if we suppose that one who is learned in Language never reacts in Language forms without at first taking counsel with himself and asking "What do my principles tell me about this matter?" If he did so, he would be what is called a prig. Nearly all our behavior is impulsive behavior; we act without deliberation. We should be lost in the mazes of our own thinking if we did not. It is no different with impulses founded on personality from what it is in organic impulses. In learning good diction and composition, good grammar and good logic, we undergo what has almost always been called discipline, but the discipline is a body of content in personality and not the sharpening or training of a psychical instrument called the mind.

CHAPTER IV

MATHEMATICS

WE COME to the second of the great symbolic institutions, content in pure thought or abstract thought, to the science of number, the science of form, the science of function. We learn to think in part by learning Mathematics.

I. AS INSTITUTIONS

Number and Measurement originated as did Language in the inescapable relationships between individuals which we call Society. Not much likelihood that either will emerge unless there is somebody to talk to and the possibility of speech. With the savage, as with us, intercourse does not get very far until there is some common understanding touching matters in which quantity and space forms are involved. Thus the folkways tend to get put together that way, in crudity and with great lack of precision no doubt, but still altogether preferable to a condition in which there is no possibility of intercourse in that field at all. It is a far cry from measuring distance in terms of so many pipes-to-be-smoked to measuring it in terms of light-years, but the difference is one of degree rather than one of kind. The folkway once established, it survived because of its social utility, became institutionalized, the institution became organized into systems of number, gave rise to Mathematics and thus to the most indubitably universal of all institutions, a system of thought which is self-verified.

Whether or no we feel confident that God is a mathematician, we can be sure that highly civilized Society is in fact mathematical, wherever quantity and spatial form are involved, and even beyond. The civilized individual is in command of the elements of the institutional mathematics of his time.

Once in the folkways, a number system made progress possible in various of the major institutions, certainly in Commerce, Industry, Husbandry, Science, but also in Prudence, Veracity, Good Faith, Property, Punctuality and what Punctuality implies in the synchronization of the acts of individuals. It was also an important instrument in enabling the individual to form concepts of himself and his own as apart from his community and his family. It defined, identified, and made conceivable things which were otherwise vague and indefinite. It still does. I suppose the principle is clear enough in respect to most of the above, but perhaps not so clear in respect to Veracity and Individuality.

Veracity.—In respect to Veracity, we can easily find the story in our own experience and in that of our neighbors. The psalmist remarked in his haste that all men are liars. Now that is a statement of fact, and the element of quantity is involved. David could not know anything about it, even if he had made the statement at his leisure, unless he had caused a competent census to be made and we are not told that he had done so. If he had stated that he had seen Jonathan or Bathsheba that morning, we should presume him to be a competent witness, for no question of quantity would be involved.

We are apt to give as our opinion that 90 per cent of the people are fools or at any rate generally incompetent. Perhaps they are, for it often looks that way. Sometimes the books say something like that. But there is no veracity in the statement unless we can claim to have applied valid tests to a fair sample of the population and counted up the results.

We can, however, say that it is altogether probable that in the year 1918 at least 25 per cent of our population could not read in any true sense. The army tests were valid on that point; the results could be counted, and reasonable statistical conclusions drawn. Both things were done. Those who make the statement can do so veraciously.

For ages, likely enough, there has rankled in the minds of uplifters and literary people the belief that "the rich are growing richer and the poor poorer." Historians, sociologists, and politicians have accepted the saying uncritically and made it part of their dogmatics. And yet there could be no veracity whatever in the statement unless and until competent income statistics could be gathered. As soon as that was done, the statement was shown to be false in both the American and the European studies.

Individuality.—It seems like a far-fetched idea to hold that number had anything to do with the emergence of concepts of individuality, of selfhood, and yet the evidence is fairly clear that the institution did have that effect.

Outside of family communism which is inherent in the Family itself, there was widespread communism, in the sense of common ownership of goods, only in primitive times. Property became conceivable, and especially land in severalty, only when it had become possible to measure and count. So long as the measure was indefinite "heap," it was pretty hard to tell how much was Strong Arm's and how much was Wind Storm's. It does not require a complex ideology to identify the results of a drive for game as being common property. Measurement had nothing to do with it. If you insist on privilege, your insistence is not in pounds of meat but in particular tidbits.

Maine, in discussing the customs of ancient Romans and other Indo-Europeans, made it clear that the individual man apparently could form no conception of himself as an individual apart from his membership in a village commune or in a family. He began to feel himself when number and measurement had so far penetrated the mores as to enable him to identify something that he could call his own and trade with others who were like minded.

So in its very inception and early stages Mathematics is a major and universal institution. It is such because it appears everywhere among advancing peoples, because it in fact has expanded, become organized, and refined in the culture of all peoples whom we rate as highly civilized; and because we can rationally see how it is that it is an essential factor in the art of successfully living together.

EVOLUTION

The history of number and numerical language, of organized concepts of form, and of extension into higher mathematical fields is quite beyond the scope of this work. Perhaps the best account in English can be found in Smith's *History of Mathematics*.[1]

Suffice it to say that what Breasted calls the first recorded date in history,[2] more than four thousand years B.C., finds a progressive people in command of the most difficult of all common measures, a calendar, and that calendar with modifications is the one which we still use. It is inferable that progress in number and measurement must have been a long story in prehistory.

Processes.—On the other hand, evolution in processes, content in thought, Arithmetic, Geometry, and Algebra, was slow. We find Arithmetic among people far back in the historical period, but it was clumsy and not likely to develop into a true mathematics of quantity. Even the Egyptians, when they had already found a calendar of 360 days, still found it impossible to deal in generalized fractions, i.e., fractions with numerators more than unity—a fifth-grade matter today.

The Greeks made a great deal of progress in Geometry, so much so that their work is what we still teach in school. They were apparently the first to make of Arithmetic something more than a method of computation. Nevertheless, they never made much progress in the science of quantity, for they never developed a mathematical language which could be managed by the commons at all, or used by the learned with facility.

Mathematics of quantity became manageable as science, and progressive as doctrine, when a usuable language of quantity appeared in western Europe, transmitted by the Arabians from oriental sources. That language was, first, the Arabic number system and, second, Algebra. In less than three hundred years the world had modern Trigonometry, Cartesian Geometry, and the Calculus. By the year 1700 the structure of elementary or institutional mathematics was virtually complete as we know it.

[1] David Eugene Smith, *The History of Mathematics* (New York: Ginn & Co., 1923-25), Vols. I-II.

[2] James H. Breasted, *The History of Egypt* (rev. ed.; New York: Charles Scribner's Sons, 1912).

IS HIGHER MATHEMATICS INSTITUTIONAL?

If one of the tests of an institution is in the principle that it must have emerged from the needs of the common experience and be at least potentially a part of common experience, then it seems to me to be clear that Mathematics beyond the Calculus is neither elementary nor institutional, and therefore no part of the Curriculum of the Common School. It is a valuable part of Culture no doubt, but it is culture made possible by elementary mathematics rather than the institution itself.

The reader may wonder why Trigonometry, Cartesian Geometry, and Calculus are called elementary; in school circles they are usually called advanced. Anything, I take it, is elementary when it is fundamental and comprehensive in import. Mere difficulty does not make anything advanced. As to the institutional aspect, it will perhaps be convenient to leave that issue to be discussed in connection with the several branches, reserving only the following general comment.

If we rest our theory of the Curriculum on practical individual needs as they are observed in the transactions of individuals, then anything more than the mere rudiments of ciphering and a few commercial processes is scarcely to be justified. The same argument could be applied to pretty much the whole Curriculum, leaving only an effective primary school as the common individual need. But the consequences would be, and indeed are, a succession of cycles of societal disruption, for lack of adequate intelligence in the mores.

INTELLIGENCE

The supreme contribution to the element of Intelligence in Civilization, to understandings of how the world is put together, *and to reflection on such understandings*, comes from Mathematics. It does not "teach us how to think," but it is in itself pure thought within its sphere and, by its symbolism, often beyond its sphere.

For example, the attitude of the individual toward the world of mechanical culture who has no conception whatever of how specialists go to work to achieve what are to him their miracles is the attitude of the tribesman in the presence of his shaman. The attitude of one who knows how they can do it, even though for lack of skill he could not do it himself, is that of a civilized rational being. The one attitude widely prevalent in the mores means a low level of public intelligence; the other means a high level—and by that route accretion to the security of social existence. But to understand and appreciate the Machine in its broadest sense is to be able to use the language in which machines are explained. For all but the simplest, that language is Mathematics.

As we have repeatedly seen, both in this volume and in its predecessor, not everything can be taught in school. It is impossible, for the sum of human knowledge is too great. It is undesirable, for the effect, even if it could be done, would be to destroy individuality and regiment a whole population. But the school can breed into the individual, and by that route into the mores, the general intelligence which makes further learning possible and determines, so far as may be, that what shall be learned will be sound learning and not fallacy or delusion.

By far the greatest resource in this direction is still the printed page. To keep up with the progress of Science is to read books— not the juveniles of popular science, but the substantial volumes of reputable scientists written for educated readers. Very few of these can be read unless the reader is in command of elementary Mathematics, not as a professional mathematician but as an educated person.

Mathematics is often called a tool subject. In one sense that is true. In a much wider and more fundamental sense, Mathematics is interpretation of the world, the supreme science in itself.

In our more serious reflection, we constantly think in mathematical terms without knowing it, even when no actual quantity is involved. Thus, "constant and variable," "factor," "reduced to lowest terms," "in the last analysis," "function of," "limits of attainment"—and many others are frequently employed by cultivated people. In so far as the thinker is in fact aware of the actual principles themselves, in that proportion his thought is clarified and released from the rule of verbal stereotypes.

In all this argument based on the development of General Intelligence, it is easy to be misunderstood. From the time when a sixteenth-century work was entitled "A Whetstone of Witte," teachers of Mathematics more than most have adhered to the dogma of *mental training* in the organic sense of the expression. Since the theory has lost its force, there has been a marked tendency to turn "open minded" and liberalize the most fundamental discipline in the Curriculum into a mere accomplishment of doubtful appeal. But breeding Intelligence is in no defensible sense the same thing as training the mind. Every new and valid idea is an accretion to Intelligence, but mind remains the same. In other words, Intelligence is a body of content and not an organic trait. In developing Intelligence, there is no valid analogy to the training effect of exercising a muscle.

II. ARITHMETIC

In the history of the race, number and then arithmetical processes came first. They had to; in experience they are primary. So it is in the education of the pupil. It does not follow, however, that the modern pupil must learn all of Arithmetic before advanced concepts are introduced into his thought.

I. THE NUMBER SYSTEM

There is no Arithmetic as a system of thought until there are number concepts and some sort of a number system. An ordered curriculum begins with the number system upon which modern Mathematics rests, that is to say, the Arabic. In school parlance we call it Notation and Numeration.

The practical consideration here is that pupils shall form concepts of number as number and not be allowed to learn figures instead. Figures are the language of number, and, unless the pupils are prevented, many will stereotype their Arithmetic from the beginning. In my day, as teacher and inspector, I have seen many an instance.

Numeration includes counting and counting by groups. Later on, it includes concepts of fractional parts and of fractions. It includes, not at first but early, some valid concepts of large numbers, particularly in an age when people speak jauntily of billions.

An American cabinet minister once stated in my presence that he thought that the average Congressman could include about four hundred thousand in his conceptual system of quantity, but beyond that dealt in figures. I have seen an institute speaker use space on the blackboards of a schoolroom for the purpose of trying to reduce the word "million" to some sort of imaginative concreteness, and have noted from the gasps of the teachers present that "million" had been but a word with them. Concepts are the material of thought; there is no Arithmetic, which is a system of thought, except it be based on valid number concepts securely held.

Notation is the writing and reading of number and symbols of process. It is easily taught, and perhaps therein the danger resides. Notation, in any system of trillions and so on, is useless, for outside commerce and government even billions are replaced by exponential expressions.

Now Notation as a pedagogical matter includes number combinations in all four fundamental processes, that is to say, the tables. Given number concepts, and those of adding to, taking from, multiplying and dividing by, the ready use of tables becomes a language form; it becomes an instrument of facility. It is something a bit more than numerical spelling. Hence the number facts expressed as figures are drilled until use becomes automatic.

Finally, Notation as the language of Arithmetic must continuously be taught and learned as new principles and new processes are opened up.

2. THE FUNDAMENTAL PROCESSES

It goes without saying that second in the content of the Curriculum in Arithmetic, and indeed in Mathematics, are the four fundamental processes of addition, subtraction, multiplication, and division of integers.

In a study of the Curriculum such as this, many pages might well be devoted to the curricular analysis of the details of these processes. That is, however, needless, for many excellent studies of the problem have been made and the results published. The issue is important; but in this volume we are concerned chiefly with valid conceptions of the processes themselves as components of the Curriculum.

No doubt the layman is chiefly interested in computation. That is indeed important. It is useless to pretend that one who seems to be saturated with arithmetical doctrine, and yet cannot be trusted to foot up a column of figures or to perform accurately simple computations in division, has any right to claim that his doctrine is real and not spurious. Nevertheless, the person who is a good computist and has behind that quality no arithmetical intelligence is not in possession of even the rudiments of education in this field. He can be trusted to compute, but he cannot be trusted to think.

It follows that in a school system in which instruction in processes must of necessity come early in the pupil's career, elaborate manipulations which utilize large figures are worthless, even as assimilative material for study purposes, to say nothing of curricular objectives. I may have occasion to perform tedious computations with census tables, in which my figures are all in millions. The computations are as simple in principle as those which arise out of the monthly bills. I did not learn in school how to work any such averages and interpolations; in fact, I was never taught it anywhere. But I was somewhere taught principles in arithmetical processes. That being the case, I can think out any sort of a computation in that field. That is education in arithmetic.

Arithmetical intelligence at this lower level is emphatically the comprehensive objective, but it arises out of *problem-solving* in which there is much practice in recognizing particular arithmetical situations. The pupil who reports that he "could work the example if he only knew whether to add or subtract" may be capable of the manipulation of figures, but he is to the extent of his report devoid of arithmetical intelligence. But this is a matter of didactics or teaching and not of the Curriculum.

3. PROCESSES IN DENOMINATE NUMBERS

a) Measurement.—Much of the arithmetical curriculum in the lower school has always been devoted to measurement and to tables of measures. That is of course entirely justified on our general theory of the Curriculum. Arithmetic deals with quantity, and there is no civilized notion of quantity apart from measurement of some kind. And yet instruction which deals with measures alone breaks down, for units of measure change, and more important ones come in. When I was a boy in a Maine village, a youth was thought to be lacking in mentality if he could not measure a tier of wood in cords. Psychology was poor, but the curriculum theory was sound. Cords of firewood have been translated into kilowatt-hours—I wonder if these boys can measure in their units as well as we could in ours.

The concept of measurement itself as a count of convenient units, even of units chosen for the occasion, is greatly more important than drill in the use of measures which are conventional at the time and place. Doubtless, young pupils should take on the images of units of measure found in their own community and should be drilled in the tables of measure until the latter have become automatic in the pupil's personal use. All that not only has a practical utility, but it is assimiliative experience out of which can be built up the generalized notion of measurement itself. Nevertheless, the generalization will not register unless it is taught as such—save by chance. As further learning goes on, both as Mathematics and in the use of measures employed in the sciences, the concept can be made to broaden and mature until it becomes one of the cardinal accretions to mathematical intelligence.

b) Denominate numbers.—It is very probable that most pupils in whom mathematical intelligence is taking good rootage need no special instruction in processes as applied to denominate numbers; they would find their way as *that kind of persons*. Nevertheless, systematic instruction leaves nothing to chance. The processes are minor but essential curricular objectives.

4. FACTORS

During the last half-century or less the systematic study of pedagogy has greatly reduced the drudgery and mental gymnastics which formerly went into the teaching of factors and factoring in Arithmetic. Out of the long processes in H.C.F. and L.C.M. come no doubt some skill in manipulation, but little or no insight touching principle; and so with much else. But all that is past and gone. It is no doubt true that the whole subject is properly algebraic in character and is best dealt with in Algebra; but, since factoring must inevitably be employed in the study of fractions, it is better to call attention to the simple facts of factoring in passing. Thus is economy in instruction secured, and the all-important matter of rounding out apperceptive mass whenever possible is heeded. The pupil who reduces to lower terms by dividing both terms of a fraction by the same number follows a rule. He who is taught to identify and remove the highest common factor of the two terms makes some progress in coming to see the essential nature of fractions and adds somewhat to his mathematical intelligence.

5. FRACTIONS

Historically, the theory and practice of fractions has been one of the slowest sets of mathematical concepts to emerge; in that respect most experienced teachers would, I am sure, agree that the child follows the history of the race. *Fractional parts* is easily grasped out of the common experience of early childhood, but not so *the fraction* as a ratio and an early example of the functional character of mathematical thought.

Despite the fact that we less and less use common fractions in computation, and the further fact that in cultural evolution the tendency has always been to avoid operations in fractions by splitting up larger units into smaller—seconds and minutes instead of fractional parts of the hour—it still remains true that *doctrine* is still in common fractions. Hence mathematical instruction does not pass by the arithmetic of the fraction.

Be that as it may, it is entirely fruitless to utilize complex fractions, or fractions with large terms, for the purpose of generating the appropriate intelligence. All that belongs to the era of "sharpening the wits." Nothing is gained save drudgery and bewilderment. As much can be learned from fractions having terms of not more than two or three digits as from those which are expressed in many digits. So far as fractional computation is concerned, the latter would appear as decimals, or perhaps as exponential expressions in Algebra.

Processes.—Understanding of the principles of fractions arises out of practice in manipulating processes and apparently in no other way. You cannot enlighten pupils in the doctrine of fractions by lecturing about it. From the viewpoint of grounding pupils in principle, the important processes are:

a) Changing the terms of fractions considered as ratios, commonly called "reduction to lowest terms" and the reverse

b) Reduction of several fractions to common denominator

c) Conversion of improper fractions to whole or mixed numbers and the reverse

d) Reduction of common fractions to terms of tenths, i.e., reduction to decimal form

e) Addition and subtraction—one unit so far as instruction is concerned

f) Multiplication and division

The last is one unit and more importantly so than the preceding. There the advantage of treating as a single unit is largely a matter of simplification and convenience. Here, there is a positive pedagogical advantage, for the process of inverting the divisor makes it possible to bring out the reciprocal nature of these fundamental processes.

6. DECIMAL FRACTIONS

The utilitarian spirit in teaching leads to exalting decimals at the cost of doctrine in fractions. It is no doubt true that, for all practical purposes of computation, the use of decimals bids fair to supersede that of common fractions altogether. That is no doubt well; but curiously enough it is in part a return to the arithmetic of the Egyptians, who, as we have seen, seem never to have progressed beyond dealing with fractional parts. A large fraction was so many thirds or fifths or tenths by count. So it indeed is with young pupils, or should be. If, however, the pupil remains at that stage, his thought in fractions makes but little progress.

So it is with decimals which are at the bottom a count in tenths expressed in conventional notation. One can readily learn to apply the decimal notation, but learning to think in decimals is unlikely to appear unless the pupil is grounded in common fractions and comes to see decimals as a special case. I have collected hundreds of teachers' registers in which the teachers concerned were never able to compute percentage of daily attendance. Such expressions as .90 per cent are still common enough when the computist really means .90 or else 90 per cent. Such people have rules in memory but no thought.

Decimal notation and numeration and decimal operations in the fundamentals go without saying into the Curriculum as essentials.

7. PERCENTAGE

The foregoing may perhaps be read as a grudging admission of decimals as a concession to the utilitarian spirit of the age. Quite the contrary, the emergence of decimal processes in a workable notation has been one of the major accretions to mathematical culture. Upon it, and upon decimal measurements, depend the ready application of Percentage. When our pupils come to be able to handle the thought of Percentage with facility, they take a very important step in mathematical learning. Without knowing it, they are introduced concretely into the most important thought-process in Mathematics, namely, the function. Strange to say the thought of Percentage is at bottom much the same as that of the Differential and Integral Calculus. There is the same derivation of the value of a variable at any point and the same derivation of the variable from a particular value. We build up *thought* as we go, and never realize it—unless we turn psychologists and analyze mental processes.

The heart of decimals then as a school subject is in its applications in Percentage. The heart of Percentage and the beginning of algebraic thought is a clear notion of finding any one of the three terms when the other two are given.

School textbooks and courses of study commonly enough add Interest, Bank Discount, Commercial Discount, and Taxes as separable curricular elements in Arithmetic. They are not. The first three belong to Commerce and the last to Government. Nevertheless, all four can be used as study material in learning Percentage, without special study of the subjects themselves. An exercise which states that a rate of 2 per cent on $10,000 property value is levied and inquires what the tax bill will be requires no special study of taxation. Incidentally, the pupil will pick up at least the tax vocabulary. So with the other three and similar exercises chosen from various scientific fields. Nevertheless, both teacher and textbook-maker must be on guard lest they actually expand the Curriculum under the guise of study material.

8. RULE OF THREE

The old-time "Rule of Three" is the arithmetical ratio and proportion. Long neglected, it is still one of the readiest instruments of computation and one of the simplest instruments of thought. In its use it was simple proportional thought, but not a theory of proportion. "As a is to b, so is c to the unknown." So it ran. It was still vernacular, antecedent to algebraic language. It is interesting to recall that in the old days, when one had "ciphered as far as the Rule of Three," his days in Arithmetic were presumed to be at an end. So they were and so they are now. The old-time schoolmaster might and did include a great deal between Counting and the Rule of Three which we exclude now, either because it is obsolete or because it is superfluous, but it still remains true that in the arithmetical Rule of Three, the thought of elementary Arithmetic culminates. The next step is into algebraic thought.

THE UNIT IN ARITHMETIC AND IN MATHEMATICS IN GENERAL

The reader's attention is invited to the discussion of language-arts units found in the preceding chapter and to the explanation of teaching and learning units in general. Units in Mathematics are in character like units in Grammar and Logic, but they are still units. Let us briefly remind ourselves what that means.

Here are eight chapters, fourteen units, in Elementary Arithmetic. It is believed that they define the course. Each of them is a definite something to be learned and not a topic to be *studied about* with question-and-answer recitation to follow. But whereas in Language most of the units in courses are the courses themselves and each of them *an art to be learned*, here each of the units is a principle or body of principles to be "seen into," *to be understood*. There is nothing to memorize save in the tables and counting where the teaching process is drill; nothing to part-learn.

"Elementary" as we use the term here, and as we shall always use it, does not necessarily mean "easy" or "simple," nor does it mean the Arithmetic of the elementary school as we currently define schools. It signifies that which is fundamental, and comprehensive, and essential, as opposed to what is extended, specialized, and nonessential. It is intended to draw the line between what of itself enters into the fabric of General Education and what is a more or less interesting and useful body of culture without necessarily being educative in the generation of mature personality.

UNITS IN ARITHMETIC

    I. The Number System
   II. Addition of Integers
  III. Subtraction of Integers
   IV. Multiplication of Integers
    V. Division of Integers
   VI. Average (i.e., Arithmetical Mean)
  VII. Measurement and Common Measures
       1. Concept of measure as application of some unit of measure
       2. Common measures as illustrations
       3. Important tables in common use memorized
       4. Process in ascending and descending reduction of denominate numbers
       5. Addition and subtraction of denominate numbers
       6. Multiplication of denominate numbers
       7. Division of denominate numbers
 VIII. Factors
       1. The factorial concept
       2. Common factors
       3. Highest common factor
       4. Lowest common multiple
          As we have seen, nothing is gained by using the long processes in H.C.F. and L.C.M.

UNIT ELEMENTS

In working out the structure of courses at various points in the work, I have not thought it necessary always to list the elements in each unit. Sometimes there is but one element, namely, the unit itself. More often in science-type courses the unit cannot readily be grasped save as the pupil grasps the elements.

We have already encountered the principle in our discussion of Grammar in the preceding chapter.[3] It is doubtless well that the principle should be reiterated here.

If each unit were a topic, then the subdivisions called "elements" would be merely a table of contents. Not so. Here the elements are minor understandings which being grasped in succession give the pupils the unit understanding which is the objective. They are the points which a speaker or writer makes in developing expository discourse.

Thus in Unit IX in the foregoing, the several processes constitute the learning of the fraction as a fundamental concept in arithmetical thought. Apart from that there is only the notion of fractional parts. The essential notion of the fraction could be lectured about until doomsday, and even rather mature pupils

[3] See p. 61.

would not see what the teacher was talking about. With capable teaching of the unit as thus organized, on the other hand, the true mathematical character of the fraction passes into the pupil's stock of ideas, without any critical awareness on his part of what has happened to him.

III. ALGEBRA

Algebra is generalized Arithmetic. Partly in pursuance of that principle, instructional arrangements in recent years, both in this country and abroad, have tended to assimilate the two branches and introduce pupils wherever possible to algebraic concepts during their course in Arithmetic.

Algebra as we know it, however, is historically and logically separable. Ancient Algebra was philosophical Arithmetic, and our science did not arise until a workable algebraic language had emerged and become organized and refined. If we had today only the method of Diophantus, let alone the older algebraic thought carried on in vernacular language, the science would be teachable only in the University and would be of little or no service in technology. As it is, the refined institution is teachable in junior high school as a separable discipline, and it has been the chief instrument by which thought has marched on to the higher Mathematics.

Why teach Algebra?—The question is raised over and over again. Algebra is not strikingly "interesting," and it is not easy to make it such. Its utility to the Common Man is far from obvious. We readily grant that Language should be taught; individual utility is apparent there. And yet there have been times not so long since when there was objection to teaching any Language beyond alphabet-reading, good penmanship, and spelling. In truth, there is exactly the same reason for teaching Algebra that there is for teaching English Composition. Both are essential components of major and universal institutions, parts of civilized thought and of civilized outlook on the world.

The individual who knows no Algebra but assumes that he knows what it is and he who vaguely recalls that he once "took such a course for credit" are scarcely in a position to pass judgment on this or on any other part of the Curriculum. Nor is the woman member of a school board who remembers that she "took algebra, found it stupid, and could never see what good it did her." Such opinions in the end would leave the schools with no curriculum at all, and General Education with no content, beyond "Life!" and "Art!" much desired by those who feel no obligations to precision.

He who has learned his Algebra has taken on algebraic thought, and thereafter thinks algebraically, and for that reason more adequately, whether he knows it or not. That comparatively few pupils actually do learn Algebra is no argument to the contrary. We know that at least 25 per cent of those who have "studied reading" have never learned to read in any true sense. That is the fault of the teaching. There is no good reason for excluding Reading or Algebra—nor yet History nor Science—on the ground that either some or most pupils "never got anything out of it." It is a ground for taking *teaching* seriously.

A very eminent physicist has said that he could explain the whole doctrine of relativity without the use of a single mathematical symbol but that no publisher would accept the ponderous volume thus made necessary. We are not concerned here with the mathematics of relativity, but the small boy does but reiterate the words of the scientist when he announces, "I can do that by Algebra but not by Arithmetic." Algebra is an extension of Language and therefore of the means by which thought can be shared.

Per contra, neither Algebra nor any other part of the Curriculum is to be defined by the professional requirements of university mathematicians, scientists, or technologists. We build from the bottom up. We seek our foundations in the history of Mathematics as institution. If the professional mathematician desires something else or something more, then his university department must provide for its own instructional needs.

Algebra has sometimes been called the *science of the equation* and the *science of function*. So it is. It is useful to bear in mind that most of the processes which enter into the course in Algebra are ancillary to these two main purposes.

With all the foregoing in mind, we can proceed to the curricular content in the subject.

1. ALGEBRAIC NOTATION AND NUMERATION

a) The point of departure is obvious: it is in the use of letters or some equivalent of letters to express generalized number and of signed or directed number. Therein is much the same kind of radical advance in thinking capacity as occurred long ago when there emerged a phonetic alphabet and a language possessed of a refined grammatical structure. Thought was at once facilitated, and because it was facilitated it could pass onward into realms hitherto undreamed of.

The notion of signed numbers, that is to say, plus-and-minus quantity, actually doubles the dimensions in which we think, and it does so not only as a matter of quantity but as a matter of symbolism where there is no quantity.

b) An essential part of algebraic notation and numeration is found in the notion that there are monomial, binomial, and polynomial expressions, that each of these stands for one, two, or more single numbers taken distributively and at the same time for single numbers taken collectively; and that such polynomials are capable of being treated as if each of them were one term. Nevertheless, we can make little out of a complex polynomial unless we can see how it can be simplified, quantity itself remaining as before, and the process of simplification is itself valuable as a means of coming to assimilate the doctrine of polynomials.

Hence the subject commonly found in elementary texts, under the title, "Parentheses and Parenthetical Expressions."

c) Finally, Notation and Numeration introduces two other vital concepts, the *Coefficient* and the *Exponent*, so vital indeed that they travel into Language in connections in which there is no idea of quantity.

2. THE FUNDAMENTAL PROCESSES

The four fundamental processes of Addition, Subtraction, Multiplication, and Division seldom have the same kind of utility which they have in Arithmetic. There, their utility in computation is compelling, but one can hardly imagine anything in Algebra which corresponds to the footing of long columns in addition or to the working-out of long multiplication or division. On the contrary, Algebra comes to the relief of Arithmetic in respect to the last two through its theory of exponents and logarithms. But the four processes as *applied in thought* with simple terms are critically important, not only to algebraic processes in general, but also as the doctrine of the four fundamentals in Arithmetic. Failure to master this phase of the course in Algebra is the parent of many failures to grasp Algebra at all.

3. THE EQUATION

In the Equation we come to the heart of Algebra, the heart of Mathematics, the heart of the mathematical treatment of Science.

It is the point at which Language and Logic become Mathematics. The sign of equality is the verb "to be." In truth the Equation is a simple declarative sentence, and the whole process of clearing an equation is nothing else than a reduction to the simplest possible subject, copula and predicate. In the end, $x = a$. Here, as always, it is the doctrine of the Equation that is the important thing, the Equation as thought. An infinity of exercises in clearing equations is worthless, except as such exercises contribute to that central objective in the unit. Above all, unless the pupil has abundant experience in applying the Equation to the statement and solution of carefully selected problems, he is likely never to learn the essential thing.

The standard texts have long expounded the essentials in various forms of equations in the first degree, with both one and more than one unknown; and the quadratic. That is undoubtedly well, but it is the limit of the requirements of the Common School. As soon as we pass beyond the quadratic, we are in the field of professional mathematics or in that of higher cultural pursuits. Exercises used for study purposes which are in the nature of unusual and difficult statements add little or nothing to the attainment of the objective. The most complex of problems susceptible of final statement in the simple equation or quadratic adds no more to the pupil's understanding of the Equation than do a variety of simple statements. After all, in the end, the equation derived from one of these involved statements is but an equation.

Empirical equations.—On the other hand, a perusal of scientific works intended for the reading of educated people will reveal that the most common use of the Equation by far is the statement of laws or principles or rules in which the terms of the equations are symbols of quantitative units of the science under discussion. That is indeed what the Equation is for; therein is the place where it becomes a visible substitute for the sentence, or even for many sentences. Many years ago, forward-looking teachers produced schoolbooks in which this principle was recognized. Their work commonly proved abortive, either because of the sheer weight of scholastic tradition or because high-school and college teachers were essentially ignorant of the meaning and significance of what they taught.

Now an equation which merely states a law in the simplest possible terms, such as $s = at^2$, is hardly a subject for teaching. The pupil reads there a statement which has already been reduced to simplest terms. But when he meets a complex empirical statement and comes to see that the methods of reduction with which he is already familiar make it possible to simplify and state in few terms in equational form a law which could hardly be stated otherwise, or indeed otherwise grasped, he makes one of those jumps in thought which so frequently occur in the pursuit of Mathematics. In effect, he takes on a more refined and adequate vernacular.

4. FACTORS AND FACTORING

The processes of factoring in elementary algebra yield their principal value in the management of fractions and, of course, in the reduction of equations. Nevertheless, the concepts involved in factoring are a cardinal element in all Mathematics, and therefore *Factors* is an essential element in the Curriculum.

I suppose that scarcely any part of a needlessly discredited subject has been misused in instruction more than has been this unit in Algebra, unless it be radical expressions. Various processes have been introduced which are valid enough in themselves but which have little or no utility of any sort. Others appear which may add to the facility of the professional mathematician but which contribute nothing to the elementary doctrine of Factors. Notable are the identification of trinomial squares in complex polynomials and similar polynomials in the form of hidden differences of two squares. Again, the general expansion of the binomial has no place where it commonly appears. The binomial theorem itself is a part of university or professional mathematics. The expansion taught in high schools is little more than a curious property of Number.

Altogether the identification of factors in simple expansions of the forms, $(a \pm b)^2$, $a^2 - b^2$, $ax^2 \pm bx + c$, is all that is needful in the reading of the educated person.

The function of the Common School, I repeat, is to ground pupils in the material of Civilization, not to teach them everything. If the intellectually mature person, in his individual pursuits, requires more than need be taught in his elementary mathematics, he will readily find it for himself in the mathematical handbooks of his calling. If he cannot do that, it will have been of no use to have taught him at all.

Nor need there be separate treatment of binomial squares, product of the sum and difference of two squares, or of short processes in multiplication and division. Take five minutes for each and place it on the board marked "reserve." These are servicable in factoring and, if taught as parts thereof, not only are time and energy saved but the unit principle is heeded, and, most of all, the doctrine of Factors is clarified.

5. FRACTIONS

As we have seen, the pupil, like his primitive ancestors, finds in his early naïve experience of Number the concept of fractional parts. That is well and normal. All of us, if we would escape spuriousness, the deadly enemy of all personal life, must found our thought in concrete experience before we take wing into the abstractions which are characteristic of civilized thought. Nevertheless, mere untutored concreteness comports at the best with only a very simple cultural environment.

In Arithmetic, if Unit IX is well taught, the pupil does become capable of dealing with the fraction as thought. Nevertheless, save in rare instances, it is probably never much more than an operative process. He deals with fractions as they occur in mathematical operations, but that is about all. The fraction, algebraically expressed, however, is nothing else than a ratio, an expression of division, which can be dealt with as an expression without being processed as division, the very essence of abstract thought.

Processes.—It follows that addition and subtraction of algebraic fractions as fractions is of relatively little utility of any sort. Indeed it is a simple matter to extend and apply arithmetical notions. Multiplication and division as reciprocal means of manipulating expressions in fractional form are, however, of major importance, and both at once pass over into factoring. Anybody who has taught Algebra to high-school pupils knows that the critical matter here is to teach pupils to recognize the ratio and the factorial situation. They will tend to treat polynomial expressions in either term, but especially in the numerator, as if they were in factorial form when the expressions are merely in addition or subtraction.

Nevertheless, when the pupil has thus mastered the fraction as the statement of an actual ratio, he knows the fraction as truly as it can be learned.

Altogether, the Curriculum content here centers on three processes, the first three of those which we found in Arithmetic, the fourth being simply the performance of the operation indicated by the fraction. The practice material found in teaching can easily be so extended that it in reality introduces new and useless elements into the Curriculum, on the ground that "it helps to develop their minds." The opposite course should be followed: a great deal of simple practice material focused on the three essential elements of the unit.

6. THEORY OF EXPONENTS—EXPONENTIAL EXPRESSIONS

Here again we come upon one of the cardinal chapters in Algebra as mathematical thought.

The pupil lays the groundwork in his early study of the algebraic number system and in his use of exponents in manipulating expressions in multiplication and division. All of that should have given him mastery of the meaning of the exponent itself as a power.

As notation.—Beyond that is, in the first place, an extension of notation so that the pupil acquires facility in expressing large numbers as powers of 10 instead of as billions, trillions, etc. These are often fascinating and immensely awe-inspiring to young children, but they represent the childhood of Mathematics and especially the stage at which it was vernacular language.

Roots.—Second, the theory of exponents well taught and securely grasped releases the pupil from that profitless drudgery, the study of expressions under the radical sign. In a much-encumbered subject there have been few more vexatious instances than that whole chapter on radicals. A root is the denominator of a fractional exponent. So conceived, the notion is taken into the whole body of algebraic thought, and the management of roots is greatly simplified. It is a prime illustration of institutional development and refinement and particularly of the simplification of algebraic language.

Doubtless the pupil should be made aware of the fact that, when he sees the expression $\sqrt[3]{a^2}$, it is the same as $a^{2/3}$.

Extraction of roots.—Again, there is no point in including the processes of extracting roots. That is more or less valuable in Arithmetic as computation, no doubt, at least to the extent of the square root. It is no more valuable, however, than the computation is valuable, and that is very little—at least beyond roots which can be found by inspection. Teach here the arithmetical extraction of the square root if you will, and even the cube root, and they will promptly forget the process, since the underlying principle is remote. On the other hand, if the pupil is thoroughly grounded in mathematical thought and actually needs the process, he will look it up. If the pupil is familiarized with Logarithms, he will deal with large numbers that way or else use a slide rule or a table of roots.

7. LOGARITHMS

As David Eugene Smith has rightly urged, Logarithms is an essential element in the content of elementary mathematics, or, in our terms, of the Curriculum of the Common School.

It is an extension of the doctrine of exponents and one of those "mutations" in the evolution of Mathematics which made immediate and great advances possible.

It is doubtless an essential tool in the hands of all who practice the mathematics of mechanics in all its branches, in a great deal of modern economics and demography, and indeed in the hands of all who customarily deal with computations in large numbers or intricate processes; but that is no reason for including it in the content of General Education.

The Logarithm is, however, a great instrument of thought, and that is a horse of another color. Nobody can adequately follow the argument of many of the books prepared by scientists for the reading and enlightenment of educated people unless he can read discourse expressed in the thought of Logarithms, and that will probably be more and more true as the years go on. Unless a sufficiency of individuals can read the meaning of modern culture, there is no common expectation about it. Better suspend it all and return to subsistence agriculture and handicrafts. Possessed of the thought of Logarithms, one can follow far the thought of scientists, even though he has not worked out a computation since his school days.

Furthermore, granted the pupil is well grounded in the doctrine of exponents—in itself relatively less difficult than fifth-grade fractions—Logarithms is not a difficult subject, unless it be made difficult by poor teaching.

8. RATIO AND PROPORTION

The arithmetical Rule of Three is simple linguistic Mathematics. It is entirely valid, but it is not systematic thought. Ratio and Proportion exhibits an internal logic of principles. Like all Algebra, it is generalized Arithmetic. It has terms, and the terms are related in laws; it is a relatively advanced instrument of thought. Whether the pupil ever recognizes the fact or not, if he has the thought, he thinks in that thought.

In an extended and meticulous survey of the content of scientific studies in junior college, from home economics to physics and chemistry, Dr. J. S. Georges found Ratio to be, with one exception, the most frequently needed mathematical notion—beyond of course the elementary processes.[4] Proportion is an equality of ratios.

9. SERIES

A chapter which has little obvious importance for the "average man" but which is of superlative importance in the thought of the civilized Common Man is entitled "Series."

The management of money is not without practical importance to us all, both as individuals and as citizens. When we get much beyond cash transactions and drawing checks on monthly balances, we usually run very promptly into Series as a form of thought. Very possibly, if the intelligence implied by this unit in Mathematics were as secure in the mores—as the fascinations of speculation, let us say—we should not have such an abundance of ignorant banking and insurance laws, municipal and commonwealth bankruptcy, fantastic proposals in political economy; and the diligent but financially ignorant citizen would not so often be the victim of financial miscreants. It might even help the community to utilize securities and commodity exchanges as beneficent institutional agencies of Commerce rather than as gambling hells. Series is the philosophy of the "long run."

However, we are not concerned with the breeding of financiers but rather with the instruction of individuals and citizens who in their contacts with the financial organism in Society will be able to exercise intelligence.

More than that, however, are we concerned with the cultural

[4] The report may be found in the archives of the Laboratory Schools of the University of Chicago.

breeding of Intelligence in general, with a philosophy of life if you will. An illustration of what I mean by the latter is found in the theory of limits as it is found in converging infinite series. The notion is perhaps more concretely found in the equation of a curve which approaches an asymptote. In both instances we have in pure thought the theory of emergent evolution, as it is inductively revealed elsewhere. If our young people had long been trained in the principle, or enough of them had been, the world might have escaped the intellectual and moral chaos which seems to have been the sequel of half-digested evolutionary doctrine and unbalanced devotion to the doctrine of relativity in all things.

No more need be said. The elements in the unit are few, but there is a great deal in each element. The chief warning is that which has been sounded all along, namely, to avoid mere intellectual gymnastics and the specialized study of the professional mathematician.

10. PERMUTATIONS AND COMBINATIONS

Again one of the vital contributions of Mathematics to general Intelligence, in the presence of a world of quantity expressed in numbers, is found in the chapter which commonly appears in textbooks in Algebra as "Permutations and Combinations." We constantly encounter the situation in our daily grappling with the world and in our reading. Most people, at least in my observation, always pass the matter over as one of the inexplicables, or else, being compelled by circumstances, they endeavor to solve their problem by a sort of experimental arithmetical attack, only to find themselves in a state of bewilderment.

All such people are unaware that there is a systematic treatment.

11. PROBABILITIES—THE DOCTRINE OF CHANCE

Fifty years ago this was still a sort of mathematical curiosity, in the arms of which college students rested for a day or two following a period of arduous trapeze work on involved radical expressions. Science was physics and chemistry, with an occasional historical and descriptive course in economics or politics. The great insurance scandals were yet to come. The educated and unsophisticated still lost their money in fraternal benefit associations and modified tontines, even as their descendants still place insurance on the uninsurable.

But with the rise of statistical methods as applied to the study of sundry social concerns, and of the science of biometrics, it became clear that the Doctrine of Chance is not limited to the curiosities of gambling but is an essential part of the educated Common Man's whole outlook on the complex cultural environment in which he finds himself. Indeed it is hard to think of anything which lies more vitally at the basis of clear social thought. What lay at the base of old-time naïveté, in matters of insurance, was the inability of most people to see that a proposition may be inflexibly true of a large class and entirely untrue of any particular individual within that class—and the converse. If it were not so, there would be no distribution of risk. Similarly, it is still seemingly true that the greatest obstacle to clear thought in sociology is particularism, inability to see that what is true of a class, one of the sexes, for instance, is not necessarily true of all individuals in that class, taken distributively. One hears it argued that a characteristic asserted to be true of a given well-defined group is not true of John Doe and Mary Roe, who are admittedly members of the group, and that therefore it cannot be true of the group. The famous aphorism, "You cannot indict a nation," if we take the statement baldly as it usually is taken, is in reality similarly fallacious. It is doubtless not feasible to present a nation before a grand jury, but you can indict a nation of all the wrongs condemned by the moral law and of all the faults in logic. You cannot, however, make your indictment stick distributively, that is to say, what is true of the nation will not necessarily be true of every individual in the nation. The same kind of fallacy is likely enough at the basis of the intellection of many socialists who can seldom, apparently, distinguish between Society and individuals in the mass.

In the establishment of collective justice, we are obliged to deal with types, whereas in distributive justice we must think of individuals. The attainment of one form to the exclusion of the other often defeats the aims of both, as is notably true of the current unemployment situation. But the laws of chance distribution give us an actual mathematical statement of type, the mode in central tendency, and of the extent to which a given group is typical. In short, the whole body of concepts which enter into straight social thinking in this respect arise out of this unit in Algebra.

12. VARIATION

Variation has held a casual and uncertain place in high-school and college algebra as a corollary of Ratio and Proportion, very likely because until recently textbook writers have failed to grasp its vital relation to the key notion of *function*.

Algebra is in truth the science of function, and it is fitting that the closing unit in the Common School course should be a summing-up of the pupil's elementary conceptions of function. It is a thin unit with probably but one element, the unit itself, but it is significant of the nature of function. Otherwise the pupil is likely to miss the point altogether. Young people, or older people for that matter, seldom adopt higher generalizations unless the latter are made into units and taught. Such teaching of generalizations lies at the heart of the teaching-unit principle. To expect pupils to derive all generalizations inductively is to expect them to derive all Science anew before they are out of their minority.

STANDARD PROGRAM IN ALGEBRA

  I. Algebraic Notation and Numeration
      1. Symbolic number, usually literal number
      2. Directed number
      3. Symbols of operation
      4. Coefficient and exponent
      5. Collective number—binomial and polynomial expressions
 II. Addition and Subtraction as a Single Unit
      1. The additive and subtractive concepts as applied to symbolic number
      2. Process
III. Multiplication and Division as Single Unit
      1. The basal concepts as applied to symbolic number
      2. The operations as reciprocal processes
      3. Process

IV. Factors
V. Fractions
  1. The fractional expression
  2. Reduction to higher or lower terms
  3. Reduction of two or more to common denominator
VI. The Equation
  1. Solution or reduction process
  2. Linear in one unknown
  3. Linear in two or more unknowns
  4. The quadratic in the form $ax^2 + bx + c = 0$
VII. Theory of Exponents
  1. Positive and negative exponents
  2. The exponent as a power and a root
  3. Processes with exponents
VIII. Logarithms
IX. Ratio and Proportion
  1. Terms
  2. Laws of proportion
  3. Geometric proportion
X. Series
  1. Basal concept
  2. Converging and diverging series
  3. Determination of any term
  4. Summation of series
  5. Theory of limits
XI. Permutations and Combinations
XII. Doctrine of Chance
  1. Meaning of chance
  2. Theory of probability or risk
  3. Chance distribution of traits or characters
  4. Properties of the normal distribution surface
  5. Central tendency
XIII. Variation

COMMENTS ON ORGANIZATION

With the exhibit before us it will perhaps be helpful to note the application found therein of the unit principle in the organization of instructional material.

The units themselves are no doubt clear enough: they are the comprehensive and significant aspects of the course. But how about the elements?

It will be noted that Unit I, for instance, shows an element organization. The five elements found there are believed to constitute the unit. The pupil could not grasp the unit itself without understanding them all. They define the unit. So it is with the others in which a unit organization is shown. In Unit IV, on the other hand, no elements are shown. "Factors" is itself the only element. To be sure we might list the three important applications found in the text, but these would be only assimilative material of the guide-sheet kind. They are important as a *means* of coming to understand the unit and they are of practical importance as basis for further study; but they do not constitute actual elements of the unit itself. One could grasp the meaning and significance of Factors without them, but he could not make much progress in factoring. So it is with the guide sheet in all science-type units. The guide sheet is just as essential as the element organization, but it is not of primary importance, as is the element organization. Since the publication of the second edition of *The Practice of Teaching*, the tendency has been to look upon the guide sheet as mere busy work, or else to conceive the guide sheet as itself the unit and when completed to constitute evidence of the mastery of the unit, a fatal misconception in either case.

If under the unit "Factors" the three applications were themselves listed as units, that would indeed turn the unit into a mere topical exhibit.

Nevertheless, the course organization as shown here has no positive quality about it. The principle on which it is drawn is explained, but the exhibit itself merely represents my judgment in application of my own principle. My judgment may be poor, and teachers in practice may very likely come to work out a better application than I do myself.

IV. GEOMETRY

Geometry, like Number and Measurement, is fundamental in the structure of Civilization and by consequence in the structure of Intelligence and Intellectual Character in the individual and in the mores. Perhaps almost the earliest experience of the infant with the outward world, certainly one of the earliest, has to do with space; and among his earliest adjustments is spatial orientation.

So it has been in the history of the race. The institutional origins of Geometry are perhaps not so remote as those of Number, but in the higher stages of evolution, in organization, expansion, and refinement, Geometry far outran all the rest of Mathematics; so much so indeed that the oldest textbook in the world is Euclid's *Elements*, which is still the basis of nearly all our school texts in the subject. Geometry must be deep down in the thoughts of men and in the fabric of Civilization. That is the sufficient reason for knowing that it is a major element in the Curriculum of the Common School.

Geometry no doubt has a great deal of practical utility to the individual, and it is no doubt essential in the further study of Mathematics, but to bring these reasons forward as justifications of the school course is to get the cart before the horse, to fall back on the justification of curriculum material for individual ends, to continue the false process of building from the top down. It is to reopen the door to endless and futile debate over the questions, "What individuals?" and "What ends?" *In truth, Geometry in school is of practical use because practical utility arises out of a geometrical world;* it is essential to further study because there would be little further to study were it not for Geometry and geometric symbolism. We are engaged in the endeavor to transmit Civilization without raising futile questions as to what knowledge is of most worth. Hence Geometry has the same justification as all the rest of the Curriculum. The reasoning was good in Plato's time; it is good now; and, so far as we can see, it will always be good.

GEOMETRY AS A SCHOOL SUBJECT

The geometry of the Greeks, which lingered down through the days of the Roman Empire and the Middle Ages to our own time, was pure thought applied to space forms and magnitudes. It should be remembered that they hoped to get out of it a universal logic. Measurement and the uses of the engineer were on the whole of minor importance, at best interesting applications. So was Arithmetic which was exalted over what we should call computation. Long since forgotten, that was the general theory which determined the high-school course down to within a generation—and of course still does in some quarters.

The issue is of critical importance in our theory of the course in Geometry. Is Geometry as a school subject to be a series of propositions derived deductively from a set of common-sense assumptions called axioms, and from definitions, or is it to be empirical and inductive study of the properties of space forms?

It is perhaps worth while to recall the methodological theories which lay behind the geometry which most of us were taught.

Mental discipline.—We have several times encountered the dogma of mental discipline as a theory of education.[5] The argument from mental discipline held that demonstrational deductive geometry was an unequaled instrument for training the mind. That argument lost force when the faculty theory of mind and the physiological analogies were experimentally discredited.

Logical training.—It was also held that deductive geometry was severe training in logical analysis, about the only logic left in the schools. There was much reason in the theory. It was good, however, only in so far as teaching brought out clearly the meaning and universality of the logical method employed. Merely reciting lessons from a textbook would accomplish nothing, save by chance in the cases of a few pupils, and the chance was remote. Better than that would have been a continuation and improvement of the old courses in Logic.

Finally, even granted good teaching, the argument itself was not good, for deductive reasoning is but one of the two great forms of reasoning, and those who defended rational geometry expressly ignored induction. Sound investigation and good learning must of necessity employ both forms. Some of our current writers in pedagogy fly to the opposite extreme and base their whole methodology in all subjects of study on induction alone.

Necessary truth.—Writers have often justly urged that pupils

[5] For a summary see my *Basic Principles in Education* (Boston: Houghton Mifflin Co., 1934), p. 355.

should have some experience with truth which is, so far as it goes, necessarily and universally valid and not merely contingent and relative. But such experiences are no more true of Geometry than they are of all the rest of Mathematics. The expansion of a binomial square is of the same order of validity as the equality of angles at the base of an isosceles triangle. Even so, the notion is a matter of appreciation, of sense of value, and, greatly valuable as it is, it cannot be depended on to arise except the teacher bring it out.

Defensible modern theory.—We are then forced into the conclusion that the study of Geometry is at bottom *a study of the properties of the elementary forms which occur in space.* We find the forms in our experience, and to that extent our geometry is inductive. We define them, and from that point study of their properties is rational and deductive rather than empirical and inductive.

When we set up as our purpose the study of properties, we are at once compelled to inquire what properties are essential to the development of intelligent attitude in the presence of the spatial environment. That being done, a considerable amount of the traditional geometry at once falls away. It must be remembered that the ancients, including Euclid, greatly prized elegance, and so a great deal crept into both plane and solid geometry which was chiefly valuable for rounding out an impeccable logical structure for the reading of adults—and then they had too much leisure time. Like much else in the traditional curriculum, adult philosophical interests thus trickled down and became incorporated in the instruction applied to youth.

INSTRUCTION

The standard program in a subject, here as elsewhere, is the writer's definition of that part of the Curriculum which the subject stands for. In formulating the program, I have set up as units what seem to me to be the essential properties of space, as space is presented to the Common Man. In listing elements in each unit, I have selected as elements what seem to me to be the essential

properties of each form, through the understanding of which each unit itself can be securely grasped. The reader is warned, as he has been before, that there is nothing absolute and positive about the list. With standard texts before me, it represents my own considered inferences from the principles set forth in the general argument which has been developed. Others may select other properties and very possibly with more justification. The *principles* are the logical standard of reference and not the properties which are selected. Be that as it may, the program which follows defines Geometry in respect to content as a school subject in the Curriculum as I understand it.

UNITS IN GEOMETRY

I. Lines
    1. From point to line, from line to surface
    2. Lines and line segments
    3. Parallel relations
    4. Perpendicular relations
    5. Projection of line segments
        One of the most important concepts in the actual use of Geometry as thought

II. Angles
    1. Definitions and terms
    2. Equality of angles
    3. Angles involved in discussion of parallels and perpendiculars
    4. Measurement of angles

III. Triangles
    1. Definitions and terms
    2. Angular values and relationships, internal and external
    3. Congruence
    4. The isosceles, equilateral, and right triangles

IV. Quadrilaterals
    1. Definitions and terms
    2. Congruence in parallelograms
    3. The square and the rectangle

V. Polygons
    1. Definitions and terms
    2. Angular values and relations internal and external
    3. Congruence
    4. Area

VI. Symmetry in Plane Figures

VII. The Circle
    1. The circle as the limiting case of regular polygons
    2. Equality of sectors
    3. Angular value of arcs and circumference
    4. Chords and arcs
    5. Radius and chord
    6. Geometrical definition of tangency
    7. The three-point problem
    8. Inscribed and circumscribed polygons
    9. Ratio of circumference to diameter

VIII. Similarity
    1. Definitions and terms
    2. Triangles, quadrilaterals, polygons

IX. Geometrical Ratio and Proportion
    1. Definitions and terms
    2. Proportional lines
    3. Proportional relation in tangent and secant
    4. Ratio in areas

X. Areas in Plane Figures
    1. Equivalent figures
    2. Areas of rectangle, triangles, and polygons
    3. Pythagorean theorem
    4. Area of the circle

XI. Plane Surfaces
    1. Definitions and terms
    2. Projection of points and lines on a plane
    3. Lines perpendicular to and parallel to planes

XII. Angles between Planes
    1. Definitions and terms
    2. Dihedral angles
    3. Equality in dihedral angles
    4. Intersection of planes
    5. Polyhedral angles

XIII. Polyhedrons
    1. Definitions and terms
    2. The prism
    3. The parallopiped
    4. The pyramid

XIV. The Cylinder
    1. Definitions and terms
    2. Section of the cylinder
    3. Dimensions

V. TRIGONOMETRY

The reasoning which we have followed from the beginning of this chapter applies with undiminished force to Trigonometry. It is part of fundamental mathematical intelligence and thought, an institutional element in Civilization, and therefore part of General Education. We cannot go far in the reading of scientific literature without it. It is in the daily experience of most of us, whether we are aware of the fact or not. Indeed, the untutored frequently build up a crude trigonometry of their own, much as the youthful prodigies which we sometimes meet in school build up a novel arithmetic which they cannot elucidate. Moreover, Trigonometry is but Algebra and Geometry united and extended, and the same curriculum argument which justifies both these branches justifies this as well. It is useful because we live in a trigonometrical world.

Nevertheless, institutional Trigonometry ends with the Trigonometry of angle functions. That is where it had its crude beginnings in ancient times, probably in land surveying, and the ancient thought extended, refined, and systematized is the school trigonometry which we have today.

TRIGONOMETRY IN THE CURRICULUM

Here, as elsewhere in the whole curriculum in Mathematics, the conspicuous current need is simplification, reduction to fundamentals. That has been the motive which has controlled a great deal of curriculum study during the last thirty years or thereabouts, but the program is still far from being achieved. There are no doubt many excellent texts in high-school and college trigonometry, but they tend to suffer from the faults common to textbooks in the whole mathematical field.

1. The author allows terms to creep in which belong to higher or specialized mathematics. An example here is *radian*. An allied fault is the introduction of exercises which are matter for intellectual gymnastics rather than elucidation of the essential units of the subject.

2. He commits the common fault of expanding the Curriculum itself by introducing exercises which do not focus on a given unit but rather involve principles which have themselves to be taught in order that the exercise may be worked. It is the old story of "clock problems," "tank problems," "hare-and-hounds problems," found in the old algebras.

Nor is the reason far to seek. Apart from his own pedagogical errata, the author is bound to satisfy the requirements of professional mathematicians and engineers in the colleges. But it is no part of the duty of the Common School to give preprofessional instruction. Such requirements, however, have been increasingly customary for about sixty years. The effect is that college departments dominate the secondary curriculum, while the pupils, so far as they can, escape into the "extra-curriculum." They subsequently "demand entrance credit" for the curiosities of the latter.

THE STANDARD PROGRAM

In suggesting the standard program, I have not thought it necessary to work out the element organization of the several units. The principles involved have been explained in the preceding sections.

I. Definitions and Terms

    To state the title thus seems like abandoning the unit principle and falling back on a topical arrangement. Not so: the definitions and terms to be employed in the whole course, apart from those elsewhere provided for, is to explain the subject itself.

II. The Six Fundamental Angle Functions, and Relations

III. Equations

IV. Natural Functions and Numerical Values

V. Logarithmic Values

VI. The Right Triangle

VII. The Solution of Any Triangle

VIII. Angle Functions in the Circle

IX. Areas

X. The Spherical Triangle—Trigonometrical Properties

VI. CARTESIAN GEOMETRY

The pupil in a good elementary school, as schools now are, is familiarized with the use of rectangular co-ordinates. He constantly finds them in his further high-school studies. He has always found them in the notion of latitude and longitude. When the primitive located his cache as so-many paces east and so-many paces north from a landmark—or used other terms to signify direction—he used the same thought. It is difficult to read a newspaper, a year's issue of a current magazine, or a book in elementary science or commerce and industry without encountering the same method of reading and the same thought.

This is primary Cartesian Geometry or Co-ordinate Geometry or General Geometry, more often called Analytic Geometry. It is deep down in the thoughts of men. The science itself deals with what is clearly the experience of the Common Man in an advanced stage of Culture; it contributed greatly to the production of that stage. Moreover, it is but the expansion and refinement of Algebra and Geometry, and as such it shows the same type of life-history as do all institutions. It is an institutional element of

Mathematics, just as Mathematics is a major component of Civilization.

All this is ground enough for the assertion that it is in principle an essential in the Curriculum of the Common School. In truth, it has been in the Curriculum for several generations now, for it is traditional Freshman and Sophomore mathematics, and these years, for more than a century, with increasing clarity and definiteness, have been identified as secondary and therefore as Common School.

"But it is too hard and too advanced. We are already agitating for the dropping of Algebra." That is no doubt true. It would be equally good reason for dropping reading out of the primary school, for that is too hard for many, especially under incompetent teaching and administration. The primary question is not whether any subject matter is easily taught and readily learned but whether it is an essential or justifiable element in the Curriculum. After that comes the pedagogical problem of arranging the subject for teaching and learning how to teach it more and more economically and effectively.

And yet there is some truth in the contention of the "soft pedagogues," for the requisite last mentioned has not been achieved for Cartesian Geometry and the Calculus. Many years ago, T. J. McCormack, in arranging a work of DeMorgan for publication, remarked that "it is precisely mathematics and the pure sciences generally from which the educated public is debarred," adding that the higher levels of Mathematics particularly had taken on a "protective coloration of the terrifying sort." In truth, it is doubtful that either Cartesian Geometry or the Calculus presents ideas so imaginatively difficult for the youth who has background in the essentials of earlier Mathematics as does fifth-grade Arithmetic for the boy of ten.

Very few of our texts in Analytic Geometry do deal with elementary mathematics. One of the best of them calls the subject a "discussion of the properties of loci" and then goes on to say that it is "essentially an instrument of research." Cartesian Geometry is indeed a study of the properties of loci, and as such under a good teacher is a revealing experience. The moment it becomes an instrument of research, it passes out of the field of institutional Mathematics and enters that of specialized cultural pursuits. Study of the characteristics of conic sections as loci of moving points is elementary. Investigation of parabolic and hyperbolic functions is professional. Similarly, Analytic Geometry is sometimes described as a particular method of investigating the properties of space forms and magnitudes. On the face of such a description, the branch is professional. We already have instruments for that purpose in Euclidean Geometry and Trigonometry which are adequate—at least for the needs of the Common Man. In short, Analytic Geometry is in its intent specialized and professional; Cartesian Geometry, as contrasted with Euclidean, is institutional and elementary. Analytic Geometry is Cartesian, but not all Cartesian Geometry is analytic, in any sense different from that in which Euclidean Geometry is analytic.

I have examined all the texts written in English, which are available in a large university library. With few exceptions, they are all Analytical Geometry, obviously prepared for the training of scientists and engineers. Good texts, suitable for the uses of the Common School, have apparently yet to be written.

On the whole, the best I have found, as I think, is Olney's *General Geometry and Calculus*, a text familiar to college students in my time, although I never used it. The Preface is dated 1871. It is perhaps overelaborate, but there is in it a sweep and clarity and doctrine such as seldom appears in more recent books or indeed in other books contemporary with it. It is worth noting that the work was prepared for use of Sophomores in the University of Michigan to follow a Freshman "respectable course in Elementary Geometry, including Plane and Spherical Trigonometry, and Algebra."

In stating the curriculum then, the important thing is to draw the line, as clearly as judgment will permit, between what is professional and what is actually within the experience of the Common Man at the present stage of Culture, whether he knows it or not.

VII. THE CALCULUS

The *Cambridge Modern History* dates the beginning of the period which it treats at the discovery and early settlement of the Americas. It does so because that series of events profoundly altered men's outlook upon their world and formed the introduction to a new era in world-history. It must have been much the same as would be today the effect of a successful voyage to some inhabited planet, if there be such. And yet the identification of what it was they had discovered was a matter of three hundred years or more.

If we were similarly to seek the definite beginnings of what is in fact the modern period in Science and Industry, we should find it more clearly than anywhere else in the formulation of the method of the Infinitesimal Calculus. True enough, a long line of inductive students had made discoveries which expanded the intelligence of the learned, probably more than did the Atlantic voyages that of the Common Man of the period.

In the course of the four centuries which preceded Newton and Leibnitz, Mathematics had been greatly enriched by the advent of the Arabic number system, by the arrival of a workable Algebra, by the formulation of Cartesian Geometry. But here was something which made it possible to make the tremendous leap from plodding, wasteful, uncertain experimentation to the economy and certainty of extending established principle to its inevitable

[6] See above, p. 106.

consequences, in advance of any possible experience. In due season, industry by its aid was to pass from an age of invention to an
age of design.

And yet the Calculus must also wait two hundred years and
more to come to its own. Had it not been for the persistent
junior college teaching of a seemingly abstruse and useless subject, the final effective discovery might well have waited another
two centuries. Thus Civilization finds its way into the mores and
thence into common practice. Today, an ordinary well-trained
engineer can take on as routine assignment what a generation ago
would have required peculiar engineering talent.

IN THE COMMON SCHOOL

Calculus has long been taught in the junior college, and the
junior college is Common School. That, however, merely shows
that it can be done; it does not prove that it should be done We
have taught much that we never had any call to teach. The critical questions to be answered are: first, "Is it a major essential of
the major institution with which we are dealing in this chapter?"
and, second, "Is it part of the experience of the Common Man?"

The answer to the first query is almost obvious: the Calculus is
the summation of elementary Mathematics, or at least the final
step which makes all that has gone before in this chapter coherent
as a complete system of thought.

In answer to the second of the two questons, it may be said
that the environment of cultural products which constitutes by
far the most serious adjustment problem today is expressible for
the most part only in the thought of the Calculus.

Let us see.

At bottom Calculus is: (1) a full discussion of the doctrine of
function and (2) a method by which the value of a variable can be
determined at any instant of time or at any point in space through
which the variable passes.

The function concept is the vitally important thing in the
thought of the educated man. It is nothing wholly new in his experience. He has been familiar with at least the germ of the notion

ever since he was a fifth- or sixth-grade pupil in his use of the
principles of percentage. He encounters it definitely in Variation.
Much of the doctrine of Trigonometry is a matter of function, although not necessarily a study of function. But the Calculus is a
study of function, and therein the concept and the doctrine come
out fully and explicitly.

The concept itself is thought, and, when it has been learned explicitly, a major accretion to thought in the fabric of personality
has been achieved. It has been applied chiefly in the fields of
professional physics, chemistry, and engineering, but it is of even
greater utility in sociology and therein reaches the necessary
thought of the Common Man. Many an essential concept in
sociology is no more likely to arise in the thought of the modern student, apart from the notion of function, than it did in
the thought of Plato, Augustine, Aquinas, Locke, and others of
the great social thinkers of the past. "No more likely"? Great
ideas, like fortunate mutations or useful fashions, will sooner or
later emerge in the thought of individuals, and they do sometimes
arise apart from instruction; but all that is to rest adjustment on
chance and not on system. Without the doctrine of function as a
pregnant generalization, there is but scanty definition of social
values, and all reasoning starts with valid definition. Without
such, social inquiry remains forever a tedious matter of debate,
and what is prone to emerge, even in university classrooms, is a
political platform rather than a body of impartial principles.

For example: For a long time, taxationists and other economists have endeavored to persuade lawmakers and businessmen
that capital values are functions of income derived or derivable
from the capital and nothing else, that without that functional
conception there is no meaning to capital itself. But few are in
actuality able to think that far, not because they are dull but because they have not the appropriate instrument of thought. They
still see capital as thing-in-itself—with disastrous consequences in
Society. The United States government still continues to tax
capital as if it were income, and able men are held up to scorn because they file exactly the declarations which the law requires.

Similarly, the stock market from day to day seldom reflects values. Securities sell for much less than their true value and thus interfere with the normal course of Commerce, or else they sell for far more than their real value and thus precipitate panics.

Ever since there was employment, there has been endless conflict over wages. The conflict has been responsible for more social disruption than most things. What in fact is a fair and just wage? The question cannot be answered at all apart from a clear understanding of the complex of relationships which exist between wages and prices. When we study relationships where quantity is involved or implied, we are obliged to employ functional analysis of some sort.

Pigou, in his great work, *The Economics of Welfare*, employed the method of functional analysis and came to a conclusion, mathematical in its nature, that there is maximum distribution of income in the hands of the individuals of a nation, and maximum income to distribute, when each is receiving in proportion to his ability, native or acquired.

It is seemingly a far cry from capital, income, wages, and welfare to the structure of our school and college system; and yet the latter is inescapably a social matter, to be understood as such and its maladies corrected. Our system is what it is because we see it as a succession of things-in-themselves, namely, grades and schools, whereas effective instruction follows the relation between developing pupil native ability and developing personality.

Once more. In the modern world most people arrive at workable concepts of physical causation. They studied the physical sciences in school. Their daily experience with mechanical things helps. The idea of physical causation, however, is one of the simplest: an appropriate mixture of air and gas plus a spark results in an explosion. Nothing very complex about that. Biological events are more complex, and reasoning about them is altogether a less simple matter. However, the less one knows, the more gladly does he theorize. One has only to contemplate the wealth of theories his neighbors offer when he gets into trouble with his garden or his health. But when we turn into the domain of social events, there are few people indeed who are capable of any kind of reasoning. The logic is far too complex, and nearly all social events are clouded by self-interest of some sort.

In truth, nexus between events is not the same kind of thing as we pass from physics to sociology. In physics it is mechanical; in biology it is genetic; in sociology it is psychological. What a man *can* do is one thing; what he *will* do is quite another; what he can be prevented from doing, another still. In physics the nexus may be obscure and remote, but in the end it is simple. In biology the nexus may originally have been simple, but the genetic series soon makes it complex. Hence diagnosis. In sociology the nexus almost always occurs as a complex of relationships from the beginning. Hence it is that the whole ideology of the social studies must rest on the functional concept. An illustration will perhaps make the matter somewhat clearer.

No doubt thousands of people as I write are discussing the lawlessness of the times. They sigh over it and despair. The more dynamic have confident recipes, most of which have been tried over and over without salutary results. If the competent thinker among them states that lawlessness is a function of social disruption, meaning that it is an element in a total complex of mutually related similar elements, his hearers do not even know what he is talking about. They do not think in such terms, but only in mechanical terms. Not so many years ago our ancestors did not even think in mechanical terms; they thought in terms of magic. But given a modicum of elementary sociological principles, and the habit of functional thought, a rational interpretation is quite possible. One ceases to deal with symptoms and hunts through the social complex in order to locate the several abuses which in themselves constitute disruption. If he is a legislator, he directs his attention to the abuses and avoids the bad habit of trying to mend the community as he would repair his automobile. He knows that his program will require patience, but he knows he is right. If such methods of thought are common in the population, the people will come to follow sound thinkers rather than the quacks who are so often elevated into the place of veritable messiahs.

But functional thinking is mathematical thinking.

Processes.—Nevertheless, the heart of the contribution of Calculus to mathematical thought is in the processes of differentiation and integration of variables and what comes out of it. There seem to be two distinct values here.

The first and perhaps more important is the culmination of the thought which we have been exalting. The second is the accretion to Intelligence which always comes when a piece of the mysterious is removed. It is this last which happens when the pupil sees how it is that the appropriate engagement of two gears can be calculated and the gears designed, or how the strength of a solution which is following a gradient of weakening can be determined for any given instant, or how the position of a planet in its orbit as seen from the earth at any given instant can be computed. These are but illustrations of somewhat remote applications. There are many simpler. Indeed, the modern mechanized household is full of such. One contemplates with amusement, for instance, the mutual criminations of housekeeper and serviceman over the misconduct of thermostatic control of heat. Neither of them is a aware that they are dealing with a relationship of variables which no practicable device as yet on the market can precisely control—and at least as far as the temperature of the ordinary house is concerned. Any good text in its assimilative exercises affords other illustrations in profusion.

In general.—I might go on for many pages showing how the Calculus has lighted up many dark places in Man's thought about the world in which he finds himself. Enough has been said to show that the subject is indeed the culmination of institutional Mathematics and that it is essential to the educated man's reading of his environment of cultural products. As to the first, it belongs in the Curriculum of the Common School because it is an integral part of Civilization. As to the second, it belongs there because the adjustment theory of education requires it.

STANDARD COURSE IN CALCULUS

I. Definitions, Terms, Notation

II. Variables and Functions

III. Concept of the Infinitesimal as Less than Any Assignable Quantity

IV. Differentiation of Simple Algebraic Functions

V. Differentiation of the Function of a Function

VI. Application of Differential Analysis to the Determination of Particular Values in Variables

VII. Maximum and Minimum Values

VIII. Integration as Reverse of Differentiation

IX. Application of Integration to Known Values in Variables to Determine Variables Themselves

VIII. MATHEMATICS AS THOUGHT

Teachers and schools are rightly enjoined to teach their pupils to think. Ridiculous reports of success in doing so are often made by those who spend much time in allowing or requiring pupils to discuss matters about what they know nothing. Thinking is not an art to be learned, nor is it a faculty to be trained; it is rather *thought* to be incorporated in personality. Language is thought. When a pupil has become proficient in the right use of his mother-tongue, he has not learned to think: he has learned thought. So it is with Mathematics. In both cases the individual passes beyond the stage at which reflection is merely contemplative, as it is with the wholly untutored and primitive—and very possibly with some of the higher mammals and birds—and becomes civilized. He deals in systems of symbols and thus becomes capable of abstract thought as no true primitive ever is capable.

Mathematics is thus kindred to Language, both in the sense that it is a medium of communication and in the sense that it is thought. Moreover, as we have seen, mathematical thought does in fact pass over into advanced Language. Perhaps its greatest value in General Education is achieved when it ceases to be mathematics confined to number, form, and space and comes to be a body of terms in common language use. Nevertheless, as such terms creep into language use, the result is jargon unless the user has the mathematical concepts out of which the terms spring.

No doubt Mathematics as the science of number, function, and form is practically useful to the individual, but that utility is soon exhausted. Its supreme utility is in the great principle that the individual possessing it is to that extent a highly civilized individual, and where Mathematical concepts are common in the mores there is a highly civilized community and society. On the other hand, if the student supposes that, at every turn in his reflections on the universe, he is to pause and inquire of his soul, "What does my algebra or geometry or calculus tell me about this?" he will end only in bewilderment or disgust. But what he has taken on as mathematical doctrine reveals itself even in his intuitions: *he has become that kind of person*. I suppose that people who have actually learned their mathematics—perhaps 10 per cent, perhaps 20 per cent, perhaps not more than 5 per cent, of the whole number who have studied—usually think in terms of that learning without being aware of the fact. Therein is the germ of truth in the doctrine of formal discipline.

The reader will perhaps have gained the impression that the writer is not hospitable to proposals to drop Mathematics out of the Curriculum of the Common School.

CHAPTER V

GRAPHICS

O F THE three major symbolic institutions, Graphical Representation of Ideas seems to have been the first in order of development. If we were dealing with the History of Culture instead of with the Content of General Education, it would be natural to begin here. In Graphical Representation are the beginnings of written Language in the pictograph. Developed into Geometry, Graphics was the larger part of Mathematics down through the Middle Ages. Language and Mathematics, however, so far outran the parent-form that they became greatly more important as thought forms, that is to say, as discourse. Nevertheless, Graphics originated in the fundamental nature of the adaptive organism, in the common sense and experience of mankind, and it still occupies its original place. It has steadily evolved, become organized and refined, and even in our own time has expanded into an essential and peculiar form of concrete and economical thought. On one side, it has developed into the medium of pictorial representation as the artist employs it; and, on the other, through an extension of mathematical thought as an outcome of Cartesian Geometry into graphical analysis. It is universal not merely because logical inference leads us to that conclusion but also because it is in fact part of the culture of all peoples who are at all advanced in the scale of Civilization.

It is a major and universal institution and as such an indefeasible part of the Curriculum of the Common School. In truth, those of us who lack it are less educated than we should be if we had it.

AS SYMBOLISM

When the primitive made a pictograph, he represented in graphic form some ideas which were in his consciousness. When he made a picture of his acts or intended actions, he entered into discourse in a crude way. It was a matter of common sense, both because the picture was the obvious thing and because the picture as a cultural product was a matter of common, ready apprehension. For these reasons, a cultural product was left behind, and social experience in a somewhat advanced form was made possible. Wherever social experience becomes more widely possible, Civilization the more rapidly moves forward.

On the other hand, the primitive made pictures of his achievements, or likely enough what he wished had been his achievements, and in that way became the precursor of the modern painter of a famous battle piece, or of a landscape, or of the heart of religious faith, or of a friend who has gone before.

Out of the two, pictograph discourse and sketches of scenes or of people, we can see that the one was bound to lead to the graphical analysis of the mathematician, and the other to the art of the most compelling of our painters. There has been enormous improvement, but nothing fundamentally new. Moreover, when artists or alleged artists depart from the *representative* activity which is in the line of institutional evolution, they commonly land in absurdity.

The child is prone to make pictures, and he does it for very much the same reason that no doubt impelled his most remote ancestor—because he likes to. The grown-up child of our time finds it much easier to apprehend the meaning of a picture than that of either the printed page or numerical symbols. It is the more primitive and therefore deeper down in the ideology of mankind.

The final stage of the institution, or at least the present stage, is, first, that of an instrument for sharing thought or sentiment that cannot be shared in any other way and, second, that of an argument which can be set forth only with difficulty in any other form.

Our feeling for childhood, and the awe which goes with it for the most compelling infancy in all history, could be expressed in the Sistine Madonna as it could not be expressed in all the books on child study ever written. The epic of the Winning of the West is told more compellingly in the murals found in some of our State capitols than in all the history that has ever dealt with the subject.

Similarly, some of the thought embodied in commercial graphs, or in one of the mathematical curves, is much more easily grasped than could be the same thought in the form of vernacular language or even in a system of equations.

The mental processes involved in Graphical Representation apply to all of us.

Observe your neighbor, when he is trying to explain something, impulsively reach for a pencil, make some crude sketches, and remark, "This is the way it was." Again, observe yourself and note how often in thinking out a problem you either try to form some sort of a visual image of its elements or else take pencil and paper and make some sort of a graph of the elements and their relationships.

Now the foregoing is the practical meaning of Drawing as a school subject. When our impulses lead us to make such casts about, in the effort to find a more concrete form of thought, how much better our thought itself might be if we were in possession of an institution which long ago became organized, refined, and handed down for just that kind of thing! To be in possession means, in the first place, learning the necessary elementary forms as a graphic vocabulary. It means also learning the more or less conventionalized representations found in such things as maps. In the end, it means learning the art of mathematical graphing, the rationale of which has been laid in Mathematics.

GRAPHICAL REPRESENTATION IN THE CURRICULUM

By approaching the problem of the Curriculum in this evolutionary and institutional fashion, we can derive critical judgment not only touching the issue whether a given body of content belongs in the School at all but also touching a definition of particulars in regard to that content. In other words, we can find answers to the questions, "Is Drawing a fad and a frill, as it is sometimes held to be, or is it essential content?" and "What is justifiable in Drawing and other forms of Graphical Representation and what is not?" and "Why?"

A. DRAWING

In the light of all the foregoing, it is manifest that Drawing is not only a justifiable but an essential element in the Curriculum. But what drawing?

The Philadelphia Exposition of 1876 gave an impulse to Drawing as well as to industrial arts in our schools, such as somewhat earlier expositions had done for schools in Europe. In other words, the subject has been increasingly common in our public and private schools for sixty years or more. And yet in a long career as a schoolmaster and university professor, I have seldom seen a graduate of high school or college who could draw in any other than a childish fashion. Where, in all reason, most of the products of our schools ought to be able to represent the salient features of the visual environment as naturally and as capably as they use the art of handwriting, it is only the exceptional pupil or student who can do so. How did we get this way? Is Drawing only another instance of the principle that pupils in a democracy are not supposed to learn anything? Or is there some special factor here? The comprehensive answer is that these pupils never studied Drawing, but only what their teachers were pleased to call "art." They arranged the covers to composition papers and arranged color schemes. Something in that of value, but not Drawing.

DRAWING IN THE SCHOOLS

Drawing made an early entrance into the schools, often under the guidance of amateurs who did not know what they were about. Schoolmasters and school boards regarded the movement as a fad forwarded by importunate pressure groups, or at least that was apt to be the case. The authorities were not interested.

Nevertheless, there were professionals as well who did know what they were about, and out of the ranks of these arose teachers and publishers who by the end of the century had formulated a good many courses which were much as they should be, judged from the institutional point of view and the standpoint of folk psychology. Occasionally, a retired newspaper illustrator or other artist found a refuge in the schoolroom and taught both pupils and teachers to *draw*. But all in all, a promising movement drifted slowly away until only here and there can be found a teacher who has anything more than the most insecure grasp on the educational meaning of Graphical Representation.

Nor is it hard to find the reasons. The latter can be summed up as:

a) A false if not puerile theory of education itself.

b) A confusion between art and drawing.

Child development notion.—I have several times noted that during the last quarter of the nineteenth century there culminated a set of circumstances, in themselves liberal in import, which in the end sentimentalized all serious content out of public instruction, or at least went a long way toward doing so. Founded on a false belief in an analogy between a growing plant and a developing human being, all tended to turn in the direction of encouraging children to follow their impulses. Now, Drawing was one of the first of the school subjects to fall into the hands of these particular doctrinaires, partly because it was a new subject which tended to be left to itself by a generation of schoolmasters who knew well enough that they could not draw, and partly because it was very susceptible of that kind of treatment.

In consequence, the typical teaching of Drawing in the elementary period exploits the child's inclination to make pictures and builds on that. The child in his own fashion depicts whatever he feels inclined to—the human figure, houses with the conventional spiral twist to stand for smoke, automobiles, animals, steamboats, and what not. Doubtless the children—not pupils, for they are not *in statu pupillari* but only in the nursery—learn something, but they do not learn to Draw. They learn nothing that will contribute to their capacity as thinkers.

That is part of recent history. The other part is in the confusion between drawing and art

Long ago now, those who had been called "drawing" teachers

began to be called "art" teachers, and what had been classes in "drawing" became known as classes in "art." Perhaps there was more in this than meets the eye. Europeans had long been in the habit of upbraiding Americans for "having no art in their civilization"; and, when Europeans talk that way, a certain type of American can be guaranteed to develop an inferiority conflict. At all events, having finished the conquest of a continent, and being in a fair way to place an automobile in every family, our people began to overcompensate their art inferiorities by attempting to put art into our civilization on a mass-production basis. So the schools went about the job, and the pupils at first painted pussy willows and tulips, and then got so that they could make posters. They also designed and molded clay figures. The local superintendent of schools accumulated another budgetary worry.

And so into "creative art" in the schoolroom.

Now all this would have no justifiable place in the Common School, even if the objective could be achieved. The School is an extremely important institution, but it is not the whole of Civilization. The Common School is not concerned with specialized courses of any sort. The type of content noted is Art Institute work. There it is abundantly justified, either as professional training, or as the pursuit of a cultural enterprise for the sake of the individual satisfaction to be derived therefrom. In the Art Institute—or Art Museum—it presumably can be effectively taught, and it cannot be so taught in the Common School save under unusual conditions.

The Fine Arts themselves have an indubitable place in the Curriculum, but it is a place in appreciation and not one in the practice of the technology of any of the arts. We shall come to that later.

A corollary interest with some accomplished teachers has been the development of a sense of beauty in the visual environment and the inculcation of desire for beauty in the outward aspects of the community. That is of course well, but it is not an educational objective which can be attacked directly. It comes in the first place out of a sense of order which is the very essence of Drawing in particular and Graphical Representation in general, out of the aesthetic products of dealing in the fine arts, and finally as one of the major products in General Education.

Mechanical and Architectural Drawing.—There are often found in our high schools, as electives, Mechanical or Architectural Drawing or both. That the courses have often been fruitful for the pupils who have had them cannot be denied. Nor have they fallen into the morass of sentimentalism characteristic of many of our "elementary art" courses. One cannot sentimentalize a great deal over an accurate plan of a building or machine. But fruitful or otherwise, have these courses any defensible place in the Common School? I believe not.

A drawing of this sort contributes nothing to the general intelligence of the Common Man over and above what sound and effective capacity in Freehand Drawing backed by Geometry contributes. Doubtless this application of Graphics is part of the major institution of Graphical Representation, but, like specialized Mathematics, it is a specialized culture which the institution makes possible rather than the institution itself. A finished plan of a house or machine to be constructed is a picture in exact detail to be read, but there is no more reason for the reader's being able to make the drawing than there is for his appreciation of a great painting to depend on his having done the painting himself. The untutored individual is not at all likely to reap a full appreciation of a classic unless he has enjoyed instruction in the products of the great institutional arts, one of which is Architecture. So it is with mechanical drawing. The citizen is not likely to make much out the picture of a machine unless he understands machines as part of the cultural environment. Hence, courses in the mechanic arts are in the Curriculum of the Common School, but the reading of the structure and parts of machines is of the course in mechanics itself.

Design, posters, and advertising.—Similarly there sometimes appear in high-school courses that classify under this heading. They are properly Institute courses, either with a vocational purpose or else as accomplishments which appeal to some individuals. On either count they have no place in the Common School.

To get back to first principles, then, Drawing in the Common School is on the same kind of footing as Language and Mathematics. Like them, it is institutionally organized thought form, and as the pupil substantially learns it he is able to reflect upon the world with more facility and withal with more genuineness. He acquires something of a balance over against his Language and Mathematics which tends to correct the inclination of the former to run into verbal unreality and of the latter to run into mathematical artifact. He whose thought runs along with great facility in Language discourse is more likely to keep his feet on the ground, if he has the habit of picturing his thought in visual form when he can. The mathematician who plots a function in a curve where he can look at it is perhaps less likely to suppose that he can soar into the empyrean on the wings of an equation. But this last is beyond Drawing; it is part of a higher Graphics.

That part of Graphical Representation which we call Drawing rests for the most part on analysis of the perceptual images derived from visual sensation of space forms. It is geometrical in the broadest sense but not rational geometry. No doubt the early geometers made a good deal out of geometrical drawing, in gaining the experience on which their reasoning was founded. Some of the best modern teachers of Geometry have held that the beginnings should be in the construction of the significant figures and problems as drawings, with pencil, straight-edge, T-square, and compass. This is to found Geometry on instruction in Drawing.

The graphic vocabulary in this simple form represents a long series of discoveries, of graphic principles if you please. There is nothing conventional about it. The drawing of a cube seen from an angle is one of the things which most pupils do learn. It is familiar. Nevertheless, it is founded in the known psychology of perception; that is the way the actual cube is seen by anybody. Hence, common expectation. The accomplished artist follows the same principle in his painting; he does not make a copy of a scene, but rather paints what he knows will be the perceptual image of the scene.

This being the case, it is comparatively easy to search out and list the type forms which, with modification and management to be sure, carry the story through a great many variations in subject matter. When the forms are listed, no matter who does the listing, they turn out to be at bottom figures in solid geometry. They could hardly help being such, for, after all, space is geometrical. These are the units in the course or at least the basis of the unit organization.

But here, as always, a curriculum and definition of a curriculum in courses is one thing, and teaching is quite another. This volume is concerned with the first. Nevertheless, some consideration of organization for teaching purposes helps to clear up what is meant by units and what is not meant.

In the first place, Drawing is a practical-arts course, so far as its pedagogy is concerned.[1] That is to say, it is not a science arranged in logical form from which principles and laws are to be learned, nor is it a language in flowing discourse, nor yet a matter of appreciation, nor of drill. It is rather a process of learning how to use materials and instruments in pursuit of a purpose in action. It is deliberate and not merely contemplative as is the case in appreciation, nor perceptual practice as in language learning and some forms of drill.

Again, the units are not the geometrical forms themselves but rather type forms. The pupil does not, for example, learn how to sketch a cylinder as an abstraction, but rather he learns to draw objects which are in general in cylindrical form. More than that, he learns to draw vases, or apparatus in the chemical laboratory, which are in part cylinders, in part truncated cones perhaps. Finally, there is the great matter of teaching technique into

[1] See my *The Practice of Teaching in the Secondary School* (rev. ed.; Chicago: University of Chicago Press, 1931), p. 94 and chap. xxii.

which we cannot go here, which shows how to transform geometrical forms into drawings; and in that way gives to each unit its connotation.

The teacher who has once grasped the educational significance of Drawing, and organization on the unit principle, will soon find the elements in each unit which best complete the definition of the unit, and best bring out the application of the type forms.

But, it may be objected, the visual environment is far from being altogether geometrical, even in the most general sense. That is true enough, and there is just the point at which we pass beyond the Curriculum of the Common School and enter the field of the special interests of the Art Institute. To be able to sketch readily objects about which and in which the Common Man does his reflective thinking is one thing; to be able to draw and color living forms so as to give each its appropriate individual character is a different purpose altogether. The one is a vital contribution to education; the other is a pleasing and perhaps useful and profitable accomplishment. The second involves artistry; in the first there is no artistry. Even the sketching of anatomical material is at bottom geometrical; to catch the expression of a face or to suggest the movement of an animal or of wind and water is but remotely geometrical.

Neither here nor anywhere else in the Curriculum are we concerned with teaching pupils everything in the field which different individuals may sometime have occasion to use. When the pupil has mastered the type forms, and has gotten the hang of their applications, he has generalized, and he is ready to use his powers throughout the field in which they are applicable. He has learned thought in the field of Graphics.

UNITS IN DRAWING

Of all the texts and manuals which I have been able to find, in very few are discussions of institutional drawing as we have been studying it. Most of them instead exhibit elementary Art Institute courses, although some of them, I should think, would be repudiated by competent teachers as being even elementary. Several, however, do conform to the educational principles which have been set forth. One of the latter group, *Freehand Perspective and Sketching*, written by the late Dora Miriam Norton, sometime Instructor in Perspective, Sketching, and Color in Pratt Institute, seems to me to come closest to the appropriate Common School course, both in content and in organization. The fourth edition is dated 1916. Norton's chapters are not laid out on the unit principle, but like most good expository treatments of any sort—and good working schoolroom texts in particular—the book comes very close to a unit organization. With the consent of her publishers, I have worked out the unit organization of the course from the chapters of her book. It is perhaps unnecessary to record that I assume responsibility for the units both as to form and as to content.[2]

The list which follows is set up not as a positive thing possessed of an assumed indefeasibility, but rather as what I believe to be an adequate definition of the course implied by the principles which we have studied. Each item of the list is a true unit because each is a substantial part of an art to be acquired; and, when mastered, each of them is an accretion to personality in the form of an ability to do a particular thing.

UNITS IN DRAWING

   I. The Picture Plane and Pencil Measurement
  II. The Ellipse
     1. Section of a cylinder seen in outline at an angle
     2. Section of a cone similarly seen
 III. The Cylinder and Cylindrical Objects
 IV. The Ball and Spherical Objects
  V. The Cone and Conical Objects
 VI. Grouping Objects of Different Forms
VII. The Vanishing Point and Straight-Line Objects
     1. As applied to cube
     2. As applied to rectangular block
     3. As applied to rectangular frame

[2] Dora Miriam Norton, *Freehand Perspective and Sketching* (New York, 1916), with the kind permission of Bridgeman Publishers, Inc.

B. MAPPING

Drawing is not the only aspect of Graphical Representation. It is fundamental and primary in cultural history and in the psychological processes of the individual. In the refined forms with which we are familiar, it is ordered or systematic symbolism, that is to say, a method of representing analysis of space forms so as to form a true picture.

Next in the ideology of the Common Man is *Mapping* or plotting or charting. The word "mapping" is selected as term and title because the other two words are largely limited in this use to the United States. By Mapping we mean the art of sketching the layout of a piece of land or the floor plan of a room, house, or other building.

No doubt it is the primary approach to cartography which is the basis of geographical language, but it is not cartography as the geographer uses the term. If it were simply the beginnings of cartography, then we should be considering the subject in the later section which deals with Geography. Suffice it to point out that there is no more reason for the Common Man to know how to make geographical maps than there is for him to make the finished mechanical drawing which explains the machine in which he is interested, or to paint the landscape which he loves, or to write the poem which he enjoys. Mapping in the sense in which we are employing the term is Graphical Representation but not Geography.

Mapping means making to scale a drawing of a particular

piece of ground or of a room, and locating thereon the significant objects. Thus is the terrain brought under ideational control, perhaps the most meaningful part of the environment next to the body itself. It is part of the Curriculum of the Common School, not because we think it may prove useful to some pupils, or is in general a good thing, but because it is part of the personal structure of the civilized individual. There is exactly the same reason for it that there is for Addition or Grammar.

Mapping is not a part of Drawing as a school subject, but something specifically different. Drawing makes a picture of an object as we see the object; Mapping makes an abstract representation of the object as it is. Moreover, Mapping does not locate the various objects on the ground as pictures. When that is done, as it sometimes is, we have a somewhat primitive form of mapping, prized in some quarters today as an agreeable form of quaintness where no serious use is to be made of the map as instrument. The real map uses conventional suggestions for some objects like trees and shrubs, doorways and windows; and for others it uses crosses, circles, or other marks of identification, with legends showing the meaning of the marks.

UNIT ORGANIZATION

Mapping is mapping: there is but one unit. If the pupil learns to draw a rectangular object, that is that; he can draw a box and like things, but he cannot draw spherical objects without learning more. On the other hand, mapping a lawn and showing the paths across it is much the same thing as showing the plan of a room and locating the articles of furniture thereon, or making a street layout for a portion of a city. And yet what one has to learn in order to make a map is more than one thing. Hence, while there is but a single unit in the course, there are several elements in the unit. The element organization would appear to be:

1. A simple plat with boundaries
2. Mapping to scale
3. Locating objects on the map and writing the legends
4. Conventional representations of objects
5. Conventions peculiar to street design
6. Conventions peculiar to floor plans, such as location of stairways

C. MATHEMATICAL GRAPHICS

The term is used in its elementary sense as Graphical Representation and not in the sense of the graphical analysis of Mathematics. As Graphical Representation, it is an outgrowth, largely, of Cartesian Geometry, and it constitutes discourse. When, for example, we make a curve to show population growth since 1870, we write a piece of discourse as truly as would be the case if we told the story in Language. Discourse is thought. Such a curve is not the same thing as making a tabular exhibit of population statistics; a table is not discourse. The curve, however, is the same as if we were to write in our vernacular much as follows: "In 1870 the population of the United States was————, in 1890, ————, and in 1910, ————. The increase from 1870 to 1890 was evidently at a greater rate than from 1890 to 1910————," etc. The Language discourse requires study and analysis of the tables, and the exhibit thus made is complex and incomplete. The trend curve, however, plotted in rectangular co-ordinates tells the story with the utmost simplicity at a glance to those who know their Mathematics and Graphics. Not only that but more also, for the curve shows what the simple story in Language could not show, namely, the movement within the census intervals. So Mathematical Graphics has exactly the same reason for its place in schools as does Composition.

The subject tends to get taught as a corollary in Mathematics, whereas its systematic place is in Graphical Representation, along with Drawing and Mapping. That does not mean that it has no place in Mathematics as well, as study material in Cartesian Geometry for example, but there it is studied as principle rather than graphical application.

The question then arises, "What graphs?"

The subject is fashionable, and we sometimes find it taken for granted that all current kinds of graphs should be taught. So we have bar graphs and sundry standard pictograms. The latter run out into the vogue of depicting relative sizes of population by lines of figures of men, or by human figures of different sizes; or quantity production of grain by drawings of sacks in rows; or of comparative military strength by rows of profiles of warships or rows of soldiers. Since all this sort of thing has value only for the illiterate and those who are too indolent to read tables, manifestly there is no need of teaching it.

Now the pictogram in any form may be graphic; in fact, we have seen that written Language started in that form. But the pictogram or a series of pictograms is not discourse or thought. I have read a great many dissertations submitted by candidates for higher degrees, in which the student would exhibit competent tabular statements and then loyally repeat his tables in bar graphs, or summarize them in standard histograms. Perhaps they believed that the device made their documents look scientific; I hope they did not distrust the literacy of the faculty. In any case, their graphics meant not a whit more than their tables meant.

Even a bar graph set which shows relative magnitudes is never of any graphic significance unless the reader, either by inspection or with pencil, traces the curve made by the ends of the lines. It is this curve that tells the story, if indeed there is any story to tell. The bars are merely the ordinates used in constructing a curve.

Altogether, there are but two kinds of graphs which are of much use to the ordinary reader, namely:

1. The line graph which shows growth, either positive or negative, development, history—in short, trend.

2. The line graph which shows distribution. The most important of all, the curve of normal unselected distribution, is of that kind.

UNITS IN GRAPHICS

The unit organization follows:

I. The Trend or Historical Graph
   1. As gross descriptive representation
   2. Meaning of slope as rate of change in the quantity depicted by the graph
   3. Meaning of peaks, hollows, and other irregularities
   4. Cyclic and secular characteristics of the curve—where the period is long enough
   5. Meaning of shaded areas between the curve and its axis, where the areas are such as to be significant

IN CONCLUSION—THE SYMBOLIC INSTITUTIONS

In concluding the three chapters on the Symbolic Institutions, it is perhaps well to comment upon them in summary as Thought and primary instruments in thinking, which has been our emphasis all along.

Throughout our studies of Culture, and indeed in the common experience of life, we are constantly coming upon antithetic pairs of concepts: form and substance, theory and practice, the abstract and the concrete. Unbalanced materialism is forever exalting the second members and decrying the first; unbalanced idealism is constantly neglecting the second.

In truth, the members of the pairs are bound up together as are waves and water, or life and bodily existence. The substance is not more than the form, nor yet the form more than the substance. I suppose that all would admit that the world of physical existence, that of biological life, and that of social rightness are ultimately controlled by the solving of problems as they arise in any of the fields and bringing the solutions into application to the facts of life. Solving problems is thinking, and there is no actual thinking without Thought or Logic of some kind. Save as humans are able to think out the conditions which surround them and bring the conditions under ideational control, they are but the sport of shifting circumstance.

When we seek a basis for our thinking, we discover Thought in the external scheme of things in its formal aspect. So has the race found it in the course of social evolution, and its findings have been chiefly Language, Mathematics, and Graphics. There may be added Music, in rhythm, melody and harmony, as the Thought of the auditory environment; but that is another story. Over and over, we find in the world people who are of high mentality, and even of superior cultural attainments, and yet who do not think in any systematic form. Especially in the complex of modern society, they find it hard to separate the particular from the general, the collective from the individual, Society from individuals in the mass. But we have dealt with all that before. They do not think because they have not the formal requirements for that kind of thinking. We falsely say that they have no imagination.

Nevertheless, a sentence, or an equation, or a curve, may be formally impeccable and still have no meaning because it lacks substance. The words are stereotypes, the curve is but a mathematical artifact, the equation is no more than an abstraction. Substance is of course in the ideas which are derived out of experience, but it is still more in the experience of the race, and out of that have come Science, Religion, Morality, Art, The State, Commerce, Industry, Health. These are what are sometimes called *content subjects*, and not inaptly. Nevertheless, not a single one of them has ever arisen out of the primitive, save in terms of the formal aspects of Thought. The very fact that we are obliged to say "terms" discloses the vital significance of form in content.

CHAPTER VI

SCIENCE

PROBABLY few would question the contention that Science has a proper place in public instruction. It is equally true that few would admit that Science is essential in the fabric of General Education; otherwise the elective system of instruction would not be tolerated. Very few indeed would rightly profess any well-founded ideas as to what sciences properly enter into the Curriculum of the Common School and what do not enter. We must endeavor to find some solution of these issues in the present chapter.

I. SCIENCE AS INSTITUTION

As we read ethnological treatises dealing with the culture of the primitive world, we hardly fail to be struck with a characteristic which appears everywhere, save among the most degraded savages. The nature peoples, one and all, endeavor to find some satisfactory way of managing the external world of nature— to avert the stroke of lightning, to ward off pestilence, to secure good luck, and, not less, to use the forces of nature for the betterment of the standard of living. Along with this primitive management goes the satisfaction of curiosity about the makeup of the world and their place in it—in other words, the quest of a philosophy.

Every issue of every daily newspaper makes it plain that curiosity about the world and interest in its management are perhaps stronger than ever. Here is something in the mind of modern men which has always been in the minds of men. It must go deep down in thought.

MYTHOLOGY AND MAGIC

The primitive could form no conception of causation, but only of agency. He saw things happen about him daily, done by his neighbors, and, following the fundamental law of all learning which is ideational in character, he inferred that all things happen in the same way. If the wind blows over his hut, he personalizes the wind as an active and perhaps malignant spirit. If the season gives him a rich run of fish or an abundant yield of corn, again a beneficent spirit did it. No cause was ever dreamed of. That is, in its various levels of development, Mythology. Mythology explains the primitive's world and gives him common estimates. That the estimates are wrong is of no consequence, since they give the people a mores; better, devastation at the hands of malignant spirits, so long as you can get the people to agree about it.

But Mythology implies instrumentation, and instrumentation is Magic. Instead of using germicides on the evil spirits which torment your neighbor with an infectious disease, you drive them off with incantations.

Little by little, in the course of many millenniums, ideas of causation, or what we should call causation, appear, and they make a more satisfactory explanation of the world. Out of Mythology, Science is emerging. If a cut in the bone of the skull is made in order to remove a tumor or a bit of spearhead, it is only because the surgeon has seen a sequence of cause and effect, both in ailment and in remedy. Hence, Magic gives place to Technology. Error gives place to positive knowledge.

Well, it is a long, long story, and we need follow it no farther. What is common in the mind of the primitive and the modern are: first, the perceived necessity of managing the world; and, second, an overwhelming curiosity to know how the world is put together. What is peculiar to the mind of the modern is the perception that the world is governed by laws; that, by understanding and obeying those laws, men can reach freedom and escape not the malignant but the inexorable purposes of nature. A bit of Mythology still left in that word "purpose."

It follows that Science is major and universal part of the art of living together in co-operation in the management of the external environment. So Science is part of Civilization and not the modern conveniences which technology in Industry and Commerce makes possible. Science is indefeasible in the Curriculum of the Common School, an essential part of General Education.

II. SCIENCE IN THE CURRICULUM

All that, however, is but introductory. The issues remain: "What Science?" and "What sciences?"

WHAT SCIENCE?

The Science which we commonly find in the schools ranges all the way from Nature Study, so called, to respectable courses in Physics and Chemistry in the senior high school.

Now, in general, descriptive sciences have no place in the Curriculum save as they form the necessary ideational background for the definitive sciences. Perhaps it would be a bit plainer if I said that what is merely informational material has no place. With the rich abundance of popular books and newspaper articles, about all a pupil needs to have in order to make mere information available is the ability to read understandingly.

Ignorance takes the world for granted—and in doing so the ignorant has only himself to blame if he is intellectually swindled now and then. Wood burns; that is that, and all there is to it. That is peaceful enough, but the world cannot be managed on those terms.

On the other hand, the person who is informed that the burning of wood or coal is a process of oxidation and that it is kindred to rusting and decay has no doubt taken a step in the direction of intelligent attitude, but it is only a step. There is as yet none of the material of thought about it. But when the pupil has come to understand the elementary process of oxidation and sees the burning of fuel as a case in oxidation, then he has definition and something of the substance of thought. He can make some progress in thinking out the world.

WHAT SCIENCES?

If we look into a survey of what is taught in American schools, we shall find that in the country at large a great many sciences—and some pseudo-sciences—appear in school programs. Manifestly, if Science is essential in General Education, some criteria as to what sciences are needed are called for.

The comprehensive and significant.—We shall make a good start on the problem if we bear in mind the truism that no school system ever could teach everything. It is perhaps less of a truism to assert that, even if it could do so, the result would be merely to establish a condition of chronic intellectual and volitional retardation. The economy of the Curriculum rests on the principle of personal maturity and on its significance. If at maturity the pupil has acquired the round of the comprehensive and significant, he is in position to learn independently whatever as layman it is worth while for him to learn in the particular concerns of his individual life and career. That is part of the definition of maturity. The Trivium and Quadrivium served excellently well as the basal curriculum for a thousand years, just because the seven liberal arts were comprehensive and significant, as far as they went.

The fundamental sciences.—The best assurance we have that we are in touch with the principle just enunciated is the common consent of scientific and scholarly men identifying the fundamental sciences, namely, Physics, Chemistry, and Biology. It would be a great advantage if there were a General Sociology of the same stature as General Biology. However, we can keep the principle in mind and do the best we can to supply the lack. The foregoing are the definitive sciences par excellence. They are comprehensive and significant because all thinking in the fields of the physical and the living worlds comes to bearing in them somewhere.

From the standpoint of instruction and order of cultural emergence, however, there are two others which are fundamental, namely, Geography understood as human ecology and History viewed as an account of social evolution. If it is true that all thinking in the material world has to come to bearings in Physics, Chemistry, and Biology, it is equally true that all the adjustments of mankind have to come to bearings somewhere on the planet and somewhere in time.

THOUGHT

We have seen that the forms of thought are contained mainly in Language, Mathematics, and Graphics. It is no less true that the

substance of thought is primarily in the Sciences. We reiterate
the principle that we do not learn how to think: we learn thought.
In so doing we learn the forms and the substance. Hence, ability
to think in the material and living worlds is achieved by learning
Physics, Chemistry, and Biology. They are substance of thought.
Similarly, we learn to think in the world of Society by learning
Economics, Civics, Politics, Commerce, Industry. They too are
substance of thought.

A. GEOGRAPHY

"Geography" means "a description of the Earth." It was never
that alone, even in the beginning. It was that with the addition
of descriptive ethnology, anthropology, astronomy, geology, politics, and even archeology.

It is related that a statesman, contemplating the staff of professional geographers employed by the United States Government
on a major land-utilization project, remarked that he did not see
why they needed so many professors to tell them the capital of
Tennessee. The story is likely apocryphal, but one hopes not. It
does reflect the conception of Geography which prevails nearly
everywhere. Few people realize that Geography is anything more
than a child's subject found in the Elementary School.

On the contrary, it is properly speaking a fundamental body of
culture and an essential body of thought.

In the last two generations there has grown up in universities a
discipline which conceives of Geography as an account of the
relation of Man to his planetary environment. You cannot deal in
relationships without dealing in thought. The discipline is variously called "human geography," "social geography"—"social"
being fashionable—"scientific geography," etc. Professor Barrows has called it Human Ecology and that is the exact denotation, the only denotation under which the subject can be justified
in the Curriculum of the Common School. That is what Geography has always been, ever since Greek times, in the minds of
men who saw in it anything more than a mass of unrelated information. Columbus was that kind of a geographer and so was

Henry the Navigator, and many another of the explorers who opened up new lands in the beginning of the Modern Period.

Modern Geography under Barrow's definition sets up a well-founded claim that the Earth environment has a logic of its own in relation to human occupancy and utilization and that human well-being in Society is founded primarily upon a comprehension of that logic.

A citizen who has been a lifelong resident of Boston or London, or a cab-driver, may have become familiar through experience with the layout of the city—and may not have. By contrast, in cities laid out on the rectangular plan, or some other plan, one learns not locations but the plan. Hence, he readily forms a *conception* of the city and knows locations in terms of thought. To the extent to which the city is planned, he knows where a distant street number must be, even though he has never been there. So it is with Geography stated as a logic. The Earth has a great plan, and in so far as pupils come to understand that plan, they know what the essential features must be. They can follow leaders who have constructive programs dealing with communities and are more likely to refuse to follow charlatans or dreamers whose plans are irrational. What is more important, they come to realize that the appropriate depository of facts is the atlas and not their memory systems.

UNITS IN GEOGRAPHY

The warning that has been held forth at every point so far applies to Geography as well, and indeed to all the sciences. The list of units has no positive quality. It is a list of comprehensive and significant understandings which, so far as my studies go, seems to me to cover the essentials of Geography in the Common School, but I do not contend that the understandings are the only units or the list as a whole the best list.

I. Land and Water Forms

The common land and water forms of tradition which occur in all extensive areas—and indeed in the experience of most normal pupils. Herein is the primary ideology of the subject without which geographical thought is impossible.

The learning process is in the first place perceptual—a typical land or water form *seen* in a complex of forms, with visual aids, and illustrated so far as possible out of the experience of the pupils. The old method was definition, the cart before the horse.

It is in the second place *conceptual*—what is it that makes a river a river or an island an island? Here is definition, verbalized after the percept itself is held but not before. Definition without a perceptual basis is spurious; perception with no definition leaves no basis for thought.

Mastery is reliable and consistent accuracy in identifying the forms.

II. Map-reading

Recall also the related but different matter of Mapping in Graphical Representation (see p. 128).

Just as land and water forms are the primary ideology of Geography, so is map-reading its primary language.

Here is an art which is an ability to read out of a map land and water forms, locations and relationship of locations, communications, direction, and distance. Since the unit itself is an art, there is no understanding in the logical sense, and but one element, namely, the unit itself. In the course of teaching, isolated details come in as they do in teaching Language. Such are map conventions, or rather the use of conventions in general, use of precepts, and reading distance from scale; but these in their ready use constitute the art or a large part of it. Finally the art is learned, but it is a generalized learning product. No special teaching of particular forms of maps is required. Most of us employ the art when we use a road map on an automobile journey, but nobody would think it necessary to give a course, or set up a unit, in road maps. And yet many of us have friends who can no more read a road map than they can read Greek.

The unit bears a close analogy to the primary reading unit in Language. The pupil who has mastered the latter reads as truly as he ever will read, but he does not read Physics or Economics.

He has to take on the ideology of these subjects, his primary reading carries him into that ideology, and he eventually reads their language as well as he reads his nontechnical vernacular. So it is in Geography. Under proper teaching, all kinds of maps are in use until the course is complete, but to learn Geography is to extend map-reading.

Mastery is evidenced reliability in the pupil's capacity to read maps in the sense in which map-reading has been defined.

III. The Earth
1. Spherical character
2. Spherical dimensions
3. In the solar system
4. The solar system in the stellar universe—gross
5. Gravitation as a gross concept
6. Land, water, and atmosphere
7. The globe as a map
8. Use of Mercator projection—distortion

IV. The Atmosphere
1. Air as material substance having weight
2. Barometric pressure
3. Effect of altitude
4. Temperature and the thermometer
5. Effect of heat on air movements
6. Wind as air in motion
7. Prevailing westerlies in planetary circulation
8. Trade winds in gross

V. The Ocean
1. Extent in relation to the Earth's surface
2. Salinity
3. Effect of heat on water
4. Ocean currents in gross
5. Tides
   (The subject of the tides is a prime illustration of a principle which has several times been noted. Under reasonably good teaching, and good school management, young pupils will comprehend not only the existence of tides but in general the mechanics of tidal motions as due to the pull of sun and moon. But they cannot, needless to say, grasp the exceedingly abstruse mathematics involved, nor the behavior of tides as the navigator understands it. In neither case would anything be added to common intelligence if they could.)

VI. Rainfall
    1. Atmospheric moisture
    2. Relative humidity
    3. Sources of moisture
    4. Effect of variation in the atmospheric temperature
    5. Precipitation

VII. Weather
    1. Cyclonic movements
    2. High- and low-pressure areas
    3. Effect in relation to the direction of winds
    4. Effect in relation to strength of winds
    5. Effect in relation to daily temperature
    6. Effect in relation to precipitation
    7. Weather map

VIII. Climate
    1. The three fundamental climates
    2. Types of climate as dry, moist, high and low variation in mean temperature
    3. Types as continental, coastal, island
    4. Variations according to geographic conditions

IX. Geological Origins
    (There might easily be a whole elementary course in Geology here, and the teacher who is specially interested is apt to inaugurate such a course. That is not warranted. What is required is only enough to insure that pupils shall acquire a sense that the surface of the Earth as they know it has not always been so, and that it has reached its present form by development out of widely different forms by a process which is understandable.)
    1. Earth movements and the elevation of mountains
    2. Erosion and reduction to peneplain
    3. Sculpturing
    4. Plains as old lake and sea bottoms
    5. Glaciation as gross phenomenon
    6. Glacial erosion of land surface and consequences
    7. Development of streams and typical stream life-history
    8. Order of time requirements

X. The Soil
    1. What soil is
    2. Chemical and organic nature of soil
    3. Origin of alluvial and glacial soils, loess and desert
    4. Soil as Man's fundamental resource
    5. Destruction of the soil
    6. Conservation

XI. Forests
    1. Geographical conditions which make forest possible
    2. Different types of forest, where they are, and why
    3. Forest products, vegetable and animal
    4. Man's dependence on forest products
    5. Conservation

XII. Ores and Minerals
    1. Definitions
    2. Chief ores and minerals—iron, oil, copper, gold, silver
    3. Rare earths as essential minerals in making certain metals
    4. Why certain minerals, notably oil, occur in some places and not in others
    5. Depletion—a special instance of the problem of conservation.

XIII. Drainage
    1. Water finding its way to storage basins or to the sea
    2. Lake and river systems as drainage
    3. The forest floor and lakes as storage basins
    4. Run-off
    5. Ground water and capillarity of the soil
    6. Consequences of ignoring the effects of stream flow

XIV. Day and Night
    1. The planet in its diurnal revolution
    2. The Earth in its orbit
    3. Inclination to the ecliptic
    4. Equinoxes
    5. Solstices

XV. Change of Seasons
    1. Earth with inclined axis traced around orbit
    2. Relative positions of Northern and Southern hemispheres with respect to sun's rays at different points in orbit
    3. Seasonal opposition of Northern and Southern hemispheres

XVI. Latitude and Longitude
    1. Use of rectangular co-ordinates in locating points
    2. Latitude in degrees with reference to the Equator
    3. Longitude in degrees with reference to prime meridian
    4. Effect of spherical character of Earth on size of degrees measured in linear units along the surface.
        (In this unit the temptation is strong to pass over into spherical astronomy on the ground that "they need to know it." The elements given are Geography; determination of latitude and longitude is navigation and spherical trigonometry.)

XVII. Time
    1. Measuring elapse of time by diurnal movement of Earth
    2. Prime meridian and local noon
    3. Circumference of the Earth in degrees
    4. One hour is revolution through fifteen degrees
    5. Local time by clock
    6. Standard time and time zones

XVIII. Geographical Communities

There are innumerable geographic responses, most of them so obvious as to be no part of instruction. For example, heavy clothing in winter is a geographic response.

The location and the character of local communities are geographical responses or adjustments on a grand scale, especially if "adjustment" be taken in an algebraic sense so as to cover maladjustment. In short, any local community is conditioned by its geographical relations. In effective response to them it stands or falls as successful Community. Be it recalled that, when we speak of Society, most of us mean Community.

Herein begins to be the culmination in Human Ecology of what Geography in the Curriculum means as an element in Science. Most people take communities for granted without any awareness that they have any explanation or any logic; and yet every community has an explanation, even though the latter be no better than the circumstance that a prominent and able man happened to live there.

It has just been observed that communities are geographically conditioned. A large part of the social history of the last three centuries—a period in which population has been more and more mobile and communities more and more fluid in their ups and downs—can be written in terms of adjustments and maladjustments in community commitments. If a local community has grown up in a coal-mining region or in one in which the chief resource is lumber, then its whole structure becomes a series of commitments to the continued existence and utility of the resources upon which it depends. Man can fix his dwelling place where he will; but he cannot eat the cake of his free choice and have it too in the shape of favorable commitments. He may establish himself on a river flood plain, but if he does so he must expect periodical washouts. The people, unintelligent in the inevitableness of geographical cause and effect, expect to bear the burdens of the flood-plain dweller indefinitely as if he were the victim of the unpredictable. A population may, contrary to the warnings of those who know, settle a whole area which is unfit for settlement; but they pay the penalty of their wilfulness and lack of intelligence—and almost invariably expect the larger community as a whole to bear their burdens. Thus are societies disrupted.

Geographical intelligence widely spread in the population and widely applied to this matter of community planning would probably in itself solve a large proportion of our social problems. It is of little consequence that some individuals should understand. They do now. No social product emerges until enough individuals understand to affect the Intelligence present in the mores.

ELEMENTS[1]

1. Fundamental notion of the local community as a population dwelling together on a given area and related to each other in securing subsistence and social satisfactions
2. Trading center and outlying area
3. Size and shape of local communities as determined by geographic circumstance
4. Resources on the land or by virtue of position
5. Climatic controls as determining possible manner of life
6. Relation to trade routes—water, land, and air
7. Natural and manufactured products
8. National community
9. Metropolitan cities and why
10. World community—the ecumene

XIX. Transportation

Without transportation there can be frontier families living on a self-subsistence basis, but there can be no Community, either local, regional, or national. In truth the community has been expanded and life thereby rendered more secure through instruments of transportation, especially through escape from famine

[1] See also Sec. F of this chapter.

in all its forms, including, of late, medical succor at a distance. Moreover, social progress itself, as we understand social progress, has been accelerated through the expansion of the Community and out of the wider learning from social experience thus made possible. Per contra, social regression has been made much more possible and rapid, through inclusion in the enlarged Community, and in local communities, of peoples living at lower stages of Civilization.

Indeed, there is much reason for holding Transportation to be a major institution itself, on a par with Commerce and Industry. On the whole, that view of the matter is, I think, hardly to be justified, for Transportation is meaningless apart from community life and the operations of Commerce and Industry. It is institutional, but it is constituent rather than major.

Nevertheless, Transportation is determinate: we cannot run a railroad wherever fancy dictates and make much out of freight and passenger receipts. Moreover, a transportation system badly conceived can arbitrarily ruin whole communities. Trade routes are at bottom geographically conditioned, and while new forms of transportation call for new applications of old principles, it is still true that even the airplane often responds to the conditions which once determined the most economical caravan routes. The arguments once urged by Washington on General Forbes still apply to the route followed by the Baltimore and Ohio Railway as compared with that followed by the Pennsylvania.

ELEMENTS

1. Meaning as conveyance of persons, goods, and messages
2. Method, from marching to airplanes and wireless
3. Trade routes and persistence of many, even from prehistoric times (The Mohawk Valley in New York is an excellent illustration.)
4. Trade routes as determining local communities.
5. Ocean routes and air routes as determined by trade relations
6. Railway transportation—limitations and advantages
7. Highways and byways in relation to different methods of transportation
8. Internal waterways
9. Waste in transportation through geographical maladjustment and bad regionalization

XX. Regionalization

Regional study has been called by Barrows the culminating branch of Geography. It is very much in the foreground in the belated community-planning of today.

Bowman, in a footnote to his chapter on Regions, remarks, "We live, produce, and trade regionally. To some extent, we even think regionally."[2] He need have said no more. Such is an economic region whatever may be its geographical explanation, and Geography sometimes shows that what is in fact an existing economic region is a bad geographic region.

When we come to the study of the distribution of wealth, which is Commerce, we shall find that a large element in price is transportation, so much so that wealth has sometimes to be destroyed because of the cost of transportation to the points at which it could be used. Excessive transportation costs are often traceable to failure to recognize and develop geographical regions. Transportation is extended beyond its natural haulage.

So a region in the sense in which we are using the term is a larger or smaller portion of the Earth's surface which has distinctive geographical characteristics, usually dominated by some particular feature. Thus the Mississippi Valley is one of the largest regions in the world, and it is dominated by the river itself. Throughout the whole valley are to be found similar geographical characteristics and, since it is so large, great diversity of natural resources. But even so, the whole great valley is a complex of smaller regions similarly determined.

Thus far we should have little more than handy descriptive formulas, were it not for the fact that definitive and dynamic considerations flow from the economic and cultural consequences of discovering true regions and being led by the regional logic involved. So we may say that people tend to be most prosperous and happy when they live in a well-defined region in which there can be a maximum of regional production and a minimum of regional importation. In this conception the United States is geo-

[2] Isaiah Bowman, *Geography in Relation to the Social Sciences* (New York: Charles Scribner's Sons, 1934).

graphically the most favorably situated region in the world, with the possible exception of Russia. We come nearest to being able to live a prosperous national life without dependence upon external production. But the United States is of course made up of many constituent regions, and the well-being of the nation as a whole is at a maximum when each of the constituent regions has been found in which internal economy is at the maximum and external economy at the minimum. Indeed that is the presumption upon which our Federal Republic is based.

It is the very fact that such regions do exist that makes Human Ecology possible. There can be no "ology" of any sort unless there can be discovered valid principles of analysis in which thought can be found.

President Bowman asserts in the passage quoted, "To some extent we think regionally." That is profoundly true and upon the principle hangs more than economic well-being, or at least something which antedates economic well-being. When one of these natural regions gets accepted and exploited, there tends to develop for better or worse a common culture and common internal institutions. That is conspicuously true of the Mississippi Valley. A century ago, when the chief method of long-distance communication was by way of river steamboats, the northern and southern ends of the valley differed radically in internal economy, in culture, in institutions. Since the advent of the north-and-south railway, and more especially since the coming of the automobile and improved highways, the region has come more and more to a common basis in all three respects.

In the last analysis, the whole surface of the Earth is to be understood as a complex of regions. We thus bring the surface of the planet within human *comprehension* and more or less under human *management* as the common heritage of mankind.

The fact-finding, analysis, and mapping of regions is a task far beyond the capacity of any layman, but a clear insight into the principle itself is not beyond the layman, even the young layman.

SUGGESTED ORGANIZATION OF THE UNIT

1. A geographic region is an area having common geographical characteristics, usually integrated through a dominant feature
2. An economic geographical region is one in which internal economy can be at the maximum and external economy at the minimum
3. Whole nations are sometimes good economic geographical regions
4. Whole organized states are sometimes but segments of geographical regions, and that is one of the chief historic causes of war
5. Large areas sometimes form true geographic regions which are economically impossible
6. Regionalization is the process of discovering, organizing, and utilizing economic geographical regions

In the process of classroom procedure, typical regions in different parts of the world are to be studied as assimilative material, and that is a matter of pedagogical as well as geographical judgment. Of course we sorely need schoolbooks.

FACTS AND INFORMATION

The reader will perhaps have come through to this point, wondering where a place is made for training in the accumulation of geographical facts. The answer is nowhere and everywhere.

Ever since thinkers began to ponder on education, the one thing about which all of them have conspicuously agreed is that information is not learning, nor even a mark of enlightenment. William Shakespeare has never to my knowledge been rated as an "educator," but he gave us in the character of Juliet's nurse the perfect example of the "well-stored memory," and what it amounts to.

So it is that an individual might be able to yield up on demand every fact between the covers of a considerable text in Geography and yet know no Geography. Delivery of information on demand is machine-like; in fact, I doubt not that if it were worth while some mechanical genius could invent such a machine, much as it has been done for mathematical operations. But no machine ever has been or ever will be in possession of Thought.

And yet there is no doubt that educated people do show knowledge of geographical facts as well as geographical intelligence. Where did they get the facts? Did they not set to it and memorize them? The question may be answered by asking another. Where does anybody get the facts about his home town? Did he memorize deliberately the street numbers of the homes of all his friends, the location of the city hall, the post office, the railway station, the several churches? We know very well that he did not; we know that he became *familiar* with them and recognizes them in the same way as that in which he recognizes his acquaintances.

So it is with the geography of the planet. The traveler, the navigator, the professional geographer is stored with information concerning that with which he has become familiar in his studies. His information is much more extensive than that of the well-educated common man, but it is of the same kind. But the professional has not been in search of information as his ultimate goal but rather the understanding which has arisen out of the experiences which have given him his information.

So it is with our pupils, in three years perhaps, of geographical study. If they have been adequately trained in the use of maps and have been habituated to the use of maps in study, then they will have become familiar with much of the surface of the Earth. They will deepen that familiarity in every unit in the course, culminating in the last three units. Best of all, perhaps, they will have learned to use an atlas in looking up the location of relatively unimportant places and features. Moreover, in this way, their familiarity with the planetary surface will expand as they grow older.

Nevertheless, this is not presenting a ready-made excuse to the ignorant. The student who turns up in high school, college, or later life and professes ignorance of the Rocky Mountains, or the Hudson River, of the location of China, or the fact of the reverse of seasons between the Northern and Southern hemispheres, who knows nothing of London, New York, and Calcutta, will merely exhibit evidence that he has never studied Geography in any true sense, no matter what his credits may show.

Next in point of evolution and scope is History, an account of the past, and like Geography, the background of the social studies, and as we have repeatedly seen, the name of a major method of inquiry, contrasted with the experimental. Here, again, we must specify what it is we mean by History as a school subject.

Historia meant "inquiry" and not merely a chronicalistic record. As such, it had perhaps as good a title to be called the origin of modern scientific method as had the philosophy of the Ionian school. And that is what we mean by History as a school subject; that is to say, an inquiry which reveals the past as an understandable course of events resulting in the emergence of societies or social orders as we find them about us in the world today with all their defects and maladies. In that sense, History is not an organized science which can be learned as science as can Physics and Chemistry, but it is an approach to the large movements of the past which envisions them as intelligible rather than as a mere record of events to be noted and memorized in one way or another. Whatever is understood rightly is a contribution to Intelligence, in the person of the individual and in the mores.

Now the great historians of other days have prevailingly dealt with History in that spirit. When Gibbon entitled his great work *The Decline and Fall of the Roman Empire,* he challenged the understanding of men, so much so that the very title has become a part of Culture, and whenever things seem to be going wrong men still ask, "What happened in Rome?" When the work of Francis Parkman could be characterized as a study of the forest politics of North America, it was given a setting which has made it leisure-time reading for two generations of able men, even men who had no pretensions to historical scholarship. When John Fiske developed his thesis entitled *The Critical Period of American History,* he fixed in the minds of all students an essential element in an understanding of the United States as we know it.

Others have written History as a more or less charming narrative in which we see individual men and women as character portraits and the drama of their acts. All that is History as Literature rather than History as Science. The pupils in their reading find a great deal of it and the more the better; it is valuable background reading. But it is not what we mean by History as a school subject.

Again, professional historians devote themselves to a highly organized, systematic pursuit, in which they endeavor to find historical facts and to infer the bearing of such facts on the correct interpretation of whole periods or whole movements. We utilize their results in setting and correcting our school courses, with such pedagogical judgment as we can apply, or at least should do so; but that is not what we mean by History in the Curriculum of the Common School. We do not set pupils to discover for themselves the story of the past. We expect to utilize the story of the past in making them see how and why the present has come to be what it is.

Finally, there have been times when historians have aspired to make out of History a logical and definitive science in itself, comparable with Physics or Biology. Hegel tried to do that in the Philosophy of History. Henry Adams raised much the same issue in his famous communication as President of the American Historical Association. We do not pretend that there is any such discipline to which we can submit our pupils.

History in our schools and colleges has seldom been History; it has been Annals or else Antiquities—and occasionally cheap scandal. That is good for encyclopedic purposes but not for instruction. I venture to say that nobody ever learned anything out of the traditional academic History, unless by chance he acquired a historical interest which led him for the rest of his days to read History over and over until he became familiar with the past in the same sense as that in which he became familiar with the route from his home to his place of business. Even so the normal result in such instances is erudition and not intelligence.

Happy is the youth who has had for a teacher a historian and not an annalist or an antiquarian.

HISTORY OF CIVILIZATION

The conception of History as an implement in instruction which has been set forth is nothing new. As we have seen, great historians have followed that conception, and the list of names might greatly be extended.

But while theories are evolving, practice sometimes writes the theory. So it has been with our subject. A course has gradually been emerging, largely under the influence of professors of special method in teaching, called the "History of Civilization," and that term defines History in the Curriculum as we have presented the argument. It is conceived as an attempt to understand the evolution of Civilization in terms of the evolution of the universal institutions which as we believe constitute Civilization.

But school people as a class are avid of new things. The name was new; and the name produced a demand. It was easy to employ academicians to write all the annals of all the nations, necessarily very much boiled down, and call the result History of Civilization—a hodgepodge of indiscriminate narrative. Needless to say, that is not what is meant.

NATIONAL HISTORIES

National histories as such have very little place in the subject as taught in school. The several nations participate in social evolution, but in the story as a whole very few of them appear in any important way. Rome does, but we study what came out of the Roman experience rather than the History of Rome. It would be a poor course that failed to note the contributions of the Near East and of Greece, but that does not imply Egyptian, Babylonian, and Greek History. So it is with the History of England, France, and Germany. Specialists and adult readers will make much of it all, but there is contribution to General Education only in the sense which has just been mentioned.

On the other hand, the national history in the country in which the school is carried on necessarily comes in as a course, not so much for reasons connected with the Curriculum in History as for matters of pedagogical necessity. Pupils will not make much out of The State, Commerce, Industry, Community, unless they have that which lies nearest at hand in their own experience as their body of reference. Manifestly, however, national history should be taught as History of Civilization. In our own case, that means that the Winning of the West is more important than the campaigns of our wars, and the development of commercial institutions more important than the ups and downs of political parties.

EDUCATIONAL SIGNIFICANCE

If one's reading of history and learning from it stopped with school courses, that would be something but not all there might be. The well-taught pupil would leave school with a sense of social evolution, with a sense of the continuity of human experience and thought. He would have learned to be somewhat less credulous about new eras. Educated people have done just that. But General Education fails in one of its essential implications unless the result is the generation of abiding interests which more or less dictate the reading of a lifetime, and in that way generate wisdom in the mature person. History is no different in that respect from all the rest of the Curriculum. The individual can scarcely be called educated if the wisdom of seventy is destined to be only what was learned in the schools of his minority.

SOCIAL SIGNIFICANCE

All the foregoing proclaims the social meaning of History on the face of things. If we need to be more concrete, all we have to do is to recall the history of the last twenty years. In a topsy-turvy world, popular interest in history has become absorbing. One is amazed to see how much historical erudition has emerged overnight in newspaper offices. Everybody who has a scrap of historical learning at his command comments on Babylonian New Deals, on the Peruvian totalitarian State, on Diocletian's economic autocracy, on dictatorships of the past, on French national workshops—and so on. All this is very interesting but very much belated. If it had all been made part of the equipment of the rising generation as a matter of course, as much as is, let us say, the elementary principles of Physics, the mores would have selected very different kinds of leaders in one of the world's troublous periods. Conversely, people would have been disinclined to be quite so optimistic as were Americans in the post-war decade, and less pessimistic than most peoples are today.

In putting the course or courses in History together, two methods are logically inferable from our premises.

First, we may use the major institutions as the basis of the unit structure of the course, and then employ the great historic movements as assimilative material in teaching. That is theoretically the best method. It has been the method of a great deal of historiography. Thus we have History of Literature, History of Commerce, History of Science, History of Religion, History of Medicine, and much else of the same kind. The defect is in the principle that any such course must either be very scrappy or else be able to command the devotion of a lifetime.

The alternative method is the selection of comprehensive and significant movements or events—such, for instance, as the "Empire of Alexander" or the "Rise of the American Republic"—and study them in terms of the great institutions. That is the method which we seek to employ. Here the institutions are not studied in themselves but are rather the framework of constant reference in the teacher's thought.

Units in History are units of understanding and not units of information. It follows that the course cannot be laid out chronologically. The black beast of pupils, dates in history, for the most part can be learned only by memorizing them. Most of them are of little importance; some are essential to give chronological setting; and some are landmarks. Like formulas in Physics or often in Mathematics, the important dates should be displayed prominently on charts in the classroom and appear in a conspicuous place in the textbook. If the reader will consult the list of units which follows, he will see at once that important movements have a way of overlapping chronologically other equally important movements.

The following list is proposed as being representative of true units, if rightly conceived, and of a suitable organization of the past for instructional purposes; but there is nothing positive and absolute about it.

UNITS IN HISTORY

I. The Prehistoric World
  1. Hunting, herding, and primitive agriculture
  2. Primitive industry and commerce
  3. Universal mythology and magic
  4. Tribal and clan organization
  5. Customary law
  6. Ancestor worship

II. River Valley Societies (Egypt, Mesopotamia, India, China)
  1. Geographic reasons for rapid social and cultural advance in river valleys
  2. Recorded language
  3. Advanced commerce and industry
  4. Labor as slavery
  5. Art in its pre-Greek forms
  6. Religion and ethical philosophy
  7. Juristic documents
  8. Oriental despotisms

III. Greece
  1. The land of the Greeks
  2. City-states
  3. Classes in the community
  4. Greek government
  5. Greek commerce and industry—monetary system
  6. The foundations of art as we know it
  7. The beginnings of science
  8. Greek religion

IV. Conquests of Alexander
  1. Extent and rapidity
  2. Consequence of neglect of national character and of national defense
  3. Failure of oriental despotism and of Greek democracy

V. Hellenistic Monarchies
  1. End of the city-state in the East
  2. Egypt and the Near East brought under advanced form of government
  3. City-founding in western Asia, comparable to American Winning of the West
  4. Hellenistic commerce and industry
  5. Hellenistic culture including organized schools and universities
  6. Advance of science

VI. The Roman Republic
 1. The Roman Republic as city-state
 2. The Roman constitution and law
 3. Military organization
 4. Roman agriculture and commerce
 5. The old Roman family
 6. Classes in the community
 7. Government in the Republic
 8. Consolidation of Italy
 9. Conquests of the Mediterranean world
 10. Effect of conquests on society and on government

VII. The Roman Principate
 1. Collapse of Roman society under the dictators of the first century B.C.
 2. The principate of Augustus and his successors—middle ground between democracy and absolutism
 3. The demoralization of free labor by slave competition
 4. Unemployment and Roman relief
 5. Growth of the latifundia
 6. Increasing burden of taxation

VIII. The Monarchical Empire
 1. Military government—the pretorians and the army
 2. Position of Septimius Severus
 3. The burden of military defense
 4. Collapse of ability to meet taxes
 5. The barbarian invasions
 6. Disappearance of civil government in the West

IX. The Byzantine Empire
 1. The City of Constantine
 2. Geographic eligibility of Constantinople for commerce and strategy
 3. Roman law under the great jurisconsults
 4. The code of Justinian—*The Civil Law*
 5. The Byzantine Greco-Roman Empire persists until 1453
 6. Establishment of the Ottoman Empire

X. The Rise of Christianity and the Church
 1. Appeal of the Christian faith to the commons
 2. Contrast with pagan morals and social structure
 3. Conflict with paganism—the persecutions
 4. The great Church Fathers
 5. Irenaeus and the Catholic church
 6. Conversion of Constantine—Christianity the imperial religion

7. Power of the church in a disordered world
8. Rise of the Western monasteries—Benedict

XI. The Dark Ages
  1. A world for centuries without permanent effective government and ordered society
  2. Submergence of civilized peoples beneath the power of peoples living at a lower stage
  3. The church as the only dependable element of social order left
  4. The monasteries as relief agencies and carriers of ancient culture
  5. The short-lived empire of Charlemagne

XII. Islam
  1. Mohammed and the Muslim faith—the Koran
  2. Military power
  3. Conquests and contact with Roman and Frankish peoples
  4. The rise of commerce, industry, and the higher culture among the Islamic peoples
  5. Transmission of ancient learning to Europe

XIII. The Middle Ages[3]
  1. The rise of Feudalism and structure of feudalistic society
  2. Law and order under several great popes
  3. Renaissance of the Roman law
  4. Beginnings of the English Common Law—Magna Carta
  5. The rise of cities and medieval commerce and industry and transportation
  6. The cathedrals and medieval Christianity
  7. Rise of the universities and the learned professions
  8. Awakening in inductive science and the beginnings of literature in modern languages

XIV. The Monastery
  1. A community organized on a communistic basis under church auspices
  2. A vigorous and critically important institution for a thousand years
  3. As religious community
  4. As landholder, industrial organization, and self-subsistent community

XV. The Manor
  1. The economic and juristic aspect of feudalism
  2. Lord of the manor and proprietor

[3] Often confounded with the Dark Ages and made to extend from 476 to 1453 or 1492.

[4] Not the history of the Reformation but the movement in gross as part of the times.

5. The beginnings of chemistry
6. The Industrial Revolution
7. Credit economy

XX. The Autocracy of the Bourbons
   1. Personal rule—able ministers of the monarch
   2. Submergence of the courts and the law
   3. Ruinous taxation to support foreign conquest and the luxury of the court, the church, and the upper class
   4. Misery of the lower classes
   5. The French Revolution

XXI. The Rise of the United States of America
   1. The reactionary government of George III
   2. Invasion of ancient English political liberties
   3. English mercantilist economics
   4. Triumph of the Franco-American alliance
   5. The Constitution and the Critical Period
   6. American ocean-borne trade and its struggle for existence
   7. The Second War for Independence
   8. Adam Smith and the beginnings of modern economics

XXII. The British Empire
   1. The conquest of markets by an industrialized nation
   2. Great trading companies—semisovereign
   3. The British Raj in India
   4. Settlement of Australia and New Zealand
   5. Canada on Dominion status
   6. South Africa
   7. The British Commonwealth of Nations

XXIII. Napoleon Bonaparte
   1. Recovery of law and order at the close of the Revolution
   2. French dictator and emperor
   3. Conquests and defeat
   4. Napoleonic inheritance among politicians

XXIV. The Progress of the Industrial Revolution
   1. Dislocation of industry and agriculture in England after the Napoleonic Wars
   2. Misery of the factory workers
   3. Failure of English jurisprudence to keep pace with economic changes
   4. Remedial legislation and the beginnings of the humanitarian era
      (It is hardly possible to place too much emphasis on this element in coming to an understanding of the first phase of the In-

dustrial Revolution. It is apt to be treated as a piece of rather mawkish sentimentalism and indiscriminate condemnation of employers, whereas the significant historical fact is that, down to a period which is still not very remote, concern for the lives and suffering of other people was seldom in the mores anywhere.)

5. The joint-stock corporation and corporation law
6. The growth and significance of labor unions
7. Rapid expansion since the arrival of electric motors and the the gasoline engine
8. Great expansion in the commercial and industrial employment of women

XXV. The World-Community

1. Transportational development brings the whole Earth into a commercial and industrial community
2. Spread of books, newspapers, and reading capacity
3. Telegraph, telephone, and radio
4. All these things knit together peoples into an ideology which is more or less common
5. Failure to develop a world-state capable of administering the Law of Nations and of policing the world

MASTERY

Little needs to be said touching the matter of mastery that has not already been said in connection with Mathematics and Geography. Each unit is a definite thing to be *understood*, and mastery is held to have been achieved when there is evidence that the several understandings covered by the elements have been grasped and integrated into the whole understanding which the unit entitles.

History is History and not journalism. For that reason, events which have occurred since the turn of the century are scarcely to be made matter of instruction, save in the university, and university work proper is not to be understood as instruction leading to General Education. At the end of the course as suggested, the pupils have presumably reached educational maturity so far as The History of Civilization is concerned. They will read newspapers both before and after graduation and profit the more from them, but they will not be the sport of every propagandist who arises.

In respect to the history of our country, or to that of any other fatherland, two courses are open. You can attempt to get it all as a matter of information—and then most pupils will soon forget—or still better as a matter of intellectual interest. The latter implies the reading of a lifetime, an eminently worthy pursuit, but not a matter of instruction. Or you can select for teaching and study the great movements and events in which is embodied most of the explanation of what the United States is today, or might be. In conformity with our general principles, that is what we undertake to do.

UNITS IN UNITED STATES HISTORY

I. Discovery

(The typical textbook relates more or less completely the story of the early voyages of discovery which can only be memorized and forgotten. Doubtless, the pupils are aware that the country must have been discovered sometime. The tale of the voyages, instead of contributing to intelligence, leads to misconception. The process of discovering America lasted for something over three hundred years.)

1. The East coast comes within the ken of civilized men
2. Finding the West coast—from Drake to Lewis and Clark
3. La Salle and the Great West
4. The hunt for a way through

II. Men of the Stone Age

1. Contacts chiefly with Iroquois, Algonquins, and Mobilian stocks
2. Hunters and primitive agriculturists
3. Tools and weapons at Stone Age level of culture
4. Tribal organization and the totemistic clan
5. Mutual understanding between Whites and Indians difficult if not impossible
6. Frightful consequences of putting primitives in control of the appurtenances of an advanced culture

III. Colonial North America

1. The three great colonizing nations
2. Contest for the rule of a continent
3. Subsistence, and semisubsistence, farming in New England and the Middle Colonies
4. Pressure of Indian tribes on the frontier

5. Home industry
6. Plantation economy in the South based on external credit
IV. Breaking Away from the Old World
   1. The English conquest of Canada and relief from Indian pressure
   2. Revolt of the English colonies and Independence
   3. The Louisiana Purchase
   4. Annexation of Florida
   5. Independence of Central and South America
   6. The Monroe Doctrine
V. Establishment of the United States Government
   1. The Colonial governments
   2. The Continental Congress and the Confederation
   3. Defects as form of government
   4. The Constitution and the federal government
   5. The Bill of Rights
   6. Conflict over State rights
   7. Issue settled by the Civil War
   8. The Civil War Amendments to the Constitution
VI. Evolution of Popular Government
   1. The Federalist theory of government
   2. The Jeffersonian theory and the election of 1800
   3. The election of 1828 and Jacksonian democracy
   4. Representative democracy until after 1900
   5. Development of primary democracy
VII. The Westward Movement
   1. Land hunger and adventure in an open country
   2. Eastern industrialization and escape from unemployment
   3. The homestead acts and school grants
   4. Effect of lack of gold and silver on the monetary system
   5. The precious metals in California, Colorado, and Nevada
   6. Highways, canals, and railroads
   7. Establishment of new States
   8. Industrialized Western agriculture
VIII. The Agrarian Problem
   1. King Cotton and slavery
   2. Economic effects of slavery
   3. Effect on free labor
   4. Emergence of single-crop agricultural economy
   5. Premature development of railways
   6. Development of two debtor regions and single creditor region
   7. A history of bad regionalization

IX. Industrialization
1. Beginnings of the factory system—family owned and operated by neighbors
2. The protective system of Hamilton and Clay
3. Home market for infant industries
4. Importation of cheap labor
5. Increasing use of machinery in quantity production
6. Growth of the industrial corporation as form of ownership of capital
7. Unprecedented production and distribution of wealth
8. Unemployment

X. The Labor Movement
(Labor as a phase of institutional Industry belongs elsewhere. The American labor movement as a unit in United States History belongs here.)
1. Slow development of trade-unions for mutual aid and improvement
2. Relation to early humanitarian movements
3. Relation to growth of industrial corporation
4. Knights of Labor—all-trades union
5. Effect of unrestricted immigration and depression of 1873
6. Emergence of craft union—American Federation of Labor
7. Collective bargaining and why

XI. The Population
1. Economic and political reasons for original immigration
2. Racial composition at time of first census
3. Influence of Irish famines and Continental political upheavals on immigration in the Middle Period
4. Appeal of unoccupied land to peoples under the pressure of over-population
5. Steamship and factory exploitation at the period of greatest immigration
6. Restrictive legislation in the period following the war of 1914-18

XII. American Foreign Policy
1. Effect of the geographical situation
2. "No entangling alliances"
3. The Monroe Doctrine
4. Conquest of California and the Southwest
5. Cuba and the Philippines
6. Intervention in the war of 1914-18—why?
7. With a single possible exception, and that exception disputed, we have engaged in no war with a civilized nation for aggression and conquest

No reference is made to Washington and Lincoln or to any of the Founders other than Hamilton and Jefferson. They will all necessarily come in as study material provided by adequate texts and teachers. Biography is not History, albeit it often contributes to History. The lives of our great national heroes, for the most part, contribute but little to an *understanding of our history;* but they do in some cases contribute greatly to an *appreciation of our society.* History is humanistic; the other principal contributions to Science are not. Hence, biographies of some of the great ones of the past give us realizations which we never get out of purely intellectual approaches. But this is Literature, and it is to be read long before, during, and long after the course in History. More than that, Washington and Lincoln are pre-eminently figures which enter into our national celebrations. They are great characters, to be commemorated in auditorium periods at least once a year as long as the pupils remain in school.

C. GENERAL SCIENCE

Let us remind ourselves again that in the formulation of the Curriculum in Science, we are concerned not with sciences as such but with that which contributes in the most elementary and fundamental and comprehensive manner to Science in the person of the Common Man. Pedagogically speaking, there is the further all-important matter of ideational background, of apperceptive sequence.

It is difficult to understand the place of Science in the Common School apart from a glance into the history of our school system. I wish there were space for more than a glance.

In the old middle-class secondary school of our Middle Period, the academies and local high schools, there was almost everywhere what was called natural history which covered not only plant and animal life but geology and mineralogy and astronomy as well. There was natural philosophy, what we call Physics. Now that school was not preparatory; it was terminal. It sometimes rejoiced in the designation "people's college." Altogether it is one of the most interesting institutions in our social evolution.

The sciences taught, however, were what may be called "elementary informative."

The old city grade school frequently called "ward school," always definitely a lower-class school, was not the common school of the early national period which was continuous up to the end of General Education as it was then understood. The grade school too was terminal and not preparatory, since down nearly to the turn of the century there was no assumption that any of the pupils would go on to high school. There was no science in it.

Now then, with the beginnings of the progressive period, the name "Elementary School" began to become accepted for the eight grades, and the curriculum began to become "modernized." In our present concerns Nature Study was the significant thing, exceedingly comprehensive and exceedingly infantile. In short, in that closing decade or two of the nineteenth century was the place in which the rising generation began to be swindled out of its cultural inheritance by half-baked sentimentalists.

The college science, which had finally found a place in the sun, was what may be called elementary definitive—or, perhaps better, rudimentary definitive. It suited the needs of prospective physicians and engineers, which in that period were not great. In the nineties, however, the impact of Harvard and Johns Hopkins doctors on the colleges began to be noticeable; and anybody who was in college at that time must have vivid recollections of how the students went down before the new teaching of real Physics and Chemistry. The students had either no background at all or else only the background of the informative sciences of their schooldays.

Meantime, about 1890, high-school texts of the order of Gage and Avery had secured a footing in the high schools and, generally speaking, pupils devoured them. They were all, and more than all, that most of the colleges had complacently been teaching ever since sciences had come into the Curriculum. They were elementary definitive in the sense that they embodied the teaching of principles but had little or no mathematical treatment. They supplied the material of thought but little of the form of thought.

By the time the century was a decade old, the process of breaking up the old class terminal schools had begun in the junior high school movement. In principle, the junior high school substituted for the sterile and futile seventh and eighth—and in New England, ninth—grades of the old ward school what was called "enrichment." Enrichment took the route of comprehensive courses, much as the universities since the war have been intrigued by "comprehensives." One of these comprehensive courses was called General Science. The word "comprehensive" was, however, switched out of its true meaning and made to mean everything. History of Civilization as it appeared in texts is another instance of the same thing. Community Civics a third.

"General Science" is not a good term. Its verbal meaning is "general" as distinguished from "specialized" science. It might even be identified with Metaphysics. Nevertheless, the term has come to have a scholastic denotation, and in this volume it will be kept. It will signify the elementary definitive stage in Science. The course will deal with what is *primary* in Physics, Chemistry, and Biology, and not with all the sciences. A great deal of what is ordinarily taught in senior high school and junior college belongs here. That is true, for example, of nearly all that is taught as primary machines, chemical change, elements and compounds, most of hydraulics, hydrostatics and pneumatics, and much of heat, sound, light, and electricity. Some of the rest of senior high school Physics belongs in shop courses in machines, and of that later. Some of it is elementary engineering, for example coefficient of expansion and determination of specific heat, and does not belong in the Common School at all. Elementary ideology in the field of living creatures and processes belongs to the course in General Science. The fundamental ideas in Sociology, however, are covered in History and in the course on the Community. The fundamentals in Geology and Astronomy are part of Geography.

PLACEMENT

In principle, the course can begin rather early in the secondary period, fifth year or sometimes a little earlier, and be carried on much as it would now be in junior high school, or even in many four-year high schools. For a long time there has been a pronounced tendency to coddle and baby children, and thus to preserve their infancy, under the delusion that "their minds have not yet reached the power to reason." If one cares to look for significant facts, instead of resting upon unverified assumption, he will find that children who are but eight or nine years of age often have common sense enough to follow a simple course of syllogistic reasoning. I have known infants of apparently ordinary mentality to exhibit an awareness of cause and effect, or at least of antecedent and consequent, before they had learned to talk. I have seen fourth-grade children in our laboratory, who had learned reading and were under a competent teacher, follow the study of Geography much as junior college students were doing it at the same time. This is not to be taken as advocating Logic in the kindergarten and Physics in the nursery—but even that would be preferable to the systematic pap-feeding which is now well into its third generation.

TEXTS AND UNIT ORGANIZATION

The greatest single fault in science texts of all sorts, including texts in General Science, is overelaboration, and that usually amounts to arbitrary extension of the Curriculum.

It commonly takes the form of extended and irrelevant information; introduction of purely professional detail; indiscriminate applications. The writer is likely to try to balance this abstruseness by converting his discourse into a sort of advanced "baby talk." Exactly the reverse process is called for. The course organization should stand out in clear units of understanding to be developed; informational material should be selected which illustrates and applies the principles being taught and is not in the book for its own sake. The discourse should be that employed by the educated adult, but not the scientific specialist. Nevertheless, where technical expressions are required by the necessities of definition, they should be used and explained. One can define the atom as a "wee bit of something so small that we cannot see it," or he can define it as "the smallest particle of matter which can enter into combination." The first means nothing, chemically speaking. The latter requires explanation, but that is nothing else than teaching the rudiments of Chemistry.

In the organization and economy of the Curriculum, particularly in an age of rapidly expanding knowledge, the great need is *simplification*, and the beginning of simplification is *organization*, which is nine-tenths of teaching.

UNITS IN GENERAL SCIENCE

I. Living Creatures
 1. Inanimate matter and living creatures
 2. Difference between plants and animals
 3. Forms of lowest life which are neither plants nor animals
 4. Relation of plants, animals, and microbes to one another in the economy of nature

II. Food
 1. Quest for food determines behavior in all the lower forms and is extremely important in humans
 2. Food in plants and its assimilation
 3. Food in animals and its assimilation
     (Both 2 and 3 should be treated in gross, without attempting to teach the whole physiology of digestion and assimiliation.)
 4. Assimilated food as tissue
 5. Assimilated food as energy

III. Classification
     (The young pupil, even in the preschool before he is a pupil at all, is familiar with the fact that cats are different from dogs and cows from horses and that they are nevertheless both animals. Not much later he becomes aware that many animals are of the cat kind and others of the dog kind. There is the beginning of naïve thought in the world of living things. It remains to extend that knowledge short of the systematic taxonomy of the botanist and zoölogist.)
 1. Animal classification: Phyla, Classes, Orders, Genera, Species, Varieties, Individuals
     (The essential thing here is understanding of the meaning and method of classification, through simple practice in noting the classification of some representative forms. I not long ago came across a school in which a class had been required to memorize the technical names in order, down to species, and apparently not much else. The exercise would contribute little or nothing to intelligence.)

2. Plant classification

(Similarly treated, but the teacher cannot go far before he is in the specialized study of the botanist.)

3. Man as animal at the top of the scale

IV. Life-History

(The heart of the matter is a realization that every living organism goes through a life-history from a germ of some sort to some form of reproduction and some form of death.)

1. In unicellular creatures
2. From seed to plant, pollination, fruiting, new seed, and withering and death of the plant
3. Metamorphoses in insects
4. Length of life in different forms
5. Annuals, biennials, and perennials in plant life
6. Corresponding life-history in animals
7. Oviparous and viviparous animals

(Teachers with a sense of humor as well as delicacy are required for this unit. Lack of such qualities has made the "facts of life" fit material for the humorist. Children who have thus been well taught, at least in my own recent observation, talk about the whole matter in an entirely natural way, with very much more actual delicacy than was common when they were entirely untaught, and when most boys, and a good many girls, were obscene and secretive little cads—and sometimes never got over it.)

V. Like Tends To Produce Like

1. Dogs do not have kittens
2. Good bodily traits in parents tend to appear in their offspring and the reverse
3. Breeders of plants and animals produce better stock by
   a) Selecting parents which have good traits
   b) Destroying individuals which have bad traits in order to prevent progeny
4. That has been done by nature in the course of millions of years through the survival of stock which is better fitted to survive, and the elimination of the unfit

VI. Matter in Its Composition

1. Matter and nonmatter
2. State and change of state
3. Molecular structure of matter—in simple form
4. Elements and compounds
5. Atomic structure of elements but not structure of the atom

6. Atomic weight

(All that is required is the concept itself in its simplest form. A good teacher places the list of elements somewhere on the board or a chart with their atomic weights and makes no attempt to hold pupils responsible for the figures themselves.)

7. Metals and nonmetals

VII. Chemical Substance and Chemical Change
   1. Physical and chemical properties
   2. Physical and chemical change
   3. Preparation of food as chemical change
   4. Living processes as chemical change

VIII. Oxidation and Reduction
   1. Tendency of oxygen to enter into combination
   2. Decay, corrosion, and combustion as oxidation
   3. The combining process in each
   4. Physical and chemical products in oxidation
   5. Reduction as reverse process

IX. In Living Processes
   1. Oxidation of food in digestion
   2. Heat of oxidation essential to bodily health and activity
   3. Air as source of oxygen
   4. Discharge of products of oxidation in blood stream, respiration, and excretion
   5. Opposite process in plants having chlorophyll

X. Solution and Solvents
   1. Solution and mixture
   2. Solvent and solute
   3. Molecular process involved
   4. Gross facts concerning solubility and properties of different solvents

XI. Simple Equations of Chemical Processes

(Reading and writing chemical processes expressed in simple equations. This is science and, as such, understanding is involved, but the understanding or thought content has already been found. The unit itself is a language art, and the objective is ability to read a simple process in equational form. To carry the matter beyond that is to enter the field of theoretic chemistry.)

XII. Primary Machines
   1. The inclined plane and its derivatives
   2. The lever
   3. The wheel and axle and derivatives

4. Mechanical advantage
5. Why "primary"?

XIII. Mass and Weight
1. Mass conceived as amount of matter in a body
2. Weight conceived as measurement of mass
3. Density
4. The pull of the earth commonly called gravity
5. Gravitation as a general principle of attraction between bodies

XIV. Air Pressure
1. Weight of atmosphere
2. Balanced against a column of mercury or water
3. Vacuum and limit to which a pump can draw water
4. Air pressure on moving planes; wind load
5. Convection currents

XV. Water Pressure
1. Gravity pressure in a liquid
2. Seeks its own level—weight of one column against another
3. Pressure in a vessel
4. The hydrostatic paradox

XVI. Specific Gravity
1. Body displaces its own weight
2. Relative weights of substance and equal volume of water expressed decimally
3. Flotation

XVII. Pumps—air pumps and water pumps
1. Principle on which lift pumps and exhaust pumps work—weight of air and water—pumps do not "suck"
2. Force pumps—air chamber for regular flow
3. Arrangement of valves
   (This unit goes more often astray in teaching than any other in the course, and the teaching is one of the surest tests of the teacher's grasp of the unit principle. I have seen a teacher devote weeks to a vain attempt to secure mastery through memorization of the valve action in all sorts of pumps, and in the end the pupils were no nearer mastery than in the beginning. On the other hand, if the pupils come to *understand principles*, they will always see what the valve action in any kind of pump must be, and in fact such pupils do see.)

XVIII. Fluids
1. Molecular condition
2. Diffusion

3. Absorption
4. Surface tension in liquids
5. Capillarity

XIX. Heat
  1. Nature of heat as molecular activity
  2. Intensity of heat measured in degrees—thermometry
  3. Quantity of heat measured in thermal units
  4. Specific heat
  5. Sources of heat—solar radiation, friction, chemical action, electricity

XX. Heat Action
  1. Radiation
  2. Conduction
  3. Expansive effect
  4. Anomalous effect on ice and certain metals

XXI. Change of State
  1. Melting-point in different substances
  2. Quantity of heat required to pass melting-point
  3. Vaporization point
  4. Quantity of heat required in vaporization
  5. Release of heat involved in liquifying and solidifying
  6. Vapor pressure
  7. Relation of external and internal pressure in determining boiling-point

XXII. Sound
  1. Source in vibrations set up
  2. Transmission in sound waves
  3. Propagation in different media
  4. Sensation and sensory apparatus
      (Texts commonly introduce at this point the anatomy of the ear, only to confuse the pupil and set up a pretense of learning. It is doubtful that anyone really understands the ear as sensory apparatus, unless through the aid of some particularly ingenious model or else through dissection. Even so, adding the anatomy of the auditory nerves, not even expert physiologists know how it is that purely physical vibration has a specific effect in consciousness, for that is still one of the enigmas of Science. The gross fact that there is an apparatus which takes up vibrations and makes them audible is comprehensible and sufficient.)
  5. Pitch
  6. Intensity

7. Quality
8. Physical difference between musical notes and noise

> (Tradition following topical arrangement in high-school courses usually embarks on elementary musical theory at this point. That is to confuse objectives. In General Science we are concerned with mastery of the elementary concepts of Sound and not with their applications in a technical subject.)

XXIII. Light
    1. Wave motion in medium called ether
    2. Sources of light
    3. Rays and beams
    4. Refraction
    5. Refraction in prism—the spectrum
    6. Color
    7. The lens as special case of the prism—effect on seen object
    8. Reflection in seen objects—form and color
    9. Diffusion and consequences to us
    10. The eye as an optical instrument
    11. Mirrors—images and focusing

> (The subject of lenses and mirrors might well be not only two units but an entire course in optics, if we were setting up a preprofessional course, but we are not. The assimilative exercises commonly found in high-school texts do little to develop the unit; they rather expand the Curriculum.)

XXIV. Static Electricity
    1. Electrical charge on a body
    2. Positive and negative electricity
    3. Attraction and repulsion
    4. Potential
    5. Discharge

XXV. Magnetism
    1. Magnetic condition
    2. Polarity
    3. Attraction and repulsion
    4. Lines of magnetic force
    5. Earth as a magnet

XXVI. Current Electricity
    1. Generated by chemical action
    2. Generated by electromagnetic induction
    3. Flow in a conductor
    4. Resistance—heat effects—unit of resistance
    5. Potential as determing flow—unit of electric pressure

6. Circuit
7. Current strength—unit of strength
8. Electrolysis as reverse of chemical generation

XXVII. Induction
1. Simple induction in parallel conductors
2. Magnetic effect of solenoid
3. Electromagnet
4. A whirling coil in a magnetic field—current in the coil
5. Alternating and direct currents
6. Induction coil and potential in primary and secondary circuits
7. Device for stepping up or stepping down voltage

On account of the prominence of electrical applicances in our mechanical environment, teachers of General Science and writers of textbooks are prone to carry the teaching units in Electricity to great lengths, to the confusion of the essential purposes of instruction. The foregoing are enough. Beyond these units come: individual reading as interests dictate; further study by pupils and by adults; the higher concepts and systems of thought in Physics, Chemistry, and Biology for those pupils who continue in school; shop work in the courses in Industry.

UNITS AND MASTERY

The same principles apply here which we have found in Mathematics, in Geography, and in History. Each unit is an elementary comprehensive and significant aspect of the organic or inorganic environment of the Common Man. Mastery is found in the assured comprehension of each unit as defined by its elements, which are in themselves minor understandings, and which form the structure of the argument about which the assimilative material is to be organized.

D. PHYSICS AND CHEMISTRY

In their contributions to Science, Physics and Chemistry are not two sciences but one. Together, they deal with the inorganic world and with its transitions to the organic. They are concerned with matter and its forms and transmutations, with motion, force, and energy.

Now these are par excellence the organized, logical, definitive sciences. They are the content of thought about the realm with which they deal, and, when taken into personality through the learning process, they constitute almost complete adaptability or intelligence in their own field.

It is not very far wrong to assert that modern Physics came into the world with the enunciation of the law of falling bodies. Now that in itself is but one of many contributions to phenomenology, even though it be superlative in its implications. But the law had nothing like the importance of the broader generalization which defines acceleration of moving bodies under constant and under variable forces. It is the existence of comparatively few great principles like that which constitute the maturing of Physics as institutional Science.

So it is with Chemistry. Men have always dealt with things chemical. Long centuries ago men who were intellectually inclined speculated about the nature and structure of matter, and in the end some of their conjectures were surprisingly good. Modern, logical, definitive, normative Chemistry came into being with the positive definition of chemical elements and with the disclosure of the nature of the elementary constitution of matter. Therein emerged a logic, a system of thought about an aspect of the world, a discourse. The supreme achievement in modern Chemistry is not in "discoveries," although they undoubtedly make news, but in the fact that the chemist has acquired thought in advance of his discoveries—even if he thinks poison gas. There would seem to be almost an ethnic period between the methods of Edison and his time and those of the young chemist who deliberately designs a substance which shall possess certain desired physical and chemical properties.

No doubt the chemist can lead us a mad dance with his hydrocarbons and biochemistry and the intricacies of atomic structure; but in the end his science, like that of the physicist, rests on a comparatively small number of great generalizations.

INSTRUCTION

It is only occasionally that one can find a textbook in either Physics or Chemistry which is suitable for the purposes of General

Education. That is particularly true of texts in Chemistry. Time was when the text was in truth elementary, made up of the pertinent and essential generalizations appropriate to the understanding of the Common Man. The science itself has made remarkable progress since those days, and the new enunciations cannot be ignored in the Common School. Nevertheless, current texts in pursuit of the pseudo-practical often become an unorganized mass of industrial information, and the principles set forth tend to be those appropriate to the engineer. The books can be read, but it is absurd to suppose they can in most cases be economically used as the basis for teaching. One cannot digest a handbook.

An example of what I mean can be found in the principles of chemical equilibrium. I suppose few things in Chemistry are more pertinent to the uses of the industrial chemist than this, and yet it is in its whole tendency and utility specialized and not general. It certainly contributes something to our understanding of the behavior of matter under transformation, but after a short paragraph we find ourselves in a study of processes which will run through to completion and others which will not. The Common School is not concerned in studies of industrial processes; it is concerned with enlightenment touching the great matter of how the world is put together.

On the other hand, principles here, as elsewhere, cannot ordinarily be assimilated by the learner except by the use of the teacher's supreme device of illustration. To illustrate anything whatever is to bring the unknown into ideational relations with the known. The known is in the pupil's body of experience, either as a matter of common experience or else because he has previously acquired simpler principles in school somewhere. Some industrial processes which are familiar to all, or else to some in particular communities, may well serve the assimilative purpose to which we have referred; but no industrial process is of any consequence for study purposes when the pupil must learn the process itself before he can use it in arriving at an understanding of a principle which is being expounded.

Finally, one finds scattered through texts sundry scientific principles which are simple enough in themselves, but which contribute little or nothing to General Education. Some of them—qualitative analysis is a good example—are worth presentations at the hands of the teacher without being made units or parts of units for study and mastery.

The reader should bear in mind that what follows is set forth under the presumption that pupils have background in General Science. The course belongs not earlier than in the senior high school or junior-college level.

I. Energy
   1. Definition
   2. Energy of position—not merely local position
   3. Energy of movement—not necessarily movement of bodies
   4. Different forms of energy
   5. Measurement of energy
   6. Conservation and transformation of energy

II. Matter
   1. Definition
   2. Physical properties of matter
   3. Transformation of matter into energy

III. Valence
   1. Elementary forms of matter entering into composition recalled
   2. Valence as a law governing combination
   3. Valence of an element defined in relation to combination with hydrogen
   4. Degrees of valence
   5. Valence in a radical
   6. Valence in writing the formulas of binary compounds
   7. Law of multiple proportions
      (If chemical equations are the language of chemistry, then valence is the grammar. Moreover, it is one of those concepts which under an inspiring teacher enable the pupil to see that the ideal transcends experience. It helps him to catch a vision of the principle that Chemistry is a science of design as well as of experiment.)

IV. Ionization
    1. Ion defined as a chemical unit
    2. Electrical imbalance in the ion
    3. Positive and negative ions
    4. Behavior in solution between electrodes
    5. Ionized gases
    6. Electrolysis

V. The Periodic Law
    (The periodic law in its complexities is professional Chemistry, but in its main outline it is comprehensible to older pupils. It is greatly significant. It is pre-eminently thought. When a science has reached the point at which it can be said, "We now know what there is left to be discovered in this particular area of our field," then the science has become as normative as Logic.)
    1. Atomic number
    2. Periodic change in properties as atomic number increases
    3. Mathematical function involved
    4. Missing elements

VI. Nitrogen as Unstable Element in the Economy of Nature
    1. Does not readily combine
    2. Instability of compounds
    3. Significance in explosives
    4. Significance in foods

VII. Carbon in the Economy of Nature
    1. The carbon-dioxide cycle in living processes
    2. Complexity of carbon compounds
    3. Hydrocarbons and carbohydrates
    4. Carriers of energy
    5. Significance in complex molecule of living tissue

VIII. Acids—Bases—Salts
    (Since the three are intimately related, it is the relationship between the three that constitutes the heart of the unit.)
    1. Acids
        a) Oxides of nonmetals that will combine with water
        b) Essential characteristics
        c) Tests
        d) Naming acids
    2. Alkalinity
        a) Compounds which have the power of neutralizing acids are alkalis

    b) Most common alkaline metals

    c) Mutual neutralizing actions with acids

  3. Bases

    a) The hydroxyl radical

    b) Some metal in combination with hydroxyl group or groups

    c) Essential characteristics

    d) Tests

  4. Salts

    a) Compound in which the hydrogen of an acid has been replaced by a metal or metallic group of elements

    b) Physical and chemical characteristics

    c) Naming salts

  5. Acids, bases, and salts in living processes

IX. Inertia and Force

  1. Newton's first law

  2. Force as a term in mechanics

  3. Moving bodies

  4. Momentum and striking force measured

  5. Analysis of forces—graphing and combining

X. Power and Work

  1. Terms learned and defined

  2. Units of work done

  3. Units of power applied

  4. Input and output

  5. Load in resistance overcome

  6. Friction as resistance

  7. Efficiency of machines—total import equals total output

  8. Useful work done

XI. Force

  1. Newton's second law

  2. Force defined in equation of motion

  3. Acceleration

  4. Acceleration under constant force in terms of space, force, and time

XII. Force in a Revolving Body

  1. Centrifugal and centripetal

  2. Measured along radius of revolution

  3. Measured in other than a circular revolution at any point

  4. Conditions under which a body moves in a fixed orbit

XIII. Acceleration
  1. Positive and negative
  2. Constant and variable
  3. Velocity at the end of a given time in motion
  4. Average velocity
  5. Space passed over in unit of time under known acceleration
      (Law of falling bodies. This is one of the numerous cases in teaching science and mathematics in which drill on a formula until it is learned as a correct spelling of a word is learned helps to make a given understanding available for many years. $s = \frac{1}{2}at^2$ and $s = \frac{1}{2}gt^2$ when thoroughly memorized do not add to the understanding of this unit, or take the place of understanding, but when association calls them up in memory, the whole argument is made readily available as it otherwise would probably not be.)

XIV. Equilibrium
  1. Newton's third law
  2. Force acting on a body balanced by force acting in the opposite direction
  3. Center of gravity in a body
  4. Stable, unstable, and neutral equilibrium in terms of center of gravity

XV. Thermodynamics
  1. Heat as energy
  2. Equivalence of heat and work
  3. Absolute zero
  4. Relation of work done to fall of temperature between source and condenser
  5. Thermodynamic balance
  6. Entropy tends toward a maximum

XVI. Light
  1. As wave motion
  2. Electromagnetic theory
  3. Dispersion of beam in spectrum
  4. Absorption
  5. Doppler effect
  6. Polarization

XVII. Radiant Energy
  1. The electromagnetic spectrum
  2. Hertzian rays
  3. Heat
  4. Visible light

5. Ultraviolet
6. X-rays
7. Radioactive substances
8. Cosmic rays

The course as thus laid out, on the principles adhered to in this whole volume, in the first place defines the place and scope of Physics and Chemistry as a Common School subject, according to the conceptions of the author. The units further constitute the *argument* of the course, and the elements of each unit the argument of that unit. Mastery of each unit is comprehension of the unit, to the extent defined in its elements.

Teaching to the point at which there is real comprehension is a difficult matter, since it implies not only grasp of the unit principle, pedagogical insight in laying out study material, skill in supervising study and following the mind of the pupil, but also artistry in presentation. But these are the art of teaching.

The element organization is the structure of the argument in presentation, which of necessity is always brief—never a lecture. The organization constitutes the chain of successive points which the teacher makes in developing the theme. The books which profess to be set up on the unit principle are seldom clear in their presentation, or overview as it is sometimes called. The reason commonly is that they do not follow their elements but ramble. The best of our newspaper editorials are admirable illustrations of clear, concise, forceful presentation. I have often admired health articles in the current journals for the same qualities; they are very commonly the equivalent of straightforward presentation of a unit in Physics or Chemistry. If one will consider some of them, I suspect that he may be surprised at the lucidity with which essentially abstruse matter is presented—and presented in such a way that probably few readers are ever aware that they have been reading anything other than the simplest of discourse.

E. BIOLOGY

There has always been Biology in the form of experiential learnings from various pursuits, and some notion of the meaning of biological phenomena. When some Indian farmer noticed that, if you put a fish in a hill of corn, you got a better hill, he was practicing Biology. The fact that there were in prehistoric times domesticated animals which differed materially from their feral kindred is evidence that prehistoric man practiced eugenics, at least in his farm animals and perhaps in his sporting animals. To be sure, they had no scientific explanations of what happened and why it happened, and so they could not reason biologically. That side of culture was still in the bosom of spiritism. In the early historic period there was medicine and perhaps some cure of disease—certainly some difficult surgery—but no systematic medicine. There was physiology, but it tended to be mystical, fanciful, or at the very best highly empiricist. Down to very recent times the history of Biology was the history of evolving scientific Physiology.

We are accustomed to believe that modern scientific Biology came in with the Linnaean system of classification in the eighteenth century. So it did, but the science had still a long road to travel before it, like Physics and Chemistry, had reached its comprehensive and significant generalizations which explained rather than merely classified, which defined rather than described. Among these generalizations were the cell theory of living tissue, the adaptive meaning of the nervous system and of various physiological processes, the mechanisms of heredity, and the origin of species by descent with modification.

Biology is one of the three fundamental sciences, in the sense that it deals with one of the three sets of conditioning circumstances under which we live. Physics and Chemistry taken together deal with the inorganic world and its forces; Biology, with the world of living creatures; and Sociology, yet to be developed, with Society. Moreover, like all the sciences, it has become a *form of thought* as well as in its principles *substance of thought*. A large part of the thinking of the modern world is done in terms which are derived from Biology. The terms have become symbols and are used conveniently even where there is no biological substance involved.

The school tradition is that Biology is to be defined as a course in Botany followed by one in Zoölogy. Neither of them has any defensible place in the Curriculum of the Common School, beyond what is implicit in General Science and in Biology. Beyond that, both rapidly become specialized and professionalized in content.

Visit any high-school classroom in Botany and note its microscopes, its drawings, its intimate study of plant morphology and physiology, its elaborate classifications and nomenclature. You are in effect in a university laboratory peopled by young people who are still immature pupils and not university students. Similarly, visit a high-school class in Zoölogy, or a college class for that matter, behold its bones, its aquaria and terraria, its dissecting tables and preserved cadavera, and ask yourself what sort of a class it is that you are visiting. The reasonable answer is that you are observing premedical work if anything.

True enough, botanizing and the study of animal life about us may prove to be richly rewarding avocations, but it is no part of the business of the Common School to provide people with ready-made interests. If instruction results in General Education, it will have provided its pupils with the instruments of access to all cultural interests. But we have no interests unless we are able and willing to find them for ourselves.

Human physiology.—Time was when pupils pursued a substantial course in human physiology. In the movement which held that whatever requires effort is abominable, it disappeared into teacher talks on hygiene—not without their use certainly—and then into a sort of nebulous enterprise called "physical education." Now Physiology as a contribution to Science is in its nature an extension of Biology, specialized and preprofessional in tendency. As the foundation of instruction in Health, it has definite meaning and significance, but that is another and later story.

UNIT ORGANIZATION IN GENERAL BIOLOGY

Nothing need be said touching the characteristics of good textbooks in Biology, or the principles of good organization, which has not already been said in connection with our study of General Science and of Physics-Chemistry. The guiding principle here, as there, is simplification and reduction to the essentials which constitute elementary thought in the field. Here, as there, the unit organization defines the course as a justifiable element in the Curriculum, and it further outlines the argument of the course.

I. Cell Theory
  1. The cell defined and pictured
  2. Protoplasm
  3. Nucleus and cell structure—in gross—not a course in histology
  4. Capture of food energy in the cell
  5. Digestion
  6. Growth and reproduction
  7. Unicellular forms of life

II. Organisms
  1. Metazoa
  2. Bodies with specialized cells
  3. Forms specialized for preying, flight, and conscious activities
  4. Specialized sexual reproduction

III. Energy in Plant Food
  1. Direct capture of solar energy in photosynthesis
  2. Source and character of food material in plants
  3. Availability
  4. Circulating medium
  5. Capillarity and osmotic pressure
  6. Elaboration of starches, fats, and proteins
  7. Expiration of oxygen
  8. Energy output in plants—longevity

IV. Energy in Animal Food
  1. Chemical in origin
  2. Made available in the animal body as input
  3. Fats, carbohydrates, and proteins in bodily economy
  4. Metabolism
  5. Output in repair of tissue, growth, and bodily activity
  6. Elimination of waste
  7. Critical difference between plants and animals in their use of energy

V. Growth in Individual Animals
  1. Conjunction of male and female cells
  2. Embryological development in gross
  3. Dependence upon and independence of mother

4. Meaning of prolongation of infancy
5. Elaboration of structure and function during ontogenesis
6. Development of personality in humans
7. Involution
8. Physiological death

VI. Internal Economy
1. Capture of oxygen
2. Digestion of food—in gross
3. Blood stream
4. Assimilation
5. Homeostasis
6. Glandular growth control
7. Emergency apparatus

VII. Racial Adjustment to Environmental Circumstances
1. Getting on in the world in which one lives
2. Adjustment by adaptation contrasted with mechanical adjustment
3. Evolution of organs
4. Survival of vestigial organs
5. Adaptability

VIII. Individual Adjustment in Environment
1. Adaptive organism in Man
2. Little or no inherited adjustment
3. Hands, voice, and brain
4. Learning from experience
5. Learning from the results of racial experience

IX. Heredity
1. Chromosomes and genes
2. Pairing of sets of genes
3. Unit characters
4. Mendelian law
5. Dominance and nondominance
6. Hybrids and thoroughbreds
7. Mutants
8. Noninheritance of acquired characteristics
(The issue has long been debated. Whatever issue is left is largely a matter of definition of true biological inheritance. The important thing in General Education is the principle that effects in education, either normal or perverse, are not biologically transmitted. They are socially transmitted through upbringing and instruction.)

X. Organic Evolution
1. Descent with variations in individual organic traits

2. Some variations favorable to survival and some less favorable
3. Artificial selection of desired traits by breeders
4. Natural selection by survival of advantageous variations
5. Incidental traits which have no survival significance
6. Evolutionary history defines the species and normality within the species
7. Origin of Man as animal form
8. Civilized Man becomes less and less animal

F. SOCIOLOGY

The world of physical inorganic things. Then the world of living organisms. Finally, the world of social existence. These three cover the conditioning circumstances under which man lives. Physics, Biology, Sociology. From the standpoint of our theory of knowledge, these three are in truth the comprehensive and fundamental areas of Science. Doubtless the three will sometime be on the level of scientific equivalence. When we use the word "sociology," however, we have in mind a pursuit which has gone under that name for just about a hundred years. Is that pursuit Sociology, a full sister to Biology? I believe not.

Our test of what belongs in the Curriculum as Science, and what does not, rests on the issues: Is the science or scientific pursuit an organized, definitive, logic; is it in its nature, at least in its elements, appropriate to the requirements of nonprofessional, nonspecialized education; or, finally, is it necessary phenomenological background for sciences which in themselves belong to the Curriculum, and which are definitive and logical?

Academic sociology as we know it meets none of these tests. Particularly does it fail on the first. If such fundamental and fruitful concepts as folkways, mores, customs, institutions, culture, and civilization were in actuality the subject matter of a recognized academic discipline, then it could be said that there was in existence a Sociology on its way to take its place by the side of General Biology.

An examination of the titles in any large library under the caption "sociology," supplemented by inspection of the standard texts and treatises available, and of the course descriptions in university catalogues, must convince anybody, as it seems to me, that sociology, much like academic education, is the name for a field of discussion and investigation rather than an organized science. As such, it is no doubt a useful academic pursuit, but it is not available for purposes of instruction looking toward General Education.

On the other hand, just as Astronomy and Mechanics long preceded Physics, and Physiology preceded Biology, so Law, Jurisprudence, and Economics, which are Sociology, long antedated any science under that name. The former dates back four thousand years or more, and fragments of Economics are nearly as old. The Civil Law is more than fourteen hundred years of age as an organized system, and Economics as an organized body of thought is at this writing something more than one hundred and sixty years old—older than Biology.

ETHICS

Ethics is pre-eminently a social discipline, but there is nothing in it which can be learned as an organized body of thought in contribution to Science. Doubtless, there have been various bodies of theory touching the origin and evolution of ethical concepts, but these do not constitute Ethics any more than the history of culture constitutes Science and Art. Ethics rests on Morality, and that is not a contribution to Intelligence but to something else entirely, namely, Conscience. Ethics is not in itself a body of necessary truth, save as it is related to Jurisprudence, which takes us out of the domain of Science and into that of The State. The most notable of all ethical treatises, the *Nichomachaean Ethics* of Aristotle, was essentially an introduction to Politics and felt by him to be such. Ethics is rather a term in Literature, in which some of the best and wisest of our philosophy of conduct has been enshrined. We thus have an ethical literature which is one of our most precious possessions, perhaps more precious than all Science put together, but it is not Science.

THE SOCIAL STUDIES

In what is perhaps a sort of belated surge of conscience over past neglects, "social science" has broken out like an attack of the

measles all over the school system. Examine the school prospec-
tuses and visit the school. You will find, perhaps, ventures into
almonry conventionally known as "social service"; into penology;
into vague and uncertain "social economics" dealing with such
vast questions as capital and labor. Children are induced "to learn
how to think socially" by "discussion of modern problems," thus
being taught to cultivate opinion in advance of knowledge.

There are doubtless a great many social questions which seem
to some of us to need settlement, but they cannot be settled by
discussions in high-school and college classrooms, nor yet by inducing pupils to believe that Sociology has arrived at the stage at
which the teachings of a high-school textbook can be accepted as
expositions of natural law. If the pupils undergo a course of instruction in such social approaches as we have, then when they
come to their maturity and accumulate such wisdom as is not
learned in the schools, very likely they will be able to arrive at
reasonable conclusions touching most matters of social import.
At all events, they will have been equipped in school with the
rudiments of social intelligence in the place of the bad habit of
following blindly the prescriptions of every medicine man with a
glib tongue who comes along.

What have we then?

Well, in the first place we have Civics and Politics vitally fundamental to an understanding of organized society. But these are an
affair of The State and not of Science. There we shall come upon
some elementary notions of Law, of civil agencies, of the Public
Defense, of Constitutional Government, and of Taxation.

Next we have a great deal of organized material which touches
us daily and hourly in the institutions of Commerce and Industry,
in regard to which the educated have always been distinguished
by their ignorance.

Finally, we come to two courses, pertinent subject matter in the
present chapter.

THE COMMUNITY

The first is the Community—local, regional, national, and
world communities—which as descriptive subject matter makes

the background of Economics, The State, Commerce, Industry, and indeed of all our thought in matters social. It is here that the contributions of academic sociology have been of the greatest value. The course is usually placed at junior high school level, and it could probably be placed even lower.

ECONOMICS

"Economy" means "housekeeping" in its original significance. And so the word was long used to mean whatever we do that enters into the practical arrangement of our affairs, among which business stood out as pre-eminent. It has even been a term in theology where "economical" is contrasted with "ontological." It is not so very long ago that the term "political economy" was pretty nearly a synonym for "statecraft" or the "art of government."

We still speak of "national economy" to signify the way a social order is put together in its economic aspect, or even the resources of a nation and its organization for utilizing them. In this meaning, the better terms are the "human ecology" or " geography" of a nation, or perhaps "the national community."

But we are concerned with a science which is said to be "the science of wealth," with a logic which defines wealth and its production and distribution. Most texts and treatises on Economics are in reality quite as much concerned with Commerce and Industry as with Economics. Now, these are institutions in their own right which have had an institutional history quite apart from Economics and Science in general. To hold that Commerce is derivable from Economics is to get the cart before the horse; Economics has been derived in large part from Commerce. True enough, Commerce must conform to economic principles, but it must conform to many other principles which are not economic in their nature. Economics has been derived also from experience with The State, but The State, like Commerce, goes far beyond Economics. True enough, again, the conduct of Government, where economic concerns are involved must conform to economic logic.

So most of what will be found in the ordinary school and college text in Economics belongs properly to Commerce and Government and Industry; and under our conceptions of the Curriculum what properly belongs in those fields is there discussed—in later chapters.

Economics has still a debatable place as a school subject. It has never found any secure place in the Curriculum of the Common School and, as a college subject, has tended to occupy that precarious place which is the destiny of subjects of which it is said, "They ought to know something about it." The natural consequence is that economic intelligence in the mores is an exceedingly nebulous thing.

In times of depression students flock to the economics courses in high school and college with the vague idea in mind that, if they go through the ritual of taking a course or two, all will be well with them.

On the other hand, a considerable number assert with confidence that the subject belongs to the superstitions and folklore of the past, on the ground that economic law "did not prevent the depression." As well give up Chemistry on the ground that the laws of combustion do not prevent a house's burning down if the owner gets careless with fire.

Finally, the destructive radical finds fault with Economics, as he does with everything else, his chief stock in trade being that the "law of supply and demand does not work," that prices are whatever the traffic will bear, and in short that there is no logic about wealth, its production and distribution. Such people commonly confuse the much-vexed law of supply and demand as an economic principle with the same law in Commerce as determining price. Their whole line of reasoning would apply equally well to medicine and the cure of disease, since a patient will likely enough die if he consults a quack, or alternatively refuses to follow the advice of a competent physician.

Not long ago, I came across a high-school text presumably written and published to meet the demands of the "liberals"—an instance by the way in which supply and demand evidently did work—in which occurred the remarkable statement that "economic law is always changing." If that were true, evidently there would be no logic and no science. No doubt our knowledge of economic principles undergoes changes as more facts accumulate, and as new developments occur; but that is not to say that the principles themselves are always changing, or that a principle formerly held was necessarily in itself untrue. Since my time in college, pretty much the whole structure of Physics and Chemistry has been altered; but we do not for that reason announce that bodies no longer fall in in accordance with the formula $s = \frac{1}{2}gt^2$, or that acids are no longer sour but alkaline. The new has been built on the old, and our confidence in the physical sciences is stronger than ever.

ECONOMIC INTELLIGENCE

People expect too much of all the sciences. They are but systems of thought. Credit for a course or two, or many courses, is no guaranty that the individual will use thought in reflection. The most we get out of any science is intelligence of a particular kind.

So it is with Economics. It is an analytical science. It is not experimental but it is empirical, in the sense that it is founded upon observed facts. It deals with a subject which is indefeasible in all human relations. He who faithfully cultivates the subject can hardly fail to acquire the logical outlook on what is in the end the food supply, and the supply of other necessaries, and the supply of luxuries as well. Logical outlook constitutes intelligence.

Nor is the system of thought here set up implicated with the "capitalistic system" so called. It deals with subject matter which is indefeasibly human and universal. A communistic autocracy, if it hoped to extend the Great Escapes, would rest on exactly the same fundamental laws as those which govern the success of free enterprise working in a money economy as a social order.

THE COMMUNITY

To become familiar with and to understand the Community as a social organism is to embark on the study of General Sociology, even though the pupils never arrive at a definitive course bearing that name.

Most people take the local community in which they live for granted; to them it is just "my home town." Few realize that every community has an anatomy and physiology of its own, much as does the physical body. The analogy breaks down in the principle that the body is a product in evolution, while the Community is not. Community is not institutional; it is normally a natural geographical response. People have come to live there because of the quality of the land, of the climate, of communication with the outside world, of natural resources available.

It is normally a natural geographic response; but many local communities are merely accidental in character. In this, the origin goes back to the casual settlement of some man or men who gathered others about them. In this community the origin may have been in possibility of martial defense ages ago, and the community persists by sheer tradition. In still another, it is a group of people who have been driven out of more favored regions and are doing the best they can in meager circumstances. But healthy community life depends in the first instance on the issue whether or no there is any natural excuse for its existence.

It follows that communities can be planned, that is to say, set in order and guided in the direction of normal community functioning. Societies or social orders cannot be planned; they are the outgrowth of the spread of Civilization in the mores.

UNIT ORGANIZATION

It is of course imperative that pupils should have by them for study and reference examples of typical communities set forth in descriptive and analytical accounts. In other words, the inductive approach in illustrative factual material is as necessary here as it is elsewhere in the sciences.

I. The Natural Community
   1. A group of people settled upon a given area and engaged in the production and distribution of needed and desired goods and services

    2. There must be natural resources sufficient in variety and quantity to support the population

    3. In the natural community, there is always a minimum of imports and exports

    4. So long as the natural community is local, the life which goes on therein will tend to be meager, although there may be little poverty

    5. Social conditions are at their simplest

II. Specialized Communities

    1. A specialized community may grow up about a single community enterprise, to which everything is subsidiary

    2. Types of specialized communities: farming, mining, manufacturing, residential, entrepot, military

    3. Specialized communities are not normal and therefore tend to create abnormal societies

    4. Expansion into larger communities is always an effort to recover the balance found in the natural local community

III. Geographical Origins

    1. Resources

    2. Climate

    3. Water supply

    4. Trade-route relations

    5. Topography

IV. Extent and Boundaries of the Local Community

(The intent here is to "find the community" in principle. The tendency is to consider the municipality as the community.)

    1. Center—commonly a village or city, itself semicommunity and subsidiary to the wider community

    2. Farming area using the center in commercial and other social activities

    3. Mining, forestry, and other activities similarly centering

    4. Hierarchy of communities centering upon regional and national centers

V. Economic Production

    1. Husbandry and extractive industries

    2. Public utility services

    3. Manufacturing and processing

    4. Source of raw material

    5. Home consumption of products

VI. Division of Labor

    1. Primitive conditions in which the only division is between the work of women and that of men

2. Little division in our frontier communities
3. The rise of a trading class—middle men—trading centers
4. Craft specialization
5. Specialized community and regional production
6. Economic advantage of division of labor
7. Diminishing advantage beyond certain points

VII. External Trade
  1. Some or all of the raw materials of manufacturing must be imported
  2. Goods not produced locally and desired for local consumption must be imported
  3. Goods produced in excess of local needs must be exported
  4. In the long run, all imports must be paid for in exports

VIII. Distribution within the Community
  1. Stores and merchandising
  2. Economy in merchandising—superfluity or inadequacy of enterprises carrying on distribution
  3. Dealing in home products
  4. Dealing in external products
  5. Essential goods and services
  6. Luxury goods and services

IX. Financial Services
  1. Banks
  2. Building and loan associations and similar enterprises
  3. Checking accounts and use in the community—clearing checks without use of money
  4. Savings accounts and investment of savings by banks
  5. Export of savings—in purchase of domestic and foreign
  6. Credit services to merchants, manufacturers, and farmers

X. Nonindustrial Production and Distribution
  1. Churches and allied enterprises
  2. Schools other than trade and commercial
  3. Fraternities, clubs, and unions, for sundry purposes
  4. Theaters
  5. Community music
  6. Community recreation
  7. Estimate of sufficiency, insufficiency, or superfluity of nonindustrial enterprises

XI. Classes within the Community
  1. Enterprisers
  2. Managerial

3. Wage and salary earners
4. Professional
   a) Salaried
   b) In private practice
5. Official

XII. The Necessitous Man
1. The humanitarian impulse to care for the needy
2. Charitable organizations and their professional setup
3. Private charity and limits of its justification
4. Mendicancy
5. Tax-paid charity
6. Charity not an individual right
7. Family obligation to care for its own

XIII. The Population
(The intent here is to come to an understanding that there is in every community a population justified by community functions and that excessive population means, in the long run, demoralization.)
1. Population required in the productive enterprises
2. Population required in commercial enterprises
3. Population required in governmental service
4. Population required in servicing enterprises
   (Bear in mind that the bulk of the population in a normal community occurs in the first two classes.)
5. Birth rate and death rate
6. Housing—adequate or inadequate for justifiable population

XIV. Delinquency
(The intent here is to come to an elementary notion of the meaning and destructive effects of delinquency in the Community. The whole matter appears again in a later course on police protection in the study of The State.)
1. Malicious mischief, larceny, robbery, arson, murder, kidnaping
2. Violation of ordinances and regulations—misdemeanors
3. Prevalence of crime in the United States as compared with
   a) Canada
   b) England
   c) Scandinavian countries
   d) Holland and Switzerland
4. The different states compared
5. Cost of crime to the community in
   a) Economic loss
   b) Misery and unhappiness of the people affected

6. Chief sources of the criminal class
   a) Broken, negligent, and incompetent homes
   b) Lax school discipline
   c) Vicious reading matter
   d) Incompetent police

XV. The Municipality
   1. A chartered corporation set up by The State covering a local community for the purpose of local self-government
   2. May or may not be coextensive with the community but is not the community—difference
   3. The city charter or village act of incorporation
   4. Difference between a municipal ordinance and a statute
   5. Municipal enterprises
      a) Fire protection
      b) Water and sewerage works
      c) Public parks and recreation grounds
      d) Maintenance of streets
   6. Local government has two main functions:
      a) To exercise regulatory powers over community life
      b) To administer municipal enterprises

XVI. The Great Community
   1. Test of any community is that it is an area upon which people are settled in homes and have become organized for carrying on in cooperation the great social functions of production, distribution, regulation, and reproduction
   2. The community does not owe its origin to law; the municipality does
   3. Great regional communities tend to form after the pattern of the local community
   4. A nation like the United States or Canada is a national community before it is an organized State
   5. Since people trade and travel the world around, the whole world is more and more a community.

XVII. Community Planning
   1. Putting things where they belong
      (The expression is taken from Haig in the *Report* of the New York Regional Survey Commission. It means, I take it, arranging the apparatus of the community geographically so that there will be engendered the minimum of inconvenience and waste, and the maximum of the peace of the City Beautiful. The expression amounts to a definition of the unit.)

2. Zoning
3. Restricted districts
4. Sections for different types of merchandising
5. Sections for different types of manufacturing
6. Residential planning
7. Railway stations and yards
8. Airports
9. Wharves and docks
10. Parks and parking
11. Architectural control

The reader should bear in mind that this course is elementary and preliminary. It is a study of the Community as such and not a study of what goes on in the Community. Later we shall come to The State, Commerce, and Industry, which are concerned with what goes on in the Community.

UNITS IN ECONOMICS

One of the most difficult problems in teaching Economics as a social science, or indeed in studying it either as pupil or adult, is in the fact that it is difficult to use the language with precise and constant meaning. For that reason, I have thought it well, in suggesting a unit organization, to treat the elements in explanatory paragraphs in some cases rather than merely to give the titles as has been earlier practice in this volume.

I. Economics Is Impersonal and Objective

In some respects, Economics is the most teachable subject in the Curriculum, and in others the hardest to teach. It is teachable because the ideology is more or less within the experience of everybody. It is hard to teach because in no science does the teacher have to encounter so much predisposition to wishful thinking, and so many situations in which inherently subjective attitudes prevail.

Hence it is that Unit I is establishing objective attitude. The unit is in appreciation rather than in understanding. It cannot be mastered before going on with the rest of the course. It begins the first day, and the teacher may well be at it with some when the course is brought to a close.

II. Changing Economy and Changing Economics

    1. Economy originally meant housekeeping. Hence it comes to mean sometimes the way a community keeps house in the production of economic goods and services.

    2. Economics is the Science of Wealth without regard to the kind of wealth being produced or the method of its distribution.

    3. After the Middle Ages it is said that the nations of western Europe changed from a manorial to a money economy. That means that nations which had been organized on the basis of the production of wealth largely by serfs, and distribution according to the good will of the lord of the manor and the custom of the manor, advanced into an economy in which labor was paid for in money and goods were bought and sold for money.

    4. But the laws of Economics were the same in one economy as in the other, except that the laws of money appeared in the new economy and that nobody knew much about economic law anyway.

    5. Again, we speak of the frontier economy of the United States and say truthfully that such an economy has long since passed away.

    6. But the laws of economics were the same in one period as in the other, save that we have learned more about the laws. Looking back, we are able to understand the frontier period better with the aid of the laws which we do understand.

    7. The present might be called the automobile age, or automobile economy, and the whole community setup is very different from what it was before the automobile came.

    8. But the automobile has changed no economic laws. If they were true before the age came in, they are still true, albeit we may have to think out new situations with them.

        a) Supply and demand governs as it always did. The producer cannot sell a car unless there is somebody who desires it enough to buy it. If prices become lower through greater available supply, then more people will desire cars.

        b) Revolutionary changes in national economy in a country which still distributes under a money economy or its equivalent do not alter the laws which govern the value of money.

III. Wealth

    1. Wealth is the limited material possessions which we enjoy, consume, or use as capital or land.

    2. We have possessions which are more valuable to most of us than any wealth, for example, love of friends, self-respect, capacity to enjoy nature and art; but these are not material things. Hence, they are not wealth.

3. Wealth is also our title to services which require labor or the use of capital. Slavery is morally wrong and economically unjustified, but the services of slaves was wealth. So is the enjoyment of services of others for which we pay a wage or fee. The money is not wealth; the services are wealth.

4. Wealth presumes scarcity or at least limited supply. Air is material, it is in the possession of everybody, but it is not wealth.

  a) Water is sometimes unlimited in supply, and everybody has free access to it. In that case, water is not wealth. In settled countries water becomes limited in supply and thus becomes wealth.

  b) Even land is only potential wealth in a country in which it is unlimited in supply. As soon as somebody acquires the legal right to fence it in, or seizes the right without regard to law, it becomes wealth.

5. Wealth implies labor and effort somewhere in production and distribution. Even wild land does not become wealth until there has been labor performed in fencing it in or in excluding trespassers.

IV. Capital

  1. Capital is wealth which is used in the production of more wealth.

  2. Goods used in subsistence and laid up in reserve are wealth but not capital, except when they are to be used in the subsistence of workmen engaged in production.

  3. Capital is betterments on land in productive use, factories, machinery, railways, etc.

  4. Shares of stock are not wealth or capital, but evidence of ownership in capital; they have only the real value that the capital has.

  5. Capital originates in production which goes beyond the requirements of subsistence. The greater the thrift, the more the capital.

  6. Savings in savings banks, insurance companies, and like enterprises is capital in the sense that savings are convertible into real capital.

  7. Accumulation of capital is the economic foundation of Civilization.

V. Use of Capital

  1. The use of capital is Interest.

  2. Interest is part of the product of capital set aside for the use of the capital.

  3. Upon interest hangs the support of most colleges, many schools, hospitals, endowed churches, the whole system of insurance and support of old age, and indeed most institutions which are concerned with immediate human betterment.

  4. To ignore the use of capital is economically much the same as it would be to ignore wages of labor.

5. All large-scale communist, and semicommunist, orders have broken down, in large part because of the delusion that the use of capital can be ignored.
6. Rate of interest is determined by:
   a) Supply of available money to be loaned, and demand for it
   b) Risk involved in investments

VI. Destruction of Capital
   1. Capital is slowly accumulated.
   2. All capital is subject to depreciation in utility. If the depreciation is not made good, the capital ceases to exist.
   3. Capital may be destroyed by war, fire, and mischances of nature.
   4. What is destroyed is the actual capital or wealth, not the commercial value of capital alone. Sometimes commercial value of capital after a devastating war is even greater than before, and people are deluded into the belief that capital has not been destroyed.
   5. War especially destroys capital by utilizing wealth which ought to have gone into extensions of capital or into making good depreciation.

VII. Land
   1. Land, comprises not only terrain but the resources in soil, water, and other minerals.
   2. Land in use is wealth, analogous to capital but not strictly capital.
   3. Land is the most limited of economic goods, for there is only so much of it on the surface of the planet.
   4. The use of land is much the same as the use of capital, but as Civilization advances and capital accumulates, the use of capital tends to cost less; but, since Land is limited in supply, the use of Land tends to cost more.
   5. The use of Land is Rent.

VIII. Money
   1. Money is not wealth but money, a medium in which wealth can be exchanged and reckoned.
   2. A sound monetary system *rests upon* wealth, that is to say, upon something that has economic value in itself, usually precious metals.
   3. The pecuniary unit is primarily a measure, and economic values are expressed in terms of the unit.
   4. But if all the wealth in any country is reckoned in money, there is never more than a very small portion which is in actual monetary wealth, that is, metallic money or specie.

5. If a rich man is estimated to be worth a certain amount in money, all it means is that all his wealth can be exchanged for some other wealth of equivalent money value, if there is anybody able and willing to exchange.

6. The real value of wealth is in the satisfactions it yields and in the utility in production which it has.

IX. The Distribution of Wealth

1. The distribution of wealth means the proportion of the total wealth of a country in the hands of the individuals of the country considered severally.

2. Not the proportion of the total money.

3. If the average man can have twice the goods and services he had in some previous time, the total amount of wealth remaining the same, then wealth is twice as well distributed, even if earnings in money are no more.

4. Increasing wages and other forms of income at the lower levels do not necessarily improve the distribution of wealth, since such increase is more than likely to lead to increased prices and diminution of what income will buy.

5. Human betterment does not consist in distribution of wealth but rather in more equitable distribution of the satisfactions which come from usable and enjoyable goods and services. Men were no better off when wealth was more evenly distributed, and there was not enough for anybody.

6. Hence, production of enough to go round is quite as important as distribution of what is produced.

7. Distribution is at a maximum when each secures wealth in proportion to his ability to produce, directly or indirectly, for in that case the maximum for distribution will be achieved.

X. Income

1. Real income is the amount of enjoyable and consumable goods and services an individual receives in a given time.

2. Income in money is the total return received as:
   a) Wages and salaries
   b) Interest
   c) Profits, including dividends
   d) Professional fees and other fees

3. National income is the total of all individual incomes.

4. National income is not:
   a) The revenues of government
   b) A fund which can be drawn upon by individuals

5. There is no national income which does not appear first as individual income.

XI. Noneconomic Production
    1. The product of churches, libraries, theaters, schools and universities, and like enterprises is not wealth.
    2. In general, the product of government is not directly wealth.
    3. Nevertheless, most of these indirectly produce wealth since they make production of wealth more possible, and distribution as well.
    4. Such enterprises come into the economic order because they must necessarily consume wealth.
    5. Hence, part of the wealth of the nation must be set aside to maintain them.
    6. Such enterprises cannot, however, be maintained indefinitely on an economic basis unless their work does in fact produce indirectly the equivalent of the wealth they consume.

XII. Value
    1. Value in use—utility.
    2. Law of diminishing utility.
    3. Real value of particular forms of wealth is in satisfaction it gives.
    4. Hence, values change as Civilization spreads through the population. Some things are desired more and others a great deal less.
    5. Value in exchange or relative desirability of forms of wealth to different individuals.
    6. Money value is Price.

XIII. Risk
    (One of the most ancient and fundamental experiences of life is risk. Sumner called it the aleatory element in life. One of the prime marks of the level of Civilization among a people is the extent to which risk is avoided or distributed. One of the sure marks of the individual primitive is the appetite for playing with risk, that is to say, gambling.)
    1. Saving or thrift against an uncertain future—generally established habits of thrift are a powerful safeguard against long-continued business depressions.
    2. Insurance—life, fire, accident, any casualty.
    3. Profit is risk-bearing in venturesome enterprise.
    4. Investment banking as distribution of risk.
    5. Corporate enterprise is economical distribution of risk.
        (The unit appears here as a general principle in economic society. It will appear more in detail in the chapter which deals with Commerce.)

XIV. Supply and Demand
    (The average graduate who has had but scant study of Economics is prone to believe that all of Economics revolves about supply and

demand, in fact that it is all there is to Economics, save what is reserved for Ricardo's long-forgotten "Iron Law of Wages." In truth supply and demand has but little place in Economics. It has an important place in Commerce, but even there its place is by no means all-important. It is included here because it has some importance.)

1. Demand for a particular good or service will always condition production, even where there is no question of exchange.
2. Similarly a large supply will stimulate demand up to the point at which demand is becoming sated.
3. Elastic demand
    a) Can do without
    b) Can find a substitute
4. Inelastic demand the opposite, and has a great deal to do with intelligent public policy relating to ownership of the means of production, notably water supply.
5. Influence of education upon demand.

XV. Prosperity
    1. Is in abundance of goods and services available.
    2. Is in maximum distribution of goods and services consistent with maximum production.
    3. Maximum distribution in the long run depends not on the intelligence and character of individuals but on Intelligence, Conscience, and Taste in the people.
    4. Hence, in the long run, continuous prosperity depends upon the level of Civilization to be found in the people.
    5. Prosperity is not in terms of money: an extremely high national income may be the sign of insidious malady in the body politic.

FINAL COMMENT

In discussing this course, I have been at pains to distinguish between Economics as the science of wealth and Commerce as an institution in its own right. Economics has nothing to do with Ethics. It describes wealth and its production and distribution, without regard to the desirability of a given form, or to the justice of a particular distribution. On the other hand, like all the sciences, it gives to Ethics much of its substance. It is one thing to desire to do right, and quite another to find the intelligence which will tell us what is right. Hell is paved with good intentions, at least so we are told.

But Commerce, if it is sound and socially useful, depends quite as much on Morality and Ethics as upon Economics.

Since Economics as a fundamental science makes no pretense of passing upon ethical questions, it manifestly cannot concern itself with such matters as the rightness or wrongness of distribution. It leaves that to Jurisprudence; but it is in a position to say whether this legislation or that decision can or cannot have the effect intended.

The course which has been discussed, if properly reduced to textbook form and adequately taught, should be sufficient to generate the elements of economic intelligence in the Common Man. But economic intelligence is but a part of general intelligence, and it will avail not much unless it is integrated in personality with other fruits of instruction looking toward General Education.

G. OTHER SCIENCES

All the foregoing suggests the query, "Does the list of sciences as discussed complete the count of those which belong in the Curriculum of the Common School?" Others are taught and have traditionally been taught. I have known schools which had courses in Mineralogy and Crystallography. Psychology is sometimes taught and in earlier days was taught in another form than that in which it appears today.

Publicity will frequently bring subjects into the Curriculum because they attract the interest of some teachers and some parents. Local professional enthusiasm for a particular subject often leads to agitation and inclusion in the program of the local schools, and the elective system makes it easy to persuade school authorities to sanction new subjects. I have seen Jewelry recorded as an accepted entrance credit in an indubitably first-class university, to say nothing of sciences and pseudo-sciences which in all probability had somewhere been nothing more than responses to the importunities of minority pressure groups.

In this chapter there has been developed a body of principles which give us an impartial foundation from which to judge what sciences are essential contributions to fundamental Science, to basal Intelligence, and for that reason are in principle indefeasibly parts of the Curriculum. The principles have been stated and reiterated. Once more, they are in brief summarized.

That only is justified which is in principle essential and fundamental, comprehensive and significant. That test being applied, the only sciences which qualify are those which seem to have reached the stage at which they are organized bodies of the substance of thought; and those which are necessary phenomenological foundations in instruction for the organized sciences.

The exception is in Geography and History, which we have shown to be background of all practical, intellectual apprehensions of the environment, especially in all that concerns Society.

We have also seen that portions of the ideological fields cultivated by some of the sciences belong to the Curriculum, not for their own sake but because they are essential parts of sciences which do belong. The most notable are Astronomy and Geology, which in their rudiments are part of Geography; and Botany and Zoölogy, which appear in General Science. We have also noted that it is impossible to pursue any of the four last named very far before one finds himself in specialized study which is appropriate to the University.

As to a multitude of other sciences, it can hardly be maintained that none of them would contribute to the intelligence of the pupil. They would indeed, but it would be far within the region of diminishing returns.

Again, it may well be urged that the elements of Civics, Politics, and Jurisprudence are properly sciences, that they are very significant, and that they belong to the instruction of the Common Man as citizen. They do indeed, but they belong not as contributions to Science but rather as contributions to The State. Both Science and The State are contributions to our ultimate intellectual attitude toward the world, which we call our Philosophy.

Finally, the function of the Common School is not to teach everything but rather to generate that adaptability which makes the pupil capable of learning by himself whatever his needs and interests in mature life determine. One of the logical marks of the transition out of the *status pupillaris* is an awareness that one does not necessarily have to "take a course" to learn something. That awareness is indeed one of the Great Escapes—escape out of the domination of the specialist.

CHAPTER VII

RELIGION

FOR three chapters to come we turn sharply away from the argument of the last four, away from logic, from the forms of thought, from thought in content, to what is not thought but sentiment, not understanding but appreciation, not reason but the reasonable in human experience; away from Science to what have been called the Humanities.

I. INTRODUCTION TO THE HUMANITIES

The persistent fallacy of what was once called the Age of Reason, and is now worshiped as the Wonders of Science, is that nothing is learned save by the exercise of a mythical *faculty* called the Reason, and that there is no certainty save in what is logically justified.

The adaptive process which we call learning, in all forms of life, rests on experience, and there is no learning save out of experience of some sort. There is no inborn faculty which gives us anything; there is adaptive capacity which is characteristic of the human, one of the organic conditions of existence. The question then forces itself on our attention, Is there any valid learning product, in the race or in the individual, which arises out of unanalyzed experience, or are the sentiments and their organized products sheer fancy and delusion?

EMPIRICAL METHODS AND DIALECTIC OF THE RACE

So long ago as the Stoics at least, the distinction came to be drawn between experience in the gross as all men find it and selected experience focused deliberately on particular inquiries. The latter we know as the *empirical method*. It is the method used by scientists the world over in the search for scientific truth. It may be observational, when the search for facts is nonexperimental. It may be experimental, when a hypothesis founded on facts observed in experience is formulated, and selected further facts are observed in order to see if the latter are what they logically should be in the light of the hypothesis.

In the use of the empirical method there must always be the element of rational analysis, dialectic, which in substance is seeing why the facts are what they are. Otherwise, the result is termed *empiricist*, and our reaction is, "Maybe so; maybe not." In other words, the empirical method in any of its forms is inconclusive apart from logic, that is to say, conformity to the forms of thought.

But dialectic is also used where the inquiry does not admit of empirical investigation at all. In Logic and Mathematics there is nothing empirical and no experimentation, save sometimes in a subsidiary sense. Conclusions depend upon sheer internal necessity. If *a* is equal to *b* and *b* is equal to *c*, then *a* must be equal to *c*. Nothing empirical about that. Nevertheless, there is experience which arises out of social intercourse in disputation, for there must be meeting of minds to give an opportunity for the elimination of fallacy. So good logic too is learned out of experience, but it is not empirical nor yet experimental.

NONEMPIRICAL EXPERIENCE

We remind ourselves then that there is an abundance of experience which is in no sense empirical in the strict use of words and cannot be. Aside from that which is dialectic, there is the common uncritical experience of life. It is the source of our values as distinguished from our rational insights, of what we call the Humanities. A religious or moral conviction arises that way; so does an aesthetic conviction. The experience herein of any one individual in the quest of assurance is insignificant compared with the experience of the race. In empirical investigation the experience of an individual can stand against the experience of the race, and necessarily has done so, for there is no common experience in empirical matters. Common sense has no experience of the structure of the atom, or of the mechanics of the solar system; but common sense does have experience of Justice, of Righteousness in general, of the Beautiful, of God. Intelligence is positive; what goes into it can be logically demonstrated. Conscience and Taste are not positive, but they are no less real. Conviction does not come through demonstration, but directly out of affective experience. All the treatises on nutrition ever written would be incapable of arguing the young male of the species into liking spinach, but they may persuade him that it would be expedient for him to acquire the taste. Our moral and aesthetic convictions are acquired tastes.

This estimate of appreciation as being nonrational is sometimes challenged, on the ground that we can and do analyze our sentiments. It is true that we analyze. We are constantly analyzing property right and asserting that this is and the other is not property. We analyze a painting and say that here form is good and color barbarous. Or music, and prefer the rhythm of this and the melody of that. Or a poem is picked to pieces, and aesthetic judgment decrees that it is good here and bad there. Ethical and aesthetic analysis is the basis on which a large part of instruction in appreciation is carried on, and the naïve appreciation of the child or the untutored lifted into the critical appreciation of the educated. Nevertheless, such an analysis is merely breaking down a whole into its constituents; in the end each of the latter is under appreciation. There is nothing in the analysis which is the same as what goes on in ratiocination. There is no "if this, then that"; no relation of cause and effect; no antecedent and consequent. One analysis is in appreciation and yields directly a series of felt results; the other is in understanding and yields rationally apprehended results.

The point of the whole matter is that the Humanities in the end rest on the same basis as that on which Science rests, that is to say, on experience, but experience differently apprehended and differently managed. Their products in Culture might well be called the outcome of the *dialectic of the race*. What has long persisted in the sentiments of men has again and again disappeared and then reappeared, has been found in one form or another everywhere or nearly everywhere, is probably valid, right, basal, in all human experience. The reasoned conclusions of individuals on the other hand, are as likely to be wrong as right, except they are capable of demonstration and are in fact demonstrated.

II. RELIGION AS INSTITUTION

Perhaps on the whole the most conspicuous of social phenomena over the ages, and in point of influence the most dynamic, is what we call Religion. We can hardly escape the inference at the outset that it is major and universal institution. But let us see, and first of all let us find out if we can, what it is that we are talking about.

RELIGION IN EVOLUTION

We have all along seen that the evolution of an organ or an institution as a functional entity defines that organ or institution. Hence we turn first to the evolutionary story in our search for definition.

The starting-point in our inquiry is to be found in Spencer's precept: "Whatever is common to men's minds in all stages must be deeper down in thought than whatever is peculiar to men's minds in higher stages; and if the later product admits of being reached by modification and expansion of the earlier product, the implication is that it has been so reached."

Ordinarily the precept is taken as a warning not to ignore the earlier stages. In our present subject, and often elsewhere, the warning is equally pertinent not to ignore later stages. Students in Spencer's time had been much impressed by the identification of the rock scratches made by existing Alpine glaciers with similar scratches presumably made by ancient glaciers in the long ago. Agassiz started from the known phenomena of a later stage. If we ignore the stage with which we are familiar, we are likely to land in false assumptions touching the earlier stage out of which the later has descended. We encounter a primitive institution in which there is a superficial resemblance to one with which we are familiar, and identification of a genetic connection between the two may lead us into mischievous conclusions.

So it is with Religion. Ethnologists have, as it seems to me, sometimes indulged in a good deal of false evolution, because they have assumed that what is little more than verbal resemblance appears in both primitive folkways and modern religious cults. That is notably true of the connotations which surround the word "spirit" and its cognates. It is argued that because we find everywhere in the primitive world belief in spirits which animate objects, and sorcery intended to control the activities of ghosts, therefore Religion originated in spiritism and ghost worship. As well say that railway ties are animate because they are sometimes called "sleepers."

What is there then that we can say is common, and fundamentally common, to religious cults as we find them today? In order to find an unprejudiced answer, let us turn to the work of men who have devoted themselves to the study of Religion as institution.

In Friess and Schneider's *Religion in Various Cultures* occurs the following statement: "The German theologian, Rudolph Otto, on the basis of both the psychology and anthropology of religion, has maintained that the sense of the 'numinous' is a unique and ultimate quality of experience, and that when this immediate sense of the uncanny, the sacré, is developed by moral regulation, it produces the sense of the holy or the sacred."[1] I suppose it is fair to say then that the kernel of religious feeling is reverence.

Now, wherever we go in the primitive world, we find an entirely comprehensible animism or spiritism. The savage entertains no ideas of cause and consequence. The law of learning which we find everywhere leads him to explain the unknown in terms of the known. What he is vitally aware of is himself as organism, and his dreams and the reflections of his face in still water give him a plausible notion of spirits. Hence, he accounts for an extremely perplexing world by assuming spirits indwelling in objects and controlling what we should call natural forces. Grafter that he is, he performs incantations for the sake of pleasing or terrifying the

[1] Friess and Schneider, *Religion in Various Cultures* (New York: Henry Holt & Co., 1932).

spirits. In that way, he manages his world, or supposes that he does. It is a far-fetched idea to call the incantations worship, or to call the specialist who gets the job of interpretation and of wielding the magic a priest. And yet it is commonly done. There is nothing resembling worship about it, or sense of the numinous, or of the sacred. You do not worship a ghost or revere it; you drive it away if you can.

But all this is the precursor of something, and if we have grasped the idea of institution and of institutional function and utility, it is not difficult to see what that something is. The animating spirits in sticks and stones, wind and storm, drums and bells, fecundity and vitality, are the ancestors—many, many times removed—of energy, electrons, hormones, chromosomes, medicine, and engineering. In brief, all this shamanism and magic is far down in the roots of the family tree of Science and not in that of Religion.

And yet, what seems to be capital error in evolutionary thinking is not surprising if a start is made with a superficial scrutiny of many modern cults, including not a little Christian ritual. Therein may be found survival of a great deal of spiritism and magic. So it is with mysticism which is, as it seems to me erroneously, supposed to be of the essence of Religion. It is maintained here that the process by which we reach experience of God is as natural and nonmystical as that by which we have experience of material force, but vastly different in quality and form. Apparently, when the beginnings of Religion occurred, Civilization had advanced far enough for rather advanced qualitative mutations to appear. From that day to this it has been in reality a great deal harder to keep scientific notions out of Religion than to keep religious notions out of Science. Cults are constantly tending to regress toward the materialistic.

On the other hand, we do find the beginnings of what is truly reverence and worship far back in the primitive world. It appears in sun worship and in the pantheism which was more or less common among our Indians. We find it in universally prevalent ancestor worship. No doubt it appears in the cult of local divinities

which was common in our Aryan racial line. Wherever you find
sense of reverence and feeling of the sacred, that whose guidance
rather than material intervention is sought, in short whatever
tends to lift man out from under the curse of his original egoism
and self-love—there you find that which is common in the sentiments of the primitive and the modern.

DEITY

Sense of the numinous is reverence, feeling of sanctity, of holi-
ness. But such feelings do not exist in a vacuum; they must have
a source in experience, and they must have an object. The latter,
moreover, must be personal or quasi-personal as distinguished
from mechanical and material. Certainly we may admire a machine, but we do not revere it. Hence the search after God. Sometimes people find God in the spirit believed to dwell in the moun-
tain of their old homeland; sometimes in dead-and-gone heroes
who have seemed more than human in their wisdom and ability;
sometimes in personified ideals of beauty and power; almost
everywhere at some time in the immortal spirits of their ancestors. At length in the incarnation and personification of ultimate
reality in the Ideal of Goodness and Wisdom and Justice and
Mercy and in a belief that men and women can rise into communion with that Ideal and thereby realize their true selves. These
findings are what we call Faith.

Faith has often been lost, even as Science has been lost and The
State and Civilization itself, even as Music was apparently lost
after a good beginning in prehistoric times until the historic period was far advanced, always because the generations either
could not or would not transmit their Faith or State or Science or
Music.

Men have believed all sorts of things *about* God, because reverence had been lost in curiosity, and have futilely tried to run Him
into the channels of logic and creed, unaware that Religion is not
Science, not even theological science. Having taught their contemporaries that reverence is belief, the descendants have lost
their Faith as soon as the thing believed became incredible.

Men have found God and then lost Him in the deified magistrate, in the chief engineer of the universe, in the impersonal abstractions of the philosopher.

There is another germ to Religion, the one which gives it its name—for "religion" means "a binding"—and the one which survives still in dynamic Religion. It is this: that right and justice, the good which is actual in the customs which are primitive law, are seen and accounted for as the will of revered ancestors, as the will of national heroes, as the will of God. All that is the germ of the idealistic philosophy by which civilized peoples are governed today, if they are justly governed at all. It is to accept conduct as resting on principles and not on expediency or pragmatic conclusions. Time was when the highest encomium to be bestowed on a neighbor was to say that he was "a man of principle." There is no accounting for the world without it. It is Religion and especially Christianity.

We can find the actual process here in the revelations of emergent evolution, but that only satisfies our curiosity; it gives us no affective compulsion. Hence it is that men who have been valiantly good have usually had faith in a personal God.

WHAT IS NOT MEANT

It would be preposterous for us to attempt to completely delimit the concept with which we are dealing, but we can at least consider what seems to be within Religion as product in human experience and what is often confused with Religion.

Not theology.—Theology is properly an inquiry into the nature of God and into the reality of God. It is then a logic, a body of thought, an aspect of Metaphysics. But it is not and never was Religion, either psychologically or institutionally considered, any more than Physics is energy, or Biology life. It assuredly has no place in the Curriculum of the Common School, at least not on the principles argued in this volume. It is an intellectual and not a humanistic pursuit; it belongs to the University.

Not the tenets of particular cults.—I was once lecturing on this part of the Curriculum, and after class a student came to me to say that she could not accept my argument at all, since she did not believe in Hell. Manifestly there was need of enlightenment.

Religious communities have always built up cults. A given cult may be expressed partly in ritual, partly in mystic beliefs in all sorts of doctrines, partly as irrelevant anthropology and cosmology. In the student's utterance was a fragment of the older Christian materialistic eschatology as she had probably found it in the cult in which she had been brought up, and then had rejected it—and along with the rejection had gone her religion altogether, or at least she supposed it had.

No cult, either ancient or modern, is Religion any more than instruction is education, or democracy the thing it is supposed to achieve. The confusion is an example of one of the commonest of the foibles of the untrained thinker, the fallacy of hypostasis, the most mischievous of them all unless we except *post hoc* reasoning. In principle, cults are, or once were, methods of furthering religious experience. Whether a given cult accomplishes that result or not is in principle a positive issue: it either does or does not. Most cults become hypostatized into what they should accomplish. There have been multitudes of them and still are—"different good roads to heaven," which is another fragment of materialistic eschatology. They range all the way from the primitive and the perverse to the activities of great communions composed of essentially civilized persons. But no cult is Religion.

In the religious freedom accorded to all in our country, innumerable cults have grown up. Some of them, probably most of them, are merely the absurd expressions of the untutored and undisciplined. Viewed purely as social phenomena, as objectively as possible, it is not hard to see that the effect in the community is so divisive as well-nigh to paralyze Religion as an institutional influence. It is nothing else than what statesmen in all the ages have recognized, and their cure has commonly been the State Church. State Churches have probably worked a good deal better than the popular beliefs of the day are willing to concede. Whether they have worked or have not worked is aside from the question. In truth, there is no room for such civil institutions in our country. Congress is constitutionally forbidden to set up anything of the sort, and the States which had them have long since given them up. They are repugnant to the sentiments of practically all who make up our body politic.

The alternative is effective instruction of the rising generations in the whole field of General Education, and noncredal religious instruction in particular. Indeed, it is likely that in the past it has been failure at that point which has permitted State Churches to become eccentric, topheavy with priests and priestcraft, and finally moribund.

Not scriptural.—The major religious communities have had scriptures of some sort in which the essentials of the faiths have more or less been recorded—and much that is not Faith at all, but history, ethnology, anthropology, cosmology, and what not. But scriptures are not Religion. Since they are always in more or less fixed form, they tend to check the evolution of Faith. The result is that presently a generation finds itself without any faith at all. The Bible is by all odds the greatest of all scriptures, perhaps the greatest and richest single body of recorded wisdom the race has ever had. And yet the Bible is not Religion, but rather one of the richest sources out of which institutional Religion can rise in the individual or in the population. Intimate familiarity with its precepts has undoubtedly led to the development of character and wisdom; and incidentally to the establishment of three great literary tongues.

But the hierarchies of certain religious communities insisted on decreeing that the Bible is the literal word of God—the magisterial idea—and therefore a rationally infallible book. Bibliolatry became substituted for Religion—with the usual unhappy results of such inversions. The Church had earlier made the same mistake with respect to the structure of the stellar universe; it meddled with what did not concern it. But the Earth did move, and the Bible was not what some of the churches said it was. The ancient trouble: Religion confounded with Science, and bad science at that, the record of experience substituted for what comes out of experience.

Not Morality.—We commonly say that the ethical religions are the highest in point of religious evolution, and so they are. Indeed we might go farther and assert that the others have been late survivals of the mythological stage, and thus not Religion at all. As we look back over the road that Religion has followed, it is easy enough to see that moral experience, right for right's sake, is so kindred to religious experience that it is difficult to draw any distinction. Moreover, common sense could hardly fail to seek a justifier in an experience which is compelling pretty much in proportion as it is nonrational. Nevertheless, Religion is far more potent than institutional Morality, and mistaking one for the other has often led to the decadence of both. That is especially true when a church centers on morality, or what its book of discipline calls morality. It begs the question and makes moral conduct the test of Religion. It naturally follows that the public applies the test and estimates the reality of Religion by the conduct of church members.

Morality is a distinct institution, and while the Church, like the Family and the School, may and must do its part in the inculcation of moral standards and in maintaining them, its responsibility for doing so is no greater than that of either School or Family, and not nearly equal to the responsibility of The State in its definition of crime and pursuit of the criminal.

Religion, like Morality, contributes to the inculcation and maintenance of Conscience, and it does so in the notion of *sin* as repugnant to God and a degradation in the individual. Men who profess no faith, or suppose that they do not, often have the very root of the religious attitude in them in their reverence for what they call honor, and in their contempt for baseness and meanness of every kind and sort. That is apparently where the notion of sin enters.

The Church has certainly denounced certain acts as sinful, and very generally such have also been infractions of moral principles as such, just as the Law has reprobated infraction of moral principles as crime. Nevertheless, the idea of sin goes beyond the moral law. Attitude and conduct are often felt, and rightly felt, to be sinful which nobody could possibly suppose to be immoral or unethical.

Perhaps a clearer and more pathetic expression of the feeling of sin has seldom been uttered than that passage in the "Lament for Quinctilius" which has comforted the grief of many a Christian, made it possible for him to accept his grief and become reconciled, albeit the author was a Roman poet who was a curious mixture of Stoicism and Epicureanism:

> Durum; sed levius fit patientia
> quicquid corrigere est nefas.[2]

Nefas is almost an exact equivalent of our word "sin."

So Religion, in which there inevitably develops the feeling of sin and the sinful, exercises its own controlling influence over conduct. It can scarcely be doubted then that Religion contributes to Conscience quite as critically as does Morality.

If we turn back into recorded history for our facts, it soon becomes manifest that wherever Religion has been strong and vital, there co-operation in the face of peril and sacrifice has ordinarily been at its best; and Morality, as Morality was felt at the time, has been most secure in the mores. A wise judge once said to me, "I disbelieve that I can administer justice effectively, unless the churches can succeed in bringing back a feeling for the sanctity of an oath."

Shallow pragmatic tests.—Theology, often very crude, and always more or less irrelevant; cults of varying degrees of enlightenment; scriptures; codes of conduct—these all get so woven into the mores that men are wont to apply them as pragmatic tests of Religion. "If that is theology, then I want nothing to do with Religion"; "Look at Blank, and yet he is an ardent church member. Don't talk to me about Religion"; "More cruelty has been perpetrated by Religion than by any other one agency"; "The Bible is not only patently wrong, but parts of it are indecent." No doubt the facts often are as stated, but the conclusions drawn merely betray lack of education in the theorizer. As well argue that, since some college graduates turn out to be rascals, educa-

---

[2] Horace *Odes* i. 24. Connington translates thus:
> "Ah, heavy grief! but patience makes more light
> What sorrow may not heal."

tion must be dangerous. If all graduates were consistently ignorant rascals—which they are not—even that fact would be no
reproach to education. Logically we should be constrained to
overhaul the instruction.

In truth, then, there is scarcely any of our major institutions,
save perhaps Language and Number, which shows so clear an institutional history as Religion. It is indefeasibly part of Civilization and as such an element in the Curriculum of the Common
School, having the same sort of justification which Language and
Mathematics and Science have.

IN EDUCATION

In the development of individual personality, the significance
is not far to seek. We have seen many times in this work and in
Basic Principles in Education, especially in chapters vii–ix in the
work last named, that the core of the maturing process is the sublimation of organic egoism, the elimination of self-centeredness.
Without that educational achievement, the individual becomes
incapable of learning much, since he can see the world only as a
reflection of himself. In the infant the significant revelation of the
trait is *negativism;* in the adult it is *arrogance* and *egotism* in some
form. The thoroughgoing egotist can apparently see the world
only as something to do as he pleases with. Now, whatever may
be his professions, the egotist is essentially the Godless person, for
he is his own God. Common appraisal of contemporaries and historical characters who are and have been felt to be saints has
invariably assigned to them the quality of humility. The individual who in truth has found his God, however imperfectly it may
be, is not likely to be burdened with self-conceit.

IN SOCIETY

To demonstrate the principle that Religion is of the fabric of
Civilization is to state its significance in Society.

Nevertheless, few things or institutions have been so questioned
in respect to their social utility as Religion. Indeed it has often
been plausibly argued that it is a perverse institution, essentially

antisocial in its effect. The argument has invariably been an instance of the fallacy to which reference has just been made—the fallacy of hypostasis.

Some of the bloodiest and most devastating of wars have been the so-called "religious wars." Cultist and credal differences have split families, neighborhoods, and communities, and thus contributed to the disruption of social orders.

The third volume of the great *Cambridge Modern History* is entitled *The Wars of Religion*, meaning the long succession of European conflicts which began with the Reformation and culminated in the devastation of the Thirty Years' War.

And yet there was not a war of religion in the whole period.

There were wars to enforce on peoples the cult of their sovereigns. There was fighting in defense of the right of peoples to their own creeds. Far more, however, was there warfare in support of the lust of power of individuals who made cultish issues their excuse. The whole period was one in which Civilization had not fully been recovered, and warfare was still the sport of kings. On the other hand, men have fought for their food supply for countless ages, and the fact that they would fight bitterly in defense of their creed—what they had as Religion—is rightly conceived to be evidence that they valued Religion next to and perhaps above their food. To call such periods "Wars of Religion" is to suggest that Religion itself is a baneful influence, instead of recognizing that wars over credal issues have reflected the same lack of Civilization which all wars reveal on one side or the other or else on both sides.

We have sufficiently seen that to impute divisive influence of credal differences to Religion is to impute to the latter what ought in all reason to be imputed to lack of Religion—and of civilized attitudes as well.

Next there is cited the sorry story of ecclesiastical corruption and inferences drawn to show that corruption is inherent in Religion. As well deny the utility of all Government and revert to anarchy on account of the well-known fact that governments among many peoples and in many climes have been notoriously prone to corruption. It may well be rejoined, "Ah, but the priests told us that Religion protected them from malfeasance, that they held the keys of Heaven." No doubt the priests told their parishioners what was not true. Nevertheless, the argument rests on exactly the same kind of fallacy as that which we meet in school circles every day, which holds that a Doctor of Philosophy is made wise by the degree itself.

Fundamental to all social values attainable through effective instruction is one to which we have referred again and again, perhaps at tedious length, namely, escape from the domination of the specialist. I know of no better illustration than escape from the domination of priestcraft—unless indeed it be domination of the educationalist. Few things have been or are more destructive to Religion and Education, respectively.

Therein is one of the tragedies of Society, for there are few individuals in the Community who in the nature of their calling can be more influential for good than the priest, and few have been more conspicuous benefactors than have been individual priests in various faiths. If there were in the mores a great bedrock of the Religion of the race, the effect could scarcely be other than socially salutary, both in the direction of restraining the vagaries of sectarianism and of pseudo-faiths, and in that of supporting the leadership of those who are genuinely priests of the Most High, whatever may be their credal professions. But this is only to repeat the argument set forth touching the fundamental social utility of instruction in Science, the same argument which will appear in connection with instruction in Art, in The State, in Commerce and Industry, and in Health.

THE CHURCH

Much of this institutional argument may be resisted, and even resented, on the ground that the Church universal at least should be fixed upon as institution, and Religion treated as merely the name for a way of life. But there is no church universal.

The Church, as Christians use the term, is Community and not institution. If there were space, the statement could easily be demonstrated on historical grounds. So it is with the nearest equivalents of the Church in non-Christian faiths, notably Israel and Islam. Churches, as we know them in America, are in reality in most cases guilds, or unions, or associations. They do not claim to be anything more. Others are parts of international communions, notably the Anglican, the Lutheran, the Roman. As we have seen earlier, a church is often a national institution and sometimes has been an ecclesiastical State.

III. INSTRUCTION

We have to remind ourselves at the outset that in our own national polity, instruction in Religion cannot be given in tax-supported schools. That is our misfortune. National polity does not establish what in principle is right, and in working out a theoretical Curriculum we are under no restrictions derived from constitutional and statutory considerations. Religion, however, is not repugnant to the Federal Constitution, but only laws affecting the establishment of Churches or cults. We live in a domain of entire ecclesiastical liberty.

COURSE

Religion is basal in the Humanities. As in all the rest of that field, there cannot be laid out didactic courses of the type to be found in the subjects we have thus far studied. Nor are there institutional *forms* in which the subject appears, as is the case in Morality and Art. If there were such forms, then there would be a historical course in Comparative Religion but not one in Religion.

It should perhaps be noted that writers on what is called Religious Education tend to make the whole matter chiefly Bible Study and descriptive accounts of the great world-faiths. That is no more the pursuit of what is implied in the course as we have conceived it than is the general history of the United States a course in Civics and Politics. The Bible is a record of religious experience over a long range of development, but it is not altogether that. It is in part early Hebrew conceptions of cosmology, in part the laws and history of an interesting but politically and economically unimportant people, in part a contribution to the secular literature of the world. But it is also, from the Psalms through the prophetic and apostolic writings, perhaps the richest single body of religious experience in existence. That part of the Bible is valuable *instructional material* to be put along with much else. Finally, the King James Version, in English-speaking countries, as a great classic, belongs to Literature in several units of the latter.

UNIT AND MASTERY

These observations might be taken as meaning that there is no such thing as a definite object in view. If a definite objective is taken to be a thing defined a priori by the tests and measurements which the instructor designs to apply, and to be treated as an item of credit toward academic or scholastic attainments, then such a view of the objective would be even more ridiculous than it elsewhere is.

But to say that there is no objective at all is equivalent to saying that Religion is not susceptible of being used in instruction. The objective, it is true, cannot be defined with the precision which is possible with respect to a unit in Language, Mathematics, or Science; but inability to define with precision is not inability to define at all. If we take a broad view of the essentials of Religion as it has been under evolution, it is not difficult to arrive at a sufficiently clear understanding of what the single unit in the course is. I take it to be:

a) A sense of the sacred and the holy as it is found in various situations in life. Acceptance of the moral way of life, that is to say, doing right for right's sake and further acceptance of the institutions which make up institutional morality as part of Civilization, may very well go far toward the establishment of Conscience. But such acceptance is a poor thing, relatively speaking, when compared with the addition which is made when the individual acquires a sense of the sacred in the obligation to observe moral principles. One may be convinced of the obligation to Loyalty, but when he feels the meanness of disloyalty, there as entered a feeling of the sacred. One may be convinced of the social obligation of keeping faith, so much so that he senses a feeling of disgust at bad faith; but when he experiences what he phrases as "my sacred word," breach of his own promises amounts to a self-insult. In every way, for untold centuries, that upon which morale chiefly depends, namely, Respect for Sex, is vitally religious in import, in that a sense of the hallowed surrounds the relationship between men and women.

b) A sense of dependence upon, and communion with, a Supreme Being who is the impersonation of the Ideal and the Right, and whom we call God.

And so there may be the principle of mastery, which means here, as it means everywhere else at bottom, actual attainment. But to assert that there can be mastery in any of the Humanities of the same sort which is to be found in Language, Mathematics, and the sciences is mere nonsense.

In discussing the principle of mastery in my various writings, I have sought to make plain what I understand to have been the meaning and significance in schoolcraft wherever the word has in the past been in common use. There have been in mind two aspects or phases of mastery.

First, I have used it to mean actual learning in contrast with mere acceptable performance of school tasks.

Second, in some cases, I have used the term to mean complete learning of a unit as contrasted with half-learning. This aspect requires some elucidation.

If we take as our unit trustworthy ability to handle the English sentence with correctness, then there is the possibility of complete learning. The issue is positive; the individual has become reliable, or else he has not. Moreover, he can be tested, or at least clear evidence can be found. Even so, we have reference only to the *mastery of a unit;* we do not include all there is to be learned *about* the sentence, nor do we include the skill and style in the use of sentences which is the achievement of the professional writer. There can be complete learning of a unit of the Curriculum, but not exhaustive learning about a subject, not perfect skill in the use of the thing learned.

Again, the unit may be the equation in Algebra, divested of qualifications and extensions. Genuine and complete mastery is possible and a positive issue. The junior high school pupil who "gets the notion" or acquires the "knack" of handling equations knows the unit in the same sense as that in which the mathematician knows it. He does not know all there is to be known about equations, nor does he possess skill in applying the equation to material which is in itself beyond his knowledge.

Perhaps the illustrations will suffice. They could be carried out to the same intent in Science, The State, Commerce, Industry, and much else beside.

On the other hand, in the Humanities, the first aspect of mastery must appear, if there is to be any real learning at all. But the second cannot appear, for in appreciation there can be no positive standards. We can set up as our objective in Music or in Literature some reliable sense of the difference between the good and the cheap and tawdry, and preference for the former. We can collect evidence which shows or tends to show that taste has been formed, but there is nothing positive about it. We cannot define a unit in the Humanities with the same precision as that with which we define Acceleration in Science, and keep at the teaching until we are sure that the pupil has fully taken in the notion; or else we are sure that he has not. We can set up as a unit the Drama, in Literature, and in the course of time come to the conclusion that the pupil's taste in that direction has been formed; but we cannot assert that even in respect to this particular unit is there any such thing as completeness in appreciation. In respect to Acceleration, we should conclude that our teaching had gone for nothing if somebody enunciated some absurd theory and the pupil accepted it. But if the pupil in Literature never deepened or qualified his taste for the drama beyond what he had learned in school, we should equally feel that our teaching had gone for nothing.

In the Sciences and their derivatives, and in Language, we look for completeness; in the Humanities we look for reliability in preference.

So it is in Religion. The idea of mastery in the first aspect is entirely valid, but there is no possibility of getting positive evidence bearing upon any notion of completeness. Even so, any ordinary method of testing and credit is not only an impertinence but ridiculous. Apply either one, and you would get those most hateful of human traits, cant and hypocrisy. But failure to get positive evidence is not failure to get any evidence at all. The behavior of the pupils, and especially of the school as minor community, is always revealing to the discerning schoolmaster, and it is evidence.

SOURCES

Religion is a product of the experience of the race, refined and extended, lost and recovered. Such products in experience have been richly recorded in the Music, Literature, Painting, Sculpture, and Architecture of mankind. One need not be above getting a bit of edification even out of some of our Indian legends, but not many.

We may list the general types of source material as follows:

I. Liturgical—invocations, prayers, Christian collects

We must, however, distinguish between liturgical material proper and ritualistic material. The latter may indeed be useful, but it is cult and not instruction.

The liturgical material goes back a long way, some of it to be recovered from very ancient sources. A great service might be rendered through the systematic collation of such for school use.

II. Religious Poetry, Essays, and Oratory

The great source of this material is the Hebrew and Christian Scriptures, but much of it can be found in great sermons.

The difficulty here is to distinguish between what is Religion as such' and what is Religion with ritualistic and theological additions.

III. Sacred Music

Music is, of all things, the most useful source, chiefly because it registers so deeply in the affective life. Even in ancient Egypt, apparently about the only good music they had was the temple music. Necessarily, the bulk of sacred music is Christian in origin, since it was Christianity which gave one of the two principal impulses to organized music as we know it. Music, however, is a kittle institution; and of all it is the most subject to degeneration. Selections for school use ought to be in the hands of people of cultivated tastes, and especially of sound musical tastes. One sometimes hears gospel hymns so called which have apparently been neither more nor less than stimuli to erotic excitement.

IV. Sacred Painting and Sculpture

 Much, but not nearly so much as there is of sacred music and literature.

V. Religious Architecture

 Of that below. However, apart from the architectural setting of school audience rooms, reproductions of great religious edifices in pictorial form is part of the course in Architecture.

PEDAGOGY

Nearly all the teaching, as apart from general religious influence, belongs to what in Gary parlance is appropriately called "auditorium periods."

We are not without experience here, for schoolcraft long ago fixed upon the appropriate setting for religious teaching and erected the school chapel. That is as it should be, for religious experience is, and almost always has been, in the end expressed as some form of worship. Happily, the prejudice which formerly surrounded all forms of artistic support has largely disappeared. Even the denominations which a generation ago aspired chiefly to an audience room devoid of all save the appurtenances of a comfortable lecture-room are not now content to erect a new church building except it be given a religious setting. In some cases, great services have been set up which in former times would not only have been anathema but impossible for lack of setting. A great service builds a religious atmosphere and yields in vicarious form religious experience.

Hence, a school chapel, not necessarily a Christian chapel even, is at least as appropriate to religious teaching as is a demonstration table, or laboratory if you will, to instruction in Chemistry.

SERMONIZING

In an extremely sophisticated age, the sermon has more or less fallen into disrepute, and yet some of the greatest oratory of the past has been in that form. It is an instrument, and properly used can be very effective. When a good principal makes a serious auditorium talk on a moral subject, he is preaching whether he calls his discourse by that name or not. Great heads of schools have often wielded their greatest influence that way.

INDIVIDUAL CONFERENCES

Our best principals do a great deal of meeting pupils to talk over individual problems in the classroom—and moral and spiritual difficulties as well. If one either cannot or will not do it effectively, then he is no head of a school. If the ideal of the principal is to surround himself with all the office gadgets he can hear about, and try to be a good manufacturer, then he has mistaken his calling.

When I speak of individual conferences, I have no reference to any kind of a system in which the pupils are periodically called into the principal's office to see if all is right with their souls. As well pull up the garden plants once a week to see if they are growing.

SCHOOL CHAPLAIN

Suitable organization has often included an executive associate in the form of a school chaplain, responsible for the religious life of the school and a force in its discipline. Some of the great English Public Schools have in the past made effective use of such an officer. I have known the function to be unwittingly performed by a director of school sports, although of course without any direct religious implications.

Nevertheless, the principal cannot successfully delegate any of the functions which inherently belong to him as principal. The principal whose main reliances are the typewriter, mimeograph, a bevy of office girls, and membership in a downtown service club is not very different from the manufacturer or merchandiser or politician who is so essentially ignorant of his job that he surrounds himself with engineers, economists, lawyers, and "social workers," to do his work for him, forgetful of the principle that, if he is ignorant of functions which have to be carried out, he can scarcely trust himself to select the functionaries.

IV. THE SCHOOL AND THE CHURCH

All the foregoing may read like an argument leading toward the substitution of the School for the Church. That cannot be done.

The Church, the Synagogue, the Mosque, the Temple, are,

and have been in varying degrees, communities or at least associations for participation in the pursuit of particular faiths through particular cults. They are groups of people, each of the groups clustered about an edifice and a priesthood of some sort for participation in the religious life. They may be productive or they may be weak and poor and even vicious. Whatever they are, that is the function which they have in the Community. The School is concerned with instruction; the Church is concerned with teaching a faith and with something that goes beyond instruction. Least of all is the Church or are churches fragments of the School for lectures in sociology, psychology, and politics—the less so in that such churches commonly teach but an indifferent Science.

The School and the Church are the supreme agencies in the transmission of Civilization. Their functions, however, are complementary. The School will not go far in the administration of General Education unless it has the support of a vigorous Church; but it is equally true, on the record as it seems to me, that the Church in any community will tend to run the scale of the fashionable unless it comes to rest on the basis of nonecclesiastical religious instruction contributing its influence to the mores.

CHAPTER VIII

MORALITY AND MORAL INSTITUTIONS

IN RECENT years there has been—for obvious reasons perhaps—a renewed concern for what is known as "character education" in the schools. The term, like a good many terms for qualifying education, is in itself meaningless. Education is education, and valid General Education is not to be qualified by announcing that there are to be considered various "educations," such as "education for citizenship," "education for right use of leisure," "education for character," etc. Where the elements that make for Conscience are left out, there is no complete education. The character-education movement is, however, a reminder of neglect in the conduct of schools, and the leaders of the movement attempt a systematic attack on the problem, in the place of accepting the casual influence of teachers who may or may not be strong and good men and women.

I. METHODS OF APPROACH

From the beginning of our national period at least, the management of schools has seldom had any clear social purpose in the ordering of curriculum and methods, and Morality, which is the basis of ordered society everywhere, has tended to be only incidental to the maintenance of order in the schoolroom. But that is not to say, in the first place, that it has been consistently ignored; or, in the second place, that school government and administration has altogether been devoid of foundations in principles touching the whole matter. The student can rather clearly distinguish three stages in our instructional theory touching what today would be called character-building.

A. FROM ETHICAL THEORY

In the first place, in one form or another, there has been approach from the assumptions of ethical theory, with inferences drawn deductively concerning both curriculum content and general school procedure.

The most conspicuous instance, explaining what I mean, is the influence of Christian ethics. Now Christian ethics as a body of ethical principle touching what is right, as all ethical principle does, is doubtless the highest form which the race has yet seen. Moreover, it contains, as perhaps no other system does, what is disclosed in systematic study of the evolution of Morality in the race. But Christian ethics is not basal Morality; it is rather an outgrowth and high interpretation. To make this or any other system the content of the Curriculum in breeding Conscience is to get the cart before the horse, to cultivate adherence to symptoms of mature character rather than to apply the discipline through inculcation of the great moral and volitional principles which generate genuine character if anything does. To develop a preference for the teaching of the Sermon on the Mount in advance of sound discipline as thus defined is almost certain to breed either rebellion or else cant.

During the last thirty years or thereabout, ethical theories of instruction seem to have evaporated into political liberalism and to have come to rest on a belief in democracy itself as a system of ethics rather than a form of government.

No basis found in ethical theory is a sound one. The logic is bad, since it starts from assumption and inference rather than from facts. The moral history of the race is factual; valid ethical theories are rational inferences and applications.

B. TRAINING ETHICAL JUDGMENT

A corollary of the preceding, as it seems to me, has been the development of actual moral laissez faire, which, stripped of fine words and specious reasoning, means: Leave the pupil in the school and the child in the home to do as he pleases, in the expectation that he will learn wisdom from his own follies. The minor is expected to learn in twenty-one years, out of casual experience alone, what the race has acquired in the same manner with untold misery and suffering in many thousands of years.

And yet the dogma has its appeal as a sort of mystical democracy until with many school people it amounts to a credal obligation—and with others as a blessed excuse for inability to discipline Young America, and the youth of other lands as well. Wherein are its fallacies, apart from those which are revealed by common sense?

In the first place, it rests on long-discarded educational psychology. It assumes that there is a faculty called judgment which can be trained through exercise to make discriminating and accurate decisions whenever the individual finds himself in the presence of an ethical situation. As well claim that the pupil can learn to think accurately in arithmetic, without reference to learned arithmetical principles and processes, by sheer experience in arithmetical situations.

The whole pedagogical theory is a far cry from that of the intransigents who a generation ago held rigorously to formal discipline and automatic transfer, but at bottom the modern liberal and his intransigent parent rest on the same erroneous principle. In some strange way the horse has changed his color, but he is the same horse still.

C. ANALYSIS OF MORAL TRAITS

A third approach consists in the collection of mention of desirable moral traits and statistical treatment of frequency. In that way, a list of objectives can be built up arranged in a hierarchy of assumed relative values. The method is certainly far more defensible than either of the preceding. It seems, nevertheless, to have the defects which are characteristic of the job-analysis type of approach in all studies of the Curriculum.

It is easy enough to question a thousand persons and ask them one by one what they believe to be right principles, and keep on until we find nothing new. Statistical analysis will then give us some assurance as to what people really think about it, at least those persons whose opinions are presumably worth anything. That is factual, but it is not good speculation; it is examining without pondering sufficiently. Most speculators ponder without examining at all. The difficulty is partly in the principle that a thousand opinions are opinion still, and partly in the principle that the method does no more than explore the current mores. Ten years hence the mores will have shifted more or less, for the better or the worse. The mores can make anything *seem* right; but they never determine what *is* right.

But let us remove this objection by applying the same method to the great teachers of all time. Let us explore the Egyptian and Babylonian monuments, inquire of the Chinese and Hindu sages, consult the Hebrew prophets, the wise men of Greece and Rome, and carry the inquiry down to the latest moralists. We shall certainly get an imposing list of the virtues which have been extolled, and with equal certainty find an astonishing consensus. We shall perhaps be surprised to learn that what in fact we supposed to be very modern is in fact very old.

But in the end, critical analysis will show that most of the virtuous traits named are only symptoms of something else. Some of the traits which we value most highly today, and which have been valued for thousands of years, have never proved to be capable of institutionalization. As we shall presently see that is the test of the fundamental and teachable.

Thus, *honesty*, which we prize most highly, is not a unitary trait at all. It is a mark of the educated person, and it rests not merely on Respect for Property, but on Good Faith, Veracity, Obedience, Respect for Sex—and indeed on the whole structure of civilized personality. You cannot teach a pupil to be honest; you will get only a bewildered individual if you try to. But you can carry on his instruction in various institutional units, so that in the end he will be honest.

A surprising instance is found in Altruism, which in these days we extol above honesty even. And yet if Altruism had ever become institutionalized, the results would appear in organized charity, but the latter has had a sorry history down to this day. A good many years ago, one of our most eminent sociologists, Professor Giddings, remarked that the history of the English poor law had demonstrated that any nation can have all the poverty it is willing to pay for. From the Roman *annona*, down through medieval charity, to the English dole and American relief, history has a doleful tale to tell and it is a record of demoralization and social disruption. In the quest for "social justice," ordinary, vital, saving Justice has usually been lost.

Altruism in the individual is but the sign of sublimated egoism, and the latter is the heart of mature personality. Civilized man is compassionate, merciful, considerate, generous, just; but in our instruction we do not attempt to produce these traits. If we do, we get only outward show. The civilized community will assuredly refuse to abandon its unfortunates and incompetents, but the community is thereby but admitting its failure in the diffusion of Civilization.

So it is when we turn the picture and examine the traits which have been reprobated over the centuries. Nearly all of them are negative, marks of the absence of Civilization in the makeup of the persons affected.

Some evils are, however, actually institutionalized, so basal are they in the grown-up infant and primitive in the community. Lechery and gambling, for example, go back into the primitive world as far as any of the moral institutions. They have, and always have had, institutionalized apparatus and agencies. Murder has at times similarly been institutionalized, and robbery. These do not, however, meet the rational test which must be applied to constituents of Civilization; they are not rationally comprehensible as essential elements in the structure of progressive societies, but rather the contrary.

Altogether, then, the approach to the problems of character education in the Curriculum by the method of collating admired traits is bound to prove fallacious.

D. INSTITUTIONAL MORALITY

In conformity with the principles upon which this whole work rests, we turn to the basal moral institutions in the fabric of Civilization, identified on the principles set forth in chapter ii, and we shall expect in that way to discover whatever is objectively fundamental and valid in accordance with the doctrines of Emergent Evolution. But first we shall need some definitions.

II. PRACTICAL MORALITY

The word "morality" seems in a way to have fallen into disrepute, so much so that the pseudo-intelligentsia seem to be of the opinion that there is something barbaric about it. You will hear them assert, "I am no moralist" as if there were something about the assertion which is very much to their credit. "Moral" and its cognates have had, at least since Cicero's time, a meaning which is almost exactly translated by the English "righteous" and its derivatives. But here again we fall into difficulties. For three hundred years past, a false connotation has been fixed on "righteous" and "righteousness" by some of the irresponsible literary nuisances. Doubtless, the reason has some intelligibility about it, for the hypocrisy of the later English Puritan movement left a sinister taint on everything it touched. Our old friend hypostasis again, coupled with perhaps not a little wishful thinking and playing to the gallery. One sometimes sympathizes with Plato's ultimate belief that litterateurs should not be allowed within the confines of the Republic.

In this chapter we use the word "Morality" as being the equivalent of "Righteousness" as that word is used in the King James Bible.

If once more we turn back to the historical and genetic point of view, and read as much as we can of the dissertations of the moralists, on the one hand, and of the history of conduct, on the other, we can hardly help seeing that there is one common denominator in all discussions, ancient or modern, save now and then the discussion of a utilitarian of one sort or another:

Since a remote antiquity some men have more or less been doing what they believed to be right because in their eyes it was right, without regard to expediency, to the hope of reward, or to the fear of punishment.

Consider the *Mahabharata.* "Draupadi complains of the hard lot of her righteous husband, and charges the Deity with injustice; but is answered by Yuddishthira: 'Thou utterest infidel sentiments. I do not act from a desire to gain the recompense of my works. I give what I ought to give—whether reward accrues

to me or not, I do to the best of my power what a man should do—
It is on duty alone that my thoughts are fixed, and this, too,
naturally. The man who seeks to make of righteousness a gainful
merchandise is low. The man who seeks to *milk* righteousness does
not obtain its reward—Do not doubt righteousness; he who does
so is on the way to be born a brute.' "[1]

In brief, Morality so conceived seems to be, more than most
things, service to the Ideal, regardless of the ethical question
whether what is believed to be right is in truth objectively right.
When an individual so acts, we say that his act has *moral quality*,
whether he be a poor savage visiting the grave of his father because he believes it is right to do so, or an American businessman
paying his just debts, despite the fact that he has been discharged
by a court in bankruptcy.

III. INSTITUTIONAL MORALITY

Conceivably, a whole population might be made up of men and
women whose conduct was consistently affected with moral quality, and yet no Civilization would appear, since there could be no
common expectation. That is exactly what happens when the
dogma is set up which holds that a man's morals are his private
affair. The result has over and over been demoralization and progressive anarchy. Especially in periods in which there exists an
advanced cultural accumulation, Society itself breaks down as a
going concern because there is not enough common moral expectation in the mores to make the culture manageable.

There is then something more than *moral quality* in conduct.
That might serve the purpose if there were no such thing as Society as one of the conditioning factors in existence. Socially
speaking, Morality, moral orders, codes, the moral law, were inevitable. The tendency toward moral quality in the acts of individuals was bound from the beginning to generate content and
substance, and that is what we call Morality.

So it has come to pass that the moral order is put together in
terms of moral institutions which are valid in that they are the

[1] Taken from Herbert Spencer's *The Principles of Ethics* (2 vols.; New York: Appleton & Co., 1927), I, 320–21.

products of long ages of variation in the mores and folkways, and hence in the customs. Each of the institutions has followed the typical history of major and universal institutions which we have so often studied. They must be the fundamentals of the Curriculum in respect to education in moral character.

In attempting to identify them, I have followed the method outlined in chapter ii. In applying the tests, not a great many clear cases turn up, but those which do appear are wonderfully comprehensive and significant. Each of them is discernible in its beginnings in very early times; it has survived as recognized value in the innumerable vicissitudes of social change because of its social utility; it shows a history of expansion and refinement; and it is rationally comprehensible as an element in the structure of stable and advancing societies, in the art of living together. Indeed in one way or another, all of them in the course of centuries have crept into the Law, either civil, canonical, or martial, or all three.

But here, as is true of all the products of social evolution, *a surviving institution is socially useful because it is right and not right because it is socially useful.*

A. CLEANLINESS

About the first in order of emergence which looks like a germinal stage of Morality is *bodily cleanliness.* Well, we are told that cleanliness is akin to Godliness. It is a true instinctive adjustment in the higher mammals, and especially in the carnivora. It is found among peoples who on other counts would rate as savages, although most savages, and backward peoples generally, are filthy. It is true enough that cleanliness is not always found among peoples who are rated as civilized. Neither are all of the other moral qualities, nor all of Intelligence and Taste, but to the extent that they do not appear in folkways and mores and customs to that extent such peoples are uncivilized. Nevertheless, the ablest of all advancing peoples, the Greeks, the Romans, the English, have been conspicuous for their cleanliness. A very considerable part of our own total production goes into the effort to keep clean.

To the primitive and to us, body is self in the concrete, and the beginnings of self-respect are in respect for the body. Once respect for the body is established, self-respect goes far—into respect for orderliness in self and others and in surroundings, into modesty, eventually into refinement and good taste. In selecting men or women for employment, or for other kinds of close association, discriminating judges commonly look to the candidate's personal *tenue*, the way he "holds himself." The well-set-up young man wins confidence as compared with him who is slovenly, not to say dirty. The confidence tends to be justified.

Symbolism.—In each of the institutions we have thus far studied we have noted that some of them are essentially symbolic, formal, while others carry the substance and content of thought. But we have also seen that the substance which is in Mathematics—although the latter is chiefly formal and symbolic—and in the sciences, becomes symbolic and a form of thought outside of either Mathematics or Science. We say that we think "in chemical or biological or mechanical terms." So it is here. Cleanliness, once established in the folkways and awareness of mankind, at once became more or less symbolic and helped to reduce to manageable terms discourse that had to do with matters altogether outside the immediate implications of bodily cleanliness. In the first place, there was ritual cleanliness, the meaning of which was perhaps wholly symbolic. But symbolism went beyond ritual and to this day is used in metaphor for the sake of clarity and emphasis.

The Hebrew and Christian scriptures are full of it.

In suits at equity we find the maxim which holds that both parties must come into court with "clean hands." There is no relief at equity for litigants whose acts in the premises are themselves tainted with inequity.

The politically righteous demand an honest ballot and say "let us have a clean election."

We shall find this tendency for moral substance to serve also as symbolism and form all through the chapter.

B. LOYALTY

Far back in folk history emerges Loyalty to a person, certainly as far back as the totemistic clan and perhaps at its most intense in the patriarchal clan—loyalty to the kindred, even the symbolic kindred of the totem, loyalty to the chieftain, to the head of the house, to comrades. Whatever its origins may have been, it is in all ages one of the most enduring of social cements. To this day, people will say, when speaking of a neighbor's character, "But he is not loyal"; and you can usually sense that they feel that disloyalty leaves nothing whatever of the moral fabric intact.

C. OBEDIENCE

Next in order of emerging Morality, I shall name recognition of and respect for authority. Viewed from the personal standpoint, it is willing conformity to rightful authority.

Authority is the core of The State and of that later, but more than that it is the heart of all ordered societies. In its higher aspect, it is logic and reason and acceptance of an ordered universe and its compulsions. Willing conformity to rightful authority! What does that mean?

In the first place, it is contrasted with subservience, which is conformity to force, out of fear of consequences or hope of reward. Subservience is merely contemptible, and the old-time schoolmaster who could get that and nothing more was getting worse than nothing at all, for he was breeding the spirit of the slave, of all things the meanest. More to be respected is the lawless soul who defies the policeman than is he who looks over his shoulder to see if an officer is in sight before committing a violation of the law which he knows to be a violation.

In the second place, it is conformity to rightful authority, and there is the rub, especially in the cases of many Americans, most of us for all I know. Rightful authority, in the first place, is presumptive authority, and that extends to parents, teachers, and the Law. When the individual reserves the right at every step to question what is rightful authority, it is the same as if there were no authority. If he feels imposed upon by usurped authority, he has recourse to the courts and ultimately to the legislature. "I will obey all that seems reasonable to me" is often heard. That is the negation of Obedience. We do not obey a given behest because that behest is a reasonable one, but because it is reasonable to obey. Unlimited right to question the lawfulness of authority or the reasonableness of every ordinance or statute is not liberty but lawlessness. The consequences do not lag. When that spirit enters the mores, the reign of unrightful authority promptly begins, always has, and always will. It does now.

Over and over again, students have put up to me what they call the right of rebellion. Of course there is no such right, either moral or civil. The wielding of unrightful authority, that is to say, authority outside the law, or wielding it in a brutal or otherwise tyrannical manner, is both immoral and illegal. In our theory of government it is of none effect, null and void. It is no doubt true that patriots have often banded together to resist unlawful authority, but the burden of proof is on them. It is a far cry from the resolution and courage and deliberate choice which actuated Washington and his compatriots in resistance to the unconstitutional ways of the Government of George III, to the self-will of every person who disobeys any law whatever on the ground that he "does not believe in it."

A misbegotten liberalism in some current theories of instruction treats authority and "authoritarianism" as if they were necessarily inventions of the Devil.

Authority in its social aspect is institutional. It originates in the common sense and experience of mankind working toward co-operation in achieving the Great Escapes. It is the essence of one of the great social functions, namely, Regulation. Its rise, internal adjustment, and refinement have been a long, long story, because, more than any other of the moral institutions, Obedience has to work against native egoism; and the sublimation of egoism into self-respect is perhaps the greatest difficulty encountered in the processes of Civilization and Education alike. Self-will stands in the way of all the moral institutions, but in the way of Obedience most of all. Here, more than almost anywhere else, regression has its greatest opportunity.

Respect for authority is not, however, likely to arise unless those who wield authority are themselves respectable. Especially is that true of officers who persistently feed their own egoism in the exercise of authority. Every senior schoolmaster, industrialist, and military man knows how hard it is to find subordinates who know how to hold authority. Conformity is within the capacity of us all; respect depends upon externals. One can promise to come to tea at four o'clock, but he cannot promise to be hungry at that hour.

The reign of law.—The ultimate refinement of the institution has been in the substitution of the authority of Law for the authority of men, organized law declared as well by rational interpretation of social relationships as by legislation reflecting the will of the body politic.

Beyond that even is individual conformity and personal adaptation to moral and intellectual truth. As such, rational Obedience is decidedly part of the intelligence structure. One of the commonest marks of intellectual infantilism is the oft-heard claim to right of opinion. Nobody has any right to hold an opinion on matters about which he knows nothing and cannot be assumed to know anything. To refrain is Obedience to truth and to reason.

D. FORTITUDE

A long period of feminism in the upbringing and instruction of boys, it sometimes seems, has had the effect of breeding pusillanimity into the highly schooled part of our population. It is normal in the male of the species to fight, and the individual boy who fails to learn to fight—and lose as well as win—is handicapped for life. More than that he contributes to the submergence of his class beneath the heels of a turbulent rabble which will fight. Many a boy has been turned into a semi-psychopath because in a boyish encounter he was allowed to run whimpering to his mother, or teacher, or foolish father, rather than be told sternly to go back, stand his ground, and submit to a mauling if need be.

Beyond all questions of physical bravery is the issue of moral courage in standing up for one's convictions, so fearful is the prospect of becoming unpopular. That is singularly fateful in democracies, where so much depends upon the courageous expression of well-founded convictions by the people who are best qualified to hold convictions.

E. PATRIOTISM

Patriotism is "love of the fatherland." With us it is quite as much love of the home town and home State. It is probably organic in origin, for it represents about the most concrete early experience outside the home in which self can expand and become distributed. It is highly affective in character and therefore highly dynamic in action. Nevertheless, it is also institutional and, like Fortitude, it has long been in the mores and customs of advancing peoples. It is no doubt originally an adjustment derived from martial sources. It is, however, an adjustment and emergent, and it still has its appeal to all of us—unless we are so sicklied over with the pale cast of thought as to have become semi-psychasthenic.

Patriotism in modern times, at least with us, has long outlived its original significance. As cultivation of what is still essentially martial thrill—of an exceedingly vicarious kind—it degenerates into mere thrill-hunting, which is always bad. Martial Defense is still one of the major institutions, as we shall see later, but it ought to be divested of emotionalism rather than fed on emotionalism.

SOCIAL CONSCIENCE

On the other hand, normal love of country is potentially the most vigorous trunk upon which to graft *social conscience*. By social conscience we mean not only concern for the common good but a great deal more for the going sets of relationships which constitute civilized society, and which lie at the basis of the commonweal and the lot of the unplaced and the wretched. If a little of the patriotic enthusiasm felt by Americans at the beginning of the last war could be applied continuously to warfare on indecent literature, on political incompetency, insincerity, and dishonesty, on dishonesty, recklessness, and ruthlessness in business, our country might indeed be made safe for democracy, or rather democracy made safe for our country.

Morality is the inclination to do right because it is right, but it is quite another thing to know what is right. The morally finest of the race have sometimes acted like bandits because they knew no better. Most of the foundations of our Ethics are found in the sciences, and especially in Civics, Politics, Commerce, Industry, and Health, as intellectual disciplines.

F. PRUDENCE

Prudence means foresight and adjustment to contingencies, escape out of the rule of chance. In economic affairs it is *thrift*. It is one of the readiest and most reliable indices we have touching the advance of Civilization among various peoples. Lack of it is one of the plainest marks by which we can identify peoples who are lacking in social development, and individuals who are the least educated and most infantile. A connotation of Prudence is awareness of consequences of one's own acts—what one "asked for"—and it is therein one of the connections between Conscience and Intelligence.

The history and ethnology of Prudence are fortunately clear; we have no long and involved quest for the institutional thread which tells the story. From the universal improvidence of savages to their crude preparations for winter, to the development of husbandry and the storage of surplus food, to foresight which appeared as the early stages of Science, to the final stages in the instruments for the distribution of risk in modern societies—it is all a tale of consistent progress. That is not to be taken as asserting that there never has been regression or that improvident individuals and whole communities no longer exist; but there is little evidence that there ever has been such ethical skepticism of Prudence as to remove it out of the structure of progressive societies. Such failure as there has been, and now is, is evidence of true regression and not of changes in the fabric of Civilization.

The prudent and the thrifty are the real carriers of social progress. The family which sets aside a portion of its income as a rainy-day fund is, other things being equal, higher in the scale of

Civilization than the one which does not. Such families maintain purchasing power for a long time in periods of depression and help to tide over the severities of the onset. If there were enough such families, depressions would be mild compared with what they have come to be; the amplitude of business cycles would be less. Again, other things being equal, the relative proportion of savings-banks deposits and paid-up premiums on insurance policies is a mark of a relatively high stage in Civilization attained by the people of the community which have them. Finally, cities, school districts, industrial corporations, and States, which hold adequate reserves against a period of dwindling revenues are more civilized than those which do not. Some of our great corporations, which prior to 1929 did not intend to pay off their debts, but rather to carry on a policy of perpetual refunding, were as shiftless as families which bought on the instalment plan regardless of savings. Such families and such corporations were regressing in the general direction of economic savagery.

G. VERACITY

Curiously enough, while speaking the truth as a valued virtue goes back in the history of the race at least into the Stone Age, it does not seem to have expanded into Veracity until Greek and Roman times. It has often been noted that the Hebrew Decalogue limited its prohibitions to "thou shalt not bear false witness against thy neighbor."

In Homeric times, '*alētheia* meant chiefly the truth as opposed to lying, and the Homeric poems leave us with the impression that telling the truth was taken in a strictly Pickwickian sense. By the Athenian period, it had come to stand for reality as opposed to appearance.

The Romans made much of *verus*, which meant at bottom "true," "real," "actual," "genuine."

Ethnology, and even the history of early times, is full of instances in which peoples who were otherwise relatively advanced made of skilful lying a virtue. In short, the institution has shown a slow development, and in the form which is recognized by moderns, a late development.

Among our people, lying, that is false representation, has commonly been held in peculiar contempt. Calling a man a liar has been fighting talk. Analysis of the psychology of lying, however, has shown that most of it is a mark of immature personality, mostly to be identified as either defense reaction or else as inferiority compensation. But abstention from even deliberate, knowing, and vicious lying is only a small part of Veracity. The meaning of *verus* is comprehensive. Veracity is devotion to the true as opposed to the false; to the real as opposed to the mystical; to the actual as opposed to the romantic; to the genuine as opposed to the spurious. Veracity means then not only telling the truth, but acting the truth, and being the truth.

The critical social significance is manifest. There is no ordered society anywhere, except as the individual can presume that the statements of his neighbors in all walks of life mean what they say, and will so be made good, and that their acts are what they purport to be.

H. RESPECT FOR SEX

Men and women are organically, and so irretrievably, different, the greatest and most far-reaching difference found in human existence. In normal personality they are different because temperamental differences determine, or tend to determine, what individuals of each sex are likely to learn and the quality of the learnings. Men and women do not see the world from the same angle, never have, and probably never will. The two sexes are complementary and not the same in social as well as in racial functions. That condition always has existed since there was sex, at least in the warm-blooded animals, and will doubtless continue as long as sex remains a fundamental conditioning circumstance of existence. Violation of the condition inevitably tends toward social disruption, and the more so as societies become more and more complex. The sexes are not equal, each to each, but they are equivalent. One of the chief products of advancing Civilization has been the establishment of that equivalency in custom and in the civil law.

There are doubtless many factors involved in reconciling the ways of life which are appropriate to men with those which are appropriate to women, but whatever they are, they all rest, it seems to me, on the moral consideration for which I believe the most comprehensive term is Respect for Sex.

That means, I take it, in the first place respect for the fact of biological sex itself, a reverence for it, and an abhorence of making light of it in any way.

It means, in the second place, honorable insistence upon respect for what each sex at its best holds sacred in its peculiar social functions.

It means, in the third place, reverence in each for its own functions and place in the world decreed by the conditioning circumstances of its existence.

Observe that I do not say "respect for the opposite sex." That depends upon the circumstance that the opposite sex is respectable.

In the literature.—Of all our studies as studies, this is perhaps the most complicated, and the one in which it is most difficult to find the thread which runs through the history, and which may be supposed to be the story of institutional evolution. There are at least two good reasons.

In the first place, sociological writers have always tended to confound several entirely different things, notably marriage, chastity, the family, and the fundamental institution which affects them all and much else beside.

Second, the subject is the one above all others in which the attitude which we call pruriency leads astray writers who in respect to the institution itself are still at the juvenile stage of development. As one reads the great mass of anthropological and ethnological literature, he all too frequently is justly impressed that what he reads has little more scientific significance and reliability than what one might hear in the smoking-car of an old-time lumberjack train or in rather a caddish city club.

Marriage.—Marriage is a civil institution, or a canonical institution. We sanction ecclesiastical weddings in our laws—probably on the whole prefer them—but for the purposes of adminis-

tration, the clergyman is a civil officer. Respect for sex entails
reverence for Marriage, a feeling for its sanctity and for its relatively indissoluble character. There is not necessarily anything
sacred about a church wedding, but the ceremony helps to the
establishment of a feeling for its sacredness. The thing is important, and not the instrument by which it is achieved, even the
best and most promising instrument. Apart from the normal conviction of sanctity, Marriage is a mere civil contract and looked
upon as an easily voidable contract. It is worth noting that the
country which has the worst divorce record in Christendom has
also the worst criminal record.

Chastity.—Chastity is definitively respect for marital status and
nothing else. A polygamous person is not living in unchastity,
even though he have as many wives as the Grand Turk of other
days. A polygynous person may or may not be. It is not likely
that a person whose Respect for Sex is nil, or nearly that, will
remain chaste. Nevertheless, unchastity is not necessarily a violation of the institution which we have before us, for people who
are entirely guiltless on the count, and are perhaps living well-
ordered marital lives, may nevertheless have a respect for sex
which is altogether below that of some of the unchaste. Chastity
is rather an implication of Good Faith, Respect for the Rights of
Others, and perhaps above all, of social conscience in general.
More than that it is an implication of a quasi-religious regard for
the purity of womanhood. All in all, then, the quality is a symptom of character and refinement rather than an institution in
itself, perhaps the supreme symptom of all, but nevertheless a
symptom.

The practical inference for instruction is that chastity is not
one of the things that can be taught. Effective General Education
must carry the quality along with it, especially if the more comprehensive quality which we have under discussion is established.

Nevertheless, the school management in its pastoral function
can do much to restrain the wayward boys and girls. In that respect it is indeed *in loco parentis.*

Origins.—All along from primitive levels in Civilization, long before the establishment of the patrilineal family, and long before there is any serious regard for chastity, either marital or premarital, there appears again and again in advancing peoples a sense of the uncanny or *sacré* in the presence of sex, a sort of proto-romance. It becomes elaborated into cults and as such persists long, sometimes in forms which are repulsive to us. It turns up in chivalry, and out of chivalry grows the personal dignity which is found in the mutual respect which keeps both men and women in their proper places. It is a large part, perhaps the largest part, of the substance of Literature and pictorial Art. In the form of mother worship it appears as a powerful element and motive in Christianity. Altogether, then, it is following this thread which leads us to the fundamental and substantive institution.

Moreover, provided we do not get it mixed up with something else which we cannot teach, nor with the physiology of sex which has nothing to do with the matter, it is one of the easiest of the moral units in instruction. The latter is not much more than driving off perverse influences and maintaining a wholesome regimen in the school as minor community.

SOCIAL CONSEQUENCES OF DISREGARD

Current events, especially since the war of 1914–18, unfailingly illustrate the social consequences of disregard. Pornographic literature and painting, lascivious and suggestive shows, journalistic dwelling on the subject of sex, popular preoccupation with pseudo-science on the subject, reckless teaching in colleges, suggestive feminine costume, regression to barbaric levels in bodily adornment, seem to be producing the effects in society which they probably always have produced, escape from which is the explanation of the development of the institution in the culture of the race. Among the consequences are:

First, increase in the crime of rape, and popular indifference to rape, presaging a renewal of the age-old degradation of women.

Second, and parallel, disappearance of that kind of respect, if not reverence, for womanhood, which in enlightened times has been a veritable part of the function of regulation in the Community.

Third, a decadence of the Family as civil institution, and hence a sort of creeping paralysis in authority. It is mere sociological prating to assert that the "wonders of science" will ever find a substitute for the Family. A great nation, more gifted than any other in capacity for radical upheaval, tried it on a great scale and found that "the experiment was a failure."

Fourth, the widespread desertion of the Home by women and invasion of gainful employment by them has set up a vicious circle of tragic unemployment for men, failure of marriage and the establishment of new homes, more unemployment for men, and so on round again.[2]

If relatively weak nations and inadequate States desired to take the only feasible method of subverting strong nations and powerful States, such as have been found in England and the United States of America, they must do exactly what has more or less been done, namely, subvert their morale by the use of the influences named above.

I. EQUITY

A very ancient norm of conduct is what we commonly call *fair play*. It appears in the Golden Rule. It has always the connotation of equality, impartiality, due warning, avoidance of prejudice, or corruption in special favor. It appears in primitive declarations of war, such as throwing a spear over into the enemy's country, or sending him an embassy and ultimatum. We find it in the code of sportsmanship. It has long been part of the code of civilized warfare. In Commerce we hold in contempt the trader who takes unfair advantage of his customer or competitor. Its essence is in its mutuality, in its give and take.

It is, as much as any institution, at the basis of civilized conceptions of Justice. Indeed a whole branch of Jurisprudence has grown up to deal with Equity as such, where the positive law could not render justice.

---

[2] For pertinent facts as of 1932 see S. P. Breckinridge in *Recent Social Trends in the United States* (New York, 1933). See also comparative employment statistics by decades in the fifteenth census and earlier, and in the sixteenth census, at this writing under way.

No doubt, there always arises the query, "What is fair?" That is the ethical problem. Nevertheless, the feeling comes first. No use to theorize as to what is Equity in a given situation if there is no sentiment about the matter to start with.

J. GOOD FAITH

Keep your promises. On no other of the moral institutions does Civilization, the art of living together, so obviously depend, for it is at the heart of common expectation in matters in which contract appears. And yet, the institution is comparatively a newcomer, at least in the form which is required by the circumstances which arise in an advanced culture.

Maine remarked, "No trustworthy primitive record can be read without perceiving that the habit of mind which induces us to make good a promise is as yet imperfectly developed, and that acts of flagrant perfidy are often mentioned without blame and sometimes described with approbation. In the Homeric literature, for instance, the deceitful cunning of Ulysses appears as a virtue of the same rank with the prudence of Nestor, the constancy of Hector, and the gallantry of Achilles." Even today we come upon callous indifference to promises made, and, worse than that, upon casuistical justification of such, on the ground that the end justifies the means, or by appeal to that hoary catch-all of iniquity, "The greatest good of the greatest number," which logically might justify the massacre of 49 per cent of the population by 51 per cent.

Such things are, however, plain instances of regression, for elaborate laws relating to contract date back more than 2000 B.C. They are to be found in the Code of Hammurabi, and that was only an elaboration of much earlier customs and laws. It was not primitive.

We have thus far been speaking of promises definitely made. That is but a legalistic conception. Good Faith goes beyond that, into the region of promises implied, into general fiduciary responsibility. Under modern social conditions, we are constantly involving ourselves in the obligations of Good Faith, far beyond any legal definition.

"Thou shalt not steal." Moreover, "Thou shalt not covet thy neighbor's wife, nor his manservant, nor his maidservant, nor his ox, nor his ass, nor anything that is thy neighbor's." That is a penetrating statement of certain ideas which the ancient Hebrews had learned. But it was nothing new in the world when it was first set down, but only more definite in thought in an advancing language. Others as well had discovered the principle in their experience of life and had come to accept it as the only basis on which Society in that sort of relationship could go on. The principle is emergent, not only a declaration of rights but right in itself. There was set up a prohibition of depriving a man of his specified property, and then the further injunction to respect several rights of the neighbor, and finally the comprehensive command to respect whatever is his neighbor's. Whatever is one's own seems to be in a fundamental and moral sense *property*, although Law specifies certain kinds of legally recognized property.

In truth most rights are reducible to property rights. Property is *proprius*, what is one's own, special, particular. Property is extension of the self, and self cannot be destroyed save under pain of disintegrating personality, and hence society as going concern. And so property as a moral concept extends far beyond land and chattels, but does not exclude them. The concept of property covers presumptive rights in husband and wife, in children and parents, in body and life, in reputation, in one's job, in his place in the world, in his privacy, as well as in land and chattels.

Those who talk about "placing human rights above property rights" are merely talking nonsense—frequently as a prelude to stealing something. Property rights are human rights, the greater part of all the human rights there are. Property as such has no rights; rights cannot inhere in an abstraction.

L. LABOR

To name Labor is at once to suggest labor unions or at least Labor as an industrial institution. Not so. Before that is Labor as a moral characteristic of civilized man.

It is often said that our Indians for the most part had not arrived at a conception of the dignity of labor. That seems to have been true enough, and it is more or less true of all primitive races—and of infantile adults among highly civilized peoples. As soon as a people has come to take self-initiated labor for granted, it has become well started on the highway of rapid advance in Civilization. The reason is not obscure; labor means that true cultural products are created and left behind as the generations move on. One of the numerous critical marks of personal maturity is the establishment of the moral quality in question.

Labor as moral institution comes in when there has entered the mores and normal personality the conviction that productive work of some sort is worth while for its own sake, regardless of initial appeal, that such an attitude is *right*. It is identifiable in the individual when personality has so far matured, volitionally and morally, that he or she will undertake whatever needs to be done as a matter of course. The attitude is justified when the individual discovers for himself that such a course is capable of yielding abiding interest; in other words, he has found that he is a free man, and she that she has found self-respect. Play and drudgery have alike given place to Labor.

Those who have had much to do with children, and young people prior to maturity, in the home, at school, or under employment, know that the childish attitude may be summarized as follows:

1. They will not work at all unless they are interested. Their response to injunctions to work is *"Why* do I have to?" They are incapable of seeing any reason about it all until they have acquired the work attitude itself, and even then there is no answer of a rational sort. The conviction has come by way of appreciation.

2. They will not finish a job unless they are made to, and making them finish is the only way in which they can gain the experience of what a finished job is. The power of sustained application has to be built up by parent and school—patiently and firmly and with final insistence.

3. Even when that is all done, there is still failure in the moral side of craftsmanship. They have no notion of doing a good job; good enough is sufficient. That too must be learned as part of the maturing process.

Children who are not brought up to work are spoiled, arrested in volitional development. As they reach high-school and college level, and adult employment as well, their seniors observe their ways and observe that "they don't know what work means." So they do not, never having learned.

Nor need we expect that such children and young people will ever follow through any adequate curriculum whatever. The latter signifies work, and they will not work—save in the exercise of ingenuity in explaining why they do not, will not, and ought not. In case the arrest in actuality dates from true infancy, that is to say, from two years or less, negativeness will probably have become established as a personal trait, and then the child or youth in truth cannot learn.

Strong families have known all this from time immemorial and have brought up their children to take all needful work as a matter of course, as part of the normal order of things.

Strong schools have followed the same course, but the school's most available pupil experience for the purpose is study, teaching how to study, and training pupils into the capacity of prolonged study and into the capacity of following an argument for many hours, instead of the capacity for noting and memorizing the gist of a statement in perhaps ten minutes.

M. PUNCTUALITY

As Civilization has advanced from the meager and casual ways of barbarian existence, and complex societies have become more and more the rule, the root of ordered existence comes more and more to be in the synchronization of activities. Hence the use of timekeepers and the rise of Punctuality as being in the nature of a moral institution.

Understanding timekeepers and their use and care, and methods of determining time itself, are matters of Intelligence; keeping appointments is a matter of Conscience. Many a person of otherwise impeccable character goes far to spoil it all by failing to realize that Punctuality is as much a matter of morals as is Veracity.

As we look back over the history of Culture, we find that as soon as people have collected in large communities, and considerable division of labor has taken place, measures of time become part of the whole complex. There could be no full and reliable expectation of what one's neighbor would do, unless the two neighbors were both aware of the lapse of time in accurate measure, and were willing to keep appointments. More than that, in common with all other elements in Civilization, common expectation can in the long run be found only in right expectation as the common denominator. From the clumsy and inaccurate timekeepers found among the ancient Egyptians and Babylonians down to our instruments of great precision, standardized every hour through radio signals, there is a long and typical story of institutional development. Nevertheless, Punctuality in Egypt, three thousand years before Christ, was the same virtue which it is today. It is more imperative today in ordered societies, and individuals need not waste so much time by reason of defective timekeepers.

N. CO-OPERATION

Co-operation is the great word in Civilization. Nearly all the universal institutions have grown out of the necessity of making co-operation possible, those which have not have arisen out of the necessity of harmony. The moral institutions when they have bred into personality and into the mores convert the possibility into an actuality, provided always they are supported by intelligence as to what is right.

At first blush we are perhaps disinclined to believe that there is any institution here, but only the name for a critical part of social functioning. Perhaps that is right. It is, however, true that what we call today "team work," "playing the game," in short, conformity to the ways of the group, is the matrix out of which the other institutions have, in important instances, grown.

When we succeed in getting back to the orig.
prudence, we are pretty apt to find that recogniz
as resentment at the nonconformist, the renegade, ι
er, the rogue, so much so that we find what is appare.
feeling among some species of lower animals. Much th
ing is today found in normally operating communities:
the individuals who decline to play their parts in commun.
tivities. There is then institution, or at least the equivale.
universal institution, in which there is oughtness. It touches community life as such much as does Patriotism in its modern phase
touch Society. In Co-operation and Patriotism are the two chief
elements in Social Conscience.

IV. IN PERSONALITY

In Language, Mathematics, Science, there has been emphasized
the principle that, when great structural learnings in these fields
have become established in the fabric of Personality, the individuals affected become linguistically capable, intelligent, rational; but they do not at every moment drag up out of their memory
systems the principles appropriate to whatever is being thought
or done at that moment. They are not all the time saying to
themselves, "What is the correct way to write this?" or "What
does my Algebra or Logic or Biology say about that?" The educated person acts upon intelligent and rational impulse in nearly
all his experience; but he does on occasion stop and ponder, and in
that case he has the thought in both form and substance with
which to ponder.

So it is with the moral character which is securely built. The
person has not to pause for an ethical judgment at every turn. He
has become the kind of person whose impulses are usually right
and sufficient; he is conscientious here as he is intelligent and rational in the former case. And yet, not infrequently, he has to
form an ethical judgment in an unaccustomed situation. He desires to do right, but what is right? He commonly ponders, and in
pondering he tears down the new situation into its approximate
elements and recognizes the bearing of the principles which have
become a part of him.

But that is not all. The wholly moral, but ignorant, man or woman might well go through life, showing moral quality in every act and yet never engage in moral conduct save by chance. He or she means to do right, but the situations encountered are strange and are not even recognized as being strange. There is no analysis, since the individual is ignorant of the terms of the analysis. The action may be that of a buccaneer for the reason that the actor knows no different. So, as we have seen, the physical, biological, and social sciences, and the substance of thought which is contained in them all, contain pretty nearly all the data of practical ethics—all the data which are not a lucid part of the daily experience.

V. INSTRUCTION

We have thus worked out the units in a course—fourteen of them. But the course cannot be given didactically in a classroom setup, for a particular year or term or semester, under a particular teacher or department of teachers. The influence of the school is a general influence, and the course lasts until maturity. The units give us the broad definition of the content of the course, the systematic bases for directing the influence of the school, a means by which the administration can check up and estimate progress, and terms under which ways and means for applying new influences can be studied. After all, every school is a community, and the influence of the school spirit on the individual pupil is, for better or worse, stronger than the influence of the individual pupil in most cases upon the school spirit. Even so, there are exceptions, for every school has influential pupils, and it is the responsibility of the management to see that their influence is sound and constructive and not the reverse.

The chief instructional influences are:

1. Sound, sympathetic, wise, firm discipline—applied unremittingly by all teachers—intellectual discipline as well as volitional and moral.

2. Example: both that of educated, mature, experienced, teachers themselves and instances and characters drawn from good literature in various forms.

3. An important, if not the most important, influence is to be found in what Professor Groves has called "moral sanitation," the exclusion of vicious influences, especially that of vicious books.

4. The selection of activities, especially in intramural sports, which are best calculated to afford experiences out of which some of the units can emerge. The playground director has more potential influence than most members of the teaching staff.

5. Individual and collective exhortation applied *as occasion suggests*. Our greatest breeders of youthful character have usually been men who could exercise a salutary influence through the spoken word.

6. Pastoral relations with the homes, not those of a perfunctory visiting-teacher setup, although good visiting-teacher work decidedly has its advantages, but the immediate personal influence of the head of the school.

7. Psychiatric counseling, which I mention with reserve. Hardly anything the school does in the way of personal service is capable of more salutary results than is this service when it is applied by well-educated and trained men and women of sense and taste. If the school management cannot be tolerably sure it is attaining these ends, better leave it alone altogether. Nevertheless, the moral structure in personality is so intimately bound up with the sublimation of organic passions that many of our most stubborn conduct problems are psychopathic in their nature and origins.

8. Finally, skill and ingenuity in discovering the immediate pedagogical objectives which contribute to the ultimate curriculum objectives. In unit terminology, these are the elements. It is futile to list such, and it would be misleading to the student to attempt to do so. In the subject-matter courses the elements of units are inherent in the subject-matter itself; here they are inherent in the pupil. They vary according to the school, the locality, and indeed the pupil. In order to show what I mean, however, I name two such which are probably common enough.

The first of these is *caution* in daily life as one of the contributions to the attitude which we call Prudence. The city schools commonly do a good deal with this element, particularly in their campaigns for safety in respect to the perils of automobile traffic.

Another which has impressed me in case work has been what may be called *right attitude toward criticism and correction* as a contribution to Obedience. Resentment here seems to be a trait which lingers indefinitely in children and young people, unless it is altered. It is probably a survival of infantile egoism. Where it exists, it is obviously an obstacle to instruction in nearly every field.

All these represent the necessity of continuous thought in problem-solving which marks off the profession from the trade, and which is not to be escaped in the person who assumes the obligation of leading a body of teachers and governing for their betterment a body of pupils. The resources which are likely to be a support to the natural acumen and experience of the schoolmaster are found in a hundred good books dealing with the lore of the craft, in educational psychology, in the suggestions of psychopathology, in the theory of education itself. All that spells professional growth.

CHAPTER IX

ART

IN THE history of instruction, Art is a very old subject, if we are not particular as to definitions and content. Running back so far as we have any historical reports, we find Music and Literature but not much else. Altogether Art, as we know it today, must classify as instructionally modern and as an element in the Curriculum which has hardly yet found its place. And yet in one form or another it is now found nearly everywhere, periodically running the gantlet of an anti-fads-and-frills campaign.

We must then, in the first place, find out what it is that we are talking about, and inquire on general principles what if any justification there is for Art in the Curriculum and what Art. The terms "art" and "art education," as they are used in our schools today, usually mean Drawing, and what has grown out of Drawing; and latterly appreciation in the pictorial and plastic arts. Seldom are Literature and Music comprehended as parts of Art; they appear as separate disciplines.

A. INTRODUCTION TO ART IN THE CURRICULUM

ART AND ARTS

The word "art" in itself is one of the most difficult in the language if one has occasion to use it in any exact sense. At bottom the meaning is "a method of doing." Language is an art. We speak of the art of the physician, or the teacher, or the craftsman. As method of doing something, it gives rise to "artificial" as opposed to "natural."

Again, it means the distinguishing characteristics of a particular artist or craftsman.

Finally, it means the accumulated products in Culture of the methods, ideas, principles, and works of artists during the ages; and that for our purposes is the important meaning.

PRACTICAL ARTS AND REPRESENTATIVE ARTS

The Practical Arts are usually defined as those which have as their object production which tends toward some practical utility. And yet production in the Practical Arts also inclines always toward the fine and the beautiful as well as the useful; any good job well done tends to have in it elements of beauty and refinement. It is no doubt true that articles of domestic utility or personal utility commonly respond to a demand for the beautiful as well as for the useful. That is notably true of tableware, furniture, and articles of dress and bodily adornment. Distinction here is sometimes drawn between a thing for which beauty is not particularly required, like an old-time cookstove, for example, and other things for which there is a demand which includes beauty or at least that which satisfies the buyer as beauty. So we say that a fine piece of the silversmith's art is veritable Fine Art; and yet there is no categorical distinction between Fine Art as so conceived and the art of the portrait painter, let us say. Both are examples of fine workmanship beautifully conceived.

The distinction which is much more fundamental is that between Practical Arts, whether beautifully conceived and executed or otherwise, and Representative Arts, which have a story to tell independently of the technique of execution.

The Practical Arts have no place in the Curriculum of the Common School, in the first place because no one of them is comprehensive, and, in the second place, because in their nature there is little substance in them. Moreover, to include them is like attempting once more to teach everything, forgetting the principle of the comprehensive and significant.

INSTITUTIONAL ARTS

If we turn back into the history of the race, to the origins and evolution of Civilization, we soon note that from a remote period there have been forms of activity in the Community in which great thoughts have been recorded, action urged, events memorialized, beautiful scenes and beautiful persons made permanent and transportable, great men made visible for succeeding generations, a god or a government or a family adequately and sig-

nificantly housed. Out of all this has sprung up, become organized, refined, and extended, five great arts: Music, Literature,
Painting, Sculpture, and Architecture.

The five in their history show the typical institutional development with great clarity. Above all others, they are the media in
which the whole fabric of Civilization has been transmitted and
ordered societies made possible. If they are not yet in the mores
in terms of appreciation and taste, the society is crude and limited. If they disappear out of the mores, or themselves become
corrupted, society becomes sorely crippled, somewhat perhaps as
impaired circulation of the blood hurts the vitality of the whole
organism. If they fall into the hands of degenerates and miscreants, the whole Community tends more or less to become
demoralized. In them somewhere is the possibility of the dis-
courses which make Science, Religion, and Morality effective; and
not these only but The State, Commerce, and Industry as well.

In each of them we shall come to see that the kernel of their
institutional character is in the principle that each of them is a
particular method of conveying meaning or the substance of
thought.

They are indefeasible elements in the Curriculum of the Common School, for precisely the same reason that has led us to include Language, Mathematics, and Graphics, and also for the
same reason which has led us to include all the rest that we do
include. They constitute Art in the Curriculum, just the same as
sundry of the important sciences constitute Science.

BEAUTY

So far as my observation and experience go, most of our art
teachers and a good many artists have been and are devoted to
the doctrine that Art is a quest of the Beautiful as an abstraction.
Not so. The great arts are representative of reality, and they do
not express anything, save incidentally. I note the caveat that I
am using "reality" in the philosophical sense and not in that of
current politics and art. When a painter leaves us the portrait of
a beautiful woman, he does not express Beauty; he represents a

THE CURRICULUM

woman who is beautiful. So with a landscape painter. True enough, representation may be in a beautiful mode.

Greek and Gothic art did not build beautiful temples and churches; it did things adequately and appropriately, and we call the result beautiful. The Gothic cathedral did not express a pre-existing Beauty; it was an adequate, dignified, majestic church and turned out to be beautiful in our eyes.

Great Music has often been anything but concerned with Beauty. When melody came in as an early stage in institutional evolution, it was not merely a concourse of sweet sounds—the subjective apprehension; it was "a tune," something which had musical meaning. The meaning might be passion, religious or patriotic aspiration in some form, or else the quieting alleviation of passion.

One of the great periods of Art in its social significance was the Middle Ages, when illiteracy and lack of printed material meant that feeling, and indeed apprehension, had to be conveyed through Painting and Sculpture. It would be far fetched, for example, to say that Matthias Grünewald's great painting of the Crucifixion was concerned with Beauty.

GENERAL OBJECTIVES IN INSTRUCTION

Every individual who is above the level of a veritable clod formulates some kind of a philosophy for himself in which his attitudes toward the world in which he lives are more or less formulated. One of the important contributions of instruction in Science is assurance that some part of that philosophy will be sound, and the purpose of public instruction in Science is to generate a common philosophy which shall be a sound philosophy. So it is with Religion and Morality. And so it is with Art.

Herein is accumulated and sorted out a great body of feeling and sentiment, digested out of the experience of the race in the intercourse of humans. Out of all, there may be added to the common philosophy sense of the appropriate, sense of balance, humor if you will. What it contributes or may contribute is background against which both Intelligence and Conscience may be brought to bearings.

What is not in the objectives.—The Common School is not University, nor yet Conservatory of Music, nor Art Museum, nor School of Design. Instruction which in its nature is special training is foreign to the institutional purpose of the School. It makes no attempt to produce "creative artists," nor skilled performers, nor critics.

CLASSICS

Nothing is good because it is old; some things are old because they have always been good. They have stood the test as truthful interpreters of human experience a long time and under varied conditions of life. The race does not tire of them because they are forever new. The significant facts in the Humanities are the tested survivals, since the very name "humanity" imports human experience which is without time limitations.

We do not read classics, or listen to them, or contemplate them, as an exclusive diet in adult life; but if we have been brought up on them, our preferences tend toward modern art productions which are rich in human values, as compared with those which have little or no value at all, other than their capacity for creating sensation and some form of sensuous enjoyment. In other words well-bred tastes incline us toward vicarious experience which is wholesome in character, tending toward the enrichment of personality. So education goes on and on all the way through life. Our tastes have been formed on universal values, and we enjoy that which does in truth keep our ideals alive. Where tastes of that sort are in the mores, there can be common estimates, and those estimates most likely to be right estimates. Therein is the social value of instruction in this whole field.

As always, another and vital social value is the breeding of a public the tastes of which can make great artists of all sorts possible. No difference here from the Intelligence diffused in the population which makes great scientists and great jurists and other statesmen possible, great merchants and industrialists. There has probably never been a time when there was so much production which classifies as Art as there is today. There were never so many facilities. Pretty much anybody, apparently, who feels so inclined can compose a jingle or write a book; write for the newspapers or wield a reckless brush. These people are accepted by an utterly uncritical public as "artists," unaware that an artist is first of all an able and competent man or woman, capable of great conceptions as well as possessed of a competent technique.

B. MUSIC

"Let me make the songs of a people, and I care not who makes the laws." History goes far to substantiate the claim. Revolutions have been organized through songs, kings sung off their thrones and presidents sung into office. Most wars have been stirred up and carried on to the tune of martial music. Religious feeling and thought as well have been embodied in music. Better see to it what kind of songs are made. The only way in which that can be done is through breeding civilized musical taste into the mores.

Like other institutional arts, Music expresses meaning in a particular form, just as Language, Mathematics, and Graphics express meaning in the most generalized forms. It seems to be one of the most difficult things in the world for people to see that not all meaning is expressible in any one form. And yet we all illustrate pluralism in thought forms in our ordinary conversation. We use Language to convey our meaning, but we realize intuitively that the language used does not in itself convey full meaning. The form is there, the sentences are accurately phrased and impeccably grammatical; but as spoken discourse there is often a wide gap between form in Language and clarity of meaning. So we fall into undeliberate cadenced utterance to satisfy our feeling for clarity. That is rudimentary Music. Meaning is made clearer, or at least given force. So it is in written discourse; most of the marks of punctuation are in reality musical devices to suggest cadence. Poetry is Music. It is said that Augustine, who was temperamentally intellectual and rational or nothing, once related that he lost his grip on some articles in his philosophy until they were brought back in the music administered by Ambrose.

THOUGHT OF THE AUDITORY ENVIRONMENT

We recall the argument of chapters iii–v, in which we were dealing with the symbolic institutions. We saw that Thought, as distinguished from reflection or thinking, is order and coherency in ideas, spatial forms, events; in other words, that Thought is the pattern which our civilized perceptions of an ordered universe take on. When one takes Thought as thus understood into Personality, and comes to be satisfied with mental life on those terms, he becomes orderly in the core of his personality. He can think.

So it is with Music. A given tone may be sensually pleasing, but that is of little account; so may much else. But when tones are put together in melody, and especially in modern harmony, musical discourse results. There is ordered tone, just as there is elsewhere ordered space, ordered number, ordered ideas in general, ordered events. Indeed, as one listens to great music, he is tempted to say that here is the supreme achievement of the race in the formulation of order. Subjectively, the result may be the immense majesty of the *Fifth Symphony*. Noise is auditory chaos, beloved of early childhood and infantile adults.[1]

Appreciation of good music is then the addition of a phase of Thought to Personality. He who has it is inevitably better educated than he could be without it. That is not to say that Music can ever take the place of Language and Mathematics. Still, able mathematicians have a curious habit of being accomplished musicians as well.

MUSIC IN SOCIETY

Music has had in the past, and may still have, two somewhat distinct offices in the relationships between humans, a direct and an indirect.

The direct influence has always come as a means of creating *community feeling* through individual participation in songs, not only the great community but minor communities as well, such as churches and schools. So it was with the great chorals of Bach in the Lutheran churches of his time. So it has been with national

[1] The whole matter is developed from the standpoint of the musical scholar by D. N. Ferguson in *The History of Musical Thought* (New York: F. S. Crofts & Co., 1935).

anthems and revolutionary songs. Old-time harvests were gathered that way, old-time boatmen and sailors won strength and endurance and co-operation in their chanteys.

In less simple times, as communities have grown larger, and passed beyond the singing of the whole community, the social influence is indirect and more like that of the other arts and sciences, namely, the setting-up of common standards of taste in matters in which there is bound to be individual interest of some sort. In Music that means appreciation of great music. But, more important than that even is the consideration that common tastes in one of the Arts leads to common estimates of value, and those estimates right estimates; in other words, contributions to Taste.

IN INSTRUCTION

Music is thus unquestionably institution if there is any such thing. On both the historical and the rational counts, it is universal institution, one of the major elements in Civilization. It is thus indefeasibly part of the content of general education and an element in the Curriculum of the Common School. That is our justification for teaching it. The fact that the majority think it a good thing is no justification at all; in a few years there is just as likely to be a majority who regard it as superfluous.

Almost from the moment when education began to be thought out from the theoretical standpoint, in Plato's time, Music was made an essential element. It will be remembered that in the first of all curriculums, the Trivium and Quadrivium, Music was made part of the Quadrivium.

Granted the argument for the place of Music in our educational purposes, the question then arises, "What music?"

I. THE SINGING VOICE

Most children like to sing, and they come into the singing voice naturally if they are not spoiled by the inhibitions which are so common in language-arts pedagogy. Especially is it true if they have been launched on their singing careers before the appearance of the self-critical attitude, which is likely to come on at about nine or ten years of age.

Unit.—Learning to sing is learning to sing, that is to say, the acquisition of an utterance art which has the characteristics of singing and which has them consistently. That is the unit, and the pupil has mastered it when he can and does at will readily employ the singing voice. That does not mean that he can sing anything assigned him, any more than that the primary-school pupil who has learned to read can necessarily read advanced physics. Such attainments come with experience and with expansion of ideational content in the memory system.

The unit once learned, singing experience passes into *school singing*. The course is still singing, but not in the sense that school singing is a systematic part of the program of studies with units to be mastered. It is rather experience-getting, plus the direct social effect to which we have referred. Nevertheless, it is not perfunctory; it is under the direction of the singing teacher, and standards of improvement in performance are in his or her mind. It either does or does not have its normal and proper effect; in other words, teaching problems are involved. The teaching problem does not, however, focus primarily on the individual pupil, but rather on the school or class in its collective musical activity. The element of appreciation as well as of performance is involved, and that implies that good songs should be selected.

II. SCALE AND STAFF

In the routine teaching of singing, when there were few trained teachers or none at all, the logical thing to do seemed to be for pupils to learn the scale and then to put together the tones in songs. The same notions of teaching led to the teaching of the alphabet first, then the recognition of words, and finally words in sentences. No competent teacher does either today. Children learn to read by reading and to sing by singing. That principle once established, however, there is a tendency to treat the essential formal elements in a cavalier fashion. So it was with spelling and grammar, after a more intelligent method of teaching reading came into vogue. There has perhaps been some tendency to deal lightly with musical notation.

There is an exact analogy between grammar and the scale and staff. We do not learn grammar in order to learn expression in language: through grammar we learn something that is in Language. So it is with scale and staff in Music. The pupil can learn to sing or play an instrument without them. Indeed, he learns better that way. But having learned musical performance, the language of music gives him the orderly statement of the thought which is in civilized music, of which we have made much.

Unit.—Learning scale and staff is the precise analogue of learning the printed page; it is learning to read music. It is a language art learned through practice and not through analytical methods. There is but one unit. Mastery is attained, not when the pupil reads perfectly, for nobody does that, but when his use of the auditory-visual apparatus has consistently the characteristics of sense of tone and interpretation of the graphic symbols of the staff.

Harmony.—Herein too are the elements of Harmony, but the rudiments do not extend to the great logic of the subject. The latter goes beyond the Common School.

III. CHORUS

Where the school becomes organized into part-singing, with leaders and instrument or instruments, then we have, or may have, the essence of choral music and its characteristic common participation. It is one of the means of developing sense of co-operation. The school as thus organized undertakes not merely what is comprehensive school-singing, but it undertakes a repertoire of substantial pieces.

The chorus is not a course, at least not a systematic course. There are no units. If there were, there would be a specialized course.

One of the best periods in American music, at least best from the social standpoint, came when it was common for community choruses of adults to be organized for serious work in practice. It not only yielded the direct social values to which we have referred, but it had the further utility of affording a worthy and

useful avocational interest in the place now occupied by endless
cards and golf. It was cultivation of one of the great arts.

MUSICAL APPRECIATION—THE CLASSICS

The other side, that of the indirect social influence, the upbuilding of familiarity with and taste in the great classics, can of
course make nothing out of participation in performance. The
artistry of performance is of necessity beyond the reach of all but
the highly trained specialist. All this side of Music was in effect
closed to the commons, until the arrival of phonograph and
broadcast. Herein was social progress indeed.

Hitherto, the classics had been within the reach of royalty,
within the reach of individuals able to pay for expensive tickets
of admission to performances, at the best within the reach of those
privileged to attend a few municipal and State theaters and opera
houses. But all that is changed. The phonograph makes possible
in school a kind of instruction which would literally have been
impossible at any earlier period in musical history. With the aid
of the phonograph, instruction in the world's classics is possible in
every school in which a competent teacher can be found.

Musical appreciation is therefore comparatively a new thing in
schools. So far as one individual's observation is worth anything,
it seems to be true that the bane of such courses is lack of teaching.
The record is played without comment other than some remarks
on the life and place in Music of the composer.

On the other hand, in a few instances, and there are doubtless
many in the aggregate, superb teaching of musical appreciation is
found, enough to make it evident that it might appear everywhere, given teachers with genuine personal background and adequate scholarship in music. Such teachers must indeed be musical
scholars, beyond the well-rounded personal development which
comes out of general education—not composers nor yet accomplished performers, but scholars. Our higher schools have been
exceedingly slow in producing such. The reason may be found in
the fact that our universities have been slow in organizing adequate departments of music. Musical training at higher levels,

save for the few who could study abroad, has usually been in conservatories of music in which the emphasis is upon performance. The training of teachers on the other hand has largely been in teachers'-colleges, where young people are shown how to teach singing and direct brass bands in the public schools. Neither the conservatory nor the teachers college form of training is likely to produce scholarship save by chance. A justifiable change in teachers'-college policy would be training students more adequately in the subject matter which they are to teach.

COURSE ORGANIZATION

There is not likely to be any systematic result, if courses are merely dubbed "musical appreciation" and allowed to go at that. There has to be organization, so that the pupil can begin somewhere and end somewhere. Moreover, the body of musical culture itself must as a whole be brought into integration, so that in the end the pupil may have acquired some degree of musical taste, and not merely a liking for some particular form or composition. In other words, there must be a unit organization.

At bottom, the whole principle of unit organization is not different in Music from what we have found it to be in subjects previously discussed. In Language, in the several mathematical fields, in the sciences, in Morality, the unit organization is the definition of the course or courses, and of the content of General Education in the particular field. The units in Algebra are in themselves Algebra in the Common School. The several moral institutions which we have found constitute Morality as we see it. So it is in Music, and so in Literature, Painting, Sculpture, and Architecture. If it were not so, then these arts would be excluded from the Curriculum as nonteachable and pupils would properly be referred to nonschool enterprises.

We might seek to organize our course as Literature has sometimes been organized, by study of works of great composers, or even of the evolution of musical forms, but that would lead into one-sided and immature specialization; or else into the history of Music, an intellectual purpose rather than one in appreciation.

In any of the Arts, the problem of unit organization is to find the most general forms in which the content of the Art is expressed and transmitted. In that way the pupil learns as the race has learned and what the race has learned; he follows the evolution of the art, although not necessarily the historic order of forms. Music, as we know it, is the youngest of the organized arts, despite its ancient history as institution. For that reason, it is not so easy to be confident of right choice of forms as in Literature, where the only form added since Greek times is the Journal and possibly the Treatise.

With the foregoing apologia, the following are suggested as the units in Musical Appreciation:

   I. Song
        In popular usage, all vocal music is thought of as song. Here we have in mind the technical use of the term as short lyrical or narrative poem with musical setting.

  II. Hymn
        A religious or sacred song and also in the present use a national song. Familiarity with the great historic national songs.

 III. Anthem
        Particularly as integral part of Anglican church service.

  IV. Choral
        We have met the form in school-singing. It belongs also in appreciation because some of the greatest music is in the form.

   V. Sonata
        Because there is an important body of classical material in the form.

  VI. Oratorio
        A great historic form, perhaps doubtful for present use.

 VII. Opera
        At present there are serious limitations, though not necessarily obstacles, to attempts to use Opera in schools. It is drama as well as music; the visual element ought to be present, especially for those who are not already familiar with some of the operas. And yet of all the forms, Opera has perhaps the best title to prospects of permanency, save the Symphony. It has lived for something over three hundred years and seems to be growing in favor rather than declining. It is a cardinal principle in our study not to exclude anything from the Curriculum because of present lack of feasibility, provided it in principle

belongs to the Curriculum. We can look forward to the time when the cinema and phonograph will make Opera possible in every school.

VIII. Symphony

Greatest perhaps of all the forms and happily now one of the most available.

IX. The Mass

Again a great form especially in its full elaboration.

MASTERY

Mastery is fundamentally the same kind of thing in the Humanities that it is in the other fields studied. It is actual learning of the kind contemplated, in contrast with mere measures of performance. On the other hand, mastery here is a very different thing as a matter of definition and identification. In Language, Mathematics, or Science, we are identifying an established language capacity or else an understanding of some principle or principles. The unit can be taught and retaught until mastery is established and evidenced. In all the Humanities, including the major arts, objectives are in the form of discrimination and preference. We get evidence of mastery, that is, of actual learning, when we can infer from tests applied to discrimination, or from behavior as evidence of preference, that learning is taking place. We can even at the end of the pupil's career conclude that taste is probably what it would be in an educated adult, but there is nothing of positive exactitude about it either in terms of definition or in those of identification of learning in the pupil.

INSTRUMENTAL MUSIC

Is there any place for instrumental music in the Common School? On the principles which have been developed, I believe not.

That there is a place for Music, both as singing and as appreciation of great music, we have demonstrated. But the place is social and not individual, save as the individual is himself a social being. Civilization is social and not individual in import, and the paramount values to be derived in all general education are social values. The individual becomes civilized.

Instrumental music, so far as performance is concerned, is of necessity specialized, both with respect to the instrument concerned and with respect to learning. The only common instrument is the vocal apparatus; other instruments are particularized. The piano is not the violin nor yet the cornet, and so on through the list. Hence it is that, while individuals commonly learn singing as a group, no instrument is ever learned that way.

Further, the greatest educational value in instrumental music is found in the appreciation of great music rendered by competent artists and not by school children.

It is often said that everybody should know at least one instrument. I have often heard it said that everybody should know at least one language other than his own, but I never heard any good reason given for the statement. I have heard it urged that the personal use of an instrument is essential to the appreciation of music rendered on that instrument. If the plea could be sustained, it would prove too much: all the instruments in an orchestra must then be learned before one could appreciate a symphony. If that were true, the attendance at concerts would be small indeed. That competency in one of the major instruments is desirable from the individual point of view is undeniable. It is a resource, but so are many, many things individual resources. All such must be administered elsewhere than in school if they are administered at all. Here, as in the case of foreign languages and many specialized vocational subjects, is an opportunity for organizations like the Y.M.C.A. to supplement the school rather than duplicate it, as they all too often now do.

Has instrumental music no direct social utility, such as we have found in singing? Concert activities at once suggest themselves; but these have direct social utility only for those who take part. A good school orchestra is a most appealing affair, and we are prone to permit our admiration to bias our judgment. So it does and more also with the school brass band. Most boys—and a good many girls who are trying to be boys—sooner or later have an urge to tootle a horn. Add to that the glamour of a uniform and of marching in procession, with free trips to distant cities, and the recent consuming interest in bands is easily accounted for. Less appealing is the hard work essential to elementary mastery of the more civilized violin, and other strings.

C. LITERATURE

Of all the arts, by far the most important in the fabric of Civilization is Literature. The greater part of transmission and diffusion is effected by Literature. That has not always been true. Time was when Painting, Sculpture, and Architecture were more important. It has, however, increasingly been true since (a) the emergence of an alphabet which made it comparatively easy to learn to read, and which was readily capable of carrying the thread of continuous discourse; (b) the invention of printing; (c) the very recent spread of the art of reading among the masses of the population; and (d) the growth of public libraries and the publication of inexpensive books and periodicals.

SOCIAL SIGNIFICANCE

The form and content of civilized music is, as we have seen, experience of the race recorded and transmitted in a particular meaning; at least classical music is of that order. So it is with Literature. Kindred to Music, it is much more comprehensive, primarily because it is expressed in the abstract form of thought found in Language, supplemented by the thought of the auditory environment found in Music.

Hence it is that the fruits of the experience of the race are recorded in Literature far beyond what is true of any other art. Common participation in literary tastes gives us our chief access to common estimates in Intelligence, Conscience, Taste. But observe that, in making this statement, Literature is envisaged as a whole and not merely as what is sometimes called belles-lettres.

AS CULTURE

Literature builds a cultural environment which is in our time more pressing than any save the natural, industrial, and mechanical environments alone. The mores, at least the superficial mores which determine current conduct, come into adjustment with this environment or tend to do so. If the prevailing tone of current literature in any age is romantic, then the common outlook on life will tend to be full of the ideology of glory, honor—in its less reputable aspect—hero-worship, in short, cult of the emotions. If the prevailing tone is cynical, then we find that reckless unconcern for values of any sort tends to become characteristic. And so on with sensationalism, prurient curiosity, lasciviousness, and what not. On the other hand, where the tone of current literature is that of our best books and journals, the mores will tend in that direction, and usually, if not always, the really basic mores will tend to come to the surface.

In so far as adjustment to the literary environment amounts to a repudiation of the intellectual and moral institutions which lie at the core of the fabric of Civilization—rational outlook, morality, citizenship, respect for the Family and for sex—the adjustment is, like a great many more in both the organic and the social series, bad—maladjustment. The social effect is more or less social disruption, which is only another term for collapse of social order. It appears as flaming-up of crime, widespread frivolous divorce, breakdown in Family and in ordered Government, in the end as economic "depression." The inclusion of the last in the series of maladies traceable in part to a perverse literary environment may seem far fetched at the best and ill founded at the worst. On the contrary, while most depressions have as an element in their causation crass ignorance of economic and commercial principles, the recent instances in particular show also a patent causation in the belief that it is not respectable to be respectable, and that prevailing practice is to be looked to for justification and not eternal principles of right and wrong. Such has been the teaching of an immense amount of recent literature, but business cannot be done on that basis.

Censorship.—Of all the foregoing, statesmen, both civil and ecclesiastical, have been well aware for centuries. Their recourse has ordinarily been some form of censorship. Indeed, until within a little more than two hundred years, censorship was assumed to be one of the attributes of sovereignty. The assumption was not bad in itself but bad rather in the principle that, as in other forms of autocracy, you could not be sure of your censor.

The true principle here is to recognize that cultural products form an environment, that there inevitably will be adjustment to that environment, and that the natural method of combatting maladjustment is the use of public instruction to breed taste for the good rather than allow each younger generation to grow up untutored and a fertile field for literary scalawags.

But this is merely to repeat the argument of our whole study as it is related to the use of public instruction in General Education.

VALUES

It is scarcely within the scope of this work to develop a theory of literary criticism. Nevertheless, in order that we may know what we are talking about, it is perhaps worth while to look briefly at a few of the qualities which mark off good literature from bad.

Good literature does not demoralize.—Good literature transmits Civilization; it does not demoralize its readers and by that route the public. If the contrary were true, and if everything which suited the whims and appetites of the writers were literature, there never would have been any such thing as Literature, for Society would never have risen to the level at which civilized literature became possible. The facilities, arts, enterprises, through which and by means of which books and newspapers are published are characteristics of ordered societies. They emerged and endured because on the whole Literature was contributing to the art of living together and not contributing to disruption. As I am writing these words, my attention is attracted to a characteristic statement in a widely read current work of fiction in which the author develops the thesis that what he calls respectability is only for the weak. If believed in and seized upon by the readers as an excuse for evil living, it contributes to regression toward savagery.

Veracity.—Good Literature, like all good art, is *veracious*, even though it be in the form of fiction. It does not trade in unrealities, unless the reader is warned in the beginning that the tale is of intention fantastic. *Alice in Wonderland* did not offend veracity.

The romances of the last two hundred years or thereabout have been chronic offenders, in that they have often depicted people and situations which never did exist in any kind of a sane world, and never ought to have existed in any world. That long series led young people into the bad habit of dramatizing themselves as inhabitants of an unattainable world. It is tragic to recall the many thousands of women especially who must have lived wasted lives because of romantic rather than idealistic notions of marriage. I have no doubt, although I cannot prove it with census figures, that a very considerable proportion of our childish and shameful divorce record is traceable to the fact that silly middle-aged people often dramatize themselves as participants in the "triangle" of current fiction.

Still worse is the mendacity of the "scientific" novel.

Theme must be worth recording.—The subject matter is quite as important as the artistic skill found in the technique. The latter must be taken for granted, although we may turn aside in our reading to admire the skill employed. The great writer or great artist in any field reveals himself in the conceptions which form his subject matter. The issue must be worth setting forth. No doubt a poet could be found who is skilful enough to set forth as pathos the dying lamentations of a hog, but the result would not be Literature.

IN EDUCATION

Wherein then does Literature enter into the educational process going on in the individual?

All learning arises out of experience; and, in the modern world, the bulk of civilizing experience is necessarily vicarious rather than direct. The educational function of all literature is in the principle that it makes vicarious experience on a wide scale possible. If we were limited to the immediate experience accumulated in our individual lives, we should scarcely have done more than emerge from the higher levels of barbarism. We read books largely in order that we may associate with imaginary people, and indeed historical people, whom we come to like and admire; in order that we may live over again the past; in order that we may be stimulated by high ideals or by witty sayings; in order that we may enjoy the music and the dignity of beautifully arranged discourse.

It is, I suppose, safe to say that by far the greater part of the wisdom and moral sense of highly civilized persons has come out of the experience which they have found in Literature. They might have found all their breeding in association with their contemporaries, but nobody living in the advanced stages of Civilization has ever had contemporaries enough for that. Moreover, our contemporaries, like ourselves, live only in a cross-section of time, unaware of human experience that has gone before. But Literature is of all time.

IN INSTRUCTION

Literature is in the Curriculum of the Common School because it is indefeasibly institution, major and universal, part of the fabric of Civilization. That is reason enough.

No doubt the impulse of most people is to take it for granted that Literature in the schools means the vernacular literature. Since we have found instruction in foreign languages, to say nothing of instruction in all languages which have literatures, to be unwarranted, it follows that the literature read and studied in school must be in the vernacular. That, however, by no means closes the door to literature native to other tongues. Literature is Literature, however, wherever, and whenever it is or has been written. From Homer to the present day, great literature is human and not of any race or nation. Happily, translations of most of the great literature of the past, and of the present world, exist, and the translations themselves are often great literature. No doubt there are advantages in reading a great piece in the tongue in which it was written, but that is true only of those who have acquired sense of the foreign tongue itself. It is mere pretense that such is ever the outcome of language instruction in the Common School on any scale large enough to be socially, or indeed culturally, significant.

UNITS

In looking for unit organization, the same principles apply which we have found in Music. Unlike Music, however, Literature has had time enough to become thoroughly constituted in its forms. Many of them are prehistoric, and most of them went through their organizing period in Greek times.

Unit organization is as essential to systematic instruction here as elsewhere. One of the most banal of teaching proposals seems to me to be that which appears under the head, "Appreciation in Literature." Such courses begin nowhere and end nowhere.

MASTERY

Mastery means actual and genuine learning of the appreciation type, in contrast with merely satisfactory performance on a series of lesson assignments, estimate of which is verified to the teacher by some kind of pertinent evidence. The objective is, in the first place, familiarity with all the different literary forms. Many a person has lived to an advanced age before becoming aware that there is such a thing as poetry capable of yielding satisfying experience. The objective is further awareness of the difference between the good and the tawdry or bad, and preference for the good. Testing is not measurement, nor can formal tests be applied to the full objective for each unit. Tests can be made and have been made to apply to the pupil's powers of discrimination, and the more of them there are the better. But a test which shows consistent discrimination cannot show the other side of appreciation which is preference. That can be reached only through evidence drawn from unsupervised behavior. People ought not to deceive themselves by believing that positive evidence of the mathematical type can be secured; but, on the other hand, they ought not to allow themselves to believe that teaching can go on without any evidence of learning at all.[2]

The forms suggested as units follow.

I. ORATORY

Probably the oldest of all, particularly if we give the word its root-meaning, spoken appeal. Oratory changes in style and has done so through the ages, but the characteristics of eloquence,

---

[2] I have discussed the theory of testing in chap. xix of my *The Practice of Teaching in the Secondary School* (rev. ed.; Chicago: University of Chicago Press, 1931).

good argumentation, sincerity, and effective appeal are as good in one age as in another. A superlatively good piece of invective delivered today would use a very different idiom from that which appears in the *Philippics* or in the *Orations against Antony*, but the veritable frame and argument of both of them could be used today in our idiom in America.

The objective is to make pupils aware of the characteristics of good oratory, or just plain public-speaking if you prefer; to lead them to discriminate between sincere appeal and scholarly presentation, on the one hand, and crass demagoguery, fallacious argument, and mendacious statement, on the other—and to hate the latter.

It is hard to imagine a service which would contribute more to good citizenship than this, and good citizenship is a social value.

II. DRAMA

Next in order, probably in historic development, and, with the exception of the Journal, certainly in the current literary environment, is the Drama. The Drama of today is the cinema. The latter can improve until it becomes one of the most useful social forces in existence—one of the most useful that ever has existed—or it can be one of the chief contributory factors in demoralization. Before it can realize the potentialities of the Drama, it must assuredly be made over from a cheap money-making enterprise into one which produces a fair proportion of great artists. So far, in all the years of its existence it has produced perhaps three artists comparable to the best of those of the Stage, and one of them was never allowed to realize himself. Whether it does improve or not will depend chiefly on the issue whether public instruction can succeed in developing dramatic taste in the rising generation.

III. EPIC POETRY

In some sense, the Epic is the greatest of all literary forms, perhaps the greatest of all artistic forms. There are few great epics, probably because epic conceptions require great men, and especially men of competent and vivid historic sense. The four works which have contributed most to folk appreciation, the *Iliad, Ae-*

neid, Divine Comedy, and *Paradise Lost,* were all epics. Rarely we find a work in history which is a prose epic, but prose can never take the place of poetry. It is one thing to read history and study it and make social generalizations out of it, but it is quite another and vastly more important thing to be able to see the epic in phases of a national history and then to place the epic in epical form. Happy the nation that can breed such a poet!

If it be true that valid literary taste is formed primarily on the classics, then certainly the Epic is an important unit in the long course in Literature.

IV. THE BALLAD

A sort of minor epic. Narrative poetry which misses the epic theme.

V. THE LYRIC

The poetry of song and, in its various forms, still the largest part of the body of poetry.

VI. THE NOVEL

Apart from the newspaper, and possibly the cinema, the bulk of the leisure-time literary contact of our population is through some variation of the Novel. The form goes back to Roman times at least, but in its present conception it is hardly more than two hundred years old, and in its current phase less than a generation.

In large part, the ideology of our day arises out of the reading of stories. The untutored and immature requires action and movement, and, like his musical ancestors, he demands stimulation of his passions. To that purpose, the current novel is very adaptable; like the cinema, it is very sensitive to the mores.

The Novel is assuredly a unit in the course, and the objectives are not different from what they are in other units. There is, however, the addition which can hardly be treated in this connection, namely, the generation of taste to the point at which the individual desires less story-reading.

VII. HISTORY AND BIOGRAPHY

History is Literature as well as Science. In the latter we study History for the sake of the logic of human events; in the former we read History as one of the most rewarding of avocations. Biography is History, but it is a special variant of History as a literary form. As such, good biography is to be preferred to the novel as a source of personal culture, and perhaps we can estimate maturing literary taste in the reader by the extent to which he gives up novel-reading in favor of biography.

The attack on the problem is twofold. We do not teach History as such for the primary purpose of appreciation; we teach it for the sake of making the past intelligible. But in the teaching of History as Science, if the teaching be effective, we exert some indirect influence in the creation of a critical attitude toward historical writing. That is one of the important things in the appreciation of History as a literary form. The approach in literary appreciation is in the direction of building up right attitudes toward History as a form of leisure-time reading, including detestation of works obviously intended for destructive or propagandist purposes.

VIII. THE JOURNAL

History suggests the Journal, for journalism is but current historiography. In historical order of development, the Journal is by far the most recent of the literary forms, so recent indeed as hardly to be recognized as Literature at all. Therein, perhaps, is explanation of much that we have to deplore in our newspapers.

Nevertheless, the Journal is in essence a literary form, an institution, for it has followed the social history of all the forms. Moreover, it holds a peculiar place of privilege in our modern commonwealths under the polity of freedom of the press. Hence, newspaper-publishing is in its nature a profession and subject to the ethical obligations of all professions.

As I write this section, there comes an article in one of our periodicals, from the pen of a competent journalist, asserting that the bulk of the capital, energy, and space of our newspapers is devoted to the exploitation of crime, sex, sports, and sensation. He might have added that few newspapers, either metropolitan or provincial, can avoid the temptation to make Roman holiday of the reputations of citizens, whether public or private, for the delectation of the rabble. Nor are newspaper faults peculiar to American journals.

Over against the statement just referred to, might well be placed the cynical statement of another journalist, this of a few years gone by. This man remarked that newspaper writers are in much the position of the keepers in a zoölogical garden who feed the beasts what the latter seem to desire, but do not necessarily select the same food for their own dining-rooms.

The last statement has in it the crux of the whole matter in which we are interested. If we are to continue to cherish blindly the doctrine of unrestrained liberty of the press, the salvation of society evidently rests in large measure upon public instruction in this literary form, until there shall cease to be such a thing as a newspaper rabble to be fed. If our schools had for a generation past been as effective in teaching Literature as they have been in teaching Science and Health, our newspapers would very likely today be a great deal more valuable to the community.

IX. THE ESSAY

Much of the older philosophical writing, and nearly all of the modern which is not in systematic form, is in the form of the Essay. In fact, every editorial is a short essay.

If we were to collect and study the reading of an educated person of a generation or two ago, we should probably find that the bulk of it was in the Novel and the Essay, with poetry scattered along as casual and desultory. The great epoch of the periodical was one in which the Essay was the heart of the latter. Cultivated persons were not common but they were numerous, perhaps proportionately more numerous than is the case today, despite the greater number of graduates in the present population. Educated leaders in politics were possible, because there was an informed and educated following. Much of that was due to the quality of the essay-writing. We should find it hard today to find periodicals of the caliber of the *Edinburgh Review*, the *Fortnightly*, the *Westminister* in Britain; the *Revue des Deux Mondes* in France; the *Atlantic Monthly*, the *Forum, Scribner's, Harpers*, in America.

We have some of them still, it is true, but restricted as compared with what they once were, and running a desperate struggle in competition for existence with pictorial sheets.

The Essay as a unit in Literature would in all probability yield to instruction, even if the latter were nothing more than convinced and resolute determination on the part of schoolmasters and of teachers in Literature that all pupils should be made familiar with this literary form. Above all, the public effect might well be that more people would become capable of being *convinced by argument*, which sometimes seems like a vanished trait.

X. THE TREATISE

The Treatise is a more extended and more systematic Essay. Where the Essay is typically personal comment on a particular subject, the Treatise is a prolonged and logically arranged and supported argument. And yet John Locke's Psychology was entitled *Essay Concerning Human Understanding*.

It may seem strange to the reader that I should name the Treatise as among the literary forms at all, and yet, other than in its current scientific phase, it is one of the oldest forms. The intellectual life of the race has centered on the Treatise. Time was when it was taken for granted that educated people would read notable works as naturally as they read newspaper or periodical editorials today. To confine ourselves to modern times, in the closing years of the seventeenth century and long afterward, men did not feel that they must be professional physicists and mathematicians in order to read the *Principia*, albeit that great work would hardly rate as light reading at any time. Blackstone's *Commentaries* was read as a matter of intellectual interest by men who had no thought of practicing law. *The Wealth of Nations*, *The Origin of Species*, the *Synthetic Philosophy* of Herbert Spencer, and *Ancient Law* are instances of notable treatises which were treated as Literature.

That the public interest in treatise material has not entirely perished is evidenced by the success of a considerable amount of semipopular scientific writing within the past few years. A great deal more and a great deal better might be brought out if the schools would do their duty in equipping their pupils to read something more exacting than mystery stories, or intensely dogmatic problem novels, or the latest shallow and misleading popular science. It is, however, a Sisyphean task, so long as the textbook method of instruction survives. The school textbook is usually a particular form of the Treatise, and in principle it serves an indispensable function in instruction. But so long as young people have become habituated in all their school days to getting up scrappy assignments, they are not like to endure readily the severe application required in treatise-reading.

NOT HISTORY OF LITERATURE

The foregoing may easily lead to the misapprehension that appreciation of Literature is information about literature. Indeed, that has been the conception of teaching prevalent among the eruditionalists in the past, and in some quarters it still is. To raise the question is to answer it: information about works, authors, times, and places, and ability to make prompt and ready attribution of passages is not to know Literature. It is quite true that people of cultivated literary tastes will usually do all this, but it is incidental and a by-product and not the essential thing.

NOT FORMAL STUDY

Since the literary forms were first proposed as units, some teachers have misinterpreted the proposal to mean that the technical structure and characteristics should be the objective in each unit. Not so. That would be to throw Literature back among the sciences, and to emphasize the informational, even the professional, point of view. The units are units in appreciation, and they are valuable because they give the whole field coherency and manageability. It is no doubt true, on the other hand, that, while an understanding of the critical character and structure of the lyric adds but little to an appreciation of lyric poetry, a sense of the Lyric as a differentiated form of poetry does help to put the pupil in the way of orderly appreciation. Systematic Botany in itself gives no appreciation of the beauty of flowers as a matter of value, but we are undoubtedly helped to a full appreciation of a rose if we know it is a rose and not a dandelion.

D. PAINTING

Painters and writers on Painting, and writers in general literature as well, habitually appropriate the word "Art" to the exclusive behoof of Painting and Sculpture. With most people, apparently the connotation of Art is Painting. Dealers in "art supplies" are engaged in the merchandising of materials chiefly for painting. So it is in schools. Consider the typical school prospectus and note the pages devoted to Art. In most cases they refer to Drawing or else to embryo and misplaced museum courses in Painting. Now all this is entirely unwarranted. Painting is no more Art than any of the other four, no more truly fine art than are much of carving, jewelry, furniture.

Painting must, in the first place, be distinguished from graphical representation.

In graphical representation or Drawing, various type forms are used to symbolize the external world, not because there is any pictorial representation involved, but rather because such type forms objectively correspond to percepts which are the same in all. The type form for a cube in space will serve as an illustration. The artist, on the other hand, must indeed draw and *represent* space as it veritably is, but, it he does no more, he is merely practicing a form of applied mathematics, checked by some elementary principles in perceptual psychology. But the pictorial artist does more than that. He deals not in symbols but in representations which he finds in his own genius and artistic skill. He sometimes, with what seems to us marvelous skill, creates the perception of a face with a line or two, perhaps with a single line, and the result is a *picture*. The cube symbol is a *graph*. Altogether beyond that the artist creates a totality of composition, texture, color, which we perceive as totality, which appeals immediately to the feelings, and we get a particular kind of meaning which is not derivable otherwise. He can "make us see" what neither draftsman, nor musician, nor poet can make us see. He represents but does not copy. The newspaper cartoon is an excellent illustration of what is meant.

So much for the term as used in Art. It is commonly applied to painting in color, but it applies as well to line drawing, etching, engraving, in so far as these achieve pictorial representation.

AS INSTITUTION

Happily, we can find in ancient remains what must have been close to the beginnings of Painting as recognizable institutional art. We can get no similar remains in any of the other Arts save perhaps Sculpture. We have to infer musical and literary beginnings from the ethnology of contemporaneous primitives. Architectural remains out of the primitive world are scanty or nonexistent because of the perishability of building materials and structures. But the Stone Age paintings from the caves of Europe are unquestionable, and the line of institutional descent is clear, especially when we bring to bear contemporary ethnological evidence.

The purpose of these Stone Age murals has been under dispute, but, whatever the purpose was, the fact remains evident that they were representations and neither copies nor symbols.

The canons of good Painting from the institutional standpoint are of course not essentially different from those of Literature.

It is probably true, perhaps certainly true, that outside religious pieces, Painting has been held back in development by its dependence for patronage on rich vulgarians, not to say reprobates. True enough there have been rich and powerful patrons who were the reverse of vulgar, and they of course must have been of great service. Music, for a similar reason, appears to have suffered a long period of arrested development in the societies of the ancient Near East. It was used chiefly by the wealthy for entertainment. Western music, on the other hand, at least since early Christian days was fundamentally of the folk, save in so far as in modern times the higher forms have been more or less under the patronage of cultivated as well as wealthy upper classes. Literature has on the whole been exempt from the kind of arresting and debasing influence which has been mentioned, perhaps because in its formative stages the vulgar rich and powerful have tended to be illiterate. Sculpture and Architecture have always tended to have a saving civil and ecclesiastical patronage, and after all a building must stand up.

If the foregoing be true, then one of the chief cultural uses of public instruction in Painting should be to give it the same kind of footing which Literature and Music enjoy by turning it into a folk art.

IN EDUCATION

The educational significance of the acquisition of taste in pictorial art is precisely the same as in that of the other arts. It puts the individual in contact with a body of humanistic meaning which is peculiar to itself. In simpler terms, it makes him aware of a great body of experience which he hardly knew existed. That is especially to be considered in our own national economy, since we are beginning to have an extent of art museums, and guilds for the cultivation of pictorial art, which for the first time in our history make available to millions of our people great paintings. Moreover, as awareness of the existence of art treasures expands, people in modest circumstances begin to buy for their own homes pieces which are excellent, even though they are hardly to be called great masterpieces.

There are, perhaps, two levels of educational interest, at least in our own country and in our own time.

In the first place, we are surrounded by a pictorial environment which is, in the gross, scarcely above the infantile level of those who "like to look at pictures." Newspapers and pictorial periodicals cater to this level of taste, and one has only to observe with discerning eye in order to see how it contributes to demoralization. Indeed, pictorialism has gone so far as to make it rather a serious question whether reading among the masses will not presently disappear as a lost art. The educational problem here is to bring about such a change in public taste as will induce the public to realize that there is abiding satisfaction in worth-while pictures, a satisfaction which is not limited to the casual glance but one which endures day by day and year by year for the remainder of a lifetime. Our journals could print reproductions of great works about as well as the trash they do print if there were a demand. They sometimes do it now, but demand would lead them to do more of it and do it better.

In the second place, there is the same kind of educational objective which we find in the other arts, and indeed everywhere else in the Curriculum, namely, the cultivation of taste which will tend to control the kind of paintings made, and make a background of support for artists of real genius and perhaps in the end for great artists.

IN INSTRUCTION

Just as is true of Music, public instruction in Painting on the side of appreciation is possible today far beyond what it has ever been. Photographic reproduction of great works is carried out on a quantity basis, and were there a market so large as that created by the needs of twenty-five million school children and young people, production would expand and improve beyond what it is now. As recently as a generation or two ago, about the only instructional material available for most schools was composed of lithographs of the New England authors, of a few American statesmen, of Horace Mann and Friedrich Froebel. Even so, a few of us did what our financial and aesthetic resources would permit in the purchase of a few good etchings and reproductions for the schoolhouse walls. That was something. Today, it is doubtful that there is a single schoolhouse, large or small, in the United States and Canada combined, which cannot be equipped with a fairly good supply of reproductions for purposes of study, provided there is a teacher in charge who is sufficiently enlightened to know them and to use them.

General and not specialized.—The Common School is not the place for specialized instruction of any sort. That applies with peculiar force to "creative work" so called in Painting. Somebody has a large accountability for the thousands of young people who are wandering about the country today without places and with no likelihood of ever winning subsistence save on a basis of

charity, either private or public. Many of them have been seized
in their school days by the glamour of the life of the artist, with
all its supposed attention-compelling eccentricity and moral special privilege, and encouraged by teachers who have identified
"talent." No doubt there must be, among the teeming millions
who attend our schools, the normal amount of potential genius;
but it is entirely safe to say that not one art teacher or drawing
teacher in a thousand would know budding genius if he or she
saw it. Genius has a way of finding its own, and we are not told
that its pathway is either easy or glamorous.

UNITS

Precisely the same principles apply to the organization of the
course in Painting that we have found in Music and Literature.
We look for the forms of content which constitute culture in the
field, just as we have found corresponding forms elsewhere for the
same instructional purposes. But we do not look for the technical
organization as the artist sees it. We shall not go very far wrong
if we fix on the following:

I. ILLUSTRATION

By all odds, the most common form of content in the pictorial
arts is Illustration. We are familiar with it under its name in
books, but most newspaper and periodical pictures are in the
form—and it runs all the way back to the beginning. The essence
of Illustration is in the principle that it sets forth in pictorial form
the artist's conception of an event or a situation which may elsewhere be the subject of discussion in Language. The newspaper
cartoonist, for example, in a striking illustration sets forth conceptions of a man or a policy, or the meaning of an event, for
which a writer would need a whole volume.

II. PORTRAIT

On the whole, the form which we seem to value most is the
Portrait. The common impulse, especially if the portrait of a well-
known person is to be painted, is to desire "a good likeness."
Well, people who are paying the bill have some right to satisfaction in the picture; but it is a pity that more people are not of

sufficient discernment to see that a good portrait-painter is likely to know what is really a good likeness better than the family and friends. Painting is representative, and, since portraits are likely to last over into the next generation at least, it ought to be the inwardness of the subject which the painter has a way of discerning which is transmitted rather than the individual as his family and friends saw him—or think they did. Happily or unhappily, most of us are not worth painting; all there is to us is a likeness, and a photograph will do well enough for that.

A good portrait is the summation of a good biography, and yet the painter sometimes sees and brings out what the biographer would never reach.

III. LIFE—ACTIVE AND STILL

The books make mention of Still Life or "stills." It seems to me that a better if somewhat awkward designation would be Living Things. Dead organisms are outside the purview of Art, unless you are willing to include as Art the fish and game which one sometimes sees hanging on the walls of dining-rooms. There is no representation in them—save as an artist can bring out the perception that they are "awfully dead." On the other hand, the skilful artist who is blessed with the conceptual as well as the perceptual capacity makes a vase of flowers or an animal stand out as something more than a copy. The picture is a substitute for the actuality, and the latter is thus made abiding and transportable.

IV. LANDSCAPE

Favorite for many generations, not because of the aesthetic pleasure the painting gives us, but because it is vicarious experience of an actual landscape. What makes a landscape canvass Art is usually, first of all, in the choice of subject.

V. DECORATION

Decorative painting is commonly associated with and conditioned by architecture, not only the physical structure but the functional purpose of the building. Save for the fact that this relationship ought to be appreciated, there is not much point to setting up the form as a unit. In content, a mural may conceivably be any of the forms.

VI. GENRE

Representation of the common life in its common and significant activities is Genre. In its cultural implications, it is one of the most significant forms into which Painting falls. The artist reveals himself as artist at a high level, for it takes a good deal of a man or woman to identify the common and significant as humanistic material. The tendency of some modern painters of what might be classed as Genre seems to be to fall into the error of confounding either sociological material, or else illustration for an industrial prospectus, with what is truly Genre.

VII. SYMBOLICAL PAINTING

No doubt the greatest of all the forms is Symbolical Painting, comparable with Tragedy and Epic in Literature. Much of religious painting is of necessity in the form, but the form is far from being limited to serious or pathetic themes. Botticelli's "Pieta" and his "Spring" are both classical examples of Symbolical Painting.

PHOTOGRAPHY

The question naturally suggests itself, "Is not photography a form of modern pictorial art to be set up as a unit in this course?"

That photography in the hands of a skilful operator may be and frequently is a fine art is beyond question. That it serves a useful social purpose can hardly be doubted. That it may sometime become an adaptation of Painting as an institutional art we cannot deny, for we do not know what the future may bring forth. But even at the best it is but feebly representative as yet, and representation is at the heart of Painting as institutional art. Save in the hands of skilful operators, photography is but part of the sense perception of the times. Whatever is photographed is but a thing, whereas the great painter presents us with the Ideal which may lie behind the thing as type.

Be all that as it may, there is nothing in the appreciation of photographic products which is not also appreciation in Painting, and it is hard to see how photographic material—save of course as reproduction of paintings—could be used in the essential contribution to Taste which Painting itself makes possible.

E. SCULPTURE

Sculpture is institutionally allied to Painting. In defense of it as part of the Curriculum, and in outline of it as working course in instruction, not much needs to be said that has not already been said in the preceding section. The units are much the same. It differs from Painting, so far as our interests are concerned, at three chief points.

IN THE BODY OF CULTURE

Save where circumstances have preserved cave murals, the Painting of ancient and prehistoric times has been lost. We have, consequently, little or nothing in visible form which serves to trace for us the evolution of the art. Sculpture, on the other hand, has usually been done in durable material; hence, not only are a good many of the works of antiquity preserved to us, but archeology recovers the tale as it was in the prehistoric world. The series of prehistoric figures and figurines gives us a singularly interesting scale by which to judge the validity of many modern and recent adventures in "new sculpture." If, for instance, we note the resemblance of the works of a "new school" to figurines found in the Congo Valley, we suspect that the departure may be regression instead of progress.

IN TECHNIQUE

The sculptor has not only to deal in stubborn materials, but, if he models animate figures, veracity demands that he shall know much of superficial anatomy. While he uses his art for symbolization, he can make but scant use of the painter's great device of suggestion. In Sculpture what we see is the thing itself, while in Painting we are aware only of our perceptual interpretation. Hence, there is a resemblance to Music and Architecture.

BEFORE THE PUBLIC

Finally, the characteristic use of Sculpture in all the ages has been in some way to influence the folk, the commons. Feelings of awe, of respect, of reverence, have been the objectives of the greater part of Sculpture as we know its history. Such purposes are not achieved by placing a statue in a museum or in the home of wealth; it must stand out in the open, or in a public building, before the gaze of the public. Hence it is that the institutional significance of the art differs somewhat from that of any other. A visible embodiment of a god, a hero, a king, a service, is quite a different thing from a song, an ode, a portrait, a temple.

So it is that Sculpture has been of great and vital service as a carrier of the memories and traditions of a people, and hence of their mores. It has on the whole been of service in preventing people from losing grip on their ideals; and, as the body of culture has grown, it has been instrumental, other things being equal, in enabling people to move on to more advanced ideals. A people neglects its sculptured memorials at its peril. A bridge, a playing field, a public building, is not converted into a memorial merely by calling it such.

IN INSTRUCTION

Material for instructional purposes in Sculpture is hard to come at. In order to supply schools with material comparable to what can readily be furnished in Music, Literature, and Painting, it would be necessary to turn every schoolhouse into such an art museum as has never existed, at least in this country. Lorado Taft conceived a huge building arranged to show the complete story by centuries with reproductions to be made by competent sculptors. It was a monumental conception worthy of a great sculptor who was also an aesthetic statesman. It was never achieved. It is impressive to reflect that even Taft's great idea can actually be achieved in the first three arts in every school.

The time-honored—and very much begrimed—reliance has been on plaster casts. Even if the latter did really stand for Sculpture, the field would be very limited. Perhaps some ingenious enterpriser will sometime give us something that will do for Sculpture what the phonograph has done for Music, but it is hard to imagine how it could be done.

So we frankly fall back on photographic representations as the best available approach there is; and, while it will always prove inadequate, still much can made of it.

In the larger cities there are numerous great works in which the social function of Sculpture is at its best, and Sculpture itself at its near best. Classes should be taken to see them. Not infrequently, a fine modern piece exists in the smaller places, especially in cemeteries. Still and all, it is the familiar experiences of the schoolroom which count, even if they are but photographs. The units suggested follow with no other comment than has been made in the case of Painting.

UNITS IN SCULPTURE

I. Life

II. Genre

III. Decoration in Buildings

IV. Portrait

V. Memorial

(Note, however, that a heroic statue is usually a portrait even though it be also a memorial. The memorial proper is usually more elaborate. Examples are the Lincoln Memorial in which the statue is the central figure and the rest is building. A better illustration of pure sculptural memorial is the Robert Gould Shaw Memorial on Boston Common.)

VI. Symbolical

F. ARCHITECTURE

The individual may grow up unaware of Music save as jingles of one sort or another. He may even turn off the radio when classical music is heard.

He may be illiterate and without direct experience of Literature.

He may never have seen a piece of Painting or Sculpture.

But nobody since a very remote period has ever lived in settled communities without being aware of Architecture of some sort. All cultural products form environments, but Architecture is part of the physical and mechanical environment. On the adjustment theory of Education alone, Architecture deserves a place in the Curriculum of the Common School, even without appeal to the institutional theory of the Curriculum.

Here we come to an art which bears close resemblance to Music.

As we have seen, modern civilized Music is in itself the thought of the auditory environment. Architecture of necessity adheres to the form of the visual environment and is a large part of the substance, the latter moreover reduced to terms of community existence. When architects depart from this logic, and betray the integrity of architectural thought—by using columns in decoration, for instance, which could not conceivably support the entablature which they pretend to support—they do so only at the cost of what Russell Sturgis called an unwholesome frame of mind,[3] or in current terms, bad mental hygiene.

IN EVOLUTION

Happily, there have come down to us from a remote antiquity examples of buildings the world over, and archeological exploration has restored for us buildings which long ago disappeared. It is in seeing what we can make out of that long tale of facts that we get our feet placed on the bedrock of reality, and escape the temptation to conjecture and hypothesize and ultimately to build up a mystical philosophy.

Exactly as in the case of organic evolution, evolution in architectural forms has been possible because progress had to take the path of adaptive species and varieties. The species appear as architectural forms and the varieties as architectural styles.

Let us see.

DWELLINGS

Men must have dwelling-places. In the long run, a dwelling-place becomes a home and the domicile of a family. Human interest centers on it, and the dwelling becomes an extension of the self. Security is felt. Without such, there is, other things being equal, but an inadequate self, and the tendency is toward an unstable personality. So it is that statesmen have long recognized that home-ownership makes for social stability, and in their politics have endeavored to remove obstacles. It is worth recalling that Jefferson's ideal was a Monticello for every man suited to his needs, abilities, and tastes. The Family is the heart of the Com-

[3] *The Appreciation of Architecture* (6th ed.; New York: Baker & Taylor Co., 1903), p. 124.

munity and the basis upon which rests The State as going concern. But a family is but an indefinite and insecure thing until there is a dwelling in possession. So dwellings do, and have tended to, become what people like; likes evolve, and common estimates emerge. So it has been with all the forms.

TEMPLE

On the whole, the next human interest has been Religion, perhaps in effect even before the Home.

While not all forms of Religion have required buildings for worship, most of them have. Hence the Temple was one of the forms of Architecture earliest in existence and most consistent in its evolutionary course. The *style* which the form takes from age to age tends to be the one which best suits the requirements of the worshipers, and that style is the one which survives and undergoes adaptive changes. Such adaptation is, however, no elusive matter: it is, rather, traceable to such concrete and practical circumstances as the nature of worship, the place of the temple in community life, the needs of worshipers, etc.

The difference between a Greek temple and a Christian church building, for instance, is the difference between priestly worship and congregational worship. When a Christian church is made to look like the Parthenon, the architecture merely discloses an "unwholesome frame of mind."

So is the difference between a church building and a meeting-house. The church building belongs to a ritualistic form of service. The old New England Meeting House has been much admired as a style, and legitimately so, since it renounced ritualistic services. A "churchly" building, on the other hand, is merely ridiculous when the service centers upon a preacher and a quartette choir.

Thus does evolution determine rightness in form and style and yield an idiom which is capable of translation when purpose changes or new needs arise.

PALACE

Palace, so far as the name goes, was originally the Palatine Hill in Rome. Augustus had a fine house there, and the name got at-

tached to the imperial residence and later to royal residences. Of
course, the thing itself goes back into the dim ages as the dwelling
of the king and what we should call his offices as well. So Palace
as form is official residence, a dwelling which the claims of prestige
make as imposing and magnificent as possible. Moreover, official
residence is more than dwelling; it is also a place of entertainment
for the court and visiting officials, a housing for the appurtenances
of royalty; a seat of Government. That seems to be the essential
meaning of the form.

With the increase of wealth in the later Middle Ages and the
early Modern Period, Palace became also the name for the great
residences of magnates, and some of the palaces, especially in the
Italian cities, reveal great elegance of design and execution. In
our own period after the Civil War, American millionaires for a
generation or more vied with one another in erecting palaces, in
New York City especially. In these buildings apparently the only
palatial meaning left was the maintenance of prestige. That period seems to be all past and gone, in the United States at least,
and rich men no longer build palaces, not because they cannot
afford them, but apparently because Taste has sufficiently become
disseminated to make them undesirable and meaningless. Fine
houses if you will, but not palaces as mere elaborate buildings.

Civic building.—Nevertheless, the original meaning of the form
persists, translated into Civic Building—city halls, post offices,
State capitols, courthouses, etc. Now observe that, when an architect senses the idiom in which he works, he produces in a new
village post office the real meaning of the royal residence of old.
When we see one of these buildings so conceived and placed, while
we may grumble "pork barrel," a better spirit leads us to say,
"There indeed is the Great Republic in visible and elegant form in
this small town." We recognize the Post Office when we see it,
just as we commonly recognize the Public Library. The Palace
has traveled far from royalty, but the form is still present in
extreme democracy—apparently it is most likely to appear in
extreme democracy.

Name and style vanish; the form abides. In so far as the architect feels all that, he gives us an appropriate building, an elegant and dignified part of the community.

MARKET

For the sake of a single term, "market" is used, but, if the reader pleases, we will understand that the expression refers to commercial buildings in general, and not to a city square with its booths, hitching-racks, or parking-places which is sometimes called "the market."

Commerce in the later Middle Ages came into the mode of housing itself well, of respecting itself. So, although the practice long lapsed with the rise of utilitarianism and a world-bourgeoisie, banks and shopping places have been coming into their own again—so far as Art is concerned, becoming civilized.

Market, like Civic Building, has had a history, and the idiom in which it is now treated may belong to a set of obsolete conditions. Nevertheless, nothing can be entirely new, and an old idiom has sometimes to be translated into new substance. Here, as elsewhere, intelligence consists largely in awareness of transitions.

When the medieval guildhalls which are so much admired rose, the transition was from a community in which the church building was trading center as well as church. In fact, the Temple in most of the religions had tended to be that. Hence, much the same as the Civil Building later had strong proclivities to transverbalize without translating the Palace, so the beautiful guildhall was likely to copy the style of the church building. Why should not the merchants so do? They were merely removing by specialization one of the functions of the religious edifice. But it is anachronistic to erect in America a Gothic department store—or would be if it were ever done—merely because the owner and his architect have admired some Flemish guildhall on a European trip. Even so, that would be no worse than the practice of erecting Greek temples to do duty as American banks.

Morrison relates that Sullivan was once called in to design a bank building. Being entirely familiar with what banks mean in communities, after studying location, he presented a sketch.

Whereupon the directors asked him to stick some pillars in front of the building, because that was what they were used to. Whereupon the architect rolled up his sketches and disappeared. Fortunately, the directors trusted him, and he eventually erected the building and did it right.[4]

These cultural anachronisms merely turn the outward and visible community into unintelligible chaos. One of the fruits of public instruction in this great art should be to make people wary of desiring a design merely because they like it or think it beautiful or otherwise pleasing. They ought to realize that the building will probably outlast their time. One recalls the horrors of the post-bellum parlors of the eighties and nineties. The owners thought them very attractive; today they are derided by a generation which has acquired better taste. A little earlier the mansard roof was fashionable, and many a fine colonial dwelling was remodeled to include it; today it is cliché to look back on that style with horror. What has long endured in cultural history, has undergone modification and adaptation to new uses but still retains the idiom which has gone with the form through the ages, is likely to be right and, being right, to keep on being pleasing to succeeding generations.

CASTLE

The strong place for martial defense has been architectural form ever since natural defensive positions ceased to be sufficient. It is an expression of one of the primary constituents of The State, and of the Community long before there was any State. But the feudal castle is also subsidiary architectural style which has lasted down to our own time, long centuries after the castle ceased to have any meaning. Hence, battlements and loopholed windows are bad taste, not because we have ceased to like them but because our liking—if any—has no substance in it.

And yet, since community defense is still a social function, there must always be buildings which house the defenders. Hence, functionally speaking, an armory, a police station, a fire station

---

[4] Hugh Morrison, *Louis Sullivan: Prophet of Modern Architecture* (New York: W. W. Norton Co., 1935).

even, is the modern equivalent of the Castle. The form abides. The style disappears, and a new idiom must be found to express not only the social function but the architectural requirements of the offices as well.

One of the most ancient of architectural forms is the Memorial, indeed as primitive as ancient. We at once think of tombs and then of Egyptian pyramids, and then again of prehistoric tumuli.

A memorial building is not one which is dedicated to some person. Most of our school and college buildings are that, and they are not memorials but school buildings. To call a building a Memorial Library does not make it memorial. To be that, it must have no other function. The Lincoln Memorial at Washington qualifies indeed, but, the Monument comes short, for its real function in use is that of a public observation post.

Architectural memorials are commonly tombs, sometimes beautiful and significant structures in cemeteries, and sometimes great tombs like the Taj Mahal or the Mausoleum of Hadrian. The social function is much the same as that of the corresponding form in Sculpture: a great or a dear memory is kept alive, a great tradition or ideal is kept in mind. But the function is sometimes prostituted. So it is when the Memorial is but witness to the immortal self-love of an individual, or to the mob passion for sanctifying a demagogue. In a less offensive sense, the function goes wrong when the memory of soldierly devotion and sacrifice is made the excuse for building a bridge or a schoolhouse or a playing-field. None of these is made Memorial architecture by attaching a tablet which certifies that that is what it is.

Industry has scarcely begun to house itself with any heed to the appropriate, so long as the utilitarian purpose is served. That is perhaps the chief reason for the horrible ugliness and maddening inhumanity of the old mill town. It must, however, be remembered that modern industry is still very new; and that, after all, the modern factory has no architectural idiom in its background which it could translate. That means, I take it, that the intelligence which has led to the modern community must turn to the rescue of the Community from ideational chaos. In part that implies an architectural intelligence derived from the past which can think out an idiom for structures for which there is no precedent. And so in fact, Industry does begin to give heed, as it was bound to sooner or later, and for a reason which is no different from that which lay at the back of the earlier forms, namely, the ultimate determination of the race to escape from the meaningless and the chaotic. In so far as aesthetically appropriate factory buildings are being erected, and they are, industry is becoming civilized, even as Industry is part of Civilization. In proportion as public instruction in Art is administered to the rising generation, the progress will not only be expedited but secured.

TRANSPORTATION

The story is much the same with Transportation. Save for bridges, which have had a well-nigh established form, architecturally considered, since Roman times, Transportation has never until the appearance of railways, automobiles, ocean liners and freighters, and airplanes, required architectural treatment of the kind found in modern terminals and local stations; nor until recently has it become a vital, integral part of local communities. Hence it is that eclecticism comes in and styles are used for great railway stations which express merely the grandiose—"handsome buildings."

RECREATION

Buildings for recreation have been features of community structures since Greek and Roman times at the least. The form persists in stadiums, gymnasiums, fieldhouses, country clubs. No doubt the form is still in process of adaptive change and evolution; but, in so far as we are intelligent and appreciative about architectural meaning in evolution, abortive changes will be at the minimum.

OTHER FORMS

Certain well-recognized modern community functions like schools, university buildings, libraries, and museums have scarcely more than begun to find their architectural expression, apart

from traditions which have come down to us, chiefly from ecclesiastical associations and those of Civic Buildings.

WHAT CAN WE MAKE OUT OF IT ALL?

1. There are no *forms* which have existed in the past and come
to have an established place in the universal conditions of community life which do not exist today in adaptations. Sometimes,
style has persisted; more often it has disappeared into new styles.
An understanding of the story as evolutionary process gives us our
basis for architectural intelligence and rationale. Intelligence in
architecture, more than is true of the other arts save Music, arises
out of the close connection of Architecture with primary forms of
thought. There can be no good taste in Architecture which is
offensive to architectural logic.

2. There are new agencies, if not new functions, in the Community. While it is true that forms cannot be invented, in the
proper sense of "invent," the intelligence derived from the forms
in stylistic evolution is equivalent to understanding Architecture
as institution, constituent of Art. Out of that intelligence and the
taste that goes with it can emerge valid new idioms, and so they
do emerge. Therein seems to be our chief critical resource when
confronted with radical departures.

3. Forms evolve because community needs evolve, and because
taste applied to a particular form and style in that form also
evolves, even when the community adjustment of the form itself—
Civic Building, for example—is good, that is to say, when there is
no need other than the eternal aesthetic need. Nevertheless, since
evolution is by way of fashionable variation, fashions will always
keep within a much narrower range when the general level of
taste in the community is high than will be the case when it is
low. In the latter case, progress is slow because so much time,
energy, and capital are wasted on variations which are beyond
normal range of adaptability. A two-headed calf is an organic variation, but it never gives rise to a two-headed species. The reason
is in the fact that any such variation is beyond normal or natural
range.

Styles which, however, have become obsolete because the form itself—Temple it may be—has become adjusted to progress in community culture have often left values which appear in modern buildings because the values themselves are valid and universal. The best example is the Parthenon, perfect as a building and obsolete as a style, but containing principles which are still used in the design of the most modern buildings.

4. Finally, a grasp upon the evolutionary principle can save us from aesthetic as well as from ethical anarchy. The plea of the modern sophist and pseudo-liberal is apt to be, "That is only your taste. If you had been brought up in that kind of building, you would like it, and taste in one style would be as valid as taste in the other." It does not follow that tolerated habits are right habits, or that habituation to domestic monstrosities makes such styles right. In the humanities it is the experience of the race which counts and not that of the individual. The evolutionary method saves us from the greatest of all fallacies, that which held that "man is the measure of all things," that there is no Ideal or Right save that which men from time to time create or prefer.

FUNCTIONALISM

The evolutionary argument which we have been following leads straight into justification of what architectural scholars call Functionalism. The building must express the function in the community in which it is placed which it is intended to serve, or at least must not express some other function. It must look the part.

In the community—social significance.—Hence we come back to the final problem in General Education, the transmission of sense of the orderly, which lies not only at the basis of rational living but even at the foundations of mental hygiene.

Great architecture has always represented the race's expanding sense of the adequate, the beautiful, the worthy, the dignified, as they are found in the abiding-places of families and community enterprises and civil functions. These are but the order which is *Thought* apprehended in appreciation. But Thought is everywhere the groundwork of capacity to interpret and manage the environment.

A building occupies space to the exclusion of anything else. Further, its utility for any particular purpose depends upon its relations to other buildings and to the functions in the community which they severally serve. So the peace and efficiency of community living depends in the first analysis upon the principle that things must be where they belong; and things in the gross are buildings and their appurtenances. We have met the issue in part in the units in "The Community" and in "Regional Planning" in Geography. In Architecture we find ourselves turned again to the same problem in respect to aesthetic values.

Altogether, we may talk about "solving our social problems" until the crack of doom, and never solve them until we come to live in understandable and appreciable communities. There is no possibility of either understanding or appreciating chaos.

INSTRUCTION

CLASSICS

As elsewhere in Art, the classics are of necessity the groundwork of instructional material, but they are not the whole of teaching. We have constantly to bear in mind the pedagogical maxim which warns us that we learn from experience but do not learn experience. We can learn from the classics, but, if we deal with classics alone, we shall have converted a course in appreciation into one in history, probably into decidedly sterile history at that.

Scattered down through the ages there have been good buildings, great buildings, even noble buildings, and there are still. These are the material with which the teacher has to work. But, it must be remembered, there are also monuments of hideous oppression, the regressions of successive waves of barbarism and near-barbarism, and perhaps, most deceptive of all, the memorials of the irrepressible egotism of monarchs, magnates, plutocrats. No building is great, any more than a poem or a painting is great, unless it has a great and noble subject.

Hence, in using any building whatever for study purposes, the central question ought always to be, "What was the purpose of this building in its time?"

STYLES

By "style" we mean a structural and decorative treatment characteristics of the buildings of an architect, a period, or a national culture. Any style is always in principle conditioned by the form of the building, as Dwelling, Civic Building, Market, Memorial, etc. There are of course many styles, too many in fact to be mentioned here or studied in the classroom. Some of them are scarcely to be dignified as styles; they are rather fashions or even fads. Nevertheless, the idiom of Architecture is in the great historic styles. These may perhaps be identified, as far as Western Architecture is concerned, as Egyptian, Greek, Roman, Romanesque, Gothic, Renaissance, Neoclassical, American Colonial, and Modern.

We thus get a plane of reference against which to arrange the units proper.

The historic styles have tended to serve not as background for scholarship but rather as repertoire out of which artists could draw plans for their conceptions. Many attractive buildings have no doubt resulted, but few of them have made the beholder feel a sense of conviction of the validity of what he sees.

UNITS

Touching the instructional meaning and significance of units in the appreciation of Architecture, nothing need be added to what has earlier been explained in connection with Music, Literature, and Painting, except this.

Architecture is peculiar in that Art is conditioned by Mechanics, even in the apprehension of the layman. Hence a certain rudimentary vocabulary of mechanical terms is needed before the art proper can be understood. There are three introductory units which are thin science units involving understanding rather than appreciation. The reader is warned not to take the three so seriously as to suppose that pupils require the same kind of instruction as that which would be required in a professional school.

I. Elementary Structure
   Roof, walls, and floor
   Stairways
   Post and lintel
   Entablature
   Column
   Arch, vault, and dome
   Fenestration

II. The Building on the Ground
   (The objective here is an understanding that no building is just an erection but that every building is inescapably related to the ground on which it stands.)
   Stability made apparent in placement and appearance
   Adequate vertical support that makes the building look as if it would carry its roof and roof structures
   Balance
   Main axis
   Subordinate axes
   Orientation

III. Ornamentation and Decoration
   (Meaning of each term as distinct from structural characteristics of the building. The two will appear in the study of all buildings.)

IV. Dwelling

V. Temple

VI. Memorial

VII. Civic Building

VIII. Castle—But not exclusively the feudal castle as style

IX. Market—Including Banks and Financial Enterprises

X. Factory

XI. Bridge

XII. Railway Terminals and Station Buildings

XIII. Airport

XIV. Recreation

XV. Schools and Academic Buildings

Styles are to be arranged to parallel the units as reference material. A suitable arrangement would be to have typical buildings in each of the styles in pictorial illustration on the classroom walls.

Finally, the usual warning: this is a course in appreciation in the Common School, not a course leading to scholarship in the University, not a vocational course for builders, not even a pre-vocational course.

CHAPTER X

THE STATE AND CIVIL INSTITUTIONS—CIVICS

THE State and Civil Institutions bulk very large in human affairs. About all the positive security there is anywhere in a perilous world is ultimately under their shield. That being true, it would seem like a foregone conclusion that Civics would everywhere be central in public instruction; and yet, so far as I know, it has seldom been even marginal. Certainly, the great Curriculums of the past have never given it any place at all.

In our country the only single element in the subject which has been of even common occurrence is a single, elective, vocational course in commercial law. In the allied field of Politics a single memoriter course in Civil Government has been common. In other lands, where the subject has appeared at all, it has been prone to be in the main a propagandist course or series of courses extolling the merits of the Government of the time and place. With all our faults, that malpractice can seldom with truth be laid to our charge.

And yet, in the democracies at least, the people who have passed through the schools manipulate the agencies of The State through their votes. It would seem reasonable that all should know enough about The State to be able to understand what it is that they are about.

Aside from the practical consideration, the present chapter and that which follows are founded on the conviction that here is one of the most important of the intellectual pursuits of mankind, out of which there has grown a rich body of cultural material, that in the Common School as much space should be devoted to Civics and Politics as are given to the whole field of Science, in the same spirit of serious study which is on the whole characteristic of that subject in our best schools.

A. THE STATE AS MAJOR INSTITUTION

The word itself is one of those which make it hard to follow the social sciences with precision of meaning at every step. It is a common noun, the meaning of which has no relation to civil affairs. It is also a transitive verb. The State as civil institution is usually described as "a population organized for the purpose of governing and being governed." That is the sense in which the term is used by historians and publicists. They thus speak of England, France, Italy, and the United States as *States*.

In American usage our commonwealths are called States, with the exception of Kentucky, Massachusetts, Pennsylvania, and Virginia, where the official designation is "Commonwealth."

Finally there is The State as abstract term, which is the form which we shall mostly use. Hence, when we have in mind an American commonwealth, we shall write "State" or "a State"— of Illinois, for example. When we have in mind the abstract term, we shall write "The State."

In accurate thinking, we cannot do much with descriptive expressions; we must turn to definitions. Hence we turn to a working definition: "The State is coercive power acting upon a whole population." Let the definition stand as tentative if you will, until we can answer in factual terms some of the questions which the definition will at once raise.

I. ORIGINS AND EVOLUTION

Even in the proto-societies which exist among the lower animals, some one will always emerge as leader of the pack or as leader of the herd or flock. So, as we have seen in chapter ii, is it under normal circumstances in human relationships. The leader is one whom the others will follow, either because he has superior prowess, or is thought to have superior wisdom and skill, or because he can compel others to follow. So it is in smaller groups, regardless of the justification of the group purpose, all the way from a city gang to a committee of college teachers. Wherever you find leadership well established, you tend to find some kind of capacity and strength and safety which supersedes weakness, some kind of order which succeeds chaos, even though capacity and order be devoted to an evil purpose. People prefer it that way; it has social utility. A fine instance of what has probably happened over and over again is contained in the legendary call which brought Rurik to Russia: "So the Chuds, the Slavs, and the others, said to the *Rus*, 'Our land is great and rich, but there is no order among us; come then and govern us.'"

Here is, then, one thing that we can make out of the story: everywhere in organized groups there is some sort of *coercive power* in a head, whether the head be a strong man who rules by dint of physical force, or another kind of strong man who rules by power of personal influence.

CUSTOMS

But one does not read the story very far upward among the more advanced primitives before he finds a different kind of phenomenon, namely, *the power of custom*. The customs of the tribe have come to have far more compelling force than have the commands of the leader or ruler. The latter still exists and doubtless has his way when he can, but he has to observe the customs. Even at the later stage when strong men have gathered to themselves supreme power, they almost always keep their purposes outside the customs which rule the intimate side of the common life The ruler levies soldiers and lays taxes, but he does not interfere with marriage or the descent of property or the transactions of commerce—except, it may be, in special and occasional instances.

Here, then, are two more features which seem significant.

The first is the reign of custom, and historical jurists tell us that custom was primitive law and that valid modern law still has in it a large element of custom. Moreover, the customs seem to keep apart from the evolution of rule.

The second is the *recognition of right* in kingship of some sort or rulership. Men at the stage of our Algonquins and Iroquois had only a vague recognition of such right. Their leaders were still the men who could lead and whom others would follow. Recognition of right in the fact of rulership bestows *sovereignty*.

These two elements in coercive power had come into existence in prehistoric times. They are sometimes found by ethnologists among people who have had no literature or other means of recording their culture. The story from then to now is of course a highly complicated one with which we have no concern in the Common School. Roughly, it is a story of the evolution of custom into law, and of personal rule into Civil Government.

AS INSTITUTION

The State is thus universal institution. It arose out of human nature, out of the common sense and experience of mankind. It has been under an evolution which we can trace historically; it has come to be organized and refined, and is in the end rationally understandable as a principal factor in ordered Society, an element in the fabric of Civilization.

Only one institution.—But The State is only one institution among many. Among them all, it is head dominance in a social organism, but it can no more exist as sovereign, apart from Language, Morality, Science, Commerce, Industry, and all the rest of the structure of Civilization, than the human head can exist and function without heart, lungs, nervous system, organs of digestion, etc.[1]

THE CIVIL STATE

The transition to the Civil State rests again on two marked changes which have occurred in Law and Government.

Lawgivers and their codes meant written law in the place of traditional law. In the ancient world we sometimes find revolutions centering about the demand for written law, so that the people could know what to expect. Obviously, no such demand would arise until the ability to read had emerged and had become somewhat widely diffused among the commons. Written law was down in black and white to be pondered. Second, law began to be a body of principles to be used *in thinking out* juristic and political situations. Government came to be definitely Government in ac-

[1] For the notion of head dominance see my *Basic Principles in Education* (Boston: Houghton Mifflin Co., 1934), p. 133, where the principle is taken particularly from Charles M. Child, *Physiological Foundations of Behavior* (New York: Henry Holt & Co., 1924).

cordance with law, what we call constitutional Government. The Civil State is thus a State of citizens rather than subjects. It is also called Juristic State, that is to say, one in which Government is presumed to be carried on in terms of principles of right and justice.

SOVEREIGNTY

So we return to our definition and see that what has been evolving all along is *Sovereignty*, and that Sovereignty is supreme coercive and restraining power recognized as existing of right.

The important thing about Sovereignty for our purposes is in what lawyers would call its residence: Does Sovereignty reside in the king, or in the laws, or in parliament, or in the people? The residence of Sovereignty determines the Form of The State, not the form of its Government but of The State itself.

II. Forms of the State

1. MONARCHY

When the leader of a population had merged into the accepted king, held to be king by some sort of right, Sovereignty resided in an individual, and that individual was a Monarch, a single ruler without restraint of a legally constituted council or parliament, holding by right of birth. Now in strict thought, Monarchy runs through two phases:

a) The monarch is a *Despot* or, in more recent terms, an Autocrat. He rules by law, but he himself makes the laws, which are more properly decrees. Still, he is governed by the laws he himself has made, and he promulgates what is more or less system of law for the guidance of his officers. When the monarch refuses to so govern, and his caprice becomes the only law there is, then he is said to be a *Tyrant*.

b) The monarch is still accepted as such, is held to be the fount of justice, conducts the executive Government, is commander-in-chief of the forces, and may veto an act of his legislature; but he is subject to the reign of law and law originates in a lawmaking body. We call the system Constitutional Monarchy, or Limited Monarchy.

2. REPUBLIC

In contrast with Monarchy is the Republic. Now the heart of the distinction is not, as many suppose it to be, in the difference between the rule of one man and the rule of the people. It is rather in the substitution of the *General Welfare*, the Commonwealth, for the glory and advantage of the monarch. It seems strange to us, who have never had any experience of Monarchy in a personal sense at all, that the concept of Government as apart from royal prerogative and advantage could ever have been difficult to understand. It is nevertheless true that for the last seventeen hundred years or thereabout it has been an exceedingly hard notion to grasp—that is to say, down until the last century and a half. "General Welfare," as the term is used in our Constitution, is a good translation of the Latin *res publica*, from which "Republic" is derived.

The *rule* in a republic normally belongs to elective magistrates of some sort, since the very notion of kingship is repugnant. No doubt the Republic tends toward Popular Sovereignty, but so does Constitutional Monarchy. Neither of them necessarily tends toward Democracy as Form of Government.

3. FEUDALISM

Alongside Monarchy, and the Republic—and Democracy even —stalks Feudalism through the ages. It arises whenever an established State has broken down, and the older the State the more complete is apt to be the collapse. The defining characteristic of Feudalism is the rise of many local lords who take upon themselves sovereign functions.

The Feudalism in which we are particularly interested, however, is that which arose after the breakdown of the Roman Empire of the West and the subsequent disintegration of the barbarian States which succeeded it. Western Europe was plunged into the Dark Ages of anarchy, which lasted with occasional light spells from, say, A.D. 400 down to the rise of the strong popes in the latter part of the eleventh and the twelfth centuries. It would be most useful if pupils could read some reliable graphic accounts of that period, in order to see what a world is like when the only rule is the rule of lawless violence.

Feudalism began with the surrender of individual liberty and lands to the strong man, the baron, in return for the protection of the latter. A legal concept called *commendation* was the name of the process. The individual became liege or vassal, and in most cases serf. He was expected to form part of the military forces surrounding the lord.

Economically, Feudalism rested upon the Manor, or the lord's estate. The commended serfs carried on the labor of the estate, and the lord exercised sovereign powers over them.

The important thing about it is that vassalage tended to become organized into an hierarchy of larger and smaller vassals, until all recognized themselves as vassals of the medieval king and the king as in theory the owner of all the land in the kingdom.

Feudalism created a society of status rather than a society of contract, as we know society in America. The former is one in which every individual is born into a place in a scale of rank, and finds it very difficult to rise out of it. The latter is a condition in which each may rise to any place to which his abilities entitle him. The romantic tales of European nobilities which have for long so appealed to the daydreams of many portray a life which was characteristic of the Feudal State and of the inheritance which descended from it.

I believe it to be important to include a unit on Feudalism, both because it helps the pupils to form adequate ideas of The State as institution and extends their conceptions of Society and because of two other reasons which are of practical importance to an American's understanding of his own country.

The first of these is the principle that where cities are weakened by corruption in various forms, and by ignorance and incompetency in the city government, there appear in our singularly enlightened land precisely the symptoms which revealed themselves after the collapse of the Empire of Charlemagne. "Protection money," or submission in any other form to racketeers, is no less than the commendation which marked the beginning of Medieval Feudalism.

The second is the principle, which seems to me important, that the real American Revolution was not in the Revolt of the Colonies but rather in the disappearance of the last vestiges of Feudalistic ideologies, first in the teaching of Thomas Jefferson and his followers, and second in the substance of the Federal and State Constitutions.

4. POPULAR SOVEREIGNTY

We are thus brought to the form of The State toward which all evolution in the long run tends, namely, Sovereignty residing in the mass of the people, or rather in the body politic. And yet Popular Sovereignty does not necessarily imply a Democratic Form of Government, although that is the form which is doubtless likely to arise. In Belgium, England, Holland, and the Scandinavian countries, Sovereignty has certainly come to reside in those who are entitled to vote for members of Parliament; but none of them is in form a Democracy. They are in form constitutional monarchies, and in substance republics in which there is a hereditary chief magistrate. The Government in all of them is ministerial and not democratic, but of that presently.

It may be well to linger on the point briefly.

In recent years, we have fallen into the habit all over the Western world of grouping all these nations and the American democracies together as "the democracies," in contrast with the existing despotisms to be found in Germany and Russia particularly. I suppose it to be a journalistic device. In an important sense, it is unfortunate. We attribute to democracy freedom from arbitrary government, reigns of terror, wholesale executions, when in reality what we have to bless for our security is established Civil and Juristic States, where law reigns instead of men. Democracy has seldom shown any peculiar reverence for the reign of law.

To continue a step farther. Republics of the French type are not democracies. They are ministerial republics, in which the chief magistrate is chosen by the Legislature, or Parliament. But they rest on Popular Sovereignty.

IN THE MORES

We have discussed Sovereignty in terms of political and legal theory, where definition rests upon recognized right to rule; but, after all, how and why is right recognized? That brings us to the ultimate political power, the mores existing in any people.

There may be lack of concern about rule, and in that case the final outcome will be despotism in some form.

The bulk of the population may be slaves. Now, while slaves never have political rights, and at the best but few civil rights, they are human beings, individuals, persons, members of the Community. As such they contribute their part to whatever is the content of the mores, and slave mores are not likely to support Civil Government.

There have been few autocrats of any sort who have ruled in entire disregard of the mores, for so to do is well-nigh a psychological impossibility. They may have rested on a priestly caste which had the commons in tutelage. They may have in reality been popular leaders themselves. They may, so far as they could, have ignored the rights and well-being of the people; but they have seldom ruled without one eye on the mores and the other on the customs. Even the despots who rule over much of Europe today surpass the most accomplished proprietors of build-ups and smears in the propaganda which they diligently cultivate.

In the end that is recognized in admitted Popular Sovereignty which has always in truth existed as ultimate political power.

The principle is of capital importance, for upon it rests the truth that the School is an organic part of The State, and it makes incontrovertible the proposition that only impartial, objective, effective public instruction can in the end support the Civil State in which Sovereignty is in actual effect in the body politic.

III. FORM OF GOVERNMENT

It is hardly worth while to go back and show that Despotism as Form of The State is also Form of Government. We are interested only in forms of Government in the Civil State. We might go back to Greece and Rome and the medieval republics and study emergent forms, but that too is not worth while. So we confine ourselves to the forms which exist in the modern Civil States, specifically to Democracy and to Ministerial, or Parliamentary, Government.

1. ARISTOCRACY

First of all, let us come to grips with the notion that Aristocracy is or ever has been a Form of Government. For something over a hundred years Americans have been indoctrinated with a notion of Aristocracy which is little better than raw head and bloody bones. You can always appeal to the fear of some people that somebody may be better than they are.

Now, Aristocracy is a perfectly definite political term, a good deal like a term in Physics or Biology. It means Government by the Best, that is to say, the wisest and most competent. It cannot mean anything else. It has no reference to blue blood or wealth. I suppose that the term originated with Plato's philosophy of Government as expounded in the *Republic*. Weary and contemptuous of the demagoguery and ignorance of Athenian governments, he expounded the notion of Government by qualified men, and he had in mind the word which meant then what it means now.

To most of us, I suspect, the connotation of the word is derived from the feudalistic States of Europe, in which there has been always a good deal of what is accurately to be called Caste Government. The English House of Lords is a reminiscence of old days in which there was conflict between Government in the interest of a ruling caste and Government in the interest of the General Welfare. But there is not, and never was, anything that could properly be called "aristocratic" about that.

I suppose everybody who has any sense of Patriotism desires that the best and most qualified and competent men should be in the Government to legislate, judge, and execute. Our country started life as an aristocratic republic, and in principle that is what it still is. Only, the problem with the Founders was the same as it is with us and was with Plato: How are you going to get your aristocrats?

The English of the eighteenth century had no doubt that aristocracy was born in the blood, like a hooked nose. Our founders, familiar with the English royalty and gentry since Stuart times, simply did not believe that you could get the best that way. Genetics has tended to show that they were right about it.

If not that way, then, said they, let us try the experiment of seeing whether the people themselves will not tend to pick out the best and most qualified to be their Government. On the whole for a hundred years it worked out about as the Founders had hoped. Let us bear in mind that differences between good Federalists like Adams and Hamilton and good Democrats like Jefferson consisted chiefly in the fact that the Federalists were skeptical about the people of that day or any other day doing any such thing; while Jefferson felt confident that they *could be educated to do it*. If anybody thinks that Thomas Jefferson believed in proletarian rule or anything like it, that person simply must have failed to read Jefferson.

So the difference between Democracy and some other social and political system is not in a contrast between Democracy and Aristocracy, but between Democracy and Caste Government, on the one hand, and Democracy and Proletarianism, on the other.

2. MINISTERIAL GOVERNMENT

Ministerial Government is far more modern than Democracy, but it may be helpful to consider it first. Let us take England as example for study, for England is the prototype of the form, just as the United States is the prototype of modern Democracy.

The Head of State is the hereditary king, who is said to reign but not rule. Acts of Government are carried out in his name. He can on occasion rule as well as reign, but he does so as a matter of personal influence. In his executive capacity, he acts under the advice of the Prime Minister.

The Prime Minister is the leader of the majority party in Parliament. He is not elected, but comes into office by force of the circumstance that he is accepted leader. He is also head of the ministry which he has organized, part of which forms the Cabinet.

Parliament is the lawmaking body, composed of the House of Commons, or the elective branch, and the House of Lords, which holds place without election by virtue of elevation to the Peerage. Lords are today created by the King on the recommendation of the Prime Minister in office. Now, nearly all bills introduced into Parliament, all important bills, are introduced by the Ministry. So long as the Ministry holds the confidence of the House of Commons, it continues in office. As soon as it has lost confidence, as evidenced by rejection of one of its important bills, it resigns, and the King calls upon another leader, presumably in opposition, to form a new Ministry.

Or the Prime Minister, confident that he and not the opposition represents the desires of the electorate, may advise the King to dissolve Parliament and issue writs for a new election. At the election, the Ministry may be sustained or the opposition may be. If the former, the existing ministry goes on. If the latter, it resigns, and a new ministry is constituted.

Thus the people *approves* or *disapproves* the policies of its Government by the known character and opinions of the members of the House of Commons whom it elects. But the people does not originate, nor on important issues, do its representatives in the House of Commons. The House of Commons is representative only in the sense that an agent with revocable power of attorney is representative. The House of Lords is not representative at all, and yet recent history has more than once shown that the Upper House estimated the desires and opinions of the electorate better than did the elective Lower House, as evidenced by election returns.

3. DEMOCRACY

Democracy is typified by the United States and the American republics which have patterned after this country. We shall postpone discussion of the Form of Government until the next chapter. Suffice it to say that in our theory of Government our executives and legislators are supposed to do what the voters themselves would do if they were present and acting, and were fully informed. There is no such thing as ministerial responsibility. What the English would call private bills are in many instances with us the important bills of a session. We recall how measures enacted by Congress are often known by the surnames of their individual sponsors.

That there is sore need of instructing our young people in the elementary doctrines of Democracy hardly requires argument, for inattention or incompetent attention at the hands of our schools and colleges seems to have left the notion to grow up that Democracy is pretty much the justification of whatever one likes in the world.

Democracy means the participation of the folk or people in the conduct of Government and nothing else. Like "aristocracy" the term is as definite as a term in the natural sciences. *Democracy is not:*

a) *"Social democracy,"* for such an expression is meaningless. All government is a social matter. If what is meant is that all are equal before the law, then that is a matter of juristic principle true of all civilized States.

If an American is presented in the home of royalty and is charmingly greeted by King and Queen, it is meaningless to call the latter "democratic" rather than well-bred, delightful people, unless indeed they have confided in their visitor that they intend to abdicate and run for the House of Commons.

A professor does not become "democratic" by smoking a pipe and telling fish stories; he merely discloses a gregarious nature and an interest in fishing.

A hostess does not achieve "pure democracy" by inviting all hands to dinner; she merely exhibits deplorable lack of consideration for the mutual congeniality of her guests—and a probable intention of running for office.

In brief, a snob is not the opposite of a democrat; he or she is merely the opposite of a self-respecting person.

b) *Rule of the classes which are lowest in wealth and intelligence,* for the people is all of us. There is no particular sanction attached by democratic principle to the wisdom of the ignorant or the virtue of the impecunious. Such views are but the resources which political buzzards employ for the sake of advancing their political fortunes. They have been doing it from the time of the Athenians to that of the Americans. Nor is there attached to the learned and the wealthy special privilege; on the contrary they have to pay nearly all the direct taxes, and they are seldom allowed any part in Government beyond their votes.

c) Not even universal suffrage.—Democracy no doubt by definition involves the elective principle, for you cannot have Government by the people if officers hold by right of birth or position. And yet there is no soundness in the old contention that everybody has a natural right to a voice in the choice of those by whom he is to be governed. If that were true, then it would follow that children should be given the ballot, and that prisoners should elect the warden of the penetentiary. Nor is it any rejoinder that these are excluded because they are incompetent; for if that be the principle, then the process should go on and all the rest of the incompetents be excluded. The natural-right argument resolves itself into an argument that only the competent and responsible should be allowed to take part in governing others, in other words, should possess voting privileges.

d) Not a system for setting up "mandates."—Lack of instruction is seemingly responsible for the delusion that Democracy is a method by which a majority can give a mandate to its elected representatives to carry out any kind of action at all. Ever since there were any political thinkers, even the most ardent democrats among them have recognized the principle that a majority can be even more tyrannical than a despot. Democracy is participation in Civil Government, and Civil Government is Government by law and not by men, not even a majority of men and women.

e) Voice of the People not the Voice of God.—At least it has never been revealed that it is, so far as I know.

Democracy is valuable just in so far as it succeeds in securing the just ends of all Civil Government, namely: establishment of justice, guaranty of domestic tranquillity, maintenance of the common defense, security in Civil Liberty. In so far as it fails consistently and systematically, some other form which succeeds better is to be preferred. There is no more Divine Right in a People than there is in a King.

REPRESENTATIVE DEMOCRACY

Democracy can be primary, that is to say, immediate participation of the commons in the conduct of public affairs, when conditions are so simple that one man is likely to know as much about them as another and to be about as well qualified to administer them.

Democracy ceases to be primary when affairs have become so complex and remote that there is no possibility of each voter's being competent to administer them without special devotion to them and study of them. In that case Government must become *representative*.

Now this word is used in two different senses:

First, it means delegated authority to do all things needful.

Second, it means "typical." For example, "This is a typical collie dog"; or "That poem is typical of Elizabethan times."

American Representative Democracy rests on the first of the two meanings. It signifies, or should signify, to all voters something like this: We are selecting these men to be President, Governor, members of Congress and of the State Legislature, because we have confidence in their wisdom, honesty, and skill, to enact laws which they shall find ought to be enacted or to take action which they find can be taken and ought to be. When we have done that, it is boy's play to keep pestering our representatives with letters and telegrams instructing them how to vote. If they did what we could not blame them for doing, they would answer, "You sent me down here to do my best according to my own judgment in the light of what I can find out on the ground; now I want you to stop instructing me in my duties, or else to elect somebody else in my place—if you can—who is willing to be your errand boy."

But it sometimes seems as if our people had forgotten what

Representative Democracy is and had concluded that it is the second meaning of "representative." So in a great many instances apparently they pick out men for whom to vote who are as nearly like themselves as possible. In that way there tends to be Government made up not of trustworthy Representatives but of typical men. It is safe to say that probably no country has as yet reached the level of Civilization at which competency and integrity in Government could be secured that way.

In England, typical of ministerial government, the House of Commons governs with the consent and approval of the people. In the United States, typical of democracy, the people govern through their representatives in Congress and the State Legislatures. In both, The State is a popular sovereignty—In England in substance, in America in both form and substance.

UNITS IN THE STATE

I. The State
  1. A population organized for the purpose of governing and being governed
  2. More exactly, coercive and restraining power acting upon a whole population
  3. Customs growing into laws
  4. Personal rule growing into Civil Government

II. Civil State
  1. Appears with Government by Law
  2. Head of the Civil State is not above the law
  3. Lawmakers are not above a higher law called Constitution
  4. People are not above the law

III. Sovereignty
  1. Recognized right to rule
  2. Location of Sovereignty determines the form of the State

IV. Monarchy
  1. Sovereignty is in a single individual, typically a king
  2. Monarch may be:
    a) Absolute—rules by law but makes the law himself—a Despot
    b) Despot who rules by mere personal caprice—a Tyrant
    c) Constitutional monarch who reigns over a Civil State but is not above the law

V. Republic
  1. Means Commonwealth, that is, rule for the ends of the General Welfare and not for the glory of the Monarch or State
  2. Is contrasted with Monarchy
  3. Of necessity then is governed by elective magistrates and legislators
  4. Does not necessarily rest on popular sovereignty
  5. Modern constitutional monarchies tend to be monarchy in form and republic in substance, having hereditary chief magistrates

VI. Feudal State
  1. Feudalism is commendation of lands and liberty to the strong man in return for protection
  2. Arises when Civil State or Despot becomes so weak as no longer to be able to govern
  3. The manor, vassalages, and serfdom
  4. Rackets incipient feudalities
  5. When the feudal State emerges, the monarch is in theory owner of the kingdom, the lords his vassals, and the commons their vassals

VII. Popular Sovereignty
  1. Sovereignty in the mass of the people
  2. Political power is always potentially in the mores
  3. Hence the world tends toward popular sovereignty
  4. Not necessarily a republic—constitutional monarchy tends toward popular sovereignty—through Ministerial Government
  5. Does not necessarily involve democratic Form of Government

VIII. Aristocracy
  1. Means "government by the best"
  2. Not a Form of Government
  3. How to select the best:
    a) By birth, but that gives only a caste system; the noble born are not necessarily the best
    b) By popular suffrage, expecting that the commons will select the best to govern; but that depends upon public intelligence and character

IX. Ministerial Government
  1. King or the elected President summons the leader of an elected branch to organize an administration
  2. Becomes Prime Minister and holds so long as he can hold his leadership
  3. On encountering a vote of lack of confidence, may advise the King or President to dissolve Parliament and appeal to the people in a new election of members

    4. Or may resign and give place to a new ministry

    5. If the election gives the Prime Minister a majority of the new members, he continues

    6. In a ministerial form nearly all measures adopted by the Parliament are proposed by the Ministry

X. Democracy

    1. Not Form of State but Form of Government

    2. Means rule of the folk or people and nothing else

    3. Necessarily involves suffrage, but not necessarily universal suffrage

    4. Not:

        a) Equality in social prestige

        b) Condescension in acknowledged superiors

        c) Rule of those lowest in intelligence and wealth

        d) Arbitrary rule of a majority

XI. Primary Democracy

    1. Direct rule of the people in primary assembly

    2. Election of all officers by direct vote

    3. Passing upon all appropriations by direct vote

    4. Transacting all business by direct vote

    5. Possible only in a small population and simple society

XII. Representative Democracy

    1. Government by individuals chosen to represent the people in governing

    2. All administrative and minor political officers appointed by the elected representatives.

    3. Lawmaking, appropriation of money, and public business transacted by representatives

    4. Represent primarily persons and not opinions or desires

    5. Representatives properly chosen because of confidence in their honesty and superior competency in Government

    6. Not representative because they are average and typical

B. LAW AND THE LAWS

The heart of the Civil State is the Law. To understand Civics is to understand what Law is in principle.

I suppose that, when most of us hear the term or see it in print, we at once think of a professional calling practiced by attorneys and counselors. With that we have nothing to do, any more than we are concerned with professional Mathematics in the Common School, or professional Music or Painting or Medicine.

Next after that would probably come in the minds of most of us the statement frequently heard, "That is the law," or the question, "What is the law?" For such matters, we consult a lawyer. The old adage has it, "A man who is his own lawyer has a fool for a client." We are not concerned in giving a law course in the Common School.

Finally, we often hear it said that such and such a law is bad—and so it often is. We are concerned in an elementary way with what is sometimes called the body of the law, or the system of law, or jurisprudence. It is essential that the Common Man should have some means other than his own prejudices of forming an opinion on such matters, or in other words of acquiring lay intelligence about what is the nature of the civil law as contrasted with natural laws.

I. Social Need of Public Instruction in the Nature of Civil Law

Law is always breaking down in palpable injustice, always has been for that matter. I do not mean here injustice in the scheme of things in an imperfect world which no civil law can correct, but rather ridiculously unjust and even barbarous conduct of cases in court, and absurdities in the substantive law, which no amount of legal sophistication can explain away. Perhaps "barbarous" is a harsh word to use, but I know of nothing milder to apply to such practices as bullying the witness which appears to be well-nigh universal and apparently is seldom rebuked by our judges. Periodically there is an outbreak in popular periodicals about the whole matter, and instances are exhibited through many pages of grievous faults in both the substantive and the procedural law, or at least in practice.

I am referring here to faults which are within the competency of judges or the legal profession to correct at any time, much as did Medicine clean house after the Flexner Report in 1910.

On the other hand, laws are very largely made by legislatures somewhere in the form of statutes, and that means that they are indirectly made by the people who choose the legislators. Such laws will be good law only in so far as the intelligence of those who make them is capable of making good law. Otherwise, they will handicap the courts and will generate injustice. In an electoral system the intelligence of lawmakers is not likely to go far beyond the intelligence of those who elect them. One cannot vote intelligently for a representative to go to the State Legislature and assist in making the laws unless the voter himself has some elementary intelligence about what Law is.

On both counts, the neglect and sloth of the courts and the profession, and the ignorance and casual ways of legislators, we come back as the corrective to awakened lay intelligence in the Commons. But in no different sense than has been true of pretty much the whole round of human affairs. I am prepared to argue, for example, that the modern awakening in the field of Medicine would not have appeared for a long time if ever, had it not been for a generation of instruction in the natural sciences in the high schools, sufficient to create a lay intelligence which in the end would no longer tolerate sheer incompetency in practitioners. Similarly, our extraordinary intelligence about things mechanical is recognized by other peoples if not ourselves to be due to long-continued and widespread instruction which has fairly bred mechanical sense into the mores.

WHAT HAVE THE SCHOOLS TO DO WITH IT ALL?

In order to answer the question, let us in the first place remind ourselves that the system of Law under which Americans have everywhere lived, save in the State of Louisiana, is itself a folk system. Therein, far more than in universal suffrage, inheres our democracy It is not a system like the Romanesque which prevails nearly everywhere on the Continent of Europe, which is derived from the finished Civil Law of Imperial Rome and which starts from assumptions which are in some fundamental senses radically different from the assumptions of our system. The principle that ours is a folk system is enough to start a chain of reflection in answer to the question, or ought to be.

But let us take a look backward in our history.

In 1790, when the first census was made, 95 per cent of our

people were of English descent. As a race, they were singular in
their genius for law and lawmaking, so much so that it is sometime said that self-government under law was born in the blood.
Hardly that, but rather that the evolution of the English Common Law and English Equity was just the kind of thing that
would follow the actual mores, and in turn mold the mores and
the abiding public sentiment which grows out of the mores everywhere. Moreover, they had for centuries been keen for the redressing of injustice. The English Law transplanted to this soil
was of the folk in a vital social sense, and it did not have its
sources primarily in the decrees of authority.

Down until near the end of the nineteenth century, in the
settled sections, there was proportionately a great deal more
private litigation than there is today, in the sense that more individuals would go to law for redress of grievances. The jury system was in one of its best periods, and that tended to keep the
application of law on a folk basis—as a good jury still does.
Lawyers were likely to be the big men of most local communities.
Jurymen—and service on juries was a good deal more general than
now—listened to the expounding of Law and discussed the expositions afterward, until a good many of them had the equivalent of
public instruction in the elements.

In the South, court day was the occasion of joyful gatherings,
and many a man found a cultural interest in listening to the
lawyers. Earlier still, gentlemen read Blackstone as one of the
most rewarding of avocations. So here too was a sort of "adult
education" in the law, enough to generate a modicum of legal
intelligence in the mores.

And then there was the Winning of the West and the erection
of thirty-three juristic States west of the Alleghenies, the true
American epic. From Kentucky in 1792 to Arizona and New
Mexico in 1912, men carried our law westward until, with a similar
Canadian movement, it embraced the greater part of a continent.
They built States around the Law; and not the Law around the
States. The commons were accustomed to that way of looking at
the Civil State.

But all those days are now of the long ago, and the culture and society which then existed are as extinct as the carrier pigeon.

Among the boys of the original stock there is little more than a vague awareness that there is such a thing as law. They know that some men are lawyers, and then there are murder trials and divorce cases "in the papers." Some of them are going "to study law," and for the most part they will learn only how to win cases —and no doubt to draft legal documents.

Meantime, the great folk movements of the last century brought in many millions of immigrants nearly all of whom came from countries in which there had been little of a folk basis in the law for centuries. To them law had always meant command and obedience and nothing else. A State which cannot enforce its commands is to them merely beneath contempt. Their system has been founded on the doctrine that what is commanded is right; ours on the doctrine that what is right is commanded.

In short, the old days had vanished by 1900, and the schools and colleges had done next to nothing to supply what had been lost. What of it? Only this, that there can be no effective democracy on legal conceptions which are suited to autocracy. On those terms, self-government merely becomes a lost art.

II. The Nature of Civil Law

It may be said in the first place that laws exist to control and prescribe relations between individuals in the interest of order and justice where common intelligence, conscience, and good taste cannot be trusted to control.

The layman is apt to be confused and misled by several different meanings of the same word. We are likely to hold to the attitude that law is law and that is all there is to it. Many of us, perhaps most of us, suppose that all laws are made by the State Legislatures or Congress or the city councils. The last make no laws at all, and it is far from true that all true laws either are or could be made by the other two combined. So in the first place we shall need to get clear some distinctions in terminology.

POSITIVE LAW

First of all is what lawyers and political scientists call *positive law*. That means the law as it is directly applied by the courts and enforced by their officers. It is the law with which we are familiar and is what we ordinarily refer to when we use the expression, "That's the law." Where does the positive law come from? That is where we begin to go astray.

STATUTES

An act of a legislature making a law is called *enacting a statute*.

In the first instance, the positive law arises out of statute-making. A statute is always written law; but it has to be interpreted and applied by the courts. That is so, first, because no legislature could apply and enforce its own acts, unless it be in a very small State and very simple society. It is so, second, because it is beyond the wisdom of men to draft a statute which is so perspicuous in form of statement that it will apply itself in the great variety of cases which may arise under it. Hence the courts interpret what they call the legislative intent and thus apply the substance of the statute. One readily sees that court decisions must become quite as important as the statutes upon the bearing of which decisions are made.

Now it is important to bear in mind that not all acts of the State Legislatures and of Congress make law, although they are lawmaking bodies. The great bulk of the business of all of them is in providing for the conduct of the affairs of Government, authorizing public works, making appropriations, providing for army and navy, laying taxes, etc. All such acts are said to "have the force of law," but they are not laws in the sense in which we are using the term. They are not devoted primarily to determining the relations between individuals or groups in the interest of public order and the establishment of justice. The latter are the real statutes.

Now statute-making would go far to place all our affairs on the "best and surest foundations" if legislators and persistent pressure groups were intelligent about the nature of law. As it is, organized pressure and good-natured lawmakers can place almost

anything on the statute-books which is not positively unconstitutional. The result is the negation of system, of anything resembling an understandable legal policy. Hence, it is often well-
nigh impossible for anybody to tell "what the law is." Civil law
is a body of regulations put together in coherent and understandable fashion; nothing else is Civil Law. When lawyers are reduced
to the extremity of keeping posted on what all the legislatures
have done, they cease to be members of a learned profession and
become mere secretaries.

COURT DECISIONS

So the second, and indeed immediate, source of the positive law
is found in court decisions.

Now in applying the legislative intent, perhaps as much coherency is brought into the body of statute law as is possible; for
the courts will analyze, interpret, and elucidate, and in reading the
decisions you come to see *why* the court decides as it does. In that
way, there is gradually built up a body of legal doctrine which is
good for at least that jurisdiction. Doctrine can be learned and
more or less used for thinking purposes. Nevertheless, so far as
justice is concerned, if the court is to apply a constitutional
statute, it is powerless; for the court is bound by the plain intent,
and that may conceivably be as far as possible removed from
justice.

So we can see why it is that American trial lawyers are immensely preoccupied with court decisions, sometimes to the extent of estimating, as it were statistically, how a given case is
likely to go in court. Once more, the effect is to turn what was
once perhaps the greatest of the professions into something a bit
higher than clerkship.

THE COMMON LAW

Individuals frequently feel that they are wronged by their
neighbors to the point at which they deserve legal relief and yet
find nothing in the statutes to cover the issues. Nevertheless, they
do get relief. The court applies the principles of what is known as
Common Law. Indeed, if we were reduced for relief to what is

made and provided in the statutes, we should be in sorry case. Most of the major crimes even are said to be "indictable at common law." That means that if murder itself were not mentioned in the statutes and penalties affixed, nevertheless a court would take cognizance, try the case, and probably hang the murderer if he were convicted and hanging were part of the customs.

The Common Law is a great body of legal and juristic principles which has in the course of centuries of study and experience in the relations of individuals in the Community emerged as common in human nature and Society. It is a body of legal truth which is capable of constantly being refined and of growing to meet new situations. It has been called refined common sense, and again called pure reason. Whether it does grow or does not depends upon the ability, learning, and juristic statesmanship of lawyers and judges. It is the perfect example of an institution as we have studied institutions. Whenever a judge so conducts a trial or writes a decision as to administer justice in a case, otherwise than by applying a statute, he is applying the Common Law of his time. If he writes an illuminating decision, the latter may perhaps be listed among lawyers as a *ruling case*, presumably an accretion to the body of legal and juristic principles known as The Law, or perhaps a correction.

The decision itself makes positive law. The reasoning behind the decision demonstrates that the decision is good law. And there is no good law which is not also justice.

The Common Law in its very nature is capable of growing to cover all possible issues under changing conditions of Society. Justice itself does not change; our knowledge of Justice does expand as new applications of old principles arise, and the applications themselves clarify the principles more and more. That is the way with all knowledge, which is Science.

WHAT THE COMMON LAW IS NOT

There appears from time to time so much misapprehension as to what the Common Law is that it is worth while to note some of the more flagrant instances.

Not the customary law.—Once upon a time, not many years ago, in a conversation with a young lawyer, I referred to the Common Law. After a pause, his rejoinder was, "Oh, you mean the customary law." Now, it is true enough that the Common Law as we know it arose out of the old customary law of England many centuries since. So did all civil law, the Roman, for example, arise out of custom somewhere. But the Common Law has been a system of legal thought, more or less, these seven hundred years and more. It is true enough that it arises out of conceptions of the Civil State which have been particularly English conceptions down until this day. It is further true that rightly conceived it may be developed as a body of jurisprudence by statutes which originate in the convictions of the lay public, and even now and then may be influenced by the common sense of the verdict of a jury.

Not the English law.—Ever since the beginnings of American jurisprudence, there have always been those, even among the English element in our population, who exhibit an unreasoning prejudice against everything English. In the early days their cry was, "Let us be independent of England and have a law of our own." Such people were not unlike many of our modern graduates, ignorant of the very nature of civil law. If they had had their way, it is doubtful that we should even yet have any law, other than a chaotic body of statutes.

What we call the Common Law is in reality the Anglican system of jurisprudence. Today, it has elements drawn from American experience and from the experience of the British self-governing Dominions. It long ago took on elements from the canon law, particularly in the field of domestic relations and other applications of Christian ethics. In our country it has taken on elements from the Spanish Romanesque where they were better applicable than old Common Law principles. The most famous instance, I suppose, has been in rights in stream flow as brought out by geographical conditions in the arid West.

Finally, it has been enriched by being drawn back to the folk in such statute-making as workmen's compensation acts, restatement of the whole master-and-servant doctrine, limitation of working hours, practical annulment of the old doctrine of *caveat emptor*.

Not a law of precedents.—Finally, one hears the young liberals especially decry the *hoary law of precedents*. Perhaps the poet with his eloquent "broadening down from precedent to precedent" has been responsible for the idea. No doubt there have been many judges who have been either so lazy or so lacking in imaginative capacity that they either could not or would not think in any system. We find such men in every calling. They, of course, find comfort in precedents. But what really comes out of preceding cases in which a particular principle seems to apply is the reasoning of the judge and not the form of his decision. Reasoning can never be run into the channels of static precedent; otherwise there could be no professions.

THE COMMON LAW AND THE STATUTES

We have thus seen at work what is a system of thought, that is to say, a science, particularly as a guide to the courts in the administration of justice. We have also seen that statutory law tends to become incoherent and chaotic, for lack of any consistent principle governing enactment.

Social progress consists in very large part in the rational development of jurisprudence, under which more and more there is attained an approach to perfect justice in the relations of individuals and of groups. Many individual judges and jurists have been diligent in building up such a jurisprudence.

Legislators seldom have co-operated, chiefly because most of them are unaware that there is any such thing as rational law; nor will they be likely to be aware of anything of the sort until public instruction shall have brought into the lay mind as much legal intelligence as it now has mathematical and mechanical intelligence. I fancy that if any State legislator today ventured to propose that the value of π in that State should be a convenient 3.0, he would be laughed off the floor. There is enough mathematical intelligence abroad to know that such things cannot be done. There might be enough legal intelligence similarly generated to

make possible a legally coherent structure of statutory enact-
ments. If our legislatures and courts could co-operate in such an
enterprise; and if the former could be persuaded to give over attempts, while so doing, to make over Society and the order of
nature by statutory enactment, likely enough in a generation
their hearts' desires would be added unto them, and much that
they never conceived of as well.

III. EQUITY

One definition of law is to contrast it with Equity. The distinction is unhappy, since "equity" is about the only name we can
find for one of the great moral institutions. The technical distinction thus made is prone to be taken as an admission that law has
nothing to do with justice. Equity, however, may also be defined
as a particular judicial process applied in the interest of justice
when the ordinary suit at law could not render justice.

Suppose, for example, that you have a much-prized tree and
that lawless men come along and propose to cut it down, with no
warrant at all for doing so. At law, you could afterward collect
money damages, but the money value is not great, and, after all,
the tree is gone. But being duly advised of what is going to
happen to you, you resort to a judge, state your case, and he
issues his injunction to the depredators. If they ignore the injunction, they will be imprisoned for contempt of court. An injunction is a writ in equity. That is perhaps the most familiar use
of equity, but of course there is a great deal more.

So there grew up equity courts or chancery courts alongside
law courts, a clumsy and costly system. In due season, intelligent
and progressive lawyers began to see that something could be
made out of it all, and thus Equity became organized into a
system of principles by which men could think out, better than
they had done before, the applications of justice. In that way,
law became more and more transformed from a system of order,
which all law was in the beginning, into a system of justice as well.

IV. JUSTICE

For ages men have been trying to define Justice. The quest is
not unlike similar quests for definitions of such things as life, con-

sciousness, energy, value. When we get to the primary terms of existence, definitions are hard to come at. About all we can do is to describe Justice by saying that Justice is the application of Conscience, especially fair dealing, awarding to each man his own, the guaranty that what one has a right to expect will be achieved.

We are ordinarily preoccupied with justice as it is related to laws and courts, but it ought to be reiterated that only a fragment of Justice can be incorporated in law and be applied by the courts. By far the greater part of it depends upon the presence of Ethics in the mores, in the relations of individuals. Moreover, there will be little justice in the laws, unless there is justice in the mores. When men and women commonly seek only the gratification of their own desires, are habitually unfair in their dealings with one another; when they are grasping, unscrupulous, and even murderous, save as they dread the law, the time will soon come when there will be no law to dread.

One of the most common forms of ignorance about the law is that law and justice are distinct. People often assert, "That may be good law but it is not justice." No law is good law which awards injustice. As we have seen, not all law is concerned with the award of justice to either individuals or classes, for many of our laws are nothing more than the carrying-on of Government; but no law which works injustice is either good law or good government.

INTELLIGENT ATTITUDE

It is quite true that courts sometimes render what is but a travesty on Justice. It is more often true that legislatures enact laws which are unjust, and neglect to enact laws for the abolishment of injustice. That is only to say that men in power sometimes act unjustly, either because of lack of intelligence or because of lack of good will. The fault is not in Law but rather in laws enacted by men.

Nevertheless, there is hardly any issue in life which is so deeply colored with partiality and subjectivism as our attitude toward justice when our own interests or passions or prejudices are involved. All are prone to define justice in particular instances as that which suits their own desires. Few of us can see ourselves and our interests in an objective light. To that extent, we are uneducated. Apart from prejudice, most of us are inclined to desire a sort of rough-and-ready justice which is more than likely to render grave injustice at the best, and to completely demoralize the systematic administration of justice at the worst.

It is far more reasonable to suppose that men experienced in the law, and sitting in an impartial tribunal, will be more likely to render justice, or see that it is rendered, than that the rest of us can reason offhand about matters to which we have never given any special study, and in which we may be prejudiced. One of the most nonsensical ideas in the world is that the will of the people is itself justice. The public may require that justice be done, but it will not achieve its end save in countries where the public is sufficiently moral to know what justice is.

V. Procedural Law

We have thus far been concerned with what lawyers call the substantive law, that is to say, with the law which lays down what is right and what is wrong, what is forbidden by The State, what public policy requires and in what way. But there is another side, the *procedural law*, or, if you are in love with logical symmetry in terms, the adjective law, the law which prescribes how things shall be done in the courtroom. It deals with all matters of process, from the requirement of three witnesses to a will to the jury system and the rules of evidence. It is quite as important as the substantive law, and it cannot be treated in the cavalier fashion with which laymen would often like to treat it— and get back to the office. It has required a great deal of experience in court work and fair dealing to find processes which will disclose vital evidence, will be effectual as compulsion, and will not work more injustice than justice.

Procedure in American courts is often bad. It is in that field that most of the "technicalities of the law" occur. The public is often impatient because of its ignorance of what justice to litigants requires, because of its failure to recognize the principle that even the worst malefactor is entitled to a fair trial, and because of our bad habit of allowing the newspapers to try cases. When a newspaper states that not one person in ten believes that A is innocent, it merely dwells on the irrelevant. Not one person in a good deal more than ten knows enough about the law, or of the requirements of a fair trial, or of the uncolored evidence that is before the jury, to be entitled to an opinion.

Nevertheless, procedure is notoriously full of needless delay, and at times the delays have been scandalous, full of lax discipline in the courtroom, pedantic involvements of evidence, timidity in judges with respect to the behavior of lawyers and with respect to the judge's own courage in his own convictions. If judges had less fear of being overruled by higher courts, the science of law might well make better progress. I do not know where Physics, Biology, and Medicine would be today, if Galileo, Darwin, and Pasteur had been afraid of being overruled. If there were a more intelligent public, fear of such a fate might well be less poignant.

Apparently it has long been true, for the race has been under the domination of the specialist for a long time. I quote a passage from Sir Henry Maine's *Early History of Institutions:*

"If, says Gaius [Roman jurisconsult], you sued by *Legis actio* for injury to your vines, you would fail: you must call them trees, because the text of the Twelve Tables spoke only of trees. The ancient collection of Teutonic legal formulas, known as the Malberg Gloss, contains provisions of exactly the same character. If you sue for a bull, you will miscarry if you describe him as a bull: you must give him his ancient juridical designation of 'leader of the herd.' You must call the forefinger the 'arrow finger,' the goat the 'browser on leeks.' "

In the substantive law the legislature is perhaps more often to be blamed for miscarriage than the courts, but in procedure, the courts, or at least the profession as a whole, have things in their own hands. Occasionally, a strong presiding judge takes the bit between his teeth and in a few minutes turns the stream of justice in that State into right channels.

VI. Branches of the Law

We have thus far been dealing with law, with the science which lies behind law and laws, with Justice and Jurisprudence. Our individual contacts with law are usually with some branch of law. We go to an attorney, what the English call a solicitor, if we are wise, in order to avoid signing a cutthroat contract, to avoid leaving our meager property to somebody we never heard of, or to thwart the humorous ways of tax collectors. That is ordinarily routine, but a skilful man is required even for that.

The branches of the law appear as commercial law, with which we are involved almost every day; police law; laws of domestic relations; corporation law, which we are sometimes led to believe is the invention of the enemy of mankind; admiralty. Then there is international law; canon law in vestigial fragments; martial law, which in these days we may encounter at almost any time; and, finally, constitutional law.

In the process of public instruction, we could not go very far into any one of the branches without attempting to train lawyers. Some of them we shall encounter in subsequent sections and chapters.

VII. Ordinances and Bylaws

Another class of regulations, commonly called laws, are not laws at all. I refer to the ordinances of municipal corporations and to the bylaws of other corporations. In driving along the highways, one frequently observes signs of warning with the legend, "State law." Of course, there is no law which is not State law, and with us sometimes Federal law. Apparently the highway management believes that they thereby induce users of the highway to give particular heed, supposing that ordinances or rules of the highway commission will be understood only in a Pickwickian sense.

Ordinances are acts of the councils of municipal corporations intended to control the burghers or indwellers in community life. With infrequent exceptions, they require only what an informed and courteous citizen would do or not do anyway. By the statute setting up the corporation, they have the force of law, but otherwise they are no more law than are the regulations of country clubs. They have no systematic structure, they are not bodies of principle, there is nothing about them to understand.

Bylaws are regulations of industrial, commercial, and other corporations, applied to the conduct of their own business or other function. Observance is usually a matter of contractual obligation.

VIII. INSTRUCTION

All the foregoing sets forth the reasons wherefore Law is in principle part of the Curriculum of the Common School, and to some extent it explains at length the indicated content of such instruction. It will perhaps serve as suggestion for textbook-making. There follows an appropriate unit outline which will make the whole matter more definite.

UNITS IN LAW

I. What Law Is
1. Control of conduct—commanding what is right and forbidding what is wrong
2. Establishment of defensible rights
3. Setting up civil and martial authority

II. Positive Law
1. The law which the courts enforce
2. The law as we know it
3. May be good law or bad law
4. That depends upon the intelligence and character of people, legislators, and judges
5. Embodied in Constitution, statutes, and court rulings

III. Ideal or Rational Law
1. Rational Law is a great body of principles arising out of human experience, revealing what is just law, and what law can and cannot do
2. A *body of thought* derived largely from Jurisprudence and from Political Science and Economics
3. Because it is a body of thought, it is sometimes called the scientific law or the philosophical law
4. The test of good positive law is in its conformity to Rational Law

IV. Jurisprudence
1. Jurisprudence is the theory of Justice
2. Justice is at bottom fairness, impartiality, apportioning to each what is his right and what is his own

3. It is based on good conscience and good reason
4. So Jurisprudence is applied Ethics
5. In the Civil State it is also sometimes the name for a system of law
6. The Rational Law is based in part on Jurisprudence
7. The Positive Law is supposed to be

V. Statutes
1. An act of a legislature making a law sets up a statute
2. Always written law
3. Always valid positive law, provided it conforms to the Constitution
4. But not good law unless it conforms to principles of Justice and Good Government

VI. The Common Law
1. The body of legal principles which in most English-speaking countries judges are presumed to use in thinking out decisions when decision is not a plain matter of applying a statute
2. One of the three great systems of law—Anglican, Romanesque, and Islamic
3. Has grown up out of Anglican notions of right and justice in the community and in relation to natural conditions
4. English and American popular sovereignty or self-government has grown up largely within the principles of the Common Law
5. Unlike statutes, the Common Law is not written law
6. In its nature it is a growing system of legal and juristic thought when it is in the hands of able and accomplished judges and is not paralyzed by needless statute-making

VII. The Courts in Two Functions
1. As umpire
   a) Authoritative settlement of disputes
   b) Decision binding as positive law, unless reversed on appeal
2. As lawmakers
   a) Where decision is accepted as establishing reasonable rule
   b) Decision is no more binding *as good law* than the reasoning of the court which makes it

VIII. Equity
1. A body of principles and processes which apply where a suit at law could not award justice
2. Writes of injunction and mandamus and quo warranto are illustrations of equity processes
3. Formerly, in our legal background, a separate jurisprudence, with separate courts
4. In maturing systems of law, equity and law coalesce into a single system

IX. Substantive and Procedural Law
   1. Substantive law is what is actually commanded or prohibited, or right or authority set up
   2. Procedural law is what governs procedure in court
   3. There must be orderly procedure, and it is difficult to secure that and not deprive accused persons or litigants of their rights
   4. But procedure is a means and not an end in itself
   5. Nothing which actually imperils the attainment of substantial justice can be good procedure

X. Ordinances and Bylaws
   1. Regulations set up by municipalities and other corporations
   2. Sanctioned by the charter which is a statute, or else by the general law
   3. Have the force of laws but are not laws
   4. Not systems of law but individual rules
   5. Have application to members of corporations concerned and to those who partake of their advantages

C. THE PUBLIC DEFENSE

"In order to secure domestic tranquillity—provide for the common defense."

If we were to look for the one function of The State which we recognize today, and which can be traced farthest back in the civil experience of mankind, it would probably be the Public Defense. About it have clustered some of the most compelling forces which have led to the evolution of sovereignty out of its loose beginnings in tribal communities, and finally into that reign of law which defines the Civil State. By Public Defense is meant defense from violence, either the violence of the martial invader or the violence of the criminal. Hence it is that this section is part of the Curriculum in Civics.

I. THE MARTIAL DEFENSE

Martial defense means warding off the invasions of enemies. Is, then, invasion limited to breaking in upon the national domain? We commonly believe that it is. And yet some reflection will convince anybody that there may be invasion where no territorial inroad is involved, invasion of natural rights in a world-community. It is futile to talk about not fighting until there is actual violation of boundaries. When essential rights are invaded without sharp remonstrance in martial demonstration, it commonly happens that a long-drawn-out war is the consequence.

It is difficult to discuss the subject in public schools, or even in a book dealing with schools, for the current world is in a state of emotional upheaval over the whole matter. Nevertheless, since Martial Defense is part of the apparatus of Civilization, and will continue to be such until the whole world is civilized, the subject is part of the Intelligence, Conscience, and Taste of civilized persons.

Furthermore, it is expedient that those who will in any case talk largely about the causes of war, the horrors of war, militarism, pacifism, oaths of resistance, entangling alliances, leagues of nations, world-courts, should at least know something in their own right of what they are talking about. It is prone to be true that there is about as much valid individual opinion about such matters as one might find in a concentration camp or a Russian high command. So long as there are barbarous nations in the world, equipped with the enginery of modern war, it is idle to talk about the end of war.

INSTRUCTION

I take it that in instruction we are concerned mainly with the development of intelligence concerning war and the martial defense and with an appreciation of the inherent liability of able-bodied men to martial service. Behind it all lies General Education, of which martial intelligence is but a part. Much resides in Morality, on both the volitional and the ethical sides, in perception of right and rights, in Patriotism, Loyalty, Fortitude. But specifically we are concerned in the present course with: first, awareness of the causes and consequences of war; and, second, some understanding of the nature of our own national defenses. As nearly everywhere else in the Curriculum, the practical end in view is to train pupils up to the point at which they can read intelligently on the whole subject.

Some very sketchy consideration of the first is perhaps called for here, in the interest of clarity touching what is meant. Our own martial history is full of evidence revealing the consequences of popular ignorance about the subject. We have fought five international wars, and we were not prepared for a single one of them. For the first, the War for Independence, our ancestors could hardly have been expected to be prepared. In every subsequent instance, including our only civil war, our people were profoundly ignorant of what war means, of what precipitates war, of the manner in general in which it ought to be conducted, at least to the extent of realizing that ward politicians and country lawyers are not likely to be endowed with military talent by special dispensation of Heaven.

"Preparedness" means at least two things, both of them of vital importance.

In the first place, it means some elementary but adequate intelligence of what modern war is—and what it is not—something which goes beyond the lurid sensationalism of anti-war propaganda, and something quite different from the patriotic fervor which is so easily stirred up when war impends. It further means a public intelligence which will make it unprofitable for Congressmen to interfere with the strategic plans of land and naval forces. One of the best reasons for keeping out of war is in the principle that a state of war means surrender of civil liberty to autocracy, and the rule, at least at the front, of naval and military men. Nevertheless, if a country cannot keep out of war, it is the wildest folly to meddle with the intensely specialized function of conducting war.

In the second place, preparedness means discipline against "war talk" before the event. Patriotism at such times is apt to evaporate into mere self-gratulation founded upon one's awareness of his membership in a large group—and probable individual exemption from service. All such tends to play into the hands of warmongers and in the end to bring about a rush into the horrors of needless armed conflict.

Only in the third place, as it seems to me, is it intelligent awareness of the nature of our martial problems and defense and of the needs of our armed forces.

CAUSES OF WAR

Some intelligence diffused among the population regarding the causes of war, as the historian sees the causes, would probably go far to amend the public sense of wrong which is the working capital of most wars; and perhaps go farther still toward the generation of effective public opinion bearing upon the prevention of war itself.

International feuds.—Since 1648 most European wars have been in the nature of chapters in international feuds. The feud of primitive life begins in a wrong or fancied wrong which leads to reprisal. That reprisal leads to rejoinder in force. And so it goes, perhaps generation after generation, until the original occasion has long been forgotten, and yet they cannot let go and stop it. Such things do not exist in civilized States, for about the earliest sign of the reign of law is assumption of retributive justice by the king's officers, the trial of appeals, the infliction of penalty for wrong, and the forbidding of private vengeance. The relations between States, however, are still primitive in the sense that there is no positive international law, no effective international court, and no international constabulary. Hence, war breeds war and in turn more war.

Since recorded history began, however, there have been only about three fundamental causes of warfare:

Cultural wars.—Between the middle of the seventh and the end of the seventeenth centuries, the most conspicuous cause of major wars, apart from barbarian invasions, was difference in religious faith. All that is past and gone, but what it was at bottom still remains. Religion is a form of Culture. Men will fight before they will be deprived of their faith, if faith is strong enough; but they will also fight assaults on their cherished way of living, on their culture—and they would be poor stuff if they would not.

In the nature of things, there is no escape from cultural wars, short of the diffusion of Civilization throughout the world. Other causes are matters of national right, or right which is claimed, and as such they are in their nature justiciable. But you can no more bring profoundly antagonistic cultures into court than the uncongenial tastes of discordant neighbors.

Dynastic and nationalist wars.—From the beginning of the emergence of the modern national States in Europe, down to the present hour one of the chief causes of war has been: first, the extension of the domain of a ruler or ruling family; and, second, refusal to recognize expatriation of emigrants. Twenty-five years ago, the first was supposed to be at an end. That was a delusion. The event was to prove, what might have been foreseen in the beginning, namely, that personal sovereignty is seldom more than the expression of the mores of a people. Depose the person, barbarously murder him and his whole family if you will, and a despot will arise to succeed him and inherit his ambitions. The second, which was the real issue in our War of 1812, is apparently, at least in the eyes of Germany, as strong as ever. And yet, since the adoption of our Constitution, naturalization of aliens has been more and more recognized national right among the nations which accept international law.

Economic wars.—But probably the most comprehensive cause, scattered as it is through all history, has been economic in its nature. "Economic" is an extensive term. It covers wars fought for richer lands, for trade privileges, for relief of crowding populations, for access to essential commodities. The whole field of economic war, or of wars in which there is an economic element, is in its nature as eminently justiciable as are the commercial practices of nations within their own economy. It is further true that of all the causes, it betokens perhaps the lowest stage of Civilization, in the aggressor nation, for nothing can be made out of it which is any better than robbery with violence. The world and its resources are the inheritance of all mankind, in the sense that Commerce knows no national boundaries; whatever nation interferes with the free flow of goods and services in exchange in the world-community inevitably contributes to the generation of armed conflict somewhere.

INTERNATIONAL LAW

The foregoing analysis ought to make it clear, if indeed any argument is needed, that there is but one way out of a condition of chronic warfare which is not worse than war itself, the way, namely, that makes it unnecessary for most of us to maintain private police. We rely upon law and upon lawmaking bodies, and upon a constabulary set up to maintain the peace.

International law is not very different from the Law which we discussed in the last section; indeed it resembles the Common Law. After all, Law in principle is as universal as Physics. It is at bottom a declaration of the principles of right and justice which ought to obtain in the intercourse of nations. It is compelling upon Governments in the same sense as that in which honesty and right dealing and respect for law are compelling upon civilized individuals in any nation, irrespective of the presence of the constabulary. People often fail to understand international law, because there is no international State with its legislature, courts, and police force. The same people fail to understand national law, in that they suppose it to be only that which is enacted by legislatures.

It is worth recalling that we Americans have lived in what has been an international State from the beginning. The Constitution is an instrument by which at first thirteen and then forty-eight States learned to govern themselves as one in foreign and interstate relations, and as individual States to exercise all the other attributes of sovereignty.

The causes of war between nations are no more ineradicable than feuds between families.

COST AND CONSEQUENCES

Everybody is aware that wars entail costs, but few realize what the costs are. When a war looms on the horizon, the first question in the minds of people ought to be, "Is it worth the cost?" Wars have seldom been entered upon after those who were most vitally concerned had counted the cost and were still determined to pay the price—the other side commonly weakens. Twenty or thirty years after a great war, the older people who have not lost sons have forgotten, and the younger generation never knew, being too young to have learned naturally and never having been taught. The actual participants in the former war, after that lapse of time, are but a small minority in the body politic. Hence the first pre-requisite of intelligence about war is that there should be instruc-tion in the cost of war.

The most terrible costs can be summarized in the list which follows:

1. The destruction of young men who have a right to their lives, and the grief of parents and families over their loss. Wars if fought at all cannot be fought by men past the prime of life, and in bodily strength and endurance prime comes early.

2. Lives which are dragged out by bodies hideously injured, escape from which even in death would be a blessing.

3. Blasted careers. The soldier survives only to find that he has no place in the world; female invasion of employment and the stay-at-homes have crowded him out. The post-war generation of young men suffers the same fate.

4. Destruction of accumulated wealth, and especially of ac-cumulated capital. Viewed ordinarily as a sordid consideration, this is one of the causes which drags on and causes misery and unhappiness in the community as a whole long after the immedi-ate grief has been liquidated in the grave.

Economic cost ought not to be taken as money cost. It is some-times hard to see the economic cost if we keep our minds fixed on the count of wealth instead of on wealth itself. There is, however, a money cost which is translatable into true economic cost through the disruption of the whole financial organization of so-ciety, and especially the levy of excessive taxes.

5. Disorganization of established social relations which were making toward orderly progress, disruption of society and all its attendant evils. We have nowhere near finished paying the cost of the Civil War in this respect.

6. Destruction of the best potential leadership, perhaps the most disastrous of all costs, and on this it is worth while to linger.

By and large, war in its very nature destroys good leadership material. First of all, it is that material which gets into the fight-ing. Second, the front lines and forlorn hopes select for destruc-tion the idealistic, the energetic, the devoted and those capable of devotion. That becomes more and more the case when there are used in warfare the fruits of advanced material culture. Weapons increase in deadliness and new weapons are added.

Modern naval war is especially deadly. In the action between the "Constitution" and the "Guerrière" in the summer of 1812, which was unusually bloody for the time, the "Guerrière" lost seventy-nine killed and wounded out of a crew of two hundred and seventy-two. When the "Queen Mary" went down at Jutland, she carried with her to death twelve hundred and fifty-eight of a complement of twelve hundred and seventy-five.

Potential leadership is thus destroyed wholesale. After the war is over, the community holds a disproportionate number of weaklings and rascals to seize the leadership and father the new generation. The consequences in politics, commerce, industry, literature, and education are what might have been expected. If there were space, I am sure that this principle of adverse selection could be demonstrated factually all the way from the Punic Wars down to and including the war of 1914–18.

THE COST OF NOT GOING TO WAR

With Kipling's people who were always crying joyously, "There will be trouble in the Balkans in the spring," and their kindred, out of the way; and war faced as a thing of terrible costs: then comes the counter consideration, namely, "What is the cost of not going to war?" In at least two respects, the cost of peace may be more terrible than the cost of war.

1. What is involved in cowardice, dread of individual death, terror of the enemy, especially when the trait is common in a population, may be even more to be abhorred than the direct costs of war already enumerated. To submit to the domination of others willingly and gladly is in every age soul-destroying. More practically, it generates cruelty in all social relations, and excesses which would not have been dreamed of in better days. People who allow themselves to be enslaved elect themselves for personal nullification.

2. A pacifistic, as distinguished from a peace-loving, attitude

in boys is apt to become next door to a chronic psychopathic condition. Normal young fellows do not say much about either fighting or peace oaths. "I did not raise my boy to be a soldier" is equivalent to saying, "I did not raise a man-child at all." The male of the species has too much racial history in his temperamental makeup to make it safe for him to doubt that one of the principal reasons in nature for his existence is fighting if need be, in defense of his women, children, and country. One of the best justifications of military training in school seems to me to be that the boys may receive something vital to them personally that their women teachers cannot give them. But the instruction which boys receive ought to equip them to estimate whether they are really asked to fight in the racial cause or only in that of some ambitious politician.

SCHOOL AND COURSE ORGANIZATION

The premises developed in the preceding pages seem to lead to the following conclusions:

First, intelligence about the martial defense is an essential factor in assimilating the meaning of The State as the head dominance of cultural institutions.

Second, it is highly important that courses leading to that kind of intelligence should be included in the Curriculum as part of instruction in citizenship.

Third, actual experience in martial matters should be part of the instruction of all able-bodied boys for their own personal needs, and as contributions to the national defense itself.

All the foregoing, in some form, have long appeared, here and there, throughout the country, in some schools.

City high schools and State colleges and universities had "military training" of some sort long before the days of R.O.T.C. It was apt to be perfunctory, too often intrusted to some local National Guard officer, and usually limited to exhibitionist practice in the school of the soldier and the school of the company. The reason why it did not come to more is, as I believe, to be found in the fact that there was no educational and instructional theory behind it. An agreeable contrast was sometimes, and still is, to be found in military academies which take their purposes seriously as something more than private reform schools.

There has never, so far as I know, been arranged and taught systematic courses for all prospective voters designed to breed into the mores intelligence about the nature of war itself, its causes and consequences, and about the organization of our forces.

a) Rational military training for all boys.—By "rational" is meant training which is well thought out as a system of giving boys some elementary experience in the proper activities of soldiers, including especially sound military discipline as the latter is conceived by our best military men. It should not be limited to the spectacular movements of marching bodies of men, and probably public exhibitions should be eschewed.

b) Rudimentary training of officers at the higher levels of the Common School.—A citizen army at the best presumes that all should have some notions of what is required of officers, even though in the nature of the case few would ever be officers in the field.

The R.O.T.C. as now constituted is under the auspices of the War Department. That makes it part of the national policy. Whether the policy is good as a defense measure we need not inquire. If it is good, it is eminently justified as Curriculum content.

Necessarily, the two courses suggested should be under the immediate oversight of military men, well suited for the purpose. Nevertheless, it is evident from the general purposes of schools that they should be under the ultimate control of the scholastic heads of schools. If the military courses in any particular school tend to become the core of the school itself, the tendency should be checked.

These have been referred to as courses. Strictly speaking, they are not courses at all, but rather parts of the school as organized subsidiary community.

CLASSROOM COURSES

A. Causes of War—Units
    I. Predatory invasion of cultural rights
        1. Religion
        2. Form of Government

3. Established way of life
4. Seldom if ever arbitrable

II. Extension of a dynastic or national domain by conquest
1. Sheer ambition for larger territory
2. Extension of a form of Government, especially a revolutionary form
3. Refusal to accept naturalization of emigrants by other States— doctrine of indefeasible allegiance.

III. Economic causes
1. Artificial restraint of trade
2. Wars for possession of natural resources instead of purchasing them
3. Wars for commercial privileges
4. Pressure of overpopulation and:
   a) Reluctance to lose sovereignty over emigrants
   b) Refusal of countries to accept immigration

IV. Precipitating causes
1. Many modern wars have no essential causes other than the fact that some people want war
2. Hence war propaganda to build up "war spirit"
3. Once in, the nation attacked uses propaganda both at home and abroad
4. Even without systematic propaganda, irresponsible "war talk" is sometimes sufficient

B. Costs of War—Units
I. In direct human misery
1. Death in camp or in action
2. Disease and crippled condition
3. Loss of career and of employment

II. In social disruption
1. Established adjustments in society are broken up and steady progress in betterment set back
2. New social problems are created
3. An already complex society is rendered more complex
4. War debts and war profiteering engender disruption in the creation of a newly-rich class

III. In destruction of accumulated capital
1. Destruction of actual capital in productive plants and housing
2. Destruction by diverting funds from needful extension and restoration of depreciation
3. Actual destruction of crop land and natural resources

IV. In destruction of potential leadership
1. In the main, the strongest and ablest young men are called into armies
2. The most perilous service tends to fall to them
3. Those who would naturally become the leaders in all fields of activity high and low are apt to be destroyed
4. Post-war periods in all times always show dearth of good leadership

V. Cost of not going to war
1. Defensive war probably the only just war
2. Defense against actual invasion of territory not the only defense
3. Loss of national independence is more costly than most of the other costs put together
4. A nation of civilized men ruled by aliens has never perhaps been a happy people
5. Society in such a nation treated as a going concern can never be normal

C. International Law—Units
I. International peace rests on the same bases as domestic peace
1. We are protected from criminal invasion of life and property by:
a) A great majority who are honest and civilized
b) The law and the police
2. International relations rest on the same bases
3. What is required by the logic of civilized existence in the world is:
a) Nations which are willing to be guided in international relations by the same principles which govern civilized individuals
b) International law as defining the rights of nations accepted
c) International forces capable of restraining criminal nations

II. Arbitration
1. Essentially an agreement between the Governments of two nations to have a particular dispute adjudicated by an impartial commission agreed upon by the two
2. Each piece of arbitration requires a compact between the two, agreeing to arbitrate and to accept the findings of the commission
3. There may be general arbitration treaties, agreeing to arbitrate all disputes of certain classes which may arise
4. Arbitration is preferable to war, but it is not settlement according to law

III. International conferences
1. Not to be confounded with peace congresses, following a particular war

2. Agreements touching:
    a) Causes of war
    b) Conduct of war, forbidding certain practices
    c) Defining blockade and contraband
3. Binding only upon the signatories
4. Amount to nonpositive international legislation

IV. International law is a rational and moral system which seeks to define the rights of nations and justice between them
    1. Not different in fundamental principles from our Common Law
    2. It arises out of civilized Law which is good everywhere, and out of specific treaties between nations, which are in the nature of contracts
    3. It has been developed by:
        a) The work of scientific lawyers
        b) The decisions of arbitral tribunals
    4. It is not as yet enforceable law
    5. For that is required:
        a) An international lawmaking body
        b) A permanent international court
        c) An international force capable of enforcing decisions

D. American Martial Establishment—Units
    I. Military forces
        1. The regular army and its branches
        2. The national army in war
        3. State troops—the National Guard
            a) As State military defense against mob violence
            b) Relation to police and sheriff's forces
            c) When the regular army can be used for the same purpose
            d) As part of the national army—first line of reserves
        4. Civilian reserves
        5. Education of officers in the regular army
    II. Naval forces
        1. Constituents of a fully organized fleet
        2. Naval bases
        3. Use of naval vessels for protecting nationals in foreign countries
        4. Naval reserve
        5. Personnel required by the fleet
        6. Education of naval officers
    III. Navy as first line of defense
        1. Minor importance of land war problems in our martial defense, since we have no powerful military neighbors

    2. Important military invasion must come by sea if at all

    3. Manner in which overseas forces are transported

    4. No such considerable force can land on our shores so long as our fleet controls the sea approaches

IV. Air forces

    1. Use of bombing planes in invasions

    2. Aircraft carriers, approaching by sea

    3. Air defenses

    4. Use of combat planes

    5. Air bases.

V. Martial law

    1. Processes of civil law inadequate to military discipline

    2. Martial law is sanctioned by civil legislation

    3. Purpose

       a) To maintain military order and control

       b) To secure justice to the personnel of our martial forces

    4. Courts martial

    5. Proclamation of martial law over civilian population

VI. Foreign policy of the United States

    1. American foreign policy is unlike that of European nations

    2. Grows out of both our geography and American political institutions

    3. Definable as a non-alliance, defensive policy

    4. Development after the Spanish War:

       a) Spain's Government in the Caribbean intolerable

       b) Cuban independence under Platt Amendment

       c) Acquisition of Puerto Rico

       d) Acquisition of the Philippines—and colonial administration

    5. Relation of policy in the Caribbean to defense of the Panama Canal

II. CRIME

The second of the two great subjects of Public Defense is Crime.

DEFINITION

In the first analysis, a crime is any act or neglect which is contrary to positive law, and positive criminal law is, with us, for the most part found in the statutes. Nevertheless, a statute is not always good law.

A more critical analysis finds that crime is objective and that its definition is to be found in the nature of Society, of the Community, and of the Civil Order itself. The function of the Legislature is not to make a given offense a crime but rather to recognize and define as crime what is crime anyway. There is no intelligent and enlightened approach to the subject unless that fundamental principle is recognized and followed.

In principle, that is crime which in fact invades the rights of individuals, tends to disrupt society, to disorganize the community, to flout the sovereignty of The State, and which is in its nature preventable by law.

Many things are falsely declared to be crime which in no way conform to this definition, but are only offenses against the tastes and whims of individuals, perhaps most individuals. Sumptuary laws have always been of that character. On the other hand, many courses of conduct do conform to the first part of the definition, and yet in their nature are not preventable by law. Discourtesy and insult are sometimes as hateful and disruptive as any crime, and yet the offenders can obviously not be brought into court and punished. That is but a sample of many forms of conduct which are not subject matter for the criminal law. The larger part of the disruptive forces in communities can be prevented only through effective upbringing and schooling, and through the influence of the churches.

GROUNDS FOR DEFINING CRIME

What means have we, then, for arriving at some certainty as to what crime is, apart from subjective preconceptions and race of opinion among the casual?

As everywhere else in our study of Society, we must, in the first place, give heed to what has been reprobated out of the universal experience of the race. For example, Bouvier states[2] that some offenses, such as murder, rape, arson, burglary, and larceny, are unqualifiedly condemned by the universal sentiment of all civilized countries. Others are also condemned, but some of the most heinous are not, largely perhaps because they are recent forms of conduct in extremely complex societies. Others still, universally prevalent for ages, are condemned among some peoples and

[2] *Encyclopedia of Law.*

looked leniently upon by others. Is that only crime then which has been offensive to the customs of many people?

Here is another instance of the rational as over against the empirical. We have experience and that is essential; there would be nothing to learn if we had not. But from experience we learn *principles*, and that is critical. Hence, civilized individuals come to recognize as crime at once even that which has never been crime in the customs. Adultery is one of the crimes not universally recognized and more or less tolerated where it is recognized; and yet Aristotle, who before all men possessed the inductive principle, placed adultery and murder in the same class as wrong under all conditions and circumstances. He had not only evidence but principle.

IMMORALITY AND CRIME

To quote Bouvier again, "Most common-law offences are as well-known and as precisely acertained as those which are defined by statute; yet, from the difficulty of defining and describing every act which ought to be punished, the vital and pressing principle has been adopted that all immoral acts which tend to the prejudice of the community are punishable criminally by the courts of justice."

Breach of trust.—An illustration is to be found in breach of trust, one of the most ancient of recognized crimes, and, in a complex society, one of the most common. Every responsible citizen knows when he is a trustee; in fact his acts make him responsible whether he knows it or not. It matters not in principle that there is no statutory enactment applying to his particular case; he knows or ought to know when he is doing wrong. In truth, before all others, the financier, merchant, or manufacturer, ought to know what is and what is not breach of trust. When he embarks on a business career, he assumes responsibility for knowing. He cannot be furnished with a statute-book which tells him what he may and what he may not do in every conceivable event. A country which pins its faith on statutes never catches up with malefactors, because the loopholes in the code never get altogether plugged up. Much the same principle applies to the acts of the various commissions which enact sundry codes of administrative law.

Two parents once left their two half-grown boys for an afternoon, having furnished them with a list of prohibitions. Climbing up the chimney and down the well were not mentioned, and the boys did both. Men are often but boys of a larger growth.

PETTY MISDEMEANORS

The increasing complexity of societies has created an immense number of misdemeanors, ranging all the way from sprinkling the lawn out of turn to exceeding the speed limit. Most of them are violations of city ordinances, some of them violations of the regulations of public commissions, some violations of statutes. Enactment of statutes to control misdemeanors is a good deal like using a naval gun for the purposes of the Chicago Stock Yards.

So far as I know, in American practice everywhere, certainly in most of the States, treason, felony, and misdemeanor are lumped together as crime. When a judge who is putting through the morning's summonses assures a scandalized misdemeanant that "coming into court on such a charge carries with it no criminal stigma," he is merely talking nonsense; the fact that the respondent is in court at all for an offense of which that court takes cognizance gives the man a criminal record—when in actuality no crime has been committed. I suppose that most of us who own automobiles or live in cities, of over 5,000 let us say, have criminal records.

In some, at least, of the Canadian Provinces and some European countries, a misdemeanant merely sees the city clerk and pays his fine. In some cases, he gets a bill on the police report. He may, of course, have his day in court, if he believes that he is falsely accused.

THE ACCUSED

We turn from crime to the accused, from the community to the individual, from law to liberty.

In all civilized countries an accused person is entitled in the elementary nature of justice to fair treatment, and that usually means unprejudiced treatment. Perhaps there are few more reliable tests of the level of Civilization prevailing in any country than this.

Under our system of law, the elementary principle in dealing with offenders is that all such are presumed to be innocent until they are found guilty. In some other countries, under other systems, the reverse is true. Not only do we conceive any other principle to be the basest injustice, but the most arrant irrationality as well.

Certain inferences flow at once from our principles:

1. If a citizen be admonished by a police officer, or apprehended, the requirement is that he shall be decently treated and not insulted and abused forthwith. In the United States it is commonly enough the reverse.

2. If a citizen be arrested for an alleged crime, he has a right to be charged at once, that is to say, to be made aware of the nature of the accusation.

3. The accused has a right to refuse to talk, and to have the services of counsel if he so desires. Moreover, he has a right to be informed of his rights.

4. Most of all, the accused has an indefeasible right not to be subjected to that relic of the darkest days of the medieval Inquisition, namely, "the third degree." Torture is unknown to civilized law. There are two good reasons, aside from its cruelty:

First, it is a monstrous violation of justice.

Second, it is grossly stupid and ignorant, since evidence secured under torture is beneath contempt as evidence.

THE PROSECUTING ATTORNEY'S OFFICE

When evidence warranting court procedure has been collected, the case goes to trial under the direction of a lawyer chosen for that function.

Now there is obviously required not only an able, trained lawyer, but one who is a specialist in the criminal law. A considerable part of our record of crime is due to the fact that the office often goes to a machine politician or else to a young lawyer who would otherwise be without clients. The purpose in the instance last named is to "give the young fellow a chance," a tribute to good nature rather than to civic intelligence.

In dealing with an accused person, from arrest to punishment, there are three and only three issues to be settled:

1. Was a crime committed?
2. Did the accused commit the crime?
3. On appeal, did the accused have a right and fair trial?

To achieve these essentials, the typical process, especially with major crimes, goes through the following stages, each in its own tribunal:

1. Was a crime committed? Inquest.
2. Arraignment of suspect. Is the evidence enough to warrant holding him?
3. Grand jury. We too think he probably did it.
4. Trial before judge and petit jury. Guilty or not guilty.
5. Trial in an appellate court on issues of constitutional right or validity of procedure in the lower court.
6. Perhaps further appeal to the State or Federal Supreme Court.
7. Finally, the convicted or his friends, may appeal to the Governor, or in Federal offenses to the President, for executive clemency, that is to say, reprieve, commutation of sentence, or pardon.

Executive clemency is a survival of royal prerogative and as such it formerly had no judicial aspect at all. Indeed, within not many years, I have known a Governor to issue wholesale pardons on the ground that his deceased wife wanted him to be merciful. That is exactly the kind of way that an old king would have looked at the process. At the best it was an opportunity for tempering justice with mercy, and that aspect is still left, rightly enough but subject to grave abuse. In our more enlightened States, executive clemency has come to be a last resource against possible injustice, especially where matters not within the cognizance of the trial court have come to light.

It should be borne in mind that a convicted man cannot be retried for the same offense.

THE TRIAL ITSELF

Aside from points of legal procedure which are too technical for our present concern, the guiding principle in the trial is that it shall be fair to the community and to the accused. The features most common which violate fair trial seem to be the following:

1. Browbeating and intimidating witnesses, which not only negatives fair play but makes it progressively harder to find people who are willing to testify as witnesses.

2. Probably the most serious defect in American trials, especially murder trials and the trials of prominent people, is the unrestrained license of the newspapers. The statement is entitled to some elaboration.

Liberty of the Press might here be, and sometimes probably is, a guaranty against abuse of the judicial process. Judges, prosecuting attorneys, and the police are but human, and in this imperfect world a judge himself may be even a miscreant. Armed with the power of punishing for contempt of court by summary process—a very necessary power in itself—a judge may conceivably become the worst of tyrants, unless there be some means of bringing his acts to the clear notice of public resentment. The Press as institution is the only reliance we have, or at least it is supposed to be.

And yet sensational newspapers have in recent years made the trial of important cases a scandal, in that the practice has grown up of trying such cases in the Press as well as in court. Doubtless, to most people the practice seems innocent enough, and it is made to look like an important extension of democracy. In truth it amounts to a reversion to the ways of our barbaric ancestors, among whom trial was in popular assembly where passions and prejudice could have full swing. The heart of civilized jurisprudence is in the principle that all causes be tried under circumstances in which objective fact can be ascertained, exalted above the influence of passion and ignorance, and where procedure can be controlled by men who are learned in its principles.

Beyond the exploitation of trials is the sensational newsmongering devoted to crime itself. Anybody who is at all familiar with the psychology of suggestion might well expect publicity given to crimes to stimulate more crimes of the same sort. That such is in fact the case appears from the statement which I quote from August Vollmer, himself one of the best equipped of our police chiefs:

"Again, the practices of most newspapers are exceedingly detrimental to enforcement. Their 'headline' publicity greatly increases the difficulties of the police and greatly aids the criminal. Epidemics of certain types of crime almost always follow the sensational publicity given to such crimes."[3]

INSTRUCTION

The nature of crime and of criminal processes in court is an essential element in the Curriculum of the Common School: in the first place, because it is major element in our understanding of The State; and, in the second place, because it has immediate practical importance in the training of responsible citizens. The second of the two reasons is open to disputation on the very principles which we have advocated.

It may be held that General Education is sufficient and that all this is in the nature of special training.

It is quite true that effective instruction, apart from all consideration of crime and police, may well be the best, and indeed only, guaranty that the individual himself will not become a criminal. To that extent, there is certainly no ground for dealing with the subject in specific courses. On the other hand, General Education, apart from this course or its equivalent and that which is to follow, contains no promise that the educated will be effective in the civil effort to control the criminal proclivities of those who are not educated. In other words, intelligence about the whole subject is itself part of General Education.

Our criminal record in the United States is perhaps most nearly an unanswerable challenge to the validity of our political institutions. Our people are little interested, save as a matter of annoyance or of entertainment, as the case may be. We return to our familiar maxim: Whatever is put into public instruction on

[3] August Vollmer, *The Police and Modern Society* (Berkeley: University of California Press, 1936).

a universal scale in one generation appears as a public interest and capacity in the next.

In the general field with which we are dealing, there is abundant book material, not counting current mystery stories—many of which are not without their value—but the material is not read on any large scale. The reason probably is that there has never been created a constructive interest and reading capacity. If such books as Fosdick's reports on American and European police systems had been read as generously and as competently as have popular and semipopular books in Science, for which the schools have created an interest and reading capacity, it is easy to believe that our police forces would have improved more rapidly than has been the case. Perhaps some dents would have been made in the mass of ignorant and stupid legislation.

UNITS IN CRIME

I. What Is Crime?
   1. Violation of a law prohibiting certain conduct or requiring certain action
   2. Crime is objective, and the function of legislation is to recognize and declare crime
   3. Not all criminal acts require definition by legislation; they are recognized in Common Law
   4. Law cannot make people moral; it can only define for punishment immoral acts
   5. Crime objectively is any action which invades the legal rights of others violently or by stealth, which tends toward the disruption of society, or the disorganization of the community, or contempt of The State

II. Misdemeanors
   1. Crime imports the shameful and disgraceful and disruptive
   2. A misdemeanor is properly an offense against a regulation which carries no stigma of disgrace or shame
   3. Multitudes of such regulations are necessary in a complex society
   4. Are properly dealt with by other than criminal process

III. The Accused
   1. Presumed to be innocent until proved guilty
   2. Has a right to decent and courteous treatment when arrested and kept under arrest
   3. Has a right to be informed of the specific charge at once

    4. Has a right to decline to be interrogated

    5. Has a right to counsel and to habeas corpus

    6. Has a right to a speedy trial

IV. The Prosecuting Attorney

    1. Begins where the police leave off

    2. Conducts proceedings before the courts

    3. Is concerned not with proving the accused guilty but with ascertaining the truth about guilt

    4. Must be an educated person, a trained lawyer, experienced in the law

    5. Ought to be a specialist in criminal law

V. Judicial Procedure

    1. Issues to be settled in criminal court procedure:

        a) Has a crime been committed?

        b) Did the accused commit the crime?

        c) Has the convicted man had his constitutional rights and a fair trial?

VI. In Court

    1. Right of prisoner to fair trial but no more

    2. Functions of the trial jury is to determine facts, chiefly the fact, on the evidence, of guilt or innocence

    3. Innocence does not have to be proved; guilt does

    4. Facts are disclosed by witnesses and by material exhibits

    5. In the interest of justice, witnesses are entitled to courteous treatment by lawyers on both sides

    6. Functions of the trial judge:

        a) To require order in the courtroom

        b) To preside over the examination of witnesses

        c) To determine admissibility of evidence

        d) To instruct jury in the law

        e) To sentence the accused if convicted

    7. Can be appealed to higher court on claim of violation of constitutional rights, or defects in trial procedure held to impair the accused's right to a fair trial

    8. The Government has no appeal in a criminal trial

VII. Executive Clemency

    1. Governor or President can intervene after conviction to:

        a) Reprieve the convicted man from present execution of the sentence

        b) Commute the sentence to a lighter sentence

        c) Issue outright pardon

    2. The President can act only when the crime is a Federal offense

3. Executive clemency is extended, or supposed to be extended, only when:
   a) Facts have been disclosed since the trial which, it may be presumed, would have altered the verdict
   b) The circumstances seem to show that mercy should be extended
4. In enlightened States, executive clemency is not extended as a favor
5. The Executive does not act until after full judicial procedure has been had
6. Note that an accused person cannot be tried twice for the same offense

III. POLICE

The agency upon which reliance is placed in civilized counties for protection from violent inroads upon the lives, persons, and property of individuals, from disaster, and from the harmful nuisances inflicted upon the many by the few, is called Police. Police service, therefore, goes far beyond the prevention of crime and the arrest of criminals. A study of the round of duties performed in the average American or European city, by the average city policeman, in an average month, would probably greatly astonish the investigator. He would find them extended from the detection and arrest of some malefactor, to helping ladies across the street, to driving an ambulance, to warning citizens to clear their sidewalks of snow and ice, to summoning a negligent citizen for failing to keep his alley in sanitary condition. In short, we should find the police to be what may be called the residual housekeepers of the town.

MEANING OF TERM

Fosdick quotes Blackstone's definition: "The public police and economy must be considered as the due regulation and domestic order of the kingdom, whereby the individuals of the State, like members of a well-governed family, are bound to conform to the rules of propriety, good neighborhood, and good manners."[4] In other words, the comprehensive function of the police is to constrain the negligent and the perverse into ways of *politeness*—to insist that individuals shall make themselves fit to dwell in the city, the *polis*.

[4] Raymond B. Fosdick, *European Police Systems* (New York: Century Co., 1915), p. 3.

Fosdick seems to object that the definition is wide enough to include the entire domestic policy of a nation. Hardly that perhaps, but still a good deal wider than the meaning of "police" commonly held. Blackstone's definition is what the student of Civics, Politics, Law, is obliged to see in the term. It defines the scope of the *police power* as constitutionalists use that expression.

Police and police power are thus to be distinguished from ordinary police forces as we know them. The latter are creations of just about a hundred years past, while the police function is as old as The State.

DIFFERENTIATION OF FUNCTION

The pursuit and arrest of criminals is but one of the police functions. Fire Department, Health Department, Charities and Corrections Department, all of them exercise police functions. Inspection of steam boilers, of steamships and steamboats, of buildings in respect to sanitation and structural safety, of banks and insurance companies, of mines and dikes, and many others, are police functions. In European countries the names "mining police," "insurance police," "dike police," are frequently used.

So, since the police function first came to be recognized by students and statesmen, it has greatly differentiated and is now exercised by many different forces. Even so, the process lags, especially in the United States, and sundry police activities are ripe to be placed elsewhere than in the regular police force. We shall consider two activities as illustrative.

VEHICULAR TRAFFIC CONTROL

Control of city traffic is an ancient duty of the police, was such even when the police were the old-time watch and ward. In truth our colonial cities had traffic ordinances which were singularly like what the automobile has brought forth. Parking was a problem then as now. Fast driving was an offense. Even regulation of the use of streets by trucks had a precursor in ordinances controlling the use of streets by heavy ox-drawn carts. But motor-vehicle traffic has given rise to a specialty, and one notes how often traffic control is competent beyond our comprehension in the same city in which the control of crime may be miserably inefficient.

One is a specialized police function suited to the conditions in which it operates; the other is of the constabulary. There is no proper constabulary in the length and breadth of the land, save the State Police forces—not the motor-vehicle police—and recently a developing Federal police.

CONSTABULARY

"Constable" originally implied a military function. Latterly, a constable is a civil officer who is equipped and trained to use force, either individually or in organized groups. In countries which have a better record in dealing with crime, as well as with minor offenses, than we have, the constabulary, either under that name or some equivalent, is set apart to deal with crime and that alone. For many years, for example, the English constabulary has not concerned itself with licensing dogs, or giving warnings of infractions of city ordinances, or controlling traffic. It deals with criminal offenses. The constable is a policeman, but not all policemen are constables. Policemen are empowered to make arrests and otherwise to collaborate with the constabulary, but that is not their main business, as with us.

Constabulary a State force.—Crimes are offenses against The State. Criminals do not operate within the confines of a single municipality, nor after their misdeeds are accomplished do they continue to reside at their usual domicile. Their first impulse is commonly to get out of town. Hence, the constabulary is in its nature a State force of men, trained for its work, properly a body of educated men, permanent in the sense of being career men, not identified with any locality or neighborhood. Nobody loves a cop —or else loves him altogether too well. He lives too close to neighbors whom he may have occasion to admonish—and that is not agreeable. Neglect to do so may be profitable.

We have made some progress in organizing true constabularies in our State Police, especially in Massachusetts, New York, Pennsylvania, and Texas, but they do not as yet work in cities by taking over the control of crime there as well as in the country. We have no Federal police or constabulary save with respect to Federal offenses.

Canada does much better. There is, first of all, the Royal Mounted operating throughout the Dominion, the Railway Police also operating in the national field on railroads and terminals, the Provincial Police, and finally the municipal police in various cities. Naturally, Canada has a far better record in control of crime than has the United States.

As between constabulary and general police, we may rightly draw the distinction that the latter deals characteristically with misdemeanors and the former with crime.

THE SHERIFF

Curiously enough, at a lower level on the spiral of progress, we had what was properly a constabulary in the County Sheriff.

The Sheriff was, and still is in principle, the Governor's understudy in the county. He is the executive head of the county which is not a municipal corporation but a subdivision of the State. He is head of the *posse comitatus* which was, and still is, a sort of police militia of which all able-bodied men are members and subject to the Sheriff's call to pursue criminals or quell rioting. The Sheriff could call on the Governor for the support of the organized militia, now the National Guard. So the Sheriff was in effect the high constable of the county.

The office often functioned exceedingly well in a frontier society, and in some States still does. Generally, however, it has become obsolete as constabulary with the development of State Police and with better organization of the National Guard.

The Sheriff was always also the chief officer of the court and as such executed the court's decrees, served writs, held sales of bankrupt's goods, and in general executed the laws within his jurisdiction. The function of course still abides, but the office itself has become obsolete. Today what is required is a very different kind of man than he who so often served admirably in earlier days.

THE NATIONAL GUARD

In principle, the whole power of the nation is behind the preservation of order and the execution of the laws. Able-bodied men of military ages are members of the militia, liable to be called

out to maintain the public order by the Governor who is its commander-in-chief.

In practice, however, the National Guard, which is a semi-
trained, volunteer army, organized and equipped for service, is
called wholly or in part whenever the mayor of a city or the
sheriff of a county applies to the Governor for help in maintaining
order. It will be remembered that the National Guard is also the
first line of reserves in the national army subject to the call of
the President in case of war.

THE REGULAR ARMY

Similarly, United States regulars may be dispatched to a spot
within a State, to quell rioting or repel invasion, at the call of
the Governor upon the President. The regular army could also
be sent by the President to maintain a republican form of Government in any of the States, without call of the Governor thereof.
So far as I know, that has never been done, but it must have
seemed likely in the time of the Dorr Rebellion in Rhode Island.
Cleveland sent United States troops to Chicago to defend the
transmission of the mails, against the objection of the Governor of
Illinois.

In truth, there is hardly any duty imposed upon President,
Governor, Sheriff, or Mayor, greater than his duty to maintain
order and call for the power of the State and Nation when
needed.

CRIME PREVENTION

Enlightened States give heed to crime prevention as well as to
the definition of crime and the apprehension and conviction of the
criminal. The latter can be prompt in effect, but it is negative.
The former is slow but positive and cumulative.

Practical police experience shows that certain activities, not
necessarily wrong in themselves, almost inevitably become fo-
cuses of crime and breeders of crime. Notable are organized gambling and organized liquor traffic.

Individual gambling on a small scale is rather a mark of infantile or primitive personality than a positive wrong. It is of im-

memorial antiquity and is perhaps most common among primitive or backward races. In this form, it has seldom been prohibited as a wrong. Nevertheless, when gambling becomes organized in race tracks, gambling dens, and perverted use of exchanges, it becomes a notorious breeder of all sorts of crime, as well as of misery in families and economic disaster in the Community.

The case of the saloon is familiar and notorious. The temperate use of liquors, which in excess may become intoxicating, has, it is true, sometimes been stigmatized as wrong in itself; more often it has been thought to be harmless and even salutary. But when an organized traffic grows up which panders to the appetite systematically, harm is done, not only to the individual but to the Community. The saloon thus becomes a breeder of crime, particularly civic corruption, or at least tends to do so.

So it is with dance halls and similar enterprises.

On the other hand, conduct which is wrong in itself, when organized by the growth of agencies pandering to it, at once begins to harm not only the Community but Society as well, that is to say, it disturbs the normal and healthful conditions which ought to exist in the relations of individuals. The conspicuous instance is houses of prostitution.

In dealing with this whole constructive side, not only from the standpoint of the prevention of crime, but also from that of the willing acceptance of law, large demands are made, not only upon social intelligence, but also upon social conscience. There are a great many people who become professional libertarians as soon as they see their own interests or pleasures in prospect of being assailed. The principle has often been cited that no law is effective law unless it finds support in the actual state of the mores; but the fallacy is often committed of inferring that no law is good law without such conformity. On the contrary, the growth of Law as distinguished from laws has been through the enlightenment of peoples so that the mores contains what is right in itself.

It follows that in the last analysis, the prevention of crime, as well as the efficient control of the criminal elements in the population, other things being equal, rests upon the effectiveness of family upbringing or public instruction in a country, or both. The converse follows in logic: the prevalence of crime is evidence that upbringing has fallen off and that public instruction has been ineffective.

Not only is it true that genuinely educated individuals are not criminals, but it is also true that genuinely educated people are intelligent and conscientious concerning the well-being of the Community and the health of Society. They are also intelligent about the police function in the State, although they are in no sense qualified to be policemen themselves.

UNITS IN POLICE

I. The Police Power
  1. Good community housekeeping
  2. Prevention of nuisances
  3. Warding off disaster and rescuing the victims
  4. Constraining the lawless
  5. Detection, apprehension, and conviction of criminals
  6. Prevention of crime

II. The Police Power Is Distributed among Many Agencies
  Among the agencies are fire and flood prevention and control, inspection of machinery and buildings and shipping and of various commercial enterprises, public sanitation, and many others
  The agencies with which we are chiefly concerned are the General Police, usually a city force; and the Constabulary, which is properly a State force

III. Traffic Police Is a Recent Specialized Agency
  Functionally belongs with the Highway Department, much as the inspection of banks belongs to the Treasury Department or to the State Banking Commission

IV. Constabulary Is the Force Which Specializes in the Control of Crime
  1. Constabulary deals with crime, while the General Police deal typically with misdemeanors, and with crime only in support of the constabulary
  2. Every constable is a policeman, but not all policemen are properly constables
  3. Constabulary is in principle a State and not a municipal force, for
    a) Crimes are offenses against the State
    b) Criminals are not limited in their operations or in their flight to the locale of the crime

4. State Police forces are constabulary, not to be confounded with highway patrols

5. We have no Federal constabulary save for Federal offenses

V. American Police Systems

Descriptive accounts of selected States as part of the effort to understand the police function

VI. Foreign Police Systems

Particularly those of England, France, and Italy. Same purpose as V

Note use of secret police and *agents provocateurs* in some foreign countries as practices abhorrent to our institutions

VII. Municipal Police Functionally Considered

1. Patrol for general protection

2. Correction of prohibited nuisances

3. Keeping order in crowds

4. Assistance in calamities and accidents

5. Co-operation with specialized police agencies

6. Co-operation with constabulary, where distinction is drawn, especially in detention of criminals and suppression of riots

7. Summoning misdemeamants to give an account of themselves before the proper authorities

VIII. The Sheriff

1. Chief civil executive of a county

2. Commander of the *posse comitatus*, or police militia

3. High constable of the county in apprehension of criminals and suppression of riots

4. Chief court officer for executing decrees and serving writs

5. Obsolete as constable where there is regularly organized State police

IX. The Whole Power of the State behind Law and Order

1. Duty of the Governor to call out the National Guard on the call of a mayor or a sheriff who certifies that disorder has gone beyond local control

2. Duty of the President to employ the regular army upon the call of a Governor to suppress insurrection or repel invasion

3. President may use United States troops to preserve a republican form of Government

4. United States regulars may be sent to protect the exercise of Federal functions when the latter cannot be protected by United States marshals

X. Crime Prevention

1. Breeding places of crime

2. Ways in which such places generate crime and criminals

3. Appropriate police laws
4. Suppression

XI. Citizens Have Rights before the Police
1. Not true that citizens have no rights save what The State grants
2. American civil institutions place the citizen's rights antecedent to The State
3. The Government decides what rights it will enforce and how
4. Police enforce laws and ordinances and have no right to arbitrary notice or arrest
5. Not entitled to abuse an arrested person either physically or mentally
6. Arrested person has a right to be charged. "You come along with me" or "Tell it to the judge" does not constitute a charge
7. Arrested person has a right to counsel

XII. Citizens Have Duties before the Police
1. All able-bodied men are liable to be called upon by a policeman for assistance
2. Property is at the disposal of the policeman if it is essential to the performance of his duty
3. All citizens are under obligation to "aid and comfort" policemen in the performance of their duties
4. Every citizen is under obligation to notify the police of criminal actions known to him; otherwise, he is accessory
5. Every citizen is under obligation to make the required legal charge when he has been attacked or criminally invaded

STUDY MATERIAL

Study material throughout the course is to be found in competent books dealing with the best American and foreign police systems and practices, as well as with the theory of what police everywhere ought to be. It ought, however, to be noted that outside the English-speaking countries police work is apt to be colored by the legal systems on which it rests. Not infrequently, policing in Continental countries is conducted on principles which we should think an unduly high price to pay even for freedom from crime and criminals.

NOT CRIMINOLOGY

In the recent interest in "social sciences," the tendency seems to be in some quarters to center not upon the nature of crime, and criminal law and policing the community, but upon the treatment of prisoners, upon prison administration, indeterminate sentences, parole, etc. I hold that all this is no part of the business of the Common School.

In the first place, it does not go to the heart of the problem, which is an intelligent attitude toward crime and the forces of Public Defense.

In the second place, while no educated population will knowingly tolerate abusive conditions in the prisons, the methods of dealing with prisoners are very much in an unsettled state. At the best, they are matters for lawyers and prison experts and not for youthful and amateur theorists.

In the third place, such matters, like a good many others which have found their way into the schools, are essentially adult interests with which his total General Education, as well as instruction in the Public Defense, qualify the pupil to deal when he shall have become a voting citizen, and without which he is likely as an adult to make mischief rather than contribute to wholesome civic progress.

I never heard the abuse of prisoners treated as a debatable matter. We have in other days had a sad record here as well as in the kindred fields of the treatment of the insane and of paupers. Nevertheless, it would be hard to show that such abuse ever existed on a large scale, save as the outcome of the appointment of superintendents, warders, and attendants on the principles of the spoils system, which has been the bane of all our politics for something over a hundred years.

The other side of "criminology" is the newspaper interest in lie-detectors, ballistics, fingerprints, and the like—in other words the detective-story appeal. Whether such matters have any superlative importance in professional police work, we need not inquire. They are assuredly no part of public instruction.

D. THE FAMILY

Law and the Public Defense are obviously related to The State; we hardly think of them in any other connection. They are forms in which The State has developed. In the cases of the Family, Corporation, and School, the connection is not so clear, albeit all the way back there are here and there implications that they are of The State. I hold that all three, no less than Law and Public Defense and Civil Government, are forms in which The State as major institution appears. Let us call them Civil Institutions.

I. THE FAMILY IN EVOLUTION

The Family, at least the monogamous, patronymic, stable Family, which is what we are talking about, is apparently a comparatively recent product in social evolution, belonging to the ages of rapid progress in Civilization. To be sure it had precursors which carried on a similar social function, and out of which somewhere along the line it has doubtless come down to us by a process of ideological descent with modification—patriarchal family, matrilineal family, mother family, the last being no family at all unless you are going to call mother cat and her kittens a family. As we found in our study of Religion, we have to be on our guard lest we assume a genetic connection where there is nothing more than verbal similarity. There can hardly have been Family in the sense in which we use the term, until the man had become aware that these were his children as well as hers, nor until the two parents sensed themselves as a pair set apart from other pairs in the joint parenthood of the children, in other words, not until the establishment of stable marriage in which the father was on an equal footing with the mother.

The last statement may seem strange is this day of the emancipation of women, but the fact is that the father has been the inferior member of the pair for a good many thousand years more than has the woman. Among our Indians in their natural state, for instance, the husband was commonly taken to the house of the bride, and, in John Fiske's phrase, "she could send him packing when she got tired of him." We are not told that she could imprison him for nonpayment of alimony.

KINDRED

It seems tolerably clear that much of what has been attributed to the Family in social genesis belongs rather to the Kindred.

That is especially true of legal conceptions, and more broadly of political conceptions where descent of rule is in the picture. Throughout the primitive world, and well down into historic times, kinship does not necessarily signify blood relationship. It signifies some form of totemistic relationship as well, and later on all who have come to dwell together. All along is the obvious mother relationship, but even that relationship is not necessarily uterine. Frequently, foster-children are on terms of blood relationship because they have partaken of the foster-mother's milk. Beyond that is adoption—not only of children, but also of brothers, and husbands, adopted but not married, to take the place of their predecessors slain in battle. In short, in the long history of Civilization, kinship has not meant what it does in the close family systems of enlightened peoples.

AS CIVIL INSTITUTION

Why, then, is Family to be called civil institution, institutional constituent of The State?

In the first place, because we can see historically that, when we begin to find strong Civil States, we always begin to find strong family systems, and usually the stronger the family system the stronger the State as a going concern.

In the second place, wherever we find Civil States which have been strong, and then have weakened as social forces, we are apt to find associated with the process of weakening the decadence of national family system—fathers who either cannot or will not govern, women who are unable to or refuse to nurse their children, slave- or servant-reared children, easy divorce, infidelity without divorce.

And we can see how it is.

In the normal patronymic family there is discipline and upbringing of children founded on natural affection and on concern for the well-being of the children. That is the ideological pattern of the *res publica*, the Republic, sovereignty applied in the interest of the governed, so much so that the Christian conception of God follows the pattern.

FAMILY AS COMMUNITY

So much for Family as civil institution. The Family is also primary Community; and as such it is the only instance of normal, natural, communism which has persisted down through the ages, and which has until recently been one of the chief factors in economic stability.

When a family is strong in affection, manifests family pride, and counts its kindred of the blood out to a reasonable degree of consanguinity, then the members have somewhat the same kind of insurance against adversity of all sorts as can be found in other situations in regular insurance companies. A nation made up in the main of such families automatically tends to enter upon periods of hard times with what amounts to consolidated savings accounts. The united influence of a family connection in the encouragement of those of its members who have fallen into discouragement is strong. Attempts to find a substitute for the Family, through doles or relief, or through converting a State into a sort of industrial manor, have thus far failed.

Again, the Family as institution makes for social stability, because it tempers wholesome individuality with collective restraint. It is a matter of common observation that where strong families are the prevailing type, there is hardly any influence, certainly not the laws, which exercises such restraint on debauchery of all sorts, as does the fear of disgracing loved and respected parents and betraying family pride.

Finally, we sometimes have occasion to observe the fate of aged people who are left alone in the world, and who have become incapable of managing their own affairs. It is rather astonishing at such times to find how difficult it is to set the machinery of Government at work for protection and relief, for the sheer reason that there remains no person who is likely to take the initiative.

The Family is then the normal primary factor in security within the Community—and the Corporation is the second. Age after age, people ignore and weaken the Family, and are then forced to fall back on the Government—never yet with abiding success. They attempt to make an institution in the great fabric of Civilization do work for which it was not evolved. I believe that surgeons can sometimes induce the intestine to take over the work of a diseased stomach, but it must be a makeshift business. You cannot do even that in Society; you cannot teach Civil Government to do the work of the Family and other institutions, because "times are changing." If the social order has broken down, the institutions which constitute the art of living together in the Community must be restored to folkways, customs, mores.

Both as civil institution and as primary community, the Family is an element in the Curriculum of the Common School.

II. MARRIAGE

Books which by their titles lead us to suppose that they deal with the Family in most cases deal rather with Marriage and with the Home in its economic aspects.

Marriage is no doubt intimately bound up with the Family, but it is nevertheless a different institution, long antedating the Family, grown up to deal with a different relationship. There might conceivably be a good family in all the substance of the Family without any marriage at all, but it is not the normal condition. Nor is marriage any guaranty that a good family will be the outcome. Nevertheless, no civilized State could afford to sanction families in which children were being born out of wedlock.

Among the more fundamental sources of social disruption all along has been the organic relation of the sexes. Marriage has evolved as adjustment in the problem. It is rather legal, civil or canonical, than familial institution. It is essential to sound family life because the latter requires stability in the relations of husband and wife.

Marriage is also religious and sacramental in its nature, and its history from early Roman times to this day shows that in proportion as it takes on the character of a civil contract the looseness of the tie increases. In other words, whatever tends to make the parties feel sanctity in their relations tends to make them take for granted that individual whims must be submerged. If they could feel that without any ceremony at all, the substance of Marriage would be present, but nobody ever knows that he does sense the sanctity. If the feeling is that they have merely entered upon a civil contract, enforceable by law, they soon find that that is one of the things the law cannot enforce. Legal marriage becomes easy, and legal divorce in the end just as easy.

Hence it is that, among the numerous social maladjustments which followed the disruption of the Church in the sixteenth century, one of the most unfortunate was the disappearance of most of the canonical law. The marriage ceremony ultimately degenerates into a mere wedding, with spectacular accompaniments, and only the ghost of a feeling of sanctity about it.

Is Marriage then properly a subject of instruction in the Common School? I believe not.

We have certainly accumulated a sufficiency of sociological fact-finding in relation to divorce and broken families. There is for the most part but one conclusion to be drawn: in all but a negligible proportion of cases, failure of marriage is due to personal inadequacy in one or both the spouses. To give instruction aimed at the comprehensive cause would be to carry out the whole curriculum aimed at General Education. People who meet the wear and tear of married life, and keep happy in the process, are people who have *become personally capable* of devotion and of forgetting self. They did not take courses in happy marriages and collect credit for them.

Sex education.—In this connection, the question of "sex education" so called will not down. Periodically, newspaper campaigners, uplifters, people with axes to grind—but seldom school people—demand definite programs of this sort in the schools.

We have already met the matter of sex and generation in our chapter on Science.[5] When we pass over into the field of human sex, we come into a region of intimacies which people of Taste will avoid. The sensible and competent teacher and schoolmaster have usually countered the urge to "include sex education" with the plea that, knowing children, young people, and schools, they are well assured that the program will do more harm than good.

[5] See above, p. 170.

Older people sometimes wish that there might be laws effectively enforced which would prevent young people from making hash of their lives through imprudent, romantic, passionate, marriages; but such elders know that no laws have yet been devised for the purpose which do not do more harm than good. So with pedagogical embarkation on the problems of human sex.

Much of the more respectable part of the demand comes in the last analysis from people who wish to shoulder off on the schools matters which in their nature are matters of parental advice, admonition, and control; or else of professional advice in medical men; or pastoral guidance; or finally of suppression of centers of corruption by the police. But the school is concerned with General Education and nothing else. In its instruction of pupils, it has to do with the meaning of sex in biology, and with *respect for sex* as part of its program of character-building. That is its part. It can best accomplish its contribution to the general result by playing its part well, and declining to take over the duties of parents, clergymen, and medical men, or of legislators and police.

THE HOME

The other side of writings on the Family which neglect the essentials is the Home. Now, Home is undoubtedly a familial institution, at least the natural home is, but Home is not Family.

Ever since the period of which "enrichment of the program" was perhaps the most characteristic description, instruction in the general domain of the Home has been common and extensive. Courses variously known as "Home Economics," "Household Arts," "Domestic Science," have appeared nearly everywhere. They have singularly well responded to our cult of the practical and to our casualness wherever matters of principle are involved. No doubt the effect of such courses has on the whole been salutary. So might much else have been. If we were to include everything in the Curriculum that can demonstrate particular value, we might keep individuals in school a lifetime, and even then they would miss education altogether. Are the courses defensible as integral parts of a defensible Curriculum?

The practical-arts side of the program in instruction dealing with the Home is usually limited to cooking, sewing, and dressmaking, with correlated instruction in nutrition, dietaries, and textiles in the best schools. This part is either special vocational training or else instruction in what the individual pupils ought to find for themselves. If it is not vocational training, it is taking over some of the duties of the families and transferring them to the schools. Nobody can reasonably claim that girls who have become soundly and adequately educated are incapable of learning to cook, sew, or carry on any of the household arts, in so far as there are any such arts left to be carried on. Broadly educated girls do just that as young housekeepers.

No doubt, courses in the aesthetic side of homemaking are capable of adding something to the Taste of pupils, but they can do so only as particularized instruction, which is out of place anywhere in the Common School. The girl who has had the instruction in Art which all pupils in principle ought to have can scarcely be said to require special instruction before she initiates herself into consideration of designs in wallpaper and dress goods.

There is no such thing as "Domestic Science," if the term means at its simplest a body of organized knowledge. What enters into that designation are fragments of knowledge found in Chemistry, Economics, and Physiology, largely. If the term means only various sciences in particular applications in the Home, then the applications are no different from other applications. We cannot give separate courses for each of the applications of the several sciences.

At the inception of instruction in household arts, one of the purposes rightly urged rested on the fact that homemakers in whole countrysides and sections of cities were often as classes devoid of capacity in the simple practical household arts. Hence, a social purpose was urged and justified. But that purpose was one in the field of Charities and Corrections and Public Health and not one in Public Instruction. If existing schools were used as instruments of instruction because they were ready and available and nothing else was, then the sensible and practical thing was to use them;

but that did not justify this field of instruction as belonging in principle to the Curriculum.

In making the list of units which are suggested below, I have tried to be governed by the principle of factual inquiry into the course of human experience which has produced the stable, monogamous, patronymic Family as we know it, and especially by the history of the laws of domestic relations.

UNITS IN THE FAMILY

I. Who Constitute Family?
   1. Parents and Children, the "immediate family"
   2. Ascendants living and dead
   3. Kindred on both sides
      (Of course the kindred fade out until well-nigh a whole nation may be composed of individuals who are remotely related. Let us say kindred up to the second degree. The prime essential is that all children shall be made aware of their kin.)
   4. Servants
      (Anciently, family included all connected with the household or even with the estate. Save where the folkway of outside help has grown up and help has become merely a part of the wage-earning class, the servant in the house is in fact a member of the family, sharing in its fortunes and feeling for its credit. Much of the ethics and indeed sociology of the servant question is bound up in this relationship.)

II. Government in the Family
   1. Head as leader, ruler, and guide
   2. A peaceful and happy group of any kind requires a head
   3. The civilized head of a family is not an autocrat
   4. The natural head of the family is the father of the children and not the oldest living male or female
   5. In the full civilized family the headship is in partnership between parents: but in civil and community relationships there has to be undivided authority

III. Place of Children
   1. Infancy and minority
   2. Rights of children
      a) To be well born
      b) To be well nourished and clothed

  c) To be kept healthy
  d) To be well brought up
 3. Rights are against the parents and not against the Community
 4. Peculiar place of eldest son
  a) Because he is oldest, he has special obligation in setting good example
  b) Is apt to be the strongest of the children because he has had more time to grow
  c) Obligation to take the place of the father in event of death or incapacity, so far as may be

IV. Family as an Economic Unit
 1. Normal income is family income
 2. Parents assume that condition when they marry
 3. Children's income is family income—spending money is a gift
 4. The family budget:
  a) Means that the family shall not spend more than it receives
  b) Rainy-day fund
  c) Provision for the future
  d) Intelligent allocation of principal expenses
 5. Presumptive responsibility of children for parents in old age
 6. Responsibility for kindred at least prior to charity

V. Descent of Property
 1. Descent of property from parents to children essential to strong family system
 2. Hence there is an element of Patriotism in it
 3. Common rules of descent in American commonwealths
 4. Testament
 5. Intestacy and consequences

VI. The Family and the Community
 1. A strong and prosperous community, city, or nation, depends on strong and wholesome families
 2. General prosperity depends on thrift and resource in the families
 3. Strong and capable families are principal resource in hard times
 4. A community can never be better than its families

VII. The Family and the State
 1. Law and order start in the family
 2 Good citizens are bred primarily in families
 3. Democracies especially depend on the natural government that is found in good families

VIII. The Home
 1. The home is essentially common dwelling and common table
 2. Good home is first of all an ordered home

3 The mother is naturally the housekeeper and homemaker
4. She is also primary teacher
5. She cannot successfully delegate her duties
6. She is therefore head of the home
7. Home implies:
    a) A dwelling-place and grounds in which a family can be separate from other families
    b) Sanitary conditions and surroundings
    c) Appropriateness in rooms and furniture
    d) Privacy for individuals in the family

NOTE ON TEACHING

In teaching, the problem in the course is double. In most of the units there is the twofold objective: understanding, in which the pupil comes to see the Family in its structure and social relations; and sense of value, in which he comes to feel the oughtness of those relations.

E. THE CORPORATION

The word "corporation" has a sinister sound in American ears, not so much so as formerly, but still the institution is under suspicion. A generation ago most people seemed to think that it was a new and sinister device, invented about 1880, to further the designs of those who were bent on making the "rich richer and the poor poorer." A good many of our leaders, whose sincerity and patriotism were surpassed only by their ignorance, were devoted to that belief and did what they could to keep it alive.

And yet everybody who cherished such beliefs, if he lived in an organized village or city, had been living in a corporation all his days. He probably kept his checking account, and very likely his savings, in the hands of a corporation; and so with his insurance policy. Very possibly he attended an incorporated church. He certainly traveled on an incorporated railway.

In truth, the Corporation in its early stages is almost as ancient as the Family which we have been studying. It apparently originated in the Kindred, which, as we have seen, was so close to the Family that the two are frequently confused. Legal corporation, or incorporation, existed among the Romans rather early in republican days, and all down through the Empire and the Middle Ages corporations were singularly like the organization with which we are familiar. Prior to that, at least in the Aryan line of descent, were joint family and house and village communities, and later the patriarchal family or clan. Judge Baldwin showed that the Roman legal corporation probably took over from the old Roman patriarchal family.[6] All these have, not a more vital meaning than the parent-children family in ordered society, but a similar and broader meaning. It amounts to this: How do you get the Community organized as a going concern? Answer: first as a system of families; second, as system of corporations. The product in adjustment in both instances has been one which led toward better order, collective security, the use of collective resources in the production and distribution of wealth, and the use of collective resources in furthering the great social functions in community not connected with the production and distribution of wealth.

Neither Queen Elizabeth nor J. Pierpont Morgan invented the corporation as a device. It was in the world already as institution.

DEFINITION

Any group of individuals organized together for the purpose of pursuing a common interest is a corporation. Thus a corporation is fundamentally a normal product in social evolution, a way of doing things together.

But we usually mean a legally endowed corporation, or, more properly, incorporation. Any such group is incorporated by act of the sovereign giving it a charter. The fateful words are in substance these: "A, B, C, M, and Z shall be a *body corporate and politic with power to sue and be sued.*" The act of incorporation is the charter, and the charter is a statute or else owes its origin to a statute covering all similar cases. There is thus defined a legal entity; that entity is made responsible in law and is given the power to protect itself collectively instead of as a group of individuals. There are also certain privileges in an industrial or com-

[6] Simeon E. Baldwin, *Modern Political Institutions* (Boston: Little, Brown & Co., 1898).

mercial corporation, the chief of which is the principle that the corporators are made liable for the debts of the corporation only to the extent of their individual investments, whereas in an unincorporated partnership each is liable for the whole debt of the firm. Certain corporations, such as railways and telephone companies, are sometimes endowed with the use of eminent domain.

It is worth noting that there are always two good reasons for incorporating a group, or at least should be:

First, that an enterprise useful in the community may be set up and made legally effective.

Second, that a group actually organized and acting may be made legally responsible for its acts.

It ought further to be borne in mind that a corporation is in existence, either actually or potentially, before it is incorporated, that the corporate entity is antecedent to law as an *organized group*, that the law does not make corporation out of something that is not corporation already.

Here are two terms, "corporation" and "incorporation." One exists naturally and the other exists legally as well. The correct term for the latter is "incorporation." However, popular phraseology does not distinguish; "corporation" commonly means the chartered legal entity. So that is the usage which we shall follow.

GOVERNMENT OF THE CORPORATION

When the charter defines a body of men as *a body politic*, it means that they are endowed with power to set up a government for themselves which shall be binding upon the corporators and their successors. The government appears in ordinances and by-laws, and it is administered by elective officers.

Now, the government of a corporation follows the simplest and most natural form of all government. It is a group of leaders whom the corporators will follow by giving them their confidence, and a leader whom the leaders will similarly follow. The commons are the stockholders, or the voters in a city; the leaders are the board of directors; the leader is the president or chairman or manager elected by the board of directors. That is the type of government followed the world over, where *administrative efficiency* is the value chiefly desired.

THE MUNICIPAL CORPORATION

It is well, perhaps, to study the municipal corporation somewhat closely, both as type of corporations and in place of treating it as part of Civil Government, which it is not, in the next chapter.

A GROUP OF PEOPLE IN COMMUNAL RELATIONS

Let us imagine a group of civilized people coming together in pursuit of a livelihood and of life. It will usually be in response to geographical conditions. They will soon find that there is much that must be done in common. The individual enterprisers— farmers, craftsmen, traders, professional men, and the like—can be depended upon to supply all the needs which appear as food, clothing, and shelter; legal and medical care; very probably recreation, and, of course, many others. But there are certain necessities which cannot be left to individual initiative. Among these are policing, streets, water supply and drainage, protection from fires, sanitation, maybe the provision of markets. Of course, the first consideration is schooling the younger generation, but more of that in the next section.

CHARTER

If these people were actually in a new country far from any established State, and the territory upon which they were settled was not within the sovereignty of any State, then a State would begin to develop. But we assume that the community is within the boundaries of a civilized country. One of the first undertakings will then be to secure from the State a charter in order (*a*) that they may exist under law and order in their own community concerns; (*b*) that they may lay taxes for community purposes; (*c*) that they may enter into business relations as community; (*d*) that they may enact ordinances for the local government of the community.

Either under a special act of the State Legislature or under the general law of municipal corporations, the charter will be granted. Very probably it will recite that all qualified voters in a certain territory shall be "a body politic and corporate with power to sue and be sued." Those are the words which define any legal corporation. Various powers and obligations will be cited in the charter, varying in complexity and extent from the simple community which we have imagined to New York City. As a body politic, the city has power to enact ordinances and tax itself for municipal purposes.

GOVERNMENT

The government of the municipality is probably specified in the charter, or else the citizens are empowered to draft their own framework, subject to approval by the State which grants the charter.

The valid framework, that is to say, the frame which makes normal and right government a possibility, is not whatever the citizens desire or think they do and the Legislature enacts. The Legislature can make laws, but it cannot make Law. The form of government in most American cities is not that of a municipal corporation which the city is but rather that of a State which the city is not.

Our State and Federal Governments are what they are because they belong to sovereign States. They make laws, levy or authorize taxes, conduct the Public Defense in both of its forms, declare war, administer justice, create corporations, and do all that the sovereign is required to do.

The municipality does none of these things, save lay taxes for its own legitimate purposes. It is concerned not with great matters but with local housekeeping and that alone. It does not govern its own population, but it does govern their municipal relations through its ordinances. In all civil matters whatsoever the population is under the Government of the State as truly as if there were no city at all.

All this being true, the normal form of the government is that normal to corporations the world over, and which we have already discussed. Those enlightened cities which use the city-manager form so called, and stick to it because they know it in principle to be right, conform to corporative principle.

The State which has fallen into the hands of corruptionists and rascals can be rescued only at election. The administration thus constituted can legally be ousted only by the very uncertain process of impeachment. The State cannot sue itself, nor can the individual sue the State, save with its own consent.

But the officers of any corporation, or the corporation itself, can be sued for malfeasance. Nearly all that a city government has to do is in its nature subject to review by the courts. In principle, a city is as subject to the appointment of a receiver as is a bank. In other countries a bankrupt or corrupt and incompetent city—not necessarily city government—can be and sometimes is taken over summarily by the sovereign or its representatives. Something like that has sometimes been tentatively done in America, notably a recent instance in which Massachusetts took away control over its own affairs from a bankrupt city. In truth, the one thing, apart from ordinary human depravity, which has tended to make our cities our chief reproach, is the delusion that a city is in some sense a sovereignty. Such it is not, but only a corporation set up for a particular community purpose. It is not, as I have heard it called, a "little republic." It exists only to provide for good streets, water supply, drainage, street lighting, sanitation, and a variety of similar housekeeping needs. When the citizen is taxed for these and does not get them, he is merely swindled—even though a majority of his neighbors did the swindling.

COMMERCIAL AND INDUSTRIAL CORPORATIONS

The municipal corporation has a particular place in the nation. One has only to reflect, and ask himself the question, "What would America, or indeed any other country which operates under the Anglican system of law, be without the organized village and city?" The answer might well be, "There would have to be something else just like them." And yet there was no need for more than a very few cities over a large part of our country, let us say, seventy-five years ago. State Government was as necessary then as now, and the citizen met his Government mainly through the civil division known as the county. Community needs as distinguished from civil needs were so simple that they could be and were met by voluntary organizations without any sanction of charters, and by free individual enterprisers in commerce and industry.

The cities multiplied because the inevitable social movement toward greater and greater complexity, as progress in the Great Escapes went on, made them increase. No doubt, in the raw nineteenth century, as a nation was coming to maturity on hitherto unsettled land, cities were under artificial stimulation. No doubt, further, that the record of our city government is not a thing to be proud of. Nevertheless, the cities would have multiplied anyway, even if there had never been a protective tariff; and the way to manage a city is to begin by understanding the city as corporation.

The commercial and industrial corporation is just as truly a product of social progress, and a factor in social progress, as is the incorporated municipality. It might have been artificially prevented, just as it was artificially stimulated. But in any case it would have come back in the inexorable march of social evolution, even if it had been forgotten for a thousand years.

Just as the municipal corporation is the normal way of organizing the local community, in order to meet some community needs, so is the joint-stock company the normal way of meeting certain other community needs. Let us see in broad lines how and why.

1. The first answer is the one commonly given.

The individual-enterpriser system, made up of craftsmen, factory-owners, merchant-traders, could never produce goods and services enough to go round, save on a low standard of living and in a community in which there was a large element of subsistence farming as a way of life. The reason was in the principle that the age-old co-operation in effort could not be achieved on a sufficiently broad scale. The industrial and commercial corporation was the response.

2. One of the forms which co-operation took was the consolida-

tion of the savings of many thousands of individuals, in a money and credit economy in which that was possible, to form the working capital in a joint effort, while it remained possible for the individuals in the joint stock to continue to pursue their individual careers—on the farm, in the professions, as public servants, as lingering individual enterprisers, often as employees. Moreover, it became possible for co-operation itself to distribute national income, or tend to do so, through normal economic return in dividends.

In principle that should, and in effect to some extent actually does, distribute ownership of the means of production in a normal and natural manner. The ownership of stock is constantly being diffused among the people. If there were space available, it could be shown how that process, in the long run, is inevitable when thrift is at a high level. So far from it being true that the bulk of ownership in the country is consolidated in a few families, it is distributed as it probably never has been before, save in very simple communities. The management of one of our greatest corporations, which by the way operates a natural monopoly, is fond of announcing that less than 1 per cent of its outstanding stock is in the hands of any one person. The time is in sight, if the normal processes come to be understood and obeyed, when the ownership of the enterprises of production and distribution will be in the hands of the people—but not in the hands of The State, even theoretically—acquired as any other property, a suit of clothes for instance, is acquired.

3. The Corporation as institution is a means of distributing risk, one of the critical elements in social progress, or rather making distribution possible.

One of the ways in which people can often be persuaded to distribute risk is by means of what is held out to them as collective security through what looks like a State, but is in reality a colossal industrial manor. No such thing gets set up until some individual or group seize the reins of arbitrary power. The risk is absolute. A mistaken policy at the capital will bring the whole community down in collapse. The eggs are all in one basket.

The opposite extreme is in the individual-enterpriser system in which the primary risk can be distributed over the whole producing and merchandising community of individuals. There the risk is distributed beyond likelihood of complete collapse. To paraphrase a well-remembered statement, "You cannot sink a raft, but your feet will be wet all the time." The wet feet consist in periodic depressions which cannot be avoided. The premiums on the risk-bearing are in high profits on each unit produced, for profit is in its nature risk-bearing. The premiums so to speak are so high that there can be little real distribution of wealth.

The corporation, on the other hand, *can* distribute risks at a much lower premium in profits per unit produced and sold. Nor can the risk be absolute where there are many corporations with stock widely distributed among an economically intelligent population. Whether a given corporation acts that way or not depends upon the intelligence, social conscience, and mercantile statesmanship of the management.

All the foregoing is, of course, the merest sketch, and for the economic mechanisms at work we shall have to wait until chapters xii and xiii.

Academic Corporations

One of the earliest types of corporation is the University, once described as "a company of scholars." The function of the University, since long before there were any universities, is the recruitment and conservation of the professions, the pursuit of culture for its own sake, and the discovery of new truth.

In modern times in America, the University has come to be so mixed with the School, quite a different kind of institution, that the true place of the University in the Community is lost to view —with, as I believe, much the same kind of disastrous effect on university government and use as appears elsewhere when the municipality has the form of a State, in spite of the fact that it is Corporation and nothing else.

On the other hand, the School, as we shall see presently, is in its nature not a corporation, but rather a part of Government. And yet we find the curious paradox that the public-school district in the United States is in law a corporation, while the University which is Corporation in its social function is more and more in much the same relation to the State as an established church.

LABOR UNIONS

The modern labor union has had precursors all the way down the ages, wherever free labor under employment in large groups of individuals could maintain itself in competition with slave labor. Since the coming-in of modern industrial organization, labor unions have multiplied beyond all knowledge, become enlarged and expanded in scope. There is exactly the same accounting as in the cases of the municipality and the business corporation. Here was a function which had to get performed, so long as labor was not slave labor, on the one hand, nor in the master-and-servant relation, on the other, the function, namely, of collective bargaining in wage agreements, and conservation of appropriate working conditions. The Union is actually, if not part of the order of nature, at least part of the order of Society, where large employers have appeared and especially the impersonal employer found in the industrial corporation.

Now, one of the two vital things contained in any incorporation is the phrase, "with power to sue and be sued." It is that which puts the corporation into The State and makes it part of the law and order which is the Civil State. The labor union is the prime illustration of those things which are corporations and yet not incorporations. In effect, it therefore stands outside the order and logic of things. It ought to desire to come in and become legally responsible. If it does not so desire, it should be made. Doubtless, in due time incorporation will be the accepted order of things.

THE CORPORATION AS CIVIL INSTITUTION

We have thus far been dealing with the subject as a study in community organization; but properly understood, the Corporation is more. It is Civil in its nature, that is to say, like Law, Family, and Government, it is part of the constituency of The State. The sovereign cannot produce nor distribute, keep the community house, nor act as the custodian of Civilization. But the sovereign through its constraint and repression can make all these things possible in orderly form, can make them all part of the "establishment of justice" and "provision for the general welfare." None of the Community functions can go forward in a great Commonwealth and in a complex Society, apart from integration. Head dominance in the social organism is in The State, and The State in action is chiefly the Government. Let those who govern, wait on governing; they will have their hands full.

UNITS IN THE CORPORATION

I. Corporation
  1. A group of persons who have become organized for a common purpose, such as:
      a) Regulation of public affairs, as a village or city
      b) Production of goods or services or both, as a manufacturing or railway company
      c) Distribution of goods or services or both, as a mercantile or servicing company
      d) Conservation and transmission of learning, as university, a company of scholars
  2. An incorporation is a corporation recognized by law but the law does not make a corporation
      Nearly all of what we call corporations are really incorporations, that is to say, natural corporations which have been recognized and given charters in law.
  3. By incorporation the corporation acquires certain legal powers, and is held to certain legally recognized duties
  4. It thus becomes in law perpetual, that is, its life is presumed to extend beyond the life of an individual; may hold property; can sue and may be sued; in short, acquires certain rights which The State will defend, and certain duties which The State will enforce.
  5. The instrument of incorporation is the charter

II. Corporation Is Institution
  1. The Corporation evolved and was not invented
  2. It has social meaning and function and does not exist for individual benefit
  3. Business corporation is only a particular instance of the Corporation
  4. It is one of the two chief institutions in which the Community becomes organized, the other being the Family

III. Organization of the Corporation
  1. The natural organization of the corporation is:
      a) A body of corporators, indwellers in the city, owners, scholars, craftsmen

      b) A small group of leaders, council, board of directors, faculty, trustees

      c) A single leader, or head, or executive

      d) Normally, corporators elect directors, and directors choose the executive

      e) The Executive appoints, subject to confirmation, minor officials and employees

   2. A corporation organized in any other form seldom works well

IV. The Municipal Corporation

    (City or incorporated village—might be any larger area which forms a true local community)

   1. A natural product which arises when a local community becomes so large and so complex that certain *social* functions cannot get performed either through The State or by individual enterprisers

   2. The municipality is concerned almost entirely with local community housekeeping—an evolution of the Home

      a) Well-being of indwellers

      b) Administration of community business

      c) Fire protection and similar defenses

      d) Regulation of building codes, zones, and markets

      e) Sanitation

      f) Police but not constabulary

   3. Municipality has no civil functions, i.e., functions which in their nature belong to The State

   4. Chief of the civil functions which are erroneously placed in the muncipality are

      a) Control of crime

      b) Maintenance of public instruction

V. Municipal Government

   1. Normally, takes the form of the Corporation and not of Civil Government, that is, State Government

   2. Normal form is

      a) Council elected by the people of the municipality

      b) Manager elected by the Council, and removable by the Council

      c) Subordinate officers and employees appointed from civil service by the Manager

   3. Elective mayor and city legislature imitates the State, whereas the city has no civil functions

   4. City Council makes ordinances but no laws

      a) Ordinances must conform to law

      b) Must not violate the constitutional rights of indwellers as citizens

VI. Commercial and Industrial Corporations
  1. Incorporated to perform social functions in production and distribution
  2. Not primarily to make money for owners
  3. Earnings on labor, management, use of capital, and liquidation of risk, are involved in social nature of corporations
  4. Corporate organization is inevitable where individual enterprisers cannot produce enough to go round at a price which makes possible distribution
  5. Ownership in corporations tends to become more and more widely diffused
  6. Resources of more individuals become consolidated

VII. Corporate Responsibility
  1. A legal corporation is an artificial person having power to sue and be sued
  2. The Corporation is a product in social evolution, and therefore every corporation is affected with a public interest
  3. But corporations are managed by fallible men
  4. Hence corporation law
    a) Corporations are governed by law under the power to sue and be sued
    b) They are not conducted by the Government
    c) Every corporation takes its powers and duties from its charter, or act of incorporation, and it has no other powers and duties
    d) But its managers are punishable for malfeasance as individuals
  5. Every group of individuals, not a family, which acts socially in production, distribution, or regulation, is a corporation, whether legally recognized or not
  6. Law and order in the Community require that every such corporation be incorporated, made legally responsible, and endowed with legal powers

F. THE SCHOOL

This whole work, as well as most works which deal with what the public calls educational subjects, is concerned with instruction as a phase of the social function of reproduction and transmission. That function is normally carried on by the Family and the School. The School is therefore vital as part of the apparatus of social existence. The subject matter of transmission is Civilization.

The immediate and practical importance of including the

School as an element in the Curriculum of the Common School is found in the principle that the School is an instrument to be used; it does not operate of itself and of its own motion. Hence, some critical intelligence as to what the School is and what are its functions must be in the mores if Civilization is to be transmitted at all, rather than be left to the ups and downs of the survival process. The School can be left to the specialists alone with even less confidence than can most other public concerns.

In order to see how needful such enlightenment is, we have only to consider prevailing public attitude toward schools. Let it be remembered, for instance, that the color of the Greek and Roman slave systems still gives to the word "pedagogy" much of its connotation, and pedagogy is the theory and practice of teaching; and that, when all is said and done, in the minds of many if not most people, teachers are essentially nursemaids, or at best governesses, charged with the care of children in order that the latter may be out of the way at home—save when the teacher vote is needed and then teachers become "pillars of society." People persistently confuse education and instruction and both with schools—a confusion which is fatal to all educational thinking. With us, it is commonly taken for granted that, where a schoolhouse is open and somebody called a teacher is in charge, education must be going on. Moreover, the better the schoolhouse the better is thought to be the education. The confusion is so widespread that publicists, preachers, current essayists sometimes, remark on the failure of education as a social force and on "our great American fetish of education," when what they really have in mind is the failure of instruction and of schools to generate education.

Manifestly it is disastrous that there should be abroad so much ignorance, or at least loose thinking, touching the essential nature of educational processes, of instruction, of the social meaning of the School. If there were no other good reason for including the School as a subject in the Curriculum, then the practical need would justify its inclusion. But there is more fundamental reason, the same, namely, which we have found in the cases of all other justifiable subjects. The School is institutional part of the working fabric of Civilization.

INSTITUTIONAL EVOLUTION

That the School is institutional in its nature can on its history hardly be doubted, if we bear in mind that the essence of the School is present whenever there is organized effort, outside the Family, looking toward the instruction of the rising generation. The instruction may be meager, there may be no written curriculum at all, no schoolhouse or regular meeting place, no defensible theory and practice of teaching; and yet, even in tribal times, the common sense of people tells them that, if things are to go on, tradition, custom, folkways, must be transmitted. Initiation and ordeal are in the nature of public instruction, since they require anticipation and preparation. There is something singularly like degree-taking in the young savage's attaining success in conflict before he is admitted to full fellowship with the men and to favor with the contemporary girls.

As institution, the School has followed the normal life-history; it has become organized, has expanded, become refined, and, in the minds of thoughtful people, it is seen to be the ultimate instrument in the perpetuation and extension of the art of living together as ordered society.

CIVIL INSTITUTION

Not so often is the School seen to be a veritable part of The State, although we shall presently see that our whole tax-supported public-school system rests upon the fact that the reasoning of our courts has led to that conclusion.

Organized schools go far back into history. Indeed, Egyptologists tell us that an important historical source for them is in the pupils' notebooks which occasionally turn up. But, so far as we can make out, down until modern times, the schools were not understood as having a critical social significance. They were for individuals as such, and typically vocational. One sometimes suspects that some of the Roman emperors may have been impressed with the civil nature of the School; but, if they were, it never came to anything, more that what we should call today State aid. The efforts of Charlemagne have often been urged as a premonition of what was to come, eight hundred years later, in our modern State school systems, but I cannot see that there was anything more in mind than the hope of securing an educated priesthood and bureaucracy. We find chantry and cathedral schools in the Middle Ages, half school and half university, but it is hard to see anything of a social nature in them beyond finding likely poor boys and giving them a chance, and in general finding recruitment for the offices of the Church. Certainly, the gentry and nobility of those days were not keen and thirsting for education.

When we come down to the Reformation, however, a change becomes manifest. In the Calvinist and Lutheran phases at least, the individual man was lifted into a place of terrible responsibility. No use to open the Bible to an illiterate laity, however; and, as soon as you teach people to read, you will presently have to show them how to use that liberal art. Whatever may have been the conscious intentions of the reformers, the whole movement was headed toward popular sovereignty; and popular sovereignty is rule of the mob unless the enlightenment which goes with general education is spread abroad in the land, to say nothing of self-discipline.

I suppose that it can safely be said that the organic foundations of the American public-school system have their concrete origin in the Massachusetts Act of 1642, in which it was ordered that local officers should see to it that "the children can read and understand the principles of religion and the capital laws of the country, and that they are put to some useful work." In a revision, a few years later, a preamble recited, "For inasmuch as the good education of children is of singular behoof and benefit to any commonwealth. . . . ."[7] At least, the act was motivated by a conception that the Commonwealth (bear in mind that Massachu-

[7] George H. Martin, *Evolution of the Massachusetts Public School System* (New York: Appleton & Co., 1908).

setts is not a State in our American use of terms) was deeply concerned in public instruction. The Act itself came close to a declaration that the School is Civil Institution.

IN THE EYE OF THE LAW

In our country the motive of universal schooling has prevailed greatly, but chiefly because it has been assimilated as conferring individual opportunity. Universal schooling means tax-supported schools, and the taxpayer in self-defense has always challenged every departure that spelled more taxes. Moreover, universal tax-supported schooling imports civil control of instruction. That total situation has led to judicial interpretation of the logic thus set up, if there be any logic. There could be but one such interpretation, namely, that schools exists for the defense of an enlightened State from the menace of an ignorant electorate, and for the well-being of the Community. We may take it that, so far as American law goes, it is a well-settled principle that the School is Civil Institution.

Of all the multitudes of court decisions which there are, all of them tending toward the same conclusion, I have seen none which seems to me to say so much in such short compass as does the following from a Kentucky case: "If it is essentially a prerogative of sovereignty to raise troops in time of war, it is equally so to prepare each generation of youth to discharge the duties of citizenship in time of peace and war."[8] Observe that the court held the Public Defense to be inherent in sovereignty itself and Public instruction as well. I can think of nothing in the way of legal theory which could more effectively declare the contention maintained in this section.[9]

Apart from legal reasoning, the argument of this whole volume, based as it is upon the institutional character of the fabric of Civilization, shows at every turn that the quality of any social

---

[8] *Louisville* v. *Commonwealth for School Board*, 134 Ky. 488.

[9] For an elaborate discussion of the whole matter as found in the judicial literature see Newton Edwards, *The Courts and the Public Schools* (Chicago: University of Chicago Press, 1933).

order must depend in the last analysis upon the quality of the public instruction administered in the preceding generation.

PRIVATE SCHOOLS

Moreover, in law there are no private schools which are not parts of a school system which is in itself Civil Institution. Parochial and private schools exist under the sufferance of the States, and the statutes commonly prescribe that they shall give instruction equivalent to that given in the tax-supported schools. No doubt Legislatures have acted, and ought to act, in a rational manner and avoid all taint of arbitrary action; but if the power of the sovereign to control the school system entire is denied, then the alternative is to commit the function of public instruction to the whims of individuals and to set up a multitude of independent powers at the very heart of sovereignty. Whoever controls the schools today can determine the public policy of thirty years hence or less, and even the form of The State.

THE SCHOOL DISTRICT

The basis of our school government is in the local school district, ranging in size from the area and population surrounding and supporting a one-room country school to our greatest cities. At least our theory of support and government is contained in the school-district system. It is in form a corporation, or, as the courts commonly describe it, a quasi-corporation, an "as-if" corporation. Such is the thing in form, a vestigial remainder of the time when schools and even villages were isolated and remote. In substance, however, it is, like the county, a civil division, that is to say, a division of a State which carries out the State's policy in public instruction, both by fiscal support and by the election of the boards of control.

Like the county, it is long obsolete, something left over from quite a different kind of community organization.

The tendency has long been for the several States to support and administer their public-school systems directly as an arm of the State Government.

INSTRUCTION

Schoolmasters and students of educational processes have long contended that in the Common School there should be instruction in the nature and purposes of schools, and to some extent perhaps in Education, to the end that the product of the schools might have some measure of critical intelligence touching the place of schooling in the national and world-economy.

UNITS IN THE SCHOOL

I. Education a process of personal growth which for better or worse goes on anyway

II. Instruction a school process intended to insure that education be normal and right

III. A school is a group of pupils and teachers organized for purposes of instruction

IV. A school is also a minor community in which teachers, pupils, and others live together for part of their lives

V. Undergoing instruction is not necessarily getting an education—the latter depends on the instruction

VI. Going to school and college is not getting an education—that depends on the school or college and the use which pupils make of their time

VII. The school exists primarily for the transmission of Civilization to the rising generation

VIII. Good citizens are educated citizens

IX. American school system
1. No Federal system
2. Forty-eight State school systems
3. The State school system is basically headed by the Legislature which makes the school laws, and by the Courts which apply the laws
4. Superintendent of Public Instruction, usually elected by the people
   a) Not an executive officer—not the head of the school system
   b) Holds certain ministerial duties which vary from State to State, chief of which is apportionment of school funds appropriated by the State, approval of schools, hearing of appeals from rulings of county and local officers in some cases
   c) Has, however, important powers of personal influence and persuasion
5. State Board of Education, either elective or appointive, in many States takes the place of the Superintendent of Public Instruction
   a) Acts through the Commissioner of Education who is usually appointed by the Board

  b) In addition to powers and duties belonging to the Superintendent of Public Instruction, is usually the governing board of various schools maintained by the State directly

  c) In a few States, State Board of Education tends to take the place of local boards

X. Local systems

  1. Are carried on under the authority of the several States

  2. Authority is sometimes in the general school law, and sometimes in a city charter, which is itself a law

  3. In principle, local systems are not the property of the local community, but rather a method by which the State aims to get public instruction carried out

  4. Among their chief powers is the levying of taxes to support schools

XI. Organization of local systems

  1. The governing board is the Board of Education, or School Board, or Board of Instruction, or School Trustees

  2. The duties of the board are governmental but not supervisory and directory

  3. The executive officer of the School Board is the Superintendent of Schools, whose duties are executive as head of the system, directory and supervisory

  4. The real key to efficiency in the schools is the school principal, who is essentially the head teacher in each school

XII. County system

  1. In most States no true county system

  2. County superintendent, elected by people, is chiefly an understudy of the Superintendent of Public Instruction

  3. Duties are ministerial rather than supervisory

    a) Computes distribution of school funds among local systems or school districts

    b) Examines and certifies teachers

    c) In some cases hears appeals from the orders of local trustees or school boards

  4. In the newer County Unit so called, there is County Board of Education which displaces local boards in all but chartered cities

CHAPTER XI

POLITICS

THE word "politics" started life as one of the noblest in any language. It meant "those things which pertain to the *polis* or city," that is to say, Public Affairs. It came to mean the theory and practice of Government in the City-State of antiquity. So it is today *the art of governing a people in the application of sovereignty.* That is its denotation. In the self-governing nations we are all of us politicians in spite of ourselves, provided we have the electoral franchise. The real meaning of the term has, however, become lost in sinister and irrelevant connotations, such as dishonesty, intrigue, trickery, corruption, demagoguery, racketeering. Now a politician may be engaged in any or all of these; but so may a physician, a merchant, a mechanic, a priest, a schoolmaster, a professor. We do not set up the notion that medicine is synonymous with quackery because some physicians are quacks; or that commerce and dishonesty are one and the same thing because some merchants are rascals; or that occupation of a pulpit or a teacher's chair is demagoguery and chicane because we find plenty in both callings who are guilty of both. The effect of all this loose use of words is that we have no respectable word in common use to define the art of government. Straight thinking and ordered community life begin in the right use of words.

It does not follow that, because all voters are in the nature of their franchises politicians, they are necessarily professional politicians, expert in the art. Nevertheless, Patriotism requires of all who are entitled to vote at least two things:

First, that they shall vote.

Second, that they shall make themselves free from the delusions which permit them to be led by demagogues. The demagogue, ever since the day of Cleon the Tanner, is more than any other miscreant the keystone of most things which make Government

bad. He flourishes on the ignorance of the "educated." Trace the
career of any demagogue you please and you will find that he
appeals to the electorate in proportion to the latter's ignorance
and selfishness, and especially ignorance of Civil Government including Taxation, of General Economics, of Commerce and Industry in their constituent institutions.

Organized parties are the condition of successful application of
popular sovereignty. In principle, parties ought to stand for organization of those who on the whole think alike in public matters. Through all the vicissitudes of political credos there lingers
everywhere in bodies politic, always has and probably always will,
the cleavage between those whose temper is to try all things and
those whose temper is to hold fast to that which is good. We call
them Liberals and Conservatives.

The great popular sovereignties, which on the whole do understand the art of self-government, have on the whole adhered to the
two-party system. Those countries which have tried self-government and then have regressed into some form of absolutism have
almost invariably been destroyed by breaking up into multitudes
of minor parties or blocs. Rank individualism not only is incompatible with the exercise of popular sovereignty but is one of the
surest marks of personal infantilism.

A. CIVIL GOVERNMENT

I. ITS NATURE

Civil Government is The State in action or, perhaps better,
being applied. It is not, however, like the other aspects of The
State which we have studied, universal institution. Indeed it is
not institution at all, although it is founded on national institutions. It differs in form from country to country, not only according to the genius of the people who are governed but according to
the extent and character of the territory, and various other factors.

We study Civil Government because it is essential to our understanding of The State so to do. It is not merely part of "edu-

cation for citizenship," but rather instruction leading in part to the education of a person possessed of Intelligence.

NOT MUNICIPAL GOVERNMENT

Civil Government does not include city or village government. That is an affair of the Corporation, a business matter, in which there is no room for politics, not even in the correct use of that abused term. Municipal government is business and not politics; Civil Government is politics and not business. We have had more than one Governor, and perhaps a President or two, who turned out dismal failures because of their well-meant but mistaken aim to give a State or the nation "a business administration."

CIVIL GOVERNMENT IS NOT ADMINISTRATION

It is critically important to draw a distinction which is seldom noted, namely, that between Government proper and Administration of public enterprises which are sanctioned by Government. The enactment of legislation, whether it be lawmaking, or declaration of public policy, or the sanction of a public enterprise, or the appropriation of money and the laying of taxes; the establishment and control of the Public Defense; the establishment and correction of the monetary system; the judicial application and executive enforcement of the laws—all these are examples of Government. The erection of a public work, the distribution of the mail, the minting of money, the collection of taxes, the management of fleets and armies, the conduct of the public schools, the direction of the constabulary—these are examples of Administration as distinguished from Government. Nearly all municipal and other corporation affairs are in the field of Administration.

The critical difference between the two comes in the principle that Government deals with *policy*, whereas Administration *applies objective facts and principles* without regard to policy. It makes no difference whether Conservatives or Liberals, Democrats or Republicans, are in power, the laws of mechanics, the navigation of ships at sea, the delivery of the mail, the computation and extension of taxes, the management of public instruction, are the same under one party as under the other. But the very heart of popular sovereignty is in the power of one party or the other to determine policy.

CIVIL SERVICE

Civil Service organization so called rests upon this distinction which we have been discussing. It means that all administrative officers will be sorted out in terms of essential function and be placed on a permanent list, to receive appointments on grounds of personal merit and efficiency, without regard to the party affiliations of the officer, or his influence with the appointing power. Once in, the civil service appointee holds for life and is removable only for cause impartially determined.

A corollary is that the major political functionaries should also be sorted out, and these should be the only positions which appear on the ballot. All others should be appointive—the administrative officers under civil service laws. To illustrate the meaning, the following list is appended of officers properly to be voted for in the typical State:

1. President and Vice-president, voting for electors
2. Senators and Representatives in Congress
3. Governor, Lieutenant-Governor, and members of State Legislature
4. County Commissioners, and Sheriff if any

City elections are essentially meetings of stockholders or members of the community rather than citizens, that is to say, they are that in principle. The only appropriate elective officers in a city or village are the members of the council. They in turn appoint the manager. Of course, major matters of business are properly referred to the community for decision.

THE JUDICIAL SERVICE

By far the most vital service we have is the judiciary. Judges are governmental officers, but they are not policy-determining officers. On the contrary, they administer justice, and justice is rational and impersonal and impartial; it has nothing whatever to do with policy. Judges do not pass on the wisdom of acts of the Legislature; they interpret and apply on legal and juristic principles.

To elect a judge, or to appoint him for a term, is to put him under bonds to administer his office in accordance with the desires of the majority or the interest of the appointing power. That is the negation of Justice. Two of our States and the United States appoint judges for life, subject to removal by impeachment for judicial misconduct. That does not make them perfect; but it does make it easier for them to be judges rather than politicians, and it does make judicial office more attractive to able men.

FINALLY

There is no intelligence about Government, if instruction be limited to memorizing the framework of our Government, from that of the United States to that of the township, and conning the names of the offices and the duties attached to them, from the office of President to that of poundkeeper. *The basis of intelligence about anything is an understanding of its principles.*

II. FORM OF GOVERNMENT

One of the prominent handicaps to intelligent behavior in the present age is in the fact that most of us seem to be mechanically minded. We have seen so much of foolproof machines, perhaps, that we are prone to cherish the delusion that a form of Government can be invented which will also be foolproof and will yield us all that heart can desire. It is very common with us to suppose that government can make "business" good, whereas governmental interference in the conduct of business usually makes business bad. Nay, people sometimes go farther and suppose that a change in the government in power, or even a revolution in the form of Government, will change the order of Nature. It is perhaps the supreme political delusion. Form is put in the place of substance, just as it sometimes is in the cases of Language, Mathematics, Religion, Art. In the end, the substance of Government is mainly in the maintenance of order, the distribution of justice, the public defense. Ignorance and vice and shallowness of character in the sovereign never produced good Government or allowed good Government to exist—and never will.

And yet form is as essential as substance. Theory without practice is dead; but practice without theory is casual, muddling, and without purpose. Form is no guaranty of honesty and competency, but unless there be a comprehensible form, logically valid, in the prevailing theory of The State, the Government cannot be *understood* and cannot, therefore, be rationally carried on.

Hence it is that this part of the course in Civil Government deals entirely in form, whence comes a large part of practical political intelligence.

FORM IN AMERICAN GOVERNMENT

Our form is that of a Federal Republic constituted as a representative democracy and carried on as a Government in which the three essential branches of all Civil Government, the legislative, the judicial, and the executive, are kept separate and distinct, save in two particulars, namely, the veto power of the Executive on legislation, and the constitutional power of the Executive to recommend legislation. If we keep that form in mind, we have the beginnings of understanding upon the basis of which we can cherish valid opinion and operate the Government *intelligently*. If we discover as matter of fact and principle that the form is in some respects fallacious, we are so constituted as a body politic that we can change the form without revolution. Nevertheless, here as always, valid form is logical and objective and not the product of the *desires* of a majority or even of the whole people. If we desire an illogical and unreasonable form, a two-thirds majority in both houses of Congress and a three-fourths majority of the States can have its way, but the result will be disaster in the fundamental functions of the Civil State.

A FEDERAL REPUBLIC

We are first of all a Federal Republic, that is to say, the Government of our nation is a General Government plus forty-eight State or Commonwealth Governments acting upon the whole people. We are a Republic because we recognize no personal sovereign and because Government is for the sake of the governed, *res publica*. We shall refer to the General Government as the Federal Government, for that is our custom, but in reality the whole thing is a federal government.

Dual sovereignty.—The United States, the Federal State, has exactly the same body politic as do the several States combined, save for the unimportant qualification that the United States holds sovereignty over Alaska and certain island possessions. Dual sovereignty consists in the principle that the United States governs in a broad field of civil functions wherein the several States do not, and in the nature of the case could not, govern; and conversely the States govern supreme in all other functions, each over its own territory and in its own body politic.

It has been said by very eminent men that there is no such thing as State sovereignty, as the expression is used in America. That would be true if the United States had one jot of power over the States themselves, but it does not. It holds authority over the people of each State in Federal matters, for example, bankruptcy; but no power whatever over the State itself. If the Legislature or, a Convention should enact laws repugnant to the administration in power at Washington, no United States marshal could be sent to arrest the members. Nor does the Federal Government have any authority whatever over the people of a State in State matters, for example, domestic relations.

Federal principle.—The form of Government laid down in the Constitution was no arbitrary fancy of a group of men. It conformed to reason based on experience, and the intelligent attitude is that it is still so based. The federal principle was clearly seen by Franklin and others more than thirty years before 1787, when there was no United States. It is this: that *those political functions are committed to the Federal Government which in the nature of things could not be performed by the State Governments acting severally.* The several States could not severally conduct foreign relations without destroying the United States, nor could they regulate interstate commerce, nor provide comprehensively a monetary and banking system, nor conduct the national defense. As the national community has expanded and become more closely knit, other functions have sprung up which did not exist in 1787.

CIVIL DIVISION

Sovereignty resides in the people of the United States and of the several States. But we have a third element in our framework of Government which is not sovereign, that is to say, the Civil Division in the States which we call the County. It is the creature of the State in which it exists, it exercises some of the functions of Civil Government, and it is equipped with officers elected by the people of the County.

In the early days there were two good reasons for setting up counties.

First, when communication was slow and difficult, it was impossible for citizens conveniently to reach the State capital in order to have deeds and mortgages recorded, wills probated, courts held, courthouses and jails erected; and there was not business enough of that sort in the townships to have it done there.

Now all that was and is administrative and not political in character, but our forebears had no glimmering of the distinction and no notion of a career civil service. Today with efficient communication established, the several States could set up offices for the transaction of such business wherever they might be needed, under permanent, appointive officers.

Second, the capital city was too remote to be the center for the control of crime. Hence, the county defined a *posse comitatus* and provided for a chief constable in the elective Sheriff.

The Sheriff and his deputies in their constabulary function have long been replaced by the State constabulary in some States, and should be replaced in all. The *posse comitatus* has given place to the organized National Guard. In truth most people are unaware that there is any such thing.

As rural municipality.—In most of the States, however, especially in the West and South, the county organization does for the rural sections what the organized municipality does in urban centers. It would seem to present no insoluble problem to make over such counties into true municipalities.

BRANCHES OF GOVERNMENT

We pass then to a somewhat more particularized consideration of our form of Government. We shall use the Federal Government for the purposes of study, for it would be impracticable and perhaps needless to take the several States one by one. Schools ought, of course, to follow out in their study programs the analogies and differences in detail between the Federal Government and that of the State in which the particular school is located. The States, however, follow the form of the Federal Government in general, despite here and there minor differences. The Governor in general corresponds to the President, and the State Legislature, whatever its official designation, to Congress. In essential function and procedure, the Judicial Branch is the same in both.

THE EXECUTIVE

The American President is armed with constitutional executive powers beyond what has commonly pertained to constitutional monarchs or to the presidents of republics which are under ministerial Government. The principle is that there shall be a chief magistrate, who is representative of all the people, and that he shall have powers requisite to the exercise of his functions.

Veto.—Through his veto power, he participates with Congress in making the laws and determining public policy in general. In that way he can impose a check on what in his view is either unconstitutional or unwise. But the veto power is not absolute: a veto can be overruled by two-thirds vote in both Houses of Congress.

Recommendations to Congress.—The veto power is positive so far as it goes, that is to say, it stops legislative action unless it is overruled. But the President has another legislative power which is moral rather than positive, namely, the power derived from the Constitution to recommend to the consideration of Congress such measures as he shall judge necessary and expedient. Well, any of us could do that—with no effect whatever in most cases. But with the President it is a right which is part of the Constitution. A determined President, especially in the presence of a subservient Congress, can extend his power over legislation until it is as great as that of an English Prime Minister with a heavy majority in the Commons at his back.

Enforcement of laws and oath.—He is charged with the enforcement of the Federal laws, and on his inauguration makes oath that he "will faithfully execute the office of President of the United States, and will to the best of my ability, preserve, protect, and defend the Constitution of the United States."

Commander-in-chief.—He is commander-in-chief of the Army and Navy, and can, if he will, use the armed forces of the United States for pretty much anything armed forces can be used for, restrained only by the somewhat remote contingency of organized mutiny. It must be remembered that the President is not subject to ordinary court processes in restraint. Not that he is specifically exempt by the Constitution, but that he is an independent Branch of Government. The chief obstacle to arbitrary use of troops is in the power of Congress to appropriate money.

Maintenance of republican form of Government, repelling invasion, and quelling insurrection.—Constitutionally, it is probable that the Executive can use troops to guarantee to each State a Republican form of Government, although the power has never been actually tested.

He can, however, use the armed forces to repel invasion and quell insurrection on the call of the authorities of any State so menaced.

Cleveland used troops in Chicago to prevent the interference of rioters with the due conveyance of the Mail.

Pardoning power.—He may grant pardons and reprieves for offenses against the laws of the United States, but not, as is sometimes supposed, against the laws of the States. He cannot, for example, pardon murderers, unless the crime was committed on an American vessel on the high seas, or in territory subject to the jurisdiction of the United States. He cannot pardon officers under impeachment.

Appointment.—He appoints, subject to confirmation by the Senate, Federal officers, save some whose appointment is otherwise provided for.

Treaty-making.—He makes treaties with foreign nations, and, when approved by two-thirds of the Senators present at the time the vote is taken, any such treaty becomes part of the law of the land.

Directs the Government.—He directs the administrative side of Government. In that capacity, while he cannot alter the Form of Government set up by the Constitution, he can by executive order materially alter the *conduct* of Government. Notable illustrations are the extent to which Cleveland and Theodore Roosevelt covered appointive places into the Civil Service by refusing to appoint save under Civil Service rules or on Civil Service principles.

Proclamation.—The President or any Governor has an important informal power which sometimes serves the purpose of issuing decrees. The power of making proclamation is inherent in the office. Sometimes laws are made effective only when they are proclaimed, but it is the informal power with which we are concerned.

Both the Federal and the State executives do on occasion proclaim a course of action and urge it on all good citizens, when an emergency exists and the common consent sanctions the proclamation. In the winter and early spring of 1933, for example, forty-eight governors and finally the President proclaimed the closing of banks in order to prevent disastrous runs and panics. Nearly everybody knew that the action was needful and salutary and nearly everybody was quite willing to conform. Such proclamations do not, however, have the force of law.

In this connection, it must be noted further that the mere prestige of the Presidential office is very great. Some of our Presidents have used the prestige to carry the country through times of crisis and confusion by sheer power of persuasion.

The President has great power. However, he cannot control the forces of Nature, nor forgive sin. Some seem to think he can do both.

Restraints.—The executive is subjected to certain constitutional restraints, and a good deal of natural restraint.

In the first place, he is elected for a term of but four years, and most of our Presidents have been candidates for re-election.

He is subject to impeachment for high crimes and misdemeanors, in which the House of Representatives brings the indictment, and the Senate under the presidency of the Chief Justice tries the issue.

Despite all checks, however, the President is in the last analysis restrained chiefly by his good conscience, and the intelligence and character of the electorate exhibited in the kind of man whom they chose. An able and ruthless man, devoid of scruple, could in effect elect himself term after term, and defy the impeachments of Congress, if any. There is no orderly legal power of a positive nature which could restrain that kind of President. There is nothing in our Constitution, nor in any constitution which could be written, which could protect us from the kind of absolutism which in times past has been common in the Latin-American republics. The only final guaranty we have is in the kind of man we have chosen, the character of the people who have done the choosing, and the repugnance to our mores of absolutism in any form.

"MANDATES" UNKNOWN TO OUR INSTITUTIONS

The notion that the President is elected to carry out the popular will, as revealed, or thought to be revealed, in an election, is foreign to constitutional democratic principles. It would be to set up an absolute democracy, and absolute democracy can be even more tyrannical than absolute monarchy. The President is given a mandate to be a good President under his oath of office and nothing more.

THE AMERICAN CABINET

Our Cabinet is a body unknown to the Constitution, save as the latter refers to heads of administrative departments and authorizes the President to require in writing their opinions in matters relating to their offices. From the first administration, however, the Cabinet began to develop institutionally as the President's board of advisers and official family. Since then, Congress has from time to time added new administrative departments and created new Cabinet offices. As the President's advisers, the Cabinet is a political body; as heads of administrative departments, they are administrative officers. Separate administrative heads, like the English Permanent Secretaries, are unknown to our system, although Assistant Secretaries sometimes hold office a long time, despite changes in the party in power. They know the routine and technique and cannot be dispensed with.

Since 1886 the order of succession to the Presidency after the Vice-President has been in the Cabinet officers in the order of the creation of their departments, beginning with the Secretary of State.

CONGRESS

Congress is the Federal lawmaking power. It is not, as many suppose, in the nature of a board of directors charged with the duty of conducting the nation's business, having the President for its executive officer. The President is quite independent of Congress, save in the principle that, like all magistrates in civilized States, he can enforce no laws which do not exist, and Congress makes the laws. Nor can he spend money which Congress does not appropriate. The President is not above the law, but the source of his power is the Constitution, in the same sense and no different sense from that in which Congress also derives its powers from the Constitution. The Government of the United States is not the government of a corporation. The President is not responsible to Congress but to the electorate in the next election.

Congress is also a policy-determining body.—Congress is the lawmaking power, but it is also the policy-determining power. The greater part of the business of Congress, and of the Legislatures as well, is not lawmaking in the proper sense, but rather the direction of the activities of the State. Shall there be war with England, Mexico, Spain, Germany? That is a matter of policy. Shall there be erected an Interstate Commerce Commission? or a revision of the tariff on imports? or a bimetallic currency? or a Federal Reserve banking system? Shall a battleship be authorized and money appropriated therefor? or Federal aid in the construction of highways be provided for? or an interoceanic canal settled upon? And so on for the greater part of the business of a session.

Similarly, the State Legislatures are occupied. All this has the force of law, for it is the command and sanction of the sovereign, but it is not law governing the relations of individuals in the furtherance of justice.

Composition.—Congress is composed of two Houses, the Senate and the House of Representatives.

In theory, the Senate represents the States and the House represents the people directly. Each of the States has two Senators, the same for Nevada and New York. The Representatives are apportioned among the States in proportion to population. Senators are elected for six years and Representatives for two.

In theory, and on the whole in practice, the Senate tends to be the conservative element in Congress, and the House of Representatives the radical. The reason in practice is found in two facts:

First, the Senate is not apportioned according to population, and the House is so apportioned.

Second, the Senators are elected for a term longer than that of any single Presidential term, while the Representatives are elected twice during the Presidential term.

The effect in the long run is that members of the House are more sensitive to current public opinion; the Senators less likely to mistake popular excitement for public opinion.

Able Senators are in long enough, especially when they are returned term after term, to become men of large intellectual attainments in the field of Government. We have had many Senators who became better qualified, through experience and study, as ministers of foreign affairs and finance especially, than anybody at that time in the Executive Branch.

In principle, then, both historical and current, there is reason for the Senate of the United States which does not exist for the State Senates, and never did exist, save as the State constitutions make senatorial terms longer than any one gubernatorial term and longer than terms in the lower house, and save as the people have fallen into the habit of returning their State senators for several terms.

The relation between the Senate and House at Washington is

one of the checks and balances which make us a limited democracy, much as the kingdoms of a hundred years ago were, some of them, limited monarchies.

The President as participant in lawmaking and policy-determining.—We have seen how the President has legislative as well as executive powers. In the present connection, let us in brief recall them:

1. He recommends legislation, and our strongest Presidents have effectively urged it.

2. No act of Congress has any validity until it is officially approved by the President, except as two-thirds may after ten days re-enact.

3. He may veto acts of Congress, giving reasons for his disapproval. If a bill reaches him within less than ten days of the adjournment and he fails to approve, the effect is the same as if he submitted a veto message.

THE JUDICIARY

The judiciary is everywhere a substantial part of Civil Government. Indeed, it may be contended with a good deal of truth that Government grew out of the redressing of wrongs which would otherwise be redressed privately.

But with us the Federal and State Judiciaries are not only courts but co-ordinate Branches of Government, that is to say, they are not subject to the control of Congress or of the President, save through the appointing power of the latter.

The essence of judicial action is in its presumptive and substantial quality of impartial, objective, independence. When judges are elected for short terms by a body politic which is still far from being made up of philosophers and logicians, the judiciary will not be, or at least is not likely to be, independent, objective, impartial, in its deliberations. On the other hand, a Governor or a President can use his appointing power, where the judges are appointive, to debauch the courts. Here, as everywhere else in our democracy, substantial purity and competency in the Government rest in the last analysis on an intelligent, enlightened, moral electorate. The quality of Government reflects the quality of the sovereign, whether the latter be a monarch or a people.

The Federal Judges are appointed by the President and confirmed by the Senate, for life, and they are removable only by impeachment.

The Judiciary as co-ordinate Branch of Government is peculiarly an American contribution to Government, although it has tended to be copied elsewhere in democracies and ministerial systems which have been set up since 1789. While the President may veto legislation on grounds of its wisdom as well as of its constitutionality, his veto is not absolute. The Courts, on the other hand, and finally the Supreme Court of the United States, must constantly pass upon the issue of conformity of legislation and other acts of Congress and of the State Legislatures to the Constitution, which is in fact the supreme law of the land. If the Court finds on its investigation in a law suit carried on appeal to the Supreme Court that a certain act is not in conformity with the Constitution, then its decision in that case has the effect of making the act a nullity. The decision of the Supreme Court is absolute up to Amendment of the Constitution itself.

We shall return to a further study in the next section of this chapter.

TRIAL AND APPELLATE COURTS

When a case comes to trial on the issues involved, whatever they may be, it appears in a United States District Court, if it is a case under the laws of the United States, or between citizens of different States. Otherwise, it appears in a State trial court which bears various titles in the different States. It may have originated in a probate court and been settled there, or even, in small suits, in a local justice court. We are speaking, of course, of civil suits; criminal actions have already been dealt with. In civil suits at law, the Federal and the State constitutions fix a limit in the amount involved at a small sum below which the suit may be brought and settled in a minor court. If the amount involved is in excess of that sum, then the suit is brought in a jury court.

In the latter, as in criminal cases, the jury passes upon the facts; and the judge determines on the rules of evidence what evidence is to go to the jury, instructs the jury in the law, requires order in court and fair and decent conduct in the lawyers. The verdict of the jury is final as to the facts which they find, but there is appeal to a higher court on the ground that constitutional rights have been invaded or that erroneous procedure has resulted in an unfair trial.

If it be so contended on either count, the case goes to an appellate court where the legal issues are reargued. The merits of the case as to the facts are not in issue on appeal, but only whether or not the verdict has been improperly reached, either because irrelevant and misleading evidence has been allowed to go to the jury, or because the case has been prejudiced on some other ground, or finally because the verdict is not one which could be found by reasonable men on the evidence presented. If the court sustains the appellant, the verdict is set aside and a new trial is ordered. If the appellate court finds the verdict just on the facts presented, but that the result is to deprive the appellant of a constitutional right, or otherwise to contravene the Constitution, then the case is at an end.

There is further appeal to the Supreme Court, of the State or of the United States as the matter at stake may determine, usually on the constitutional issue. The supreme courts are sometimes known as "courts of last resort." The intermediate courts of appeal, both Federal and State, are chiefly devices for clearing up and expediting business, for saving the time of the supreme courts for the more critical issues. Some of the smaller States require no intermediate courts, cases being taken directly from the jury courts to the State supreme courts.

The Supreme Court of the United States acts almost entirely on issues wherein the constitutional rights of citizens are involved. But it has original jurisdiction in certain matters which are interesting: "In all cases affecting Ambassadors, other public ministers and consuls, and those in which a State shall be a party, the Supreme Court shall have original jurisdiction." Moreover, "the judicial power shall extend to . . . . controversies between two or more States.''

The last has furnished a method by which States can settle their differences without going to war. Again and again have disputes arisen between States which anywhere else in the world would inevitably have led to diplomatic exchanges and in the end very probably war. Save in the case of one horrible exception, disputes have been made justiciable, until such action has become a part of our customs, at least for the most part. It is practically unthinkable that any dispute could arise between two States which would be accepted by their citizens as a sufficient cause for armed clash. Probably most of the citizens would not be aware that it could be done. Nevertheless, the States are in fact sovereign, and it is not absolutely inconceivable that they would go to war under extreme provocation. One can imagine conditions under which any Federal troops which could be assembled would be unable either to hale State authorities before a Federal court or to execute the decrees of the Supreme Court. After all, war itself is not necessarily uncivilized; failure to find methods of settling disputes without the use of force is uncivilized.

OTHER OFFICES AND OFFICERS

The traditional text in Civil Government included a great many subordinate offices and officers, mostly administrative in type, ranging all the way from the Treasurer of the United States down to the township fence-viewer. Such encyclopedic courses cannot be taught, for there is little or nothing in them to be understood. The pupil can memorize and forget. Nevertheless, he will in his study encounter such officers, and he should be taught as part of his training in study to find out in passing what such officers or commissions are for. He may remember or he may forget. He follows them up as he meets them in his efforts to arrive at an understanding of Civil Government. He will encounter them, and probably a good many new officers, as he reads the daily newspapers, and, if he understands Civil Government proper, he will sense what the officers are for. I doubt, however, that there are more

THE CURRICULUM

than a very few professional lawyers in the whole United States who could list offhand the officers of their own States, or give offhand the duties of all of them. If the professional wishes to know, he consults the annual register of his State, or some directory, or perhaps the *Statesman's Year Book*. That is the purpose of such works of reference.

COURSE IN CIVIL GOVERNMENT

I. Government
1. Personal control of individuals in some organized community or enterprise—good or bad
2. Mere compulsion of individuals apart from some organized purpose is not government but trespass

II. Civil Government
1. Civil Government is the Civil State in action
2. Respects rights of individuals
3. Is the reign of law rather than of persons
4. Consists in the making of just laws, the just application of laws, the just enforcement of laws
5. Maintains law and order and justice in the community
6. Not municipal government
7. Not corporation management

III. Government Is Not Administration
1. Government makes laws, applies and enforces them, determines public policy, authorizes public works, lays taxes
2. Hence politics and party politics are essential in Government in a democracy
3. Administration carries out works and services
4. Government in a democracy applies the public will, be it wise or unwise
5. Administration goes on from that point, assuming that the public demands only honesty and efficiency in its works
6. Politics of any kind have no place in Administration

IV. Civil Service
1. Civil Service is the administration of the State or of a municipality or other corporation
2. Civil service principles require that public administration of all sorts should be officered and staffed without reference to political considerations
3. Putting a position in the Civil Service is sometimes accurately called taking it out of politics

4. Civil Service means permanent appointment on technical merit to all administrative positions

5. It is necessarily a career service and not subject to change with changes in the party control of the Government

V. The Politician

1. Is skilled in the art of Government

2. Is intelligent in the science of Government—an ignoramus is no politician, even though he may be a party boss

3. All voters are politicians in function, since they take part in Government

4. An ignoramus has no moral or natural right to vote and thus take part in Government, whatever his legal rights may be

5. Demagogues, corruptionists, tricksters, grafters, are not politicians but rather malefactors and frequently criminals

VI. Party Government

1. There can be no Government under popular sovereignty without organized parties

2. A party is an organization of the like-minded in public affairs

3. Anything beyond a two-party system tends to be disruptive in representative Government

4. The machinery of party government is found in:

   a) Party organization

   b) Primary, including direct primary, for selection of candidates to be supported

   c) Convention of delegates for final nomination of candidates and formulation of party platform

VII. Form of Government

1. A formless government is unintelligible

2. Form in itself does not produce good Government

3. There must be substance as well as form

4. Substance is in the political intelligence and character of the voters

5. Good form with good substance makes good Government easy, bad form with good substance makes good Government possible but difficult; bad substance makes good Government impossible whatever the form

VIII. A Federal Republic

1. Mutually exclusive sovereignty between United States and the several States

2. Same body politic for both—each of us is a citizen both of his own State and of the United States

3. Federal Government in principle acts in all matters in which a State cannot well act, or not act at all
4. States govern in all other matters
5. The United States holds no authority whatever over any State, but only over the people of the State in Federal matters

IX. Civil Division
1. Territory and citizens set apart by Government for carrying on certain phases of Government—a sub-State
2. County is the best illustration
3. City is commonly made civil division, but wrongly so, since the city is in its nature municipal corporation
4. County is not sovereign, but it is made self-governing in electing its officers and laying its taxes
5. There are no county laws; the laws are of the State

X. Typical County Government
1. Administers the transmission of property, especially land, according to law in the
   a) Registration of deeds, mortgages, and testaments
   b) Probating of wills and settlement of estates
2. Apportions and collects the taxes, especially property taxes within the county
   (Levy of taxes is, however, usually by municipalities and school districts, save taxes required by the county for its own uses)
3. Maintains the courthouse and jail, and sometimes elects judges
4. Sometimes administers the care of the poor and the insane, and maintains a county hospital
5. Constructs and maintains highways, save where it is done by modern State Highway Departments—not byways or city streets
6. Defines the *posse comitatus* and elects the Sheriff
7. Usually maintains the Coroner's office and elects the Coroner
   (In the more progressive States, the Coroner has given way to the medical examiner, an appointive officer)
8. The executive board of a county is usually a board of County Commissioners

XI. Branches of Government
1. All Civil Government everywhere has three main functions:
   a) Lawmaking
   b) Judicial interpretation of the laws
   c) Executive enforcement of laws, and direction of civil and martial agencies
2. In the United States and the several States, these three functions are lodged in three distinct, co-ordinate, and independent

Branches of Government—the Legislative, the Judicial, and the Executive

3. The Judicial Branch interprets and applies the Constitution which is above all three Branches

4. Contrasts with Ministerial Government in which Executive and Legislative are in effect combined, and in which the Judiciary is not usually a Branch

XII. The President of the United States

(For the most part, the Governors of States have powers similar to those of the President)

1. The President is not the agent of Congress but is a co-ordinate Branch of Government

2. May veto legislation as a check and compel further consideration, subject to having his veto overruled by two-thirds vote of both Houses

3. Appoints justices of the Supreme Court, and of inferior Federal Courts, subject to confirmation by the Senate

4. Is commander-in-chief of the Army and Navy

5. May use United States forces to quell domestic insurrection or repel invasion, upon application of the Legislature or Governor of the State affected

6. May use Federal troops to defend Federal services from violent interruption

7. May summon and adjourn Congress

8. May grant reprieves and pardons for offenses against Federal but not for offenses against State Law. Most criminal law is State law

9. May negotiate treaties with foreign countries and, with consent of two-thirds of the Senate, make treaties

10. A treaty thus made becomes part of the law of the land

11. Appoints Federal officers, with some exceptions otherwise provided for, subject to confirmation by the Senate

12. Can control conduct of administrative departments, not independent commissions, by executive order

13. Sometimes issues proclamations, as do the Governors, about matters of public interest, but such are binding only on those who desire to conform. The United States is not a Government by decree

14. Is representative in executive capacity of all the people, but popular mandates are unknown to the Constitution and to our institutions in general. The people is as much bound by the Constitution as is the President, except in that they may have Amendments by orderly process.

15. The President is held in check by:
    a) The prospect of the next election as bearing upon himself and his party
    b) The power of Impeachment reposed in Congress
    c) His own conscience

XIII. The Cabinet
    1. Composed of the heads of the Administrative Departments, from time to time created by Congress
    2. Cabinet officers are ordinarily political heads of Departments chosen for their importance in the party returned at the last election
    3. No regular permanent administrative nonpolitical heads as in the English system
    4. Forms the advisory council of the President
    5. Cabinet does not constitute a ministry, and there is no ministry in the English and Canadian sense

XIV. The Legislative Branch—Congress
    1. Is the lawmaking power
    2. Is the policy-determining power
    3. Holds the power of the purse
    4. Is entirely independent of the President, save in the qualified veto power and the President's power over assembly and adjournment
    5. Has the power of Impeachment over the President and other executive and judicial officers, in which the House of Representatives brings the indictment and the Senate tries the issue

XV. Principles of Representation
    1. Members of the House of Representatives are elected every two years by Congressional Districts
    2. Is intended to be directly representative of the people by districts, and Representatives are apportioned in accordance with population, save that every State must have at least one
    3. All bills for raising revenue must originate in the House
    4. The Senate is in theory representative of the States, and the several States have equal representation in the Senate
    5. Senators serve six years, one-third being elected every two years
    6. The Senate is relatively a more permanent body, and is intended to be the conservative element in Congress

XVI. The Judiciary
    1. The Supreme Court and the subordinate courts are the Judiciary
    2. The Judiciary is a Branch of Government co-ordinate with the President and Congress

3. The three Branches take their powers independently from the Constitution

4. The Federal Courts administer justice in cases arising under the Constitution and laws of the United States

5. Since the Constitution is the supreme law of the land, the Federal courts, and ultimately the Supreme Court, have to pass on the constitutionality of Acts of Congress and the State Legislatures, in cases which arise under the Constitution

6. An unconstitutional act is not repealed by the Supreme Court; it becomes null and void so far as enforcement is concerned

7. The Federal courts do not pass on the wisdom of legislation or legislative acts, but only on their constitutionality

8. The State supreme courts perform a similar function with reference to the State constitutions

XVII. Court Procedure

1. The court of origin in lawsuits, where the amount involved is small, usually cases before State courts, is some local tribunal, as justice court or a magistrate's court, where facts are found and law applied without a jury

2. Jury is an ancient device, a body of lay citizens, supposed to find and interpret the facts as the common man sees them

3. In civil cases where the amount involved is considerable, the case is brought in a jury court, bearing different official names in the different States

4. In criminal cases the accused has the right to a jury trial if he so elects

5. In this jury court the jury finds the facts and renders verdict thereon; the judge instructs the jury in the law, and controls the presentation of evidence. It is his duty to see that there is a fair trial in all respects

6. The judge has power to punish summarily disturbance at a trial, or contempt of his rulings in the trial, or of his writs either before or after trial.

7. From this court there may be appeal to an appellate court on the interpretation of the law, on the procedure in the trial court, and on constitutional rights

8. From the first appeal, there may be further appeal to the Supreme Court, either State or Federal as the case may be

9. The prime essential of any trial is that it shall be fair, that witnesses shall not be intimidated, that the jury shall not be prejudiced, influenced by public sympathy, or by any other matter unrelated to the finding of the truth about the relevant facts.

10. Civil suits which arise under the Constitution and laws of the United States, or between citizens of different States, appear in a Federal court. All others appear in State courts, but may be appealed to the United States Supreme Court where issues under the Constitution are involved.
11. The United States Supreme Court has original jurisdiction, that is, suits are brought before that Court in the first place, when they are:
    a) Suits between States
    b) Suits in which public ambassadors, ministers, and consuls are concerned

B. The Constitution

Once upon a time I found it my duty to oversee the enforcement of a statute requiring that the Constitution of the United States and that of the State concerned should be read at least once by all pupils before leaving the eighth grade. What the children were likely to get out of the documents by reading them once in the fourteenth year of their lives did not appear. The Legislature evidently believed that there should be some kind of instruction of future citizens in the Constitution under which most of them would live. The school people had never done anything about it.

Why should there in the Common School be more thoroughgoing elementary instruction in the Constitution, and in that of at least one of the States?

In the first place, because on our principles The State is an indefeasible element in the Curriculum of the Common School; because the study of Civil Government is one of the ways in which we come to understand The State; and because the Constitution is the documentary setting-forth of our form of Civil Government.

In the second place, because Law is also an indispensable element in arriving at a valid conception of the Civil State, and some elementary study of the meaning and nature of laws is therefore essential. The Constitution and the constitutions of the several States are statements of fundamental principles to which we have agreed that our statute-making and judicial interpretation must conform.

In the third place, since the validity of the Constitution as a modern document is frequently challenged, and since Amendments are frequently proposed, it is just as well that responsible and presumably intelligent people should know what it is that we are proposing to amend, and thus avoid the emptiness of manufactured opinion.

In the fourth place, the Constitution is an indispensable element in Political Science. Since 1789 it has served as the model from which most other constitutions the world over have more or less been drawn.

I. WHAT IS A CONSTITUTION?

A constitution in general is the way in which an organism or a political body is *put together*. Thus, we commonly speak of a certain individual as "having a good constitution," meaning that he seems to keep well and recover from sickness or injury where other individuals do not. When we set up a club, we write and accept a constitution for it.

A civil constitution like ours is likewise the way in which a State is put together, but put together in terms of Government and Law. Such a constitution, if it is to be effective, must be obedient to certain principles.

Must conform to the actual mores.—First of all, it must conform to the actual mores. If the mores of a people are not adequate to constitutional Government, then popular sovereignty is impossible with that people. They will inevitably fall back into some form of despotism, nowadays known as dictatorship. The principle is recognized by the Constitution when, in the amendment process, not a mere majority of votes is required, but an overwhelming majority—two-thirds in the Congress which proposes the Amendment, and three-quarters of the States which adopt. A great majority is ordinarily more likely to reflect the mores than would a mere technical majority.

The principle has been obeyed in all the Amendments, save the Fifteenth, conferring nation-wide suffrage on negroes, and the Eighteenth, setting up prohibition of the trade in intoxicating liquors. Neither of them proved effective in the States in which they did not suit the mores.

Constitution a body of general principles.—The second of the cardinal principles which are in a workable constitution is that it shall be a document of general principles, and not a body of laws specifically commanding right conduct and prohibiting wrong conduct. The latter is the field of statutes and even of municipal ordinances.

Of all the Amendments to the Constitution, the Eighteenth was the only one which offended against this principle. It was in form a police ordinance, a prohibition of a certain line of conduct. If it had been limited to giving Congress power to enact laws in control of the liquor traffic, it would have been at least correct in form.

II. FORM AND POWERS OF GOVERNMENT

The Constitution sets up the framework of the Federal Government, and through its grants and denials of power defines the relations between the Federal Government and the Governments of the several States. With the framework of Government we have dealt in the preceding section.

I. SETS UP LIMITED DEMOCRACY

The Constitution grants certain powers to the Federal Government and denies exercise of other powers which had been used by other Governments than our own. It denies certain powers to the State Governments, and the State constitutions grant and deny powers to their own.

Thus there is set up throughout the land a limited democracy, just as there might have been set up a limited monarchy. That does not mean that other powers than those granted are to be exercised by a king or a ruling class, but that they are not to be exercised at all. Another way of putting it is to state that the people themselves in the orderly process of constitution-making have limited themselves and their representatives in the use of sovereign powers.

The Preamble to the Constitution declares: "We the people of the United States, in order to form a more perfect Union, establish Justice, insure domestic tranquillity, provide for the common defense, promote the general welfare, and secure the blessings of Liberty to ourselves and our posterity, do ordain and establish this Constitution for the United States of America.'

The expression "general welfare" occurs but once in the body of the document, in Section 8 of Article I: "The Congress shall have power to lay and collect taxes, duties, imposts and excises, to pay the debts and provide for the common defense and general welfare of the United States."

What does that mean? On the face of it, it looks as if the Constitution authorized the President and Congress to do pretty much anything, provided they said that they were doing it for the general welfare. Common sense and the rest of the Constitution tell us that such could not have been the meaning. To be guided by what "the Constitution plainly says" is apt to be like the behavior of a heedless boy who being sent on an errand gives scant heed to his instructions and no consideration at all. The document must be studied as a whole, and, not only that, it must be studied in the light of the history of its writing and of the times in which it was written.

The Preamble is what its name implies, a brief declaration of the theory of The State and its functions upon which the Constitution is based.

First of all, it was for the sake of forming a more perfect Union. The circumstances which called for the Constitutional Convention were lack of Union and conspicuous lack of means for providing for the *common* defense and the *general* welfare of thirteen commonwealths.

In the second place, to set up general welfare as one of the cardinal functions of The State under the Constitution was the same thing as a declaration that the Constitution was setting up a Republic in the ancient and not the medieval sense of the word, that is to say, a *res publica*, a Commonwealth. The countries with which the Framers and the people were familiar were based on the theory that Governments exist for the glory of the king and the maintenance of the established classes derived from the Feudal State. To say that the Constitution being set up was, among other things, "to promote the general welfare" was to repudiate the whole existing European theory of The State.

Historians and courts have commonly held that the General Welfare clause in Article I is restrictive and not a grant of power, that it restricts the activities of Government to (*a*) purposes which are for the general and not for some individual, class, or local welfare and (*b*) purposes which are elsewhere in the Constitution declared to be within the powers of the Federal Government.

3. EMERGENCY POWERS

There seems to have grown up a belief that emergencies and the General Welfare clause together sanction the abandonment of constitutional restrictions, that the President or a Governor can declare an emergency and then legally rule without the law.

The Supreme Court has recently said, what every interested and informed student knew well enough anyway, that an emergency creates no powers which do not exist already. Nor does an emergency sanction an abandonment of rights guaranteed to citizens, save in the instances and by the methods provided in the Constitution. We shall meet some of them.

4. WAR POWER

Similarly, the delusion has grown up that Congress can endow the President with war powers which he does not already possess.

Congress alone can declare the existence of a state of war. When it has done so, the President as commander-in-chief acquires by force of circumstances great accession of power, but no additional powers. Lincoln emancipated the slaves in territory occupied by Federal troops. That was an exercise of power incident to his military character; slavery was abolished by the Thirteenth Amendment.

Congress can suspend the writ of habeas corpus "when in cases of rebellion or invasion the public safety may require it." Suspension of the writ means that persons can be arrested and held without trial—legally so. If the territory in which the privilege of the writ is suspended is occupied by troops, the civilian population can legally and constitutionally be placed under martial law.

In times of peace as well as in times of war, private property can be taken for public use, but the seizure must be by due legal proceedings.

"Congress shall have power . . . . to provide for the common defense; to raise and support armies . . . . ; to provide and maintain a navy; to make rules for the government and regulation of the land and naval forces; to provide for calling forth the militia to execute the laws of the Union, suppress insurrection and repel invasions."

Moreover, the Constitution defines treason. In a state of war or of organized insurrection, sundry acts and forms of conduct, which in times of peace would not be illegal, becomes treasonable and punishable as such. Some constitutional rights become qualified by the very circumstances of the state of war or insurrection, notably free speech. If the reader is interested in following the matter up, he will do well to read a series of decisions of the Supreme Court on cases which arose during the war of 1914–18.[1]

Finally, the Court has roundly and unanimously said that Congress cannot constitutionally delegate its powers to the President.

So the notion that Congress can constitutionally endow the President with war powers to the extent of suspending the Constitution is myth. He already has war powers, both in his capacity of commander-in-chief and in that of chief magistrate. Congress is given very complete war powers, but they are specific and not general, and they must be exercised in an orderly and constitutional manner and not in an arbitrary and autocratic manner.

---

[1] Alfred Lief, *The Dissenting Opinions of Mr. Justice Holmes* (New York: Vanguard Press, 1929). In these decisions Justice Holmes was not in dissent.

5. DEFENSE AGAINST CORRUPTION OF CONGRESS BY THE EXECUTIVE

"No Senator or Representative shall, during the time for which he was elected, be appointed to any civil office under the authority of the United States, which shall have been created, or the emoluments whereof shall have been increased, during such time; and no person holding any office under the United States, shall be a member of either House during his continuance in office."

The history of representative Government had abundantly shown that an Executive would, if he could, use appointment to lucrative or honorable office as a method of controlling legislation, and in that way of governing arbitrarily. We may reasonably infer that corrupt practices of any kind are repugnant to the Constitution, albeit but one kind was specified. Most other forms are recognized crimes in themselves.

6. INTERSTATE COMMERCE

"Congress shall have power . . . . to regulate commerce with foreign nations, and between the several States, and with the Indian tribes."

The Interstate-Commerce clause is really the heart of the Constitution as a purely political document. There, as nowhere else, save in the matter of the common defense, does the Federal principle come out with clarity. The necessity of regulating commerce between the States and with foreign nations had been one of the chief motives for calling the Convention. Without such regulation, the only possible method would have been through treaties between the States and between individual States and outside countries, both of which would have been incompatible with any national integrity whatever.

No doubt what was chiefly in mind in the Convention was the use of harbors and navigable waters under the control of the Federal Government, and prevention of the erection of obstacles to the free flow of commerce between the States. Nevertheless, the Constitution is a body of principles as well as written law, or rather behind the forms lie principles which are as good now as they were a century and a half ago. We can hardly doubt that the principles which actuated the makers in 1787 would still actuate them, could they have lived over into the age of automobiles, airplanes, radio; into the times of the factory system, chain stores, modern banking, modern susceptibilities touching the reach of collective justice. The principle lives on; the particular substance which the principle clothes changes. It is one of the numerous instances in the body of the instrument which have endowed it with a flexibility which is so hard for foreign commentators to understand.

Allied to, and really a part of, the power to regulate interstate commerce are the following:

1. Power to coin money, regulate the value thereof and of foreign coins
2. Power to fix the standards of weights and measures
3. Power to establish post offices and post roads
4. Denial to the States of power to coin money or emit bills of credit
5. And of power to lay duties on imports or exports or on tonnage
6. And of power to enter into treaties and alliances
7. "No preference shall be given by any regulation of commerce or revenue to the ports of one State over those of another; nor shall vessels bound to, or from, one State, be obliged to enter, clear, or pay duties in another."

7. FISCAL POWERS

"Fiscal" means "pertaining to the public purse, or treasury." Fiscal matters are also financial, but not all financial matters are fiscal. I suppose the first thing the first king learned was how to lay and collect taxes. Of all civil powers, it is the one most liable to abuse. One of the chief reasons, however, for the rise of the United States under the Constitution lay in the fact that under the Confederation there was no effective national power of taxation and collection of necessary revenue. Hence:

1. "Congress shall have power to lay and collect taxes, duties, imposts and excises."
2. "But all duties, imposts and excises shall be uniform throughout the United States."
3. And it shall have "power to borrow money on the credit of the United States."
4. And "to pay the debts and provide for the common defense and general welfare of the United States."

The *credit* of the United States is different in degree, but not in kind, from your credit and mine. It is nothing more than the confidence of men throughout the world that the United States can and will in the end pay its bills. If confidence fails, there is no longer any credit—and commonly not much business of any kind.

5. Congress cannot lay direct taxes, other than income taxes, except it be in proportion to the population of the several States.
6. It cannot lay duties on exports.

8. ADMISSION OF NEW STATES

"New States may be admitted by Congress into this Union"; thirty-five have so been admitted. "But no new State shall be formed or erected within the jurisdiction of any other State; nor any State be formed by the junction of two or more States, or parts of States, without the consent of the Legislatures of the States concerned as well as of the Congress."

West Virginia is the only State formed within the jurisdiction of a State. At the time, Virginia was in secession, and the loyal western counties, supporting the only Legislature held to be legitimate, gave consent to the partition of the State.

9. POWER OVER TERRITORIES AND DEPENDENCIES

"The Congress shall have power to dispose of and make all needful rules and regulations respecting the territory or other property belonging to the United States."

Congress has in the past erected, and still does on occasion erect, Territories as civil entities but without the sovereign qualities of States. Legislatures have typically been elective, and the Governors and judges appointive by the President.

10. "THE UNITED STATES SHALL GUARANTEE TO EVERY STATE IN THIS UNION A REPUBLICAN FORM OF GOVERNMENT"

The power has never to my knowledge been used. It would not have required any great stretch of the language of the Constitution to have used it several times when States fell into the hands of political despots who governed arbitrarily for a time.

"And shall protect each of them against invasion; and on application of the Legislature, or of the Executive [when the Legislature cannot be convened] against domestic violence."

11. IMPLIED POWERS

Finally, Congress has power "to make all laws which shall be necessary and proper for carrying into execution the foregoing powers, and all other powers vested by this Constitution in the Government of the United States, or in any department or officer thereof."

This is one of the most important of all sections in the Constitution. It is an extremely difficult thing to set up a written charter of Government for so complicated a thing as a modern State and avoid making it so rigid that it will break down on the first test, and at the same time avoid making it so flexible that it ceases to have any restraining power at all. On the one hand, lay the paralysis of the severe restrictions found in the Articles of Confederation, and, on the other, parliamentary sovereignty which had been the underlying cause of the revolt of the Colonies and the War for Independence. The clause has stood the test, *our people having been what they have been*.

POWERS DENIED

Powers granted suggest powers denied, of which there are many. Some we have already met in connection with powers granted. Most of the powers denied, however, properly belong in the next section, which deals with the Constitution as Fundamental Law. One is impressive.

12. CONTROL OF PUBLIC MONEY

"No money shall be drawn from the Treasury, but in consequence of appropriations made by law; and a regular statement and account of the receipts and expenditures of all public money shall be published from time to time."

POWERS DENIED TO THE STATES

In setting up a Government for the nation, the principle was consistently followed of granting powers to the United States and denying them to the States. The States were already sovereign and needed no grants of power. They must, however, be denied powers in order to make the Union possible. The United States was brought into existence as sovereign by the Constitution itself as a grant of powers. That understanding was confirmed in the Tenth Amendment, "The powers not delegated to the United States by the Constitution, nor prohibited by it to the States, are reserved to the States respectively, or to the people."

We have already found certain powers denied to the States in our attempt to understand Interstate Commerce in the Constitution. Others will be found in our study of the Constitution as Fundamental Law. Three, however, contribute to our understanding of the Form and Powers of Government, albeit two of them are perhaps quite as much Fundamental Law.

13. NO STATE SHALL "EMIT BILLS OF CREDIT"

Bills of credit are instruments which can be made to circulate as currency. Their intrinsic value rests only on the ability of the issuing authority to redeem them, and on confidence that it will do so. Such action always demoralizes Commerce and results in hard times, which can become extremely hard. The Founders had had bitter experience with "Continentals," whence the expression "not worth a continental," and that currency still outstanding was one of the most serious social problems incident to getting the new Government established. France was presently to learn something from her *assignats*. Greenback currency issued during the Civil War is still a fading memory to the generation born during the war and soon afterward. Russian rubles and German marks are recent instances. To allow the States to liquidate their debts and carry on their Governments that way was to embark on a short road to economic destruction. On the other hand, it is not safe to deny the war-making power that recourse in times of prolonged war, in which the national existence may be threatened. Even so the expedient must be used with great care and great restraint lest the remedy prove worse than the disease.

Nor is this ancient history. Periodically, some weird proposal for issuing "script" as a modern method of getting something for nothing is set up, and the habit will probably last until our system of public instruction is effective enough to justify its existence.

14. NOR "MAKE ANY THING BUT GOLD AND SILVER COIN A TENDER
IN PAYMENT OF DEBTS"

The States are denied the power to coin money, but, were it not for the present clause, the State Governments could ruin creditors by making depreciated commodities legal tender in satisfaction of debts. To the insolvent debtor the bankruptcy courts are open. To destroy the creditor, the man who has trusted you, has always been viewed by many as a triumph of virtue, going far to justify the doctrine of total depravity.

15. NOR KEEP TROOPS OR SHIPS OF WAR IN TIME OF PEACE . . . . NOR ENGAGE
IN WAR, UNLESS ACTUALLY INVADED, OR IN SUCH IMMINENT
DANGER AS WILL NOT ADMIT OF DELAY"

The provision does not apply to the National Guard, to State Constabulary, to sheriff's posse, or to the organized militia which in the old days used to be kept up.

These are civil forces employed for the suppression of disorder. When the National Guard is called into the service of the United States, or drafts are made on the militia, they become Federal troops.

16. AMENDMENTS

The notion that the Constitution is fixed upon us as an inflexible charter of eighteenth-century ideas, and designed to perpetuate social conditions then existing, can scarcely be held by any reasonable person who will take the trouble to inform himself of the bearings of Article V. Nor was this one of the articles forced into the Constitution as one of the first ten Amendments. On the contrary, the Framers themselves in the Convention saw that they could not hope to draw up an instrument of Government nor a body of Fundamental Law good for all time. Hence the Amending power committed to Congress and the State Legislatures and the people. We can perhaps do no better than to have the whole article before us.

The Congress, whenever two-thirds of both Houses shall deem it necessary, shall propose Amendments to this Constitution, or, on the application of the Legislatures of two-thirds of the several States, shall call a Convention for proposing Amendments, which, in either case, shall be valid to all intents and purposes, as part of this Constitution, when ratified by the Legislatures of three-fourths of the several States, or by conventions in three-fourths thereof, as the one or the other mode of ratification may be proposed by the Congress.

In other words, Amend whenever it seems necessary, but do not amend until you are sure it is necessary.

III. THE CONSTITUTION AS FUNDAMENTAL LAW

Of course, the Constitution as a whole, including all that we have thus far studied, is fundamental law, for this is a Government by law. Nevertheless, in a more precise sense it is fundamental to our jurisprudence, that is to say, to our system of justice. It needs however to be emphasized that the Constitution is not all of Law, as we have studied Law in the last chapter, for Law is universal. It is our belief and our pride that the Constitution has been founded on Law.

It is perhaps not too much to say that the Constitution as Fundamental Law is chiefly a guaranty of Civil Liberty, and that brings us to a consideration of what liberty and Civil Liberty are, for we are exceedingly prone to misunderstand the whole matter.

1. CIVIL LIBERTY

The Preamble recites that one of the purposes of the Constitution in the beginning was to "secure the blessings of Liberty to ourselves and our posterity."

We use "liberty" in common parlance as "freedom from restraint." We say, You are at liberty to do this and that, meaning that there is nothing to prevent. I have observed immigrants, as I suppose others have, who definitely believed that American liberty, about which they had heard so much, meant that they were free to do pretty much anything that suited their convenience and their consciences. We not infrequently hear people whose ancestors have lived on this soil since the beginning protest vigorously against laws which they do not like as "interference with personal liberty," naïvely unaware that what they seem to desire would be anarchy.

Now liberty in that sense has been more and more restrained

since there began to be any Civilization at all. Courteous treatment of others is self-deprivation of liberty. The whole body of Science and all of Morality is restraint of personal liberty, but thereby we attain personal integrity.

The term as used in the Constitution, in lawbooks, in all the liberty documents which enter into the body of the world's culture, has a particular and definite meaning. It means the liberty which is guaranteed by the Constitution and by the laws made in conformity with the Constitution and with basal morality. It is Civil Liberty or Liberty under the Law.

Civil Liberty, in the first place, is protection from arbitrary enslavement and imprisonment. That is where we get the word itself. The Latin *liber* means a free man and is contrasted with *servus*, which means a slave. "Freedom" and "free" man mean precisely the same, but they are of Teutonic origin. But neither *liber* nor *freeman* ever meant an individual who may do anything he pleases.

In the second place, Liberty means freedom from the domination of other men, freedom from the power of other men to determine one's course in life, even though they be officers of Government. In truth one might say that a large part of the development of Jurisprudence has been a history of the discovery of Liberty as the foundation of Justice. So much remains to be done that one sometimes feels that legislatures and courts the world over would save time in the march toward the millennium if they would give over attempts to make the world better by adopting appealing economic devices, spend a century or two in discovering ways in which men still dominate and exploit other men, incorporating their discoveries in the structure of Jurisprudence; and in finding ways of preventing enslavement by enacting the ways into the body of positive law.

The Civil State, as we know, arose out of the process of doing just that, and substituting government by law for government by men. We do not suffer deprivation of Liberty when we are required to do that which we know, or might know, is right. So far as Government by law is right, as it presumptively is, there is no denial of Liberty by requiring us to do certain things and forbidding us to do other things. That is just the way in which we are protected from the affronts and invasions of our neighbors. So that is what due process of law means, the reason why it is made so much of in the Constitution. It is one of the advances which have been made in the development of the institution which we call The State.

In short, we can generalize and say that Civil Liberty, as it appears in the Liberty documents back through the ages, has been a guaranty of a condition of existence, usually by interference with conduct. If we establish freedom from slavery, we do it by forbidding men to hold slaves. If we establish freedom from industrial exploitation, we do it by forbidding employers to work their help unduly long hours or to throw their employees out of a place in the world as a matter of individual caprice and self-interest.

People will come to enjoy complete Liberty when the time shall have arrived when they will be completely in enjoyment of all the rights which are in principle theirs as human beings, so long as they are able and willing to take on also the obligations which go with all rights. That is equality before the law and guaranteed by law, the only kind of equality we know anything about, or believe to be possible, so long as humans have to live in a state of nature. That is as far as Civil Government in its administration of justice can ever go. Government can never by law make a man what he is not, or save him from the natural consequences of his own acts.

What, then, are the bases of our jurisprudence in so far as they are found in the Constitution?

2. SUPREME LAW OF THE LAND

First of all, the Constitution is the supreme law of the land. On first analysis, the Constitution is written law, and it specifically states in sundry places where it does and does not apply.

In the powers apportioned to the United States and in those which are denied to the States, the Constitution is supreme and is binding upon State courts in their application of the law, anything in their own constitutions and laws to the contrary notwithstanding. Nevertheless, State constitutions may go far beyond, and may be materially different from the Constitution, and still not conflict with it. We hear so much about our Federal Constitution that we are apt to forget that there are forty-eight State constitutions, and to ignore the fact that by far the largest portion of our daily existence in the common concerns of life—the holding and transmission of property, the protection of the criminal laws, marrying and giving in marriage, the regulation of the family, even death and burial—is passed under the protection and control of State constitutions.

On the other hand, the principles which lie behind the Constitution as Fundamental Law we hold to be of universal validity. They were recognized by civilized men all the way back, some of them in Egyptian and Babylonian and early Chinese times, before there was any Constitution. Many of them appeared in the existing State constitutions in 1787. We hold that these principles ought to be imbedded as matter of course in the State constitutions, and so for the most part they are.

3. CITIZENSHIP

Citizenship is defined with precision. Citizens are "all persons born or naturalized in the United States and subject to the jurisdiction thereof." They are "citizens of the United States and of the State in which they reside." A baby born in Maine becomes a citizen of the United States and of Maine at once, unless he is the child of a foreign consul or of some other person not subject to the jurisdiction of the United States. If he moves to California when he grows up and resides there, he becomes a citizen of California, albeit his voting status may be determined by the law of California, provided the latter does not discriminate on account of race, color, or sex.

4. MOREOVER, "THE CITIZENS OF EACH STATE SHALL BE ENTITLED TO ALL PRIVILEGES AND IMMUNITIES OF CITIZENS IN THE SEVERAL STATES"

We are not aliens anywhere in the United States. The Maine man who moved to California could no longer vote in Maine after he had acquired a voting residence in California and voted there, but Maine could not retaliate for his desertion by treating an estate which he left behind any differently from the estates of lifelong residents. Nor can California restrict the rights and privileges of doing business there to native sons.

5. "FULL FAITH AND CREDIT SHALL BE GIVEN IN EACH STATE
TO THE PUBLIC ACTS, RECORDS, AND JUDICIAL PROCEED-
INGS OF EVERY OTHER STATE"

A man living in New York, for instance, against whom there is a judgment for debt, found in a New York court, cannot run away to Illinois and escape judgment, or force his creditor to begin all over again in an Illinois Court.

Nevertheless, the section does not enable a man to attain a certain legal status in one State and then claim that status in another State, if such status is repugnant to the public policy of the second State. One cannot for instance acquire a teaching or a medical license in Wisconsin and claim the privileges of licensure in Michigan under the Wisconsin license, unless Michigan consents. Nor can a person claim a divorced status in his home State by going to a State with notoriously lax divorce laws and getting a divorce there, unless the home State consents.

6. EXTRADITION

A fugitive from the justice of one State found in another State is returned to the authorities of the first State by the process known as Extradition. The Governor of the State of origin applies to the State of refuge for arrest and return of the accused. The latter is arrested and held pending the arrival of officers from the State in which the crime was committed. He is then delivered up to be carried back. That is the ordinary course. Nevertheless, the State of refuge is sovereign, and there is nothing to compel the Governor to accept the extradition papers. There may be a hearing and the decision reached that substantial justice will not be done by return.

A similar process is carried out between the United States and a foreign country with which there is an extradition treaty. A treaty, be it remembered, is part of the law of the land.

7. NATURALIZATION

Congress shall have power "to establish an uniform Rule of Naturalization."

We are so preoccupied in many schools with "Americanization" and preparing aliens for first papers and the like that we seldom reflect that in this power was a distinct contribution to international jurisprudence.

In 1787 the prevailing doctrine was that nationality is indefeasible. We fought the War of 1812 in part in defense of our right to make citizens of English sailors. Today, Germany is the only great power which has consistently held that no migration to another country, even though the latter took place centuries ago, can release persons of German origin from some sort of allegiance to the Reich.

In connection with Naturalization, our children at an early age ought to be taught that, *when their parents or grandparents became naturalized, they became Americans and ceased to belong to other nations.* Hyphenated Americans still create some of our most formidable problems through their reserved devotion to their racial homes. Generally speaking, the English, Jewish, and Negro elements in our population are the only ones which as classes are not tainted with the fault. The first of the three can scarcely be charged with hyphenization, since they have fought two wars with the mother-country and have come to the verge of three others. Unless the schools can breed this taint out of the population, we shall always potentially be involved in every European quarrel that springs up.

8. INTERNATIONAL LAW

There has been a system of International Law viewed as a science, a system of thought, for more than three centuries; but there has been no international legislature and no positive law. Nevertheless, the Constitution established our attitude toward justice between nations in the beginning, and in general our foreign policy has lived up to it. The Constitution began with Naturalization. It continued with the following:

Congress shall have power "to define and punish piracies and felonies committed on the high seas, and offenses against the law of nations." Thus, a sovereign power from its inception recognized that there is such a thing as international law, and in substance announced that, if no international legislature and tribunal were possible, nevertheless, so far as its own citizens were concerned, it proposed to incorporate principles of international justice into its own law.

9. BANKRUPTCY

One of the historic problems of Justice has been, "How shall debtors be dealt with?" It is a triangular problem. On one side is the debtor himself, sometimes a vicious specimen, more often a specimen of frail humanity, frequently the victim of misfortunes beyond his control. On another is the creditor whose rights are in a nexus with the failures of his debtor and who is easily condemned as grasping and avaricious when he desires only what is his own. On the third side is the community which may easily be paralyzed if debtors can find no relief, and equally well if credit, which is trust, ceases to exist. One version of the Lord's Prayer seems to make forgiveness of sins dependent on the penitent's willingness to release his debtors. Two difficulties had to be met and two problems of a practical nature solved:

In the first place was the harsh treatment of debtors, which in ancient times involved being sold into slavery, and, at the time of the Convention and long after, involved the stupid as well as harsh treatment of being imprisoned until payment.

In the second place, was the imminent likelihood that under popular government the State Legislatures would practice wholesale discharge of debtors without regard to ability to pay.

The possibility is as lively today as it was a century and a half ago, for untutored human nature is much the same today as it was in 1787. The whole matter was made a Federal concern by giving Congress power to make "uniform laws on the subject of bankruptcy throughout the United States."

10. OBLIGATION OF CONTRACTS

Similarly, the Constitution seeks to lay the foundation of commercial integrity by forbidding any State to make any "law impairing the obligation of contracts." No such prohibition needed to be placed on Congress, since matters involving contractual relations are normally in State legislation. But Congress may not impair the obligations of contracts into which the United States has itself entered.

Then comes a series of provisions establishing more definitely the foundations of Civil Liberty as against Congress and against the State Legislatures.

11. TREASON DEFINED

"Treason against the United States shall consist only in levying war against them, or in adhering to their enemies, giving them aid and comfort. The Congress shall have power to declare the punishment of treason, but no attainder of treason shall work corruption of blood, or forfeiture except during the life of the person attainted."

In England the doctrine of constructive treason was held, that is to say, Parliament could define treason at any time—and still can. But Congress cannot define treason and never could. What might have happened, had Congress the power, in times of excited political animosity, we do not know; but Congress has not the power. We hope that we have always been too humane ever to have indulged in blood purges and bloody assizes, but recent events suggest that it is well that we cannot constitutionally do so anyway.

The States are sovereign, and there can be treason against a State. Nor does the constitutional provision which we have under discussion affect the States.

12. "NO BILL OF ATTAINDER . . . . SHALL BE PASSED"

An English bill of attainder had been a special law passed in order to reach and punish an individual who could not be reached by due process of law. Of course such bills were the very negation of Justice and of Civil Liberty. The prohibition extends to the States.

13. EX POST FACTO

Both Congress and the State Legislatures are forbidden to enact ex post facto laws. Such a law makes an act a crime which was not a crime at the time of the occurrence, or widens the definition of a crime after it has been committed. The provision is, of course, merely the assurance of elementary fair play.

14. HABEAS CORPUS

The writ of habeas corpus is the cornerstone, or one of them, of our Liberty. In times of public stress and danger, when emergency measures are called for, one of the first steps is for Congress to suspend the writ, either in part or, conceivably, over the whole country.

Time was when persons could be arrested and locked up in prison during the king's pleasure. It was a Continental rather than an English malfeasance, for such practices had been repugnant to the Anglican jurisprudence for centuries. Well down into the nineteenth century cultivated men languished in prison in some supposedly civilized European countries, charged with no crime but sequestered because of their political activities.

Habeas corpus means "You may hold the body" or in current phrase, "All right, I will let him out if you will be responsible for him." A person arrested and lodged in jail can through a friend, or more likely an attorney, go to the nearest judge, state the case, and apply for a writ. If the judge is satisfied that the accused will be presented for trial, a writ of habeas corpus is issued which is in substance an order for the release of the accused, until such time as his trial is set.

15. DOUBLE JEOPARDY

"Nor shall any person be subject for the same offense to be twice put in jeopardy of life or limb."

When a person accused of a crime against the United States, involving the consequences specified, has been acquitted by a jury, that is the end of it. He cannot be tried again and again until he is convicted. Nor can the prosecution appeal the case to a higher court, but the accused can appeal if there is ground.

16. DUE PROCESS

Here is another of the cornerstones. "Nor be deprived of life, liberty, or property without due process of law: nor shall private property be taken for public use, without just compensation."

This is the Fifth Amendment and a restriction on the powers of
the United States. The Fourteenth Amendment extends the same
restrictions to the States.

For a hundred years nobody had any doubt what due process in
the Fifth Amendment meant. It reinforced the prohibition of bills
of attainder and regulation of the suspension of habeas corpus. A
good many persons have been deprived of life for murder on the
high seas, or in the Territories, or in the District of Columbia; others have been imprisoned under the finding of a Federal court, and
have been deprived of property, either in fines or because the
Government needed a piece of property for public use. But that
has all been done by United States marshals executing judgments
of courts, after the individuals had had fair hearings in court, or
before a judicial agency of some sort. That is what is meant by
due process of law. It contrasts with arbitrary seizure of property
or imprisonment or killing by an officer of the Executive Branch,
or confiscatory legislation in Congress or Legislature.

But the Fourteenth Amendment applied to the States. It was
proclaimed adopted in 1868. It was aimed primarily at establishing civil rights for the freedmen, but it was found that it did much
more. What was due process between 1787 and 1868 seldom found
any application in concerns which fall under the purview of the
Federal Government, but as soon as it was extended to the States
as a definite part of the Constitution, it ran into all the complex
field of relationships which had grown up around the modern
organization of industry. States were legislating, or soon began to
legislate, on such matters as the control of corporate activity in
business, on property rights in industrial property, on sanitary
control of production, on the welfare of wage-earners, and a
variety of other interests of the kind.

Some of the State supreme courts, and in some cases the Supreme Court itself, found some of these acts unconstitutional, on
the ground that they deprived laborers of the right of freely con-
tracting their services, and deprived employers and producers of
their property through impairment of their right to make money
in their accustomed manner—in both classes, deprivation of due

process of law. That was a remarkable extension of what due process had been understood to mean for a century.

If the States could not make laws depriving anybody of his liberty, then they could make no laws at all. If they could not make laws regarding the use of property, then anybody could instal a pigpen on his city front lawn, or erect a slaughter-house in a residential district, or build a boiler factory next to the courthouse. Either the States, or cities holding corporate charters from States, have brought all such matters and much else under the control of their police laws, and rightly so. General laws applied to *classes* of people engaged in *particular kinds* of things are no violation of due process. That element comes in when the Executive or the Legislature arbitrarily arrests an individual or confiscates his property.

17. SEARCH AND SEIZURE

"The right of the people to be secure in their persons, houses, papers, and effects, against unreasonable searches and seizures, shall not be violated, and no warrants shall issue, but on probable cause, supported by oath or affirmation, and particularly describing the place to be searched, and the persons or things to be seized."

Arbitrary invasion of one's domestic retreat was peculiarly hateful to the men who lived in the time when the Constitution was adopted, and it is still hateful to those who have no taint of slavery in their souls. Search and seizure impartially decreed to be a public necessity and duly warranted, we ought cheerfully to endure, but unwarranted invasion is unendurable. The guaranty is, or at least has been, frequently violated by agents of the Federal bureaucracy, and citizens submit, either because they do not know their rights as free men or else because they cannot afford the cost of legal protection. The Congress itself has sometimes outrageously violated this provision. If we cherish our constitutional rights, we ought to be careful whom we send to Congress.

18. TRIAL BY JURY

"The trial of all crimes, except in cases of impeachment, shall be by jury."

"In suits at common law, where the value in controversy shall exceed twenty dollars, the right of trial by jury shall be preserved."

This of course in United States courts, but since trial by jury is one of the most ancient muniments in our system of law, the same provision or its equivalent appears in the States which are under the Anglican system.

People grow impatient at the frequent farces of jury trials and wish to abolish the system. They do not realize that jury trial on the facts of a case is as fundamental to our whole polity as is representative democracy itself. Impatience with the futilities of schools might equally well lead us to the conclusion that education itself is useless. Where juries are bad, it is our place to get them reformed.

The jury under the guidance of the judge finds the facts touching the law. Often the facts are the whole essence of the issue, and the law is entirely clear, granted the facts. Did this action in fact occur? Was this man responsible for injury? Was he neglectful? Was there contributory negligence? etc. In many and many a case, a jury has done justice where a stupid or barbarous law would have done injustice, or where the law does not and cannot permit taking circumstances into account. The lying verdict of coroner's juries, "death by suicide while of unsound mind," has often saved a family from the injustice of an obsolete statute, and still sometimes from the humiliation inflicted by popular prejudice. In truth, the history of the institution leads us to make what is perhaps an extravagant statement, but one with at least some truth in it, that juries have on the whole contributed to the development of jurisprudence as truly as have courts and legislatures. Our law, be it remembered, rests on a folk basis, and the jury is a folk method of assisting in securing justice.

The faults of the system are faults in the kind of men who are allowed to serve on juries, in the kind of men whom we allow to empanel juries, in the judges who conduct trials, in the often barbarous ways in which juries are treated.

19. SPEEDY AND PUBLIC TRIAL

"In all criminal prosecutions, the accused shall enjoy the right to a speedy and public trial, by an impartial jury of the State and district wherein the crime shall have been committed . . . . , and to be informed of the nature and cause of the accusation; to be confronted with the witnesses against him; to have compulsory process for obtaining witnesses in his favor, and to have the assistance of counsel for his defence."

Well, that's fair enough. I suppose that not many people in the United States would question the constitutional fair play to which every criminal is entitled. Perhaps the Article is valuable chiefly as a historical landmark—but we sometimes come upon landmarks on the way back.

Note the clauses one by one, and then recall that our forebears who were responsible for the Bill of Rights could remember times when in English law, as it then was, an accused person was not entitled to the rights found in a single one of the clauses. On the contrary, his trial might be long delayed; it might not be before a jury of his neighbors (the leaders in the War for Independence, at a certain stage, would probably have been sent to England for trial if they had been caught); he might not necessarily know what he was charged with; he might never know who were the witnesses against him; he had no means of securing witnesses who could testify in his favor; and, far from being furnished with counsel for his defense, it was not so very long since accused persons were not allowed any counsel at all.

Guaranty of a public trial meant protection from the outrage of a secret trial. To our eyes now a secret trial would be evidence that the prosecution had no case that would bear the light of day. Such trials exist in certain European countries still, where the accused is tried and sent to the firing squad, or the guillotine, or the beheading block, with no more notice than the Government chooses to give out.

The guaranty does not, however, mean that newspapers have a constitutional right to make every trial an opportunity for sensational exploitation, until the case is not in substance tried before judge and jury, but is rather tried in the newspapers until all the essence of attainder is present, or, in reverse circumstances, a jail-clearing. The good citizen ought to bear in mind that any case as it is presented in court looks very different from his own impressions derived from journalistic reports.

20. "EXCESSIVE BAIL SHALL NOT BE REQUIRED"

A vindictive and cruel judge in a United States court, in the absence of this provision, could, to all intents and purposes, suspend the writ of habeas corpus.

21. "NOR EXCESSIVE FINES IMPOSED"

By excessive fines a judge could easily defeat the principle of ex post facto, that is to say, impose fines which would amount to ruin, far beyond the penal assumptions attached to the crime.

22. "NOR CRUEL AND UNUSUAL PUNISHMENT INFLICTED"

It was within the recollection, or at least within the horrified historical knowledge, of our forefathers, that a criminal could be hanged, cut down while still living, and cut to pieces. In some of the States, even those accounted the most civilized, long after this restraint was set up for Federal courts, women could have their backs bared and be flogged until the blood came for minor thefts. To this day, even among our most enlightened people, we frequently hear it said of an heinous criminal, "Hanging is too good for him." Well, happily, we are limited to hanging in both Federal and State courts.

RIGHTS

The first ten Amendments, or more accurately the first nine, are commonly called the Bill of Rights, but in truth the whole Fundamental Law as found in the Constitution is an enumeration of rights. Nevertheless, certain rights are specifically enumerated as such, and with these we ought to deal. Be it remembered that they are rights guaranteed against the United States Government and not against the Governments of the States, although they may exist in the State constitutions as well.

23. RELIGIOUS FREEDOM

"Congress shall make no law respecting an establishment of religion."

An established church was one legally recognized by the Government, supported by general taxation, membership in which was a condition precedent to holding public office, and even to admission to the universities. The Church of England had been established in colonial Virginia, and the Congregational Church continued to be established in some of the New England States for some time after 1789. The Mormon Church has been at times to all practical purposes an established church in Utah.

It is long since there has been a legally established church anywhere in the United States, but we sometimes find the substance of establishment in one of its most hateful forms, namely, the restriction of office-holding to members of a particular faith.

24. "OR PROHIBITING THE FREE EXERCISE THEREOF"

So obvious a piece of civilized right scarcely requires comment, save in one particular. The guaranty does not extend to ritualistic or moral practices condemned by the general sense of our people and the prohibitions of our laws.

25. FREEDOM OF SPEECH AND OF THE PRESS

Congress shall make no law, "abridging the freedom of speech, or of the press."

The right exists for two good reasons:

First, it is repugnant to our notions of Civil Liberty that we should have to resort to counsel for legal advice every time we wish to make a remark, or to keep looking over our shoulders in a crowd in order to be sure who is listening.

Second, it is quite out of the question to carry on Government on the basis of popular sovereignty, unless all citizens are free to criticize the Government and its officers. Public men expect it, and most of them would not have it otherwise.

But in truth, freedom of speech and of the press never meant what we are daily led to believe that it means.

We make remarks about our neighbors on our own responsibility. We may be committing slander or, if we write, libel, for which we can be held to account.

A due consideration of the language of the clause, even apart from its historical setting, must convince any unprejudiced reader that it means only that Congress shall make no laws restraining publication, shall establish no censorship and no licensing bureau, or authorize the suspensions of journals for recalcitrancy. After publication, an editor or publisher or author is as responsible for his conduct as he is for any other kind of conduct. A book may be refused transmission in the mails by reason of its immoral nature, and the author may be punished, but the book itself cannot be censored as a condition precedent to publication.

That is our way of dealing with an evil which has, more or less sporadically, blazed up from time to time in all the ages. One of the principal reasons for the evolution of Literature as an institution is its compelling influence on the mores. A medical work can discuss all the matters in which the most extreme of "sexy" novels deals, and there is no taint of the salacious about the whole thing. It is the power of a literary technique which turns cold facts into suggestion which may be, and frequently is, demoralizing. The Athenians, to go no farther back, made corruption of youth a capital offense, and in all civilized ages there has been a legal presumption against anything which contributes to demoralization. The courts sometimes denounce as a matter of Common Law what is adjudged to be *contra bonos mores*.

What is immoral is a fact to be found by a jury, for the laws enumerate no catalogue of vices as distinguished from crimes. The jury finding may be extremely offensive to our literary and artistic friends, but jury findings on the facts are part of judicial procedure in a democratic country. Curiously enough, we cannot make authors the judges of the social character of their own work, either individually or collectively.

26. ASSEMBLY AND PETITION

Nor shall Congress pass any law, abridging "the right of the people peaceably to assemble, and to petition the Government for redress of grievances."

"Peaceably" to assemble is the heart of the matter. Congress is not inhibited from making it unlawful to riot in the District of Columbia, or to block the streets, or to appropriate the use of private property to mass meetings. That is about as far as Congress could go, save in respect to treasonable meetings in wartime and perhaps in respect to interruption of Federal offices, such as carrying the mail—and both the last two would probably be an Executive responsibility.

In the nature of the case, regulation of public meetings is an affair of the police powers of the States in nearly all cases in which public meetings could be held. Most of the States have similar provisions in their own constitutions, but whether they do or not, the principle lying behind the Constitutional prohibition is of universal validity in all civilized lands. Few things are more patently obnoxious to the very idea of Civil Liberty than the arrogant appropriation of public streets and public places by a rioting mob, or an organized mob determined to thrust to one side all the forces of law and order.

Nevertheless, there is nothing in the spirit of the Constitution which can be interpreted as sanction of the prevention of public meetings, even where there is advocated overthrow of our form of Government, provided the meeting does not riot—nor are opponents of such views inhibited from expressing their own estimates of them.

The right of petition is now more of a historical landmark than a guaranty of present right. If there is anything we do with great facility and freedom, it is the drawing-up of petitions.

27. SLAVERY AND INVOLUNTARY SERVITUDE

"Neither slavery nor involuntary servitude, except as a punishment for crime, whereof the party shall have been duly convicted, shall exist anywhere in the United States, or any place subject to their jurisdiction." The famous Thirteenth Amendment.

The Amendment goes a long way beyond the abolition of chattel slavery, for involuntary servitude covers various possible outcomes of labor contracts, and the Amendment limits the penalty

for breach of such contracts which the States might set up. Any
form of peonage is as truly prohibited as slavery in the strict
sense of that term.

28. RESERVED RIGHTS

"Enumeration in the Constitution of certain rights shall not be
construed to deny or disparage others retained by the people."

Thus was the way blocked to courts which might hold that
enumeration excludes things not enumerated.

Our philosophy of law and Government has always been based
on the doctrine of natural, ethical, rational rights, unalienable
rights as they are called in the Declaration, however much ma-
terialists may deprecate the idea that there are any such. The
law is in part an institution or complex of institutions which in
our theory discovers rights and does not create them. Congress
and the State Legislatures are left to work out a jurisprudence.

29. RIGHT OF THE MINORITY

Perhaps the most important right of all is specified nowhere in
the Constitution. The very fact that there is a written Constitution as a body of positive law, rather than a mere body of recognized custom, means that law is above Government in all three
Branches, and above the people even. Not even an overwhelming
majority of voters can legally and constitutionally deprive the
minority of rights guaranteed by the Constitution or recognized
in the common conscience of civilized people. There is no such
thing as a popular "mandate" in our theory of Government,
either express or implied. Conceivably, a majority of voters might
amend the Constitution so as to sanction the confiscation of all
property, reduce all of us to the status of slaves of The State, and
massacre all of us who ventured to oppose. If they did, there
would no longer be any Government capable of commanding the
allegiance of anybody. Society would be reduced to its earliest
savage form, and human nature would probably bring into play
the most fundamental of human passions, namely, that of self-
preservation. Such a thing, we have confidence, will never happen
here; but the Constitution in its theory of rights gives us some

ethical basis for estimating rightly the acts of other peoples who do just that. They sow the wind and reap the whirlwind in giving themselves over to the reign of brute force.

IV. THE SUPREME COURT AND THE CONSTITUTION

Perhaps the most vital and constructive thing about our Constitution was the creation of three mutually independent Branches of Government, and provision for judicial application of the Constitution itself. Ever since the final establishment of the Constitution, the power of the Supreme Court to interpret and apply has been challenged. It has certainly been a controversial question. Nevertheless, until this day our people have cherished the power of the Supreme Court as the most important practical defense of our Liberty and of civilized Government which we have. Within a few years of this writing, an adverse report of the Judiciary Committee of the Senate, on a proposal to nullify the Court by making it dependent upon the policy of the Administration in power, made one of the ablest and strongest State papers in our history. Opposition has been based on such patent misinformation, and lack of understanding, both of Law and of Constitution, that it seems to be time that the principles involved be made part of public instruction everywhere in the United States, as well as a unit in Political Science courses elsewhere.

JOHN MARSHALL

It has been said, with pointless reiteration of obvious misinformation, that John Marshall, Chief Justice of the United States, usurped a power which is not mentioned in the Constitution. It is true enough that the great judge had the resolution to bring into play the actual provision named below. In so doing, he proved himself to be one of the greatest of our statesmen in that he set up a landmark in the evolution of the Civil State. The section from which the power of the court is derived is the following:

"The judicial power shall extend to all cases in Law and Equity, arising under this Constitution, the laws of the United States and treaties made, or which shall be made, under their authority."

"Arising under this Constitution" is, of course, the vital expression.

Moreover, "this Constitution, and the laws of the United States which shall be made in pursuance thereof; and all treaties made, or which shall be made, under the authority of the United States, shall be the Supreme Law of the land; and the judges in each State shall be bound thereby, any thing in the constitution or laws of any State to the contrary notwithstanding."

Without these clauses, the Constitution would be but a preachment. Men whom Dicey, the ablest of recent English constitutionalists, calls "the ablest any country ever possessed," and a great Chief Justice in the following generation, were not likely to leave an instrument like the Constitution without means of enforcement; nor did they. The clauses turn a code of political wisdom and morality into positive law.

In the end, any act of Congress or of a State Legislature which has legal consequences can be challenged in a United States court, or in a State court, by any person who believes himself to be denied his constitutional rights thereby, and if need be, he can carry his case to the Supreme Court of the United States. Observe, however, that the powers of the Court arise only from *suits at law* arising under the Constitution. If the reasoning of the Court shows that the Federal or State law, from the ruling of which the suitor seeks relief, is in fact and principle contrary to the Constitution, the suitor is given relief. The effect is to make the law in question of none effect, so far as enforcement by the courts is concerned. The individual is awarded justice against those who made the law, even against the people who desired it.

The State supreme courts similarly administer constitutional justice in respect to laws enacted in contravention of the State constitutions.

Nor is it to be assumed that there is any quality of infallibility in either the Federal or a State Supreme Court. As civilized people, we accept their decisions, because it is better to do that than to attempt to exist in the community without any court at all. In reality, it is the reasoning behind the decision which nullifies the statute. We accept the decision even if the reasoning seems to be bad, but impartial justices of the quality of those who have commonly held seats in our supreme courts are far more likely to reason correctly and soundly than are people who are not impartial, and who have no learning and trained intelligence in either Constitution or the Law.

SUPREME COURT NOT A THIRD HOUSE OF CONGRESS

One not infrequently meets with the belief that the Supreme Court acts as a check in general on the rightness and wisdom of acts of Congress and of the Legislatures. Not so; the President and many of the Governors do that through the veto power. The Supreme Court does not spend part of each year scrutinizing the session laws like a teacher correcting examination papers. Cases get to the Supreme Court only as juridical issues. Somebody must have been wronged by an act of a legislative body, or conceivably of an executive. Even so, the Supreme Court is not conducting a question box to satisfy the curiosity of people as to what laws are and what are not constitutional. The questioner must come into court with a case.

A little-noted consequence of this last principle is that it adds appreciably to the flexibility and folk character of the Constitution itself, to substance rather than to form. A law may well be unconstitutional, but if it does no substantial injustice, it will never reach the Supreme Court on constitutional grounds.

Again, the third-house delusion constantly leads people to suppose that the Supreme Court sets up its opinion against that of Congress. Congress is a political, that is to say, a policy-forming body. It is morally bound to consider the constitutionality of its acts, but after all that is not its first interest or concern. Conversely, the Supreme Court is not concerned with the wisdom of lawmaking or of policy. It is concerned in this connection only with the constitutionality of laws or acts. The Court does not set up opinion on matters which are an open question; it sets up a course of reasoning touching the validity or nonvalidity of acts of the other Branches as constitutional measures. Much legislation which we may think unwise, and some which we may think dishonorable, is nevertheless entirely constitutional. In many a decision the Court has in effect warned the people that, if they desire wise legislation, it would be well to elect wise legislators.

NO DIRECT CONTROL OVER PRESIDENT AND CONGRESS

The opinion is sometimes expressed that there is set up an ultimate despotic authority in the Supreme Court. Such opinion ignores the touchstone of despotism, which is personal rule rather than rule according to law. If that be despotism, then the Supreme Court is the negation of despotism. It is quite true that the Supreme Court might be converted into a despotism, or made the instrument of despotism, by appointing ignorant and vicious men as justices, men who not only knew no law but knew no sanctity in an oath.

It has no direct control over the acts of the President. It cannot summon him into court, nor make its writ run against him. All that is provided for in the impeachment process. The courts can interfere with the execution by agents of an illegal order of the President, but they cannot forbid his issuing the order. The President is restrained by his oath of office, if at all.

Similarly, Congress has repeatedly acted in an unconstitutional manner, but the Court cannot send a marshal to arrest Congress and confine it until it promises good behavior. The Court can render of none effect unconstitutional laws enacted by Congress, but it cannot prevent Congress from enacting them. Congress is restrained not by the Court but by the oaths of the members.

SUPREME COURT NOT THE ULTIMATE RECOURSE

We are apt to suppose that we are completely protected in our constitutional rights by the Court. In the ordinary course of our history, that has been true. The Supreme Court, nevertheless, is but one of the Branches of our form of Government. In the last analysis, we are protected only by ourselves acting as voters. A Governor elected by the people, with the connivance of a Legislature also elected by the people, has upon occasion arbitrarily ejected the entire personnel of a State supreme court, and replaced it with appointees subservient to himself. A President and Congress could accomplish the same result with the Supreme Court of the United States.

Moreover, large numbers of the electorate have on occasion desired legislation obviously repugnant to the Constitution and to Justice. Doubtless, there are always in any population elements which are anarchistically inclined, but it is fairly evident that most people who adhere to proposals to override the Constitution do so out of ignorance of what the Constitution is and what are the functions of the Supreme Court under the Constitution. They have never been taught this veritable foundation in good citizenship.

NOT THE ONLY INSTANCE IN THE WORLD

Another objection sometimes urged is that the power of the Supreme Court is unique; but the Constitution itself was unique in 1789. Most of those which have emerged since those days have been more or less modeled upon our own. The power of the Supreme Court, it is true, does not appear in some of them. It is interesting to note that very few of those which do not have the power have long maintained a stable Government, while those that do have the power have been relatively stable. That does not prove a great deal, for after all not a great many of the constitutional States of the world have proved to be capable of self-government. That is a matter of the people and of the mores. The very existence of a constitution of our type presumes a method of instrumenting it.

England.—The instance most often cited is that of England, but the citation is immaterial, for England has a civil constitution only in the sense that every Englishman has a bodily constitution, the way he is put together. It is the English constitution which is unique in the world.

Parliament is supreme, and, as one wit put it, can do anything save make a man into a woman or a woman into a man. The result is a Parliamentary absolutism, checked only by the indisposition of the party in power to carry on in the face of adverse public opinion; and yet no English constitutionalist would deny that a parliamentary majority is capable of doing just that, even in the face of an adverse election. The Crown has become largely a symbolic institution, and yet commentators are fond of pointing out that a strong and determined King could legally, if not grasp the reins of Government, at least prevent anybody else's carrying on the Government, and indeed alter much of the social structure of England. Similarly, the Parliament could abrogate Magna Carta, the claims of the Petition of Right, the declarations of the Bill of Rights, with no better sanction at the best than the will of the popular majority existing at the time. The rejoinder that no King and no Parliament would act that way is no rejoinder to an American. The English constitution is a natural growth of a thousand years, a great body of national institutions rather than a legal instrument. So far as compelling and restraining force is concerned, the English State is not a Government of Fundamental Law, but rather a Government by force of circumstances.

So much for a suggestion of what the English constitution is, as you find it in the authoritative treatment of works like those of Bagehot, Dicey, Maine, and Lowell. But pass to the other side of the picture and look at it from the angle of a detailed history of legislation running for half a century, such as is found in a work like John Morley's *Life of Gladstone*. There, one notes again and again the protests of eminent citizens, even of the Universities, at the *illegality* of acts of Parliament. If people get to calling acts of Parliament illegal, it looks to an American as if his kindred across the sea had much the same constitutional ideas as his own, but had neglected to find a practical method of enforcing their rights.

Certainly, nothing in the English practice can be urged as valid objection to the American power of the Judiciary. Rather, in the long evolution of The State from personal rule, pure and simple, to the reign of law, principle, and right, pure and simple, the American conception is a full stage farther along than the English.

The English Dominions.—On the other hand, the self-governing English Dominions have substantially our form or constitutional Government under judicial control. They are under a supreme law of the land higher than their parliaments can enact, and their supreme courts in general pass on the constitutionality of legislation and other acts of the Dominion or Commonwealth, Provincial or State Governments, substantially as does the Supreme Court of the United States. True enough, the Dominion constitutions are likely to have been acts of the Imperial Parliament rather than acts of a constituent assembly. Not even that, however, is true of Australia.

The foregoing is all of it brought forward to set in true form the argument against the power of our Supreme Court as being unheard of elsewhere. Of most of the countries which most resemble our own, and which have our system of law and jurisprudence, the statement is not true. Of England it proves too much for the comfort of the critics. Nevertheless, the logical and historical validity of our form of Government is in no sense dependent upon what other countries do or do not.

V. INSTRUCTION

The Constitution can be read, not once in the eighth grade, but many, many times throughout a lifetime. The unassisted layman thus reading it will not be likely to see the doctrine and principles lying behind it, unless he reads along with it historical and juristic explanation. With pupils in the Common School, we might spend half a year on it, having them study it line upon line and precept upon precept—and still fail to lead them to understand and appreciate. For that reason, it is needful to select those parts which may chiefly contribute to an elementary understanding of the bases of our form of Government and of our national jurisprudence. This I have aimed to do in discussing the document at length for the special purposes of teachers, and perhaps as suggestive of the lines to be followed in schoolroom texts or in teaching without specially prepared texts.

There is much in the Constitution which was merely incidental to the initial establishment of Government and to reconstruction after the Civil War. There is much that is detail, such as the constitutional requirements concerning birth and age qualifications of officers, which can at best be remembered but hardly understood. Some of it has become obsolete, such as the provisions concerning the electoral college and the granting of letters of marque and reprisal. If I have erred in my selections, I believe that the error has consisted in including too much rather than too little.

Even so, as a handook for study purposes some simple but complete manual of the Constitution is requisite. For this purpose, I have never seen anything so good as Norton's book on the Constitution. I presume that Mr. Norton designed his volume to meet the needs of adult readers, but it is admirably fitted to be used as a body of assimilative material for pupils anywhere in the high school or junior college levels, provided it is used under the direction of a competent teacher.[2] This work, or some similar publication, would serve as material to be in the hands of every pupil, for study purposes. It is not, however, a textbook. If there is a competent teacher in charge, a textbook proper is not an absolute necessity, but it is a great help, especially if it is well organized for teaching purposes. Aside from the foregoing, I think every class should have for ready reference and for reading McLaughlin's *A Constitutional History of the United States*. This work is the latest and probably altogether the best. It is not a lawyer's book, although doubtless law students can use it, but rather a book for the educated layman. Along with McLaughlin should appear in the classroom Dicey, *The Law of the Constitution*. The English constitution is meant. It is valuable for students—and senior high school and junior college pupils could use it with profit—for the reason that it gives an authoritative idea of what the English constitution is, and for the further reason that the author in sundry passages draws some illuminating comparisons with the Constitution of the United States, often, if not usually, to the advantage of the latter.[3]

[2] Thomas James Norton, *The Constitution of the United States: Its Sources and Applications* (Boston: Little, Brown & Co., 1925).

[3] Andrew C. McLaughlin, *A Constitutional History of the United States* (New York: D. Appleton–Century Co., 1935); A. V. Dicey, *The Law of the Constitution* (8th ed.; New York: Macmillan & Co., 1915).

UNIT ORGANIZATION OF THE COURSE

I. A Good Constitution
   1. Constitution in general is the way in which anything is put together
   2. The Constitution of a Civil State is properly a legal document framed in terms of positive law
   3. Must conform to the ways and customs and convictions of the people
   4. If the ways and customs and convictions are not capable of supporting a civil constitution, then that people is not capable of self-government
   5. Must be a body of general principles and not of particular laws or ordinances

II. General Welfare in the Constitution of the United States
   1. The Preamble says that one of the purposes of Government under the Constitution is to promote the General Welfare
   2. That is the same as saying that the Government exists for the sake of the people, and not the people for the sake of The State
   3. It does not mean that Presidents and Congresses can do anything they please so long as they say it is for the General Welfare
   4. Activities of the Government are limited by the Constitution to:
      a) Purposes which are for the general, and not for some particular local, class, or individual welfare
      b) Purposes which elsewhere in the document are sanctioned

III. Sets Up a Limited Democracy
   1. A Government resting on popular sovereignty according to law
   2. That makes a limited democracy just as other countries have had limited monarchy instead of despotism
   3. Unlimited democracy would be Government by a despotic majority
   4. Constitution and laws are above both officers and people, for the people have placed them there
   5. Failures in other democracies have usually been due to the power of the majority to tyrannize over a minority

I. POWERS OF GOVERNMENT

IV. Derived from the Constitution
   1. There is no power which either one of the three Branches can constitutionally exert which is not derived from the Constitution either directly or by fair implication
   2. The purport of a constitution under Civil Government is that there shall never be arbitrary or personal rule

3. There are no powers in the hands of the President derived from the nature of his office alone

4. There are no powers inherent in Congress on the theory that Congress is a governing board to do whatever it thinks is expedient

5. If it were otherwise, then Presidents and Congresses would soon come to be governing according to personal caprice

V. Emergency Powers

1. There are no emergency powers other than those provided for in the Constitution itself

2. If a President or a Governor had power to declare emergencies and suspend the reign of law, then he would have power to proclaim himself a dictator at any time

3. Presidents and Governors have great natural powers of personal influence to persuade people to do willingly what everybody knows ought to be done

4. Presidential or Gubernatorial proclamations often do that, but nobody is legally obliged to obey; in times of crisis or in following ancient custom, everybody does obey

5. Congress can legally give the President no powers which he does not already possess

VI. War Power

1. Congress alone can declare war

2. Can suspend writ of habeas corpus in case of necessity and thus make martial law over a civilian population possible

3. Can raise and support an Army and Navy, and enact codes of martial law for governing them; but even commanders in the field or at sea are restrained by martial law

4. The Constitution defines Treason, and in time of war the definition of Treason overrides many rights which exist in time of peace

5. President has martial powers as commander-in-chief of Army and Navy, and they may extend to civilian population in territory occupied by troops

VII. Constitutional Power of Congress

1. Legal control of interstate and foreign commerce, and related power to make commerce possible through:
   a) Power to provide for the coinage of money
   b) To fix standards of weights and measures
   c) To establish and provide for carrying on a postal service
   d) To make uniform laws in control of bankruptcy

    2. Taxation of all the people for Federal purposes
        Property taxation is limited to apportionment among the States in proportion to population
    3. Borrowing money on the credit of the United States
    4. Admission of new States
    5. Enactment of laws governing Territories, the District of Columbia, and dependencies
    6. Proposal of Amendments
    7. Powers implied by powers granted

VIII. Powers Denied to the States
    1. States are sovereign and hence need no grants of power
    2. Federal Government acts under powers granted, and all powers not granted are reserved to the States and the people, through the State constitutions
    3. Can emit no bills of credit to circulate as money
    4. Cannot coin money
    5. Nor make anything but gold and silver coin legal tender in payment of debts between individuals
    6. Cannot maintain a war establishment, but can maintain State troops for maintenance of law and order

IX. Amendment
    1. Constitution can be amended but only by process laid down in the Constitution
    2. Can be proposed by two-thirds in Congress
    3. Or on application of Legislatures in two-thirds of the States, Congress is required to call a convention for proposing Amendment
    4. Is adopted by the Legislatures of three-fourths of the States, or by conventions in three-fourths of them if Congress so enacts

II. AS FUNDAMENTAL LAW

X. Constitution as Fundamental Law
    1. The powers and prohibitions in the Constitution apply only to the United States Government
    2. Except the State Governments are expressly included, as they are in attainder, ex post facto, and due process
    3. We know the Constitution to be positive law by act of the sovereign, and we believe it to be rational Law as well
    4. Hence, the legal principles embodied in the Constitution should be in the State constitutions as well, and most of the State constitutions do so embody them

XI. Civil Liberty
1. Whole purpose of the fundamental law is to serve as a general guaranty of Civil Liberty, and to make its extension possible
2. Civil Liberty is freedom from slavery and arbitrary imprisonment
3. Freedom from arbitrary action of the Government or of its officers
4. Protection from arbitrary control by other persons
5. Civil Liberty is not infringed by just laws duly enacted
6. Is a large part of Justice

XII. Constitution Is the Supreme Law of the Land
1. Where any act or law of Congress or a State Legislature, or any act of the Executive, either Federal or State, conflicts with the Constitution, the Constitution rules
2. Where anything in a State constitution or in a decision of a State court is in conflict with the Constitution, the former must give way

XIII. Citizenship
1. All persons born or naturalized in the United States are citizens of the United States and of the State in which they reside
2. Citizens of each State are entitled to the privileges of citizens in other States; we are not alien anywhere in the United States
3. Full faith and credit must be given in each State to the public acts of other States, chiefly in legal proceedings
4. Persons accused of crime and fleeing to another State can be arrested and returned through Extradition; the same process applies to fugitives from foreign countries with which we have extradition treaties
5. Aliens can be Naturalized and thus admitted to full civil and political rights and privileges

XIV. Obligations of Contracts
1. State Legislatures are forbidden to make any law impairing the obligations of contracts
2. In part an extension of the power of Congress over interstate commerce
   There would be very little free flow of commerce between citizens of different States, if any State could authorize the breach of contracts at will
3. Also a defense of commerce within the States—an illustration of the application of the General Welfare clause
4. It is further denial to the States of the power to impair one of the three most important foundations of Justice

XV. Eminent Domain and Due Process

1. Complete power over everything is said to be one of the attributes of Sovereignty

2. But Congress and the State Legislatures are forbidden to pass any bill of attainder

A legislative bill of attainder was a special law directed to a particular person, depriving him of life, liberty, or property

3. The United States and the State Governments are forbidden, moreover, to deprive any person of life, liberty, or property, except after due trial in court and conviction of crime, for which death, imprisonment, or fine may be the penalty

4. But the Federal and State Governments can and do take property wherever it is needed in the public interest; otherwise, individual interest could thwart the General Welfare at every turn

5. However, Government can take property only by condemnation proceedings in court, in which the owner is awarded fair compensation

6. Due process applies to individual persons, either natural or corporative, but does not apply to whole classes. A State may by law forbid the practice of a certain business by anybody, or practice in a particular way; but if an individual or company is singled out, due process is violated

XVI. The Writ of Habeas Corpus

1. Habeas corpus means "You may hold the body"

2. An order of a judge releasing an accused person on bail, or some other recognizance, for his appearance in court for trial, or even because the judge recognizes arrest as frivolous

3. The purpose is to prevent officers from arresting and holding persons indefinitely without trial

4. Perhaps the fundamental guaranty of Civil Liberty

5. Congress may suspend in times of public peril, or a State may, and martial law takes over

XVII. Search and Seizure

1. All are constitutionally guaranteed against arbitrary invasion of their premises, and seizure of persons, papers, and effects by Federal officers

The State constitutions correspondingly guarantee against similar action by State and municipal officers

2. Officers must secure warrants from a judge authorizing the search and seizure

3. A warrant can be issued only by a judge of competent jurisdiction and then only for probable cause shown

XVIII. Rights of Accused Persons
    1. Trial by jury of the vicinage
    2. Speedy and public trial
    3. Right to be informed of the charge
    4. And to have witnesses summoned
    5. And to counsel for defense
    6. Cannot be tried a second time for the same offense when once acquitted
    7. Judges are forbidden to require excessive bail or to impose excessive fines
    8. Or to impose cruel and unusual punishments

XIX. Ex Post Facto
    1. Both Congress and the State Legislatures are forbidden to make laws ex post facto
    2. An ex post facto law is one which makes an act a crime which was not a crime when the act was committed
    3. Or expands the definition of a crime or broadens the penalties after the act was committed

III. RIGHTS

XX. Religious Freedom
    1. Congress is forbidden to make any law prohibiting the free exercise of religion
    2. Does not extend to ritualistic or other practices which as conduct involve acts prohibited by law
    3. May not set up an established church
    4. An established church is one
        a) Recognized by law
        b) Supported by taxation
        c) Membership in which constitutes eligibility to office
        d) And confers certain privileges
    5. No religious test as a qualification for office or public trust under the United States can be set up

XXI. Freedom of Speech and of the Press
    1. Essential under a democratic form of Government that citizens shall be free to criticize their officers and representatives
    2. Does not sanction malicious and injurious speech
    3. Freedom of the Press exempts the publishers of books and newspapers from securing a license before publication, and from any other political control of publication
    4. Does not empower newspapers to invade homes and the privacy of individuals in the search for news

5. Both individuals in their conversation and correspondence, and authors and publishers in their publications, are subject to prosecution for slander and libel

6. The Constitution guarantees nobody any right to publish immoral and obscene material; theatrical producers are publishers within the meaning of the law

XXII. Slavery and Involuntary Servitude

1. There can be no legal slavery anywhere in the United States

2. Nor can individuals be held to servitude in labor contracts—peonage

3. Nor imprisoned for violation of a labor contract

4. Does not apply to imprisonment at hard labor for crime of which an individual has been duly convicted

XXIII. Reserved Rights

1. The Constitution does not create rights; it only guarantees certain rights

2. It is expressly declared that rights not enumerated are reserved to the States and to the people

3. Rights guaranteed in the State and Federal constitutions are guaranteed against the Government

4. Other rights are recognized by law both Common and statutory as against the fellow-citizen

5. Most of the rights which we enjoy cannot be guaranteed by constitutions or laws; for them we depend upon association with civilized people

XXIV. Rights of the Minority

1. Government by law under a recognized constitution is in itself protection of the rights of the minority

2. Popular "mandates" to override the guaranties of the Constitution are unknown to American institutions

3. A Government in which the majority through its representatives can take the lives and property of the minority is everywhere a tyrannical Government

IV. THE SUPREME COURT AND THE CONSTITUTION

XXV. The Supreme Court Interprets and Applies

1. "The judicial power shall extend to all cases in Law and Equity, arising under this Constitution, the laws of the United States, and treaties made, or which shall be made, under their authority"

2. If a citizen believes that his constitutional right is invaded by an act of Congress or of one of the Legislatures, to his hurt and injury, then a "case under the Constitution" arises

3. If the Supreme Court in the end finds that he is right, then the Court grants him relief, that is to say, renders justice under the Constitution

4. The effect is to make the act in question null and void

5. So it is with acts of State Legislatures before the State supreme courts

6. The Supreme Court does not "declare unconstitutional" acts of Congress or the State Legislatures; it declares justice to citizens who are wronged by such acts. It passes on constitutionality only when a law suit arises under the Constitution itself

7. Nor does the Supreme Court pass on the wisdom and morality of acts of the other Branches, but only on their conformity to the Constitution

XXVI. Not Peculiar to the United States

1. A civil constitution is without force unless it has judicial interpretation and enforcement

2. England does not have it, for England is not governed by law, but by men and women in Parliament. The latter may or may not be governed in their own consciences by the legal institutions of the realm

3. The English Dominions have it

XXVII. Supreme Court Not a Complete Guaranty of Constitution

1. The Supreme Court guarantees our rights under the Constitution, so long as a violation can issue in a law suit against a person or company other than the President or Congress

2. The Supreme Court cannot control the acts of the President which it finds unconstitutional, for he is a co-ordinate Branch of the Government

3. For the constitutionality of his acts, we have to trust the man that he will keep his oath of office

4. Nor can the Court prevent unconstitutional legislation, but only the effect of it when the rights of individuals or corporations are violated

5. The ultimate support of the Constitution comes from the voters in the kind of representatives they elect to the Executive and Legislative Branches

C. Taxation

One of the principal attributes of sovereignty, and the one which touches most people most of the time, is Taxation. It is an attribute, not because any sovereign whether monarch or people has made it so, but because there can be no Government without economic support. As long as The State implies Government and Government implies Taxation, the last is an inescapable element in our understanding of The State. That is in itself a sufficient reason for asserting that it is of necessity part of the Curriculum of the Common School. As we have so often found, in the present chapter and the last, there is moreover a critical reason of practical importance for its inclusion, in the principle that the good citizen must have some intelligence about taxation, not only for his own protection, but for the protection of the Community from the mischief of his own ignorance.

The United States has long been held by competent taxationists to have about the worst tax system in the civilized world. While a good many improvements have been brought about in the last thirty or forty years, our legal tax system is still utterly unsuited to the needs of modern industrial society. The American Tax Association, which has been very effective in securing improvement, has long recognized, or at least many of its members have recognized, that there is not likely to be fundamental and lasting improvement until the subject has been for some time a universally accepted part of public instruction. Not long ago the United States Commissioner of Education reported that he could not find a single school in the United States which was giving any instruction in the subject, beyond what is incidental to Arithmetic.

The subject is one of the most difficult of dispassionate discussion for two reasons, both of them deeply rooted in human nature.

A very large class of citizens personally benefit from the expenditure of tax money. They may be office-holders or public employees, and they are likely to magnify their offices. Others may be recipients of public charity, and others still may be cultivating political careers which depend upon their ability to persuade the electorate into voting for representatives who will raise more taxes.

A variant here is interest in some cause which has become very dear to individuals, and most such causes are prone to require tax support. Unlike the motives of the classes first mentioned, the advocates of causes can seldom be called selfish, but they are seldom dispassionate and their taxes behave the same as if they were raised for the most selfish reasons in the world.

A second class is composed of those who are acutely aware of the taxes they pay. These too have a selfish motive which gives their rational capacity scant chance to operate. Here are those who groan over oppressive taxation; and others still who would pay no taxes at all if they could help it.

The social effect of schooling on all these classes is perhaps as dependent upon the upbuilding of Intelligence, Conscience, and Taste in general as upon particular instruction in the principles of Taxation. And yet the latter is an essential part of the former.

TAXATION IS A NECESSITY OF CIVILIZED EXISTENCE

Undoubtedly the very first thing our pupils should learn is the principle that we pay taxes for the privilege of living in civilized communities; and that, conversely, if the community then fails to exhibit signs of Civilization, we have been swindled, or have swindled ourselves.

Over against this necessity of taxation must be set the principle that all true taxation is more or less a drag on production and distribution.

TAXATION FOLLOWS ITS OWN LOGIC

People are likely to suppose that when a tax is laid and collected by some governing authority, that is the end of it until next year. The tax may be either generous or oppressive in its appeal to different individuals, but, when the deed is done, its effects have passed into the stream of history, leaving at the worst some unpleasant memories. So they think; but not so. When a tax is levied, the act begins to have consequences, and when it is collected, an additional set of consequences begins to operate. The Legislature, or some local authority empowered by the Legislature, can start the ball rolling, but all their resolutions and laws can neither guide its course nor prescribe the limits of its effects.

The methods employed by the taxing power, and the extent to which taxes can safely be laid, are therefore more critically dependent upon intelligence widely diffused among the people than anything else which enters into the courses upon The State.

TAXES DEFINED

A tax is usually defined as a compulsory contribution exacted by Government. The definition differentiates true taxes from charges made by Government which are called taxes but are not taxes.

For example, we pay city water rates and frequently refer to them as "water taxes." But the bill rendered is a charge for a service rendered and no more a tax than the bills rendered by our provision dealers. To be sure, we are obliged to have city water, since the city in its health ordinances makes it necessary. We could hardly exist without it, even if the city did not compel us to have it. The water bill is not a compulsory *contribution*.

We pay gasoline taxes so called, but they are not true taxes. If the proceeds are set aside for the maintenance of highways, then in effect we are paying for a particular service set up by Government. We are paying roughly for the use of a portion of the highway for a certain number of miles on a particular trip. The payment is in substance no different from the payments we make for the consumption of tires, oil, wear and tear on the car. If, on the other hand, the Government diverts the revenue from gasoline taxes to ordinary Governmental purposes, then it becomes a true tax.

We may pay fees for the registration of a deed, or for a marriage license, and in so doing we pay for a service which is necessary to the security of our property, and perhaps to the authenticity of our marriage. But there is no true compulsory contribution about it.

I never heard postage called a tax, but it is just as much a tax as all this class of things which have just been mentioned.

ECONOMIC EFFECT OF TAXES

In the broadest sense, the economic effect of all true taxes exacted by Government is to reduce purchasing power as applied to the goods and services which make up the standard of living.

Such is in general the effect. If, however, taxes are being wisely levied and the revenue from them efficiently and honestly expended, then there may well be saving to the individuals who make up the community more than enough to offset the taxes as compared with what would be the case if there were no Government at all or very poor Government. The ills of society—crime, ill-health, injustice, ignorance—are expensive. Nevertheless, even under ideal conditions there is reached a level above which taxation does operate as a drag on purchasing power and therefore on production and distribution.

TAXATION IN KIND

In ancient Egypt, in the Middle Ages, and in some regions far down into the nineteenth century, commodities and services were collected in satisfaction of the tax bill. The collector took so many quarts of wheat out of a bushel, or the man worked on the highway a certain number of days. That is taxation in kind. It is long obsolete. It is worth remembering, however, that in a money economy like our own, the basis of accurate economic thinking is to be found in our perception that the meaning of our taxes is that they are still indirectly paid in kind. The collector takes the equivalent of so many quarts in a bushel or so many days labor, because we have to give up money which would buy the wheat, and because we have to work so many days in order to earn the money with which to pay the bill. *Money is not wealth, but only the means of estimating wealth.*

GENERAL SOURCE OF TAX REVENUE

The next of the major ideas for pupils to grasp is that The State creates through Government little or nothing of an exchangeable economic sort. The social meaning of The State is regulation and not production.

Many people, perhaps a great many people, act as if the The

State could create wealth out of nothing and give it to us. They seem to suppose that their lot in life is directly awarded to them by The State, and that they can improve their lot in life by electing men who promise to give them their hearts' desires. No doubt that attitude accounts for the prevalence of the word "underprivileged" as applied to the poor. It is true that many a poor man is poor because injustice has been meted out to him, much of which wise and capable Government could prevent; but that does not mean that he is "underprivileged" or that the successful are "overprivileged" or indeed privileged at all. Privilege means "by special or particular law." But to return, ask these people where it is all coming from, and they will usually vaguely say "from taxes." If asked who pay the taxes, they reply, "The rich."

Whatever is spent in the name of The State comes from taxes of one sort or another, either present or prospective. To sell bonds does not yield revenue; it only arranges for prospective taxation. The only exception to the statement has regard to money received in return for Governmental services and from inconsiderable enterprises conducted by Government, such as local water and lighting systems sometimes conducted by cities for profit.

The rich are doubtless the most heavily taxed and should be, but if all the income of all the rich, above a modest allowance for living expenses, were to be collected, the sum total would fall far short of meeting the total expenditures of Government—Federal, State, and local—and there would be nothing to collect the next year. The rich could not support the Government, for there are not enough of them.

The great bulk of the tax burden everywhere is carried by people who have moderate incomes, well above the poverty line but far short of the income of great wealth. The burden falls on them, because there are a great many of them. It is to be doubted, however, that they pay any more in proportion to ability to pay than those who carry on a constant struggle with poverty. The poor are numerous, and they carry a heavy burden of taxes attached to goods and services sold, indirect taxes.

Whatever the Government costs, the people pay the bill, always have, and, so far as we can see, always will, under any system. But let us bear in mind that the people is all of us, and not merely the relatively poor.

FINANCIAL SOURCE OF ALL TAXES

All taxes are paid out of income, either present, past, or prospective, save the capital levy which is sometimes exacted by Government in inheritance and estate taxes. The great bulk of the taxes for any one year are paid out of the earnings for that year. The earnings may be in the form of great profits and interest earnings enjoyed by the very rich; in the form of profits, salaries, interest on savings, received by the middle economic class; or in the form of wages. All forms contribute, either directly or indirectly.

INDICIA

We are familiar with different kinds of taxes, such as property taxes, income taxes, estate taxes or inheritance taxes, excises, customs. These are what the taxationist calls *indicia*, that is, ways of measuring how much the individual shall pay out of his income, or sometimes in the case of estate and inheritance taxes out of his capital.

General property tax.—The most common kind of taxation in the United States is what is known as the *general property tax*. Therein, the tax charged to the individual is estimated from the real or supposed value of:

a) His real estate
b) His chattels, such things as livestock, machinery, goods in trade, household furniture, office equipment, and so on through a long list
c) His intangibles so called, that is to say, securities

But he pays out of income, either income derived from his property or from some other source, chiefly wages and salaries and profits.

Income tax.—The kind which next stands out conspicuously is the *income tax*. Here the tax is based directly on the amount of income, and the tax bill is of course paid out of income.

Estate or inheritance tax. When estates pass to heirs after the death of the owner, Government usually in these days lays a tax on the estimated value of the estate as a whole, or else on the amount received by each heir. The tax may be paid out of income when the estate is not large; or it may be necessary to realize upon the property by selling it in order to settle the tax. In this last case, the tax is in reality a capital levy; the Government takes not a part of earnings merely, but in effect a part of the estate itself. Most of us never have any personal experience with this tax, for it is only estates of considerable size that are taxed.

Excises.—Sales taxes, gasoline taxes, corporation taxes, in short any tax which is laid on goods and services in exchange, or upon the process of trading and doing business is called an *excise*—not an "excise tax," but an excise.

It sometimes happens that what is in form an excise is in substance a public service charge, which we have already encountered.

Customs.—In our usage, a customs is a tax laid upon imported goods at a port of entry. In our policy it is not primarily a source of revenue, although a good deal of revenue is incidental, but rather part of our system of protection to industries from foreign competition.

Licenses.—A *license* is an authorization to carry on some kind of business or profession or to perform some act. It is not a tax, but a license. In principle, it is not a source of revenue in intention, but primarily a method of controlling a business or class of acts. Saloon licenses, licenses to keep explosives, car and drivers' licenses with automobiles, are examples. A great deal of incidental revenue may result, but that is not the primary purpose.

The license is outrageously abused by diverting it from its original and proper purpose, and requiring all sorts of businesses to take out licenses, merely as a means of imposing additional taxes.

Fees.—A *fee* was the original public service charge, in days when the registration of legal documents, and court services in

general, was about the only public service for which one could
pay directly and individually. It was subject to great abuse, perhaps more than it is now, for it furnished a ready means of charg-
ing fees on a great scale in order to make out of a public office a
semi-sinecure for party workers, much as European countries
followed the custom of appointing Court favorites to places to
which salaries were attached but no work.

INCIDENCE

The most important term in the whole theory of taxation is
incidence. It means, Where does the tax fall? Who bears the burden of the tax? While the problems of incidence in its more remote reaches is perplexing and difficult enough, the working elements of the matter are simple.

When a taxpayer settles his bill, he commonly supposes that
he pays the tax. Sometimes he does, and sometimes he does not.
More important than that, the individual who receives no bill
at all usually supposes that he pays no taxes. It is therefore easy
to persuade him that, if he will vote for a spending program, he
is only laying a burden upon his successful neighbors, whom he
very likely envies anyway. In a very large proportion of cases,
indeed in almost all cases, people who receive no tax bill nevertheless pay taxes without knowing that they do.

1. Every merchant selling goods pays a tax levied upon the value
of the building as real estate, upon the value of goods in stock,
and upon the appliances used in the business. So does every
manufacturer pay upon his land, buildings, machinery, and stock
in hand. Both of them probably pay excises on their franchises
or charters if they are corporations and very likely they must pay
for one or more expensive licenses. All this is as much a part of
the cost of doing business as are the wages paid to operatives,
salesmen, clerks, janitors, and other help. The taxes have to be
made good in the prices charged for manufactured goods and
upon the same goods again when they are merchandised. Moreover, from the point at which the tax is first laid, through the
different businesses involved in manufacturing and distribution,
up to the point at which the goods finally reach the consumer,

there have accumulated many of these burdens to be added to the final prices.

Nor can a State Legislature alter the force at work by calling the tax something else and prohibiting passing on the tax in the price charged. If it could do so, it would only result in destroying the business affected, thus increasing unemployment and creating the need of more taxes.

Nevertheless, the manufacturer and dealer escape no taxes. They pay their individual taxes on income and private property like everybody else.

That is a simple illustration of the whole process of "passing on the tax."

2. A much clearer, and indeed obvious, case arises out of sales taxes with which nearly everybody is familiar today. Here the tax is not a general property tax, or a franchise tax, or a license, but a specific excise laid upon the value of each article sold, and added to the price which would otherwise be charged. The salesman says that the price is so much "plus sales tax." There, of course, the purchaser pays the tax and knows that he does. The ignorant are often led to believe that a swindle has been perpetrated, and that the dealer has wantonly charged them with a tax which he should pay. Such people are often numerous enough to induce deluded legislators, or demagogues in the Legislature, to enact laws requiring the dealer to pay the tax himself, and forbidding him to pass it on. They might as well attempt to regulate rainfall by statute. Again, if all merchants and manufacturers obeyed such laws, there would be no business at all.

The whole process, wherever it appears is called *indirect taxation*.

ALL TAXES TEND TO DESTROY THEIR BASES

The *tax base* is the particular value upon which the tax is laid.

Real estate is the base upon which some taxes are laid, but different classes of real estate—residences, stores, factories, farm land, forests, mines, and quarries—behave differently in respect to the effect of taxation on the base. Some of them are more sensitive to impairment by taxation than others.

Stocks, bonds, mortgages—in short, securities—are the base in one form of personal-property taxes. Household appurtenances is another kind of base in personal-property taxation. Farm equipment, livestock, factory machinery, stock in trade, store and office furniture, are other classes of personal property and tax bases.

The values to which excises are applied in the sales tax and in franchise taxes are still another classes of tax bases.

Finally, income itself is a tax base.

Now any tax whatever *tends* to make its base less valuable than it otherwise would be. Excessive taxation makes the base so much less valuable that it can pay less and less taxes and finally can pay no taxes at all. Excessive taxation, from the fiscal standpoint, is always killing the goose that laid the golden eggs.

Personal-property taxes laid upon the market values of securities and billed at the same tax rate as other property would nearly always confiscate the income from the securities, or so much of it as to make the property worthless. Unhappily, this tax has long been one of the most destructive of all, not because it destroys the value of the base, but because it generates callous indifference to honesty in public affairs. The property-holder perjures himself annually until perjury has penetrated the mores as a venial sin and even as an index of the taxpayer's sophistication.

Happily some of the more enlightened States have abolished the personal-property tax on intangibles, and substituted income taxes on the income earned by the securities. In other less enlightened States, enlightened tax assessors have used their powers so as to remove the chief fiscal objections—although it is doubtful that they have any legal power to do so.

Forest land is especially sensitive. A real estate tax on forest land assessed at the same percentage of true value and at the same rate percent as that laid upon farm land will often force the owner to cut his forest long before it is fit for cutting, and thereafter that land will pay no taxes at all.

Real estate in general is sensitive, and farm land most of all.

The reason is that land and buildings are economically valuable only for the sake of the income derived from them. If the tax confiscates the income or a large part of it—and that is actually the case in a formidable percentage of the farms—the value is destroyed and that property is thereafter worthless for tax purposes. The owner gives it up and allows the State to take it. The State can thereafter derive no revenue from that parcel of land, unless the Government operates it for profit—and Government operation of anything has had a sorry history.

On the other hand, in recent years, a great many buildings have been pulled down because the owners could not pay the taxes out of the income derived from the buildings. An immense amount of farm land has been deserted, or maintained only by Government subsidy, because it could not produce enough to pay the taxes.

Incomes are subject to destructive effects of taxation laid upon income, but they are not nearly so sensitive as most bases. Nevertheless, the normal use of income is payment for subsistence, plus savings which are invested and become part of the working capital of the nation. It follows that excessive taxation of incomes tends to cut down purchasing power, reduce savings, cripple industry, decrease employment, and make the total national income subject to taxation less.

Experience with income taxation has, however, been unfortunate ever since it came into vogue. The legitimate use of income taxation, which is in principle the most equitable, the most rational of all, is to relieve the other bases of destructive and unproductive taxation. That has seldom been done. On the contrary, the income tax has commonly been added to other taxes, with little or nothing of the cure of our fiscal system which it was designed to effect.

Indeed this property of taxation, under the operation of which all taxes have a tendency to destroy their bases, goes far to justify Jefferson's maxim, "That is the best Government which governs least."

ABILITY AND BURDEN

A great deal of theorizing has been done in the past regarding the just method of distributing the burden of taxation. One school has held that the burden should be apportioned according to ability to bear, while others have held that the measure of benefit received should be the test. Extended experience has left very little ground for doubt. True taxes, that is to say property and income taxes, must be levied according to ability to pay, on both economic and ethical grounds. If people were taxed according to benefit received, there would be very little revenue, since those who benefit most have least with which to pay. On the other hand, one of the ethical canons of taxation is equality; but equality is far more a matter of burden than of actual equality in the tax bills. A tax of $100 for a man who has an income of $1,000 is evidently a far greater burden than the same tax upon a man who has an income of $10,000.

Hence, property and income taxes are laid on the ability principle, which appears in the familiar tax rate per cent. That is *proportional* taxation.

Nearly all legitimate excises, licenses, and fees, however, are of necessity laid on the benefit theory, for they are in substance charges for services rendered or privileges allowed.

PROGRESSIVE AND REGRESSIVE TAXES

The conspicuous exception to the above statement is the sales tax, the most unjust of all, and a relic of the days of Bourbon kings. It is not contingent on benefits received, nor on ability to pay; it is merely a very productive tax, easily and certainly collectible, and supposed to be relatively "painless." It bears hardest on those who are least able to pay. The general principle of equality of burden is involved here, and we are led thereby to draw the distinction between *progressive* and *regressive* taxes.

A progressive tax is one which increases not in proportion to increase in the value taxed, but more than proportionally. A clear illustration can be found in the Federal taxes on individual incomes in vogue not so many years ago.

The tax was laid at 4 per cent on the first $4,000 of net income, and then at 8 per cent on the next $4,000, with surtaxes beginning at $6,000. Thus a taxpayer having an income of $8,000 paid a tax of $480, exclusive of surtaxes. His neighbor who had an income $4,000 paid $160. The higher income was twice as high as the lower, but, instead of paying twice as high a tax, it paid three times as high, in addition to surtaxes. A proportional tax would make the higher income pay $320, while a progressive tax made it pay more than $480. The surtaxes rapidly increased the tax paid by the incomes which were above $8,000. Now, the ethics of the matter consists in the fact that $160 taken from an income of $4,000 is probably as great a burden as is the $480 paid on $8,000, very likely a greater burden. Progressive taxes are an attempt to bring about some approach to an equality of burden. In this particular case, however, it ought to be remembered that the higher income, in addition to income tax, probably paid considerably higher general property taxes—or at least ordinarily should have.

A regressive tax, on the other hand, creates a greater and greater burden as the income grows less and less. For example, a wage-earner who receives $1,000 a year, very likely spends $700 for food and clothing and other items subject to sales tax. If he paid the latter at the rate of 3 per cent, then in his $700 was included a tax of $20.39. That is something more than 2 per cent of his income. A well-to-do bachelor with an income of $10,000 very possibly pays no more than $700 for primary subsistence including the same sales tax. The latter is but little more than 0.2 per cent of his income. Moreover, the poor man's tax is a very considerable problem with him, while the other's is a trivial matter. Thus, the principle of regressivity in taxes.

Nevertheless, while the foregoing demonstrates the injustice of regressive taxes, it must not be forgotten that the wealthier man has taxes to pay which the poor man is not burdened with. His Federal income tax alone is probably $840 at present, and he likely enough pays as much more in State and local taxes. So that in the end he pays out in taxes of all kinds maybe 17

per cent of his income, whereas the poor man may escape with
no more than 4 per cent all told, including the indirect taxes of
which he is not aware.

Thus is a rough equality of burden worked out, but the burden
is not equal and never can be where the taxes themselves are
unduly high. If the high incomes are taxed to the point at which
there is actual equality of burden, that point will be long past
the point at which the tax base is being destroyed and the revenue falling; for the money which should normally go into investment will be paid out in taxation. The lesson for our pupils to
learn is that high taxes must always bear a good deal harder on
the poor than on the rich, and that the principle is beyond the
power of Legislatures to abrogate. The only just taxes are low
taxes.

Nor is that all. So far, unequal burden on the poor man has
been dealt with only in respect to the taxes which he actually
pays, either directly or indirectly. When, however, the property-
owners' investments are being destroyed by taxation, unemployment begins and mounts to huge proportions. Unemployment
demoralizes the poor and creates dire tragedy for those who normally belong somewhat higher on the income scale, notably the
well-equipped young men. The Government is forced to inaugurate the Dole in England and Relief in the United States. That
means still higher taxes and so the vicious circle is completed.

WHY ARE TAXES HIGH?

Why are taxes as a general thing higher and higher?

In the first place, the obvious explanation is the high cost of
modern war, in which sheer self-preservation drives Government
to bid farewell to all considerations of prudence. When the war
is over, debt has accumulated and engenders an enormous interest and general debt service charge; and there is no offset. But
that is all, so far as direct tax cost is concerned. Taxes would not
be so high if there had been no war, but they would nevertheless
have been on the increase.

Second, taxes are high because in so complex a society as exists

in modern industrial communities, the cost of Government is necessarily high; and it is well known to students of Public Finance
that even legitimate cost increases faster than population increases, at least when the latter has passed beyond a certain
critical point. And yet, in this class of causes, provided Government is honest and capable, increased cost is in its nature likely
to be offset by increased values in the tax bases and hence by
increased revenue at the same tax rate.

Third, and more important than either of the foreoging is the
cost of bad and unintelligent Government; and there we can distinguish certain subcauses:

a) Sheer lack of capacity in Government and Administration.
Functions which are essential in The State, and which normally
generate economy, do not get carried out well enough to yield
their legitimate return. Along with this illustration goes financial
ineptitude; in other words, while there may be no real waste in
expenditure, the public money is not well managed. Needless
indebtedness is incurred through mere ignorance of the working
of the financial organism in the community, and the burden of a
needless interest charge is carried. Parallel is lack of understanding of the management of capital, and needless investments are
incurred.

b) Then there is waste in the ordinary sense of the word, that
is to say, the community does not get its money's worth for the
expenditures laid out. Goods and services are dribbled away,
needless and relatively useless enterprises are set up, and other
enterprises which are no concern of The State or the Municipality.

c) And finally *graft*. We mean by graft, I take it, the dishonest
expenditure of public fuhds. Dishonesty implies a motive, and
the motive ranges all the way from downright stealing to the
employment of needless and incompetent public servants in recognition of friendship or in payment for party services. Beyond
that is what is called "pork-barreling," or the expenditure of
public funds either locally or on a national scale purely as a bribe
for votes.

But the question is analyzed and yet not answered. Why do we have destructive tax burdens traceable to bad management, waste, graft? Is it inevitable in a democracy, as is sometimes charged? That cannot be, for some of the worst instances in all history are to be found in absolute monarchies. Moreover, there has probably never been cleaner and more competent Government than there is today in some of the democracies. We have these things because we are the kind of people who directly or indirectly, as a body politic, like them. In the case of corrupt grand-dukes, there is an out, for they cannot be said to be representative. But our officers are representative; that is our faith and our pride.

Our people are apparently still fond of the frontier, town-meeting formula that one man is as good as another—if not better; and that any American is fit for anything, provided he is *elected*. The ballot seems to interrupt the course of nature and endow the recipient with genius. Today, Jim is just one of us, the more so the better, claiming no special knowledge about anything but his regular job and likely enough modest about that. Elect him to the local school board and tomorrow he is an "educator," inspired by popular acclaim with exact knowledge of what ought to be taught and how it should be taught. Joe is run of the mine in the village or the ward. Elect him to the State Legislature and tomorrow he is a lawgiver and statesman. The corollary is that our notion of representative government has become, "Choose representatives who are as like ourselves as possible," where it was once, "Choose representatives who in our opinion are best qualified to help govern." It is all reflected in the tax bills and unemployment.

And so it comes back to us, the people, the electorate. Our representatives are the choice of a majority of us, and they are probably as good or better than the average of the majority.

Hence, we return to our time-worn proposition that economical, as well as effective, honest, just, Government depends upon the character of public instruction—and there is no other recourse. If Government, in our democratic republic, is poor and burdensome, it is because the schools and colleges are, or have been, poor and ineffective. If we are met with the rejoinder that our schools are also made by the people, then the only realistic response is, Let the people take the schools out of the range of primary democracy and put them where they once were, in strictly nonpolitical boards, composed of the admittedly best rather than of typical citizens. Whether we can do that or cannot is the ultimate test of democracy as a form of Government in our hands. If we cannot, Mother Nature will resume sway, and her ways are anything but motherly.

UNITS IN TAXATION

I. Taxation a Necessity in Civilized Existence
1. People cannot live in Society without protection in their rights, justice, defense from marauders, enjoyment of a rising standard of living
2. The name for that protection is Government
3. Government necessarily entails costs in economic goods and services
4. Such costs are met by taxation

II. What Is Taxation?
1. A tax is a compulsory contribution exacted by Government
2. A true and just tax is a contribution exacted by Government in its maintenance of the general welfare under the Constitution
3. Some exactions made by Government are not true taxes, but rather charges made for services or privileges, e.g.:
   a) Water rates
   b) Postage
   c) Gasoline taxes where the revenue is applied to the building and maintenance of highways
   d) Fees
   e) Licenses

III. The Language of Taxation
1. The *levy* is the total amount set up by the governing authority for collection
2. *Assessment* is the value which an officer or a board attaches to the property to be *levied upon*
3. *Inventory* is the total amount of property to be taxed in the tax district
4. *Assessment ratio* is the fraction of the true value of property which the assessors propose to use in billing the tax

5. *Tax rate* is the levy divided by the inventory corrected by the assessment ratio. It is the percentage to be applied to each taxpayer's property in order to determine his bill or tax

6. The *tax* or *tax bill* is what a given taxpayer must pay

IV. The State Creates No Wealth

    1. It may make possible the creation of wealth

    2. Whatever the Government does has for the most part to be paid for in taxes

    3. The sale of bonds creates no revenue; bonds and interest charges must in the end be met by taxation

    4. Directly or indirectly, everybody pays taxes

    5. If we confiscated *all* the income of the well-to-do and rich, there would not be anywhere near enough to pay all taxes

    6. And they could pay no taxes the next year

    7. The rich pay or should pay in proportion to ability like everybody else

V. Taxation in Kind

    1. Taxes were once paid in commodities and services

    2. No modern State could so exist

    3. We pay taxes in money

    4. But it is the same as if we still paid in kind

    5. When we pay taxes in money, it means that we can buy that much less, or else the tax bill is equivalent to so many days' labor

VI. Indicia

    1. All taxes save capital levies are paid out of income

    2. The values which determine how much is to be paid are called *indicia:*

        a) Real property tax paid out of income according to value of real estate.

        b) Personal-property taxes paid out of income according to the values of:

            1) Securities

            2) Furniture and appurtenances

            3) Livestock

            4) Machinery

            5) Stock in trade

        c) Income tax paid out of income according amount of net income

        d) Excises on goods in trade according to value of goods, or on business processes according to estimated value of the process

        e) Customs according to the value of imports, or specific charges made on unit quantities of imports

    3. Licenses and fees are not true taxes, but charges made for privileges and services

4. Inheritance tax according to value of inherited estates, when the tax can be paid out of income. When the estate has to be sold in order to pay the levy, the result is a capital levy

5. Whenever any tax is so high that the property taxed has to be sold in order to meet the tax, there is a capital levy

VII. All Taxes Tend To Destroy Their Bases

1. The value upon which the tax is laid is called the base

2. Any tax whatever tends to destroy its base by making the latter less valuable

3. An offset is found in the principle that an economically sound tax, the revenue from which is economically spent, tends to enhance prosperity and hence improve all values

4. An excessive tax, the revenue from which is unproductively spent, does impair or destroy its base, leaving less or nothing to be taxed the next time

5. Some bases are more easily destroyed than others. In order from most easily to least easily these are:

    a) Forest land
    b) Securities
    c) Farming land
    d) Machinery and plant and stores
    e) Rented houses
    f) Private residences
    g) Incomes

6. When a base is being destroyed, the tax is confiscatory

VIII. Incidence

1. Upon whom does the tax fall?

2. The taxpayer is not always the taxbearer

3. Taxes upon property in manufacturing and trade, licenses and fees attached to trade, are necessarily part of the cost of doing business

4. Hence they must be recovered in prices charged, called "throwing off the tax"

5. The purchaser pays all these taxes in *indirect taxation*

6. Excises such as sales tax are specific direct taxes collected by the dealer and paid to Government, except where they are concealed in the price and not notified to the buyer

7. Farmers dealing in crops the price of which is fixed in the world-market or the national market cannot throw off local taxes

8. City landlords cannot throw off property taxes by adding them to the rent, save in peculiar situations when building is catching up with a shortage

IX. Proportional, Progressive, and Regressive Taxes

    1. Equity requires that taxes shall not be equal but *in proportion* to the ability of the taxpayer to pay

    2. But that is not enough, for real equity is according to *equality of burden*

    3. The lower the ability to pay, the higher is the burden for the same tax bill

    4. Hence *progressive* taxes are laid, not in proportion to ability, but more than in proportion

    5. In *regressive* taxes, by themselves considered, the burden becomes greater and greater as ability becomes less and less. The sales tax is the most vicious example, by itself considered

    6. Bad effects are more or less offset by the fact that persons of higher taxpaying ability have additional and higher taxes to pay

X. Limits of Progressive Taxation

    1. Progressive taxation at higher income levels reaches the point at which the tax base is being destroyed long before there is anything like equality in burden borne by high and low incomes, respectively

    2. When the income of the well-to-do and wealthy is taken in excess, industry is interfered with and hard times come

    3. That means lower wages and unemployment

    4. Hence, high taxes always bear hardest on the poor, because:

        a) The burden of indirect taxation and sales taxes hits them hardest

        b) Hard times are generated

    5. The only just taxes are low taxes

XI. High Taxes Arise Out of High Expenditure

    1. High expenditure is unavoidable, because

        a) Of the cost of war

        b) Complex society requires much Government

    2. High taxes are avoidable by

        a) Electing men better qualified for good fiscal management

        b) Elimination of waste in expenditure and needless expenditure

        c) Elimination of dishonest expenditure

CHAPTER XII

COMMERCE

WE PASS more and more into the field of institutions which are the outgrowth of the fundamental institutions in which Intelligence, Conscience, and Taste have their origins—the symbolic institutions, and Science, Religion, Morality, Art.

Commerce and Industry in practice are hard to separate; there is nothing to distribute until something has been produced, and, when something has been produced, it commonly is for sale. Commerce, however, in its early development far outran Industry, and modern Industry is a thing of two centuries past or less.

COMMERCE IS INSTITUTION

One has to go back to stages in human experience found only in the lower levels of savagery before he arrives at a point at which he can find no traces of Commerce as we understand Commerce. Indeed, among people so primitive as some of the South American river tribes, we find illustrations of the working of principles governing price which are at bottom fundamental to trade today. In the remains uncovered by archeologists dating 2000 B.C., early forms of metallic money are found. Commercial forms are found in ancient Babylon which served the same mercantile function as bills of lading, promissory notes, and agreements in contract with which we are familiar. Commercial Law is perhaps the earliest common law of nations.

Moreover, Commerce is universal today as always, despite the fact that, in periods of dark ages when Civilization disappeared out of the mores, trade regressed to lower forms. In short, Commerce originated in the common sense and experience of mankind; it survived because of its social utility, became organized, expanded, and refined; and is, finally, rationally comprehensible as a method of enabling people to live together in ordered societies. It is a prime element in the fabric of Civilization.

On our principles, Commerce would be an element in the content of General Education, even though there were no practical utility in it. Since it is part of Civilization, it is part of the foundations of Intelligence in the presence of the modern cultural environment. But we can see in it practical utility of the most fundamental sort, for everybody who lives is directly or indirectly affected by Commerce, by far the larger part of us directly. Every time we make a purchase, or sell an article, or draw a check, or make a savings deposit, or sign a contract, we are personally engaged in Commerce.

Economics and Commerce.—We have already met Economics as a course in Science. It is commonly confused with Commerce and Industry. These latter are economic in import, but they are much else besides. They are ethical as well, whereas Economics has nothing to do with Ethics, since it is a discipline by itself. If they are valid in Society, they also rest on the idealistic way of life. Commerce deals with the exchange of goods and services; Economics deals with the goods and services themselves, in their nature and in their social meaning.

A. EXCHANGE

In order that we may have before us in considerable detail what ought to enter into the Curriculum in Commerce, it is desirable that the whole field should be sketched out as a matter of content, much as it might appear in a textbook, although greatly expanded in the latter. In order to do so, we begin with the basal commercial concept, namely, Exchange.

BARTER

Commerce is fundamentally exchange of something that one does not want for something he does want, or exchange of something he wants less for something he wants more. In its simplest form, that is *barter*. We seldom encounter it today in the concerns of adult life, save in unusual and unimportant circumstances. We can, however, easily picture the Algonquin exchanging the hide of some beast he has killed for a pair of moccasins and throwing in the meat for the maker's labor. Therein is an epitome of both Commerce and Industry. Barter is no longer workable, it is too inflexible for the extensive production and distribution of things which man wants in his standard of living. And yet the logic of Commerce is still in the principle that all legitimate trade is in the end on a barter basis. We deal in goods and services and not in money.

MANORIAL OR NONCOMMERCIAL ECONOMY

Economic existence can go on with no commerce at all. It has done so in one form or another, at one time or another, over a large part of the world. The outstanding illustration is what we shall call *manorial economy*, from the name assigned to a setup in the Middle Ages. Something very similar existed in the plantation economy in some parts of the Old South.

Here was a little feudal State, vassal to some higher sovereign perhaps, and perhaps not. The lord was owner of the land, administered justice—such as there was—and dispensed food and clothing and shelter to his subjects. Among them prevailed division of labor, so that mechanics and others could be found to carry on the various activities of the manor. It necessarily entailed serfdom and sometimes slavery. In the pure form each man worked and was awarded what the lord, or the latter's subordinate, believed to be his just and sufficient due in food, clothing, and raw materials. In that kind of economy there was directed distribution but no exchange and no commerce.

The so-called totalitarian States of today are not States but rather industrial manors on a huge scale.

MEDIUM OF EXCHANGE

Barter in its various forms is direct exchange between individuals in particular articles or particular services. It cannot be generalized; there is no *price* and no common expectation.

But suppose there is a commodity which everybody values, which everybody would be glad to have at any time, something in universal demand. In that case, wherever there are goods to be exchanged for other goods, exchange can be effected *in terms of* the commodity which is in universal and constant demand. That is common sense. If, for example, anybody will give a bushel of corn for a beaver skin, and five beaver skins for a good canoe, then a canoe can be priced at five bushels of corn. Beaver skins have become the medium of exchange; exchange has acquired the beginnings of a logic.

All sorts of things have been used as mediums of exchange— cattle in the ancient world, tobacco among the Virginia colonists, beaver skins and wampum among the Indians. But observe that, even here, the heart of the medium used consisted in the facts (*a*) that it had value in itself and (*b*) that it became the basis of a *count*.

MONEY

Many thousands of years ago gold and silver came to be used as the universal mediums whenever they could be had. They were in universal demand, since they had utility in the arts, the supply was relatively constant, the value in use was so great that a considerable value could be packed in a small space, and the pieces used were thus readily transportable. They are still the best medium, and especially gold. If they were not, a better medium would have displaced them. The latter is not likely ever to happen, since, as we shall see, metallic money is less and less needed in quantity in highly developed commerce.

So society goes onto a price basis instead of barter when it has become folkway to exchange commodities and services of all sorts for a single valuable commodity. If the people could keep that simple principle in mind, the way would be open to understand the larger part of the working of the currency.

COIN

Gold and silver in their unprocessed state, bulk metal, are called *bullion*. Stamped into a regular form and inscribed with and identifiable image and superscription, bullion becomes *coin* or *specie*. Save for minor coins, fractional currency, we do not see much of it, for reasons which will presently appear.

Coinage is said to be a "prerogative" of the sovereign. Better than that, it is one of the necessary attributes of sovereignty, for it is one of the things that none else than the sovereign can do. There can be no common estimate in the coinage unless The State sets up the common estimate. In truth, it is typical of what makes The State an institution. One of the powers reposed in Congress by the Constitution, we recall, is the power "to coin money, regulate the value thereof, and of foreign coin." To regulate the value is to define the pecuniary unit in terms of the actual amount of metal by weight which it shall contain.

The thing to be kept in mind here is the principle that it is beyond the power of any Government to make a piece of money more valuable than the world-market price of the metal which it it contains. Our Government can undoubtedly declare the dollar to be worth fifty cents of the former value, but it can do it only by reducing the gold content to fifty cents' worth, or else by manipulating the world's gold market.

CREDIT MONEY

Time was when nearly all transactions everywhere were carried on in coin. In fact, many people who are still living can remember when, in parts of our own country, nobody would accept payments of any sort except in coin, and often only in gold coin.

Paper currency.—The first and most common form of credit money with us is composed of bank notes, gold and silver certificates, and United States notes.

The silver certificate of the United States read thus:

This certifies that there is on deposit in the Treasury of
THE UNITED STATES OF AMERICA
ONE DOLLAR
in silver payable to the bearer on demand

Gold certificates, when they are in circulation, bear a similar device.

A bank note certifies that the ———— Bank of ———— will pay to the bearer on demand $———— in gold.

The United States Note is money left over from the Civil War.

It is the Government's promissory note without interest and payable on demand in gold.

Gold basis.—A country is said to be on a gold basis when its outstanding obligations in currency will be settled in gold.

VALUE OF PAPER MONEY

Now the value of all this paper money rests entirely on public confidence that the Government or the bank can and will keep its promises. If the Government should refuse to pay in specie— and our Government has done so in respect to its promises to pay in gold—or to settle its greenback account, the paper money would be valueless save as a means of speculating on the future course of Government. So long as there is no reason to think that the Government, or a bank, will not settle, demand is not made. The sheer folkway in the use of paper money is, however, with us so strong that it would probably carry us a long way, but in the end paper money would be only as valuable as the paper itself.

All through commercial transactions of any sort, right functioning in the end *depends upon confidence that people will keep their promises.* Commerce is as much Ethics as Economics. When moral laxity of any sort enters the mores anywhere, bad business conditions will soon appear, depression and misery. Society has in part been disrupted.

BANKING CREDIT

All modern advanced commercial nations carry on transactions more and more by creating bank credits in deposits and checking accounts. We do so much more of it than any other nation that abnormal currency conditions with us are very materially modified and lightened in their normal effect. Something like 90 per cent in value of all American transactions are settled without the intervention of money in any form. We pay our bills by sending our creditors our checks, having previously placed the bank in debt to us by depositing checks which somebody else has paid us.

Clearings.—All the banks in a city of any considerable size *clear* daily through a Clearing House or Clearing-House Bank,

and regional clearings are similarly effected for the whole nation—
in this way:

All the banks are debited at the Clearing House with checks
drawn against them and credited with checks drawn in their
favor, or indorsed to them. Each has thus a daily balance—or
whatever may be the accounting period—either debit or credit,
as the case may be. Ordinarily, over a period longer or shorter
these balances must tend to cancel out. In that way, by far the
largest part of the business of the country is done without any
actual exchange of money of any kind at all. Money becomes,
not a medium of exchange, but a system of reckoning. Even so,
the integrity and normal working of the whole system depends
upon the honesty of the pecuniary unit, that its value shall be
the real value which it purports to be.

MONEY MADNESS

We sometimes hear the expression "money madness" used.
There is much to justify it when people place money above
wealth.

It appears when rich men are supposed to have their wealth
in vast hoards of specie and paper money. We call them "money-
bags." It is easy to persuade the untutored that such is the situation and that the Government can force them to disgorge and
"distribute the wealth."

It appears in the craze to "make money" with little or no
thought as to what the money is to be used for. If the individual
succeeds, it only too often happens that he or his wife have to
"get rid of it" in riotous and destructive living, not being intelligent enough to invest in useful productive enterprises of some
sort.

It appears among wage-earners in endless efforts centered upon
increase of wages, unaware that their success would and often does
result in their having less wealth, because of the increased prices
which they generate.

Altogether, this conception that money is not in itself wealth
is about the most important thing our pupils can learn about

money, that it is merely the medium through which wealth is produced and estimated and distributed.

INFLATION

The term *inflation*, frequently heard, much dreaded, and, I fear, little understood, is usually associated with the currency.

In reality, inflation occurs anywhere in life where existence goes on in unreal terms. The word means a state of being "puffed up." Many of the certified insane are in a state of personal inflation—and many who are not certified. The college faculty is inflated when it is composed of degrees rather than persons possessed of what the degrees are supposed to stand for. In Commerce there are many forms of inflation, aside from the dreaded inflation of the currency, many of them about as pernicious as the latter.

Modern advertising and high-pressure salesmanship are manifest examples. In Commerce, advertising is *notice* that a dealer has certain goods or services for sale. If the reader notes the advertisement and judges that he *wants* those goods, and a sale is thus consummated, the whole transaction is within the scope of economic advertising. If, on the other hand, whether in advertising or individual salesmanship, it becomes the practice to use all the devices of suggestion, and especially fear, to persuade people to buy what they do not need and cannot afford, then that commerce is inflated and a menace to the well-being of the community. If the rejoinder is, "That is the only way in which my business can be kept going," the surrejoinder is, "In that case, your business is not necessary to the community."

Currency inflation occurs whenever the pecuniary unit of a country cannot be exchanged for its reputed value in metallic money. It takes more dollars or shillings or francs to buy the same goods, despite the fact that no increased scarcity has occurred. Prices have risen by reason of the issue of inferior money.

Credit inflation occurs whenever we borrow money for a utility beyond any reasonable and justifiable expectation that enhanced income from the utility can retire the debt, or when it has become the practice to pay debts by incurring other debts. Credit inflation was a large element in the crash of 1873 and again in that of 1929.

CURRENCY INFLATION AND PRICES

All inflation is bad and will entail its penalties in commerce or anywhere else, since it is unreal, abnormal, unhealthy; but the inflation which we most dread is inflation of the currency. We dread it because of the effect it is capable of having on the prices of commodities. We recall the inflation of the German mark in recent times, and we have heard of French assignats and our own Continentals, Confederate money, and Civil War Greenbacks. And yet for most people the process of inflation is a tantalizingly elusive concept, or set of concepts. Let us see what we can make of it as bearing on Curriculum content.

For that purpose it will be convenient to deal with several elementary cases.

1. When a nation employs for the most part a metallic currency in all its transactions, then quantity of money in circulation is directly related to prices. That is to say, prices will be higher or lower, quite apart from the relations of supply and demand in the commodities themselves. If money is insufficient in quantity to serve its normal function as an instrument of the exchanges which will normally be made, then a given amount of money will buy more goods, and so all around the circle of commodities. Prices will fall. If the opposite situation exists, then prices will rise. But note that, when a country has long in fact had a relative scarcity of money and the quantity is increased, prices will rise for a time; but supply of commodities will increase and the markets will adjust themselves to the trade which the new supply will justify. Money will again become relatively less plentiful and prices will fall. There is nothing mysterious about it: we all know that a sudden access of expendable income will usually start any one of us on a spending program, thus increasing demand. If we all do it, demand gains on supply and prices rise. And conversely.

2. The case in which a nation uses mostly credit money, that is to say, paper money.

a) As long as the Government is solvent and banks are solvent, each paper unit is the equivalent of a metallic unit, since paper can readily be converted into coin, and everybody knows it—and therefore does not attempt to present paper money for redemption. The situation is assimilated to that of the first case, except that real money scarcity is a good deal less likely to occur. It does sometimes occur regionally, and then the cure is ordinarily an improvement in the banking system. That was the reason for the erection of our Federal Reserve System.

b) When the Government is unable to redeem its promises to make good in coin on demand, then prices in the paper money rise not because there is more of it but because people speculate on the prospect that the Government will sometime resume specie payments. They will let goods go *at a price* in paper, the price being proportioned to their estimate of the prospects of ultimate resumption. The speculators stand to make a good deal of money —or to lose all—but in reality they save the situation when the Government is rather embarrassed than insolvent.

FIAT MONEY

3. Fiat money is irredeemable paper. Its only relation to the real pecuniary unit is the denomination printed on the face. I suppose there are still a good many people who believe that the engraving of George Washington and the words ONE DOLLAR make a dollar. There are certainly not so many as there were in the seventies, eighties, and nineties.

Now fiat money practically always produces disaster—in this way:

There is so much of it printed that the process explained in the first case operates. People buy, and prices rise not because of any demon in the money but because of supply and demand in commodities. The government prints more, but prices rise still more. Presently a panic starts, and, when one is paid his wage or salary, he rushes off and converts it into goods, in anticipation of tomorrow's rise. Demand is enormously increased, and prices enormously rise. The Government printing presses pour out more of the stuff, and in due season prices are computed in astronomic figures until all values are destroyed and the whole economy collapses.

4. When a nation's transactions are prevailingly through bank clearings, effect of inflation is minimized.

In that case, very little money is used. Goods and services are exchanged against other goods and services through the banks. Ordinary currency inflation can do little harm and have little effect on prices. We depend far more on banking integrity.

Nevertheless, a fiat money program would inevitably produce the same effect in the United States, the greatest of the bank-clearings countries, as it has had in the past in the countries which had no bank-clearings at all—but the effect would come more slowly.

QUANTITY OF MONEY

Before leaving this important subject, we must consider one more subject, namely, quantity of money in circulation.

A little reflection will make it apparent to anybody that there need not be a dollar of currency for every dollar transaction. A single coin or piece of paper passes from hand to hand through many transactions. That is what is meant by *circulation*. Now quantity in circulation is made up of two elements: absolute quantity and speed of circulation. While these two elements introduce a variable in the amount required, it is nevertheless true that there always is an actual, objective amount required to make possible normal transactions in any community. Beyond that amount, transactions are not increased by additions to the quantity. That is particularly true of countries which are on a bank-clearings basis. Two principles at once follow, both of them of cardinal importance:

1. Increasing the amount of money in circulation will have no effect on prosperity unless in fact there has not been enough to

make possible the transactions which commodity demand and supply justify.

Men still labor under the eighteenth-century delusion that money is wealth, and hence some of them are obsessed by the false notion that the amount of money or of the precious metals in bullion is an addition to the wealth of us all.

2. Quantity of money has nothing to do with price inflation save incidentally and temporarily. Inflation of prices is not a matter of demand and supply where money is one of the elements of supply.

In short, there is nothing mysterious about Money. Nothing happens to it that is not a part of the daily life of all of us. It is said to be the root of all evil. That is not a true bill. The roots of evil are in humans, and their names are Cupidity, Bad Faith, Greed of Popularity, Ignorance.

INSTRUCTION

The reader will have asked himself, "All very interesting perhaps, but what has it to do with the Common School?"

The answer is that six generations of Americans have had to vote on the issue either directly or indirectly, and are still voting. It is time that rudimentary intelligence about the matter be bred into the mores, to the end that the public may have a right to entertain opinions.

"But is it not impossibly difficult for young people? I have known Doctors of Philosophy who admitted that they could not understand it." Doctors of Philosophy are no different from other people; they are ignorant of that about which they have no knowledge. The concepts with which we have been dealing are difficult only because they are unfamiliar. Mentally, they are not nearly so remote as most of high-school science and mathematics.

There are few fields in our lives as citizens in which the charlatan can do so much damage as here, and do it so readily. The only check upon him and his kind is intelligence widely diffused in the population—general intelligence arising out of particular intelligences like this.

Another chapter in the general subject of Exchange which seems to be a hopelessly bewildering mystery to most people, including many who deem themselves educated, is Foreign Exchange. And yet the elements are within the ready comprehension of the high-school pupil who is and has been blessed with good teachers or well-informed parents or both. Let us see what can and should be learned by all prospective citizens, and by those who are ambitious to become educated in the modern world.

Even this great mystery is a singularly good example of occasionally getting back to barter, even to swapping jackknives for fishing tackle, in order to clarify our ideas and get a fresh start. International trade is at bottom barter of exports for imports and nothing else. Moreover, interregional trade within a great nation amounts at bottom to the same thing.

Why so? Why not settle a bill for goods ordered from England by mailing a check or post-office order, just as we do when we order from a Sears-Roebuck catalogue? There are at least three good reasons why we cannot:

First, and most important, different currencies. They are not the same and are not under any common governmental control. Moreover, there is no internationally controlled banking system, like the Bank of England or our Federal Reserve System.

Second, and related to the foregoing, no merchant has any way of being sure of the value of checks drawn on banks in foreign countries.

Third, when we pay through buying an Express order or an order of the American Bankers Association, there is an assumption involved, as to American credits on the other side. So the bank clerk looks up his bulletin to see what exchange is on England or France or Sweden, as the case may be. In so doing, he opens up the whole subject.

Now the really cardinal principle at work is this: *Commerce knows no international boundaries; it works under a logic of its own. Whenever Governments flout that logic, so much the worse is it for the General Welfare.*

1. If we cannot, or do not wish to, raise coffee in the United States, and still desire coffee, we must buy it in Brazil or some other coffee country. Directly or indirectly, in the long run, we must exchange for the coffee something that Brazil cannot produce, or cannot produce so well and cheaply as we do, or else does not wish to produce at all. Conversely, Brazil must be willing and able to buy from us in order to sell us her coffee. So it goes all around the world-community. *No exports without imports* is the economic foundation of sound international trade.

All around the world. That coffee bill may be settled by a shipment of office furniture direct, or by shipping typewriters to England, whence machinery is shipped to France, and finally wine to Brazil.

FINANCE OF FOREIGN EXCHANGE

2. But actual shipments of goods would be clumsy. The American importer of coffee can perhaps find an exporter of furniture who has a bill due from some Brazilian, and arrange to pay the exporter so much of his bill as the coffee comes to, with the understanding that the exporter's correspondent in Santos will pay the Brazilian coffee exporter. One side of the transaction is thus settled in New York. They notify their Brazilian friends of the arrangement. The latter are glad of it, for that is the easiest way. So all are happy without the use of any money at all.

3. Still, international trade would be a slow business if it were all actually done that way.

Instead, all the importers in a country in effect arrange with all the exporters through *bills of exchange*, the former always needing to buy such instruments and the latter to sell. Hence a market is created at the banks. Exporters always have orders on their foreign correspondents to sell; and importers, orders to buy.

Now if for a time the value in gold of all American exports to England is exactly equal to an equivalent value of all imports from England, then exchange is at par, assuming both countries to be on the gold standard. American dollars can be converted into English pounds in terms of the gold value of each respectively. American exports are used to pay for imports from England through the medium of bills of exchange or drafts, and no money of any kind passes.

Let us suppose, however, that America is exporting more than she is importing. In that case, exporters will have more bills to sell than the importers will need. They can take their choice between accepting a discount in their accounts and importing the balance, not disposed of in bills of exchange, in gold. Within limits to be discussed presently, the latter does not pay. The exporters have to accept less than the face of their accounts. The importers are for the time happy, since they can buy exchange at less than the face of their accounts; they receive more than the latter.

In the reverse situation, the importers need more bills than the market affords and therefore must choose between exporting gold and paying a premium to the bankers for exchange.

GOLD POINTS

The points at which gold will be shipped in or shipped out are determined by the cost of shipment in express charges and insurance premiums. In normal times these gold points remain fairly constant.

Such is the heart of the matter, sufficient for the needs of pupils. Grounded well therein, they will be able to read further in the subject. The first interest they would be likely to encounter would be the characteristics of world-exchange; and the second, the way in which exchange affects the relative values of national currencies.

INSTRUCTION

There is scarcely any part of the Curriculum which is more remote from the needs of individuals than this. Not one pupil in a thousand will ever be concerned with foreign commerce as an individual, and these will be guided by their bankers. For special interest, University Schools of Commerce are their recourse. But let all that go. Few things are more important to people as citizens and as members of the community. If schools yearn for courses in "social science," here is social science at its most comprehensive.

UNITS IN EXCHANGE

I. Barter
1. Direct exchange between individuals of goods and services or both is barter.
2. Exchange of three meals for a day's work is exchange of goods for services.
3. Exchange of an automobile for a motor boat is exchange of goods for goods.
4. Barter is normally exchange of what one wants less for what one wants more, with somebody whose wants are inverse.
5. Barter is primitive commerce and is what all modern commerce comes to in the end if commerce is on a useful social basis.

II. Medium of Exchange
1. Where there is some commodity in universal demand, all kinds of commodities will be bartered for that.
2. The commodity in universal demand is, then, the *medium of exchange*.
3. All kinds of commodities then tend to become related to one another in value, according to relative value in terms of the medium of exchange.
4. Value in the medium of exchange is *price*.
5. Cattle, wheat, beaver skins, tobacco, and many other things served as a medium of exchange before there was any money.

III. Money
1. Precious metals have long been the civilized medium of exchange.
2. Because:
   a) They have long been in the most universal demand.
   b) They are not perishable.
   c) They have a great deal of value in small compass.
   d) They are therefore easily transportable.
3. Money has no value in itself save its intrinsic value.
4. The State cannot make anything valuable by decreeing that it shall be valuable.
5. When a community has passed beyond barter and manorial economy, it is said to be on a *money economy*.

IV. Manorial Economy
1. Economy founded on ownership of the land by a lord who had civil powers was economy in a *manor*.
2. Workers were apportioned goods and services by the lord or his agent according to the lord's judgment of their needs.

3. This was directed distribution of goods for services and not free exchange—no price and no commerce—not a money economy.
4. Workers in a strict manorial economy were necessarily serfs.
5. Communism is manorial economy on a national scale where the lord is replaced by political government in the community.

V. Subsistence Agriculture
   1. Formerly, farming people met nearly all their economic needs from what was raised on the farm under family cultivation.
   2. There was little exchange save for neighborhood co-operation in difficult undertakings.
   3. What little exchange there was consisted in export of surplus products to the cities once or twice a year.
   4. There was but little money and little need of money.
   5. Individual freedom and independence were probably at a maximum.

VI. Coin
   1. Metallic money stamped into regular form and inscribed with an identifying image is *coin*.
   2. Coinage is prerogative of The State because nothing else can set up a common medium in coin.
   3. The *pecuniary unit* is *defined* by prescribing the number of ounces of gold or silver it shall contain.
   4. Our pecuniary unit is the dollar as thus defined by Congress.
   5. The pecuniary unit is thus a measure of commercial value.

VII. Credit Money
   1. We use very little coin, but prefer credit money because of its greater convenience.
   2. A bank note certifying that a particular bank will pay on demand in gold the face of the note is credit money.
   3. A silver or gold certificate promising that the United States will pay on demand the face of the certificate in silver or gold is credit money.
   4. A promissory note of the United States payable on demand in coin without interest is credit money.
   5. No credit money has any more value than the confidence of the public that the Government or the bank can and will keep its promises.

VIII. Bank Credit
   1. Deposits create a debt owed by the bank to the depositor who is the creditor.
   2. Accounts between individuals are settled by bank check without the intervention of money.

3. Banks clear their own debits and credits, thus set up, through a clearing-house or clearing-house bank.
4. Clearings normally tend to come to a balance in any community.
5. Thus the great bulk of transactions in the United States are settled without the use of money at all.

IX. Inflation
  1. Inflation is anything that seems to be more than it really is.
  2. Lurid advertising or high-pressure salesmanship tends to create general commercial inflation.
  3. Credit inflation occurs when people run in debt for utilities, the income from which cannot be expected to retire the debt.
  4. Currency inflation occurs when
     a) There is more money in circulation than the requirements of normal transactions justify
     b) When the Government or the banks either cannot or will not keep their promises to redeem paper money
     c) When fiat money is printed
  5. Inflation of any kind is bad because it is artificial, abnormal, unhealthy.

X. Inflation of the Currency and Prices
  1. When the pecuniary unit is actually exchangeable for the number of ounces of gold or silver which it is defined to be, the currency is said to be sound. Prices will vary only in response to variation in supply and demand in respect to commodities.
  2. Otherwise the currency is inflated.
  3. In a country in which buying and selling are done chiefly in currency, commodities tend to be exchanged for the real value in gold.
  4. Hence, prices in the inflated unit become higher, irrespective of demand and supply.
  5. Rise is governed by confidence in the Government's ability and intention to restore specie payments.
  6. If there is loss of confidence, earnings in currency will at once be spent in purchases of goods.
  7. That increases demand, and prices rise from day to day until complete collapse in the value of the inflated unit occurs.
  8. When fiat money is issued, the process is made inevitable and rapid.
  9. When exchange is heavily on a bank-clearings basis, the effect of inflation is greatly retarded and lessened.
  10. Nothing, however, will protect the community from the effect of fiat money.

XI. Quantity of Money
  1. There is not needed a dollar for every dollar transaction—money *circulates*.
  2. Where there is potential demand, equivalent supply, and insufficient money, increasing the quantity of money tends to make possible exchanges which could not otherwise have been made.
  3. But no direct addition is made to the wealth of the country.
  4. In our country the needed volume of money is largely adjusted to varying needs through the Federal Reserve System.

XII. Foreign Exchange
  1. Normally there are no exports without equivalent imports.
  2. Accounts between citizens of different countries are normally settled without the use of money by balancing import transactions against export transactions. That is foreign exchange.
  3. Bills of exchange, or foreign drafts, are simply commercial devices by which this is done.
  4. Exporters always have bills to sell, and importers always have bills to buy.
  5. Hence a market is created which is like any other market, and bankers deal in bills of exchange.
  6. If there are more export bills than can be sold, the price of exchange bills falls, and exporters must accept less than the face of their accounts at the banks.
  7. If there are more import bills demanded than the supply, the price will rise, and the importer must pay the banker more than the face of his account.
  8. When the value of imports and exports balances, exchange is at par.
  9. If world-trade is not hampered by legislation or calamity, the tendency is toward par of exchange the world over.

XIII. International Gold Movement
  1. Gold bullion is the only universal medium of exchange.
  2. International accounts can always be settled by shipping specie or bullion instead of balancing export and import payments through bills of exchange.
  3. But that is expensive, for express charges, insurance, and interest cost while in transit are involved.
  4. Hence, specie will not be shipped until the cost of shipment is less than premium or discount on exchange.
  5. Gold must normally flow toward a country which is a heavy exporter until discount is so heavy as to discourage export and encourage import.

6. A country which persistently maintains an export balance sooner or later loses export trade through development of competing sources.

7. Similarly, a country which persistently imports necessities which it could produce itself tends to lose its gold.

8. But a war or some similar cause may so dislocate international trade that gold persistently flows for a long time toward some one country, thus causing a world-depression through loss of an international medium of exchange.

B. PRICE

In dealing with Exchange, we have been studying the heart of Commerce as institution, and, if no other course were set up, pupils would still have learned its elements. There do, however, arise certain other matters which are essential to a working lay intelligence concerning this aspect of Civilization—matters with which we are in constant contact and which are of profound social significance. The first of these is *Price*, that is to say, the value in the medium of exchange at which goods and services are distributed.

It is an extremely complicated subject, and we cannot go far into it without becoming involved in technical considerations far outside the scope of the Common School and pertinent only to those who are professionally engaged in Commerce and Industry. Nevertheless, the elements of Price, an understanding of which makes the difference between the person who is intelligent about the matter and the one who is still in an attitude of passive acceptance, or, more likely resistance, are readily to be imparted in a short high-school course.

COMMON ERRONEOUS NOTIONS

People who have never given much study to the subject are commonly unaware that there is any such thing as a logic of price which, as communities become established in a money economy, determines a *price structure*, which itself rapidly evolves and from which neither buyer nor seller can escape. One meets two conspicuous errors in looking at the whole matter.

The first of these is the widely prevalent idea that price is merely a matter of the relative generosity or greed of the dealer, that it is a personal matter outside the influence of the logic of circumstances.

The second is contained in the notion that the producer ought as a matter of justice to receive back what it has cost him to produce, "plus a reasonable profit," the latter to be settled very much on a subjective basis. The world is simply not put together that way, neither in Society nor in Nature. There is no such thing as a personified being called Society which can give to each what he believes he ought to receive. In fact, there is no *oughtness* about it. There is no oughtness about bodily health, no question of justice. We keep well if we live according to natural laws. If we fall into sickness, we get cured, not by legislation but by observing and obeying natural principles, the logic of Nature. Justice is, on the other hand, deeply involved between producer and consumer in that each shall be fairly and honorably treated by the other, that advantage shall not be taken, and that fraud shall not be practiced.

I suppose that we shall not go very far wrong if we see the whole subject of price as an understanding of the origins and evolution of *price structure*.

OUR SUBJECT MATTER

We shall concern ourselves, for purposes of illustrating principles, with the retail prices of staples; but what is true there is at bottom true of the producer's price as well. By "staples" we mean goods and services which are in common and universal use. They are largely within the area of necessities, but we include in our thought also those services which were once luxuries and have now become, if not necessities, at least essentials in the fabric of the community, the most notable of which is telephone service.

Labor is not part of our subject matter, save incidentally.

Nor are we concerned with luxury prices, in which there is often a good deal more psychology than logic. We sometimes see people who, to all appearances, pay high prices simply out of vanity.

HIGGLING

What might perhaps be called the primitive stage in Price is called *higgling*, or sometimes dickering. We still see it, but mainly where single articles, not part of a stock, are being sold. In the typical bazaar trade higgling is still the rule; the whole stock is higgled off piece by piece with loud protests of despair and ruin.

SINGLE PRICE

The contrasting stage is that in which a single price is set up for a whole supply or line of goods of a given grade and quality, or a series of single prices for different grades within a single supply. In it appear signs of definite organization, refinement, logic— a system of thought as well as a system of practice. It rests upon a a basic principle, namely, that price shall be fixed at such a point, or series of points for different grades, that the whole supply will be sold. Progress in mercantile skill is at bottom progress in estimating and securing that price. Vendors of all sorts can still be found who are so lacking in mercantile knowledge and skill that they cannot seem to price their goods and services at points at which more than a small portion can be sold.

Single price tends to become single for a whole community for a single line. To be sure, there will be variations dictated by the kind of customers a dealer has, but in general such variations will follow a relatively narrow range.

PRICE LEVELS

Price levels, on the other hand, are determined by general supply and demand in the world or regional market. There may be wide differences in the price at which men's suits of a given quality can be purchased, but we do not buy them for $1.00 nor do we have to pay $1,000. The price level is settled by the world's supply of textiles and by manufacturing and transportational costs. Wealth cannot be distributed until it is produced, but in the last century or two, and especially in the last generation, the amount of distributable wealth has been enormously increased. The reason at bottom is chiefly to be found in the spread of geographical intelligence.

Still, in our study of Price, we are concerned not with price levels but rather with the behavior of prices at given levels.

DEMAND

Another factor in price is obviously *demand*. On that issue, many chapters can be written and many books, but for our purposes we need to keep only two or three characteristics in mind.

First, we must bear in mind the two primary elements in demand, *desire* and *purchasing power*, or "what I would like" and "what I can afford."

Second, the qualities of *elastic* and *inelastic* demand.

Elastic demand exists when:

a) Desire for a given piece of goods or services is mild, something one would have if there were no consideration of purchasing power or inconvenience in purchasing.

b) When desire is not to be questioned, but one can do without.

c) When desire is urgent, but thrifty use reduces the quantity needed.

d) When desire is imperative, but one can find substitutes.

Inelastic demand exists when a given goods or service is essential and inescapable. In modern times there are few such which are absolute. The air we breathe is one such, but air is not economic in character, for there is no scarcity. And yet the latter statement is but relative. Air that is conducive to health, especially in congested cities, is scarce and therefore economic. But it is not vendible and therefore not commercial. Perhaps city water would be the best illustration of inelastic demand, but even there absolute inelasticity exists only in respect to minimum needs.

THE PRIMARY PRACTICAL FACTORS IN PRICE STRUCTURE

If we now give our minds to a picture of an actual group of dealers in an actual local community, and try to see what factors will operate on them in their price-fixing, we shall note two which overshadow all others.

The first is that the price must be one at which the whole stock will sell. That means that there must be a clientele of purchasers. Merchandisers therefore compete for the market, not by price-cutting, but by skill in cutting costs, and in salesmanship. Price-cutting in itself is merely ruinous.

The second factor is inherent in the first, namely, the cost of merchandising. No dealer can long survive if he consistently sells goods for less than they cost, including the cost of selling.

In the long run, these two factors must come into balance, and that process of equilibration determines the evolution of the price structure as a social process to be understood.

SUPPLY-DEMAND SCHEDULE

Price in the administration of the intelligent dealer tends in the first instance to settle in terms of what is called the supply-demand schedule, that is to say, the point at which there is the greatest return for a given volume consistent with meeting costs. That perhaps needs some elucidation.

If one has goods to sell, and is interested, as all are, in the greatest net return from his business, he can sell at a high price for a small volume or at a low price for a large volume. Now there is a point at which there is the largest net return between the two possible extremes. That is the balancing-point of the supply-demand schedule; it will be less than the highest price at which a considerable volume could be sold, and a good deal higher than giving the goods away.

But the low price will be checked by the cost of doing business.

So in a given community the skilful and competent will capture the market and survive because it is they who best understand the process at work. They will sell at low price and secure volume, while the others drop out for lack of trade. Wealth, or at least usable wealth, is distributed by low price, furthered by low-price levels in world-supply. That is success in one of the fundamental social functions, namely, distribution.

COST OF DISTRIBUTION

The price cannot be lower than cost justifies, and volume cannot be greater than price induces. Let us then turn to an examination of costs by surveying the costs which in general enter into the selling of goods.

1. Cost of the stock which the dealer buys from the producer or wholesaler.

2. Interest on the money invested in stock for the time it remains unsold. Recall that interest is a cost to the merchandiser whether he invests his own money or borrows the money.

3. Rent of the premises used in the business. Rent is the cost of the use of real estate or appliances. It exists, as interest exists, even though the dealer may own the plant entire. If he does not earn interest and rent on his own, his capital at the best is lying idle.

4. Depreciation on premises and appurtenances. Whether the plant is owned or leased, the depreciation must be made good in the returns from the business.

5. Taxes, real and personal. Taxes levied upon the merchandiser's business, and upon the property used in the business, can be passed on to the buyer, but that can be done only by covering them in price.

6. Insurance on goods and store from fire and other calamities.

7. Labor of clerks, salespeople, deliverymen, and personal services in general. If the merchant himself engages in selling goods, keeping books, or in any other service which classes as labor or store management, rather than enterprisership, then his own labor is part of the cost of doing business. Hence the remark often heard from dealers, "Well, I am making day wages."

8. Transportation of the goods from point of production.

9. Advertising.

10. Bad bills on charge accounts. Where a trader is compelled by local competition to carry charge accounts, there will always be a certain proportion of customers who either cannot or will not pay their bills. This is part of the cost, and the cost has to be recovered in prices charged. In other words, the thrifty and honorable have to help support the unfortunate and the shiftless and the dishonorable.

11. Interest on customers' charge accounts for the time they remain unpaid.

Inevitably, the intelligent and skilful dealer tries to cut costs, in order to make possible lower prices to consumers, in order to increase the volume of trade, and in order to secure the largest possible gains from the business.

Unhappily, there are several points at which the temptation to unethical practices is particularly strong:

1. Misrepresentation of goods, that is to say, offering inferior or adulterated goods as standard. Fortunately, that is somewhat antique, for dealers of any considerable experience and imagination know that Good Will, one of the most important of their assets, is thereby sacrificed. The Federal and State Governments and local ordinances have for many years been trying to stamp out such practices. A related fraud is short weight or short measure.

2. Intrigue with public officials for preferential treatment in the billing of taxes.

3. Insurance frauds—occasionally.

4. Preferential treatment by railway companies in the matter of freight rates. That was at one time the conspicuous illegitimate method of squeezing out competitors. Apparently, it has been stamped out, at least on any considerable scale.

All these and many others are instances of obvious wrongdoing. The perpetrators know that they are indulging in immoral acts.

There are, however, other malpractices which are to be rated as antisocial, that is to say, unethical, without being so obviously immoral, at least at the present stage of our customs.

Labor.—The labor element in merchandising is important as cost, but not nearly so important as in Industry. Nevertheless, the labor problem in Commerce has distinct social implications. The wage-earners are hard to organize, and competition with other dealers sometimes brings out some of the worst features of raw human nature, especially where Commerce is still at the individual-enterpriser stage. The early stages of large-concern organization, on the other hand, have often been singularly ruthless in exploiting labor. Sweating has taken place, men have been replaced by girls and by women with income-earning husbands, girls are paid ridiculously low wages, all of which has disastrous effects upon total male employment and upon the Family as institution.

The unethical effect is seen in the consequences just noted. It is further manifest in reduction of purchasing power in a large element of the population. Human nature being what it is, it is very difficult for any of us to subordinate our actual present self-interest to that self-interest which is bound up in the interest of the group to which we belong and that of the community. Any single employer, even a large one, can cut wages to the bare subsistence level, or below, without much effect upon the purchasing power of the community. He does not employ a sufficiently large number. But when everybody in the commercial setup of the community is compelled by his competition to do the same, then the purchasing power of the community is noticeably impaired, the social benefit of more widely distributed wealth is lessened, and, it may be, destroyed. Low prices are relative to the purchasing power of the people who have prices to pay.

We hear a great deal about "social injustice." It would be hard to find a more patent instance than in the contemplation of those who make their purchases at low prices which they must see are made possible, in part at least, by the callous manner in which the merchandiser treats his help.

Advertising and pressure salesmanship.—The cost of advertising is an important element in the cost of doing business, but that is not all. Advertising of the scientifically deliberate suggestive sort, and salesmanship which co-operates with advertising in inducing people to buy what they do not want and cannot afford, contribute to the production of general commercial inflation, which, as we have seen in our study of money, is in this country more to be dreaded than currency inflation.

THE LARGE CONCERN

We left the evolutionary process at the stage at which there appeared the capture of the local market by enterprises in which there had been learned the theory of the supply-demand schedule.

That stage was premonitory of another and larger development. To that we now come.

The large mercantile concern, whether we find it as department store, mail-order house, or chain-store corporation, rests upon its superior use of the supply-demand schedule and specifically upon reduction of costs of doing business. It arrives at the point at which the profit element *in the cost of each article sold* has been reduced to the minimum, and returns to the business consist in the *great number of units sold*. But great volume sold means low price per unit sold, and that is the same thing as greater distribution of wealth.

a) They can in the nature of their organization greatly reduce costs in proportion to sales.

b) They can distribute risks of all sorts through many branches in different localities, or else through dealing in a great range of lines of goods, or both.

First of all, since they buy in great quantities, they can buy most advantageously in respect to both price and variety. They can pick up job lots and articles which rate as seconds but which are still functionally as good as the best (for example, tableware which is slightly warped or off-circle), and thus wealth is distributed which was once destroyed.

Second, they can move goods on their shelves much more rapidly and thus cut down interest cost of investment in the stock for sale.

Third, and perhaps most important, since their business is not entirely local, or at any rate is impersonal, they are not under the compulsion to carry charge customers as the small individual enterpriser is apt to be. They will do either a mail-order trade or else a cash-and-carry trade. If the customer desires an account service, he pays for it in a small financial charge month by month. They thus save both the burden of bad bills and the interest cost of deferred payments on charge accounts.

Fourth, they can refuse to make free deliveries, and, if deliveries are desired, they can make a charge for the service.

But the end of it all is greater distribution of wealth.

THE MERCHANDISING CORPORATION

Such enterprises commonly become too large for individual ownership or that of copartners. Hence, the normal course is to set up corporations. That has or may have interesting social implications.

Corporations, when they are well managed and in themselves justified, can normally be expected to pay dividends. Dividends are in the nature of distribution of profits—and, economically, profit-taking is distribution of risk. The history of American corporations shows that in a thrifty and enlightened community, the normal tendency is for ownership in corporations, that is to say, stockholding, to become diffused. Moreover, when a corporation has become well established, and its stock has gone through the "ripening" process, its dividends will normally pay something like 4 per cent on their market value. That means that not only is the mercantile effect of large volume and low price to distribute wealth, but the financial effect of the joint-stock company is to distribute income.

FAIR PRICE

We often speak of "fair price" and "reasonable price." It rarely happens that anybody ever means by these terms anything other than the price that suits him. To use the adjective "fair" is gratuitously to introduce into economics a term which belongs to jurisprudence. It is therefore a misnomer to use the expression in its ordinary connotation

There is *economic price*, and this section has been devoted to showing how economic price evolves out of a situation in which there is no price structure at all into one in which price is progressively lower, even to the limits fixed by national and world-supply in relation to popular desires.

There is, however, one sense in which "fair price" can accurately and pertinently be used. In that sense, fair price is the price paid when there is no interference of craft, deceit, fraud, ignorance, or unethical practices on the part of either buyer or seller.

UNITS IN PRICE

I. What Is Price?
1. Price is the value in terms of a medium of exchange in which goods and services are distributed
2. In a money economy, price is value of goods and services in money
3. In highly civilized societies, price is a system determined by a logic from which neither buyer nor seller can escape
4. Prosperity depends in large part upon general understanding of that logic

II. Higgling and Single Price
1. When buyer and seller settle the price of each purchase by agreement, the process is called "higgling"
2. Higgling is primitive and obsolete because there is no fixity about it
3. Hence, goods cannot be produced and sold on a great scale
4. Single price is price advertised for a whole present stock in a particular line
5. In principle, the price is estimated to be such that the whole stock will be disposed of

III. Price Level
1. The level at which goods are priced depends
   a) Upon the available world-supply of the goods themselves or of other goods which enter into their manufacture
   b) Upon demand
2. In luxury goods the level is always high; that is all that makes them luxuries
3. But demand tends to lead to supply unless there is natural scarcity, as there is in gems and the precious metals
4. Hence many goods and services which were once luxuries become staples
5. Staples are goods and services which are in common consumption

IV. Demand
1. Has the two elements of desire and purchasing power
2. Is elastic when
   a) It does not apply to necessities
   b) There is possible large range of economy in use
   c) Substitutes can be found
3. Is inelastic when there is an imperative minimum need

V. The Price To Be Set
1. Depends upon the market in which goods can be sold
   Hence dealers are normally in competition for the market

    2. Depends upon the cost which must be made good in the price charged

    3. Depends upon the two coming into balance at a price which will make good the cost and will still command a market

VI. Supply-Demand Schedule

    1. High price tends to lead to low volume and low price to large volume

    2. There is a balancing-point at which the largest net returns are found in the presence of a given demand and available supply

    3. That point can normally be lowered by cutting costs, and hence lowering price and increasing volume

VII. Competition

    1. Competition is struggle for possession of the market

    2. The most skilful dealer tends to secure the largest trade

    3. Skill consists in

        a) Understanding and application of the principles of Commerce

        b) Ability to lower costs and hence prices to be charged

    4. Trade always tends toward a few large concerns which hold the market at low price

    5. Low price enhances distribution of usable wealth, which is what Commerce is for

VIII. Cost of Merchandising

    (To be understood by understanding its elements)

    1. Money invested in stock

    (Not strictly a cost, but rather capital which must continuously be recovered)

    2. Interest on capital invested in stock so long as the latter remains unsold

    3. Rent of premises

    4. Depreciation of buildings and equipment

    5. Taxes—real and personal

    6. Insurance

    7. Labor

    8. Transportation

    9. Advertising

    10. Bad bills

    11. Interest on customer's accounts

IX. Malfeasance in Reducing Costs

    1. Fraud and dishonesty in general

    2. Adulteration of goods

    3. False weight and measure

4. Corruption of Government
5. Preferential treatment by transportation companies
6. Cutting wages to the impairment of producing and purchasing power
7. Artificial stimulation of demand by advertising and salesmanship
8. Regulation by law applies very largely in this field

X. The Large Concern
1. Can cut all costs save taxes, and do it legitimately
2. Hence can sell goods at lower price and increase volume
3. Can reduce profit element in single purchases to a very low fraction and earn large sums on the large number of units sold
4. Hence enhances distribution of usable wealth, which is the social function of Commerce

XI. Fair Price
1. Fair price is not what any of us believe we ought to pay or to receive
2. We are prejudiced by our own interests
3. Price is economic and objective; it is low when trade is being intelligently and honestly conducted
4. High price for staples means that local trade is uneconomic somewhere
5. Price is *unfair* when either buyer or seller is receiving benefit from something which he ought not to do or which ought not to be done

C. BOOKKEEPING AND ACCOUNTANCY

Commerce has a logic, that is to say, an understandable structure. Logic is but language applied to a given substance, and the language brings the substance under intellectual control; it can be talked about and brought into common understanding.

The language of Commerce is contained in the art of Bookkeeping, and the science of Accountancy might well be called the grammar of Bookkeeping. The two together have sometimes been called the handmaidens of Economics.

IN INSTRUCTION

In the old common school, in the day before the high school had become primarily a vocational and college-preparatory enterprise, Bookkeeping was a common subject and frequently required of all. As we recall those old courses, or come upon them in textbooks, it at once becomes apparent that they were voca-

tional in import and designed to meet the common need only in
the sense that most high-school graduates would begin life by
"clerking in a store" or by following some similar calling. Typically, the courses assumed that the pupil was learning to keep a
set of books for some small trader. He learned the cashbook, the
daybook, the customer's ledger; and then he passed on into
journal entries, double-entry ledgers, balance sheets, etc.

As high schools grew larger, and the elective system became
common, Bookkeeping became an elective vocational subject—
and a whole generation of the most highly schooled grew into
adult life devoid of any notions of systematically managing their
own financial affairs beyond what banks and the delivery slips
of traders would do for them.

What we think of today as commonplace terms in professional
accountancy were for the most part unheard of until the Federal
Income Tax of 1913 made it profitable for businessmen to mend
their ways. On the other hand, partial payments, annual interest, present worth, which are essentially terms in Accountancy,
appeared in the regular program in Arithmetic and continued to
do so down into my own early teaching days. I presume that here
and there an eighth grade may still be grappling with partial
payments.

Nevertheless, not only are the elements in this field an essential part of an understanding of Commerce but they are
equally essential in the instruction of the Common Man as competent citizen able to manage his own affairs with intelligence
and prudence, and qualified to entertain enlightened views touching the conduct of public affairs.

THE BUDGET

We shall not go very far wrong if we set up the notion of the
individual and private budget as the theme of the course in Bookkeeping. Some terms in Accountancy are required, not only because they illuminate the valid operations of any commerce and
industry but because they form the important conceptual bases
for managing one's own affairs. To decide whether it best to

resole an old pair of shoes, for instance, is at bottom to solve a problem in Depreciation.

We have here a course which in some ways bears an important resemblance to courses in the fields which we studied before embarking upon The State and upon Commerce and Industry. The course was once part of typical courses of study for a long time, and it is still found in high-school departments of commerce, indeed in more elaborate form than is required in the Common School. Hence, we have no need of the detailed discussion which has been accorded to the courses in The State and to other courses in Commerce. Nevertheless, I shall feel free to comment as units and elements are developed.

UNITS

I. SETTING UP AND KEEPING A CASHBOOK

The cashbook faithfully kept and reconciled daily with cash in hand is perhaps the first step in Bookkeeping and the foundation of intelligent thrift. Few there be who follow the practice. It seems reasonable enough to most people with whom the matter is discussed to rejoin, "But I know how much I ought to have and is not that enough?" It may be doubted that such people do "know how much they ought to have." But that is not the point. What is important is that the whole process of managing one's own affairs should be systematic and therefore socially intelligible from the beginning. The conventional cashbook with its fundamentals of debit and credit and daily balance is just that systematic procedure.

But the ingrained habit of keeping a cashbook is quite as important as knowing how to do it. In that respect we pass out of the effective possibilities of instruction and into the domain of upbringing. Parental co-operation will require children who have an allowance, or make small earnings of their own, to keep a regular cashbook ready for inspection at all times.

II. BANK CHECKS AND MONTHLY STATEMENT

1. The course of checks through the bank, distant banks, clearing-house, and return to drawer

2. Keeping the stubs or counterfoils and continuing balances
3. Reconciling the final balance with balance at the bank as shown by monthly bank statement

Of course, practice is difficult here unless the school can set up an effective make-believe bank. One high-school class which came under my observation, however, did all the bookkeeping for the school department in a city of 10,000. It invoiced and checked deliveries of school supplies including coal, and drew the checks in payment. That, however, was a vocational class. But it showed what can be done in the direction of making instruction conform to reality.

III. BUDGET

A budget is, first of all, a plan for a year's expenditures, balanced against anticipated income.

1. Description of a budget
2. The budget as the basis for the control of a particular commercial existence
3. Selection of significant classification of expenditures

IV. LEDGER SHOWING DISTRIBUTION OF EXPENDITURES

There is no valid budget unless it be based upon distributed expenditures running over a year or other fiscal period.

The distributive columns are, of course, the same as the budget classifications, indeed they are the budget. The left-hand entries take the place of the old-time daybook.

The distributions are usually food, clothing, rent, education, recreation, church and social, etc. Standard forms can be found in manuals, and blank forms are published for the purpose. But such things are death to intelligence unless the individual can rise to the point at which he sees for himself what are the significant items for his own problem.

A budget is a meaningless affair where it is based upon what an individual supposes he ought to spend. Nobody learns to manage money that way. Distribution enables the person to secure significant facts on which to base his future judgments, nay even insures that his judgment will tend to be good, even if there is not much deliberation about it.

V. INCOME AND OUTGO ACCOUNT

Income is debit, something for which the account is responsible. Outgo is credit, a record of how the responsibility has been met.

Here enters the notion of accruals. We make occasional large expenditures which come perhaps only once or twice a year. They can usually be known or estimated in advance. It is these irregular expenditures which are most apt to get the casual person into trouble. His cash and bank balance is large, that which is distant is not impressive, and he spends what ought to be reserved. When his accounts are set up on an accrual basis, irregular known expenditures are prorated month by month and income is similarly prorated. The Income and Outgo account thus takes notice not only of what is but of what must be. Current expenditures are seen in the light of larger expenditures which must later be made. Of course, in a regular business enterprise, the problem would probably be met under the captions *reserves* and *fixed charges*.

VI. SAVINGS

Savings may be grouped under two heads:

1. That which consists in building up income-producing capital as a provision for old age, for most people probably best managed through endowment life insurance
2. The "rainy-day" or contingent fund to meet the mischances of active life. More and more of this too can best be administered through insurance premiums

VII. DEPRECIATION AND DEPLETION

A science-type unit. The problem is one of coming to understand

1. That both depreciation and depletion are realities that have to be accounted for
2. That depreciation occurs both as physical depreciation and as functional depreciation or obsolescence
3. That physical depreciation is not stopped by repairs, although careful use and faithful attention to repairs lengthens the actual use of the asset
4. That both depreciation and depletion can be accounted for and recovered by good management
5. That depletion of natural resources in the community can be foreseen and provided for

VIII. OVERHEAD

One of the most useful terms in Accountacy, is *overhead*. To the Common Man it is an essential element in his understanding of the management of his own affairs and, like all the rest of the terms which legitimately enter into the Curriculum of the Common School, essential to his intelligence as a member of the community and as a citizen. Moreover, it is but a phase of the general economic concepts which are found in such principles as the law of diminishing returns and the law of diminishing utility. To pursue the notion into the refinements of analysis which the professional accountant would have frequent occasion to follow would manifestly be beyond our concern. The three elements of the unit which follow would seem to be sufficient, although in the process of instruction a good deal of illustrative material must needs be used.

1. Part of the total cost of an enterprise which is not affected by increase or decrease of the volume of business

    (The housekeeper is familiar with the principle in her observation that the cost of feeding four people in a family is not one third greater than the cost of feeding three)

2. There always are limits beyond which the increasing volume does expand the overhead element in cost

3. And eventually the overhead made necessary by increasing volume and expansion rises so rapidly as to impose a check upon expansion

IX. SURPLUS

Surplus in business management is much like what "rainy-day" or contingent funds are in private finance. The faithfully built-up and well-managed surplus of a corporation or individual enterprise enables the business to keep on paying dividends and keep men at work during periods of depression. It thus in itself tends to stabilize business in the community and to decrease the amplitude of cycles of depression. In truth, if all businesses maintained adequate surpluses, and all individuals adequate savings accounts, there would, other things being equal, be no depressions.

Few indeed of us ever have occasion to pass judgment on business surplus, on its adequacy and relation to other obligations of the enterprise. Such matters are assuredly not within the competency of the Common School, and they would not be appropriate to its purpose if they were. There is, however, scarcely anything within the field of Commerce and Industry with which Government does not at times feel called upon to meddle. Such meddling is pretty apt to be a response to public opinion, directly or indirectly. One of the recent instances has been the destructive taxation of corporate surpluses. It follows that here too is an essential element in the understanding of Commerce—essential to the understanding of the competent citizen.

All that is needed is such elementary development of the subject as will cover the meaning and significance of *surplus* in its social effects.

X. RESERVES

The individual who is not professionally engaged in Commerce and Industry has little personal concern with reserves beyond what is implied in keeping an Income and Outgo account on an accrual basis. In business, however, there are numerous obligations which have to be met sooner or later. They are as much a part of the obligations to be recorded in the accounts of the enterprise as are the cost of raw materials and wages of labor. Depreciation is one of them, and in the well-managed business a depreciation reserve is set up. This is but one of many reserves which different types of businesses have to carry. Sinking funds to meet the maturity of bonds are another common reserve. The maintenance of all of them must be provided for before there are any real net earnings.

This too in its elements is part of an elementary understanding of Commerce which ought to be the possession of every person as part of his intelligence. The individual advantage comes out of the principle that here, as we have found to be the case all the way back to the beginning, is part of the foundation of reading capacity in Commerce and Industry.

XI. BALANCE SHEET

The individual who is not engaged in business seldom requires a true balance sheet beyond what is implicit in the accounts which are enumerated in the early part of the course; but the possibility of taking a balance at any time which will show accurately the state of a business is the heart of good management. The annual balance sheet, especially in joint-stock companies, is part of the apparatus of keeping faith with the public as well as with the stockholders.

Now a complete balance sheet which shows with precision the actual state of the business is a highly technical affair, but, like most highly technical affairs, it grows out of simple elements. Some of our most ably managed corporations publish a summarized balance sheet in terms of these simple elements. It is, however, doubtful that more than a very small number indeed of the total number of adult citizens gain the least illumination from one of these reports. They have not the rudiments in mind, and therefore they cannot read, nor is there enough background in the specific intelligence required to make them curious. If large numbers of citizens were thus capable, two great social advantages would follow within a generation:

First, a good deal of indubitable rascality would be nipped in the bud, for rascality thrives on public ignorance beyond all things.

Second, we should be spared the disgrace of beholding our most cultivated citizens, or at least large groups of them, exhibiting an ignorance of commercial and financial affairs which in principle is a reproach to the intelligence of a schoolboy. Such people can read and do read the sensational works of charlatans with all the enthusiasm which an impecunious country schoolmaster learns of the marvels of bucket-shops.

The elements are:

1. Assets
    The nature of assets as resources which can be converted into money and used to meet liabilities

2. Liabilities
    The nature of liabilities as obligations which must be met
    Particularly there ought to be emphasized that imputed liabilities, such as reserves, are as real as obvious liabilities such as bills payable

The whole state of the business can always be shown in the form of a balance of assets and liabilities.

D. Financial Institutions

While Exchange is fundamental to Commerce and, since Commerce deals almost entirely in the products of Industry, to Industry as well, nevertheless the machinery used in effecting exchanges and in making existence possible in a complex economic order is almost as important to the study of Commerce as is Exchange itself. We have met part of the machinery in our study of Money. It remains to study three principal institutions utilized in effecting exchanges without the use of money; in collecting and making available in money and credits floating capital for the use of community enterprises; in making available to individuals returns on the time value of their unconsumed earnings; in liquidating risk by distributing it; in established single price and common estimates of commercial values in securities and in the primary agricultural products. These institutions are Banking, Insurance, and the Stock and Commodity Exchanges.

I. Banking

Wherever there is an established monetary system, and an established social order in which The State has become strong enough to control marauders, and Morality sufficiently developed and diffused among the population to generate Confidence, it comes to be folkway to intrust money to individuals for safe-keeping. That is the beginning of an institution.

The folkway once established, it is natural enough for it to expand. When the early bankers had found that, instead of keeping the money, they could lend it out at interest and still be able to pay any one or a modest number of depositors on demand; and, by calling in loans, to pay all depositors, banking had emerged out of a folkway into a true institution. From that point on what we shall be studying is an institution in a relatively advanced stage of evolution.

a) COMMERCIAL BANKS

Banks are all of them commercial, but the name is applied particularly to that kind of bank in which we keep our checking accounts.

ORGANIZATION

A group of individuals contribute of their capital to a joint capital. They become incorporated under the laws of the United States or of one of the States in a charter which authorizes them to do a certain banking business. They organize by electing a board of directors; and the latter choose a president as the executive head, a cashier as administrative head, and such staff as may be required. The business of a commercial bank has the following general characteristics:

1. The bank receives money for safekeeping, the original banking function.

2. It thus maintains bank credit for ordinary current transactions, such as we have found in the section on Money. In other words, each depositor has a checking account at the bank.

3. Since the management knows that few or none of the depositors will withdraw all their money at once, and most of them will keep a larger or smaller balance for long intervals, the depositors' money in part can be loaned out at interest. How much of it must be kept in reserve is a matter of banking experience in the local constituency, and a matter of law.

4. The loans are of two kinds:

a) Discounting the promissory notes which dealers bring in, having received them from customers to whom they have sold goods.

Such notes are commonly given for an amount which covers the face of the bill rendered and interest for the term of the note. Since the ordinary merchant or producer is enterpriser and not capitalist, he prefers to have the money to use in his own business. Hence, he indorses the note, which is his promise to make good if the maker does not, the bank pays over the face minus the interest, and at maturity collects from the maker. In thriving commercial and manufacturing communities, banks are thus the very condition of local prosperity. Business could hardly go on without them.

b) Banks also lend in other ways by furnishing businessmen, farmers, and others with short-term loans for current operations, largely pay rolls. That means that the relatively small balances of many depositors are collectively made available for the conduct of business in the community. Otherwise, there could be no business large or small unless every enterpriser were also a capitalist. Production and distribution would not exist on anything like the present scale, for there would not be nearly enough individual capitalists.

The current-loans feature of commercial banking is especially applicable to the requirements of farmers. While there may be so rapid a turnover of retail goods in a cash-and-carry chain store that relatively little working capital is required, the farmer is under the dispensation of nature and cannot expect returns on his crop investment until after harvest at least, and perhaps not until after two or three harvests. Hence it is that modern farming operations require relatively a large amount of working capital. This an adequate banking system makes possible, whereas without it all farmers must have large money resources in capital themselves.

SECURITY

In this connection we ought to be clear that bankers can make no loans unless they have some guaranty that payment will be made, that is to say, *security*. Now security is of two kinds:

First, it is pledged collateral securities, that is to say, marketable stocks and bonds which in the event of the borrower's default become the property of the bank. A variant is mortgage on the property of the borrower.

Second, it is the reputation of the borrower for honesty, capacity, and general good character. Some of our ablest bankers have said roundly that personal character is more essential security than either money or property.

BANKS OF ISSUE

Bank notes, which we have met in our study of Money, are also an important resource in credit, or at least have been.

We recall that the bank-note form of credit money is a promise on the part of the bank issuing the same to redeem in currency on demand. Sound Government requires all banks of issue to maintain a reserve in gold up to a certain percentage of outstanding notes, plus full collateral in United States bonds. The bonds are deposited with the Treasury, so that if the bank should fail, the Government could redeem the outstanding notes. The bonds, of course, bear interest and are thus a source of income to the issuing bank. Since 1864 State banks have not been banks of issue.

The bank then uses its notes in discounts and loans, and thus they pass into circulation as part of the monetary stock of the nation.

SOLVENCY

A bank is solvent when its assets are equal to or more than the sum total of its liabilities, including especially liability to depositors.

LIQUIDITY

On the other hand, a bank may be entirely solvent and yet unable to make good to its depositors, if they should press their claims in abnormally large numbers or for large amounts, because of its inability to realize upon its loans at once. In that case it is said to have lost liquidity.

Bank runs.—Now if suspicion spreads abroad in a community that a bank is not entirely solvent or has lost liquidity, depositors may begin to withdraw their funds at an abnormal rate. The bank can protect itself by calling in its loans if it is indeed liquid. Let suspicion become general, and a *run on the bank* is precipitated. Long lines of depositors form and clamor for their money. Deposits are withdrawn wholesale, and unless the bank is in a singularly strong position, normally through its relations with other banks, it has to close its doors. Save for the few who succeeded in withdrawing their deposits early, the depositors ordinarily lose their all, literally so in the cases of those who have been imprudent enough to carry all their eggs in one basket.

b) SAVINGS BANKS

A savings bank has a special social utility. It has likely enough originated in the patriotic purposes of incorporators who wished to provide encouragement to people of small means to save and to earn legitimate returns on their savings. Savings-bank charters, and the savings-bank laws of the enlightened States reflect that purpose. The General Government has furthered the purpose by creating the Postal Savings Bank.

The savings bank differs from the commercial bank in important respects:

1. It receives money on time deposit and not subject to check
2. Its loans are neither discounts nor short-time loans
3. Loans are rather long-term investments for the financing of sundry community enterprises in the minimum-risk class. For that reason, savings-bank laws are stringent in the character of the loans which may be made
4. The central social purposes of the savings banks are:
   a) To encourage thrift in people of small means and to guarantee to such people modest interest returns. The savings bank is thus pre-eminently a fiduciary enterprise; people who are without expert knowledge of finance *trust* the experts of the bank to make investments for them. That is what savings banks come to in the end.
   b) To collect a great mass of small earnings and make them available as capital for the furtherance of public enterprises. Many a schoolhouse or village waterworks has been made possible in this way: A school district sells its bonds and thus secures money with which to erect its building. The bonds are sold and resold until they finally become the property of a savings bank, in a distant small town perhaps. In that way, the savings of teachers, clerks, wage-earners, fishermen, small farmers, make possible the distant building. The latter in turn receive their bank earnings in part from the interest on the bonds.

   Thus is the way of co-operation and thus is society held together as a going concern.

c) TRUST COMPANIES

Third principal form of banking is found in the Trust Company. The latter is set up under the laws of a State to administer estates in cases in which the testator is disinclined to appoint individual executors; to administer trust funds set up to protect beneficiaries; to act as trustee for a corporation in the ownership of notes, bonds, mortgages, and sometimes of physical property such as railway equipment; to hold and administer endowment funds as of a college or hospital.

d) BANKS AND THE STATE

Banks have long been felt to be peculiarly related to The State, so much so that they might well be regarded as Civil Institutions.

In the first place, in time of war or other great emergency, any Government must resort to banks as instruments in the borrowing of money. On the other hand, Government must have a place in which it may safely deposit its funds. The Government thus becomes the largest single depositor, and its deposits normally make a huge and reliable basis for credit.

Second, the whole credit structure of the country depends chiefly on the banks. That means that those who control the banks can exercise something very like sovereignty over the common economic life of the community. Herein, if nowhere else, is reason for control which goes beyond that exercised over other corporations.

Government control is exercised in two ways:

First, there is control through ordinary lawmaking, which appears in the character of the charters granted banks as corporations and in the general banking laws of the United States and the several States. The laws are enforced through the office of the Comptroller of the Currency for national banks, and State Bank Commissioners for State banks, savings banks, and trust companies.

Second, direct regulatory control of national banks, and of State banks which so elect, by the Federal Reserve Board. The latter is in form the governing board of a corporation of member banks, on which the United States is represented by its own appointees.

UNITS IN BANKING

I. Banking as Institution

1. Fundamentally the safekeeping of money intrusted to an individual or a corporation which makes that a business.
2. Banking in principle can be carried on by anybody who inspires confidence and owns capital.
3. In advanced stages of social development, it is carried on by corporations chartered for the purpose.
4. A banking corporation is a group of individuals who subscribe a capital stock and who are chartered to carry on a particular banking business.

II. Commercial Banking

1. Banks which receive money subject to check, and are allowed to make loans and discounts with depositors' money, are called commercial banks.
2. In normal times a commercial bank can lend depositors' money, subject to a proper reserve, since all depositors keep balances at the bank well above the minimum balance required. Not all, or even many, will make large drafts at the same time.
3. Loans are effected by discounting the promissory notes held by dealers.
4. Short-time loans are made to businessmen and farmers to provide them with working capital.
5. Thus loans and discounts make available to the business community the whole unemployed capital of the community.
6. Borrowers pay for the use of capital instead of owning capital itself.

III. Loans

1. A bank can only lend money; it does not create money.
2. It can lend only the money of its depositors, to whom it is obligated for safekeeping, except for a prudent reserve; its bank notes if it is a bank of issue; and its capital.
3. The interest on loans is the return to the stockholders of dividends upon their enterprise.
4. Banks are solvent when the total of their assets is equal to or more than the total of their liabilities, especially liability to depositors.
5. Banks are liquid when their loans can be called in at once, in sufficient amount to meet any call from their depositors.

IV. Security

1. Banks cannot make loans without tangible assurance that the borrower will not default.

2. Security is, first of all, collateral in the form of valuable stocks and bonds, pledged with the bank to become the property of the bank in case of default.

3. Hence, the great importance to a nation of its bourses or stock exchanges which determine value of securities.

4. It is, second, in the form of mortgages on real estate.

5. Most important of all, it is the character and capacity of the borrower.

V. Run upon the Bank

1. When a bank's solvency or liquidity is suspected, depositors begin to withdraw in large amounts.

2. That quickly develops a panic, and more and more deposits are withdrawn until the bank's ability to realize promptly on its loans is strained.

3. If the bank's liquidity is so good that it pays all claims presented, the run subsides and deposits begin to return.

4. Otherwise, the bank closes its doors, and the depositors who remain either lose outright or can be paid only after a long time.

5. A good *banking system* makes it possible for solvent banks to borrow from other banks.

6. Runs are often started by irresponsible gossip.

VI. Banks of Issue

1. National banks may issue their promissory notes in monetary denominations payable on demand without interest. These are bank notes.

2. The bank notes are paid out in loans and discounts and in calls for currency; hence, they pass into the national monetary circulation.

3. Bank notes as promises to pay are secured by United States Bonds owned by the bank in the hands of the Treasurer of the United States.

4. And they are secured by a gold reserve.

5. In that way, they become as good as any other money.

6. Federal Reserve notes are bank notes.

7. State banks are not banks of issue.

VII. Savings Banks

1. A savings bank is a bank of deposit chartered by one of the States.

2. The postal savings system is the equivalent of a savings bank.

3. The deposits are time deposits and are not subject to check.

4. They may be withdrawn on order, however.

5. Primary social purpose is to provide safekeeping for small savings and insure modest but certain interest returns on those savings.

6. Deposits are loaned on permanent investments of a class permitted by law and regulated by the State Bank Commission.

7. The secondary social purpose is to make reservoirs in which amounts of capital, individually small, but in the aggregate large, can collect, and be loaned for the furtherance of sound public enterprises.

VIII. Trust Company

1. A trust company is a bank chartered to administer trust funds.

2. It administers estates where private executors are not provided.

3. It administers funds set up for the benefit of individuals; or of enterprises like hospitals, colleges, and the like.

4. It holds securities and sometimes physical property for corporations.

IX. Banks and The State

1. In modern times, banks are necessarily under the control of The State, and in part under the direction of the Government. For good reason:

   a) Government is normally the largest depositor and the largest borrower.

   b) Those who control the banks can almost exercise sovereignty.

2. National banks and State banks which so elect are in the Federal Reserve System, the essential constitution of which is

   a) Federal Reserve Districts.

   b) Federal Reserve Banks—banks for bankers—rediscount.

   c) Member banks and interrelations in the system.

   d) Federal Reserve Board.

3. The United States, however, normally owns no bank.

4. In addition, banking is controlled by Federal and State banking laws, administered by the Comptroller of the Currency and the State Banking Commissions.

   If the State and Federal bank examiners do their duty, there is not a great deal of danger of bank failures.

II. INSURANCE

Ever since Man emerged out of his savage condition, one important and comprehensive phase of his pursuit of the Great Escapes has been escape from mischance, from the menace of the unpredictable. It would be presumptuous to assign any one motive as that which has been most potent in the evolution of Civilization, but certainly here is one of the most powerful. Science and Religion, Morality and The State, have all of them been concerned in making the world more manageable and more secure from the reign of mere chance.

But the culmination of the whole process, at least in its economic phases, is the institution of *Insurance*. We do not through insurance expect to protect ourselves from the loss of dear ones, or them from the loss of ourselves. For that purpose we actively engage in the conservation of health and consultation with the medical man. We do not seek guaranties from the insurance company that our home will not be destroyed by fire. We look to the city fire department to do something about that, and must look to our own intelligence and care. But in all these things we can be insured against financial loss and can insure those who are dependent on us from economic disaster if we die.

That is what Insurance in the economic sense means.

It is hard to come to a full elementary understanding of Commerce without an understanding of Insurance. Nay more, there are few places in the whole field of Culture in which the meaning and essential processes of economic society stand more clearly revealed. It is social science, or at least a vital chapter therein.

COMMERCIAL INSURANCE

What we buy in the form of insurance policies is commercial insurance, that is to say, it is a vendible service. It is financial institution. Like all institutions, it has had a long and checkered career while the cultural product which it is has been in the course of evolution. It has been exploited by the charlatan, by the sincere but ignorant enthusiast, by the trickster; but it has steadily been forwarded as well by the study and the efforts of competent but sometimes mistaken experimenters. Out of it all has emerged what is perhaps the only exact, predictive, mathematical science in the whole field of Sociology.

Insurance is concerned only with risks, with that over which we have no control or but imperfect control. Where there is the element of certainty or that of deliberate arrangement of events, there is no insurance. There are, moreover, in insurance always two fundamental elements which taken together make it possible: first, that from the standpoint of the individual insured, a given event is entirely unpredictable or nearly that; second, that from the point of view of the insurer the sum total of such events as affecting a given population is completely predictable or nearly that.

Where the two elements are not present, there is no insurance possible, but only fraud or gambling.

RISK

Theoretically, the whole of a given population might be indiscriminately insured from loss in the event of death, and all the buildings insured from loss by fire, also without discrimination; but the insurance cost as reflected in the premiums necessarily charged would be very great, I suppose prohibitive. Why so?

The risk that a certain contingency will appear depends upon circumstances which are capable of observation as facts and capable of evaluation as to their meaning to the insurer. Thus, a young man in perfect physical condition, aged twenty-five, and known to be of good habits, is said to be a good life-risk. There is no certainty that he will not die or be killed within the year, but there is less likelihood of it than there would be in the case of a young man of notoriously bad and dangerous habits, and still less than there is in the case of a man of sixty-five afflicted with serious heart trouble. The first is a good risk at a low premium; the second is a poor risk, requiring a rejection or else a higher premium; the third is not insurable at all, for certainty dogs his steps—he must soon die, either this year or within a few years, and the risk that the event will occur this year is very great.

Now, given the great volume of all sorts of medical experience with insured people, and indeed mortality statistics concerning those not insured, it is possible, through rejection of bad risks or through adjustment of premium to risk, to reduce the total risk in the population insured to what are mathematically the exact lowest terms. That again is distribution of wealth in the form of service; for it makes possible the writing of lower premiums and the insuring of more people.

So it is with fire. The risk of fire in a city known to have a strict building code, strictly enforced, supported by an efficient fire department, is comparatively small. The risk in a city largely composed of frame buildings, about which combustible rubbish is allowed to collect, without a building code, and protected by a graft-ridden fire department is great. The risk on an isolated set of farm buildings is very great. Hence, the firetrap city and the farmhouse are insurable, but only at a premium proportioned to the risk. I suppose a celluloid filling station which distributed free cigarettes and lighted them would theoretically be insurable at a price.

DISTRIBUTION OF RISK

Insurance is not guaranty that loss will not occur. On the whole, there is about as much actual loss of life or wealth with insurance as without it. But it can distribute the burden of loss over so many people that it is felt by any one of them only to the extent of his own insurance premium. The burden of risk is assumed co-operatively by all, in a fashion exactly determined.

PREMIUM

What is the insurance cost of risk, that is to say, its price or premium?

If one individual should go to another and ask, "For what will you insure my life in $10,000 for one year?" the answer would have to be, "$10,000." In a one-to-one situation the risk would not be distributed at all, but only transferred.

If now 100 men came to the insurer and asked the same question, he might estimate that there was no likelihood of more than five of them dying during the year, and consequently that his maximum loss would probably be $50,000. He could recoup that sum by charging each of them $500 plus whatever he should think fit as recompense for his trouble, say $1,000. So the premium would be $510. If only three should die, he would have a profit of $20,000. If seven should die, there would be a corresponding loss.

The foregoing illustrates the rudiments of life insurance and of all insurance. It shows how the risk is distributed. It would, however, be expensive and uncertain. Refinement would come in somewhat the following fashion:

1. Perhaps if there were a great deal of that being done, the law would put a stop to it.

2. If now the insuring were done by a company able to employ competent actuaries, and if the company had a million policy-holders instead of a hundred, it would know exactly what proportion of them would die within the year. The inertia of large numbers would come in. The premiums could be exactly estimated. They would be much smaller than in the imaginary case, but they would still be rather large. So further refinements would come in.

3. Among the insured in the preceding assumption there would be all degrees of risk; in fact, in a million people all kinds of malady would be present in nearly constant proportions. Hence, medical examination and scrutiny of personal history and way of life, in order to reduce the aggregate number of losses in the population insured and hence the premium to the insurables. But that is not all.

4. The insured desires not an insurance for this year only, but he needs one running over the rest of his life, into and through the years when all men become bad risks.

Enters expectation of life, the facts for which are gathered primarily by the enlightened States in their vital statistics. Out of a large number of people who are aged twenty-five, it is known how many will still be living at age sixty-five, but again it is not known which ones will be living. That makes no difference to the insurer, for he and his actuaries deal in averages. The young man who takes out insurance at age twenty-five can do so at a premium such that the total premiums paid by him at his statistically expected term of life will be in general equal to the sum total of the much larger premiums paid by the man who becomes insured at fifty.

ENDOWMENT

Thus far we have been speaking of what is called straight-life insurance, or life insurance proper, in which the only risk assumed by the insurer is risk against the contingency of death. An endowment policy, on the other hand, contracts to pay the face of the policy at death or, if the policyholder survives the term of the contract, the amount contracted, in cash. So an endowment policy is not only life insurance but insurance against the contingency of a poverty-stricken old age. It may be looked upon as a continuing savings-bank account, coupled with life insurance.

POLICY

The *insurance policy* is a contract between insurer and insured. It is apt to begin with the plea, "Read your policy." Few do so, and of those who do it is safe to say that very few take in the substance of what they read—although, it is true, policies differ a good deal in the perspicuity of their language. A fairly good test of an individual's educational stature might be found in the answer to the question, "Can he read his insurance policy?" If he can, the implication is that he has a fairly good lay comprehension of Law and Commerce, and a good foundation in Language, Mathematics, and the volitional side of character, especially the capacity for sustained intensive reading.

INSURANCE CORPORATION

As so often happens in a complex social order, in a rich cultural environment, an enterprise of this kind cannot be carried on by an individual, even if The State could permit so eminently hazardous an enterprise. Hence the insurance corporation. Insurance companies are of two kinds; stock companies and mutual companies.

The stock company is an ordinary joint-stock corporation chartered for the purpose, with a paid-in capital stock. The premiums are prices paid for its services.

The mutual company is what in other fields is called a co-operative. The policyholders are in the place of stockholders, have voting privileges, and share in the returns from the business.

In either case, the reliability and success of the concern as an institutional agent in Society depend entirely upon the competency of the officers as insurance experts and upon their skill and integrity as investors of the very large sums with which they are intrusted by the policyholders through the payment of premiums.

THE INSURANCE COMPANY AS INVESTOR

Thus far, we have been considering insurance in itself. In that respect, commercial insurance is a service to be bought and sold like any other service. But it is also financial institution, similar to banking.

The treasuries of insurance companies constitute in the community a vast pool into which the capital savings of millions flow, and from which they can be drawn for the capital support of all sorts of community enterprises. Floating capital in great quantities is thus made available, for the use of which enterprisers and municipalities and Governments pay in the form of interest. The insurance companies invest in their mortgages, bonds, and other obligations. In the end the interest comes back, in large measure, to policyholders as decrease in their premiums. The policyholders, of course, hold property in liens on the property of the borrowers.

The interest thus earned and added to income from premiums is in general devoted to:

1. Building up a surplus which is a rainy-day fund on a great scale
2. Reduction of premiums, and other inducements to policyholders
3. Paying the heavy expense of carrying on the company
4. Paying a return to stockholders on their investment, or to policyholders in mutual companies

To the individual policyholder, the financial situation with respect to life insurance is about as follows:

1. If his policy is an endowment, he is given what amounts to a powerful motive to save money, in the regular recurrence of calls for his premiums.

2. As his premiums accumulate in the treasury of the company, he thereby gains a reserve quite apart from the ultimate endowment, since the loan values and the cash-surrender values tabulated as part of his contract constitute an available asset for him.

3. Much as in the case of the savings bank, in effect he employs accomplished experts to make his investments for him.

4. Even if the individual of modest means is as financially

competent as the investment committee of the insurance company, even so he can at the most buy only a few shares of stock or a few bonds. But the savings bank, and much more so the insurance company, hold greatly varied choices of securities. Again the principle of the distribution of risk: a few bonds may prove worthless, or fail to pay interest over a long period, but hardly all the securities of a large company which is well managed.

5. Finally, all the largest and best insurance companies are in States which for a generation past have had excellent insurance laws competently administered. A cutthroat policy in a company which has its home office in one of these States is practically impossible.

OTHER FORMS

We have been dealing chiefly with life insurance, both because it is typical and because it is socially the most important in that it tends to fortify the Family.

Related forms are health insurance and accident insurance and insured medical care as a supplement to both. People who seem not to understand the essential nature of insurance will say that these are nothing different from saving against a "rainy day," that is to say, establishing an individual contingent fund. They are altogether different, both in financial import and in general social import.

The individual contingent fund is merely that; there is no distribution of risk in it. Few of us, especially in our early years, could possibly build up really adequate contingent funds; but there are few of us who cannot maintain an insurance policy, or several policies. The confusion is perhaps traceable to the fact that so many fail to perceive the essential nature of Society and of life in the ordered community. The insurance company sets up what is perhaps our most striking illustration of the nature of ordered societies, namely, *the mutual character of the social existence of individuals.* The insured succeeds in making others share the burden of his risks; but he can do so only by himself sharing the burden of others' losses.

In short, any contingency is a subject of insurance, provided it meets the primary tests of insurability, namely, that it is in truth contingency so far as the individual is concerned, and certainty so far as the group is concerned.

ANNUITIES

The transition from endowment insurance to *annuity* is easy. If the former, resting upon mathematical principles, can accumulate a capital sum at the expiration of a term of years, then that capital sum can be made the basis of annual payments over another series of years.

The premium which can be written into the policy of an individual, depends in part upon his life-expectation. We have already encountered that principle. Similarly, at retiring age, let it be sixty-five, seventy, or any other age, the expectation of life for large numbers of annuitants will be fixed and certain, barring great calamities such as bombing and machine-gunning civilian population at the hands of a savage enemy. It is accordingly at bottom a relatively simple problem in series to calculate what annuity a given capital sum will support at any given age. The later the age of retirement, of course, the larger the annuity can be.

At times in the world's history, such truths as we have dealt with in this section have become so fascinating that some people have been led to attribute an almost miraculous power to compound interest and actuarial mathematics. There is no magic about it all. It is hard reasoning based upon the observed facts of life-expectation in large numbers of individuals; and the possibilities of it all rest upon the integrity and prosperity of Commerce, which maintains dividend-paying and interest-paying securities.

INSTRUCTION

It would obviously be impossible to give a course in Insurance in the Common School which would qualify the pupils taking the course to become competent employees of an insurance company. That is not our business as schoolmasters and teachers. Here, as everywhere else in the Curriculum, the happy medium must be found between leaving the rising generation ignorant of one of the most important branches of social science and attempting to make qualified vocational experts of them. The happy medium is to be found, so far as I can see, only as a matter of judgment. The units listed below, as well as the preceding pages, are the response to the judgment which I have endeavored to apply.

UNITS IN INSURANCE

I. Insurance in General
   1. Insurance in general is provision against loss in unpredictable events
   2. Insurance does not apply to certainties
   3. It does not apply to the consequences of one's deliberate acts
   4. The greater part of Civilization is concerned with insurance

II. Commercial Insurance
   1. A service for which we pay
   2. Applies only to events which cannot be predicted of the individual and can be predicted accurately of large groups
   3. Commercial insurance is, then, the distribution of the burden of loss over large groups of individuals
   4. The individual accepts a small annual loss in payment for protection from a possible large loss
   5. His annual payment is his premium

III. Risk
   1. In certainties there is no risk, whether it is known that they must occur or that they cannot occur
   2. There is risk when it is known that disaster may occur within a given period, that disaster is contingent
   3. Distribution of risk hangs on the principle that disaster is contingent for individuals and certain for groups.
   4. Hence, the loss to the whole group is practically constant and can be shared annually in relatively small premiums

IV. The Premium
   1. The premium can be looked upon as the price attached to the distribution of risk
   2. Premiums can be reduced by reducing the loss in the group insured
   3. Done by examination of persons or things to be insured for the purpose of:

       a) Refusal of bad risks, that is, contingencies which approach certainty

       b) Adjusting premiums to particular risks

   4. Also done by cities which maintain good government, particularly by reducing fire and crime

   5. Also done in life insurance by taking out policies early in life:

       a) Because the risk of death is normally less

       b) Because the young person has more years in which to pay premiums on his own ultimate death

   6. Vital statistics enable insurers to know exactly, or nearly that, how many deaths will occur in large groups, and how many will be due to various common causes

   7. Reducing risks is distributing wealth, by making the service available to more people

V. Insurance Companies

   1. Practical and safe insurance is so large an enterprise that it requires large corporations

   2. Large staffs of experts must be employed:

       a) Mathematical experts or actuaries

       b) Expert accountants

       c) Skilled examiners in various fields

       d) Expert financiers who understand investments

       e) Legal experts

   3. Two kinds of companies: joint stock and mutual

   4. Stock companies are ordinary commercial corporations chartered to carry on a particular kind or kinds of insurance business

   5. In mutual companies policyholders take the place of stockholders

VI. Insurance as Financial Institution

   1. Premiums paid in create an enormous fund of credit

   2. Like banks, the treasuries of insurance companies form great pools into which a great deal of otherwise idle capital is drawn in small amounts

   3. The accountants know at all times how much will be needed to meet losses

   4. If all the debts of insurance companies were to be presented at once, the company would probably suspend

   5. But in the nature of insurance, there is a time element in each policy; the claims cannot and will not be made until the loss occurs or the policy matures

   6. Hence, there is always a great fund in hand, awaiting payment of losses, and that fund is ready to be used wherever the community stands in immediate legitimate need of capital

      7. Hence, every insurance company normally earns a great deal of interest

      8. Its earnings go to:

         a) Payment of operating expenses

         b) Additions to surplus

         c) Dividends to stockholders, so far as the law permits, and to the policyholders in mutual companies

         d) Often, in some policies, as additions to paid-up insurance

VII. The Policy

      1. An insurance policy is a contract between insured and insurer

      2. The beneficiary is the one who benefits from payments of losses

      3. A life policy commonly provides:

         a) The premium to be paid

         b) The terms on which the policy will be settled

         c) The cash-surrender value during the several years the policy has to run

         d) The loan value, that is to say, the loans which the company will make to the insured as more and more premiums accumulate

      4. The laws of the several States in which the best companies are located protect policyholders against unfair practices

      5. But the policyholder must do his part by understanding his contract

VIII. Endowment Life Insurance

      1. An endowment policy agrees to pay:

         a) The holder's beneficiary the face of the policy in the event of his death before the maturity of the policy

         b) The holder himself a capital sum contracted for, if he survives until the maturity of the policy

      2. It is thus in effect a savings-bank account plus an insurance policy, both of which services are provided for in the premium charged

      3. Advantages as a savings account are that

         a) The premiums required form a constant inducement to save

         b) The holder in effect employs the experts of the company under bond to make his investments for him

         c) Risk of loss of funds to the company is distributed over the company's wide range of investments

IX. Other Insurance

      1. Any contingency can be made the subject of insurance, provided it is a matter of common occurrence

      2. But there can be no effective distribution of risk, where the contingency approaches certainty, and the premium must be so high as to approximate any probable loss

3. Common insurance objects are:
   a) Fire and windstorm and lightning
   b) Theft
   c) Accident
   d) Incapacity and medical bills due to sickness
   e) Liability for injuries to others

X. Annuity
   1. An annuity arises out of a contract to pay a fixed sum annually over a period of years, usually for life
   2. Any capital sum can be used to buy an annuity at any time
   3. Annuities can be paid because it is known what the expectation of life is at any age in large groups of people
   4. Hence the payer of annuities can know what capital sums he must have in hand in order to justify particular annuities
   5. Dealers in annuities must, however, have many annuitants in order to get the group reliability of large numbers
   6. The older the person, the larger can be the annuity for a given capital sum
   7. An endowment insurance policy can be written as an annuity policy or can be converted into one at maturity

III. EXCHANGES

The third of the major financial institutions is the Exchange, as it is called in America and England, or Bourse in Continental countries. This word "exchange" is, as we have seen, pretty nearly synonymous with Commerce. Here we have in mind Stock Exchanges and Commodity Exchanges; in other words, great markets organized on a regional, national, or world basis.

Exchanges are universal in the activities of all commercial nations—universal because economic society becomes organized that way. They have evolved out of the village market as Civilization has advanced and have themselves been part of that advance. They make possible common estimates touching price as a factor in going societies. That means that they have the essential characteristic of all institutions which enter into the fabric of Civilization. Moreover, their place in the modern world is so critical that the prosperity and well-being of all depends heavily upon the intelligence and integrity with which they are used and managed.

a) THE STOCK EXCHANGE

Since the stock exchanges are surrounded with the maximum of mythology, we shall deal with them first. When we say "the Stock Exchange," we mean the New York Stock Exchange, but there are stock exchanges in all the world's great commercial cities, and minor exchanges in most of our American large cities. The very word is imbedded in a body of sinister connotations. Few things have been more the subject of melodrama, and more often the bogey of demagogues of all sorts. Even the intelligentsia who deride righteousness itself speak scornfully and knowingly of those who "gamble on the stock exchange," assuming that everybody who makes an investment in securities, or embarks on a well-considered speculation, is a gambler.

Give a dog a bad name, and he will usually contrive to live up to it. So it has been more or less with exchanges. In their own language, they discount their reputation. Indefensible practices have been common enough in the history of exchanges and still are. So have they been in the history of medicine and organized religion and public instruction and still are. The great logical enemy of the human race, hypostasis, substitutes the incident for the institution, the particular for the general, the abuse for the benefit, and would "cut off the little boy's head to cure him of squinting." The outstanding and comprehensive reasons for malpractice on exchanges are two:

First, there have always been a great multitude of traders whose ignorance is exceeded only by their cupidity.

Second, the good citizen in most cases knows nothing whatever about the working of exchanges and nothing of their place in the economy of the community. When he becomes acutely aware of hard times, and goes in search of a scapegoat, he pours out the vials of his wrath on something he does not understand. He contributes to the formation of a public opinion which is rather emotional outburst than opinion. Opinion, we recall, implies knowledge.

STOCKS AND BONDS

Members of stock exchanges deal in securities, and for all practical purposes the securities are stocks and bonds.

Shares of stock constitute ownership in the capital of a corporation and nothing else. If we could keep this fundamental fact in mind, we should be able to think our way through a great deal.

A commercial or industrial corporation becomes organized when the original corporators subscribe money to a capital stock, with which the plant and appurtenances are provided, and a residue is left to be employed as free working capital. The corporation becomes an enterpriser engaged in the production or merchandising of goods or services or both. If it prospers, its earnings are or should be devoted to two things: first, the building-up of a *surplus*, which is kept in hand or invested in securities which can readily be realized in cash; second, distribution to stockholders as *dividends*, that is to say, *what is to be divided*.

The surplus undivided among the stockholders is important in sound management, because it serves as a steadying device in the value of the stock. It is very important in society because it can be used to maintain a steady dividend rate in years in which earnings are high, in those in which they are low, and in those in which they are less than nothing. The securities to which dividends are attached are widely used in supporting ordinary bank loans for working capital with which we have already dealt. That is why they are called "securities." Decreasing dividends, or the passing of dividends, causes a stock to fall on the market, and thus impairs its value as collateral for loans. In that way, steady dividend rates are important for the whole community, regardless of who owns the stock and receives the dividends. Upon them, in part, hangs the possibility of carrying on various businesses, and therefore in the end the employment of labor.

COMMON STOCK

What we have been describing is *common stock*, the foundation of the whole matter.

The capital contributions of the original corporators are given back to them as shares of stock, ordinarily in terms of some fixed *par* such as $100, so that each owns as many shares of stock as his paid-in capital divided by the par comes to. Such a business once established and successful tends to expand and need more capital. New shares are issued which represent the new capital. And so it goes, bearing in mind that *no stock is legitimate and genuine unless it stands for actual paid-in capital, or the full equivalent.* An equivalent, for example, would be what is known as a stock dividend. In that case, earnings have been great enough to yield enough to the stockholder for investment in new stock for the purpose of expanding the business. If now, the directors vote a stock dividend, so that, for instance, every holder of ten shares receives an additional share, evidently it is the same as if each stockholder received a large dividend with which he purchased some of the new stock. If the corporation were a successful individual enterpriser who desired to strengthen his business by putting in part of his earnings as capital, the policy would be called "plowing in the profits."

PREFERRED STOCK

A great many concerns issue not merely common stock but *preferred stock* as well. The latter is preferred in the payment of dividends at a specified rate. That means that if the earnings are not sufficient to warrant dividends on all outstanding stock, that on the preferred is paid. If the preferred is *cumulative*, and a series of adverse years is encountered in which there are no dividends for anybody, then on the return of prosperity, dividends on the preferred are first brought up to date. On the other hand, preferred stock never earns more than the specified rate, whereas in very prosperous years the common may earn much more than the preferred.

MARKET VALUE

When a stock is listed on the Exchange, it is traded in, that is to say, bought and sold. It is reported daily in the market reports in the daily papers. But its value on the market has no relation to the original par. It is worth what buyers will pay for it in dollars, or francs, or shillings, just as if it were a pound of sugar.

Its market value depends, in the first place, on its record as a dividend-payer. That is especially its value to the investor who is looking for income.

Its value to the prudent speculator, however, depends on much more. Among the numerous other factors may be listed the following:

a) The general business situation in the nation and in the world-community
b) The prospects of the company:
   1. Has it adequate capital?
   2. The reliability of its market: does it deal in staples or in current fads?
   3. Does the concern deal in goods for which the demand is relatively inelastic, or does it deal in luxuries for which the demand is very elastic?
   4. Does it specialize in a single line, or do its goods represent a variety of lines for which there is a good deal of elasticity in demand?

And there are many other factors which only the professional speculator could have in mind. Nevertheless, to list even this much ought to be enough to deter most people from speculating; they cannot know enough.

STOCKS ENTREPRENEURIAL, NOT CAPITALISTIC

Nobody has a *right*, either moral or legal, to dividends as such, any more than the individual who sets up a delicatessen has a right to make money. Both of them have a right to fair and honorable treatment, and a right to be protected by the law; but both of them must depend for their earnings upon their own wisdom and skill.

BONDS

On the other hand, the bondholder is a capitalist. Even though his holdings are but $10.00 on deposit in a savings bank, he is a capitalist. His earnings arise from the use of his savings as capital. If he draws rent, then we say that he is a landlord.

Unlike stocks, payment of interest on bonds is secured by the fact that the property of the borrower is liable for the payment of both capital and interest. Such a bond is a mortgage bond.

Municipal bonds are what their name implies. They have all the fundamental characteristics of bonds in general, but they are not mortgage bonds. They are issued under a statute usually called "the municipal bonds act," and the buyer must be sure of the legality of the issue. If the city or school district defaults, the courts may order the local authorities to lay a special tax to make good.

State and Federal bonds are Government bonds. Payment of principal and interest depends wholly upon the good faith of the Government.

So much for the subject matter of the Stock Exchange. Now let us come to the heart of the matter, which is the Exchange as *market* and its social function of establishing price which is approximation to true value, and therefore common expectation. In order to come at the matter as concretely as possible, let us look back for a little at the history of American business since the Civil War.

In the period following the Civil War, when the Corporation developed rapidly in the United States, sundry inventions such as the telephone were made and *promoted* by enterprisers. Informed and intelligent men foresaw the course of industrial development, and enterprises which proved to be bonanzas were organized. That was particularly true of copper, owing to the lavish use which must be made in electrical industries. After some years of struggle and organization, some of these enterprises become very productive and great dividend-payers, 50 per cent annually, I suppose, on the original investment and likely enough a good deal more.

On the other hand, some enterprises were very badly managed, because the promoters were not informed men and could not think out their course. Again, some of the latter were pirates pure and simple who had simply learned a new and wonderful method of robbery.

Still, all in all, it is the successful and well-conceived and organized industries in which we are interested.

The incorporators could and did hold on to their shares and reap the high percentage return to which we have referred. So long as they lived, year by year they were adding to their wealth and establishing great fortunes. That was in the course of nature; but it was also in the course of nature that there was an advanced ethics to learn, and there was no particular incentive to learn it. In short, there was nowhere near sufficient Civilization in the mores to control the new culture.

However, the shares eventually came on the market and were bought and sold. A given stock with a great record of dividends, once on the market, would rapidly rise in market price and did, so that a stock paying $50 dividends perhaps would sell on the market for maybe $800 a share. But, whereas the original holder would perhaps receive 50 per cent on his original investment, the new buyer would receive but 6 per cent. And so the returns estimated as percentages would fall, and in the course of time did fall, until they reached a level but little above interest on bonds. The highest rate of return on the New York Stock Exchange on the day on which these lines were written was 5.9 per cent on a stock which was selling for 152.54.

Distribution of wealth.—Thus, the social function of the Exchange as market is, in the first place, that it necessarily distributes wealth in the functional form of income. If there had been no market and no speculation, the outcome would have been continued great profits—at least until the supply of goods had fully caught up with demand, which is another matter—and closely held shares. An addition of a lasting nature would have been made to the *plutocracy* which was in those days rapidly developing. That is all ancient history now, but the financial process which appeared then, and had already appeared in some form again and again in the past, appears still and will continue to do so, so long as society is organized in normal form.

Establishes economic price.—When the gamblers and the tyros and the manipulators are kept out of speculation, the processes of speculation on the market are wonderfully effective in establishing economic price, which is true value, much the same as the supply-demand schedule does it in the merchandising of commodities. Now that has great social uses:

First, it establishes common expectation throughout the commercial world, and that approximation to right expectation, which, as we know, is the fundamental social process.

Second, it enables the stock of useful and legitimate enterprises to rise to its proper value. If it were not for the Stock Exchange, the stock of commercial and industrial enterprises would have only a neighborhood value, proportioned to the capital available locally. Mass production and low price of commodities would be impossible.

Third, it tends to eliminate the stock of enterprises which are not socially useful or reliable.

Fourth, it makes investment possible, and thereby makes possible a host of trust funds as well as individual investment. In the analogous bond market, savings banks and insurance companies on a great scale are made possible.

Makes commercial and industrial enterprises possible.—We have already seen that practically all enterprises in the country depend, and ought to be able to depend, on local and regional banks for working capital. In order to borrow, security is necessary, and the great source of banking securities is stocks and bonds. The utility of this paper is in its liquidity. The banker knows from his morning paper what a given stock was worth on yesterday's market, and, from his special market reports, what the recent history has been. He knows what he can loan, knows that he can realize if necessary, *for there is a market*, and knows when he must call on his customer for more collateral if prices fall.

SPECULATION

Of all the processes which enter into the functioning of the Exchange, the one which is most misunderstood and abhorred is *speculation*—until some neighbor is lucky enough to "clean up" and then the critic becomes, not a speculator but one of the worst of gamblers, not much better than a crap player.

"To speculate" means "to spy out; watch; observe; examine; explore." It also means "to ponder a subject in its different aspects and relations; to meditate; to contemplate; to theorize." For some reason, in things intellectual, speculation has come to be considered next door to crime, perhaps because so many men who speculate on the universe ponder and theorize a good deal more than they observe, examine, explore. And yet Sir Isaac Newton was content to speak of his studies as speculations.

Well, a good speculator on exchange is a good deal like an intellectual speculator: he examines, explores, ponders, and either buys or sells securities. He is no more truly a gambler than is the scientist who observes, experiments, concludes, and acts.

WHAT IS GAMBLING, THEN?

I take it that *gambling* is staking something of value on the turn of pure chance; or it is playing for money, that is to say, economic gain, where there is no economic subject matter involved. In either case, it is a primitive form of behavior chiefly cultivated by the primitive races and degenerate individuals.

Betting on the turn of the dice, or on a color or number turned up by a gambling device, is gambling of the first sort. Playing cards for money, or betting on a horse race or football game is gambling of the second kind. In the last, there is speculation, for the gambler estimates his own capacities as a player or the qualities of the horse or of college players. But there is no economic subject matter involved; there is no exchange of goods and services. Either form is immoral, since it is an offense against social conscience, for the act itself and the influence of the players tends to break down society as a going economic concern. Both are grossly bad taste, for they import money considerations into what is properly an adventure in friendly intercourse.

Gambling on exchanges.—There is undoubtedly a great deal of gambling of the first type on stock exchanges, but it is not speculation. The trader does not know what he is about, he knows nothing about the securities in which he gambles, and nothing about the processes of the market. He merely bets on the tips found in "dope sheets" or elsewhere that a given stock will go up or that it will go down. In frenzied times, his purchases —for his number is legion—succeed in driving stocks to several times any possible value—and then the crash inevitably comes, usually involving the whole country in a panic.

There have been numerous attempts on the part of Government, and on the part of the Governors of the Stock Exchange, to abate the evil. No doubt the efforts have helped, but in the end the only abiding cure is in the slow process of public instruction and public enlightenment. One is the more convinced, when he recalls that the last crash was precipitated by a nation-wide mob of bellboys, waiters, housekeepers, schoolteachers, dentists, physicians, small traders, farmers, and others, who ran volume on the New York Stock Exchange up to sixteen million shares in a single day, and quotations up to merely nonsensical heights. Moreover, veteran speculators and investors became deluded into the belief that a new era had dawned. Such things are strewn all through modern financial history and doubtless will be until every high-school graduate knows as much Commerce as he now knows Physics and Chemistry.

Trading on margin.—A practice which is often confounded with gambling is called *trading on margin,* found in both stock and commodity exchanges. The dealer orders through his broker a certain number of shares of a given stock, or a certain number of bushels of wheat or corn. He pays the broker a fraction of the cost, but the broker buys on exchange the full order, "carrying" the buyer for a regular interest charge until the transaction is completed. The broker in turn discounts the buyer's note at the bank, and holds the shares as security. If the market falls, the dealer is called upon for "more margin" which is in substance more security to protect the broker against loss.

Of course the practice has all the risks which attend "running in debt" anywhere. The speculator stands to make large gains in proportion to his own working capital if the speculation is successful, and large losses if it is not successful. Moreover, it is a great temptation to gamblers. To say that the practice should be used only by competent and prudent speculators is only to say that they are the only ones who should speculate at all.

However, margining gives the management of the Exchange and the Government a means of checking wild trading. The margins allowed by brokers can be increased, and the Federal Reserve Board can order the discount rate on broker's loans to be sharply increased.

b) COMMODITY EXCHANGES

Commodity exchanges exist in all great commodity centers which are the hearts of specialized farming and producing areas. If the principal stock exchange is in New York City, the money center of the country, so is the principal commodity exchange located in Chicago, the metropolis of the great areas which grow crops on a mass-production scale. Similarly are cotton exchanges, sugar exchanges, tobacco exchanges, and others to be found in or near the corresponding producing areas. All these do but reflect the parentage of all exchanges in the village market days of Europe and in the great fairs of medieval times.

In function they have the same utility as the stock exchanges.

REGIONAL, NATIONAL, AND WORLD MARKETS

In the old-time economy the village market sufficed, either the institution of market days in England, or the American folkway of selling farm products in the village trading center and shopping there for needed supplies.

But that stage had two main defects in national and world economy.

First, it was wholly inadequate to the needs of a national economy in which there were many urban dwellers engaged in manufacturing and other forms of city life. The cities could not grow much until there was a way of supplying them with food and other agricultural products. Conversely, the rural dweller could not be supplied with manufactured products as we know them today. I have just said that the village market "sufficed." Of course, it did not suffice, for anything more than the community centered on the village. It left many thousands in London and Paris to a poverty so dire that we here in America have never seen the like. Moreover, most men accepted such conditions as the normal order of nature, and the effect on the moral standards of the time was very bad. One cannot accept dire misery all about him, without at least an inward protest, and maintain his own standards of what is right and just. Most people would hardly accept the notion that commodity exchanges have been an important factor in the advance of morality without derision; but it is nonetheless true.

Second, until the development of machine industry and railway transporation, famines were of common occurrence the world over. Even so settled a state as Vermont now is had its "scarce year." Village trading-center marketing could at best serve the village and the outlying contributory area. If distant communities fell into a series of bad crop years, there was nothing to be done about it. Supply would never more than match the demands of the local communities, save as the surplus of a subsistence agriculture came in over somewhat longer distances.

Moreover, there was not and could not be any one-price system, to say nothing of a national and world price system in the great commodities, and that is equivalent to saying that there was no universal common estimate or anything like it. Cotton prices and tobacco prices, for example, were at the mercy of buyers in English and Northern ports.

The revolution, or rather rapid change, away from such conditions is usually called industrial and transportational; but it was quite as much financial and commercial. A railway will not automatically rush food to a famine area without financial instruments and inducement. And if there is no way for farmers to market their products for cash or credit, all the mills and railways in the world cannot supply the farmers with manufactured goods.

It is not to be understood that men saw the need and invented commodity exchanges full fledged. Evolution does not proceed that way. Rail and steamship companies made settlement of great agricultural areas possible because they greatly enlarged the area within which farm products could be distributed. Correlatively, they made possible great manufacturing cities in which people engaged in that kind of production could be fed. But you could not sell Minnesota wheat for delivery in Philadelphia and Liverpool until there was some way in which buyers from Pennsylvania and England could be brought into contact with Minnesota farmers, in other words, a market. Nor could the entire wheat crop of the year be collected and stored in a single place, waiting for buyers to come and higgle over the price.

But after 1859, men who made it their business to trade on the Chicago Board of Trade could begin to estimate the crop prospects, not only in one State but in all the wheat-growing States, not only American prospects but world-prospects, and estimate American demand and then world-demand. That is the first step in speculation, just as estimating is the first step in speculation on the stock exchanges or in the laboratory. These men could and did contract with one another to buy and sell wheat, very probably wheat which neither the buyer nor the seller would ever see or even own. That meant a great market. The immigrant Dakota farmer probably knew little or nothing about the reason why he could sell his wheat somewhere, but he acted on the assumption that he could do so. Normally, he was justified. He was not stupid enough to suppose that he could market his crop among his neighbors, as the Eastern farmers engaged in diversified agriculture were still doing with their products. The Board of Trade and similar commodity exchanges made great regional markets for world-supply.

Moreover, they made price, just as the stock market makes prices for stock. It was Chicago Price. Similar great exchanges developed, and in the financial pages of the present daily papers we see quotations of Winnipeg Price. The controlling price in the world-market was long Liverpool Price. But these did not stand alone; they were functions, one of the other.

The market as thus set up led inevitably to correlative activities in transportation, warehousing corporations, cold storage, and especially elevators, which could store immense quantities of commodities, awaiting the outcome of exchange operations. One feature came to be the carrying-over of stocks of commodities to prospective periods of greater demand and smaller supply, again an illustration of distribution of risk.

Finally, the grower himself could be informed by daily newspaper reports of the activities of the exchanges with relation to the prospects of another crop year and govern his projects accordingly. Fundamental to all reliable information came to be the crop reports of the United States Department of Agriculture. It must be remembered that every farmer who produces for sale is himself of necessity a speculator and can succeed only as all speculators succeed, namely, by "examining, observing, exploring, pondering." He has his choice between that and reverting to subsistence agriculture which is outside the money economy. Too often farmers see themselves only as day laborers in the employment of the nation and paid a starvation wage. The only instance in the modern world where such a condition exists, so far as I know, is in the quasi-manorial economy of the collective farms in Soviet Russia.

OPERATIONS ON COMMODITY EXCHANGES

Commodity exchanges fix price, not, as the untutored are led to believe, out of mere arbitrary decision, but as the outcome of the workings of the only organisim which can fix price, namely, speculation. Wall Street never did or could arbitrarily fix security prices, nor the wheat-pit commodity prices.

The speculator characteristically *deals in futures*. He buys or sells for future delivery, that is to say, when the crop is harvested, and the interaction of the speculators, one upon the other, makes current price. So far as producer and consumer are both concerned, the important price is that which is going to prevail when the unhurried processes of nature shall have been completed. That involves *prediction*, and the whole function of speculation is one of prediction.

If the speculator has information which satisfies him that the national or world demand, for wheat, let us say, is going to be greater than the whole visible prospective supply, he buys at current price for future delivery, perhaps in three months. His purchase merely gives him the right to such and such a quantity of wheat three months hence. If he buys largely, and especially if others buy who are of his opinion, the market price begins to advance. If his prognostications turn out to be correct, he either sells his right at the expiration of his contract or else takes the physical commodity. He profits by selling for more than he paid.

Such is one side of the process in elementary principle, but such speculation would have in it a large element of gambling, for nobody can predict the future with that degree of certitude. Instead, the prudent speculator, as the price rises, sells a part of his holdings and takes profit, and then perhaps does it again and again, if the market continues to advance, until his rights are exhausted. Such in-and-out trading tends to cause the market to hesitate every time a sale is effected. The market is thus kept in check, the advance is regulated. In principle, this continuous estimating carries the market to the objective relation between supply and demand.

But the reverse process of selling short is quite as important. The short-seller estimates that the price is high and that it must fall. Hence, he sells short at market price on a contract for future delivery. Like the other, as the market falls, he covers part of his shorts from time to time by buying at the market and delivering. He takes profit, and the latter is the difference between what he has to pay now and what he received before. Selling tends to cause the fall to halt and thus tends to prevent the bottom's dropping out, just as the stock dealers' profit-taking tended to prevent a runaway market. The interaction of the long-dealer and the short-seller, the bulls and the bears, keeps the price close to reality.

Of course, the process is strictly analogous to the method of speculation which is found on the stock exchange.

Now the operations on exchanges which deal in wheat determine the price of wheat, but they do not make it. The relations of supply and demand in the nation, and, with exporting nations, in the world, do that. If Argentina, Australia, Canada, Russia, the Near East, and the United States, are producing more than the wheat-eating nations can or will buy on existing demand and purchasing power, the price will fall until lower prices bring in more buyers and so on down to the point at which the whole crop offered is taken. The exchanges can do no more than regulate falling price and determine it.

Like the New York Stock Exchange, the Board of Trade has

been pictured as the field which decrees the standard of living of half a continent, all for the selfish interests of a few speculators who "make money by depriving little children of nourishing food." And yet millions of little children could have no food at all, except for the fact that their fathers can sell at some price, and that a price discovered and made possible by exchange operations. The father cannot load his wheat on trucks and carry it to the cities to be peddled from house to house. It could not be used even if he could do so. Once more, if you are going to engage in commercial and industrial farming in a specialized crop, you have got to be governed by the logic which belongs to that kind of enterprise.

No doubt the speculators are engaged in making good their place in the world; so are the farmers. So are teachers and professors, wage-earners and all the rest of us, including the executive secretaries of reforming organizations. No doubt, further, that grievously unethical practices occur on the Board of Trade as well as on the Stock Exchange—practices which tend to prevent it from performing its essential social function. Gamblers and manipulators play the same vicious part on commodity exchanges which they play on stock exchanges. Incompetent and ignorant speculators who are neither gamblers nor manipulators in intention make mischief as do ignorance and incompetence everywhere. Betterment depends entirely on two things:

First, upon the creation of a far better intelligence about the functions of exchanges in general and breeding it into the mores. Not long ago a distinguished schoolmaster remarked to me that he knew not the first thing about exchanges or their functions. He is an influential citizen in his home town. If he has no ideas on the subject, it is not likely that the moral and intellectual opinion of the nation exercises any very formidable restraint on unethical practices in the great markets.

Second, the progressive enactment of salutary legal controls. There are many legal controls already, but not all of them are salutary. Legal control here has the same place that it has in regulating the mutual rights and joint responsibilities of partners, or the qualifications and responsibilities of shipmasters and physicians, or what may and may not be done in making a will.

But it is not reasonable to expect much in the way of salutary legislation if ignorant voters send ignorant representatives to the State Legislatures and to Congress. We get as good legislation as our collective intelligence and character entitle us to.

COMMODITY EXCHANGES AS MARKETS

The merchandising of wheat has been our example, but we might have used any of the cereals, cotton, tobacco, and meat products; in short, nearly all commodities which are not specialized mechanical products bearing trade-names.

Adhering to our illustration, wheat is finally sold chiefly to be used for making into flour. Millmen buy it for that purpose, and in general they buy at current prices. Thereby hangs a tale, for it is a long time before a cargo of wheat bought at the elevator at to-day's Chicago price disappears into the channels of trade as flour. Before it is ready for sale, the price of flour may have fallen or risen in response to changes in the price of wheat. The manufacturer may well find that he will have to be content with a price for flour which will not cover the cost of the wheat and the cost of milling—or alternatively he may reap a price which gives him a speculative profit. He does not like this sort of thing very well, for he is a millman and not a speculator. Hence he hedges.

Hedging.—When he buys a quantity of wheat, he is long of the market by that amount. Accordingly, he sells short the same amount as he buys.

It is easy to see that he thus protects himself against a fall by sacrificing his chance for speculative profit by and by. If wheat advances, he will have to cover his shorts at a higher price, but he will sell flour at much the same higher price. If wheat, on the other hand, falls, he gains as much by covering his shorts at a lower price as he loses on the lower price of flour.

He thus protects himself as manufacturer and is content with the profit which arises out of his skill as producer.

The process has great social utility in that, since it is employed throughout that part of the whole commodity field in which the conditions are similar to those found in wheat and flour, it tends to stabilize the national economy.

Once more, we see the use of the machinery of speculation in the distribution of risk.

ARBITRARY PRICE

One might reasonably ask, "Why not have an end to all this complicated business by having prices fixed by law which would compensate everybody for his labor and enterprise?"

That certainly looks to be reasonable, and we are surprised that nobody ever thought of it before. It can be well assumed that such ideas have occurred to thousands and thousands of people thousands and thousands of times and have often been tried.

The trouble is that only that part of the crop would be sold which could be purchased at the price. Many of the producers would be unable to sell their crops, and very many purchasers would have to go without. But let then a very skilful and otherwise able administrator at Washington fix the price from year to year so that the whole crop would come onto the market. That is, of course, all that can be done. But assuming that such an administrator could be found, able enough to accomplish the result, the final price would be exactly what normal speculation on the Board of Trade would have determined. One method gives us an artificial process depending upon the more than human wisdom expected of a single individual or board; the other gives a social process, depending, like all such, upon "the interaction of many individuals one upon the other."

An arbitrary price or prices can be fixed at any time which will make all producers prosperous—if they can sell. But such a price must always mean that demand will fall off for lack of purchasing power.

INSTRUCTION

If there is to be developed in pupils any effective intelligence about Commerce in the modern world, there must assuredly be developed in them an elementary understanding of Exchanges. That is part of the cultural equipment of the educated person. It is social science. If we have regard to the adjustment theory of education, as we always must, then here is a vital part of the environment of the Common Man, even though the individual never makes an investment, let alone engages in speculation. More than that, whether the individual realizes it or not, he is likely at any national election to take part indirectly in the regulation of exchanges. Finally, one of the elements of intelligence is that beginning of wisdom which consists in being aware of ignorance: one of the fruits of schooling should be to make individuals disinclined to meddle with markets on their own responsibility. To escape from the domination of the specialist is at bottom to know who is specialist and what he does, and then to use him. For most of us in ordinary normal times, the exchange specialists are to be found in the savings banks, insurance companies, and similar enterprises.

I need not remark on the units which follow other than to point out that, like all others which we have encountered, they represent my own conception of the elementary understandings which enter into the Curriculum at this stage.

COURSE IN EXCHANGES

I. Exchanges
1. Regional, national, and world markets in which men deal in securities and commodities
2. Concerned in national and world commerce
3. Related to:
   a) Banking
   b) Transportation
   c) Warehousing, including cold storage
   d) Manufacture

II. Stock Exchange
1. Deals in securities
2. Securities are shares in commercial and industrial enterprises—stocks
3. Or evidences of ownership of interest-bearing loans—bonds

III. Stocks
1. Shares in actual capital invested in commercial and industrial enterprises and nothing else
2. Value is in present or prospective net earnings distributed as dividends

3. Value rises or falls as function of dividend-earning capacity of the enterprise
4. Yield is percentage which dividends are of price paid for stock
5. Yield on all dividend-paying stocks tends downward to a common value
6. Hence, the effect of trading in stocks is to distribute the ownership of wealth, or at least income derived from wealth
7. Stocks are common and preferred

IV. Bonds
  1. Are interest-bearing evidence of ownership in loans secured by:
    a) Liens on the property for which the loan is used or upon other property
    b) Legal liability of the borrower in a suit at law
    c) Good faith—true of Government bonds especially
  2. Interest rate is normally a function of:
    a) Supply and demand in the loanable funds available in the community—the more the money available, the lower the rate
    b) The risk involved in the loan—the greater the risk, the higher the rate
  3. Refunding bonds is properly selling new bonds at a lower rate in order to retire old bonds having a higher rate
  4. Selling new bonds in order to pay off old ones at maturity is not refunding but merely evidence of misfortune or mismanagement
  5. Incurring new debt to pay interest on old debt is evidence of insolvency

V. Securities and Business Stability
  1. Securities are the main dependence of enterprisers as collateral for bank loans for current operating capital
  2. Hence, it is greatly important to the whole community that securities should be stable in price
  3. Perhaps the most important single element is proper surplus of undistributed earnings carried by well-managed corporations
  4. Spreads dividend payments at a constant rate over years when earnings fall off
  5. Hence:
    a) Stabilizes business dependent on bank loans
    b) Tends to secure liquidity of banks

VI. Investment
  1. Is buying securities for the sake of the interest return
  2. Endowed colleges and schools and hospitals, trust funds, savings banks, insurance companies, depend upon safe investments

3. There is no ready investment save as there is:

    a) A market in which securities can be bought and sold at any time

    b) A known price at which they can be bought and sold

4. An investment security is one that has become settled into a relatively reliable and steady value on the exchange

VII. Speculation

1. Speculation is buying or selling securities in anticipation of rise or fall

2. Is an economic process which generates a price as a common estimate of value

3. Without speculation there could be no investment save in neighborhood mortgages, promissory notes, etc.

4. Long and short trading is the mechanism which determines price of securities and tends to make price conform to value

5. Buyers tend to cause the market to advance and sellers to cause the market to fall

    a) Buyers who go long of the market must eventually sell in order to make their profit. When they sell, they cause the market to halt or fall

    b) Traders who sell short must eventually buy in order to fulfil their contract. When they buy, they cause the market to tend to rise

6. Long and short selling, bull and bear movements, act as automatic regulation and prevent the market from either running away or collapsing

VIII. Speculation and Gambling

1. A true speculator acts on knowledge and judgment in a true economic capacity

2. A gambler acts:

    a) On the outcome of pure chance, in slot machines and other gambling devices

    b) On more or less valid estimate, seeking to make money where there is no economic character involved—card-playing for money and betting on games and races

3. A gambler on the exchanges buys on the chance of a rise without knowing what he is about

4. Wild gambling on the market produces a rise beyond all real value; in other words, a runaway market, which like all inflation must sooner or later break

5. If there have been enough real speculators trading to have sold short heavily, control is regained and the bottom is prevented from falling out

6. Collapse of the market in a major securities exchange causes widespread bank failures, closing of mills, unemployment

IX. Manipulation of the Market
1. Manipulation of the market means causing an artificial rise or fall for some selfish interest
2. Since all such practices involve bad faith and have bad social consequences, they are declared illegal as fast as they are detected
3. Gambling and manipulation and not legitimate speculation prevent securities exchanges from fulfilling their social function

X. Commodity Exchanges
1. Deal in wheat, cotton, sugar, tobacco, and other staples
2. Function is to determine price which corresponds to value
3. Do not *make* price, for supply and demand furnish the underlying conditions

XI. Speculation
1. Traders deal in estimates of values of harvested crops—called "dealing in futures"
2. Buying at market for future delivery gives right to sell, but trader does not necessarily own the physical goods
3. Selling at market for future completion of contract imposes obligation to buy
4. Net effect of going long or short of the market is to establish single price—which tends to be true value
5. Single price means that those who grow on a large scale can know how much they can receive for their crops
6. Without market price growers could sell only by local peddling
7. Gambling and manipulation have same effects as in the case of the stock market
8. Manipulating and cornering have been made difficult or impossible by prohibitory legislation

XII. Buying for Manufacture
1. Just as the economic function of speculation in securities is to establish eventual reliable investments, so speculation on commodity exchanges is to establish price for manufacturers and other users
2. The manufacturer buys at the market the raw materials which he needs, but by the time the manufactured product is on the market, the price may have fallen or risen
3. The manufacturer is a fabricator or processor and not a market speculator; he desires to be protected from speculative losses and is willing to waive possible speculative gains
4. Hence he hedges by selling short as much as he buys

5. Net result is that, whatever happens to the market in his raw material, he neither gains nor loses speculative profit in the final sale of his manufactured profit. His profit is solely industrial profit

6. Social utility is that hedging stabilizes business

XIII. Government Price-fixing

    1. Cannot be fixed by law since conditions of production and distribution are constantly changing

    2. If fixed by an administrative board, the following conditions must be met:

        a) If higher than commercial value, the full supply will not be sold. Producers cannot be recompensed as a class and consumers in part must go without

        b) High price means that production will be stimulated, an excessive supply will next come on the market, prices will fall below the point at which producers can be recompensed

        c) If real economic price is constantly fixed by a superlatively able board, then the result will be no different from what it is under normal speculation

    3. The solution of production is everywhere reducing costs so that an adequate supply can come on the market at progressively lower prices

E. Commercial Law

Commerce has been so extremely important in the affairs of mankind that out of it there long ago inevitably grew up governing customs between traders which determined the moral relations which must exist between men if they will deal freely with one another. The custom of merchants grew up into a body of law known as the Law Merchant. It is that, or rather its descendant, with which we have to deal in this concluding course in the Curriculum in Commerce.

In the development of Law as major and universal institution, national systems of law each for a long time took its own course. Hebrew, Chinese, Brehon, Roman, Islamic, Anglican—all of them have been variants of the great institution itself, and yet each of them has reflected the way of life and the philosophy of different peoples. Alongside of them all grew up the Law Merchant, a true law of nations, a common law made necessary if men were going to trade much with one another. I know of no instance in the

body of Culture in which the essential universality of some institutions comes out more clearly. Wherever you go in the prehistoric or the historic world, a jug is a jug if you expect it to hold
water; and an arrowhead or spear point is the same kind of thing
everywhere if you use it for the purposes of a sharp-pointed weapon. So is a contract a contract, a bill of lading a bill of lading, a
draft a draft. Until comparatively recent times, the Law Merchant was a system by itself, accepted by States as a measure of
necessity since legislatures could not invent anything that would
take its place. It has, however, become systematized until it is
part of the general body of the Law. The term "Commercial
Law" is little more than a convenience to use in describing how
the general body of the law has spread its protection over Commerce.

"Business Law," however, has come to be a great deal more than
Commercial Law viewed as a body of principles, largely because
the producer and merchandiser must keep track of a great body
of regulatory statutes enacted by Congress and the State Legislatures, violation of which is often criminal. Moreover, "Business
Law" suggests "the law with which businessmen are particularly
concerned." It is vocational or prevocational in intention and has
no place in the Common School. When instruction is desired in
that field, the individual should resort to schools set up for the
purpose and presumably competent.

In the Curriculum of the Common School we are not concerned
with the theory of Commercial Law as the lawyer must know it
and as the businessman ought to know it. We are interested in it
primarily not as law—we have given much attention to law already—but rather as a part of Commerce in the fabric of Civilization. Nor ought we to profess to answer the question, "What is
the law?" That is the lawyer's affair. If, on the other hand, the
educated person grasps the principles which underlie all Law as
well as the laws which pertain to commercial transactions, he will
readily arrive at a notion of what the law probably is. It is easy
for such a person to read useful manuals and to see more clearly
when he ought to consult a lawyer. People cannot run to an at-

torney's office every time they expect to make a purchase, or even enter upon less habitual transactions, and yet every purchase involves a contract. These are subsidiary individualist utilities, and we are convinced that everywhere the primary purpose of the Common School is the generation of social intelligence, that is to say, intelligence concerning the necessary relations which exist between individuals. Hence, we limit ourselves to curriculum content and organization upon the basis of which *principles* can arise, the stuff out of which intelligence is made.

A GENERAL COURSE

Unlike most other parts of the fields of The State, of Civil Government, and of Commerce, the present subject is one which has long appeared in high-school programs, chiefly if not always in vocational courses. There is a very considerable advantage in this historical fact, for experience has been gained in teaching and particularly in textbook-making. We should not go very far wrong if we were to say that much of what has been taught in high-school commercial courses as an elective ought to required of everybody who aspires to become an educated person. There are, however, important qualifications.

First, much which has been set forth in texts in Commercial Law or Business Law is only incidentally law. It is rather in the nature of civil institution as in the case of the Corporation, or else commercial institution, notably Banking, Insurance, and Exchanges. Real and personal property are commonly and rightly treated, and yet it can hardly be contended that the meaning of property as the law defines it is exclusively commercial or even primarily commercial. The law covers all forms of conduct and specifies what may, must, and may not be done. When the text embarks on a discussion of the law of property, the reader very soon finds that he has been led into a complicated special field. Nor is there much in the subject of negotiable paper for the non-professional save what the pupil has already found in Banking. The one critically important feature of negotiable paper which every individual ought to realize is the consequence of indorsing a note. In the first place, however, that is not done any more with the lavish insouciance in which the innocent once gave that pledge of friendship. In the second place, anybody who has come to entertain notions derived from a limited but thorough study of the three important divisions of Commercial Law—namely, Contract, Agency, Bailments—will at least indorse a note with his eyes open.

Second, much of the content of existing texts consists of essentially technical discussions of the details of various possible situations in matters of Contract, Agency, Bailments, Property. Naturally enough, since they are intended for vocational purposes. Even so, most of them are not schoolbooks, but manuals or handbooks, put together in such a way that pupils could at best secure but a memory content good until examination day and then lost forever. A manual is a very useful book which the businessman or others can keep for ready reference, and eventually, after much consultation of the book, one comes to have a working knowledge of the matters of which the book treats. But a manual of any sort cannot be taught, and it rarely leads to trained intelligence, at least not to a system of thought. A valid course good for everybody would equip the individual to read one of these manuals intelligently and much more beside.

Third, the best of these texts have a few introductory pages dealing with Law, a good deal more important matter than the ruling cases growing out of litigation in which many of the texts abound. One realizes that the authors are limited for space and hence can give little heed to this all-important matter. We have found that somewhat prolonged study of The State and of Law is indicated for all pupils, still keeping to the rudiments of that vast field.

INSTRUCTION

I apprehend that there is no occasion for the elaborate treatment of our present topic which has been given to everything since we left Art. In The State, Civil Government, Commerce, we have been dealing with matters which have no established place in the schools. Here we deal with familiar material for which there is an abundance of literature, both in the form of pedagogical treatises and in that of textbooks. Moreover, the present course is, after all, but a scholium on the larger courses in chapters x and xi. Hence, I shall proceed directly to the course organization, reserving, however, the privilege of commenting upon each unit and each element.

TEXTBOOKS AND OTHER MATERIAL

Perhaps it is well to return to a subject of which we have seen but little since leaving the chapter on Science.

A textbook is properly a treatise organized and written for the use of those who are still in pupilage. It is before all else an argument setting forth principles coherently, and illustrating them. It makes the work of teaching simpler and more effective; but, if no teaching were needed, then there would be no occasion for any school. Ideally, the teacher should require no textbook, but in a workaday world and in a country like ours which requires nearly a million teachers at work, there would not be anything like teachers enough to staff more than a very few secondary schools if all had to teach without textbooks.

A textbook suitable for this course then, or for any course in the science type of teaching, should have certain characteristics:

1. It should contain a clear and brief summary of the course as a whole, so clear and well summarized that after reading it the pupil would feel that he already knew something about Commercial Law.

2. Each unit in the course should be taken up in succession, and the treatment of each should be:

a) A brief summary of the principles involved in the unit, a bird's-eye view, an overview. Such an overview should never run to more than an ordinary newspaper column, at the outside.

b) A more extended exposition under each element of each unit, all of it focused upon each element and finally once more upon the unit as a whole.

3. An amount of illustrative exercise material also focused on each unit and on each element in succession, limited only by the feasible size of the book. In the teaching renaissance which came

at about the turn of the century, it became common to publish such exercise material in "exercise books" as they were called, or sometimes "supplementary material."

COMMERCIAL LAW

I. Founded on Good Sense and Good Conscience

1. Like all Law, the laws of commerce are merely the outgrowth of good morals. It has been said with truth that, if all people were governed by the Golden Rule and Fidelity to Promises, there would be little need of Commercial Law.

2. Most people carry out their agreements regardless of the law of contract; most people would return to its owner a lost package found in the street, unaware that they were obeying a command of the law of bailments. Occasionally, a free man is found who pays his honest debts, regardless of discharge in bankruptcy, because he believes he ought to make good.

3. One of the difficulties is that we get into situations in which with the best will in the world to do right we do not know what is right.

4. Moreover, people who have not had the discipline which goes with good instruction patently mistake their own desires and advantages for justice.

5. Hence, lawyers and merchants, judges and lawmakers, through the ages have come to see that justice in commercial transactions has a logic of its own which can be used as guidance in lawful transactions and in litigation.

II. Contract

Contract is a *legal term* definitive of a relationship between individuals. Commercial Law is nearly all of it, directly or indirectly, contract, and contract has no substance in meaning save to those who accept the obligation found in the moral institution of Fidelity to Promises.

1. A contract is an *agreement* between two or more persons; minds must meet in a common understanding.
2. There is no legal contract without *consideration*.

3. The agreement must be between persons who are legally competent, not minors or persons of unsound mind.
4. The subject matter must be lawful, not immoral and not contrary to public policy.

III. Consideration

What turns an agreement into a contract is the element of consideration. An agreement to play golf this afternoon is morally binding but cannot be enforced. It is not legally binding since there is no consideration. The law in substance says "You ought to keep all your engagements, but where they are contracts you will have to keep them or else take the consequences."

1. Consideration must be nominated in the bond.
2. Or it must be implied in the agreement, as, for instance, market price where no price is stipulated.
3. Formal contracts under seal require no consideration, for it is necessarily inferred.

IV. Subject Matter

1. Cannot be fraudulent and still remain a contract.
2. Cannot be an agreement to do an illegal act.
3. Cannot be an agreement to do an immoral act.
4. Cannot be an agreement to act contrary to public policy.
5. If under duress, there is no contract.

V. Form

The formal side of contracts, since early Roman times at least, and probably much earlier, has sought to achieve three things: certainty that a contract has been made, assurance that it is not contrary to good morals or public policy, and assurance that it will be carried out.

1. Certain contracts are almost of necessity in writing, all in which large amounts of money or other important considerations are involved.
2. An oral contract is entirely valid if otherwise a contract. Most contracts are oral. The defect is in the principle that oral contracts are hard to prove.
3. Meaning must be logically coherent and understandable by reasonable men. The *substance* must be plain.
4. Should be simple in language and so far as possible free from legal verbiage.

This quality is to a large extent the responsibility of the contractor or contractors. Purely legal terminology will of course satisfy the court, and judges are after all not teachers of English composition. But good English is not in itself illegal.

The primary essential of a contract is that minds should have met. If legal terminology makes it impossible or unlikely that the minds of the parties should meet, then the contract is not good, whatever a court may say. In contracts involving special knowledge, engineering contracts, for example, specialized terminology must obviously be employed, but that is a matter for engineers acting as agents.

The contractor can insist on plain language in his contract form or else take his custom elsewhere, having adopted the precaution when he gets a form intelligible to him of consulting his lawyer as well. Many a perfectly legal but cutthroat contract would be avoided if the parties would diligently read and make sure what each of them is obligated to do. No amount of simplication will protect the contractor who will not read or cannot read. Nevertheless, apparently plain meaning can be so buried in legalisms, either of form or of substance, that one cannot know with reasonable certainty what he has bound himself to.

VI. Warranty

   1. An assertion that goods have a certain quality is a *warranty*. It is part of the contract which must be made good by the vendor and warrantor.

   2. What goods are held out to be, even where there is no express warrant in words, is an implied warrant.

   3. A vendor is under no moral or legal obligation to see that a buyer is not making mistakes about something which is within the buyer's presumable understanding.

   4. A vendor cannot morally, and probably not legally, take advantage of a buyer's manifest ignorance of what he is about. The honorable vendor says, "You do not want that."

   5. Indorsement of a bank check or a promissory note is in substance a warranty that the maker is capable of making good and will make good. The indorser makes himself liable, if the maker does not pay.

VII. Agency

   1. Agency is an actual relation between persons which has grown up out of the necessities of Commerce, and is recognized and regulated by law.

   2. An *agent* is one who is empowered to transact business for another. The essence of agency is the power to make contracts for another called the *principal*.

   3. A servant is not an agent in that he is not authorized to make contracts. The legal term servant has no menial implication. A medical man or an engineer may in law be a servant—a matter of function.

4. The principal is necessarily responsible for the acts of his agent when acting as agent. He cannot escape responsibility for the agent's actions which result in loss through errors of judgment or through misfortune.

5. The principal cannot be responsible for the criminal acts of his agent, even though the acts in themselves be within the terms of the agency, unless it can be shown that the principal was consenting and agreeing.

6. Agency is primarily a matter of contract, but third parties can infer agency from the acts of the principal.

7. Anybody can enter into agency, either as principal or as agent, who is legally qualified to make a contract.

8. Third parties in dealing with one purporting to be an agent are bound to assure themselves that he is an agent, so far as the responsibility of the principal is concerned.

9. One who holds himself out to be an agent when he knows that he is not is subject to punishment for fraud.

VIII. Property

We have already discussed Property as a moral institution, and there we found that the term is pretty nearly synonymous with rights. Property, morally considered, is whatever is one's own, whatever it is right that the individual should enjoy without deprivation. So husbands and wives have moral property rights in each other; parents and children have property in each other; one has moral property in his own body—he cannot rightly be made the slave of another—he has moral property in his person, to be free from insult and from invasion of privacy. Now the law of property is founded upon morality, but property under the law, property as legal institution, is the property which the law will defend.

The law, however, defends a great deal which is usually called something else. It defends, for instance, marital rights by punishing adultery. It defends children against brutal treatment at the hands of their parents, and it has sometimes given aged parents rights to support at the hands of their children. It prohibits slavery absolutely and punishes trespass upon the body, or libel and slander directed against the person.

Nevertheless, property as legal institution, as lawyers commonly understand it, is largely limited to economic rights. And yet, for the sake of clear thinking, it is important to realize that we do not own our land, and dwellings, our food and clothing, but only the right to enjoy them. Thus legal property is definitively an outgrowth of moral property; it has to do with rights.

But law constantly defines *what is* property, the extent to which a thing will be recognized as property, what rights The State will protect. In so doing, Courts and Legislatures in principle act upon what is morally right, and upon what is ethically right, that is to say, upon what is conformable to existence in Society. It is these fundamental conceptions of the law of property in Commerce which the pupil should acquire, rather than information touching what the law is. For the latter he resorts to lawyers, but he does so intelligently.

LEGAL PROPERTY

1. Legal property is, in the first place, rights to the enjoyment of goods and services which The State will defend.
2. Civil institutions tend to found definitions of rights upon individual moral right.
3. And upon ethical requirements, that is to say, requirements which arise out of the circumstances of social existence.
4. But distinction must be made between *social* requirements and the needs or desires of individuals in the mass.
5. Definition of ownership in a piece of property is called title.
6. Real property is land and the betterments thereon, including buildings and fixtures.
7. Personal property is all other than real. It appears as:
    a) Tangible personalty, and
    b) Intangible personalty.
8. Constitution guarantees that acknowledged rights will be superseded only by due process of law and that fair compensation will be made

IX. Bailment
1. Transfer of possession without transfer of ownership is bailment, and the thing transferred is a bailment.
2. Bailments are notably:
    a) Pledges
    b) Loans of tangible personal property
    c) Rent of tangible personalty

d) Deposits for safekeeping

e) Found articles

3. May or may not arise out of contract.

4. Title remains in the bailor.

5. Right to use is in the bailee, including responsibility for right use.

6. Bailee must exercise the same kind of care for bailments that a prudent man would exercise for his own property.

X. Master and Servant

1. A servant is one who performs services for another, but without the power to make contracts.

2. There is no menial implication, nor any implication of inferiority of any kind—a legal relation only.

3. The master is now liable for injuries to servants incurred in the performance of their duties, whether due to contributory negligence or not.

4. The master is responsible to third parties for injuries inflicted by servants in the course of their regular duties.

5. But the servant is also responsible.

CHAPTER XIII

INDUSTRY

IT is hard to separate Commerce and Industry, save in thought. Industrial enterprises engage in the sale of their products, and in their financial relations they are not essentially different from commercial undertakings. They compete for the market, and the tendency is for the large concern to survive until the production of a whole nation is carried on by a few great corporations. Nevertheless, in social analysis, Industry is concerned with *production*, and Commerce is concerned with *distribution*.

Production is of services as well as of goods. Transportation companies are engaged in the production of services, but so are professional people and household servants. So are managerial workers in manufacturing. In truth, all of us who depend for our living upon either wages and salaries or the fees which are paid for individual services are engaged in the production of services and are therefore in Industry and in Labor. So far as his salary measures his place in the enterprise, the president of a great steel company is just as truly an employee as is his humblest wage-earner. The social contrast is not between the higher-ups and the lower-downs but between (*a*) employees, that is, wage- and salary-earners, who constitute the labor element in production; (*b*) enterprisers who organize and carry on and who are compensated in profits or fees; and (*c*) capitalists and landowners who receive interest and rent rather than wages, salaries, fees, or profits.

In the United States, and in other nations in which there is no tradition of caste or status, the tendency is for these three economic classes to overlap. In the early stages, when the individual enterpriser lay at the foundation of the whole structure, the three were combined in one. Today, enterprisership becomes diffused among several million stockholders, and capitalist earnings arise to a large extent out of the savings of wage-earners.

INSTITUTIONAL CHARACTER

If we were to take the whole field of Industry and assume that we must generate intelligence over the whole field, in its techno-logical as well as in its institutional aspects, we should embark on an impossible task.

Furthermore, it would be unnecessary even if it were possible. It contributes very little to the working intelligence of the Com-mon Man to understand the manufacture of airplanes, or hosiery, or firearms, or breakfast cereals; and yet the individual who could form no conception of the whole matter at all would be little better than a savage set down in a world of machine industry in which he must live. But the sciences, and especially an under-standing of the primary machines and mechanical processes to which we shall presently come, give the individual an outlook on what the technologists are about. He can read in the whole field, all the way from the manufacture of automobiles and the installation of electrical apparatus to the gross aspects of surgical processes. He assuredly cannot become qualified offhand as an engineer or a surgeon, but there is a world of difference between that cultural status and the attitude in which all these things are accepted in a purely passive and mystified sense.

On the other hand, there is an institutional organization of Industry which is, of course, social in its nature, one in which are involved relationships between individuals and which must be understood if one is to become an intelligent citizen as well as a civilized individual—civilized, for assuredly Industry is a major element in the fabric of Civilization. It is that institutional or-ganization of Industry with which we are in the main concerned.

I. THE ORGANIZATION OF INDUSTRY

As fundamental to the whole field, we ought then to have regard, first of all, to the Organization of Industry in its social aspects.

THE INDIVIDUAL CRAFTSMAN

The whole matter historically starts with the individual crafts-men who has his own shop and markets his won product, who is not only craftsman but enterpriser and capitalist as well. He may or may not employ other artificers than himself. Throughout a large part of history this master-workman is the basis of industry. How profoundly true that statement is may be seen from the long list of surnames which are also the names of crafts—all the way from Brewer and Butcher to Tailor and Weaver.

THE FACTORY

Where the individual enterpriser who is also craftsman prospers and expands his shop until he employs many craftsmen, a factory has become set up. The proprietor very likely devotes himself to management and thus ceases to be a wage-earner; he becomes a profit-taker. In the differentiation of function which has gone on ever since the appearance of the metazoa, the capitalist comes in to furnish shop, plant, and equipment, and interest earnings are differentiated from wages and profits.

We are accustomed to say that the factory system dates from the application of the prime motors to the driving of automatic machinery, but that is not true. The factory is ancient, prehistoric indeed; the power-driven factory under the machine system is another kind of factory but factory still.

MACHINE PRODUCTION

Nevertheless, the new kind of factory so greatly increased the need and use of capital, and in that way so greatly modified the structure of communities, that we rightly say that an industrial revolution took place, or more exactly a mutation in Culture which rapidly attained survival status. The craftsman gave place to the machine-tender, and the advantage of large plants was so great that a powerful drive was given to the growth of the Corporation in its application to Industry. And yet nothing fundamentally new was produced. Wages remained wages; enterprisership in joint-stock companies continued to be at bottom what it had been with the master-craftsman; capital was no different in social meaning from what capital had always been, save in the fact that there was more of it.

Capitalism, socialism, communism.—The fact last named is

what is commonly meant by "capitalism" when the term is employed in its ordinary current connotation and in contrast with "socialism" and "communism." The term is meaningless, for it is usually implied that there is some way of carrying on production without capital. That, of course, cannot be; even the savage hunter owns capital, namely, his weapon. It matters not in capital theory whether the good is supplied by the individual enterpriser, or by many individuals and administered by a corporation, or is supplied and administered by the community itself, capital is still in use and is still governed by the logic of its own existence. The principal term in that logic is that it must earn its keep, that is to say, interest as over against wages and profits.

Similarly, the term "socialism" is devoid of meaning and substance, for all enterprises are founded on the relationship between individuals, and that is social.

"Communism" is a better term, for it has more or less a denotation and a substance. It can be given a definite meaning without violence to language and logic. "Having all things in common" is still the traditional meaning. So far as we can make out, no considerable social order ever existed on those terms, at least not beyond the lifetime of some strong autocrat or autocratic tradition, the best illustration of which was the Inca society of ancient Peru. Small religious communities have so existed; and the normal family is a communism. On the other hand, we have come, quite properly as I believe, to use "communism" as the general term for the collective ownership of the instruments of production and distribution, in contrast with ownership in severalty. In that sense, the word supplants State Socialism, which is neither State nor Social. Even communism as thus defined is not a form of The State, at least not of the Civil State. It is rather regression to the medieval manor on a national scale. The Government replaces the lord of the manor but is not government by law and, in spite of worthy efforts, has not thus far succeeded in becoming such. If we desire an exact descriptive term, we can call this form of community organization "Sovietism" from what is by far the most considerable attempt to make it work. In this sense, a city water works or electric-light and power plant is a modified communism, grown into the fabric of a municipal corporation.

To sum up this digression, the legitimate, logical, contrast in terms is between individually owned means of production and distribution and collectively owned means or instruments; in other words, that in which ownership in severalty is set over against common ownership.

Social utility of machine production.—The social utility of machine production, the quality which has made it advance rapidly and which assures us that, in itself considered, it is a normal product in cultural evolution, is in the fact that it has enormously contributed to the production of wealth; it has made more goods and services to be distributed. But we have to learn how to live with machines and machine production. Like a great many other products in evolution, it is quite capable of destroying itself under the weight of its own excesses. It is given to rational humans to understand and to manage.

THE PROFESSIONS

The professions, industrially conceived, are developments out of individual-enterpriser craftsmanship. The lawyer or the medical man has special skill and learning which he applies to the service of his fellows in the community for a fee. He commonly owns his own tools and goes to the landowner for his office. The fact that these and others are learned professions, and in that respect of higher cultural grade than the crafts, in no way destroys their essential industrial character as producers in the community.

On the other hand, the clergyman, the professor, the teacher, clerks, and the whole list of professional and semiprofessional workers are employees of corporations, mostly of incorporations. They are engaged in production, and their livelihood comes to them in the form of salaries. In the same general class are found the managers who grade downward from executives, who have taken over the management of enterprisership in highly organized industry, and whose compensation comes in salary form rather than in profits, to administrative workers whose skill is specialized in processes and in the management of men rather than in enter-prisership in general.

Hence it is that wage-earners are not the only "workers" in indus-try and not the only ones who work.

UNSKILLED LABOR

And then comes the ancient bedrock of the personnel in In-dustry, the unskilled, the pick-and-shovel men, the coolies, who have long been disappearing before the advance of machinery.

AGRICULTURE AND HUSBANDRY

On an absolute subsistence basis, in which all consumable goods are produced and processed on the farm, Agriculture and the breeding and exploitation of animals is no part of the field of Industry, since in that case there are no social implications. The Family is the complete community and is a pure communism. But no such situation has existed since Civilization emerged into its advanced stages, save as here and there a pioneer family repro-duced archaic conditions. But Agriculture has always varied from near-subsistence farming to near-industrialization.

So the picture of the typical American farm is that of the indi-vidual craft-enterpriser stage in industrial development. The Russian collective farm, on the other hand, if it were really oper-ated as a corporation and not as part of Government, is the com-plete picture of the American manufacturing enterprise organized as a corporation.

LUMBERING AND MINING

So far as personnel and social relations are concerned, lumber-ing, mining, and quarrying differ but little from manufacturing.

In their relations in the community, however, all of them, and Agriculture as well, occupy a peculiar place in that they have a strong tendency to destroy for all time vitally important natural resources.

Intelligently conducted Agriculture and Lumbering are not destructive since they conserve and replenish the soil and forest growth. In both, however, the community has a vital interest which must in the end be legally enforced.

The situation with reference to ores and other mineral products, especially oil and natural gas, is different, since when an ore bed or oil field has been exhausted, it cannot be replenished. Legislation has lingered here, largely because of lack of geographical intelligence and because the people have as yet proved incapable of that prudence which takes into account the needs and rights of oncoming generations.

UNITS IN ORGANIZATION OF INDUSTRY

I. Industry Is Production of Economic Goods and Services
   1. Not limited to production of manufactured goods
   2. Labor not limited to wage-earners
   3. Services are produced as well as goods
   4. There can be no distribution of wealth until what is to be distributed has been produced
   5. In general, the more there is produced, the more there is to be distributed

II. The Craft Individual Enterpriser
   1. Owns his own shop or farm
   2. Makes or grows his own goods
   3. Supplies his own circle of customers
   4. Is wage-earner, enterpriser, capitalist—all in one

III. The Factory
   1. A number of craftsmen organized for the production of a line of goods or services is a factory
   2. Not necessarly a plant of power-driven machinery
   3. Involves:
      a) Enterprisership in initiative, organization, management
      b) Capital in the form of tools, buildings, land, and working reserves
      c) Labor—professional, skilled, and unskilled
   4. These exist irrespective of who owns the capital or furnishes enterprise or labor
   5. Economic returns are, respectively, profit, interest or rent, wages and salaries

IV. Machine Production
   1. That may be done by machinery which formerly was done by hand

2. That may be done by machinery which never could have been done by hand
3. The craftsman becomes operator
4. The factory becomes a mill
5. Far greater volume of production is achieved

V. Requires Large Capital
1. Machinery is expensive, wears out, and has to be replaced
2. Entails the construction of buildings which are often themselves expensive
3. Hence machine production requires a great deal of capital
4. Capital requirements tend to make the corporative form of organization the only feasible form
5. Financial functions become differentiated:
   a) Enterprisership becomes organized into a joint-stock company, receiving profit in the form of dividends, with executive and managerial staff receiving salaries
   b) The capitalist function is performed chiefly by bondholders receiving interest, but depositors in savings banks and owners of insurance policies are bond-owners
   c) Labor is performed by operatives, unskilled workers, professional and clerical workers who receive wages and salaries

VI. Professions and Semiprofessions
1. Are producers of special services
2. Those who operate on the free market for fees are developments out of craft enterprise
3. Professions and semiprofessions are often employees of corporations

VII. Husbandry
1. Pure subsistence farming is not Industry, since it has no social implications
2. As industrialists, most farmers belong to the individual-enterpriser stage
3. Russian collective farms, except for their communistic character, and American producer co-operatives are parallel to corporative manufacturing and transportation

VIII. Exhaustive Production
1. Some types of Industry tend to exhaust natural resources
2. Agriculture and lumbering are often very destructive
3. Intelligently carried on, they are conservative of resources
4. Mineral resources are not capable of replenishment; conservation requires:
   a) Elimination of wasteful methods in production

b) Legal restrictions on certain methods of development—notably oil and gas

c) Elimination of wasteful use

5. Gives rise to possible substitutes not subject to depletion

II. PRICE AND PRODUCTION

We have already studied Price as it appears in Commerce, and we need not recur to the process of price determination again. In Industry, however, there are elements in cost which bulk altogether higher than in Commerce. The industrial price lies behind commercial price, since, as we have seen, the chief element in cost which must be met in fixing commercial price arises out of the price which must be paid to the producer for the goods which the merchandiser sells. Finally, the phenomena of business cycles appear fundamentally in production.

CAPITAL COST

We have already seen that capital bulks large in machine industry, and proportionately more of it is required than in merchandising. And yet, if we cut the corners of economic categories and treat land and capital as if they were much the same thing, then capital on the farm, including the use of land, has always been a major part of the cost of production.

The heart of the situation, as well from the point of view of the community as from that of the producer, is in the principle that capital must earn its keep in order to endure as capital. Imagine a factory erected and completely equipped. It is capital. The money said to have been "invested" was not true capital until the factory appeared, ready to be put in operation. Now, if the building stays there inert, with silent and motionless machinery, it is economically the same as if there were no capital. The labor, planning, and saving which have gone into the erection have become nothing. So real capital is easily dissipated, and, when that has taken place, it has ceased to exist as a factor in a going society, much as energy is dissipated and ceases to exist in a closed thermodynamic system. Therein is the why of capital costs in business.

Interest.—Interest is the value of capital in use, or rent if we are thinking of land. In truth, we might well say that interest *is* capital in its dynamic aspect. If the capital does not earn its value as interest, then the owner and producer is giving away his substance and the community is throwing away the fruits of its labor and planning and thrift and what has gone into the making of all three. So far as we can make out, that seems to be one of the rocks upon which communistic enterprises break down. In the free community interest earned and distributed is one the major elements in purchasing power and the source of new capital.

I suppose this fundamental concept of the functional nature of interest will continue to be elusive until Mathematics shall have been restored to the ideational systems which make up the higher culture in the community.

Depreciation.—Physical structures are subject to wear and tear in use and to final dissolution. Diligent attention to repairs and upkeep may postpone the end of the story, but even at the best the end will come. The asset is said to have expired. The story of "The One-Horse Shay" is the classic illustration of the collapse of an expired asset.

So it is that not only must capital earn its keep but it must earn its own physical replacement. That is *conservation of capital.* If the owners do not attend to it, they not only injure themselves but they injure the community, for the latter is encouraged to eat itself up, as it were. Hence the mill and its machinery or the farm machinery must earn a reserve which, with interest accumulations on the loaned reserve, will replace the expired building or other asset. That is depreciation, the second of our capital costs in production.

Obsolescence.—But not only do machinery and buildings wear out; they get out of date, often long before they are worn out. The asset is obsolescent, *becoming obsolete.* Obsolescence is sometimes called functional depreciation.

Now obsolescence is capable of being exactly measured: it is the difference between the cost of production on a given machine or in a given type of building, and the cost on the most improved machine or in the most improved design of building. When obsolescence thus computed is capitalized at the going rate of interest on bank loans, and the result is equal to the investment required for a new asset of the improved type, then the old machine or building is obsolete.

Hence, obsolescence also requires an earned reserve; but clearly no manufacturer needs to set up both a physical and a functional depreciation reserve; for if a utility in its nature will become obsolete before it wears out, then the latter is covered by the former.

Depletion.—Parallel to depreciation is *depletion*, the exhausting of resources. We find it especially in agriculture and in the extractive industries. It is hardly a capital cost, but it acts as if it were one. Its most important aspect is doubtless in agriculture, where the fertility of the soil is spent through reckless management of land and through bad systems of cropping.

In the United States, in perhaps ten generations of dealing with a land in which there always seemed to be more to be occupied when the old was worn out, vicious ways of looking at the problem have become securely rooted in the mores, and it may take a good deal more than one generation of assiduous schooling to correct the fault. The attitude seems to be made up of two ingredients: first, the conviction that it is the nature of soil to wear out; and, second, that it is the business of nobody but the owner.

The first contention is refuted by the fact that much of the land of Europe has been cropped assiduously for many centuries and seems to be as productive as ever.

The second is part and parcel of our individualist notion that there is such a thing as absolute property right, that is, the right to do as we will with our own, regardless of consequences to the community.

Depletion in agriculture is in the nature of a capital cost. If it is not met as a part of the cost of production, then the land in time becomes worthless. More obviously, but no more truly, than is the case in pure depreciation in manufacturing capital, the community has a stake in the issue. Meeting the cost is not, however, a matter of reserves but rather a matter of management, and of the continuous restoration to the soil of the equivalent of the plant food used up.

Depletion of minerals, however, is a matter of reserves in one form or another.

The labor cost in production of most kinds is by far the largest cost and by all odds the most obvious cost. Despite that fact, people who are complaining about prices are usually remarkably unreflective about the significance of the labor costs. One feels like rejoicing when we hear that wages have been raised, even if they are not our wages. We forget that there is no ever replenished fund out of which wages can be paid, that the only source of wages is the income which is derived from sales. People forget, moreover, that inflated wages result in yielding to the wage-earner less in enjoyable and consumable goods and services than he had in the first place.

Hence it is that manufacturers especially have often been driven to substitute machinery for labor wherever they could, sometimes when there was no economic justification in so doing. That policy is, however, obviously self-limited, for the point must be reached sooner or later at which the capital cost of machinery is more than the labor cost which it supersedes.

With the foregoing in mind, we return without further comment to the normal process of price-fixing which we found in Commerce.

In all the foregoing we have been discussing normal commercial and industrial processes. In the long run and in the national economy at large, normal process is the actual process. But there are unhappily a great many exceptions.

Among the producers themselves, as well as among the merchants, there have been and still are occasional unethical miscreants bent on the making of money by whatever methods appeal to them as promising, rather than on the production and distribution of wealth.

Others are so ignorant of the processes at work in Society that in actuality they stand in their own light to the detriment of the community.

More often, ignorant agitators and mischievous demagogues succeed in appealing to an unenlightened public and secure passage of legislation founded on the delusion that politicians are by nature wise and virtuous in the ways of business, and men experienced in business the opposite.

These things are no reproach to Commerce and Industry as institutions and complexes of institutions, but rather to the civil law which has not kept pace with social change, and to public instruction which has had little concern with the breeding of citizens capable of living effectively in the modern world.

III. PRODUCTION CYCLES

Theoretical economists are in the habit of saying that there can be no such thing as general overproduction. Whether or not the thesis can be maintained is no part of our concerns. We are now and then made unhappily aware that there can be overproduction of wheat, or corn, or automobiles, or dress goods, or any other product. By "overproduction" we mean the production of more than can be distributed at the prices which are made by the costs of production and distribution. So overproduction is intimately related to Price.

Elderly people out of their own experience, and young people out of their reading of economic history, are aware of cycles of prosperity and adversity, which occur with considerable regularity and are individually disastrous, disastrous to the community, and socially disastrous in that they usually entail more or less demoralization.

There have been various theories set up to account for these cycles, including even the influence of periodicity in sunspots, but the commercial and industrial economist is under no delusions. He knows them as parts of movements which are typical of Society, and indeed of the world of living things in general, about which there is nothing mysterious.

Starting from the low point of a depression, after a good

deal of liquidation of small men in great places and of false ideas, times begin to get better. Stocks of merchandise have been sold out, interest cost is lowered, confidence revives, depreciation and obsolescence begin to be made good, there is renewed investment of capital and renewed employment. Incomes are augmented, prices rise because effective demand is outrunning supply, regular production expands on the renewed basis, enterprisers hasten to produce more in order to take advantage of prosperity. In the end, the peak is reached: markets are taking up as much as they can at the present standard of need and purchasing power.

Thousands and thousands of producers keep on producing, long beyond the point at which incomes are sufficient to take up the whole supply, in some cases after raw demand itself has been satisfied—in other words, "I would not have it if you would give it to me." Capital continues to be invested in new plant and new land. Inventories accumulate and interest cost piles up. Men begin to be laid off, incomes sink, demand falls off, the new-era people of the period are ruined, and so until the bottom has again been reached.

THE INDIVIDUAL PRODUCER IN THE BUSINESS CYCLE

Now let us picture to ourselves one thousand wheat growers, or textile weavers, or canners, and ask ourselves what happens as the market rises from the low point to the peak of prosperity. Every single one of them *may* know what is likely to happen, but all of them keep on producing. Any single one of them producing for family needs would stop as soon as enough was in sight. Being in competition with nine hundred and ninety-nine others means to sacrifice himself for the benefit of those who keep on over-producing.

THE CORPORATE PRODUCER

On the other hand, some corporate form of organization—it may be a co-operative, a joint stock, or even the community itself, can stop at any time just as the individual who is producing for a family can stop when there is enough. Unless prohibited by some long-obsolete law, there can be a working agreement or agreements to curtail instead of expanding when the stage of over-production is approaching. It may well be that greed and lack of prudence may operate the same with corporate management as it does with individuals, but it does not have to. Continued over-production in one case is avoidable; in the other it is unavoidable

One of the persistent popular delusions, however, is that limiting production is for the purposes of keeping prices up and "starving the poor." Price is fixed, not only by supply and demand but by the costs of production, and the market will take up only that part of a given supply which will flow into the channels of trade at that price. The residue is loss to the producer. Nor does destruction of goods affect the price, since the price was established before those goods came on the market.

Let us recall that intelligent management looks to the balancing point of the supply-demand schedule. It has no interest in keeping prices up; it has an interest in large sales at the lowest price that can be maintained and pay costs of production, the largest element of which is the wages of labor. Nevertheless, we have here perhaps the most striking illustration in all Sociology of the mathematical principle of the functional relation between two variables. While wages constitute the largest production cost, they also form the backlog of purchasing power and therefore of demand. Capital costs, on the other hand, save interest on borrowed or invested capital, contribute nothing to purchasing power. Machines have nothing of the sort and it is not difficult to understand that, when industrial processes become more and more machine processes, the producer's market is in some degree itself destroyed.

UNITS IN PRICE AND PRODUCTION

I. Producer's Price
    1. Is determined by what buyers can and will pay
    2. Single price is the price at which the whole supply will come on the market
    3. Price, however, cannot long be maintained at less than cost of production
    4. Profit is the difference between selling price and cost

II. Producer's Capital Cost
 1. Interest on capital invested in plant or land
 2. Equivalent interest on capital borrowed
 3. Interest on inventory or goods produced and not yet sold
 4. Interest must be earned before profits are estimated, or capital will be dissipated

III. Depreciation
 1. Physical plant is subject to wear and tear and decay
 2. A proportionate part of replacement value must be earned and placed in reserve each year before profits are estimated
 3. Functional depreciation or obsolescence on machinery must be made good out of earnings and placed in reserve
 4. Obsolescence is the difference between cost of production on a machine and cost on the most improved machine of that kind
 5. A machine is obsolete when obsolescence capitalized at the going rate of interest is equal to or more than the cost of replacement
 6. Depreciation of both kinds must be made good out of earnings or else capital is dissipated

IV. Depletion
 1. Agriculture and the extractive industries entail depletion
 2. Depletion is exhaustion of natural resources
 3. Agricultural depletion can be made good by skilful management of land and soil
 4. In extractive industries a depletion reserve must be maintained out of earnings sufficient to replace capital when the ore bed or oil field shall have been exhausted
 5. Otherwise, capital is dissipated
 6. Exhaustion of natural resources themselves is a matter of control by The State

V. Labor Cost
 1. The principal cost of production is labor cost
 2. There is an inescapable issue between labor costs and the capital and operating cost of machinery
 3. Labor cost appears in wages and salaries, but purchasing power also appears in wages and salaries
 4. Machines have no purchasing power and do not contribute to demand for the products of machine production

VI. Consolidation of Enterprises
 1. Normal tendency as matter of social utility is for individual enterprises to become consolidated into corporate enterprises
 2. Cuts costs and lowers price to point at which there is maximum volume of sales, consistent with costs of production

3. The profit element in unit purchases is reduced to the minimum

4. Gains arise out of large number of units sold rather than out of large profit on single units

VII. Overproduction

1. Exists when more of a given line is produced than can be sold at prices determined by current commercial conditions

2. Or when more is produced than raw demand will take up, that is, demand irrespective of purchasing power

3. When there is overproduction, the market will take up only part of the supply

4. The residue is dead loss, for it cannot be distributed at any price

5. Destroying a portion of the supply does not necessarily raise price

VIII. Business Cycle in Production.

1. Low point of a depression

Men out of work—little purchasing power—producers not meeting costs—great deal of poverty, and ruin of prosperous families

2. Weak leaders and executives tend to disappear and false ideas to be given up

3. Inventories are gradually sold out and capital costs cut

4. Consumers reach the point at which they have to replace durable goods

5. Depreciation begins to be made good and workmen are taken back

This is the *capital goods* test, and no depression is definitely on the mend until this phenomenon appears

6. Purchasing power improves, sales increase, employment improves, purchasing power still further improves

7. Production is expanded to take advantage of better times and a *boom* is likely to occur

8. Overproduction appears and the cycle starts all over again

IX. Individual Enterprisers and Overproduction

1. A community of individual producers is bound to overproduce in in good times

2. A single producer who understands and would cut production merely benefits his competitors

3. Cycles of overproduction in communities so organized are bound to occur

4. Large consolidations can control production if they are allowed to

5. In communities so organized overproduction is avoidable

X. Limiting Production and Overproduction

1. Limiting production below what the market will take up is in itself bad business policy, for it lowers the financial return below what it might otherwise have been

2. High prices do not necessarily correspond to the greatest return, but high prices can undoubtedly be generated by limiting production

3. Limiting production for the sake of high prices is unethical since it interferes with one of the fundamental social processes

4. Checking overproduction is, however, highly ethical for it looks mainly to protection of the community from disaster

IV. LABOR

We now come to what is perhaps the most important matter in Industry, to the lot of the classes of people who are employed men and women. They are not enterprisers or capitalists or landlords in the economic bases upon which their lives are ordered, although some of them, indeed many of them, may also be small enterprisers, small capitalists through the investment of their savings, or even small landlords. Lest current misconceptions of Labor mislead us, let us remind ourselves that managers, scientists under employment, teachers and professors, clerks and clergymen, housemaids and many others are also laborers. Still what we have chiefly in mind is quite properly those who are employed in money-making enterprises.

It is hard to get at any thoroughgoing comprehension of Labor as a constituent institution in Industry, and especially what is really involved in the "labor problem," so called, unless and until we have come to see industrial and commercial labor against the background of its evolution.

SLAVERY

The starting-point is to recall that nearly all those whom we here have in mind, and others as well, were in ancient times slaves for the most part. That applied in large part to professional workers as well as to craftsmen and to those who today are machine-tenders. As we all know, it is only within less than a century that slavery as institution disappeared out of the Western World—disappeared as having legal sanction and, what is more important, disappeared out of the mores as having moral sanction. Now, the real heart of slavery, at least for our purposes, was not the physical suffering to which slaves were peculiarly liable, for that may exist apart from slavery; and not crude violation of all the natural rights which men hold most dear, for those are still violated again and again in nations in which slavery is held in abhorrence—but rather the principle that *one's life and his place in the world were subject to the arbitrary whim and self-interest of another*. Until jurisprudence has evolved far enough to accord to every man employed in organized enterprises of any sort a presumptive property right in his job which cannot be denied save by due process of law, the essence of slavery is still part of the institution of Labor.

EMPLOYMENT UNDER THE INDUSTRIAL REVOLUTION

By the time of the Napoleonic Wars, the application of power-driven machinery to manufacturing and transportation had advanced far enough to cause the employment of free men to enter upon another stage[1] in which there was no escape for anybody who must earn his bread by the sweat of his brow, save emigration. Many an American family owes its origin as such to the very fact just recited. If he stayed at home, he must have a job at what the employer would pay. A great deal has been written about the evils of those days, probably with a proportionate amount of exaggeration, but the heart of the matter was in Ricardo's Iron Law of Wages, a scholium on the Law of Population of Thomas Malthus. In substance, it held that wages must always tend toward bare subsistence. Like a great deal of social theorizing it erred in not taking a sufficiently comprehensive view. On the other side, Karl Marx made much the same kind of error soon afterward.

The picture of conditions in England was somewhat as is described below. England is chosen since there was no other great industrial nation until near the close of the nineteenth century, and by that time the Industrial Revolution had passed into another phase.

The manufacturing plants and the mines were prevailingly

---

[1] The whole situation in England is described with meticulous detail by William Smart in *Economic Annals of the Nineteenth Century, 1801–1830* (2 vols.; London: Macmillan & Co., 1910).

small private affairs, commonly enough family owned. A mill in the hands of a family which had ability and traditions of service seems to have served much the same in England as similar enterprises have served down to this day in America. One gets a good picture of what such an enterprise might be in Trevelyan's *Life of John Bright*. But that was perhaps a sort of belated semi-manorial economy out of place in a new world. Railways were likewise small affairs which were just getting launched. The rule of extensive consolidation was still far in the future. Any one owner was helpless in competition for a market when it came to steady employment and adequate wage scales. He might be inclined to advance wages and eliminate the hard work of women and children, but, if he did so, his costs would drive him out of business. So it ran around the circle. The trade-unions were in the embryonic stage, and in law they were still conspiracies. Even if they succeeded in producing riotous and destructive strikes, as they often did, they accomplished nothing, for a successful strike commonly destroyed the employer and with him employment. In brief, the small individual enterpriser tended to be in much the same position with reference to wages and working conditions as are today the small American enterprisers with reference to overproduction.

The solution, or at least the possibility of solution, came when the industry of nations had become consolidated in relatively a few great stock companies, not only for the economy and intelligent management which thus became possible but because the companies *could* deal rightly with the labor problem.

COLLECTIVE BARGAINING

A correlative is in the principle that large-scale consolidations made collective bargaining on wage scales a possibility. The individual workman, through the greater part of the modern period, has been helpless in bargaining with his employer. He would, and in most cases did, receive the compelling answer to his petitions, "If you are not satisfied, I can easily get somebody else." The union, on the other hand, which includes large numbers of workmen, is in a position to speak with a force comparable to that of the employer, and perhaps to speak to a whole industry at once.

There is no bargain unless there is substantial equality between the bargainers. And yet, collective bargaining carries no divine right; bargains must be struck in accordance with commercial reality. If wage scales in an industry are bargained up to an inflated level, it is the same as the conditions which once prevailed in the early stages of machine industry; the industry will have to curtail and will be obliged to lay off men.

Altogether, while wages have been central in the whole development of the labor union, it has been very easy to overemphasize them. As we have repeatedly seen and shall see further, nominal wages in money can easily be made higher than real wages in consumable goods and services. We certainly have no concern in the Common School with the mutual criminations of employers and labor unions; but the pupil in high school or junior college who is acquainted with the historical facts and led to see the logic of the relation of wages to purchasing power is put in a position to think for himself.

INDUSTRIAL JURISPRUDENCE

A good deal more important matter on the whole is the advance in juristic principles governing the relations of worker and employer which have become part of our jurisprudence in recent years. For the pupil, the advance throws some light on the development of Law itself to meet cultural changes.

Four which are entirely or nearly accomplished fact in our jurisprudence should, I believe, be made part of the course. Three of them represent radical changes in the old master-and-servant doctrines of the Common Law.

1. WORKMAN'S COMPENSATION

First of all come what are commonly called Workmen's Compensation acts for the relief of workmen injured in the course of employment.

The advent of power-driven machinery involved new and enhanced perils to the workman who operated it or came in contact with it. The situation was nothing new in kind; workmen had been injured in the course of their work from time immemorial. Under free labor, the prevailing ideology was that if a workman were injured that was either due to his own fault or else was his own misfortune. The prevailing well-established legal principles were: (1) assumption of risk, (2) fellow-servant doctrine, and (3) contributory negligence.

The first meant that, if an individual accepted a job, he knew what might happen to him and assumed the risk.

The second meant, "Well, John, we are sorry you got hurt, but we know and you know that George was to blame. Therefore sue him and not us."

Contributory negligence meant that if the accident had been due to the victim's own fault, in a situation in which the consequences of ordinary human fallibility were multiplied a thousand fold, then the injured man had nobody to blame but himself.

Now that reasoning was perfectly good among free men, given two conditions: first, when free contract actually existed and, second, when employment involved only ordinary risks which the prudent man could avoid.

The first condition disappeared with the frontier and the end of the Westward Movement. There was substituted a *status* in which nearly all employees are in constant terror of losing their jobs. The second disappeared with the advent of very complicated and dangerous machinery.

But that is not all. Under the new conditions was the employer any more responsible than he had been before? After all, he could always be sued if the injury could be shown to be due to his neglect. The answer was "No"—no blame can be attached to the prudent employer; the burden must be borne by the public which benefits from organized industry. Hence, the burden was distributed as all risks are distributed and covered by insurance. The premiums are part of the cost of production and are covered in prices charged for goods and services.

In every enlightened State, injured workmen are entitled of

right to compensation settled as is every insured risk, without
the intervention of lawyers.

2. WORKING CONDITIONS AND FACTORY INSPECTION

Be the foregoing as it may, the workman who catches his
jumper on an exposed set screw and is whirled to bloody atoms
about a shaft is scarcely interested in workman's compensation,
nor is the payment of the death claim of much comfort to his
widow and orphans.

Hence, the second of the great steps forward, guaranty of safe
and sanitary working conditions by the Law, supplemented by
the refusal of insurance companies to carry insurance on mills
which leave machinery exposed.

3. RESTRICTION OF EMPLOYMENT

Prior to the triumph of machine industry and to the development of highly organized Commerce and Industry, employment
of free labor had no such scope as it increasingly has had during
the last century and a half—much less than that in the United
States. The Industrial Revolution changed all that, and in the
course of time folkways developed in which it was taken for
granted that employment of some kind was the normal condition
of the majority. Happy days when nobody was in terror of losing
his job, and young people never in terror lest they have no place
in the world!

Throughout the greater part of the nineteenth century, it
scarcely entered the American mind that there could be any ethical restraint on employment, on getting a job if you could at any
age, or on employing as many as one could at the lowest possible
wage, even if that involved inducing the immigration of enough
European labor and oriental coolie labor to create a labor reserve.
That was the very heart of the Liberalism of that day; modern
Liberalism takes out of kin. The deliberate production of a labor
reserve to be drawn on when times are good and to be thrown
out when times are bad seemed the normal and natural thing to
do, instead of about the most inhuman and antisocial thing conceivable by supposedly civilized men. Indeed, even before Civil

War days, the Southern slaveholders were given to twitting the North with the accusation that the lot of their slaves was better than the lot of the Northern laborer—and there was some truth in what they said.

Abolition of child labor.—About the first clear case in which a new juristic principle here appears seems to me to have been in the movement for the abolition of child labor and the restriction of the labor of minors. From the famous *Report on Manufactures* of Alexander Hamilton, in which encouragement of manufactures was advocated in part on the ground that they would make employment for women and children, to the enactment of the latest anti-child-labor statute, there has been what amounts to an ethical revolution.

Now, the history of the regulation of the labor of minors is long and a good deal involved, and we have no space for it here. However, among many motives, the one that consistently has survived is the removal of children and young people up to fourteen and sixteen from competition with adults, or in other words, from the labor reserve.

That is important in itself, but what is more important is the establishment of the principle that a whole class can lawfully be excluded from employment when the latter involves collective injustice to Labor as a whole, and detriment to the community. Nevertheless, equivalent injustice is done unless the children and young minors released from the mills are adequately provided for in the schools and in the Family.

Restriction of immigration.—Beginning about 1840, there came an increasing flood of immigrants to our shores. For forty years and more they came to take up unoccupied land as well as to work on railway building and in the manufacturing industries. There was still labor shortage instead of labor reserve. The tale of immigration after about 1880, however, is a horse of another color, little better than exploitation of the traffic by steamship companies and by corporations engaged in the heavy industries chiefly. The long story culminated in the drastic restrictions of 1924.

There had been abortive restrictionist movements all through the greater part of the 1800's, but they all came to nothing. Regulation of the inward flow of labor was repugnant to the liberal philosophy of most Americans. The act of 1924 is another step in a changing ethics, or rather a step in the clarification of ethics, which has regard to collective as well as to distributive justice, and in which it is admitted that no class has indefeasible rights to employ and be employed to the detriment of normally functioning societies. No doubt there are other specific instances which await application of the same principle.

4. ECONOMIC SECURITY IN OLD AGE

A fourth major advance in the ethics of Commerce and Industry, and the quasi-industry which we find in the employed professions, still in its inceptive stages as a matter of jurisprudence, is the right of economic independence in old age for employed people. *Right* is emphasized for the sake of denying that such independence is a matter of charity and philanthropy. In ordinary intelligent Fair Play, one who has served faithfully and well under employment for a lifetime is of moral right as much entitled to compensation in that period in which his powers are failing under the dispensation of nature as he is during the years in which he is active but is obliged to sleep a portion of every twenty-four hours.

At the time when these pages are written, the whole matter is very much a matter of public discussion. With that we certainly have no concern anywhere in the Common School. But we are concerned with putting our pupils in possession of certain elementary principles which will enable them to think for themselves about the whole matter and not be misled by fantastic financial proposals which are made in the early stages of all such movements, nor yet by intransigent opposition.

Career pay.—The whole logic of the matter seems to start in the concept of what we will call "career pay," which accepts the principle that the aged are as much entitled to retirement pay as is the youth entitled to pay for his sleeping hours. That brings us to the point of seeking some clarification about wages and salaries as terms.

"Wages" in common parlance means that compensation which is estimated and paid in terms of some short unit of time. Not long ago, it was "day wages." Now, it seems to be weekly pay. I take it that we do not begin to speak of salaries, until the time unit is at least a month and more often a year.

Now all that goes back to a period when employment was easy; a man might have several employers during a year or even simultaneously. He counted the days he worked for each. Indeed, in the building trades especially, we still count in terms of hours. All that is obviously unreasonable and antiquated, since the great mass of employed people have but a single employer, and they have to eat twelve months in the year. Hence it is that we sometimes see wage agreements written in terms of a guaranteed yearly wage. When that is done, it is evident that a reasonable folkway is forming, and that we have passed from the meaningless day wage to the time unit in terms of which nearly all financial transactions are recorded.

Nor is it different with salaries. We pass from the "eight dollars per week," which was my first salary, to the annual salary which is all but universal today, even if employers still pay once a month.

Evidently, career pay is merely the final term in that movement.

Now that is in reality all there is to the problem at bottom, as a matter of ethics and of adjustment to the conditions of modern employment. As so often happens with new ideas, we are apt to get the cart before the horse, and begin with schemes to find money for the retired without stating the issue in its raw fundamentals. Strange as it may seem the financial problem is not logically primary.

Financing retirement pay.—The financial problem reduces itself to the query, "How is the community which reaps the benefits from employment to arrange its financial program to meet the primary conditions?"

All similar problems are met through the individual's financing his own problems. Is that feasible here?

The answer is that which those interested in the retirement of clergymen found out long ago. To place the employed upon their own responsibility, and still provide for retirement, requires for the payment of annuity premiums a very wasteful increase in the annual stipend, an increase for which there is no enjoyable use by the recipient. It would be far cheaper to make retirement payments outright than to increase salaries enough to enable the employed to do it.

In the case of the industrially employed, it would involve increasing wages to enable the employed to pay premiums on endowment policies to a point at which the enhanced cost of production and merchandising would seriously interfere with distribution. In other words, it would not be economic.

If, however, the employing group allots premium payments to an invested reserve, and thus takes advantage of the time value of money, recovering the premium in prices charged, then the situation becomes like what it is in administering workman's compensation. Note that the compound amount of $1.00 invested at 4 per cent for forty-five years is $5.84.

Taxation?—The easy way to solve all such problems, or to imagine that one is solving them, is to place the burden on the taxes. It is entirely safe to say that there is no way out in that direction.

In the first place, because of the unpleasant habit that taxes have of destroying their bases.

Second, because no such public service falls within the economic scope of taxation. Taxation is for the support of Government; and this is for the purpose of completing career pay for employees in the production and distribution of goods and services which have a money return. Payment for industrial services must be kept within the economic category in which it belongs, and there it can be made.

Many employers.—But one very critical objection to the foregoing reasoning is in the circumstance that there are many employers large and small, and employees shift from one to another. If, however, we come to see that contribution from employees is no part of the financial logic involved, however much it may be in nonindustrial enterprises, half the difficulty is removed. As to the other half, doubtless The State must come in, not by way of taxation, but rather through the creation of some corporation for the administration of funds, analogous to the Federal Reserve.

Finally, the meat of the whole matter is that this is an affair of Commerce and Industry and not one to be left to a benevolent State, and an affair of the community in its consumption of goods and services.

MONEY WAGES, REAL WAGES, AND WAGE INFLATION

Finally, the employed in general are as subject to the logic of economic principles as are capitalists and the employers of labor. Wages cannot be fixed at whatever collective bargaining may succeed in extorting and still maintain the prosperity which makes wages possible at all. There can be wage inflation as truly as price inflation or any other kind of inflation. Of the following broad tests we can be reasonably sure, at least in industry which produces goods and services for sale:

1. The distinction must always be drawn between real wages and money wages. Real wages are what the employed services can be exchanged for in tangible goods and services. Money wages are what we draw from the employer. To put it another way, real wages are what money wages will buy.

2. Since wages are always the chief item in the cost of production, which is itself the basal factor in determining price, advance in wages is often the chief factor in advancing prices and consequent lowering of real wages. Where the individual-enterpriser system prevails, the effect is obscured, since real wages will not fall save when increase in money wages is general.

3. Advance in real wages, sometimes called the workman's share in the value product, seldom comes save through the general lowering of prices and distribution of wealth, consequent upon more efficient and less wasteful production and merchandising.

4. Increasing money wages followed by decrease in real wages is prima facie evidence of wage inflation. The effect is, of course, most severe on people who are in receipt of fixed incomes, and on those who are employed by The State or in noncommercial production. It is less severe proportionally on wage-earners in industry. The evidence is only prima facie—on the face of things —for there may be other causes at work.

UNITS IN LABOR

I. Labor as Industrial Institution
  1. Is contrasted with enterprisership and capital
  2. Includes all who work under employment in industry
  3. Does not include civil service personnel or that of army and navy
  4. Does not properly include household service, which is of the Family rather than of Industry

II. Slavery
  1. What is now career subject to employment was once large-scale slavery
  2. The slave was chattel, the property of his or her owner
  3. The slave in principle had no civil rights whatever
  4. Serf was not freeman, but he was not slave
  5. Essence of slavery was in the principle that a life and a career were subject to the whims and interest of another

III. Employment under Early Industrial Revolution
  1. "Iron law of wages" as wage theory
  2. Small employer could not maintain decent wages and working conditions unless all would
  3. Labor unions were in the eye of the law conspiracies
  4. Nearly always in Europe a labor reserve
  5. Hence the worker was at the mercy of his employer in bargaining
  6. Strikes merely drove an employer out of business, or at least tended to
  7. Collective bargaining for wage scales implies
    a) Strong unions able to enforce conformity to contracts upon their members
    b) Industrial consolidations large enough to make wage scales and working conditions common

IV. American Employment
  1. For a long time there was actual free contract, because:
    a) Employed could return to subsistence or semi-subsistence farming

      b) Families were strong and tended to be landholding

      c) Strong individuals could "Go West"

  2. Continued until disappearance of frontier and then employment passed from contract to status, having to have a job

  3. High wages have been folkway in America, because:

      a) Tradition became early established

      b) America has never been obliged to import necessities or even most luxuries

      c) Or been obliged to sell industrial products in a low-priced foreign market

V. Advance in Industrial Jurisprudence

  1. Old legal rules governing compensation for industrial injuries and death:

      a) Assumption of risk

      b) Fellow-servant doctrine

      c) Contributory-negligence doctrine

      d) Employer liable only if negligence on his part could be proved

  2. Compensation for industrial injuries and death established as matter of right without court action, and cost borne by consuming public as a whole, through:

      a) Industrial insurance, premiums paid by employer

      b) Premiums recovered in prices charged as part of cost of production

  3. Safe and sanitary working conditions

      a) Established as legal obligation and enforced by factory inspection

      b) Stipulated by insurance companies in insurance contracts

  4. Emergence of ethics of restricted employment in:

      a) Removal of competition of children with adults

      b) Restriction of immigration

  5. Economic security of old age accepted as matter of justice

VI. Evolution of Career Pay

  1. If people must eat for a year, they must be paid for a year

  2. From day wages to monthly salary, to annual salary, to guaranteed annual earnings

  3. Clarification of the idea that, if the employed individual's life is given to faithful service in Commerce or Industry, then he must be paid for a lifetime

  4. Retirement pay for the employed is completion of career pay

VII. Retirement Pay in Career Service

  1. Not for enterprisers, for they elect a different status in society

2. Not for capitalists, for their retirement income is presumably the same as their active income
3. For the employed, because:
    a) Their status is career employment
    b) Their stipends cannot economically be made sufficient for the purchase of adequate annuity policies
4. Can be done economically only through building up invested reserves, the employers contributing the premiums, and recovering in the prices charged.

VIII. Wage Inflation
    1. Money wages are the money received
    2. Real wages are what money wages will buy at current prices
    3. Wages follow economic logic, and the fruits of collective bargaining are not necessarily what can be paid
    4. If too high, real wages will fall as costs of production entail high prices
    5. If too low, purchasing power will be inadequate to maintain volume of trade

V. TOOLS AND MACHINES

The heart of modern manufacturing and agricultural industry is in machines, and especially in power-driven machinery. Nor is that all, for machines enter more and more into the household, and into our whole way of life. In short, the mechanical environment is perhaps the most pressing part of the total environment, especially in urban communities. It follows that on the adjustment theory of Education, without reference to the institutional organization of the Curriculum, the development of intelligence about machinery, as an essential part of general intelligence, is of necessity part of the content of General Education.

Something of this has long been part of advancing instructional practice, but without much definite organization and permanency, as I believe for lack of adequate conception of the form which adjustment takes—whether organic development or ideational accretions—and of a broad general scheme through which it may be achieved. That lack can be supplied through, first, the institutional principle which makes Tools and Machines part of the understanding of Industry and, second, the principle of the comprehensive and significant in organizing curriculum materials.

A. Recent History of Similar Courses

In order to make sure that the meaning of the courses which are here developed and their justification is made clear, I suppose we would do well to take a brief backward glance into the recent evolution of this phase of the Curriculum.

MANUAL TRAINING

The first outward manifestation of what we have in mind appeared in the manual-training movement of the last part of the last century.

The movement did have an educational theory of its own, which was logical enough if you could grant its premises in the faculty psychology and mental training. It held to the latter, with unquestioning faith. Despite its shaky foundations in exploded psychology, there was an element of sound doctrine in it, eminently capable of defense on physiological and cultural grounds.

One of the cardinal characteristics which differentiated Man from all that had gone before him was his sensitive and flexible hand and its neural connections. He did not develop the human type of brain by using tools, but the neuromuscular connections were there to be used in learning the use of tools. It is not only plausible but probable that the sensorimotor learnings involved in the use of tools would tend to stimulate flow of blood, and metabolism, in the sections of the brain involved, and thus bring about a more complete physiology in the organ. Donaldson's classic dissection of the brain of Laura Bridgman would seem to give ground for that conjecture. Even so, half-hour exercises twice a week would presumably accomplish little in a process which would imply a continuous regimen.

But the cultural phase is more important, and in that there is some left-handed justification of the notion of sharpening the wits. But the wits which are sharpened are constituted of the acquisition of fundamentally important ideas, some of which can be acquired otherwise as well as through manual training and some can be acquired in that way alone. The manual-training advocates were fond of pointing out, with truth, that the normal home and farm life of boys and girls, prior to the mechanization of household processes, and prior to the urbanization of life in general, had in it a great deal of informal educational experience of prime importance, arising out of semiskilled hand work. In fact, the boy of fifty years ago who was not handy with tools was looked down upon, as was the girl who could not cook and sew. They were acquiring ideas of several kinds which lie at the foundation of civilized personal development.

To be specific, and only by way of illustration, the boy who was taught to drive a nail straight and to do it in the right way, and who had many similar experiences, acquired *ideas* of a volitional sort which were capable of being generalized. In other words, the boy was capable of seeing, or being made to see, that much of living is like driving nails, that there is a way of doing things right and then of always doing them that way. He had had concrete experience which could be made to serve as assimilative material. He could not get the ideas from exhortation alone, for he would seldom see what the exhorter was talking about.

Moreover, in the general round of similar experiences on the farm, or under the training of a wise and devoted village father, it was possible for the boy to form right ideas about many industrial processes, so much so that he was not entirely mystified in the presence of industrial processes in general. Wherever the manual-training program was consistently carried out, and not allowed to degenerate into faddism, the result was, at least in my observation, what the foregoing would lead us to expect: boys did become handy with tools and as men they still have their handiness. Moreover, they acquired a stock of ideas which were inescapably real to serve as a fundamental part of their ideational background.

Now the present courses in Tools and Machines are in lineal descent from the old manual-training as the latter has been described; but where the old was typically abstract and aimed at little or no purpose beyond the exercises themselves, this course is definitely hand work and tool process with representative machines. When a boy has become capable of making a weld, or of mounting a shaft on the lathe and turning it down to design and dimensions, he has had a masculine kind of training, and has acquired a cultural product which is definitely related to the building of industrial intelligence.

The course is educational in import and not vocational training.

B. Instruction

In the foregoing historical survey, these motives for courses in instruction appear, none of them leading to specialized training:

1. Handiness with tools, furthering the normal development of the neuromuscular organism.

2. A rich and fundamental ideational background, particularly of volitional ideas, to be found in learning to use tools properly.

3. Intelligence about the use of the materials and appliances found in manufacturing and agricultural industry, and indeed in the common daily life.

The important problem in the derivation of the Curriculum here is not different from what we have found in Mathematics and Science and Art, in Civics, Politics, and Commerce. Instead of attempting the impossible task of covering the whole ground in thoroughgoing detail—impossible not primarily because it would be impracticable but rather because no pupil could ever assimilate the substance of any thought or logic in it all—instead of that, the problem is to find tool processes and machines which are so comprehensive in import that familiarity with them will generate as wide a spread of ideas as possible.

If we were engaged in developing skill, the contrary process would be indicated, namely, the selection of a particular process or machine and lingering on that until trade skill or proficiency had been attained. If we were planning instruction in engineering, then the mathematical and scientific processes and principles involved would be mastered in their particular applications.

It does not follow that scientific and mathematical principles are to be ignored. Here, as over the whole area occupied by Civics, Commerce, Industry, and Health, catching up with Civilization is learning to see things in the universal terms implied by scientific principles and the applications thereof.

I. Woodworking

Certainly one of the most ancient of the crafts is carpentry and its companion, turning in wood. Like everything else that has primitive origins and is still requisite in modern communities, it probably lies close to the foundations of Culture. For that reason if no other, it is comprehensive.

One has to be on his guard here against the well-meant but mistaken generosity of patrons who desire to bring the school up to date by giving automatic, or semi-automatic woodworking machinery. It is true that today nearly all shaping and processing are done by machinery, but machines do nothing that has not at some time had to be done by craftsmen. The machine itself exercises no logic. To substitute machines for craft processes is to destroy any educational utility there may be and to turn pupils into machine-tenders.

There is included especially:

1. The use of the common carpenter's tools in the common operations of construction.

    Recall that perhaps the most valuable educational product is volitional in character, that is to say, disciplinary. Nailing up a seam and doing it right, sawing a clean and straight scarf, using a plane correctly, are outward and visible manifestations of the difference between doing things right and doing them wrong.

2. The use of the wood lathe.

In the teaching of the course in woodwork, it ought to be noted that manual training has little or no utility on the ideational side unless it is worked up in projects which are themselves likely to have a use. Time was when it was not a matter of projects but of meaningless, or at least highly conventionalized, exercises; much as the contemporaneous mathematics teacher was fond of setting clock and tank problems and of requiring his pupils to extricate radical expressions from their unhappy involvements.

II. Blacksmithing

Parallel with woodworking are the elementary operations which the smith performs, including laying and keeping the fire. Even more than woodworking, there are few things which are better fitted to give the half-grown boy the concrete practical experience out of which he may learn to outgrow the helter-skelter, impatient ways of boyhood. Moreover, it is comprehensive in its industrial ideology.

III. Plumbing and Steamfitting

I know of no better name for the course, but the connotation is formidable. It suggests training in one of the few crafts which are left. It, of course, cannot be that. Extended special training belongs either to apprenticeship or else to a regular trade school.

The simple operations of the plumber, including use of the soldering iron and blowtorch, taps and dies, use of the various forms of wrenches, placing and adjusting valves, are manageable by boys, and they have much the same educational values as those already noted in other courses.

Time was when a boy who could not harness and care for a horse was esteemed a niddering; he lacked in the common intelligence of his time, at least to that extent, and was under suspicion of lacking more. So it is today in another culture. The individual who does not know what to do until the plumber comes, who cannot manage a refractory faucet or valve, does not know which way to turn up a right-hand screw, is not as well educated as he might be.

Again, there is implied the solving of problems in terms of what is learned in General Science, thinking out a difficulty in terms of the mechanics of fluids and of convection currents, for example.

IV. Electric Wiring

The same general principles apply to electric wiring. In good courses in General Science, pupils are taught the principles, but unless they have some experience in wiring for electric light and power and for bell circuits, the principles themselves are not fully learned.

V. Instruments of Precision

The whole system of modern industry rests upon the use of instruments of precision. Even if that were not true, it would still be true that the habit of precision is decidedly part of the scientific outlook. Pupils have long been given some training in the laboratory in Physics, but laboratory measurements are remote and specialized. Moreover, the laboratory itself belongs to the University rather than to the Common School.

The use of instruments is a handicraft as well as a mathematical undertaking. The shop gives opportunity for a great deal of practice which is not remote and to the pupils artificial in significance. It is hardly a course but rather a unit which overlaps all the use of hand tools and machine tools. It is emphatically volitional in character and a part of discipline and insistence.

The elements which appear to be manifest are the following:

1. Rough use as well as exact use of the linear measures. There is of course a technique in exact measurement, as well as a felt obligation to be exact.
2. The use of calipers.
3. Use of micrometer calipers and of the micrometer in general.
4. The use of verniers.

Other handicrafts.—The foregoing seem to be about all that is sufficiently significant to deserve a place in school and possessed of enough value as manual training. To state the matter in another way, there is not much of educational value in other crafts which is not implicit in the courses listed.

On the other hand, much of what has in the past crept into the schools—such things as bent-iron work, weaving, hammered metal, even jewelry—is without industrial significance. It is not important enough.

Machines and Machine Tools

The final course, or set of courses if you prefer, which seems on our principles to be indicated, is the use of common machines and machine tools.

Of the two courses named, it seems the less obvious. Its setting is an environment of whirling shafts and cranks, of grinding gears and flying pistons, a new thing in the world but foreshadowed in the first potter's wheel no doubt. We do not adopt toward that phase of our environment the attitude of stolid indifference which the primitive is said to show when he comes in contact with mechanized culture, but most of us entertain an attitude of passive acceptance. "The gadget" and "this thing" have some mysterious place in the universe no doubt, but all that is matter for engineers and mechanics. An appalling ignorance is not only admitted but apparently prized. Such people are lacking in an essential part of general intelligence, no matter how bright and clever and cultivated they may be.

No doubt it is true that the science taught in our schools, over a long time now, has contributed much to the popular level of intelligence about machinery, a contribution which other peoples recognize, even if we take it for granted. But after all that kind of intelligence is superficial, for it lacks the volitional element which is everywhere characteristic of the practical arts. When an individual can sincerely say to himself, as he contemplates a piece of machinery, "If that shaft, or slide, or gear, should break, I could make and instal a new one if necessary," he is possessed of a kind of intelligence which arises only out of doing.

The machines are especially the drill press, the grinder, the shaper, and the engine lathe. The milling machine and the bed-planer can be brought in if desired, but the first four give us the essentials. The work is found in construction projects, in the course in auto mechanics, in jobs from home and elsewhere. As a construction project, we still have in our shops a marine-type steam engine built by the boys many years ago.

So far as the manual training is concerned, then, we have five general processes involved: bench work in chipping and filing and the four machines already mentioned.

I. The Automobile

The automobile reminds us with immense vigor that it is a pressing part of the environment of all men; and that in an automobile age, men at least, if not women, who lack intelligence about the machine are but incompletely educated.

The vehicle in its nature is a veritable pedagogical warehouse. It is marvelously comprehensive. In it are nearly all the primary machines which we encounter in General Science. It is an internal-combustion prime motor, and it embodies the principles of the reciprocating engine. It is an electric generator and motor. It is a complete lighting system, and it includes a transformer for stepping up low voltage to high. It contains a whole course in light rays, reflectors, prisms, lenses. In its explosive mixture and storage battery, it reveals chemical process involved in the transformation of energy.

But to use an automobile for instructional purposes is not a book project. If the pupil can read, and if he has had good courses in elementary science, he can go on indefinitely in reading *about* cars, their design, construction, and use—and accomplish very little in learning the automobile in the educational sense of personal adaptation. To deal with the machine effectively means bringing it into the shop, taking it down, making repairs, replacing worn parts, perhaps making new parts, reassembling and placing the car under its own power.

Driving automobiles.—Does the course in principle include driving? I think not.

The School lays the bases of conduct, but it cannot take its pupil by the hand and initiate him into all possible forms of conduct. In truth, perusal of the statistics of automobile accidents discloses that other personal qualities than lack of mechanical intelligence lie behind most of them—reckless disregard of the public safety, impatience, lack of self-control, and drunkenness are causes of most of the avoidable casualties. In other words, infantilism. Drastic police ordinances and drastic punishment in court have been the fashionable methods of control. Judging from the most recent statistics, they have in the country at large been ineffective. The School as institution is responsible to the extent that many schools for many years have in large part renounced any concern for the inculcation of either self-control or self-respecting obedience to either constituted authority or to the requirements of the public good. In effect, discipline has in large part become a lost art, associated in the pedagogical mind chiefly with the legendary barbarities of the hickory stick.

The training of drivers is a police function and not a problem in public instruction. If the public desires none but accomplished drivers on the highways, then police ordinances can require that every applicant for a license shall furnish evidence of having secured his own training.

II. Stationary and Marine Gas and Diesel Engines

Instruction follows the same course as with the automobile.

III. The Steam Engine—Reciprocating

It needs no argument to demonstrate that here is a significant and comprehensive machine, and probably will continue to be such until some source of energy is found in sufficient quantities, and economically available, other than the combustion of fuel under a boiler. We begin with the reciprocating engine, first, because it is historically first; second, because the essential processes involved are clearer there than in the turbine; and, third, because it deals with initial high torque better than any other direct-connected machine. The essential elements would appear to be:

1. The boiler as a device for generating steam pressure
   (Necessarily class and book work)
   a) Essential parts of a boiler
   b) Heating surfaces—economy in exposure of surfaces to fire
   c) Boiler explosions
2. Expansion of hot steam behind a piston, final step in converting heat energy into mechanical energy
3. Valve motion and regulation of cut-off
4. Reversing gear
5. Compound and multiple-expansion engines

IV. Turbines

The turbine principle as found in:

1. Air turbines, of which the ordinary windmill is a good example
2. Water turbines
3. Steam turbines
4. The converse principle as found in fans and pumps, and in propellers for boats and airplanes

V. The Electric Generator and Motor

The comprehensive character as bearing not only on machines but on the community is obvious.

There is involved the construction and winding and other electrical characteristics; the application of electrical units of measurement; transformation of high voltage to low voltage and the reverse.

But there are also involved uses in the community for light, heat, and power, the economy of each, and the effect on the pattern of the local community.

It is difficult, and probably needless, to lay down units limiting the scope of the course. Much must depend upon the good judgment of the teacher in drawing the line between what is of the Common School and what is specialization, that is to say, engineering.

The elements in electrical principles are, of course, found in Physics, but pedagogically it makes little difference whether the principles come first or last. In experience with immature pupils, it has usually been found best to get the concrete before the abstract. In this and similar instances, the principles are taught for the sake of scientific outlook. Here they are taught for the sake of mechanical intelligence. The practical application is that, if the principles come first, they will not help a great deal in the practical-arts attack on machines; in the latter they are taught as bearing upon understanding of the machines. If practice comes first, the principles as expounded in Physics can be made to mean a great deal more.

The generator and motor as they are found in auto mechanics cover the shop work involved.

VI. Power—Electric Generators

Perhaps the most advanced use of prime motors, making possible the transmission of power to great distances, is that referred to in the title to this unit. Turbo-electric generation with water turbines is in the broad sense the significant form because it makes possible the utilization of remote sources of power. Nevertheless, steam turbines, or even reciprocating engines, would be equally significant if the energy in remote coal mines, let us say, were to be utilized.

There is little justification for such a course in Machines. There is a good deal of significance in a unit as a supplement to Regionalization in Geography.

Such sources of power, and the implied long transmission lines, have been the subject matter of a great deal of popular delusion, which has sometimes found vent in fatuous Governmental projects. The elements would appear to be the following:

1. Given a source of power, how far away can the manufacturing plants which utilize the power be located?
   a) Distance to which it is electrically possible to transmit power
   b) Ratio of distance to increasing cost.
   c) Cost of the use of the capital required
   d) Influence upon production costs and therefore on price
   e) Is the good worth what it costs, ultimately in labor, management, self-denial, and natural resources

2. In the national economy
   a) Involves rearrangement of the whole national community pattern
   b) That involves the breaking-up of established folkways, customs, investments, homes
   c) Hence, not a question of fitting a population to a transmission line, but the reverse
   d) Unlimited power can be used only up to the demands of the present community structure and what may evolve out of it

3. The national community is knit together in geographical relations
   a) Economically that means in terms of production and distribution of wealth

b) Power may be transmitted over a wire, but the products of industry cannot be transmitted over wires

c) They are transported in physical form and bulk to the area in which they can be used

d) Transportation costs are one of the chief elements in price and therefore in distribution of enjoyable wealth

VII. Automatic Machines

After all, if one side of the mechanical organization of Industry is in the prime motors through which energy can be applied to the driving of machines, and in the shop processes which have to be applied in dealing with machines of any kind, the other side is in the automatic machines which are driven.

Manifestly, it is impossible to set up in the shops for study examples of all the automatic machines which are found in industry. Nor, so far as I can see, is it possible to find particular automatic machines which are so comprehensive that they could be made to serve as units of study.

Nevertheless, in the study of the automobile, and in the general use of machines in the woodworking and ironworking shops, the principal automatic devices are found. Notably these are the cam, the eccentric which is a modified cam, gears of various types, gear chains, belts, ratchets, trip devices, etc. These serve to elucidate what perhaps may be called the elementary principles of automaticity. When their action is seen clearly, at least automatic action need no longer be a mystery.

Beyond that, typical simple machines can be set up as museum pieces, and others may be studied in their action in various industrial plants which the pupils can visit.

THE AIRPLANE

Much as the auto-mechanics course grew up, similarly a course on the airplane is frequently found. Has it any justifiable place?

There can be no question as to the significance of the machine in transportation, but as a machine it has nothing of significance which is not in the study of the automobile and the various prime motors, save that which cannot be taught in school shops. The planing feature is undoubtedly part of the study material in wind pressure in General Science, but to arrive at anything more than a book knowledge would result in a course in the training of pilots, manifestly beyond both the function and the capacity of the Common School.

VI. AGRICULTURE

Agriculture today is emphatically part of Industry. It exists in a money economy and it produces goods for sale. As we have seen, American agriculture is still on the individual-enterpriser basis, which seems to be disappearing out of manufacturing and commercial organization. The growth of producer co-operatives, on the other hand, is not unlike the use of the joint-stock company in manufacturing.

Agriculture has long been a series of courses in rural high schools, commonly with a vocational import. Thereby, as I think, hangs a not unimportant tale.

Thirty-five years ago we were interested in developing agricultural instruction in country high schools. Some of us, the present writer, for instance, were strongly motivated by our knowledge of what the old liberal arts high school had done to the countryside. We sometimes found that farmers who could be incited to loyal support of Congressmen who professed their devotion to the farmer and the cause of rural life would not support the rural high schools in their own towns despite the fact that such were a prominent part of the whole rural-life movement. Inquiry showed that they resented the idea that their boys and girls were to receive any other kind of education than other young people received. In so holding they showed themselves good educational thinkers, for certainly there is only one education, namely, that which consists in becoming civilized. "Rural education," so called, is as much of a misnomer as "secondary education," so called.

And yet Agriculture is part of the Curriculum because it is major part of Industry. In what sense, in the shape of courses, is it part?

I. In one sense, we have already treated it in this whole chapter. Nothing that comes into the logic of manufacturing industry is any different, save in details of application with which we have nothing to do, from what is found in the logic of industrialized Agriculture. The production of different crops for the market is not in essentials different from the production and marketing of manufactured goods. True enough, in Agriculture there are special problems which must be solved, but they occur in no other sense than special problems occur in any other form of Industry. Particular kinds of farming or husbandry no doubt exhibit their own particular problems, but so do particular kinds of manufacture. Management has to meet and solve problems, but that is the function of enterprisership and management.

II. On the other hand, Agriculture as a way of life, agricultural operations—preparation of the soil, seeding, manuring and cultivating, harvesting and marketing—with all the vicissitudes of flood and drought, heat and cold, wind and storm, viability of seeds, insect and bacterial pests, have much the same educational bearing as does hand work with tools and machines. Time was when all this was familiar ground in individual experience, to all but a negligible proportion of the American population. At the rate at which people have been gathering into the cities during the last three generations, the body politic has been losing in large part all vital contact with the realities under which the food supply is produced. The city dweller, born and reared in the city, or even in the large village, is not quite in the state of mind of the French queen who, on hearing that the people were without bread, proposed that they eat cake; but their comprehension of the rural problems which vitally affect the well-being of the whole nation seems sometimes to be not so very much better. At the best, it is book knowledge.

There is little *feel* for the reality of the processes of nature as they are followed in the cultivation of the soil and the exploitation of animal products, apart from actual experience in small-scale growing of crops and care of animals. Hence it is that the following-out of selected crop and animal projects, over, it may be, several school years, is the analogue of shop work with tools and machines.

Curiously enough, there is even more justification of this part of instruction in the urban than in the rural community, for young people in the latter tend naturally to get the equivalent upbringing at home. To assert that such instruction could not be given in city schools is simply to state that here is another of the instances in respect to which life in our great cities, especially, is abnormal and unnatural, and not conducive either to national well-being or to the diffusion of Civilization among the population.

Vocational agriculture.—As a precaution against being misunderstood, let it be recalled that our subject is General Education and the Curriculum of the Common School. I have attempted to show briefly that in certain respects intelligence about Agriculture in our national economy is part of the content of General Education. We have not in mind agricultural schools of secondary grade which are seriously and deliberately devoted to vocational instruction in Agriculture and its underlying sciences. They sometimes appear as county agricultural schools, sometimes as agricultural institutes. They occupy a place in relation to the Common School cultural courses analogous to that which the modern technical high school occupies in relation to shop courses. In reality, both of these latter are or should be engineering schools of secondary grade.

VII. VOCATIONAL INSTRUCTION

We have at various points encountered the issue of Vocational Instruction in the Common School and have waved it aside as having no place there because of its specialized character. It is time to come to grips with the problem itself.

NO PART OF GENERAL EDUCATION

In all our studies the universal character of General Education has been emphasized as being something inherent in human nature, living in a complex society, at a high cultural level. We have emphasized further the common or folk character of the School as institution and the Common School as belonging definitively to the Common Man in his nonspecialized, nonvocational, existence in the Community. It has been shown, at least by inference, that the Common Man in the modern world does well if he becomes ready to live a civilized life as a citizen by the time he is twenty-one years of age. To recite all this is to exclude vocational training of any sort, including prevocational, almost by definition.

WHAT IS MEANT?

In the period of about thirty-five years during which the vocational movement has been under way, the term "vocational" has had no very exact meaning in common use of school people.

It has tended to be confounded with hand work and the so-called practical subjects.

In the Curriculum as thus far discussed, we have found reason to believe that Commerce and Industry have as good a place in the Common School as have Mathematics and Science and for much the same reason. Commercial courses, however, have ordinarily been vocational and in intent specialized. And yet, there has been included in chapter xii far more than ever has, to my knowledge, been covered in any secondary vocational course in Commerce. Furthermore, it has been shown to be indefeasibly part of the intellectual equipment of the educated person. Again, we have found reason to believe that shop courses in Tools and Machines are a justifiable part of the General Education, at least of boys.

So we have to conclude that on first analysis the distinction is mainly in the substantial purpose of courses. If they are shaped up and taught with the intent of preparing the pupil for the practice of a vocation, they are vocational, and not otherwise. If the purpose is only incidentally, in the cases of particular individuals, vocational, then instruction is not vocational. For example, college courses which are of intent cultural are not made vocational by the circumstance that students may afterward teach the content to others.

CHANGES IN AMOUNT OF TRAINING REQUIRED

As Civilization itself has become extended enough to carry a society of almost any degree of complexity, so be it that enough individuals are civilized, the vocations have become progressively simplified for the most part. That is not true of the professions, but these belong to the University and are therefore outside our consideration. In the crafts, for the most part, and some of the semiprofessions, where a prolonged apprenticeship was once required, mechanical devices have reduced the period of training to a few weeks in most cases, especially for fairly well-educated workers. Bear in mind, that there is hardly any comparison between the intellectual background possessed by our beginners in industry today and the inferior intellectual equipment of the old-time apprentice. To illustrate:

The executive officer of a steamship in the Atlantic trade a few years ago told me that he could teach a young man in six weeks all the navigation he could use, provided he were a *graduate of a good high school*. I have no doubt it was true. That ship was steered by a mechanical device which took over the responsibility of keeping her on her course. She had a gyro compass which is not subject to the vagaries of a magnetic instrument The trigonometry involved had been reduced to a thing of tables and formulas. The ancient difficulty of making the longitude accurately had been wiped out by radio time signals. And I suppose there was more simplification than I realized. All that is not to say that the young navigator could rise to responsible command other than through the acquisition of personal qualities which are not capable of mechanical simplification.

To come ashore, much the same change can be seen in the achievements of our educated young woman at the cookstove. Her grandmother may have been an excellent cook of the craft sort. This young housekeeper depends upon instruments of precision in the measurement of ingredients and in the exact control of temperature. She can read what Grandma never could have read. What was once a skilled craft requiring a long apprenticeship and much experience is now an exact art calling for qualities in its operations which are chiefly attainments in General Education.

Finally, it is to be observed that young manufacturers whose fathers were moving the public-school system and the United States Government for vocational training are now expressing themselves as desiring personal qualities and "liberal education" in their neophytes.

VOCATIONAL TRAINING REQUIRES ORGANIZATION AND METHODS
NOT FEASIBLE IN THE COMMON SCHOOL

The objective in vocational training is of right intensive, specialized, leading to skilled proficiency. The objective in the Common School is adaptability and cultural attainments around the whole horizon. The two objectives are incompatible, so much so that it is not likely that both will be attained in the same school. Both are requisite, at least in principle, in all who practice vocations, and that in America includes pretty much everybody. Ideally, the pupil would finish his General Education and then pass into his vocational training. Practically, it will be long before all will have achieved a General Education, although the trend at present is undoubtedly in that direction. Many, perhaps the majority, will leave the Common School in order to prepare themselves for their vocational place in the world.

TRADE TRAINING ECONOMICALLY BELONGS ELSEWHERE
THAN IN THE COMMON SCHOOL

The great bulk of employment is in the organized industries somewhere. The total number engaged in the professions, semi-professions, and in such individual-enterpriser crafts as are still left, outside farming, bulks small in comparison with those employed in trade and manufacturing.

Now, the Common School is not a part of production; it belongs elsewhere in the economy of the Community. Trade training is part of the cost of production, as much so as are wages and interest on capital.

Further, the Bureau of the Census lists something like eight hundred different vocations, a great deal more than that if you count all the specialties in each. Even the great industrial States with help in grants-in-aid from the Federal Government can seldom reach more than thirty or forty at the outside. There is as much justification for including all of them as for including one.

Moreover, where the school selects a small round for training, it merely unbalances the whole field of employment, even as schools have already done through high-school courses in stenography and typing. Overtraining produces more than Commerce and Industry take up.

On both counts, trade training belongs to Industry in its individual enterprises and plants, as much of it is now done, where the cost can be recovered in prices charged and thus kept out of the fiscal policies of Government. The whole field is thus automatically distributed.

So far as current apprenticeship is concerned, or what is left of it, and training in the professions and semiprofessions, that is part of another story. At all events, none of it belongs in principle in the Common School.

VIII. VOCATIONAL GUIDANCE AND PLACEMENT

So much for Vocational Instruction. Vocational Guidance and Placement are, however, quite a different matter.

As we have seen in the discussion of Labor as institution, the great majority of people living in America today find their places in the world in employment, in the service of some individual or corporation, or of the Government; their primary economic place is in receipt of wages or salaries. The generation which was born during and soon after the Civil War was the last of which it could truly be said that career is open to talent, that any boy's place in the world depends upon himself, that there is room for everybody under the reign of our institutions. With the disappearance of the frontier in the midst of the practically unrestricted immigration which lasted down to the war of 1914–18, in the presence of the increasing mechanization of industry and the wholesale invasion of gainful employment by women, all that world of free opportunity came to an end. But the ideology has been slow to disappear out of the mores. It is still urged upon boys, and the latter are looked down upon more or less if they do not find places which do not exist.

Perhaps it was never true that any of us, save in rare and happy circumstances, could ever actually choose a career; but we had little difficulty in finding some kind of a career. Be that as it may, young people have to learn the conditions under which all kinds of careers must be lived, including the present demand for personal services in each, to learn for what they are best suited and accept the verdict, to renounce the glamour of the professions and still more the prospect of great wealth as the end of all earthly ambitions.

INSTRUCTION

Having consideration of the whole vocational situation of today, as it is revealed in the census tables and in special studies of employment, it appears that the following are the points to be stressed in the course, the units if you please.

I. The Lure of White-Collar Jobs

Not everybody who can contrive to graduate from high school and college can hope at once to find an important or even an attractive place in paid employment. There are far too many candidates. But the possible openings at lower levels, or what have always been considered lower, are numerous for well-educated young people. Such places are always as genuinely worthy of respect as their incumbents make them.

II. Number Required in Every Calling Is Relatively Constant

The idea is still very prevalent that there is unlimited supply of everything somewhere, including jobs. I suppose that it comes down to us from the frontier period. In truth the number to be hired in relation to population does not vary a great deal from decade to decade in normal times. On the whole, it must in the long run show a tendency to fall, so long as processes become more and more mechanized. Otherwise, processes would not be mechanized.

III. Recruitment Required by the Learned Professions

Approximate recruitment required annually by typical professions in order to make good losses due to death and retirement, and in order to extend professional service to unserviced areas or callings.

IV. New Professions or Semiprofessions

The tendency is to professionalize many callings which were formerly looked upon as requiring neither extended education nor special training. Notable are various permanent positions in the civil service.

V. Major Kinds of Commercial, Industrial, and Nonprofessional Remunerative Activities Carried On in the United States

Descriptively analyzed as to occupational conditions and circumstances and requirements.

VI. Preparation Required

Special training in each of the typical employments, where such training can be had, and what it entails.

VII. Individual Enterprisership

Opportunities left in individual enterprisership and what is required:

    a) In personal qualities

    b) In capital

VIII. Homemaking and Bringing Up Children as a Career

IX. Schoolteaching and School Work as a Career

X. Shall I Go to College?

What is meant is the Liberal Arts College, so called.

A very large proportion of the total college enrolment today is in college in the expectation that jobs will be available somehow on graduation. The secondary school has some obligation to see that the prospective college entrants among its graduates are under no delusions in that respect. No doubt the college graduate does stand a materially better chance of finding a place, but pupils should be made to understand what that means and how far it is true.

PLACEMENT

An ancient function of the School, pursued until recently in a nonsystematic but often effective manner, is vocational placement. Principals of high and elementary schools here and there have long kept in touch with local employers, or perhaps rather the local employers have kept in touch with them in quest of likely boys, and have placed many of their graduates or those who have been leaving school. But is placement a proper function of the School in modern times, not to say a responsibility?

Of course, it has no place in the Curriculum, and this is a work on the Curriculum and not on School Management. It is, however, germane to the Curriculum in the connection which we are at present discussing. Administratively, it doubtless belongs in those pupil services which are incidental to the character of the School as minor community.

Certainly it is no exclusive responsibility of the School. In the first place, because there is a presumptive responsibility on the graduate to find a place for himself; and, in the second place, the responsibility of the graduate's family undoubtedly precedes that of the School. Nevertheless, the School is the place in great range of relationships at which the younger generation makes contact with the world outside. So long as such relationships exist, the school has a function therein, and a responsibility, on the principle that where a person or institutional agency has peculiar opportunities there it has peculiar responsibilities.

But vocational placement is a heavy responsibility, for it is of necessity more or less playing Providence with the pupil. Where the function is established in a bureau, as it doubtless must be in a large school, the placement officer needs to be a big man in every sense. Our school and college placement bureaus leave much to be desired, or at least many of them do. The tendency is to turn bureaucratic as all small people do. The climax is reached in university bureaus where Masters and Doctors are turned over for their chance in the world to routinist girls. Perhaps the most conspicuous failure is likely to arise when the placement officer is not strong enough to resist petty intrigue and favoritism and to prevent them from getting a foothold in his own office.

CHAPTER XIV

HEALTH

FEW people would ever think of Health as institution. In the common use of terms, health is the name for a bodily condition. More than that, it is symbolic of normality in sundry directions, wherever in fact we sense an organic condition as distinguished from a mechanical. Thus we speak of mental health, and about that conception there have been for ages not only cults but more or less scientific discipline. We further speak of social health and that quite rightly, for, regardless of sociological disciplines, we intuitively feel that there are abnormal conditions in Society as well as normal. In truth, wherever we have spoken of a society as a "going concern," I suppose we have had in mind social normality, a healthy condition of the body politic and economic and juristic.

Nevertheless, Health is also institution. Perhaps we might better say _sanitation_, and we might indeed do so were it not for the fact that the term has acquired somewhat special connotations as a branch of Medicine.

We do not go far in our study of evolving Civilization before we come upon folkways which have had an obviously sanitary implication, even though the people studied had not the least idea of logical principle. More often perhaps, we come upon ridiculous ritualistic practices which were thought to ward off disease. Sometimes, individuals were put to death because they were believed to have had an unfavorable effect upon the health of the tribe. Throughout all the tangle of absurdities, however, runs the thread of some sense about sanitation, and everywhere the feeling for the public health. And so it goes all down the story of advancing Civilization: peoples have commonly had practices, of which quarantine is the best example, which in fact had sanitary import, whether the people knew the how and why or not; and the practices have survived because they had sanitary utility. Moreover, epidemics or widespread bodily weakness have tended to be felt as a reproach to the tribe itself, usually interpreted as punishment meted out by the gods. We had a curious illustration of the ancient social feeling, when medical examination of prospective soldiers in our last war showed a shameful percentage of bodily weakness and unfitness. We felt it to be a reproach to our community life.

So in its blundering way the race has worked out a system of ideas and practices which, originating in the common sense and need of mankind, has expanded, become organized and refined, and has eventually become a scientific system. It is so far capable of being recognized as a fundamental condition of living together in Society and in the presence of a hostile environment that the behavior of contagious diseases is the very epitome of social existence. Certainly, no less than any other of the universal institutions which we have studied, Health is also universal and a major element in the fabric of Civilization. It is that which makes it an indefeasible part of the Curriculum of the Common School.

But why justify it on these grounds? Is not the practical reason enough in the minds of all sensible people? The sufficient answer is that eminently sensible people have not considered the practical reason good enough until within a generation or less. If they admitted its importance, they did not admit its compelling force.

CURRENT NOTIONS OF WHAT CONSTITUTES HEALTH EDUCATION

The current notions of "health education," so called—and by "current" I mean the last forty years or so, with a great impulse in the years following the war—seem to be centered about the following activities:

1. Informal talks on hygiene with some physiological implications widely and persistently adhered to. Be it understood, however, that in the absence of any consistent theory of the Curriculum prevalently held, this much is in the nature of fashion, here this year and gone a few years hence.

Nevertheless, out of this phase of instruction, there can be demonstrated, as I believe, an outstanding contribution of public instruction to the social achievement of the schools. Reference has already been made to it as illustration of the social conception of public instruction making good. In truth, it is altogether probable that there have been in history but few instances of peoples among whom health intelligence has been so generally distributed as is now the case in the United States.

That intelligence is to be attributed to three school products:

First, to the reading capacity among the masses of the population, at least in the primary sense of reading. It may be doubted that as much as 70 per cent of our adult population can as yet read in anything more than the primary sense of being able to extract meaning from the printed page in short paragraphs or headlines; but 70 per cent is a great deal when it comes to definite effects upon the mores.

Second, to the production of intelligence among the masses by rather more than two generations of effective science teaching in high schools.

Third, and specifically, to the generation of health intelligence by persistent teaching of hygiene.

No doubt it might well be argued that the very passable intelligence which we now see could not have existed but for the advances in Medicine. That is doubtless true; it is equally true that there would be no mechanical intelligence, in which our people are admittedly proficient, if there were no science of mechanics and no machines. The cure of disease is no different in semi-illiterate parts of the world than here, nor are the principles of physiology and pathology different. Few, however, would claim that medical advance alone has as yet produced so high a level of health intelligence in the remoter parts of Turkey as exists here.

It is very probably true that what we have in mind could scarcely have come to exist had it not been for the admirable lay books and newspaper articles prepared by competent medical men. And yet note:

a) That the books and articles would have had no readers had it not been for the fact that the schools have taught their pupils to read. Bear in mind that our "reading public" goes back only to about 1880. Furthermore,

b) That there would have been no reading public for the books and articles themselves had not the schools produced a generation largely equipped with the health and medical ideas with which to read. For every such medical lay book, it would be easy to find one equally good in the general field of economics, but there is little economic intelligence of any sort discernible in the general public. In one field the schools have distributed the appropriate ideas; in the other, they have not.

2. Second in the list of notions which seem to constitute our current ideas of instruction in Health is Medical Inspection of schools, and in the better schools a medical officer or school nurse as a regular member of the staff.

3. Then come free clinics, and free lunches for undernourished children.

4. And then plays and games, on the theory that they furnish bodily exercise which is so essential to good health.

5. Finally, organized athletics—one of our particular national scandals.

HOW MUCH OF THIS BELONGS TO THE SCHOOLS

In clearing out the underbrush which has grown up in the schools in our present field, the first thing would seem to be to raise the question, "How much of the foregoing belongs to the School on any count, Health or other?"

1. *The purpose* found in instruction in hygiene, despite the fact that it is usually unsystematic, is evidently in itself a Curriculum purpose. Instruction would be justified in intent, even if it were not justified in its results, as it apparently is.

2. *Medical inspection* as such is thoroughly unjustified, either as part of the normal school activities or to be supported on the school budget. It is no part of instruction in Health.

Medical inspection of schools is conducted primarily in the interest of the current public health and not primarily in the interest of the health of pupils save as they are part of the public. Its primary purpose is to detect the presence of contagious diseases among pupils, to take measures looking toward quarantine, and otherwise to forestall epidemics. It is, further, police work intended to see that sanitary ordinances and laws are enforced in the construction and operation of school buildings. It is in the domain of the Health Department of Government. It differs in no essential function from inspection of other buildings where people congregate, from the reports required of physicians who are attending adults or children in sickness, from the collection of vital statistics, and from other branches of public health work.

3. *School medical service*, covering continuous oversight of children and youth in the school community, administration of first aid, assignment to the regular physician, and periodic physical examination of all pupils, is, on the other hand, eminently justified as ancillary to the formal requirements of Health as a curricular discipline. It is part of school management and one of the justifiable pupil services. I do not say that it is imperative as part of the program in Health instruction.

School medical service does not, on the other hand, import medical treatment, save for minor and casual ailments. The school exists, in this general respect: (*a*) to conserve the health of pupils while they are in its charge; (*b*) to minister to normal bodily development; and (*c*) to breed up intelligence in respect to Health.

The question may well arise, "Why discriminate between medical inspection and school medical service?" If staff members are needed, why not have them perform both services? that is to say, have the school physician or school nurse do the medical inspection? That no doubt is possible, but two fundamental issues should be clear:

a) If the school physician serves also as medical inspector, he is necessarily under two authorities which follow diverse interests. If, on the other hand, the medical inspector acts as school physician, what ought to be intensive and systematic will become casual and unsystematic. I am confident that most experienced schoolmasters would agree with me that even the best of medical inspectors seldom have any particular educational interest or intelligence. That is normal and natural, for their essential interest lies elsewhere.

b) School medical service, on the other hand, is concerned with oversight of the physical development of pupils, the detection of unwholesome organic tendencies, and indeed the effect of daily regimen upon the health and mental normality of pupils. It is neither a police function nor yet one of inspection and report.

All this is not to say that there is not abundant opportunity for the two services to co-operate.

4. *School clinics.*—A *clinic* is a regular enterprise for the administration of medical treatment to individuals. In our schools, the original clinic, so far as I know, was that for dental treatment. But once concede that dental treatment is appropriate to the activities of schools, and there is no logical stopping-place short of turning the school into a hospital.

Dental clinics were originally supposed to administer treatment only to the children of parents who were too poor to pay for the service. But once concede that the activity is appropriate to the schools, and there is no logical stopping-place short of assumption of any or all the functions of the Department of Charities and Corrections. Most schoolmasters who have had experience with such clinics know well enough that it is difficult if not impossible to prevent abuse at the hands of parents who are well able to pay for treatment themselves.

Allied to the clinic in the schools are free lunches for undernourished children. Malnutrition is no doubt one of the capital causes of inability to learn. That being the case, it is easy to take the short course and provide lunches as part of the school budget, regardless of the disastrous consequences of setting out on a road which leads to demoralization, the very thing which the school exists to prevent.

5. *Athletics.*—Parallel to school clinics, but a far greater abuse, is to be found in interscholastic athletic contests open to the public, especially in football and basketball. As we shall presently see, plays and games and organized athletics have a rightful place in the school community (related to instruction.) So in the proper

sphere have interscholastic contests. But the revival of the ancient pancration in football has its immense appeal to the battle lust which is still present in the crowd—provided it can be sated vicariously. Hence it is that what is in its nature a legitimate school activity, having within it the possibility of contribution to bodily health and normal neuromuscular development, is diverted into what is together a public spectacle. If the public desires that kind of entertainment, the proper place for it is in a public park, carried on and supported in the charge of, and on the budget of, the Public Parks Department; or else, as in the case of the much superior American game of baseball, by private enterprise.

All these things are illustrations of the working of a false principle, namely, ignoring the functional distinctions which are part of the framework of the well-ordered community. Clinics for children as well as adults belong to the hospital organization. Care for the needs of the necessitous man and his family belongs to organized charity or else to the municipal department of Charities and Corrections. Public athletic entertainment belongs to the Public Parks and much better to private enterprise.

MAIN LINES OF HEALTH ACTIVITIES IN SCHOOL

With the foregoing historical survey and critique in mind, let us turn to the content of what does belong to the school, either as legitimate and proper part of the exercises of the school as minor community, or else as directly or indirectly related to instruction in Health, including Curriculum proper.

I. HYGIENE

First of all, here is establishment everywhere of what has proved to be the most productive side of health instruction, namely, Hygiene.

The course is informal, in the sense that it cannot well be laid out in learning and teaching units. That does not imply, however, that it need be casual. It is much like what we have found in the inculcation of right habits in English Usage and Composition and in instruction in Morality, or character education. In actual content it ought to be related to and governed by the course in Human Physiology, with which we shall presently deal. In the levels of the school in which departmentalization is undesirable, in what we commonly call the elementary school, the classroom teacher is mainly responsible. At the departmentalized levels, the task falls to the personnel administration, and to the school medical service if such is maintained. All in all, the teaching must be individual for the most part, supplemented by pertinent talks to the school as a whole, or to groups.

II. HEALTH REGIMEN

Second is health regimen as part of the discipline of the school. By that is meant oversight of the pupil's ways of life as they have bodily significance. It is part of inculcation of the moral quality of Cleanliness. It includes especially:

a) Correction of posture and carriage. Lazy posture and slouchy carriage appear to be not only bad habits from the standpoint of Health, but fundamentally vicious in the moral foundations of personality. Self-respect has made a good start—and self-respect is everywhere and always the foundation of self-government—when the pupil has acquired a well-set-up posture and carriage. Setting-up exercises may be excellent instructional means, and military drill properly conducted is likely to be productive. These, however, are instructional means to an educational end. The Curriculum content is *posture* and *carriage*.

b) Oversight of hygienic individual habits in general, but including especially:

1) Care of teeth.

2) Physical cleanliness. Some schools have made large contributions here through the use of school baths. In short, the extension of the use of bathrooms and bathing in American homes has probably been traceable, in part at least, to the effect of school instruction upon the mores.

Nevertheless, school bathing facilities are a means to an end and not an end in themselves. Schools in neighborhoods in which most homes are suitably equipped need no bathrooms of their own, save as they are appurtenance of the gymnastic equipment. A dirty child may be sent home to take a bath.

3) Check-up on dietary habits at home. I have known more than one instance in which a competent principal rendered great service to families whose cultural status was not to be doubted, by calling their attention to perverse dietary practices which were having a discernible effect upon a child's school work as well as bodily growth.

4) Regular physical examination at the hands of a school health service, where such is maintained, is allied to Health Regimen. Perhaps the service ought to be given an independent status as one of the primary elements in the Health program. A fairly thorough physical check-up, at least once a year, on or near the pupil's birthday, gives us a really factual basis for the whole program in Hygiene and Health Regimen. It is worth all the standardized tests ever invented.

SPORTS

Outdoor or gymnastic sports are presumed to have a direct influence on health. The first, and to a large extent the second, are self-motivated in that they are responses to one of the four or five organic appetites, namely, that which appears as love of bodily exercise. Gymnastic exercises no doubt are sometimes a legitimate part of health regimen, but with that exception it does not necessarily follow that all of them are justifiable as organized school activities. Some are and some are not.

In any event, they are all means to an end, so far as instruction is concerned, and not ends in themselves. To make any of them the objective is to mistake instrument for desirable product. The Curriculum objective is Health and normal physical development and not sports. The objective is especially Health intelligence.

This particular form of hypostasis, of confusing means and ends, can be found, I will not say in all schools, but certainly in a great many. It appears in the kindergarten and lower school when the teachers in physical instruction feel it to be necessary to teach children to play, instead of allowing the children to follow their own unpestered ways. It appears farther up when we erect an expensive gymnasium and find that it is devoted mainly to basketball and to teaching pupils a whole round of games which earlier generations took for granted and learned as they desired them. It is found finally when a college converts itself into a country club by fostering and supporting outdoor sports which the students of the day apparently cannot manage by themselves.

Where outdoor sports apart from the school are possible, the legitimate program of instruction will encourage them, notably long tramps under all sorts of weather conditions. Supplementary to that are gymnasiums not for formal exercises but for indoor sports. Ideally, of course, every school ought to be equipped with a playing field ample in area for all the games and organized intramural athletics which can be followed by the school enrolment. I believe the best school I ever saw, from the sports standpoint, had, as I recall, twenty-two football fields for six hundred boys, a proportionate number of diamonds and tennis courts, and it supported two crews for older boys on a neighboring lake. But it had no interscholastic athletics and never appeared in the newspapers.

In short, sport is natural diversion and nonprofessional or nothing. When it comes under tutelage and direction, it ceases to be sport. Further, sport has no peculiar relation to bodily health or to Health as Curriculum content. All normal and wholesome bodily exercise has beneficial effect on bodily upbuilding, farm work as well as winter sports.

This brings us to Athletics, a form of sport which does have distinct educational bearings.

III. ATHLETICS

The etymology of the term denotes either combat or struggling for a prize. The connotation is muscular strength and attainment. In our present school use, one which has long obtained with our people, it signifies concretely various track events, baseball, football, basketball, hockey, tennis, and sundry others which have a vogue for a time and then disappear. In all these there is the idea of contest.

Athletics is institution.—In the sense in which the term is thus used, Athletics is institutional. If we organize it and make it part of the Curriculum, we properly do so because it is worth while for its own sake. What enters into school athletics today has had in one form or another a history which runs back into the Stone Age. Our Indians had it. It perhaps reached its culmination among the Greeks, but it seems to have been only less prized by the English. It is folkway which has persisted, has satisfied human need in the social aspects of the latter, has become organized. It is universal in our sense of universality, but it cannot, rationally considered, be held to be a prime essential in holding the community together, nor necessarily an element in the structure of Civilization. In other words, it is not major institution. Practically speaking, we may say that, while Athletics is not an indefeasible element in the Curriculum, properly understood and administered it is more than a useful instrument in instruction; it is an institutional element in instruction. That cannot be said of any other form of sport. Here we have something that is a branch of Aesthetics, and moreover one which cannot be practiced in its institutional sense save upon ethical foundations.

It has a culture, at least to the extent of a symbolism which has penetrated the general body of Language. We find the symbolism in such expressions as "I have fought a good fight; I have finished my course; I have kept the faith: henceforth there is laid up for me a crown of righteousness."

When we study a school which maintains a sound athletic administration, and shows appreciation of the meaning and significance of the institution, we are commonly impressed that the latter as practiced in such a school contributes quite as much to Morality as to Health. In truth, sportsmanship, as revealed in good athletics, is not far from being an epitome of Morality. Fair play is the center of its being, and fair play is Equity in the concrete. There can be no fair play in contests without the practice of courtesy to opponents. Fortitude and Loyalty are of its very essence, especially that phase of Fortitude which accepts defeat with equanimity, and so are Cleanliness and Co-operation. It does not follow that the accomplished athlete will automatically cherish these qualities outside the field of athletics. Indeed he will not do so unless he has generalized his experience and come to accept the qualities as his own. It is the function of instruction to bring generalization to pass, but there is no generalization save out of experience in the concrete; and the good school athlete has had a discipline which gives ideational background for some of the finest of human qualities. A youth can be a good athlete, even though he never wins a contest.

Per contra.—Athletics conducted as public spectacle and preparation for public spectacle, in which everything is focused on winning, into which the degradation of bought players has crept, which is featured *ad nauseam* in the newspapers, so much so that a successful schoolboy player is acclaimed in publicity comparable to that which might be awarded a great statesman—all this is as degrading and debauching as good athletics may be constructive and uplifting.

That is especially true when the player is made the sport of an excited mob. He then is reduced to the level of a Roman slave gladiator. I suppose that most college teachers who have acquired the confidence of their students have known of cases in which college players have come to resent bitterly their exploitation, after coming to realize that all the slavery they had endured during training and games was in reality to be interpreted in terms of cheap prestige and gate receipts.

Athletics and Health.—No doubt Athletics sanely and rightly conducted may contribute materially to health, both bodily and mental, but it does not follow that the place of Athletics in the recognized program of studies is primarily for the sake of the program in Health. Athletics is at bottom an aesthetic institution, and the heart of aesthetics is that the thing enjoyed is its own justification.

When the whole purpose, however, is success in winning an interscholastic contest, then such good effects as there may be are intensely individualistic, for only a small part of the pupil body receives any benefit whatever. Moreover, such contests yield constant temptations to overexertion, to strain on the heart particularly, to overdevelopment of respiratory areas and other tissues. The latter are often destined to become the seed ground of disease in after years when the active exertion of the playing field has ceased.

Altogether, the following canons may, with some confidence, be set up:

1. All pupils should participate in competitive games suited to their years and sex, except as excused or restrained through medical supervision.

2. All games which involve severe exertion should be under the strict supervision of the medical service.

3. The general public should not be admitted to school contests.

So far as bystanders are concerned, games are a school affair. If there be outsiders, they should be present only as invited guests and without paid admission. While these precepts seem to me to be logical inferences from our analysis of the place of athletic contests in the school, in making them I am not guided entirely by my own conclusions. Coaches who have been real sportsmen themselves have more than once assured me that, if the publicity attached to interscholastic contests were removed, the chief occasion for abuses would disappear.

4. So long as newspapers insist on featuring contests, then all forms of Athletics which are subject to this kind of publicity should for the time be dispensed with. Some of the best schools from the athletic standpoint that I have ever known adopted the consistent policy of restricting themselves to intramural contests, on the ground of escape from publicity alone.

5. Paid coaches as distinguished from regular teachers in the field of physical instruction should be dispensed with. After all, in sane Athletics, coaching is part of the game itself to be administered by those who engage in the game.

6. Finally, Athletics is in the school for school purposes only, and not for excellence in the world of sports. That implies that

in track events, striving for world's records should be ruled out, unless the record be one properly set up as attained under legitimate school conditions.

IV. PHYSIOLOGY

Conceive the teaching of Hygiene in the Common School and what we have called Health Regimen to be at the best, all that is requisite and proper, and suppose Athletics to be properly conducted, with due regard to bodily development as well as to the moral qualities which may come out of it, what have we got in terms of educational values?

A great deal; so much that a full generation universally so instructed would raise the Health intelligence in the mores to the level which has now been attained by the best pupils in the best schools. But it would be limited to primary intelligence, that level in which the What is seen, but not the How and Why. So far there would be no intellectual framework on which the primary intelligence could be lifted to the secondary level in which ideas of a rational sort prevail. In this way.

The pupil who well knows that a swollen and sore finger is traceable to infection through becoming the host of a micro-organism, that tissue is breaking down and pus forming, and that certain medicaments may destroy the germ and thus remove the cause of the soreness, has achieved the What and to some extent the Why of intelligence; but he has no possible means of seeing his misfortune as a step leading to an understanding of the nature of Health.

So it is when he has been taught and has learned the nature and importance of pure food and water and milk.

So when he has learned that good teeth are important, mainly in the teaching that they will otherwise become foci of infection and decay.

That is all well; he can read and profit from simple health articles, but he cannot see the bearing of the articles. Digestion is only a name to him, the lymphatic system which is so critically important at times in matters of infection is but a medical term, and calories are known to be a good thing, but that is about all.

He knows not the How and Why of things, and still less does he have in his stock of ideas any means for relating it all together.

So the culmination of the Common School course in Health is elementary Human Physiology. Nor is that all. The body is the first term in our material environment. Education itself is adjustment. It follows that intelligence about the body is required by sound educational theory, regardless of the argument from Health.

In the old secondary school which had pretty much disappeared by the turn of the century, the course in Physiology was found nearly everywhere. It was often called Physiology and Hygiene, but there was not much Hygiene about it as a general thing. There was, however, a great deal of Anatomy. Anatomy is not understandable at the school level, but it is rather matter of description and memorization. There is some éclat in being able to speak familiarly of the tibia and humerus and clavicle, to say nothing of the ventricles of the brain and the fissure of Silvius. Such people must "know a lot." Finally a good deal of what enters into an elementary course was not known to medical science itself in the nineties.

In the pedagogical revolution which came toward the end of the nineteenth century, all that was "thrown out of the schoolhouse window," to use the favorite language of the iconoclasts and pedagogical sans-culottes. There, as elsewhere in the existing curriculum, was little or no attempt to use constructive criticism based upon pedagogical insight and knowledge, and hold fast to that which was good. What was wrong with the course was:

First, that it violated the cardinal principle of the concrete before the abstract. Direct teaching of Hygiene came first.

Second, like all the school sciences of the early part of the present century, it ignored apperceptive sequence. General Science supplied the place of an introductory course.

Third, the course tended to include an unteachable subject, namely, Anatomy, and was otherwise specialized in content. One of the complaints was that the course essayed to teach more than the doctors knew—which was very likely true.

Still and all, some of those old school physiologies were veritable textbook classics; and, after all, the course did give the only course there was in animal Biology. Asa Gray's school botanies gave the other side.

The modern course is, in the first place, a science course, and it should be organized and taught in accordance with the principles laid down in chapter vi.

In the second place, it ought to be definitive rather than descriptive, that is to say, something to be understood should be set up. We can always attain that end in an elementary sense by approaching a course from the functional point of view, What is there that has to get done? How does it get done, and Why can it get done that way?

While we cannot properly make the objectives anatomical in character, Physiology without some idea of the gross anatomy of the body and approximate location of the major organs is a course in a vacuum. For the most part, however, I suggest that the gross anatomy be treated incidentally through the use of good text illustrations and wall charts, as progress in Physiology makes desirable. Anatomy is thus used as an instrument in the learning process and not as a series of objectives.

Most of the existing texts for school and college use which I have examined err in the same way in which in the earlier chapter we found most texts in Science defective. They suffer from detail poorly elaborated. Apparently it is hard for an academic writer to leave out anything. He rather simplifies his language, but includes so much that he has no space for adequate exposition and treatment in general. After all, even a writer of advanced treatises need not be illiterate in his composition. Words of more than one syllable seldom give much trouble even to school children. Too much detail unloaded in a few pages leaves us all foundered. You do that in writing a dictionary or reference book, but not a treatise or school text, which is but a minor treatise. It must be remembered that medical students require six years altogether to get a working knowledge of Physiology and what is subsidiary to it. A good text follows the principle: *Not many things, but much explanation for each thing.*

We are fearfully and wonderfully made, and natural products like the body were not made as simple and foolproof as possible. If we set up a course which asserts that the stomach does thus and so, the brain something else, the liver another thing again, the medical scientist will hold up his hands in horror at our lack of accuracy. And yet that is just what an elementary course must do, and it is accurate enough to breed lay intelligence, and that is all we need. After all, the stomach in the main does do a certain thing, the kidneys in the main carry out a certain function. The pupil is bewildered by unnecessary discriminations between cortex and medulla, and if we succeed in getting him to talk glibly about the Bundle of His or the Islands of Langerhans, we shall merely inspire him to emulate a Philo Vance mystery story.

UNITS IN HUMAN PHYSIOLOGY

I. The Skeleton or Bony Framework
  1. As framework on which the body is hung
  2. Adaptation of plan to the mechanical work of support—importance of posture and carriage
  3. As protection to organs
  4. As system of levers
  5. The gross structure of bones
  6. The bone marrow as source of red corpuscles

II. Tissue
  1. The cell and cellular structure—differentiated cells
  2. Muscular tissue
    a) Voluntary muscles
    b) Involuntary muscles
  3. Nerve tissue
  4. Lining and surface tissue
  5. Bony tissues
  6. Connective tissue for support and separation

III. The Muscular System
  1. Muscles act by contraction and relaxation
  2. Function is to carry out movement

3. Muscles which are under the control of the will—voluntary
4. Muscles whose action is automatic—involuntary
5. Immense number of them large and small for all sorts of movements
6. Connection with bony framework and levers
7. Connection with nerve trunks and fibers—innervation and inhibition
8. Principle of opposition in muscles
9. By combining actions of different muscles, almost infinitely a larger number of movements are possible than there are muscles in the body
10. Muscle is also an organ by which heat energy can be transformed into energy of motion

FUEL AND GROWTH AND REPAIR
(Maintenance of the Body as a Going Concern)

IV. Food
1. The growing body requires material with which to build new and additional cells
2. Either the growing or the adult body requires repairs to worn-out tissue
3. Even the body at rest requires tissue extension or repairs, heat energy in every cell to maintain bodily heat, and to make possible the internal movements
4. Tissue is worn out much more rapidly when the body is in movement doing work
5. The amount of energy required to do a particular piece of work is measurable, and the energy must be supplied in the form of heat units, called calories
6. Needed tissue-building materials are supplied in the food we eat, and heat units in this food and in the air which we breathe
7. The basal food materials are:
   a) Protein, chiefly for tissue growth and repair
   b) Carbohydrates—sugar and starch—for heat
   c) Fats for heat energy and for storage in body fats
   d) Sundry salts which are useful in aiding the chemical process by which foods are prepared to be taken up by the cells
   e) Minerals for teeth and bones and iron for blood
8. Accessory are:
   a) Water to act as solvent and to supply body needs
   b) Vitamins which are elements in foods, the lack of which retards growth and is responsible for certain organic maladies such as rickets

9. Food is valuable as it has the basal and accessory materials and heat units in right quantity and proportion

10. The process of preparing food for taking up by the body is called Digestion

V. Digestion

1. Digestion begins with cooking, which reduces food to more manageable form for bodily digestion

2. Bodily digestion takes place in the alimentary canal, which extends from the mouth to the anal opening

3. Mastication breaks up food mechanically, and salivation turns the starch into a sugar

4. Swallowing is accomplished by a succession of muscular contractions

5. Passes down into the stomach, where it is churned over and over, mixed with gastric juice, and by it the proteins partly broken down

6. Empties into the small intestine, where it is mixed with juice from the pancreas which further reduces the protein and reduces the sugar to simpler form; and with bile from the liver which aids in the emulsification of the fats

7. Ferments secreted by various organs appear in the alimentary canal and make chemical action possible without being affected themselves

8. The mass in the intestine is moved on by twisting motions called peristalsis

9. When the food has been reduced to a condition in which it can be taken up by the blood, digestion is complete

VI. Assimilation

1. To convey digested food to cells of all sorts, a fluid circulating medium is necessary; this the blood and the lymphatics supply

2. The minutely digested food materials pass through membranes by osmosis largely from the small intestine into the surrounding blood stream and lymph

3. The blood carries food products directly to cells and indirectly through escape of blood plasma into the lymph, in which the cells of the body are bathed

4. An essential in the process is the sweep of the blood through the liver and pancreas

5. In the liver an internal secretion turns excess blood sugar into something more resembling starch and stores it for future use, sometimes an emergency

6. The pancreas also secretes internally a substance which makes possible the complete preparation of blood sugar for absorption by the cells

7. Liver also develops protein waste into urea for passage to the kidneys
8. Proteins go to building up and repair of tissue, and the oxidation of some of it goes into heat

Fats are burned into heat, the most abundant source, and stored in tissue fat against the day of need. Sugar is burned into heat energy especially for the muscles, converted into liver sugar is stored for emergency needs, and excess is converted into carbohydrate fat.

We turn now to Circulation and Respiration, intending to come back to Fuel and Repair in Excretion and Metabolism.

VII. Circulation
  A. Blood
    1. Composition
      a) Red corpuscles—function as oxygen carriers
      b) White corpuscles
        (1) Leukocytes—defense against invading germs.
        (2) Thrombocytes—coagulating effect.
      c) Plasma
    2. Blood flows under pressure in a single direction
    3. Arterial blood carries oxygen to arterioles and capillaries and thus to cells
    4. Oxidation of food particles the chief means of producing heat energy
    5. Carbon dioxide results from oxidation of fats and carbohydrates
    6. Venous blood takes up waste products from the cells including carbon dioxide, for transportation to
      a) Kidneys
      b) Lungs
    7. Venous blood flows only toward the heart
    8. Thence it is pumped to the lungs and flows through the lung tissue, where it meets the oxygen of the air and exchanges carbon dioxide for fresh oxygen
    9. Thus it becomes arterial blood, is returned to the heart, and thence pumped into the arteries, into the arterial circulation, until it returns in the veins as venous blood
    10. The heart is an automatic muscular organ
  B. The Lymph.
    1. Character
    2. The lymphatics
    3. Circulation in the lymphatics is maintained by movements of the body, since a system of check valves prevents it from moving in any other direction than toward the heart

    4. Receives digested food products by osmosis through intestinal walls and also the laden plasma from blood channels

    5. Hence to the cells which are bathed in lymph

    6. Similarly collects waste from cells and with them flows directly into the venous circulation

VIII. Respiration

    1. Respiration is alternate inspiration and expiration of atmospheric air in and from the lungs

    2. Gross character of lung tissue

    3. Is kept up by alternate expansion and relaxation of chest walls by diaphragm

    4. Lungs are not themselves active—they fill with air when the chest expands and are emptied, except for residual air, when it relaxes

    5. Oxygen and carbon doixide are exchanged by process of diffusion and osmosis

    6. Diffusion is kept up by alternate higher and lower pressure of carbon dioxide pressure in the blood of the lungs

IX. Excretion

    1. Excretion gets rid of waste products which become poisonous if they remain in the body

    2. Waste arises:

        a) Out of the oxidation of food products in the cells in the process of liberating energy

        b) As chemical by-products in digestion and assimilation and bodily activity in general

        c) As fragements of worn-out tissue

    3. Organs take part in elimination:

        a) Water loaded with impurities

            (1) Through sweat glands of the skin, and exudate from lung passages

            (2) Through the kindeys

        b) Undigested food products through the anus or exterior opening of the alimentary canal.

        c) Unassimilated protein is converted into urea in the liver, carried to the kidneys in the blood stream, and there filtered out and discharged into the urinary bladder, and along with water discharged in the act of urination.

X. Secretion

    1. Secretion, on the other hand, is a process found in glands of various kinds by which various substances are prepared and discharged into the blood stream and alimentary canal for functions which they serve in the bodily economy

2. Some glands secrete substances which are discharged externally, notably:

    a) Milk from the mammary glands of the breast

    b) Sebum from the sebaceous glands of the skin, the function of which is to keep the skin soft and moist

3. The various digestive juices are secretions discharged through ducts

4. There are also ductless glands which prepare substances which regulate the chemistry of the body and its growth, and discharge into the blood stream through the circulation of the gland itself

5. The substances are called hormones when they serve to speed up processes and chalones when they serve to retard

6. The ductless glands are chiefly:

    a) The pancreas, which also has a duct, secreting a hormone which facilitates the oxidation of blood sugar

    b) Thyroid, which seems to control the rate of metabolism

    c) Pituitary, which regulates bodily growth

    d) Adrenals, the hormone of which increases blood pressure and directly or indirectly stimulates the flow of liver sugar into the blood stream and its change into blood sugar

        The adrenal secretion seems to be in the nature of an emergency call when great exertion is required.

XI. Metabolism

1. Every cell is constantly being built up by assimilation and then drawn down in the production of energy

2. The whole process is called metabolism or the rate at which life goes on

3. At the lowest, when the body as a whole is resting, metabolism goes on, for the internal process must be maintained, and body heat; this level is known as basal metabolism

4. Muscular exercise, or body tension as in mental work, requires great expenditure of energy; hence metabolism must rise

XII. Regulation

1. The body must work as a whole and be able to function properly at rest, under ordinary conditions of activity, and in emergencies

2. The great agency in regulation is the nervous system

3. In internal affairs, nearly all processes are automatic; they are carried on by the organ concerned without external stimulus

4. If that were all, there would be no team work among the different organs and processes

5. The nervous system as a whole reaches every part of the body and is itself put together under the ultimate authority of the brain

6. It may be said to turn a set of individual organs, each acting by

itself, into a complete organism in which each part does its work in the right order and right relation

7. So the main purpose of the nervous system is said to be integration
8. Most emergency situations arise outside the body, and so do all problems involving behavior of the body as a whole
9. That requires integration of the body and its environment

GETTING ALONG IN THE WORLD

XIII. The Nervous System

1. The *central nervous system* is concerned with making external contacts and translating them into both muscular and visceral response
2. Is composed of:
   a) The brain
   b) The spinal cord
   c) Nerves reaching eyes, ears, nose, tongue, skin, and muscles
3. Efferent and afferent nerves and ganglia
4. Ganglion is a center in which afferent impulses and transformed into efferent impulses and action; ganglia are scattered all over the body
5. Reflex action occurs when an afferent impulse is transformed into an efferent impulse in a ganglion without being transmitted to the brain and entering consciousness
6. The brain is the highest center in the body, and afferent impulses entering the brain from the sensory organs ordinarily enter consciousness. Efferent impulses go directly to lower centers rather than to the efferent nerve endings in the muscles
7. Parts of the brain also regulate directly the higher vital functions in heart and lungs
8. The cerebellum or little brain co-ordinates muscular motions, especially those engaged in locomotion
9. The *autonomic nervous system* is apart from but connected with the central system
10. It regulates the visceral functions, especially those of digestion and assimilation

XIV. External Adjustment

1. The body must not only work right in internal affairs but it must work right with reference to getting on in an external world
2. Hence organs of sensation through which news comes in from outside and organs of action through which the body responds to the news
3. The eye as organ of vision
   a) Essentially a lens for focusing light rays to make an image of an external object

  b) A screen on which the picture can appear—the retina

  c) A nerve which can transmit the appropriate picture to the optical center in the brain, whence it appears in consciousness

4. The ear as an organ of hearing

  a) An apparatus for picking up sound waves in the air and vibrating in response—the tympanum or ear drum

  b) An apparatus of small bones for transmitting vibration in the ear drum to lymph inclosed in a cavity

  c) An apparatus for converting lymph vibrations into nerve impulses

  d) Nerve connection which transmits nerve impulse to the auditory center in the brain and thence into consciousness

5. The ear as an organ for sensing equilibrium

  Semicircular canals in three planes, sensitive hairs and brain connections, which give sensation of disturbance to equilibrium

6. Tongue and nose as organs of taste and smell

  Provided with small organs which select chemical qualities in gaseous emanations, and nerve connections which give the respective sense in consciousness

7. Voluntary muscles as organs of motion and of sense

  a) Nerve impulses transmitted stimulate contraction and relaxation of muscles and thus control motion

  b) Afferent impulses from the muscles give muscular or kinaesthetic sense

8. Skin as organ of touch

  a) Nerve endings which give sense of touch or pressure

  b) Nerve endings which give sense of heat or cold

  c) Nerve endings which give sense of pain, but these are not peculiar to the skin; they occur in all parts of the body, external and internal, when notice of pain would be advantageous to self-preservation.

TEXTBOOK

  I have known teachers who could take the foregoing outline and, with the aid of reference books and pictorial illustrations, teach it. Most teachers need a textbook in the pupils' hands as background for their teaching. I estimate that such a text covering only the essentials involved in presentation and exposition would run to about 250 pages in ordinary schoolbook format. Beyond that, illustration, both pictorial and written, exercises, and applications, could well extend such a text to twice that number of pages, or justify an equivalent supplementary book.

CHAPTER XV

THE CURRICULUM AND THE PROGRAM

WE HAVE completed the task which was proposed in the Preface. There remains a sort of Epilogue intended to recur to the practical in school work and administration, stepping down in a sort of Horatian manner from the theoretical to the mundane. In other words, supposing all this to be true, what can be done about it?

Up to this point we have been dealing with the Curriculum conceived as the cultural content out of which formal General Education can emerge. We turn now for our valedictory to the Program, which means, I take it, the policy to be followed by a particular school, and often by a particular teacher, in growing up to the Curriculum.

IDEATIONAL BACKGROUND OF PUPILS

Long ago, in my early days as a schoolmaster and school inspector, what impressed me most about schools as they concretely exist was the cultural starvation of most school children. No matter how adept the teacher, it is seldom possible to use the teacher's supreme device of illustration because he or she can seldom say, "It is like this," for in the pupil's stock of ideas there was apt to be no "this" in the universe; the pupil was too ignorant to learn. Commonly enough, as the years went on, not recognizing the real cause, the teacher fell into that modern equivalent of total depravity, the doctrine of feeble-mindedness and its transition through easy stages of border-line cases and low grades to just plain stupidity.

Of the appeal to low mentality as the *deus ex machina* of pedagogical intransigence, I have shown the fallacy in chapter xi of *Basic Principles in Education.* True enough we do encounter instances of actual subnormality, but they are far from numerous

663

enough to account for anything like the total number of school failures.

On the other hand, poverty in ideational background is observable and identifiable, and its significance in the learning process is clear enough. It follows that the first article in school policy ought to be in building up the kind of ideational background that children who come from cultivated homes are likely—although not certainly—to possess.

A sensible kindergarten or kindergarten primary, provided it does not function as merely a nursery for children, is admirably adapted in form to that purpose. The building of rich background, through abundant children's reading and similar experience, needs, however, to go on all through the early years and then fade into the school library and its use.

RESPECT FOR CHILDREN'S CAPACITY

At various points throughout the work, I have written strongly of the established habit of belittling children's mental capacity, merely because they are young. At its best, that rests upon a false psychology, and, as I think, upon the feminine tendency of young teachers to baby and coddle little children. Even before the pupil has learned to read, it is astonishing to see how much they can learn of cultural material in a systematic way. The Curriculum need not seem so formidable when school people come to realize how much of it can be got out of the way by the time the typical child is twelve years of age.

SCHOOL CONTINUITY

In the third place, it would be a great help if the schoolmaster could permanently rid himself of the notion that elementary school, the several divisions and kinds of high schools, and junior colleges are things in themselves. They are not in principle, but on the contrary the normal school career is continuous, from the time the pupil has learned enough of the primary arts to be able to learn by studying, to educational maturity. Another phase of the same thing is promotion by years, or semiannually, on performance tests instead of promotion in terms of learnings acquired and tested as such.

PROGRAMMING

As soon as a class of children are started in the first year, at six years of age or younger—and children can begin to learn reading and number, earlier than that provided they have sufficient ideational background to read and count with—the Curriculum as discussed in the present volume can be followed. But note that what course comes first and what second and so on in sequence depends upon their ideational sequence and not upon any assumed process of organic mental development. And note further that not all the courses in any one chapter need to begin at approximately the same time or to be treated in sequence. For example, Bookkeeping in Commerce is relatively easy in conceptual quality for the reason that pupils ordinarily have had some experience in spending money by the time they are ten or twelve, whereas the course in Exchanges is relatively difficult since it is foreign to the experience of pupils. The experiential background in the latter must be built up descriptively as the course itself goes on.

A phase of programming is what we sometimes call pupil-programming. It often happens that pupils of meager background must be set back in order to get antecedent courses.

TEACHER QUALIFICATIONS

The fundamental parts of the Curriculum have long been taught. That is not to say that there is an abundance of well-qualified teachers available for even the old subjects, but they are more numerous than teachers in the newer and crucially important Civics, Politics, Commerce, and Industry.

Indeed, in my own judgment at least, there is needed training in subject matter more critically than in pedagogy. One who has been writing theoretical works in education as process for many years is not likely to belittle the importance of the science and art of teaching. But nobody can teach that which he does not know adequately. It is quite true that the academic notion which holds that anybody can teach anything which he knows sufficiently well is all but obviously fallacious; and the notion that teachers are born and not made is equally fallacious. Nevertheless, professional training so called, with the scientific facilities which are as yet available, to the detriment of academic preparation in subject matter, sets up a false emphasis.

TIME ALLOWANCE

We are ordinarily very sensitive as to how much time will be required for any kind of program.

It ought to be borne in mind that the issue is part of the ideology of the discontinuous school system and of the established practice of reckoning educational progress in terms of time spent rather than in terms of learnings acquired. The old American Common School had no such preconceptions, but a century of habituation to "time to be spent" has set up a sort of ingrained ideology which it is hard to break up.

If the conception of what constitutes sound pupil administration is reversed, it will in due season be found that the time problem will take care of itself. It ought to be noted that every course thoroughly learned in its units expands and organizes ideational background, and by the very fact makes it easier to master subsequent courses.

I should be ashamed to let this work pass out of my hands with time allowances altogether dismissed as inconsequential. I therefore present an estimate of the maximum amount of time that would be required by the Curriculum as presented, supposing that we could find teachers and staff qualified for the whole work.

We can get some kind of notion of the probable time consumption if we start with time actually used in good schools for the courses commonly offered at the present time or in recent times, and from that infer what would probably be needed for the whole Curriculum including the courses not commonly offered. In so doing, it is necessary to assume a time unit which can be used as a common denominator all the way from the beginning of the primary to the end of the secondary, or to the end of the junior college, as we now use that term. I fix upon the old three-month school term, or the quarter system as used in the universities which follow Harper's conception.

In the fourteen years beginning with the first year and ending with the junior college, or at about age twenty-one for the average school experience, there are 126 of these term units, during which pupils are always pursuing courses as schools now are and, if they do not suffer retardation, are completing courses. That is on the assumption that pupils are studying three subjects at a time, which is less than standard American practice.

Counting up the equivalent course allowances in the Curriculum as developed by the method of estimating which I have explained, there are 115—less than the number which are now commonly used.

Of course, this proves something touching the *order* of time requirements, but it does not prove a great deal. The outcome would probably be that the modern school would find itself on the spiral of progress immediately over but a good deal above the position of the old common school, which "they attended winters until they had got all they could." There is no special sanctity in age twenty-one, any more than there is in age eighteen or in age fourteen or twelve. The theoretically defensible Curriculum sets up no presumptions as to whether or not any particular pupil would complete it. It merely argues what is the valid cultural content of General Education.

ANOTHER STORY

But, after all, the present chapter suggests in a brief sketch what is in reality part of another extended study which might perhaps be entitled *School Structure and School System*.

SELECTED READING REFERENCES

The list here presented is not a bibliography in the common acceptation of that term. If it were, it would run to several times its present length. It is rather just what the title implies, a list of works which furnish an ample reading background for the book, which, it is hoped, will prove useful to school people in general, and in particular useful in the replenishment and extension of the libraries of teachers' colleges.

CURRICULUM STUDIES: ANCIENT AND MODERN

Trivium and Quadrivium—Seven Liberal Arts.
  Accounts may be found in the historical works of both Cubberley and Monroe.
BOBBITT, FRANKLIN. *The Curriculum.* 1918.
———. *How To Make a Curriculum.* 1924.
CHARTERS, W. W. *Curriculum Construction.* 1923.
FITZPATRICK, EDWARD A. (ed.). *St. Ignatius and the "Ratio studiorum."* 1933.
PHINNEY, ROSS L. *A Sociological Philosophy of Education.* 1928.
Report of the Committee on Curriculum Making: Being the Twenty-sixth Yearbook of the National Society for the Study of Education. 1927.
SNEDDEN, DAVID. *Sociological Foundations of the Curriculum.* 1927.

ANTHROPOLOGICAL AND ETHNOLOGICAL BACKGROUND

GOLDENWEISSER, ALEXANDER. *Anthropology: An Introduction to Primitive Culture.* 1937.
KELLER, A. G. *Man's Rough Road.* 1932.
KROEBER, A. L. *Anthropology.* 1923.
McCURDY, GEORGE G. *Human Origins.* 2 vols. 1933.
SPENCER, HERBERT. *The Principles of Sociology.* 3 vols. Appleton's ed. of 1927.
SUMNER, W. G., and KELLER, A. G. *The Science of Society.* 4 vols. 1927.
WISSLER, CLARK. *Man and Culture.* 1923.

CULTURAL HISTORY: GENERAL

BORING, EDWIN G. *History of Experimental Psychology.* 1929.
  Tantamount to a brief history of science and philosophy.

BREASTED, JAMES H. *Development of Religion and Thought in Ancient Egypt.* 1912.

——. *The Dawn of Conscience.* 1933.

DAMPIER, SIR WILLIAM. *History of Science and Its Relations with Philosophy and Religion.* 1935.

JASTROW, MORRIS. *Civilization of Babylonia and Assyria.* 1915.

JONES, THOMAS J. *Essentials of Civilization.* 1929.

JUDD, C. H. *Psychology of Social Institutions.* 1926.

LECKY, W. E. H. *History of European Morals from Augustus to Charlemagne.* 2 vols. 1929 ed.

——. *History of the Rise and Influence of the Spirit of Rationalism in Europe.* 2 vols. 1925 ed.

LICHTENBERGER, J. P. *Development of Social Theory.* 1933.

SMITH, DAVID E. *History of Mathematics.* 2 vols. 1923–25.

SMITH, PRESERVED. *History of Modern Culture.* 2 vols. 1930——.

SPENCER, HERBERT. *The Principles of Ethics.* 2 vols. Appleton's ed. of 1927.

WINGFIELD-STRATFORD, ESME. *The History of British Civilization.* 1935.

ECONOMIC AND SOCIAL HISTORY

See also JASTROW, *Civilization of Babylonia and Assyria.*

BENNETT, H. S. *Life on the English Manor—1150–1400.* 1937.

CARMAN, H. J. *Social and Economic History of the United States.* 2 vols. 1930.

CLAPHAM, J. H. *Social and Economic History of Great Britain.* 3 vols. 1930——.

GLOTZ, GUSTAVE. *Ancient Greece at Work.* 1926.

Recent Economic Changes. Report of the Committee at the President's Conference on Unemployment. 2 vols. 1929.

Recent Social Trends in the United States. Report of the President's Research Committee. 2 vols. 1933.

ROSTOVTZEFF, M. *Social and Economic History of the Roman Empire.* 1926.

SMART, WILLIAM. *Economic Annals of the Nineteenth Century—1801–1830.* 1917.

THOMPSON, J. W. *The Economic and Social History of the Middle Ages.* 1928.

WEBER, MAX. *General Economic History.* Trans. FRANK H. KNIGHT. 1927.

ART

ABERCROMBIE, LASCELLES. *An Essay toward a Theory of Art.* 1922.

ARNOLD, SIR THOMAS. *Painting in Islam.* 1928.

BINYON, LAWRENCE. *The Flight of the Dragon (Chinese Painting).* 1911–22.

BROWN, G. BALDWIN. *The Fine Arts: A Manual.* 2d ed. 1902.

DYSON, GEORGE. *The Progress of Music.* 1932.

FERGUSON, D. N. *A History of Musical Thought.* 1935.

History of Architecture. 4 vols. 1906–15. Vols. I and II by RUSSELL STURGIS; Vols. III and IV by A. L. FROTHINGHAM.

MACH, EDMUND VON. *Outlines of the History of Painting.* 1906.

MORRISON, HUGH. *Louis Sullivan: Prophet of Modern Architecture.* 1935.

PARRY, C. HUBERT H. *The Evolution of the Art of Music.* 1893–1932.

STURGIS, RUSSELL. *The Appreciation of Sculpture.* 1904.

———. *The Appreciation of Architecture.* 1903.

TAFT, LORADO. *American Sculpture.* Rev. ed. 1924.

THE STATE AND GOVERNMENT

BALDWIN, SIMEON E. *Modern Political Institutions.* 1898.

BRICE, JAMES. *Modern Democracies.* 1921.

———. *The American Commonwealth.* Rev. ed. 1921.

CARTER, JAMES C. *Law: Its Origins, Growth, and Functions.* 1907.

DICEY, A. V. *The Law of the Constitution* (English). 8th ed. 1926.

HILL, MABEL. *Liberty Documents.* 1903.

JOHNS, C. H. W. *The Oldest Code of Laws in the World.* 1903.

JUDSON, HARRY PRATT. *Our Federal Republic.* 1925.

LOWELL, A. LAWRENCE. *The Government of England.* 1908.

McLAUGHLIN, ANDREW C. *A Constitutional History of the United States.* 1935.

MAINE, SIR HENRY. *Ancient Law: Its Connection with the Early History of Society and Its Relation to Modern Ideas.* "World's Classics" series. 1861.

NORTON, THOMAS J. *The Constitution of the United States: Its Sources and Applications.* 1925.

WILSON, WOODROW. *The State.* 1899–1902.

LAW

DICKENSON, JOHN. *Administrative Justice and the Supremacy of Law in the United States.* 1927.

EDWARDS, NEWTON. *The Courts and the Public Schools.* 1933.

FOSDICK, RAYMOND B. *American Police Systems.* 1920.

———. *European Police Systems.* 1915.

IRWIN, WILL. *Propaganda and the News.* 1936.

SELIGMAN, E. R. A. *Essays in Taxation.* 10th ed. 1928.

VOLLMER, AUGUST. *The Police and Modern Society.* 1939.

WHITE, LEONARD D. *The Civil Service in the Modern State.* 1930.

WHITE, STEWART EDWARD. *Gold.* 1922.

An admirably told story of the forty-niners in California which shows the genius of Americans of that period for constituting civil government out of a state of anarchy.

ZANE, JOHN M. *The Story of Law.* 1927.

ECONOMICS, COMMERCE, AND INDUSTRY

COMMONS, JOHN R., *et al. History of Labor in the United States.* 2 vols. 1918–35.

DEWING, A. S. *Financial Policy of Corporations.* 1922.

DOUGLAS, PAUL H. *Real Wages in the United States—1890–1926.* 1930.

MARSHALL, ALFRED. *Principles of Economics: An Introductory Volume.* 8th ed. 1927.

PIGOU, A. C. *Economics of Welfare.* 2d ed. 1924.

TAUSSIG, F. W. *Principles of Economics.* 2 vols. 3d ed. 1928.

INDEX

Accountancy and Bookkeeping, 525

Accused, the, in criminal law, 358

Agency, in Commercial Law, 582

Agriculture: in industry, 629; vocational, 631

Aikens, H. A., *Principles of Logic*, 53

Airplane, in Machines and Machine Tools, 628

Algebra: language of quantity, 71; origins, 84; in the curriculum, 84; units in, 86, 96, 97; the equation, 87; course in, 96

Annuities, 549

Anthem, as unit in Music, 271

Appreciation: as form of learning, 207; in Music, 269; in Literature, 277; in Painting, 288; in Sculpture, 293, 296; in Architecture, 307

Architecture: as part of the visual environment, 295; in evolution, 296; forms and styles, 296; functionalism, 304; in the community, 304; classics, 305; instruction in, 305; units in, 306

Aristocracy, not a form of Government, 317

Aristotle, *Nichomachaean Ethics*, cited, 188

Arithmetic: among the Greeks, 71; content in curriculum, 74; fundamental processes in, 75; units in, 81 f.; elements, 83

Art: defined, 259; practical and representative, 260; institutional, 260; beauty not the object, 261; objectives in instruction, 262; classics, 263

Assembly and petition, peaceful, in the Constitution, 455

Athletics: abuse of, 614; as aesthetic institution, 649; conduct of, 651

Automatic machines, 628

Automobile: in Machines and Machine Tools, 623

Background, ideational, of pupils, 663

Bailment, in Commercial Law, 584

Balance sheet, in Bookkeeping and Accountancy, 531

Baldwin, Simeon E., *Modern Political Institutions*, 385

Ballad, as unit in Literature, 281

Bands, school brass, 273

Banking: evolution of, 533; commercial banks, 534; function in community, 534; security in bank loans, 535, 560; banks of issue, 536; solvency, 536; liquidity, 536; savings banks, 537, function of in the community, 537; trust companies, functions, 537; units in, 539

Bankruptcy, in Constitution, 446

Baron, as lord of the manor, 496

Barrows, H. H., cited, 138, 147

Basic Principles in Education, cited, 53, 100, 663

Beauty, in Art, 261

Bibliography, 668

Bill of Attainder, prohibited in Constitution, 447

Bills of credit, emission of, denied the States, 438

Biography, as unit in Literature, 281

Biology: development of as science, 182; as course in Science, 184; not botany and zoölogy, 184; units in, 184

Blacksmithing, in Tools and Machines, 621

Board of Trade, Chicago, 565

Bookkeeping and Accountancy, 525; units in, 527

Bowman, Isaiah, cited in *Geography in Relation to the Social Sciences*, 147

Breach of trust, 357

Breasted, James H.: *Dawn of Conscience*, cited, 30; *History of Egypt*, cited, 71

Bullion, 497

Bylaws and ordinances, 339

Cabinet: American, 415; nature and functions, 415; succession to the Presidency, 416

Calculus: foundation of modern science and industry, 71, 109; in the Cur-